The Byzantine and
Early Islamic Near East
Vol. 1.1

Studies in Late Antiquity and Early Islam

Averil Cameron, Lawrence I. Conrad,
John Haldon, Geoffrey King (eds.)
The Byzantine and Early Islamic Near East
– 4 Volumes Set –
SLAEI 1 – ISBN 9783959941365

Averil Cameron and Lawrence I. Conrad (eds.)
The Byzantine and Early Islamic Near East
Volume 1: Problems in the Literary Source Material
SLAEI 1.1 – ISBN 9783959940849

Geoffrey King and Averil Cameron (eds.)
The Byzantine and Early Islamic Near East
Volume 2: Land Use and Settlement Patterns
SLAEI 1.2 – ISBN 9783959940863

Averil Cameron (ed.)
The Byzantine and Early Islamic Near East
Volume 3: States, Resources and Armies
SLAEI 1.3 – ISBN 9783959940887

John Haldon and Lawrence I. Conrad (eds.)
The Byzantine and Early Islamic Near East
Volume 4: Elites Old and New
SLAEI 1.4 – ISBN 9783959940900

Robert Schick
The Christian Communities of Palestine
from Byzantine to Islamic Rule.
An Historical and Archaeological Study
SLAEI 2 – ISBN 9783959940924

Albrecht Noth with Lawrence I. Conrad
The Early Arabic Historical Tradition.
A Source-Critical Study
Translated from the German by Michael Bonner
SLAEI 3 – ISBN 9783959940948

Martin Hinds; ed. by Jere Bacharach,
Lawrence I. Conrad, and Patricia Crone
Studies in Early Islamic History
With an Introduction by G. R. Hawting
SLAEI 4 – ISBN 9783959940962

Uri Rubin
The Eye of the Beholder: The Life of Muhammad
as Viewed by the Early Muslims. A Textual Analysis
SLAEI 5 – ISBN 9783959940986

Jean Maurice Fiey; edited by Lawrence I. Conrad
Saints Syriaques
SLAEI 6 – ISBN 9783959941006

Elizabeth Savage
A Gateway To Hell, A Gateway To Paradise.
The North African Response to the Arab Conquest
SLAEI 7 – ISBN 9783959941082

Suliman Bashear
Arabs and Others in Early Islam
SLAEI 8 – ISBN 9783959941020

Milka Levy-Rubin (ed.)
The Continuatio of the Samaritan Chronicle of
Abū l-Fatḥ Ibn Abī l-Ḥasan al-Sāmirī al-Dinfī
Annotated Translation
SLAEI 10 – ISBN 9783959941044

Josef Horovitz, edited by Lawrence I. Conrad
The Earliest Biographies of the Prophet and
Their Authors
SLAEI 11 – ISBN 9783959941068

Fred M. Donner
Narratives of Islamic Origins.
The Beginnings of Islamic Historical Writing
SLAEI 14 – ISBN 9783959941105

Hugh N. Kennedy (ed.)
Al-Ṭabarī. A Medieval Muslim Historian and His Work
SLAEI 15 – ISBN 9783959941129

Uri Rubin
Between Bible and Qur'an.
The Children of Israel and the Islamic Self-Image
SLAEI 17 – ISBN 9783959941143

Josef W. Meri (ed.)
A Lonely Wayfarer's Guide to Pilgrimage. ʿAlī ibn Abī Bakr
al-Harawī's Kitāb al-ishārāt ilā maʿrifat al-ziyārāt
Translated and Introduced by the Editor
SLAEI 19 – ISBN 9783959941167

James E. Lindsay (ed.)
Ibn ʿAsākir and Early Islamic History
SLAEI 20 – ISBN 9783959941181

David Cook
Studies in Muslim Apocalyptic
SLAEI 21 – ISBN 9783959941204

Andreas Goerke
Das Kitab Al-Amwal des Abu ʿUbaid Al-Qasim b. Sallam.
Entstehung und Überlieferung eines frühislamischen
Rechtswerkes
SLAEI 22 – ISBN 9783959941228

Michael Lecker
The „Constitution of Medina".
Muhammad's First Legal Document
SLAEI 23 – ISBN 9783959941242

Andreas Goerke and Gregor Schoeler
Die ältesten Berichte über das Leben Muhammads.
Das Korpus ʿUrwa ibn az-Zubair
SLAEI 24 – ISBN 9783959941266

Robert G. Hoyland
The Late Antique World of Early Islam.
Muslims among Christians and Jews
in the East Mediterranean
SLAEI 25 – ISBN 9783959941280

Jens Scheiner and Damien Janos (eds.)
The Place to Go:
Contexts of Learning in Baghdad, 750-1000 C.E.
SLAEI 26 – ISBN 9783959941303

Note:
Volume nos 9, 12, 16 and 18 were never published.
Vol 13 was reissued by Gorgias Press.

www.gerlachpress.com

Studies in Late Antiquity and Early Islam 1.1

The Byzantine and Early Islamic Near East

Volume 1: Problems in the Literary Source Material

Edited by Averil Cameron and Lawrence I. Conrad

Gerlach Press

This edition first published in 2021
by Gerlach Press, Berlin
www.gerlachpress.com
Cover Design: Frauke Schön, Hamburg
Printed and bound in Germany

First published in 1992
by Darwin Press Inc, Princeton NJ

British Library Cataloguing in Publication Data.
A catalogue record for this book is available from the British Library.

Library of Congress Cataloguing in Publication Data.
A catalogue record for this book has been requested.

Bibliographic data available from German National Library
(Deutsche Nationalbibliothek)
http://d-nb.info/1217802711

ISBN: 978-3-95994-084-9 (hardcover)
ISBN: 978-3-95994-085-6 (eBook)

Contents

ABBREVIATIONS

AB	*Analecta Bollandiana*. Brussels, 1882–.
ACO	*Acta conciliorum oecumenicorum*. Ed. Edward Schwarz *et al.* Strassburg, Berlin, and Leipzig, 1914–proceeding.
AHR	*American Historical Review*. New York, 1895–.
AJA	*American Journal of Archaeology*. Baltimore, 1885–.
AKM	*Abhandlungen für die Kunde des Morgenlandes*. Leipzig, Wiesbaden, 1857–.
AO	*Ars Orientalis*. Washington, D.C., Ann Arbor, 1954–.
Baumstark	Anton Baumstark. *Geschichte der syrischen Literatur*. Bonn, 1922.
BBA	*Berliner byzantinische Arbeiten*. Berlin, 1956–.
BCH	*Bulletin de correspondance hellénique*. Paris, 1877–.
Beck	Hans–Georg Beck. *Kirche und theologische Literatur im byzantinischen Reich*. Munich, 1959.
BEO	*Bulletin d'études orientales*. Paris, Cairo, 1931–.
BF	*Byzantinische Forschungen*. Amsterdam, 1966–.
BMGS	*Byzantine and Modern Greek Studies*. Oxford, 1975–.
BNJ	*Byzantinisch–neugriechische Jahrbücher*. Berlin, 1920–.
BO	*Bibliotheca Orientalis*. Leiden, 1943–.
BS	*Byzantine Studies*. London, 1974–.

BSOAS	*Bulletin of the School of Oriental and African Studies.* London, 1917–.
BZ	*Byzantinische Zeitschrift.* Leipzig, Munich, 1892–.
CCSG	*Corpus Christianorum, Series Graeca.* Turnhout, 1971–.
CPG	*Clavis patrum graecorum.* Ed. Mauritz Geerard. 5 vols. Turnhout, 1974–87.
CRAI	*Comptes rendus de l'Académie des inscriptions et belles lettres.* Paris, 1857–.
CSCO	*Corpus scriptorum christianorum orientalium.* Paris, Leuven, 1903–.
CSHB	*Corpus scriptorum historiae byzantinae.* Ed. B.G. Niebuhr *et al.* 50 vols. Bonn, 1828–97.
Dict. spirit.	*Dictionnaire de spiritualité, ascétique et mystique, doctrine et histoire.* Ed. Marcel Viller *et al.* Paris, 1932–proceeding.
DMA	*Dictionary of the Middle Ages.* Ed. Joseph R. Strayer. 13 vols. New York, 1981–89.
DOP	*Dumbarton Oaks Papers.* Washington, D.C., 1941–.
EHR	*English Historical Review.* London, 1886–.
EI^1	*Encyclopaedia of Islam.* Ed. M.T. Houtsma *et al.* 4 vols. Leiden and London, 1913–34.
EI^2	*Encyclopaedia of Islam*, new ed. Ed. H.A.R. Gibb *et al.* Leiden and London, 1960–proceeding.
GAL	Carl Brockelmann. *Geschichte der arabischen Litteratur.* 2 vols. 2nd ed. Leiden, 1943–49; *Supplementbände.* 3 vols. Leiden 1937–42.
GAS	Fuat Sezgin. *Geschichte des arabischen Schrifttums.* Leiden, 1967–proceeding.

HThR	*Harvard Theological Review.* New York, 1908–.
Hunger	Herbert Hunger. *Die hochsprachliche profane Literatur der Byzantiner.* 2 vols. Munich, 1978.
IC	*Islamic Culture.* Hyderabad, 1927–.
IGLS	*Inscriptions grecques et latines de la Syrie.* Ed. J. Jalabert and R. Mouterde. Paris, 1929–proceeding.
JA	*Journal asiatique.* Paris, 1822–.
JAOS	*Journal of the American Oriental Society.* New Haven, Ann Arbor, 1842–.
JEH	*Journal of Ecclesiastical History.* London, 1950–.
JEHSO	*Journal of the Economic and Social History of the Orient.* Paris, 1957–.
JÖB	*Jahrbuch der österreichischen Byzantinistik.* Vienna, 1951–.
JRAS	*Journal of the Royal Asiatic Society.* London, 1834–.
JSAI	*Jerusalem Studies in Arabic and Islam.* Jerusalem, 1979–.
JSS	*Journal of Semitic Studies.* Oxford, 1956–.
JThS	*Journal of Theological Studies.* London, 1899–.
JWCI	*Journal of the Warburg and Courtauld Institutes.* London, 1937–.
Krumbacher	Karl Krumbacher. *Geschichte der byzantinischen Literatur.* 2nd ed. in collaboration with A. Ehrhard and H. Gelzer. Munich, 1897.
Mansi	J.D. Mansi. *Sacrorum conciliorum nova et amplissima collectio.* 31 vols. Florence, 1759–98.

MGH Auct. Ant	*Monumenta Germaniae Historica, Auctores Antiquissimi.* 15 vols. Berlin, 1877–1919.
OC	*Oriens Christianus.* Rome, 1901–.
OCP	*Orientalia christiana periodica.* Rome, 1935–.
OLP	*Orientalia lovanensia periodica.* Leuven, 1970–.
PEQ	*Palestine Exploration Quarterly.* London, 1937–.
PG	*Patrologiae graecae cursus completus.* Ed. J.-P. Migne. 161 vols. Paris, 1857–66;
PL	*Patrologiae latinae cursus completus.* Ed. J.-P. Migne. 221 vols. Paris, 1844–90; *Supplementum.* 5 vols. Paris, 1958–74.
P/W, *RE*	*Paulys Realencyclopädie der klassischen Altertumswissenschaft.* Rev. ed. by Georg Wissowa *et al.* Stuttgart, 1893–1972. *Supplementbände.* 1903–proceeding.
RAAD	*Revue de l'Académie arabe de Damas.* Damascus, 1921–.
RAC	*Reallexikon für Antike und Christentum.* Ed. Theodor Klauser *et al.*, Stuttgart, 1950–proceeding.
RANL	*Rendiconti dell'Accademia nazionale dei Lincei, Classe di scienze morali, storiche, critiche e filologiche.* Rome, 1892–.
RB	*Revue biblique.* Paris, 1892–.
REB	*Revue des études byzantines.* Bucharest, 1943–.
RHE	*Revue d'histoire ecclésiastique.* Leuven, 1900–.
RM	*Rheinisches Museum für Philologie.* Bonn, Frankfurt am Main, 1827–.
RSR	*Revue des sciences religieuses.* Strasbourg, 1921–.

SI	*Studia Islamica.* Paris, 1953–.
TAPA	*Transactions of the American Philological Association.* Middletown, Cleveland, Atlanta, 1870–.
TM	*Travaux et Mémoires.* Paris, 1965–.
TRE	*Theologische Realenzyclopädie.* Ed. Gerhard Krause and Gerhard Müller. Berlin, 1977–proceeding.
TU	*Texte und Untersuchungen.* Leipzig, Berlin, 1882–.
VC	*Vigiliae Christianae.* Amsterdam, 1947–.
VV	*Vizantiyskiy Vremennik.* Moscow, 1947–.
WI	*Die Welt des Islams.* Berlin, 1913–.
ZDMG	*Zeitschrift der deutschen Morgenländischen Gesellschaft.* Leipzig, Wiesbaden, 1847–.
ZRVI	*Zbornik radova vizantološki institut.* Moscow, 1952–.
ZS	*Zeitschrift für Semitistik und verwandte Gebiete.* Leipzig, 1922–35.

Preface

THE FIRST WORKSHOP of the *Late Antiquity and Early Islam* project, the concerns and objectives of which are discussed in the Introduction to this volume, was convened in London on 20–21 October 1989 and attended by about 50 scholars representing a broad range of interests and expertise on the history of the transition period from late antiquity to early Islam. Eight papers addressing various dimensions of the workshop theme, "Problems in the Literary Source Material", were presented, and provided stimulating opportunities for fruitful cross-disciplinary discussions which comprised the bulk of the workshop proceedings (papers were precirculated, and were not read at the workshop). The encouragement of this sort of dialogue, across traditional disciplinary lines, was in fact one of our primary aims and marks, we hope, the beginning of a trend which we seek to further in the continuing work of the *LAEI* project.

The eight papers presented at the workshop are here published in full. It was not considered feasible to include abstracts or summaries of the discussions, important though these were. Their influence, however, will be evident in many places throughout this volume, and in the Introduction the editors have sought to take account of the points which repeatedly arose over the two days of our meeting and seemed to be of particular significance.

This book comprises the first volume of *The Byzantine and Early Islamic Near East*, which will provide a venue for the publication of the proceedings of the various *LAEI* workshops. The second volume, on "Land Use and Settlement Patterns", will contain the papers of the second workshop, convened by the project under the auspices of

Dr. Geoffrey King at the School of Oriental and African Studies on 25–27 April 1991, and is being edited for publication as this volume goes to press. A third workshop, on the topic of "States, Resources, and Armies", is planned for October 1992, and a fourth will consider questions of communal identity in October 1993.

The editors would like to take this particularly pleasant opportunity to record their thanks to the various institutions and persons who contributed to the launching of the *LAEI* project, the convening of its first workshop, and the publication of this volume. The British Academy, the Leverhulme Foundation, the Wellcome Institute for the History of Medicine, King's College London, and the Society for the Promotion of Byzantine Studies provided generous financial assistance, and the Wellcome Institute and the Institute for Classical Studies graciously hosted the two days of our proceedings. Dr. Geoffrey King, who has since joined the project as director for the field of Art History and Archaeology, devoted much work to the project as research associate in 1988–89. The text of the volume was word-processed at the Wellcome Institute by Sue Hordijenko and Jacqui Canning, and the detailed index—a difficult indertaking, but crucial to a volume such as this one—was prepared by Brenda Hall, MA, registered indexer of the Society of Indexers. To all of these institutions and individuals, as well as to the many others who have given us their support and encouragement, we extend our heartfelt gratitude and appreciation.

Introduction

THIS VOLUME REPRESENTS not only the first publication in the series *Studies in Late Antiquity and Early Islam*, but also the proceedings of the first in the series of workshops on particular themes which, it is hoped, will give shape to the series and to the project from which it derives. In part, therefore, it serves the purpose of defining the range and scope of the problems to be addressed by the project, while necessarily being selective and limited in its own coverage. It may thus be useful to begin with some account of the concerns, methods, and objectives of the project as a whole, and of the aims within it of this volume and of the series itself.

The project entitled *Late Antiquity and Early Islam*, of which the present series is the publishing vehicle, was born out of a colloquium held in London in 1986, when it became very clear that while there was clearly an increasing amount of research being undertaken on the passing of late antiquity, the emergence and early development of Islam, and the patterns of change and continuity that characterized the history of the Near East from the death of the emperor Justinian in 565 until the 'Abbāsid revolution in the mid-eighth century, this work was in general proceeding in a highly compartmentalized and segmented fashion. Over the past decades individual works of scholarship in this field have increasingly tended to be defined by boundaries reflecting the limits imposed both by the individual author's general perspective (Byzantine, eastern church, Arab-Islamic, or Jewish studies) or specialized discipline (history, archaeology, religious studies, to name but a few), and by particularist considerations dictated by the political frontiers of the modern states of the Near East. This is not to assert the obviously erroneous claim that researchers in one field have not been aware that important and even vital insights might be forthcoming from the fruits of investigations in some other field or in an adjacent region. Such awareness has been evident for some time, and individual efforts to bridge the gaps among the various fields have indeed been made. But the accelerating pace of research within one's own field, the framing of more sophisticated modes of inquiry, and the more sharply defined conclusions which arise from them, have at the same time made it more difficult for researchers to keep abreast of all the developments of potential importance to them.

Such eventualities are to some extent the consequence of the rapid development and expansion of the relevant fields, and must thus be seen, at least in this respect, as inevitable. But the problems confronting anyone seeking to pursue a broader view of things are nonetheless significant and serious. Despite the long tradition of translation of Greek and Syriac texts, for example, many works remain inaccessible to researchers unable to read these languages; the difficulty is particularly acute for those with no Latin, the language in which most such translations for long traditionally appeared. In the case of Arabic, an entire field of literary material of tremendous importance is effectively closed, with only a few tantalizing exceptions, by a lack of definitive translations and supporting commentaries. The language problem further carries over into modern scholarship in that important work often presumes a thorough familiarity with the fundamentals and technical vocabulary of the field in question. An Arabist interested in obtaining a general view of Byzantine secular literature will find Hunger's standard work on the subject rather hard going,[1] while the Byzantinist wishing to gain a firmer footing with respect to Arab-Islamic historiography will not find Duri's pioneering study much easier.[2]

Other problems present different but no less intractable difficulties. One has long been posed by the still pervasive division of scholarship concerned with certain areas along lines dictated by their past colonial history, present national status, or the dominant rôles of various

[1] Herbert Hunger, *Die hochsprachliche profane Literatur der Byzantiner* (Munich, 1978).

[2] A.A. Duri, *The Rise of Historical Writing Among the Arabs*, ed. and trans. Lawrence I. Conrad (Princeton, 1983).

foreign institutes and research organizations; it is not always easy to cross over these barriers, either in practical terms or in matters of the accessibility of scholarly work. Another is raised by the tendency to demote to a level of lesser importance, and therefore widespread disregard, sources which lack the credentials (in modern eyes) for admission to the categories of "high" or "historical" literature. Disputation treatises, for example, have tended to be viewed in this manner, perhaps because they are, after all, to a greater or lesser degree literary arguments whose outcome is never left in doubt. But here, as with other neglected genres, many important insights may nevertheless be gained through methodologies which take the nature of these treatises as a starting point rather than as a conclusion. And again, the interconnection between the examples surviving from the various confessional traditions, too often treated in isolation from one another, asks for urgent exploration.

Lastly, there has long been a tendency for the study of the Near East in this period to be restricted by the canons of a historical positivism sufficiently tenacious to presume to exclude from the domain of legitimate scholarship a growing corpus of innovative research which challenges the traditional approach, this despite the fact that this new work, largely focussed on the origins and early development of Islam and the Islamic polity, is firmly grounded in modes of investigation such as literary analysis, structuralism, oral formulaic composition, source criticism, and other similar approaches, all of which have been quite commonly and fruitfully brought to bear in other historical fields.[3] Whether this more provocative research leads to a more accurate interpretation of the history of the period (either explicitly or by implication), or a truer view of the medieval literary traditions which reflect and lend expression to it, remains to be discussed and assessed in further detail; but whatever the ultimate outcome of the debate (upon which more will be said below), the fact remains that in highlighting such obviously central questions as the interplay of cultural and religious systems and their development in relation to one another, and the implications of this

---

[3]On this problem where the study of early Islam is concerned, see Andrew Rippin, *Muslims: Their Religious Beliefs and Practices*, I: *The Formative Period* (London, 1990), ix–x; and on the general issues, Averil Cameron, ed., *History as Text* (London, 1989).

symbiotic process for the modern researcher's assessment and criticism of the evidence, it is dealing with issues of obvious relevance to our concerns here.[4]

If it is clearly impossible for scholars to "know" all the material relevant to their own research, in the way that it was once possible to "know" such fields as the classics or Oriental studies, this fact in and of itself demonstrates that the more interdisciplinary approach which is obviously a primary need at this point must be sought in some other way. The *Late Antiquity and Early Islam* project seeks to achieve such a broadening of perspectives in several different ways.

First, and most generally, it attempts to facilitate and promote communication among specialists in the various fields, and thus to draw important current work to the attention of wider audiences than it has traditionally enjoyed in the past. Its series, *Studies in Byzantium and Early Islam*, will publish works of particular relevance to the subject field of the project as a whole, and especially welcomes contributions which explore and promote the possibilities and potentials for interdisciplinary research. It will also sponsor the translation of key texts, with new editions if necessary, and with commentaries seeking to facilitate the utilization of these works by researchers in adjacent fields.

Second, and more specifically, the project seeks to provide opportunities for cross-disciplinary communication. The most important of

[4]The questions of methodology and source criticism at issue are articulated at length in Albrecht Noth, *Quellenkritische Studien zu Themen, Formen und Tendenzen frühislamischer Geschichtsüberlieferung*, I: *Themen und Formen* (Bonn, 1973); John Wansbrough, *Qur'ānic Studies: Sources and Methods of Scriptural Interpretation* (Oxford, 1977), and his *The Sectarian Milieu: Content and Composition of Islamic Salvation History* (Oxford, 1978); Michael Cook, *Early Muslim Dogma: a Source-Critical Study* (Cambridge, 1981). For an assessment of Wansbrough's theories, see Andrew Rippin, "Literary Analysis of *Qur'ān*, *Tafsīr*, and *Sīra*: the Methodologies of John Wansbrough", in Richard C. Martin, ed., *Approaches to Islam in Religious Studies* (Tucson, 1985), 151–63. A different approach (cf. below, 13–15) may be seen in Patricia Crone and Michael Cook, *Hagarism: the Making of the Islamic World* (Cambridge, 1977); and subsequently, Michael Cook, *Muhammad* (Oxford, 1983); Patricia Crone, *Slaves on Horses: the Evolution of the Islamic Polity* (Cambridge, 1980); Patricia Crone and Martin Hinds, *God's Caliph: Religious Authority in the First Centuries of Islam* (Cambridge, 1986); Patricia Crone, *Meccan Trade and the Rise of Islam* (Princeton, 1987); *eadem*, *Roman, Provincial and Islamic Law: the Origins of the Islamic Patronate* (Cambridge, 1987).

these are offered by the periodic workshops, the proceedings of the first of which are published here. These workshops seek to draw together scholars from as wide a range of disciplines, perspectives, and national backgrounds as possible in order to address defined themes and issues set forth not so much in terms of specific questions as in terms of the broader problems underlying these questions. The character of the Arab conquests, perhaps the central event in our period, is very much a case in point. While such questions as the causes, nature, chronology, and success of the conquests are of vital importance, progress on any of these aspects is necessarily conditioned by and dependent upon how one addresses other larger questions—questions concerning the nature and value of the various forms of evidence, matters bearing on social, economic, and political developments, and so forth. These broader issues also condition how one proceeds on all discussions for this period; thus the point where the workshops most directly promote the interests of the project as a whole will we hope lie in relation to its effort to set the extraordinary events and developments which took place in this period within a perspective which aims for and encourages a more comprehensive view. The project takes no national, religious, or cultural slant; rather, it seeks to explore the totality of experience in which certain specific developments took shape, and aims at definition of the changing situation in its entirety.

In this respect it must be stressed that one of our primary aims is to achieve a greater degree of synthesis and integration between the disciplines of history and archaeology. While it is certainly true that the latter is of unquestioned importance for the history of the Near East, it must be noted that both Byzantine and early Islamic archaeology are relatively new fields which have only recently emerged as well-defined disciplines in their own right, as opposed to being mere adjuncts to Biblical and ancient archaeology. Even now, the study of iconography and architecture, dictated by the richness of the surviving material, still has a tendency to dominate discussion, particularly where the topic of iconoclasm is concerned. But the increasing attention devoted to the more central concerns of archaeology in the investigation of Byzantine and early Islamic sites has made significant contributions to our knowledge, and recent advances are beginning to provide a far more solid context for historical synthesis than was the case in the past. The second workshop, convened by the project on 25–27 April 1991 at the School of Oriental and African Studies in London under the auspices of Dr. Geoffrey King, concerned itself with questions of land use and settlement patterns in the period and brought together an unusually wide range of scholars in order to do so.

The other aim of the project seeks to address the need in the field for efforts to draw the disparate and widely scattered material on key issues together into manageable form. Such work is often tedious and unappreciated, but its importance cannot be doubted and is clear enough from a number of already available examples. Friedhelm Winkelmann's detailed conspectus of sources relating to Monothelitism in the seventh century is an invaluable aid to the study of this crucial topic, especially in view of the centrality of Byzantine christological disputes for understanding the religious situation in seventh-century Syria and Palestine.[5] Iḥsān 'Abbās' new critical edition, with an important introduction, of the epistles and other literary remains attributed to the late Umayyad secretary 'Abd al-Ḥamīd ibn Yaḥyā (d. 132/750) clears the way for significant new advances in our understanding of Umayyad statecraft and political thinking.[6] One fundamental contribution of Robert Schick's forthcoming assessment of the Christian communities in Palestine from late Byzantine to early 'Abbāsid times will be his corpus of sites, which collects the information from archaeological and literary sources available for all sites in Palestine and adjacent areas where Christian presence can be detected for this period, and organizes this into a compendium from which future research will clearly derive much benefit.[7]

The value of such collections in limited areas and on specific topics suggests that a major advance in the field would be achieved if a con-

[5] "Die Quellen zur Erforschung des monenergetisch-monothelitischen Streites", *Klio* 69 (1986), 515–59. Cf. also Friedhelm Winkelmann and Wolfram Brandes, eds., *Quellen zur Geschichte des frühen Byzanz (4.–9. Jahrhundert)* (Berlin, 1990; *BBA* 55).

[6] Iḥsān 'Abbās, *'Abd al-Ḥamīd ibn Yaḥyā al-kātib wa-mā tabaqqā min rasā'ilihi wa-rasā'il Sālim Abī l-'Alā'* (Amman, 1988). On this collection, see the paper of Wadād al-Qāḍī in this volume.

[7] Robert Schick, *The Christian Communities of Palestine from Byzantine to Islamic Rule: an Historical and Archaeological Study* (Princeton, 1992; *SBEI* 2).

spectus of all the literary sources for the period could be placed at the disposal of researchers, a reference work in which one would immediately have to hand information on the state of our knowledge of these sources, the historiographical and literary-critical problems they raise, whether they are available in reliable editions and/or translations, and so forth. It is not only non-specialists, students, and colleagues in related fields who would benefit from the orientation: specialists may also sometimes deceive themselves by either overestimating the accessibility of this information to themselves or their colleagues, or underestimating the volume and scope of the vast amount that is in fact available. The need for such a guide was recognized at an early stage of the project, and work is now proceeding on its preparation under the direction of the two editors of this volume. The guide will of course be heavily dominated by the literature in the three languages of most of the extant sources: Arabic, Greek, and Syriac; but this does not suffice to provide the total picture, and it will thus aim to cover material in all the relevant languages, including Georgian, Armenian, Hebrew, Coptic, and Ethiopic. In many areas it is possible to achieve complete coverage, but in others practical considerations come into play—it is not possible, for example, to include every work in the vast literature of medieval Islam which has some contribution to offer concerning the pre-Islamic and early Islamic periods—and it is certainly true that defining a "literary" source is a problem in itself, no less than that of judging a text's "historical worth". Nevertheless, the conspectus will, it is hoped, provide an enabling tool for students and scholars in the various constituent fields to gain access to the whole range of relevant literary material, at least insofar as access is at present possible. And even where such access is as yet problematic, a guide of this kind serves the useful purpose of suggesting the agenda for future critical, editorial, and translation efforts. There is indeed no less need for similar works covering documentary and other written sources, in particular the papyri, and also archaeological sites for the period; but the literary material is surely the appropriate place to start.

Certain aspects of the project call for comment at this point. One is the matter of definition, both geographical and cultural. For the overall project we have decided on the term "late antiquity" as being the most inclusive of the several possible labels for the period preceding the rise of Islam, and as pointing, at the same time, to the notion of transition, which is one of our central concerns. There is no need here to enter into the various debates about when the ancient world ended or "Byzantium" began;[8] scholars even from the same discipline use the word "Byzantine" in different ways, and the differences between disciplines are even greater—the period which would be described, for instance, as "early Byzantine" by a Byzantine historian, is "late Byzantine" to an archaeologist of the Near Eastern regions conquered by the Arabs in the seventh century. But whatever their preferences of nomenclature, most scholars would probably agree that these conquests mark the critical period of transition in the Near East. We have set our chronological parameters with this consideration in mind. The choice of the late sixth century as a starting point, rather than the conquests themselves, allows for consideration of changes already taking place in the eastern provinces and the Byzantine empire generally, as well as in the domains of the Sasanian empire to the east, which provided the context in which Arab rule established itself; the fact that these changes have recently been the subject of much scholarly attention, especially in relation to the relatively new concentration of archaeological work on this period, makes such a chronological focus timely and opens the possibility of quite different answers to the old chestnut (a hackneyed examination question in many places) of why lands of such central importance to the Byzantine and Sasanian empires fell so easily to the Arab conquerors.

At the other end of the time scale, the end of the Umayyad period makes a convenient terminus, though not one for which one might claim special status as marking a watershed of cultural or political change. It has long been recognized that "the ʿAbbāsid revolution" should more accurately be considered as the third civil war in Islam, and it has re-

---

[8]A.H.M. Jones, *The Later Roman Empire: a Social and Economic Survey* (Oxford, 1964), still the standard work in English, ends *ca.* AD 600; contrast Peter Brown, *The World of Late Antiquity* (London, 1971), who carries the period further, and for similar periodization, Richard Hodges and David Whitehouse, *Mohammed, Charlemagne and the Origins of Europe* (London, 1983). On the other hand, Alexander Kazhdan and Anthony Cutler, "Continuity and Discontinuity in Byzantine Culture", *Byzantion* 52 (1982), 429–78, argue for a "proto-Byzantine" period from the fourth to the seventh centuries.

cently been proposed, with considerable justification, that if such an expression as "revolution" has any validity at all in this case, it must be understood as referring to "the many and profound developments which followed the accession of the dynasty, not merely to the overthrow of the Umayyads and establishment of the 'Abbāsid caliphate itself".[9] But at the same time, it is equally true that the very success of the 'Abbāsid movement bears vivid witness to the extent and depth of the changes which had already transpired in the Umayyad period; and while the effort of the Umayyad régime to maintain the political unity of the Arab empire under its own auspices failed, surely of greater importance was its rôle in nurturing Islam as a world religious and cultural order and endowing it with its distinctive Arab coloring.[10] Indeed, such a terminus serves, without prejudicing either way the course of the debate, to focus attention on the key question of the extent to which the course of historical events and developments at other levels did or did not parallel the political shift from Umayyad to 'Abbāsid rule.

On the Byzantine side there is no such obvious terminus in the mid-eighth century. Yet such a choice does mark the end of a period of uncertainty, hostility, and possible influence between Byzantium and the caliphate, by leaving the former to its own internal struggle over the status of religious images, which was to preoccupy it for nearly another century, as well as to the completion of profound military and administrative changes already under way. There is also something symbolic in the fact that John of Damascus, son and grandson of officials in the administration of the caliphate, and the greatest defender of Christian images in this period, should have been formally condemned shortly after his own death by the iconoclast Council of Hiereia in 754. That so central a figure in the controversy, reinstated by the Second Council of Nicaea in 787, in fact wrote his orations in defense of images in Muslim-ruled Palestine is one of the major ironies to be addressed by our project. In the final analysis, however, it must always be borne in mind that the processes of continuity and change hold true across all lines of periodization; that such bounds, irrespective of their descrip-

[9] G.R. Hawting, *The First Dynasty of Islam: the Umayyad Caliphate,* AD *661–750* (London, 1986), 104.

[10] See Lawrence I. Conrad, art. "Umayyads" in *DMA*, XII (New York, 1989), 265–74.

tive utility and convenience, must not be presumed to acquire thereby a determinative value of their own.

Geographical limits are more difficult to set for an area of fluctuating populations and languages, and with modern national boundaries overlaying many centuries of change. Terms such as "Arab", "Hellenic", "Syria", and "Syrian" must be used with considerable caution if they are not to mislead the inexperienced.[11] For our purposes, however, the main focus is on the geographical areas encompassed by modern Iraq, Syria, Jordan, Lebanon, Israel, and Saudi Arabia, that is, the late Roman and Byzantine provinces of Syria I and II, Euphratensis, Osrhoene, Mesopotamia, Phoenicia I and II, Palestine I, II, and III, and Arabia, as well as the Arabian peninsula and the Sasanian domains in Iraq. However, no hard and fast line can be drawn; Constantinople and Asia Minor are not so central to our concerns, but can hardly be ignored. Our areas of primary emphasis are to a certain extent dictated by the confluence of evidence and modern scholarship which makes geographical Syria, Iraq, and Arabia a central focus where the main historical issues are most acutely presented; but just as these regions did not exist in a geographical void in the sixth to eighth centuries, it is hoped that the impact of other regions will receive due consideration as the project proceeds.

In the meantime, the papers in this volume represent the first stage in meeting the objectives of the project as outlined above. The workshop itself followed a pattern which proved to be both stimulating in itself and illuminating for the problems of communication which it revealed. The papers themselves were not read at the workshop, but precirculated to participants, a procedure which allowed time for discussion at length and in depth.[12] Inevitably, the discussions revealed

---

[11]The question of Arabic terminology for Syria and Syrians is an interesting one. See Gérard Troupeau, "La connaissance des chrétiens syriaques chez les auteurs arabo-musulmanes", in R. Lavenant, ed., *III Symposium Syriacum: Les contacts du monde syriaque avec les autres cultures* (Rome, 1983; *Orientalia Christiana Analecta* 221), 273–80.

[12]The model for the format of the *Late Antiquity and Early Islam* workshops was a symposium entitled "Interdisciplinary Perspectives on Text Analysis", convened by Professor James Malarkey at the American University of Beirut in 1982. A series of similar and very fruitful colloquia has been independently organized by Dr. G.H.A. Juynboll and other colleagues on the subject of *ḥadīth*, and has now

both differences and common questions pertaining to the issues and types of material raised for consideration. Some of these have subsequently been taken into account in the published versions of the papers, and some are indicated here. But it need hardly be stressed that this introduction makes no attempt at a general survey of the field and its problems; rather, we hope that both will emerge as discussions continue.

The proceedings of this first workshop represent a gathering together of current work by scholars actively engaged in the field, and they do therefore inevitably presume some familiarity with the general issues. In this, however, the papers of Averil Cameron and Michael Whitby differ from the rest in that they both attempt surveys of the material, in the first case of the Greek sources in general and in the second of Greek historical writing specifically. In Cameron's paper some suggestions are made about overall trends in Greek literature in this period, especially the substantial amount which comes from the areas in question. In terms of the history of Byzantine literature generally, this era is usually seen as a "dark age", when little of note was produced; yet this view rests on quite false premises, since, as intimated above, it largely ignores the vast quantity of writing in fields such as theology, homiletic, question-and-answer literature, and so on, which are not fields of "high" literature, and yet which can be equally revealing about their historical and social context. These and related kinds of writing, not the few works of "high" literature, belong, moreover, to the actual context against which the early stages of Arabic literature also developed. Paradoxically, perhaps, the seventh-century east saw a considerable volume of writing in Greek, though not indeed of secular literature or in the classical genres, and this is now beginning to be appreciated in its actual cultural context.[13]

---

developed into an ongoing series of meetings which convened for the fourth time in Amsterdam in August 1991.

[13]Though the patriarch Sophronius composed learned verses in classical anacreontics: see for this literature in general Averil Cameron, "The Eastern Provinces in the Seventh Century AD: Hellenism and the Emergence of Islam", in S. Said, ed., *Hellenismos. Quelques jalons pour une histoire de l'identité grecque* (Strasbourg, 1991), 287–313, with G. Bowersock, *Hellenism in Late Antiquity* (Cambridge, 1990), Chapter VI, "Hellenism and Islam". New critical editions of such important au-

Whitby's paper, on the other hand, addresses itself to a particular question, Greek historical writing as such in the period after the death of Justinian in 565, and identifies and discusses an important change which seems to have been taking place, whereby the old and very well-established tradition of secular and critical history writing of which Procopius was still in the sixth century a major exponent effectively comes to an end with Theophylact Simocatta under Heraclius (though writing about a slightly earlier period), to be replaced by Christian chronicles or other works where historical content appears in a different guise. How far this reflects current conditions, and how far it is indicative of social change in the Byzantine empire independent of and preceding the Arab conquests is clearly an important issue for the present project, and one which received a good deal of attention in the differing interpretation of the same problems in John Haldon's paper. Pursuing the implications of broad socio-economic factors, Haldon draws attention to the rôle of cities in the late sixth and seventh centuries, the availability of secular and traditional education, changed conditions of literary patronage, and the cultural expectations of the Byzantine élites. Here again the more finely nuanced view that emerges when less emphasis is placed on "high" literature becomes evident: Haldon seeks to set the *Questions and Answers* of Anastasius of Sinai not only against a background of complex socio-economic changes, but also within a context of practical literature exhibiting a strong element of oral tradition and addressing the needs and concerns of the common man. The dramatic change in subject matter, often forgotten, is rightly highlighted by both Whitby and Haldon.

In contrast, the two papers on Syriac sources by G.J. Reinink and Han J.W. Drijvers both address themselves to particular texts—the *Apocalypse* of ps.-Methodius, a much studied late seventh-century work which circulated widely in Syriac and in Greek translation, and the less well-known *Gospel of the Twelve Apostles*, related to the ps.-Methodius text but differing from it in significant ways. The divergent views of

---

thors as Maximus Confessor and Anastasius of Sinai, and of such central texts as the Acts of the Lateran Synod of 649, are making the Greek literature more accessible, and we now also have John Haldon's book, *Byzantium in the Seventh Century: the Transformation of a Culture* (Cambridge, 1990), which provides the cultural context.

scholars who have worked on ps.-Methodius as to the date and provenance of the work indicate only too clearly how much still remains uncertain in understanding the historical and religious context of this important class of Christian apocalyptic texts. As argued here, both the ps.-Methodius *Apocalypse* and the *Gospel of the Twelve Apostles* belong to the tense period at the end of the seventh century when Syrian Christians were coming under increasing pressure to convert to Islam, a context similar to that of the world history of Jōḥannān bar Penkāyē,[14] and furthermore, a period of tense relations between Byzantium and the caliphate and of great turmoil within the caliphate itself.[15] Like the rest of the papers, these reflect in differing ways the real and pressing need in this period for elucidation even of evidently central texts. Not only do many texts remain, like the *Gospel of the Twelve Apostles*, virtually unknown, even if not actually unedited (and there are plenty of these too); a high proportion of those with a claim to be more familiar still lack their own studies or remain controversial. Indeed, the papers in this volume suggest directions for fruitful exploration throughout the range of the available source material, even in the case of works assumed to be already well known and accurately understood.

To turn to the papers by Wadād al-Qāḍī and Stefan Leder on Arabic materials is to proceed into a different environment altogether, one in which the credibility of the evidence itself is subjected to fierce scrutiny. That serious problems are evident in the Arabic sources for early Islamic history is not denied by researchers in this field: the controversy arises over the nature of these problems and the extent to which they can be resolved, that is, resolved so as to allow for the reconstruction of historical events.[16] The traditional approach has been to view the sources in terms of a positivist relation to historical "facts": if one

[14] Alphonse Mingana, *Sources syriaques*, I (Leipzig, 1908), 177*–181*. For an English translation of the section of most immediate relevance to present concerns, see S.P. Brock, "North Mesopotamia in the Late Seventh Century: Book XV of John bar Penkāyē's *Rīš Mellē*", *JSAI* 9 (1987), 51–75.

[15] See ʿAbd al-Ameer ʿAbd Dixon, *The Umayyad Caliphate, 65–86/684–705 (A Political Study)* (London, 1971); Gernot Rotter, *Die Umayyaden und der zweite Bürgerkrieg (680–692)* (Wiesbaden, 1982; *AKM* 45.3); Hawting, *The First Dynasty of Islam*, 46–71.

[16] For an introduction to this difficult subject, see R. Stephen Humphreys, *Islamic History: a Framework for Inquiry* (Minneapolis, 1988), 68–98.

"trusts" the literary tradition, in the sense of assuming *a priori* that the evidence for a given object of inquiry will in most cases contain some core of historical truth pertaining to that topic in its own time and place (as opposed to how later audiences might have viewed it), then the task of the historian is to rationalize and harmonize the evidence, identifying and explaining away the errors, anomalies, and falsifications so as to expose the core of truth, though in many cases this core may itself be ambiguous or problematic.[17] In some circles an effort is made to verify the validity of this approach by bringing it to bear on vast ranges of material, the implicit point being that as the corpus of examined evidence expands there is a commensurately dwindling possibility that the coherent picture which emerges therefrom could reflect anything but the true course of events, discrete aspects of which have been transmitted accurately to later times and may now be reconstructed by the historian.[18]

Such views have in recent years been called into question by the revisionist scholarship discussed above, which argues that the Arab-Islamic literary sources to a large extent represent a retrojection of later religious, theological, and political thinking into the early Islamic period, and that such archaic material as may have survived to later times has been so thoroughly recast and elaborated as to obscure beyond recovery, in many cases, the arguments and reports with which the process began. As the Arab-Islamic literary tradition in its present state includes no works from earlier than about AD 800 (though earlier

[17]See, for example, Fred M. Donner's important book, *The Early Islamic Conquests* (Princeton, 1981), in which (e.g. 111, 185–86) the obstacles to reconciliation of the various accounts are viewed largely in terms of contradictions in chronology. Cf. also Michael G. Morony, *Iraq after the Muslim Conquest* (Princeton, 1984), esp. 13–17, arguing for a more broadly based use of non-Islamic evidence, but more as a means of supplementing the "sufficiently coherent" picture which emerges from the Arabic sources than as an alternative view which may call these sources into question in some fundamental way. For a lucid view of the sources from this traditional point of view, see the survey in Hugh Kennedy's *The Prophet and the Age of the Caliphates: the Islamic Near East from the Sixth to the Eleventh Century* (London, 1986), 350–88.

[18]See, for example, the collected studies of M.J. Kister published in his *Studies in Jāhiliyya and Early Islam* (London, 1980) and *Society and Religion from Jāhiliyya to Islam* (London, 1990).

works were undoubtedly written), the means by which the tradition can be evaluated naturally become problematic. The skeptics differ, however, as to what can be done in response to this situation. Crone and Cook have proposed a reconstruction of Islamic origins on the basis of non-Islamic sources,[19] though more recently Crone has conceded, for example, the utility of prosopographical data, the likelihood that poetry and alleged documents preserved in literary texts may be resistant to updating, and the point that the classical Islamic tradition does in fact contain material which contradicts the tradition's relevant formulation, and so may be viewed as representing survivals from earlier times.[20] The trend represented by Wansbrough, however, doubts whether viewing Islamic history from without can provide a more accurate picture either, since non-Muslims, no less than later Muslims themselves, would have portrayed developments pertaining to early Islam in terms favorable to their own perceptions and views.[21] While this radical approach does not disallow the historical study of early Islam altogether,[22] it does make historical research a task fraught with difficulties, and renders source criticism perhaps the central issue in the current study of early Islam.

Wadād al-Qāḍī's paper addresses itself precisely to this problem with reference to a particular corpus of material—the letters of the late Umayyad secretary ʿAbd al-Ḥamīd ibn Yaḥyā—which would, if the versions we now have of these letters are reliable ones, constitute major evidence for the key question of Islamic state formation.[23] In arguing

[19]See their *Hagarism*, esp. 3: "The only way out of the dilemma is thus to step outside the Islamic tradition altogether and start again".

[20]See Crone, *Slaves on Horses*, 8–17, pursuing a distinction postulated (but not established) between a religious tradition and a tribal tradition in early Islamic historiography; Crone and Hinds, *God's Caliph*, 70.

[21]Wansbrough's most explicit statement on this issue is in his *Sectarian Milieu*, 116–17: "As succinctly as possible: can a vocabulary of motives be freely extrapolated from a discrete collection of literary stereotypes composed by alien and mostly hostile observers, and thereupon employed to describe, even interpret, not merely the overt behaviour but also the intellectual and spiritual development of helpless and almost innocent actors?"

[22]See, for example, Rippin, *Muslims*; it is revealing that this work is much more concerned with historical problems and processes than it is with historical "facts".

[23]See Fred M. Donner, "The Formation of the Islamic State", *JAOS* 106 (1986),

that these letters are authentic, in the sense that they are not later creations foisted onto the name of ʻAbd al-Ḥamīd, one of course encounters the problem that while it is often possible to demonstrate that the attribution of a work to a particular person or period cannot be correct, it is usually far more difficult to prove that it is correct. Al-Qāḍī's paper demonstrates that it is precarious to address such problems from a limited perspective, not only because many of the indicators are circumstantial, but also because the context to which the material belongs is itself so complex. Political, social, cultural, philological, and religious considerations all come into play, and there are, in addition, more general questions. Of these, one of the most important is surely that of how to define the concept of authenticity itself: al-Qāḍī's analysis repeatedly reminds the reader that discussion must proceed at multiple levels which, though posing their own distinct difficulties, are all fundamentally interrelated. It is worth noting that while this problem is of course not unfamiliar to Byzantine and eastern church historians, the mechanisms and conventions for the establishment of a tradition, not to mention the overarching conceptual difficulties with which modern historians of the Arab-Islamic tradition must work, seem to be of a wholly different dimension. And this brings us back to one of the central concerns of the project: the need for more broadly based communication among specialists in the various fields.

Some of the same issues arise in relation to the paper by Leder, which concerns itself, at least in part, with the transition of originally oral material in the shape of *akhbār* into literary forms and conventions.[24] Not for the first time, one is struck by the similarity

283–96, for a discussion of this issue on the basis of non-literary materials, in response to arguments in Crone's *Slaves on Horses.* An invaluable basis for comparison is the case of Egypt: see H.I. Bell, "The Administration of Egypt under the Umayyad Khalifs", *BZ* 28 (1928), 278–86; Kosei Morimoto, *The Fiscal Administration of Egypt in the Early Islamic Period* (Kyoto, 1981).

[24]The question of oral vs. written transmission in early Islamic times is a highly controversial subject which has vexed scholars for many years. Recent discussions include Rudolf Sellheim, "Abū ʻAlī al-Qālī. Zum Problem mündlicher und schriftlicher Überlieferung am Beispiel von Sprichwörtersammlungen", in Hans R. Roemer and Albrecht Noth, eds., *Studien zur Geschichte und Kultur des Vorderen Orients. Festschrift für Bertold Spuler zum siebzigsten Geburtstag* (Leiden, 1981), 362–74; Walter Werkmeister, *Quellenuntersuchungen zum Kitāb al-ʻIqd al-farīd des*

of these problems to those presented for historians in New Testament scholarship, with the difference, however, that here the protagonists of the new system were much less concerned than the first Christians to adopt the modes of communication of the society around them or to reach it in its own terms. As in the case of Biblical materials more generally, the degree of change imposed by such a transfer from oral to literary remains tantalizingly hard to grasp; here, the various later Islamic accounts themselves assembled these individual *akhbār* units in quite different ways and with widely differing results, so that in methodological terms the effort to harmonize them, if indeed they can be harmonized, poses a broad range of major difficulties. Indeed, to pose the question of the reliability of the Arab-Islamic literary sources, of whatever genre, in terms of a historical positivism which admits only of either consenting or refusing to include a given piece of evidence among the building blocks for the straightforward construction of one's own historical narrative, is to ignore the highly specific literary characteristics of this material and the ways in which it participates in the formation of literary tradition. Leder's paper stresses the need to consider the nature of the material *before* moving to the apparently simple but actually highly problematic procedure of using it for historical reconstruction, for to seek data bearing a greater historical "sense" begs the central question of why the various accounts convey the sense they do.

In this case, the problem of oral versus literary arises again, and again acutely. Recent work on literacy and orality in other cultures may well provide insights, in particular by emphasizing that the one does not, as is commonly thought, necessarily exclude the other; as is well known already in the case of Islamic culture, oral tradition and oral teaching can continue to be of major importance long after the introduction of written records and literary accounts. The whole question of

---

Andalusiers Ibn ʿAbdrabbih (246/860–328/940). Ein Beitrag zur arabischen Literatur (Berlin, 1983); Gregor Schoeler, "Die Frage der schriftlichen oder mündlichen Überlieferung der Wissenschaften im frühen Islam", *Der Islam* 62 (1985), 201–30; *idem*, "Weiteres zur Frage der schriftlichen oder mündlichen Überlieferung der Wissenschaften im Islam", *Der Islam* 66 (1989), 38–67; Raif-Georges Khoury, "Pour une nouvelle compréhension de la transmission des textes dans les trois premiers siècles islamiques", *Arabica* 34 (1987), 181–96.

recording and memory in the seventh-century Near East (Christian as well as Islamic) invites further examination from this point of view, and in particular the use made in both traditions of authorities, including the manufacture of fictitious ones, and the claim either to eyewitness knowledge or to an unbroken chain of testimony.

With Lawrence Conrad's paper on the conquest of Arwād we meet the application to a particular problem of the differing Christian and Muslim historiographical traditions—something which though difficult to achieve is of course essential, not least because close analysis of specific literary traditions or types of material within them can sometimes cause the discussion to become wholly self-referential and to obfuscate the question of how (and to what extent) one is to move from texts to the world itself. It is of course true that different traditions pose their own specific problems, and that they often discuss topics and events on which other traditions are silent. But where comparative opportunities do exist a range of new issues emerges, among which one of particular importance is that of the relevance, or lack of it, of language in cultural borrowing, a topic which demands urgent attention from scholars. The extent to which themes, ideas, and information could be and were communicated between Greek and Syriac and between Syriac and Arabic was greater than is usually supposed, and it is especially noteworthy that the lines for such transmisisons are not satisfactorily explained by either religious or linguistic considerations. It is also striking that just as the Greek writer Theophanes draws on Syriac sources (though in Greek translation), so the Edessan Theophilus knows about the Muslim historiographical tradition and about Arab politics. Analysis of the different traditions together in relation to one problem, rather than in isolation from each other, also serves to highlight important differences between the traditions. In this case, one of the most salient contrasts is that between, on the one hand, the Greek and Syriac sources, with their strong emphasis on linearity, and, on the other, the very different way in which the Arab writers present material in the form of discrete units as *akhbār* (comparison with Leder's analysis is of course very fruitful here), which are then individually elaborated, combined, redivided, and so forth, according to the evolving priorities and questions posed by an audience becoming increasingly Islamic in its cultural orientation. Not only do the topics of interest obviously differ very greatly; so also, and importantly, do the ways in which they are recounted. With respect to the Arab-Islamic *futūḥ* tradition, we need to come to terms with the question of why it is that the more detailed knowledge which would certainly have been available on such events as the campaign for Arwād from the many who had themselves taken part in the conquest manifests so little trace in what has been handed down. In other words, the conspicuous differences between the Christian and Muslim traditions have to do not merely with the reliability or otherwise of their evidence, but also with wholly different approaches to the selection and organization of material within a literary text. At this point the question arises again of the extent of penetration of one tradition by another. It needs to be borne in mind that whereas some Christian authors may show awareness of the Arab historical writing that was being produced in their day,[25] the continued use of Greek in the early Islamic administration did not—in contrast to the comparable phenomenon in the barbarian kingdoms of the west—lead to the development of a non-Arabic literature composed in Greek, or indeed Syriac, for Arab patrons; the level of cultural transfer between Christian and Muslim literature remained not only low, but also strikingly asymmetrical.

The workshop concluded with a lively general discussion following on from remarks by Albrecht Noth, who made, among other points, the observation that while the workshop had addressed itself overtly to the literary source material, much of the discussion had still tended to center on the effort to extract historical information from it; solving the literary problems was, however, the essential preliminary to any reconstruction of history, and one which in this field is still unduly neglected. Great differences had been revealed between the Christian and Islamic literary traditions, but the disproportionate volume of the latter had perhaps not been sufficiently stressed; it is not only the conceptual problems and the weight of traditional interpretation which create difficulties for Arabic scholars, but also the sheer amount of material with which they have to grapple. By contrast, the eastern Christian material comprises a corpus which is far smaller, and further, has been exposed

[25] See Lawrence I. Conrad, "Theophanes and the Arabic Historical Tradition: Some Indications of Intercultural Transmission", *BF* 15 (1990), 1–44, esp. 4–10 on earlier discussions of this question.

to a greater degree of analysis for longer, even despite the deficiencies mentioned above. Nevertheless, the central problems of dating and authenticity affect both traditions, and in certain instances at least there is common ground—as where an author transmits material from both traditions,[26] or when a genre in one tradition finds close parallels in another or shares a common heritage with it[27]—and these connections should be as fully explored as the contrasts.

In relation to the Arabic material discussed on this occasion, the point was made that it perhaps gave non-specialists an over-negative impression, in that both papers on Arabic material concerned categories where problems of particular difficulty arise. It is also undoubtedly the case that the period of the conquests themselves, which was constantly in view in the workshop, and indeed has been so throughout the project, is by far the most difficult, for obvious reasons. On the other hand, while the later writers may seem superficially easier to approach, it must be borne in mind that such authors as al-Balādhurī, for instance, in fact appear at a comparatively late stage in a long process of development both in historical writing and in Islamic society itself. Al-Balādhurī may seem more accessible precisely because he is applying a more readily recognizable mode of historical thinking to the essentially *akhbār* material which is in fact the ultimate foundation of his knowledge, and thus presenting it in a digested—and hence digestible—form. If the main component of our Arabic material in fact rests ultimately on this substratum, there is no escape from the immensely difficult task of understanding the formation of a literary record out of such a basis. It is worth bearing in mind, however, that while this situation finds no parallel in the Greek or Syriac tradition, the possibility posed in Conrad's paper that the material on the seventh and eighth

[26] As, for example, the access to both Christian religious and Arab genealogical lore which may be discerned in the work of Hishām ibn Muḥammad al-Kalbī (d. 204/819), and the familiarity with both the traditional historiography of eastern Christianity and the emergent historical tradition of Arab Islam which is evident in Theophilus of Edessa. For the former, see Nabia Abbott, *Studies in Arabic Literary Papyri* (Chicago, 1957–72), I, 46–50; and on the latter, Conrad, "Theophanes and the Arabic Historical Tradition".

[27] See the illustrative case discussed in S.P. Brock, "A Dispute of the Months and Some Related Syriac Texts", *JSS* 30 (1985), 181–211; Geert Jan van Gelder, "The Conceit of Pen and Sword: On an Arabic Literary Debate", *JSS* 32 (1987), 329–60.

centuries in such mainstream eastern Christian historical sources as Theophanes, Agapius, Michael the Syrian, and the *Chronicle of 1234* is largely composed of recensions and versions of the contents of one lost Syriac chronicle from the very beginning of the 'Abbāsid caliphate also raises prospects for a reorientation of the historiographical agenda on these works along lines which are not without parallels in current discussions of the Arab-Islamic tradition.

Several other themes emerged from the general discussion. One obvious one concerns the need for greater awareness of regional differences when studying writers or groups of writers, and therefore greater emphasis upon variety of response. Nor is that all. Scholars often tend to write as though religious groups were themselves constant, whereas it is clear that at certain periods not only were many Christians converting to Islam, but also that there was considerable fluidity between the Christian sects themselves, as can be deduced from the prominently apologetic and polemical nature of so much contemporary literature. The seventh-century Near East was a world of fluctuating boundaries in many more senses than just the Christian/Muslim divide, as is manifest in many contemporary sources, pointing as they do also to the close proximity of Jews and Christians in the real world.[28] Religious divisions between Christians were another constant problem in terms of keeping communities together. Thus the patriarch Sophronius thought it more important in his Christmas sermon of 634 to strengthen his Jerusalem congregation in the Chalcedonian position than to describe in any but conventional terms the Arabs who had taken Bethlehem; indeed, the latter serve him mainly as the unwitting representatives of God's inevitable chastisement of weak and wavering Christians.

Within the distinct traditions certain points of special emphasis also emerged, in particular the importance of apocalyptic as a genre which can be seen both as symptomatic of and engendered by crisis. More can certainly be done here both on individual texts and on the fusion of themes and genres which seems to be taking place—the ps.-Methodius *Apocalypse*, for instance, contains the elements of revelation, homiletic,

[28] For the literature, and questions of "real" versus "literary", see now several important contributions in *TM* 11 (1991), including a new edition, with translation and commentary, of the *Doctrina Jacobi nuper baptizati*.

and world history, and we find apocalyptic elements spreading also in chronicles, in the Islamic *ḥadīth* material, and in Christian anti-Jewish polemic. Often the same key text, typically the book of Daniel, is used in different ways in a variety of works. It is tempting to see some of this material at least as a response to the tense conditions of the reign of ʿAbd al-Malik (685–705), when Muslim self-definition was itself finding expression through such means as the Umayyad building program of the 690s and ʿAbd al-Malik's policies of arabization.[29] Despite the huge volume of scholarly work which has been devoted to this period in the past, it is perhaps surprising that we still lack the kind of thick description which is needed for real cultural history. However, more detailed study of the sources from all the traditions along the lines pursued in the workshop, and especially their location in an increasingly close context, is bound to make possible a far more rounded and nuanced view even of such old and well-trodden problems as iconoclasm.

Also among the questions which kept presenting themselves were those of education and the place of literacy. But even more fundamentally, many of these sources have never been treated as literary texts, or as the products of individual writers; naturally the bias and interests of the authors are usually recognized, but less for their own sake than with a view to isolating the historical reliability of the information contained in the text. Yet not only is there a place for literary analysis of the texts themselves; there is also great scope for understanding the process whereby they were produced within their particular social milieu, that is, for seeing them as emerging from and themselves part of an evolving historical context. Questions such as those of education, literacy, audience, and literary patronage will remain as obscure as they are at present until much more of this basic study of individual texts has been done, yet these are the issues which are in fact critical to any understanding of what cultural change is taking place in this period. Even the apparently simple matter of assessing the degree of decline in

---

[29] On this see G.R.D. King, "Islam, Iconoclasm, and the Declaration of Doctrine", *BSOAS* 48 (1985), 267–77; A.A. Duri, *The Historical Formation of the Arab Nation: a Study in Identity and Consciousness*, trans. Lawrence I. Conrad (London, 1987), 4–133; Hawting, *The First Dynasty of Islam*, 1–11; Myriam Rosen-Ayalon, *The Early Islamic Monuments of al-Ḥaram al-Sharīf: an Iconographic Study* (Jerusalem, 1989; *Qedem* 28); Rippin, *Muslims*, 51–56.

the traditional Greek secular educational system and defining the results in relation to the educated classes in the late Umayyad period is actually extremely difficult.[30] A great deal is now known about the social background of the Byzantine administration which was developing elsewhere during the eighth and ninth centuries, and more of a picture is emerging concerning the severe limitations on access to books, yet a degree of learning continued all the same;[31] when the same kind of study can be applied cross-culturally to the Near Eastern provinces under Umayyad rule, there should be a better understanding of how society was actually changing.[32] We need to discover how far and how soon the very slow introduction into this established society of new and different Arab-Islamic patterns of recording and writing penetrated beyond the immediate religious and administrative needs, and not only how they developed themselves, but also what changes they brought to the place of writing in the existing religious and secular system. The suggestion is made below that there was already a high degree

[30]Some places, such as Jerusalem, are well documented and no doubt exceptional; yet whatever happened to the cities which had mainly supported it in the past, Greek learning did not even now simply come to a dramatic end. See, e.g., R.P. Blake, "La littérature grecque en Palestine au VIIIe siècle", *Le Muséon* 78 (1965), 27–43.

[31]See F. Winkelmann, *Byzantinische Rang- und Ämterstruktur im 8. und 9. Jahrhundert* (Berlin, 1985; *BBA* 53); Cyril Mango, "The Availability of Books in the Byzantine Empire, AD 750–850", in *Byzantine Books and Bookmen* (Washington, D.C., 1975), 29–46.

[32]This is not to suggest that such questions are being ignored in the study of early Islam: see, for example, Ruth Stedhorn Mackensen, "Background of the History of Moslem Libraries", *AJSL* 51 (1934–35), 114–25; 52 (1935–36), 23–33, 104–10; Abbott, *Studies in Arabic Literary Papyri*, I, 7–31; II, 5–83; Ṣāliḥ Aḥmad al-ʿAlī, *Dirāsāt fī taṭawwur al-ḥaraka al-fikrīya fī ṣadr al-Islām* (Beirut, 1403/1983). The problem is that such studies accept at face value reports which attribute to earliest Islamic times trends which may in fact represent (and in many cases must be) retrojections aiming to assert that current practice follows the example set by the Prophet and the earliest Muslims, and is therefore correct. In such a view of things all is of course reified and presented as fixed from the beginning, thus obfuscating the process of evolution and development which is precisely what we most seek to clarify. A way out of this dilemma is perhaps offered by the Islamic biographical dictionaries, which offer information on their subjects which is quite incidental and therefore less susceptible to tendentious presentation. See Richard W. Bulliet, "The Age Structure of Medieval Islamic Education", *SI* 57 (1983), 105–17.

of orality in the cultural context of seventh-century Greek literature, that is, that the balance was perhaps already changing before any real Arab-Islamic impact can be imagined. It is evident, on the other hand, that oral transmission played an enormous rôle in the earliest stages of Arab-Islamic historiographical development. If we put these two factors together, however, what is the result? At the very least, it may be that the conquest as such ceases to be the one decisive factor in cultural change that it has often appeared to be. There are certainly other such lines to explore further.

Many of the most central writings of the period are omitted here: for instance, the Qur'ān itself and the *ḥadīth*, wisdom literature, poetry, and so forth, and on the Christian side, hagiography, disputations, florilegia, theological writings as such, letters, conciliar materials, Syriac chronicles, and the like. No apology needs to be made for concentration within such a small compass. Nevertheless, not merely the list of omissions just given, but also the subject matter of some of the papers themselves raise fundamental questions of what is to count as historical evidence, or as a historical "source". A statement of our general purpose is therefore called for, which may of course be subject to later revision or limitation. Briefly, we believe that at this stage, when we are concerned with the complete process of cultural, social, and religious change, and not merely with a sequence of events, all material must be included that is relevant to the areas and the issues. Some types of writing are of course more obviously historical than others, and indeed, can be seen to belong to a clear tradition of historiography; but we do not see history as constituted only from such materials, nor do we relegate other types of writing to a lesser place. Ultimately we have to do with fundamental shifts in ways of thinking, believing, and belonging, and this as much in lands which remained under Byzantine rule as in those which passed to Arab control: if we are to come to grips with such basic aspects of changing consciousness, we must also be concerned with studying the ways in which that consciousness expressed itself.

Averil Cameron
King's College London

Lawrence I. Conrad
Wellcome Institute

1

Greek Historical Writing after Procopius: Variety and Vitality*

Michael Whitby
(University of St Andrews)

After Procopius

THE TWO GENERATIONS that follow Procopius and the emperor Justinian encompass the last phases both of Greek historiography in classical antiquity and of the traditional Graeco-Roman world delineated in these works; in the same way as the longevity and actions (even the unsuccessful actions) of Justinian influenced and overshadowed the accomplishments of his successors, so too did the historical works of Procopius loom over later authors. The magnitude of Procopius' achievement, whatever reservations we may now have about its qualities and characteristics as a history of its age, was real enough for his successors among the classicizing historians.[1] Agathias refers to the accuracy of his narrative of Justinian's reign, which made it unnecessary to treat the same matters again, and compliments him on the scale of his reading—the type of activity that Agathias found was hampered by

*In addition to the helpful comments by participants in the London workshop on 21 October 1989, I am grateful to the St. Andrews' Classics research seminar and, especially, to my wife Dr. Mary Whitby for discussion and criticism. Particular thanks are due to the workshop organizers for arranging this stimulating meeting.

[1]See Averil Cameron, *Procopius and the Sixth Century* (London, 1985).

his own need to pursue his legal career.[2] Such references should not be dismissed as "perfunctory approbation".[3] Menander was equally effusive: "It is not possible for me, nor otherwise is it pleasant, to hold up one's own wick in response to such great splendor of words. But it is sufficient for me to be involved in my own trifles...."[4] Theophylact, as in other respects, is slightly different from his classicizing predecessors in that he refers to Procopius without explicit praise: "This (the origin of the eunuch Solomon) has been recorded by the historian Procopius in the volume of his history".[5] The ecclesiastical historian Evagrius praised the diligence, elegance, and ability with which Procopius had narrated the Persian wars.[6] When Agathias ventured to disagree with Procopius, he did so with deferential courtesy, emphasizing that his own account was really based on superior evidence,[7] and noting that Procopius' opinion about the adoption by the Persian king of the emperor Arcadius' son, Theodosius II, was divergent because based on hindsight.[8]

It was, however, possible to avoid the influence of Procopius. John Malalas, in the first version of his *Chronicle* that terminated in the 530s, had produced an account of the Persian war of 527–32 which is in some respects superior to that in Procopius *Wars* I:[9] it is not distorted

[2]Agathias, *Historiae*, ed. Rudolf Keydell (Berlin, 1967); English trans. by J.D.C. Frendo (Berlin, 1975), regrettably omitting the periphrastic rhetoric to which Agathias devoted his literary talents. In general, see Averil Cameron, *Agathias* (Oxford, 1970). References: *Hist.* pref. 22; with II.9.1, IV.15.1, IV.29.5 ("sufficiently/clearly narrated"), IV.26.4 (Procopius' reading).

[3]So R.C. Blockley, *The History of Menander the Guardsman* (Liverpool, 1985), 3 n. 10.

[4]Frag. 14.2.

[5]Theophylact Simocatta, *Historiae*, ed. Karl de Boor, rev. Peter Wirth (Stuttgart, 1972), II.3.13; ed. with English trans. by Michael and Mary Whitby (Oxford, 1986). See also Michael Whitby, *The Emperor Maurice and His Historian* (Oxford, 1988).

[6]Evagrius Scholasticus, *Ecclesiastical History*, ed. Joseph Bidez and Léon Parmentier (London, 1898), IV.12; English trans. in Bohn's Ecclesiastical Library (London, 1854). For discussion, see Pauline Allen, *Evagrius Scholasticus the Church Historian* (Leuven, 1981).

[7]*Hist.* IV.30.4–5.

[8]*Ibid.*, IV.26.4–7.

[9]Malalas, *Chronographia*, ed. Ludwig Dindorf (Bonn, 1831); English trans., with

by bias in favor of Belisarius, and it provides a reasonable account of the events in which Procopius' hero was not directly involved. The continuator of the *Chronicle* working in Constantinople *ca.* 565 did not consult other parts of the *Wars*. The anonymous *Chronicon Paschale*, written in the 620s, is also silent about Justinian's wars, a reflection of its general lack of interest in military matters away from the capital.[10] It is only with Theophanes in the ninth century that parts of Procopius' *Wars* are incorporated into the chronicle tradition.[11]

Consideration of these reactions to Procopius introduces the three main categories of historical writing from the late sixth and early seventh centuries: the recherché classicizing authors Agathias, Menander Protector, and Theophylact, who sought to extend the work of Procopius; the ecclesiastical historian Evagrius, to be distinguished from these secular authors in terms of avowed subject but in fact comparable in terms of education and, increasingly towards the end of his work, of content as well; and the chroniclers represented by the continuator of Malalas and the *Chronicon Paschale*. In addition, there are fragments or descriptions of lost authors, the secular writers John of Epiphania and Theophanes Byzantinus, the ecclesiastical history represented by fragments in the *Anecdota Cramer*, and the chronicler John of Antioch, as well as indications of sources preserved through their use by later authors such as the patriarch Nicephorus and Theophanes.[12] On the fringes of historical writing are such works as the sermons attributed to Theodore Syncellus on the 626 siege of Constantinople and Antiochus Strategius on the loss and restoration of Jerusalem in 614–30, Archbishop John of Thessalonica's record of the miraculous actions of

---

notes, by Elizabeth Jeffreys, Michael Jeffreys, and Roger Scott (Melbourne, 1986).

[10] *Chronicon Paschale*, ed. Ludwig Dindorf (Bonn, 1832); English trans. and notes by Michael and Mary Whitby (Liverpool, 1989).

[11] Theophanes, *Chronographia*, ed. Karl de Boor (Leipzig, 1883–85); English trans. of AD 602–813 by Harry Turtledove (Philadelphia, 1982); see also Lawrence I. Conrad's contribution to this volume.

[12] John of Epiphania, Theophanes Byzantinus, and John of Antioch, ed. C. Müller, *Fragmenta Historicorum Graecorum*, IV–V (Paris, 1851, 1870); *Anecdota Cramer*, ed. J.A. Cramer, *Anecdota graeca e codd. manuscriptis Bibliothecae Regiae Parisiensis*, II (Paris, 1839); Nicephorus, *Opuscula Historica*, ed. Karl de Boor (Leipzig, 1880); new ed., with English trans. and notes, by C.A. Mango, *Nikephoros, Patriarch of Constantinople. Short History* (Washington, D.C., 1990).

S. Demetrius in favor of his city, and the panegyric poems of George of Pisidia, each of which describes historical events in a manner appropriate to the chosen literary medium.[13]

Thus the amount of Greek historical writing in this period is not inconsiderable in terms of quantity, and even if its quality is surpassed by Procopius it contributes very substantially to our knowledge of the Greek-speaking world in this period and of its relations with outsiders; it is the disappearance of this material after the 630s which permits the subsequent century or so to be categorized as the Byzantine "dark age". The importance of this post-Procopian material has been recognized in recent and current research, with the result that all the major works (apart from some of the fragments) are available in English translations, either annotated or with separate studies that can be consulted for elucidation.

It is clear that some people in this period of late antiquity were interested in historical information, in reading or composing it or persuading others to compose it. How wide this interest extended is, however, obviously debatable, and there seems to be no satisfactory way of establishing the range or depth of historical interest among the potential audience. There were, probably, a few people with a serious interest in the study of history, people whose enthusiasm could sustain them through the detailed accounts of the classicizing authors, and these enthusiasts would have coexisted with the educated élite. The latter would have had a less specialized interest in history, regarding it perhaps as a subject with which the educated ought to be familiar. A few people would have read the classicizing historians for literary reasons, but more would have been concerned to acquire the type of general awareness that could be obtained from the narrative in a chronicle.

It would perhaps be reasonable to assume that those with sufficient training to contemplate a career in imperial or ecclesiastical administration were more likely than not to have some level of interest in history. Where we have information about writers of history, they tend

---

[13]Theodore Syncellus, ed. Leo Sternbach, *Analecta Avarica* (Cracow, 1900); Antiochus, *La prise de Jérusalem par les Perses en 614*, trans. Gérard Garitte (Leuven, 1960; *CSCO* 203, *Scr. Iberici* 12); *Miracula S. Demetrii*, ed. Paul Lemerle, *Les plus anciens recueils des miracles de Saint Démétrius*, I, *Le texte* (Paris, 1979); George of Pisidia, ed. A. Pertusi, *Giorgio di Pisidia, Poemi I. Panegirici epici* (Ettal, 1960).

to be men with the legal training that gave access to a good official career. Agathias received at Alexandria the preparatory education for a legal course, after which he presumably moved to Constantinople for his legal training proper.[14] As a *scholasticus*, or qualified lawyer, he found that the stress of work diverted him from his historical interests: "but I, sitting in the royal stoa, unravel and study from morning until sunset many books full of judgments and business matters".[15] The quality of Agathias' education is manifest in the knowledge of, and interest in, classical culture displayed in his epigrams and collection of poems known as the *Cycle*.[16] In a preface whose frankness picks up the engaging openness of Agathias' own comments about his legal activities, Menander records that he had completed his legal studies but made very little use of this vocational training, preferring instead the excitement associated with the circus factions.[17] John of Epiphania and his cousin Evagrius were both *scholastici* in the service of Gregory, patriarch of Antioch,[18] and Evagrius informs us that he accompanied Gregory to Constantinople to assist in rebutting a variety of charges that included paganism and incest.[19] Theophylact had a distinguished legal career during Heraclius' reign,[20] and it is likely that the author of the *Chronicon Paschale* had administrative experience, probably ecclesiastical, that made him familiar with official records.[21]

Administrative service could provide the direct stimulus for composition. John of Epiphania was not the only man who felt inspired to describe events with which his career had brought him into contact: Peter the Patrician, the *magister officiorum*, produced a complete narrative of the discussions preceding the Fifty Years' Peace of 561–62

[14] *Hist.* II.15.7; see Cameron, *Agathias*, 140–41, with R.C. McCail, "'The Education Preliminary to Law': Agathias, *Hist.* II.15.7", *Byzantion* 47 (1977), 364–67.

[15] *Hist.* III.1.4.

[16] See Cameron, *Agathias*, Chap. II; R.C. McCail, "The Erotic and Ascetic Poetry of Agathias Scholasticus", *Byzantion* 41 (1971), 205–67.

[17] Frag. 1.5–17.

[18] See Allen, *Evagrius*, 2–3.

[19] *HE* VI.7; John of Ephesus, *HE* V.17.

[20] See Whitby, *Maurice*, 28–33.

[21] See *Chronicon Paschale*, 701:20–702:6; also Michael and Mary Whitby, *Chronicon Paschale*, xxvii–xxviii.

when he was the chief Roman negotiator, an account which accurately recorded the words and moods of Romans and Persians, albeit with some alleged partiality towards the author's contribution;[22] the Roman ambassador to the Turks, Zemarchus, may have published an account of his mission,[23] which might have resembled the description by Nonnosus of his family's diplomatic dealings with Arabia and Ethiopia, of which a description survives in Photius' *Bibliotheca*.[24]

Against this background to literary creativity, it is not surprising that the little specific information we have about patrons also points to the same official circles: Agathias was encouraged to turn from poetry to history by the younger Eutychianus, a man "who performs important tasks among the imperial secretaries".[25] Historians traditionally prefaced their works with allusions to the need to preserve the record of events from oblivion,[26] but it would appear that, at least until the end of the sixth century, there was still an audience with some interest in such accounts. Granted the size of the imperial administration this audience need not have been tiny, though the high-brow classicizing authors must have had fewer readers than the less demanding chroniclers. Common traditions of service in administration and practice in the law courts may have provided a unity and strength that could offset limited numbers.

Classicizing Historians

If, however, professional background points to similarities between historians, closer examination reveals considerable differences which demand that authors be treated individually within the different categories of historiography.[27]

---

[22] Menander, frag. 6.2.12–28.

[23] John of Ephesus, *HE* VI.23.

[24] Photius, *Bibliotheca*, *cod.* 3; ed. and trans. René Henry (Paris, 1959–77), I, 4–7.

[25] *Hist.*, pref. 11.

[26] Evagrius, *HE* pref.; John of Epiphania, 1.

[27] For a general discussion of historiography in the late Roman Empire, with references to further bibliography, see Brian Croke and Alanna M. Emmett, "Historiography in Late Antiquity: an Overview", in their *History and Historians in Late Antiquity* (Sydney, 1983), 1–12.

First, the secular classicizing historians. These authors are distinguished by the content, scale, and style of their works. They composed within a historiographical tradition that stretched back a millennium to Herodotus and Thucydides, the founding fathers of Greek historiography, who had established warfare and its causes, diplomacy, and politics as the main topics of historical narration. These themes could be illuminated by the insertion of appropriate speeches for participants, and the main characters would be judged by means of authorial comment; diversions for this narrative could be introduced in the form of digressions about geography, ethnography, events distant in time or space, and natural disasters (plagues, volcanoes) and other phenomena. The scale of the narrative was extensive—a classicizing author might well devote as much space to the events of 20 years as a chronicler did to 6000 years of world history—and its language was dignified in order to match the solemnity and importance of its subject matter. Such historiography was not an easy task,[28] and though any successful war quickly prompted the composition of commemorative accounts,[29] most of the writers who have survived the test of time could impose their own perspectives on the varied human events they were narrating. Modern commentators can fault the omissions and prejudices of their ancient predecessors, but this tradition did represent the supreme achievement of ancient historical narrative; it has been instrumental in shaping perceptions of the ancient world, and its importance is reflected in the number of studies devoted to it.

The daunting task of directly continuing Procopius fell, at the urging of various friends, to Agathias of Myrina, who had already established a reputation as a poet. He composed his *History* in five books during the 570s under the emperors Justin II and Tiberius, and by the time of his death had extended the narrative of Procopius from 553 only as far as 559. As a lawyer working in the courts of Constantinople, apparently with no imperial appointment since he continually had to worry about his work and the presence or absence of clients,[30] Agathias lacked the personal experience of military matters which contributes so

[28] Cf. Agathias, *Hist.* pref. 12.

[29] Lucian, *De historia conscribenda* (*How to Write History*) 2; Loeb trans. by K. Kilburn in *Lucian*, VI (London, 1959), 5.

[30] *Hist.* III.1.4.

much to Procopius' work. Furthermore, the years covered by his history were not, in spite of the lengthy treatment accorded them, characterized by dramatic military or diplomatic activity of major importance, apart from the Cotrigur invasion in winter 558–59: most of Agathias' military narrative is occupied with the tail end of the reconquest of Italy and confrontations with the Persians in Lazica, a peripheral conflict that was exempted from the truce that covered the rest of the eastern frontier. Such activity was unlikely to stimulate great historiography. Moreover, the eunuch Narses, the most successful of Justinian's generals, remained in Italy and so was unavailable as a focus for historical composition in Greek. As a result, it would be unfair to judge Agathias' historical abilities solely on the basis of his military narratives: style and the ornaments of history were what mattered more. The long digressions that Agathias devoted to the Franks and Sasanians have received detailed study, and it has been plausibly suggested that these provide the best test for his qualities as a historian: here the opportunity to compose a literary set piece freed Agathias from the constraints of straight narrative and allowed him to indulge personal interests, including a certain amount of research.[31]

Another illustration of Agathias' qualities is his treatment of the earthquakes of 551 and 557;[32] he had personal experience of both disasters, and they were clearly events which attracted his attention as opportunities for historical narrative blended with literary adornment, the mingling of the Graces with the Muses or the combination of the pleasurable with the useful that he saw as the function of history.[33] Agathias introduces the first earthquake with a temporal allusion, "About the same time, in the summer season...",[34] the vagueness of which has caused problems: his narrative has just reached the end of warfare in Italy in 554–55, but while this might appear the most obvious date, the disaster must be identified with the earthquake of 551 and the tem-

[31] See Averil Cameron, "Agathias on the Early Merovingians", *Annali della Scuola Normale di Pisa*, Ser. 2, 37 (1968), 95–140; *eadem*, "Agathias on the Sassanians", *DOP* 23–24 (1969–70), 1-150; *eadem*, *Agathias*, viii.

[32] Agathias' attitude to scientific explanations of the causes of earthquakes is examined in Cameron, *Agathias*, 91, 113–14.

[33] *Hist.* III.1.1–2.

[34] *Ibid.*, II.15.1.

poral reference interpreted as a general allusion to the whole of this particular phase of the Italian war; the correct date has been derived from chronicles, not from Agathias.[35]

He then notes the destruction of Beirut "the beautiful" which caused heavy loss of life among not only its natives, but also the young men of means who were attending the famous law school; the remnants of the law school migrated to Sidon, pending the restoration of Beirut. Agathias next introduces his own experiences at Alexandria, a city whose inhabitants believed they were exempt from earthquakes and so were extremely disturbed even by the very minor tremor which they suffered. Agathias confesses that he shared their fear because of the poor standard of building,[36] and explains that a factor in local concern was that the tremor seemed to disprove the scientific theory that underlay the city's belief in its immunity—hence an introduction to discussion of this theory, Aristotelian in origin, that earthquakes were caused by the explosive release of subterranean pressure generated by combustible exhalations; in Egypt, a low-lying country, such pressure was supposed to be dissipated automatically by seepage through the spongy terrain. Agathias comments that the proponents of this theory, perhaps an allusion to John Philoponus,[37] were not entirely devoid of persuasiveness and plausibility, but fell far short of the real truth since it is impossible for man to comprehend fully the invisible reality controlled by the divine mind and plan.[38]

Agathias now suggests that the digression is at an end: "So, enough of these things at least for me; but let the account return again to itself". But in fact this just signals the conclusion of the discussion of causation within the longer interlude of the treatment of the earthquake, since he now turns to another earthquake casualty of which he had experience, the island of Cos. Agathias stopped there during his voyage from Alexandria to Constantinople, and his account mirrors experiences of relief workers at a modern disaster. The city itself had been so thoroughly destroyed by a tidal wave that it was difficult to distinguish

---

[35] See Ernest Stein, *Histoire du Bas-Empire*, II (Paris, 1949), 757; followed by Cameron, *Agathias*, 138–39.

[36] *Hist*. II.15.7.

[37] See Cameron, *Agathias*, 113–14.

[38] *Hist*. II.15.12–13.

streets among the tangled remnants of buildings—the chaos which is still evident in the excavated remains of the agora at Cos. Few houses survived and, as at Alexandria, Agathias offers a comment on their construction technique, "only those constructed more humbly from unbaked bricks and mud";[39] the scattered survivors were in a state of complete shock, and their afflictions were increased by the pollution of the water supply. All that survived to adorn the city was the name of the Asclepiadae and the reputation of Hippocrates. An allusion to the recurrent nature of such disasters, which are rectified by subsequent reconstruction and repopulation, serves to introduce another internal digression, the history of Tralles on the Maeander, which illustrates the sequence of destruction and recovery. Tralles was obliterated during the reign of Augustus (27 BC), but was resurrected after a local peasant, Chaeremon, travelled as far as northwest Spain to seek imperial help. The rebuilt city survives to the present day, repopulated with Romans whose language, however, had been converted by the proximity of Ionia to a more Attic Greek. The description ends with an inscription in honor of Chaeremon that Agathias had seen on a visit to the city.

Now at last the historical narrative can resume with the beginning of Agathias' description of events in Lazica. The interlude of three chapters can be seen as a structural mechanism designed to separate two main narrative blocks, west and east, that also allows Agathias to show off his learning—the Aristotelian theory on earthquakes, the story of Chaeremon, the linguistic affinities of the inhabitants of Tralles, an epigram. But such a view may not do complete justice to the account. The earthquake was a major disaster which came too close to the young Agathias for comfort. He worried about the flimsiness of Alexandrian houses, he knew that large numbers of law students in Beirut had perished—wealthy well-educated youths like himself with hopes of a successful career—and he saw the destroyed city of Cos. It would be odd if such an experience had been without effect, and not surprisingly it seems to have prompted him to think about man's understanding of the natural world: the truth might be unknowable, but this does not mean that men should be amazed or perplexed, since history demonstrates both the recurrent nature of such disasters and also

[39] *Ibid.*, II.16.5.

humanity's ability to surmount them—a capacity revealed in the story of Chaeremon of Tralles, a story with a message for the refugees from Beirut waiting in Sidon for the reconstruction of their city or for the blank-faced survivors wandering in the ruins of Cos. Such belief in the power of man's will and effort has been seen as one of the factors that distinguishes Ammianus Marcellinus as a classical historian,[40] and the same judgment can be applied to Agathias. It was not impossible for Agathias to reconcile his sincere Christian beliefs with the inquisitive spirit and humanocentric interest of classicizing historiography.

The second and longer passage on earthquakes, describing the tremors at Constantinople in autumn 557, is introduced at the end of the eastern narrative and before the account of the Cotrigur invasion in winter 558–59;[41] the insertion is chronologically appropriate, but the passage again serves partly to separate two major narrative blocks. Agathias introduces the earthquake with a vague connective, "Not long before these events...", but then gives a more precise but elaborately obscure date with references to the Festival of the Names and the sun's advance towards the winter solstice and the zodiacal sign of Capricorn.[42] Agathias describes the earthquake in fairly general terms—shaking, noise, dust, fissures in earth and buildings—but with particular reference to human panic: people remained out of doors in spite of snow and frost; women, even women of status, consorted freely with men; order and respect were overthrown as slaves and the lower classes found themselves subject to the same peril as their former superiors.[43] Agathias then gives some minor details about buildings, noting that the effects were like those of other earthquakes, before turning to the human casualties with special reference to the *quaestor* Anatolius, who was apparently the only man of distinction to be killed. Anatolius, popularly regarded as an unjust administrator, was seen by some as the cause of the disaster, but Agathias could not accept that the punishment of one guilty

---

[40]See John Matthews, "Ammianus and the Eternity of Rome", in Christopher Holdsworth and T.P. Wiseman, eds., *The Inheritance of Historiography 350–900* (Exeter, 1986), 27. In general on Ammianus, see John Matthews, *The Roman Empire of Ammianus* (London, 1989).

[41]*Hist.* V.3–9.

[42]*Ibid.*, V.3.2.

[43]*Ibid.*, V.3.7–8.

man could explain the suffering inflicted on so many innocent people, or was consistent with the survival of many who were even more wicked than Anatolius.

Agathias then returns to the theme of the general panic, which produced a crop of prophets predicting apocalyptic doom and destruction—the sort of person who normally appears after such disasters and whose impiety evokes stronger condemnation from Agathias[44] than had the Aristotelian scientists with their attempts at a rational explanation. A less extreme manifestation of the fear was an onset of piety—supplications in church, correct conduct in business affairs, avoidance of wrongdoing; some people went so far as to abandon their property and become monks, churches received gifts, and the urban poor benefited from the unstinted charity of the rich. Agathias, who had himself once dedicated an icon to the archangel Michael for help in his legal exams,[45] knowingly comments that after the fear had subsided most people returned to their normal behavior.

At this point Agathias introduces another allusion to the Aristotelian theory of earthquakes as an opportunity for a digression on Anthemius of Tralles, his talented family, and his dispute with the lawyer Zeno which prompted him to invent a steam-powered device that replicated the effects of an earthquake. Agathias describes the invention, and dwells on Zeno's personal panic which of course aroused hostile reactions when he accosted acquaintances. Anthemius' exploitation of steam power appeared to offer support for the Aristotelian theory, but Agathias remained skeptical that such a toy could reveal the secrets of reality; to prove the irrelevance of such evidence he cites other mechanical inventions by Anthemius in the course of his dispute with Zeno. The digression on Anthemius ended, Agathias turns to the efforts of reconstruction initiated by Justinian, with particular reference to the rebuilding of the dome of S. Sophia. A brief description of the rebuilding is provided,[46] after which the reader is referred for further information to the *Ekphrasis* of Paul the Silentiary—Paul's education is praised, and a general summary of the poem provided. This con-

---

[44] *Ibid.*, V.5.3.

[45] *Anthologia Graeca* I.35; ed. and trans. Hermann Beckby (Munich, 1957–58), I, 124.

[46] *Hist.* V.9.3–5.

cludes the discussion of the earthquake and, after a chapter describing a recurrence of the plague[47] the narrative returns to military matters and the Cotrigur invasion.

The extensive coverage devoted to earthquakes might be regarded as another example of Agathias' inability to separate important from unimportant; after all, one earthquake is much like another, and the sober historical narrative only required a brief indication of when, where, and how many. But his decision to dwell on the disasters reveals his powers of observation and shows his awareness of the emotions and interests of his contemporaries: even if the rhetorical bombast is out of keeping with our tastes, the Herodotean richness of the digressions is still evident. Each encloses a "human interest" story, about Chaeremon and Anthemius both coincidentally of Tralles, and both stories are more than mere personal anecdotes. Chaeremon demonstrates the human determination that can overcome the worst of disasters, a sign of hope for the survivors of Beirut and Cos and a parallel for Justinian in his reconstructions at Constantinople; Anthemius and his mechanical toys point to the limits of human understanding of natural phenomena, a warning for devotees of Aristotelian theory, while Zeno's exaggerated personal panic suggests a comparison with the short-term reactions of the inhabitants of Constantinople to their real earthquake. Thus there is more than one level of interaction within these digressions, analogous to the different levels of interrelationship that have been found to operate between Agathias' speeches and adjacent narrative.[48]

It is not surprising that these disasters prompted reflections on causation and human understanding among survivors, and so appropriately in the historian. In this respect Agathias emerges with some credit: he reviews the popular scientific theory that can be traced back to Aristotle and shows how, though it has some illustrative value, it cannot fully explain the phenomena. But at the same time, he dismisses the simplistic view of disasters as punishment for specific wickedness and strongly condemns those who attempted to exploit religious superstitions. The result is a description of, and an intelligent commentary on,

[47] *Ibid.*, V.10.

[48] See Katherine Adshead, "Thucydides and Agathias", in Croke and Emmett, eds., *History and Historians in Late Antiquity*, 82–87.

earthquakes that can stand comparison with other ancient accounts of natural disasters (e.g. Thucydides or Procopius on plagues). However, this investigation also points to Agathias' weaknesses as a historian: he was a civilian lawyer with little or no experience of the remote military events that occupied much of his narrative, so that far from being able to enrich his accounts of fighting with personal knowledge, he might have problems in understanding information available to him, while his comments on the causes of such events and on human motivation inevitably seem trite.

Agathias' *History* had at least two continuators, Menander Protector and John of Epiphania, possibly a third if Theophanes Byzantinus connected his account of the Persian war of 572 with the termination of Agathias' work. Not much is known about Theophanes: his history covered ten years of war in ten books, suggesting a very detailed treatment, and it investigated the antecedents to the war in that the narrative began with events in Justinian's reign. It correctly set the contest within a very broad diplomatic context that embraced the Turks of Central Asia and Ḥimyarites of South Arabia, as well as Suania, Armenia, and Iberia, and it appears to have contained a digression on silk. The summary in Photius, which is all the information we have, makes it look like a traditional classicizing history (causation, diplomacy, warfare, and digression).[49]

It is possible to be rather more definite about John of Epiphania, since four pages survive from the beginning of his work and it also served as the basis for Theophylact's narrative of the Persian war of 572–91. He began his account with a specific reference to Agathias' continuation of Procopius, so that these predecessors at once point to his own place in the continuity of historiography and serve as a comparison for his own theme, the flight of Khusrō II to the Romans and his restoration, which is presented as the greatest event ever. John's official position as advisor to Patriarch Gregory of Antioch had brought him into contact with some of the participants, and he had served on an embassy to Persia, so that he continues the tradition of secular officials who narrate their own historical experiences. His narrative seems to have been limited to the eastern frontier, so that it was only a partial

[49] Photius, *Bibliotheca*, *cod*. 64; ed. Henry, I, 76–79.

continuation of Agathias (though consistent with the separate treatment of the Persian wars in Procopius, *Wars* I–II). Whether John included the traditional classicizing elements of speeches and digressions is unknown, but he did deal with causation (complete with a somewhat self-conscious Thucydidean reference), and appears to have produced a very detailed account of the diplomacy associated with the Persian civil war of 589–90 and Khusrō II's flight to the Roman Empire. What is perhaps most important about our limited knowledge of Theophanes and John is that they demonstrate that there was still sufficient interest in history to sustain the production of several different accounts of the same events: Menander Protector, who can claim credit as the principal continuator of Agathias, did not stand alone.

Menander too only survives in partial form, about 100 pages of text in the latest edition; we are fortunate to have so much, but this may not represent more than, say, ten percent of the original. Furthermore, most of this material is derived from one particular source, the *Excerpta de legationibus*, which means that conclusions about Menander as a historian must take into account this limited base. Menander himself tells us in his preface about his family, education, half-hearted career, and the inducements to composition provided by the emperor Maurice's patronage of literature. This preface has been described as a quirk or, more extravagantly, as a parody of the traditional preface to a historical work, but such judgments are at odds with the apparent conventionality of other aspects of the fragments.[50] It seems better to take Menander's frankness as a device to praise the generosity of Maurice, whose patronage managed to rescue even someone as indolent as, perhaps with exaggeration, Menander has made himself out to be. The result was a history that began after Agathias' death,[51] at the point where his *History* ended in 559, and continued at least as far as the capture of Sirmium in 581–82[52]—presumably to the death of Tiberius in August 582. Menander's *History* contained at least eight books, probably ten or more, so that his narrative must have been expansive in the traditional classicizing style.

[50]So Blockley, *Menander*, 2–3, 29, more cautiously at 3 n. 10; Barry Baldwin, "Menander Protector", *DOP* 32 (1978), 102.

[51]Frag. 1.26–28.

[52]Theophylact, *Hist*. I.3.5.

Although Menander's *History* is fragmentary, its importance and interest are perhaps more immediately obvious than in the case of the completely extant Agathias or Theophylact: the fragments present much sober diplomatic narrative, which modern historians tend to prefer, while the taste for sententiousness and bombast that Menander seems to have shared with Agathias and Theophylact is disguised.[53] It is probably fair to conclude that diplomatic procedure was a particular interest of Menander's rather than just a reflection of the changed circumstances of the late sixth century.[54] Roman diplomacy had been as active and complex during Justinian's reign, but Procopius did not record elaborate details about the negotiations that led to the Endless Peace of 532 or provide a verbatim text of that treaty, even though its significance for his narrative was no less than that of the Fifty Years' Peace of 561–62 for Menander's. Citation of important documents was accepted as a facet of classical historiography,[55] and in including the text of the 561–62 peace verbatim, Menander was both acknowledging this tradition and highlighting the significance of the treaty for his subsequent narrative. In Procopius,[56] the embassy of Julianus to the Ḥimyarites is narrated without the geographical and diplomatic detail that Menander preserved in his account of Turkish or Persian embassies. A late Roman historian with personal experience of diplomacy could, as with Priscus' account of his participation in an embassy to Attila,[57] reveal a wealth of detail about the context and atmosphere of diplomacy, as well as its mechanics, that would escape the notice or interest of ordinary authors.

Menander himself deserves credit for this diplomatic information, which serves to distinguish his work from those of other late classi-

---

[53]All three historians contribute roughly the same amount of material to the tenth-century Constantinian *Excerpta de sententiis*, which might indicate a similar level of sententious moralizing.

[54]Blockley, *Menander*, 16–17, tends to the view that there had been an increase in both diplomatic activity and its formality.

[55]E.g. Polybius, *Histories* III, 21–28; Loeb trans. by W.R Paton (London, 1922–27), II, 51–67, for three treaties between Rome and Carthage.

[56] *Wars* I.20.

[57]Priscus, frag. 11; ed. R.C. Blockley, *The Fragmentary Classicizing Historians of the Later Roman Empire*, II: *Text, Translation, and Historiographical Notes* (Liverpool, 1983), 242–81.

cizing historians,[58] and it would not be surprising if he had acquired some experience of active diplomacy and/or the administrative background during a career that may be dismissed rather too brusquely in his preface. At least he was familiar with official documents,[59] and his appreciation of Peter the Patrician's account of the 561 discussions suggests that he could assess quite precisely the accuracy of a published version of diplomacy.[60] As a *protector*, his official duties could have provided the necessary experience,[61] but it remains possible that Menander's title was honorary, a reward for the composition of the *History*.[62]

Another source of expertise might have been Menander's brother Herodotus (in spite of his loss of enthusiasm, similar to Menander's, for legal studies). This speculation is based on the two entries in the tenth-century lexicon known as the *Suda* for the rare word παραπρεσβεία ("dishonest diplomacy");[63] the first entry is from Menander's account of Justin II's reaction to the failure of an embassy, "and John was condemned for dishonest diplomacy in that he had not negotiated for the advantage of the state",[64] which is followed in the *Suda* by a second citation from an unspecified source: "And again: this man threatened to prosecute and condemn my brother for dishonest diplomacy". There are at least 120 extracts from Menander in the *Suda*, and this citation deserves the status of a possible fragment.[65]

---

58 In the *Excerpta de legationibus*, Menander occupies 90 pages, as opposed to 54 for Procopius, 18 for Theophylact, and only 3 for Agathias. By ignoring these writers to focus on the sequence of Eunapius, Priscus, Malchus, Menander, Blockley can suggest (*Menander*, 16) that there was an increase in the amount of diplomatic material preserved by historians.

59 Frag. 6.1.175–77.

60 Frag. 6.2.12–26.

61 Cf. frag. 26.1.15–20: preparation of tents to be used by ambassadors during negotiations. The *protectores* were originally a corps of imperial guards, but they had tended to become ornamental by the sixth century. See A.H.M. Jones, *The Later Roman Empire, 284–602* (Oxford, 1964), II, 636–40, 657–58.

62 Thus Blockley, *Menander*, 284 n. 304.

63 *Suidae Lexicon*, ed. Ada Adler (Leipzig, 1928–38), π 421.

64 Frag. 9.2.3–4.

65 This would have interesting consequences for the career of Herodotus, who would emerge as less of a wastrel than is suggested by Menander in frag. 1. Cf. frag. 34, with Blockley, *Menander*, 286 n. 328, who notes that the link phrase

The exact origin of Menander's interest is, however, of less importance than his ability to capture the spirit of late Roman diplomatic exchanges; it is this which makes his fragments an illuminating commentary on the briefer accounts of diplomacy preserved in other historians. One example from many is the narrative of Valentinus' second embassy to the Turks in 575–76.[66] In addition to his Roman companions, Valentinus took with him 106 Turks who had gradually accumulated at Constantinople as a result of the various embassies that had been exchanged in recent years (this summary reveals that Menander had not exhaustively narrated all possible diplomatic contacts). It is not clear why the Turks had remained behind, but the Romans had presumably been maintaining them in appropriate style in the hope of acquiring friends at the Chagan's court, who could be exploited now that Roman–Turkish relations had begun to deteriorate.

Valentinus' route to the war camp of Turxanthus is described, and then his encounter with the Turkish leader. Valentinus revealed the three purposes of his mission: to announce the accession of Tiberius as Caesar, to reaffirm the validity of the treaty that Justin II had made with Silzibul, and to suggest that action might be taken against their common enemy Persia. Turxanthus' reaction is an instance of the unpredictable and unpleasant experiences that diplomatic service might bring: accusing the Romans of employing ten tongues but a single deceit, he stuffed ten fingers into his mouth to demonstrate the Romans' faithlessness in their dealings with the Turks and their fugitive slaves, the Varchonites or Avars. Diplomacy often depended on such expressive gestures. Valentinus was forced onto the defensive, pleading with Turxanthus to respect diplomatic practice and not to abandon his father Silzibul's commitments.

It turned out that Silzibul was so recently deceased that the envoys witnessed the funeral rites, which included human sacrifice, and were also obliged to participate in the general grief by slashing their faces in the approved manner. After the funeral and further conversations, Valentinus was permitted to proceed east to see other Turkish lead-

"And again" in the *Suda* is not a sure sign of the identity of authorship of adjacent fragments.

[66] Frag. 19.1.

ers, though his mission had already been undermined by Turxanthus. Valentinus' achievements in the east are not preserved, but further humiliations were inflicted by Turxanthus during the return journey, which coincided with the capture by the Turks of Bosporus, the Roman outpost at the east of the Crimea peninsula.

The contrast between the informativeness of this narrative and the account by Theophylact[67] of a comparable mission to the Avar Chagan in 583 is greatly to Menander's credit. Theophylact's treatment is dominated by a long harangue by one of the Roman ambassadors that probably bears little resemblance to what was actually said, and by a rhetorical description of the Chagan's anger whose linguistic extravagance cannot compensate for the absence of the directness contained in Menander's portrait of Turxanthus. In Menander's accounts of diplomacy, the extant speeches are normally brief and focused on the issues under discussion, and the participants often emerge as real people with differing characteristics and abilities.

Another distinctive feature of Menander's work is the personal commentary that he introduces: he explains at length his decision to record as accurately as possible the 561 negotiations, and offers his personal assessment of Peter the Patrician's account.[68] He notes his lack of surprise at the transience of Gothic power, which merely demonstrates the inevitability of historical change;[69] he comments on the Turkish offer to sell iron to Zemarchus as an indication of their wish to demonstrate their access to iron mines,[70] and interprets the transfer of the title Maniach to a young son of the former holder as a result of the friendship and loyalty of the father to the Chagan Silzibul.[71] On the Gepid leader Cunimund's approach to Justin II for help, he expresses his disbelief in such shameless diplomacy by someone who was already revealed as a breaker of agreements;[72] he also comments on the inappropriate tone of Khusrō's letter to Justin.[73] Most of these personal interventions

[67] *Hist.* 1.4.6–6.3.
[68] Frag. 6.2.
[69] Frag. 7.6.
[70] Frag. 10.3.4–8.
[71] Frag. 10.3.96–101.
[72] Frag. 12.2.23–25.
[73] Frag. 18.1.20.

are in the form of "I think", and they underscore Menander's ability to offer a personal and informed commentary on the diplomatic narrative which survives from his *History*.[74] This commentary goes far beyond the shallow labelling of foreigners as arrogant, irascible, and imprudent,[75] and can point to changes of tone in diplomatic discussions as they progress from polite niceties and stock grumbles to the real substance of a dispute,[76] or include a critique of the diplomatic performance of Roman emperors, ranging from intelligence to unreasonable confidence.[77] Menander's approach to historiography reveals that there was no failure of nerve in the writing of critical history in late antiquity.

Another area of personal comment is in the field of religion. With regard to the Persian Christian Isaozites, Menander says that his admiration was such that he decided to compose a hexameter epigram on this martyr, which he then quotes.[78] Christianity was clearly an integral part of Menander's thought world and method of historical explanation: Roman failures before Maurice took command in 578 are attributed to divine anger caused by the army's maltreatment of Roman subjects,[79] but probably also to the soldiers' laziness over the construction of proper camps, a practice which Maurice had to reintroduce.[80] The Persian victory against Maurice in the 581 campaign is ascribed to the insubordination and indiscipline of other generals that wrecked Maurice's careful plans and brought divine displeasure on the whole Roman eastern army.[81] As far as one can tell from the fragments, Menander felt no qualms about discussing Christian matters: when the Romans besieged Chlomaron in 578, the Persian commander tried

[74] Thus my assessment of Menander is in contrast to that of Blockley, who characterizes him as "a worldly-wise, somewhat cynical character" who seems to become "rather bored" by diplomatic complexities (*Menander*, 2, 18).

[75] Frags. 21.43–47, 23.9.102.

[76] Frag. 20.1.34–20.2.9.

[77] Frag. 9.3, 16.1, both Justin II.

[78] Frag. 13.3. His predecessor Agathias was one of the most productive epigrammatists of the previous generation, and had accepted the similarities between poetry and historiography (*Hist*. pref. 12).

[79] Frag. 23.4.

[80] Frag. 23.3.

[81] Frag. 23.11.

to use the local Nestorian bishop and the wealth of the Christian community to purchase the city's escape, but the pious Maurice refused to be bought;[82] the Avar Chagan, wishing to impress his sincerity upon Roman negotiators, undertook to swear a Roman oath, and this is administered upon the Bible by the archbishop of Singidunum;[83] Tiberius' generous decision to return prisoners to the Persians is described as "especially pleasing to God";[84] the Persian envoy Sebukht is identified as a Christian, and his equable and reasonable words to the rash Justin are praised, his message being a plea that the Romans should not attack their co-believers.[85] Against this background, the description of Isaozites' martyrdom causes no surprise,[86] and there should be fewer doubts about the ultimate authenticity of the account of the transfer of the relic of the Holy Cross from Apamaea to Constantinople.[87]

Fragmentary remnants of historians whet the appetite for what has been lost, and Menander is no exception. His diplomatic knowledge, his willingness to offer personal opinions, and the precision and detail of much of his narrative[88] are tantalizing; even though there are some signs of lapses of organization in narrating military matters, and the sententious moralizing of the complete work may have been as irritating to modern readers as that of Theophylact, we have undoubtedly lost much valuable evidence.

By contrast, Menander's successor Theophylact survives to reveal the blemishes that would largely have been obscured if the extracts preserved in the Constantinian *Excerpta* alone existed. Although a gap of about one generation separated his historical composition from that of Menander, Theophylact saw himself as the latter's continuator, declining "to relate again what has already been clearly reported" with regard to the capture of Sirmium in winter 581–82, whose "circumstances were clearly declared by the famous Menander".[89] This perception of a his-

[82] Frag. 23.7.
[83] Frag. 25.1.77–87.
[84] Frag. 23.8.1–2.
[85] Frag. 16.1.39–52.
[86] Frag. 13.3–4.
[87] Frag. 17; see Whitby, *Maurice*, 244 n. 42.
[88] Cf. the precise date in frag. 10.2.
[89] *Hist*. I.3.5.

toriographical continuity that had been briefly interrupted by Phocas' reign should suggest that theories about a "profound change in the nature of historical writing" in the interval are misguided.[90] There are differences between Theophylact and his predecessors in the historiographical tradition, but they are attributable to the circumstances of composition and to his personal proclivities as an author, a reflection of the individuality of late Roman historiography, rather than to some more fundamental development. The most significant of these differences is perhaps indicated by the nature of modern studies of Theophylact, in which attention has been devoted, possibly to excess, to the question of his sources: where Procopius and Agathias seem to have gathered oral reports of events, and Menander probably combined his consultation of diplomatic archives with oral enquiries, Theophylact was basically a secondhand compiler who created a historical narrative by reworking, integrating, and sometimes interpreting the narratives of earlier writers.[91]

One aspect of this difference is in attitudes to human endeavor. Agathias, in his earthquake digressions, had upheld the traditional belief that the efforts of mankind would achieve results, whereas Theophylact, in his discussion of predestination, adopted a less positive compromise between the restraints of divine foreknowledge and the freedom of the individual.[92] Another difference is that whereas his predecessors narrated events that had occurred during their adult lives,[93] Theophy-

[90] Thus Joseph D.C. Frendo, "History and Panegyric in the Age of Heraclius: the Literary Background to the Composition of the *Histories* of Theophylact Simocatta", *DOP* 42 (1988), 143.

[91] See Whitby, *Maurice*, Chaps. IV and VIII; Thérèse Olajos, *Les sources de Théophylacte Simocatta historien* (Leiden, 1988).

[92] Theophylact, *On Predestined Terms of Life*, ed. and trans. Charles Garton and Leendert G. Westerink (Buffalo, 1978). The sense of uncertainty revealed in the conflicting arguments of this dialogue, and in the compromise conclusion, may be analogous to the uncertainty and insecurity detected by John Haldon in the *Questions and Answers* of Anastasius of Sinai (see Haldon's paper in this volume).

[93] This is clearly true for Procopius, whose appointment as Belisarius' secretary marks the beginning of the main narrative in *Wars* I, and of Agathias, who experienced the earthquake of 551 as a student at Alexandria. There is no evidence for Menander's date of birth, but he was able to offer informed personal comments on some of the earliest events he narrated, the 561–62 peace discussions.

lact was probably both young and living in Egypt during Maurice's reign, so that he did not have any personal information to contribute, even to his narrative of Maurice's overthrow in 602.[94] Furthermore, the most likely date for the composition of his *History* is the middle years of Heraclius' reign, when imperial military success stimulated a reawakening of interest in historiography.[95] As a result, Theophylact not only lacked personal experience of the events he was recording, but also probably found it impossible to discover many eyewitnesses to assist him. The only instance of personal involvement in the acquisition or verification of information is the assertion that he had investigated the story that Maurice's eldest son Theodosius had survived the massacre of Maurice's family in 602, only to perish a few years later in the east;[96] this does not represent a great contribution. This lack of direct contact with his subject matter may explain the obliqueness of his historical approach: Theophylact presents his narrative as the recitation of History personified, his patron the patriarch Sergius is alluded to as "the great high priest and prelate of the universal inhabited world",[97] while Theophylact's own name is only recorded in the title to the work.

Theophylact's intention was to extend Menander's *History* at least as far as the "tyranny" of Phocas' reign,[98] quite possibly as far as Heraclius' triumph over the Persians,[99] but as a first installment he produced a narrative of Maurice's reign (582–602); there is no evidence that the projected continuation was ever composed. The com-

---

[94] See L.M. Whitby, "Theophanes' Chronicle Source for the Reigns of Justin II, Tiberius and Maurice (AD 565–602)", *Byzantion* 53 (1983), 335–37. Frendo, "History", 150, ingeniously sees "definite pieces of autobiographical information" underlying the allegorical dialogue that precedes Theophylact's *History*, but there is no evidence to support his suggestion that Theophylact had already received imperial recognition as an author under Maurice.

[95] Whitby, *Maurice*, Chap. II. The reference to the Heraclidae at *Dial*. 6 does not prove that the elder Heraclius was still alive (*contra* Frendo, "History", 144 n. 10); this mythical allusion to the children of Heracles, who restored Dorian legitimacy in the Peloponnese, probably points to the younger Heraclius (the emperor) and his cousin Nicetas.

[96] *Hist*. VIII.13.5.

[97] *Dial*. 8. See Whitby, *Maurice*, 32–33; Frendo, "History", 144–45 n. 11, repeats the assertion that Heraclius was Theophylact's patron, but offers no new evidence.

[98] *Hist*. VIII.14.10.

[99] *Ibid*., VIII.12.13–14.

pleted text looks back beyond the interruption of Phocas' reign to the traditional topics of classicizing historiography, namely warfare, diplomacy, and major events in the capital. Naturally the treatment of events is influenced at points by the contemporary concerns of the 620s, since the desperate fugitive Khusrō II of 590 had turned into the arrogant destroyer of Rome's eastern provinces in the early seventh century, while in the Balkans Maurice's aggressive defense had become impossible, a dangerous provocation of the Avar Chagan who had to be conciliated by Heraclius in the absence of military forces.[100] It would, however, be a misrepresentation of Theophylact's method to view such contemporary references as the main function of his narrative or to conclude that the main purpose of the *History* was indirect panegyric of Heraclius.[101] The family of Heraclius is naturally praised when the account treats the actions of the elder Heraclius, the emperor's father;[102] but overall, the interaction of authorial present and narrative past is comparable to that in Agathias (a narrative of Justinian's reign, but composed under Justin II and Tiberius). The chroniclers demonstrate that traditional forms of historical narration were quite possible under Heraclius, at least down to the triumph over Persia,[103] and Theophylact himself had contemplated extending his own account to record seventh-century events. His work was a written continua-

[100] See Whitby, *Maurice*, 334–36.

[101] This is the hypothesis of Frendo, "History", though he has to admit (153) that it cannot be applied to the latter half of the work. Ancient authors were not usually reticent about praising individuals, especially prominent contemporaries; it seems implausible that Theophylact would have had to devise the "hitherto unexploited" technique of "panegyric by indirection" for his historical narrative (or that readers would have understood this approach). Frendo's treatment (151–52) of the actions of Philippicus is particularly fanciful: little is known about Philippicus' military command in Heraclius' reign, although the Armenian historian Sebēos describes it as a success (trans. Macler, 66–67), so that it is difficult to take Theophylact's presentation of Philippicus' actions in 584–86 as a reflection of his achievements *ca.* 614. For explanation of the Scipio parallel applied to Philippicus, see Whitby, *Maurice*, 279–80 n. 6.

[102] Compare the treatment by Ammianus of the elder Theodosius, whose son was emperor when the work was finished; Ammianus Marcellinus, *Res Gestae* XXIX.6.15; Loeb trans. by J.C. Rolfe (London, 1950–52), III, 291.

[103] *Contra* Frendo, "History", 151, who asserts that "there was no time for the lengthy and leisurely composition of a detailed chronicle of events".

tion of the literary record of his predecessors, directed at the same audience-cum-readership among the officials of Constantinople as their histories had been.[104]

Direct comparison with Agathias and Menander tends to highlight Theophylact's deficiencies. In providing an account of an earthquake, Theophylact briefly notes the occurrence and pompously alludes to the Aristotelian theory of causation (without necessarily understanding it); but there is no description of the damage, and the impact on the populace is encapsulated in an image of a teacher surprising children playing at dice[105]—the simile is not unattractive, but lacks the immediacy of Agathias' depictions. It appears that Theophylact took his information on the earthquake from a chronicle, but attempted to elevate its stylistic level and brevity into the grandiloquence expected of a classicizing author. With regard to diplomatic contacts, Theophylact shows little interest in the type of detailed account provided by Menander, and instead his main concern is with the rhetorical presentation of the arguments, whether by Romans or their adversaries.[106]

Granted these limitations, as well as the fact that Theophylact seems to have had no geographical knowledge or experience of military matters which could help him to make sense of the available source information, his significance as a historian might be questioned. His basic value depends on the fact that the Byzantine taste for his style of

[104] Frendo, "History", 147–49, regards Theophylact as an innovative author who was concerned to address an audience of hearers, not readers, but this theory is based on an excessively literal interpretation of Theophylactean imagery. Recitation by a historian of select extracts was not uncommon; all the classicizing historians of late antiquity may have done this, and it would not be surprising if Theophylact continued the tradition; but, as mortals, they would be aware of the existence of potential readers beyond their immediate vicinity or after their death. One consequence was the conflation of language denoting writing and speaking (see, for example, Ammianus Marcellinus, XXXI.16.9), which is certainly less novel in Theophylact's case than Frendo implies ("History", 148). Theophylact's careful introduction of metrical clausulae, for example in his paraphrase of Diodorus (VII.17), reflects his desire to charm not only the hypothetical immediate audience, but also the inner ear of the reader.

[105] *Hist.* I.12.8–11.

[106] E.g. *Hist.* I.5, 15; VI.11.

rhetorical exposition ensured that his narrative survived to preserve information from historical sources that would otherwise have been lost, and that his own weaknesses as a historical interpreter prevented him from imposing too many of his own distortions onto this source material. Thus his narrative of the Persian wars was based, without acknowledgement, upon John of Epiphania, and it was John's experiences as an eyewitness in the entourage of Gregory of Antioch that account for the detail and quality of Theophylact's description of the revolt of Vahrām and the flight of Khusrō II in Books IV and V. The account of Maurice's Balkan wars was in the main derived from an unknown contemporary witness. This was probably less thorough than John and had a specific bias in favor of one of Maurice's commanders, the general Priscus, who survived the revolt of 602 to prosper under Phocas and become the new emperor's son-in-law; but reasonable sense can be made of Theophylact's narrative when his evidence is interpreted in the light of Balkan geography and of the prescriptions for Balkan warfare contained in the contemporary *Strategicon* of Maurice.[107]

Theophylact's main contribution as a historian was to amalgamate these eastern and western narratives into a single account, not without some chronological hiccups, and to add literary ornament in the form of speeches, moralizing comments, complex style, and the occasional digression. In the case of Agathias, the digressions can plausibly be seen as the author's primary historiographical interest, but in Theophylact the longer traditional digressions—such as the narrative of the early stages of the Persian war,[108] or the "investigation" of the Nile flooding,[109] which is introduced as a topic of particular interest to Theophylact as an Egyptian[110]—were close copies of earlier sources (John of Epiphania and Diodorus Siculus respectively).

It seems that stories with a Christian slant appealed personally to Theophylact. Some of these were probably available in written form, since it is likely that a hagiographical account of Maurice, focusing on

[107]Ed. G.T. Dennis (Vienna, 1981); English trans., *idem* (Philadelphia, 1984); further discussion in Whitby, *Maurice*, Chap. IV, esp. 130–32.

[108]*Hist.* III.9–18.

[109]*Ibid.*, VII.17.

[110]"It is natural and not unsuitable that we should have an affinity for the descriptions of the Nile" (*ibid.*, VII.16.10).

his saintly death together with the portents that presaged it and other proofs of his goodness, had been compiled shortly after Heraclius' accession as part of the condemnation of the ousted Phocas.[111] However, it was Theophylact's decision to retail these in his classicizing *History* and to incorporate other Christian material, and they are worth examining as one of the personal contributions he made to the historical narrative. One story, the miraculous announcement of Maurice's death in 602 by talking statues at Alexandria,[112] was reported at the time to a relative of Theophylact's, Peter, the Augustal prefect of Egypt, a personal allusion which is probably intended to authenticate a story which is otherwise merely a variant of a hagiographic proof of sanctity.[113]

Some of the stories are developed at length, as for example the proofs of the miraculous nature of the effusions at two martyr shrines in the vicinity of Constantinople. At the shrine of Glyceria at Heracleia, the miracle ceased when a priest accidentally presented a silver bowl, polluted by use in pagan rites, to catch the effusions, but this in turn brought about the capture and execution of the covert pagan.[114] At the shrine of Euphemia at Chalcedon, the emperor Maurice himself, seeking to check the authenticity of the annual issue of blood on the anniversary of the martyrdom, had the shrine sealed—but the blood still flowed, evoking a repentant reaction from Maurice: "God is wonderful in his saints".[115] The former story, about polluted silver, also occurs in the *Life* of Theodore of Sykeon, where it demonstrates Theodore's

[111]For the basic outline, see the Syriac *Life* of Maurice, ed. and trans. François Nau in *PO* 5 (1910), 773–78; and for discussion, Whitby, "Theophanes", 340, and *Maurice*, 106–107. The evidence for this hagiography of Maurice is considerably better than for Frendo's hypothesis ("History", 156) that this material on Maurice originated in a life of the Patriarch John the Faster: the notion of John as a corrector of Maurice relies on two stories in John of Nikiu, who was hostile to Maurice and keen to present him in as unfavorable a light as possible. There survives one chapter of a life of John the Faster cited at the Second Council of Nicaea in 787 (see Mansi, XIII, 80e–85c), but this offers no support to Frendo's theory; it is implausible that the life of this patriarch (who died in 596) would have narrated Maurice's death in 602 with all the details that can be attributed to the hagiography of Maurice.

[112]*Hist*. VIII.13.7–14.

[113]Cf. *Life of S. John the Almsgiver*, trans. in Elizabeth Dawes and Norman H. Baynes, *Three Byzantine Saints* (Oxford, 1948), *cap*. 46, vision of Sabinus.

[114]*Hist*. I.11.

[115]*Ibid*., VIII.14.

discernment in realizing that the silver was unsuitable for use in the communion service: the chalice in question had formerly been a prostitute's chamber pot (nothing about pagans or miraculous effusions).[116] This story was clearly part of the common répertoire of miracles that could be adapted to suit particular individuals and circumstances; the fact that Theophylact knew a version of the story in which the purpose was the efficacy of miraculous effusions, coupled with the similar concern in the Euphemia story, points to a contemporary interest in this topic.

Theophylact's ready acceptance of Christian material is also evident in his military narrative, though his allusions to Christian matters tend to be much more periphrastic than Menander's, as for example in his description of a monastery of John the Baptist burned by the Persians:

> Here indeed there happened to be an academy of men who spend their lives in thought: these men are in fact called monks, and their task is to anticipate departure from the body, to be dead while living, and to transmigrate to higher things through a sort of prudent madness.[117]

God did intervene in human affairs, for example punishing the Avars with an outbreak of plague in retaliation for the destruction of the shrine of the martyr Alexander at Drizipera,[118] and Theophylact describes what was standard practice in sixth-century Roman armies, the use of prayers and icons to win victory.[119] The long Persian narrative in Books IV and V culminates, after the reinstatement of Khusrō II, with hagiographic stories: a summary of the life of the noble Persian lady, Golindouch, who converted to Christianity, and of two dedications by Khusrō to S. Sergius at Resapha (al-Ruṣāfa) in return for services rendered. The text of the dedications is also recorded by the church historian Evagrius,[120] an example of the overlap of interests between

---

[116] *La vie de Théodore de Sykéon*, ed. and trans. A.-J. Festugière (Brussels, 1970), *cap.* 42.

[117] *Ibid.*, I.14.8.

[118] *Ibid.*, VII.15.1–3.

[119] *Ibid.*, II.3.4–9; cf. III.1.11–12 (unsuccessful); also Maurice, *Strategicon*, II.18, VIII.2.1; and pref. 36–56, for the principle.

[120] Evagrius, *HE* VI.21.

the two traditions. The clutch of stories serves both to reinforce belief in the power of faith and of the saints, even in foreign lands, and to touch on a contemporary interest, since in the years 628–30 Heraclius was attempting to install the Christian Shahrvarāz on the Persian throne.[121]

With Christianity playing such a part in the *History*, it is natural that important speeches should be made by bishops: thus Domitian of Melitene celebrates the return of Martyropolis, and harangues the Roman army en route to restore Khusrō;[122] the former certainly has contemporary echoes in that it reflects the language and tone of the victory dispatch sent by Heraclius to announce the death of Khusrō in 628.[123] Two other speeches which deserve notice because they shed light on Theophylact's interests are those of the emperors Tiberius to his successor Maurice, and Justin II to Tiberius on the latter's elevation as Caesar and adoption.[124] Both contain passages prescribing the ideal qualities of an emperor.[125] The placing of Tiberius' speech (which is Theophylact's own composition) in the opening chapter of the *History* means that the issue of leadership is firmly presented to the readers—in effect, they are invited to draw up a balance sheet for the various rulers presented in the course of the *History*. The topic is brought in again when Theophylact's excursus on the earlier stages of the Persian war provided an opportunity to interrupt the military narrative by inserting an account of the elevation of Tiberius, complete with the actual speech (or part of it) delivered by Justin. The qualities of leaders are introduced once more, this time from a negative standpoint, during the "trial" of the Persian king Hormizd,[126] where Hormizd critically analyses the abilities of his son and chosen successor Khusrō II and discourses on the evils of tyranny, while his

[121]See Cyril Mango, "Deux études sur Byzance et la Perse sassanide II: Héraclius, Shahvaraz et la vraie croix", *TM* 9 (1985), 105–17.

[122]*Hist.* IV.16, V.4.

[123]*Chronicon Paschale*, 727–34.

[124]*Hist.* I.1, III.11.

[125]For a discussion which places these speeches in their generic context, see Günter Prinzing, "Beobachtungen zu 'integrierten' Fürstenspiegeln der Byzantiner", *JÖB* 38 (1988), 1–32.

[126]*Hist.* IV.4–5.

accuser Vindōē reviews the misfortunes of Hormizd's own tyrannical reign. This debate can be seen to function on more than one level simultaneously— apart from its direct relevance to its immediate context in the narrative, the passages on tyranny would bring to the mind of a Roman reader the disasters of Phocas' tyranny,[127] while the attack on Khusrō II would tie in with the portrayal of him in the 620s as "the God-abhorred Chosroes...ingrate, arrogant, blaspheming, opponent of God".[128]

Ecclesiastical Historiography

With Theophylact the succession of classicizing historians of late antiquity terminates; the reasons for this will be examined, but only after other types of historiography have been reviewed. Ecclesiastical historiography, like secular, had a recognized succession of practitioners, so that Evagrius of Epiphania, when he came to compile a history of the church in the late sixth century, related himself explicitly to his orthodox predecessors Eusebius, Sozomen, Theodoret, and Socrates in order to take up their narrative. The notion of historiographical continuity, secular as well as ecclesiastical, was important to Evagrius, as can be seen from the survey of historians at the end of Book V, which reveals the wealth of secular writers in comparison with the dearth of church historians.[129] Greek ecclesiastical historiography had proceeded by fits and starts:[130] although Gelasius in the late fourth century continued Eusebius, his contribution was ignored by fifth-century writers,[131] so that the tradition appeared to have been dormant between the 320s and the flurry of activity under Theodosius II. There was then another apparent interruption of over a century, since Evagrius seems not to have known Theodore Lector or the continuator of the 560s whose work

[127] The tyranny of Phocas was still relevant in the 620s as a means of explaining the misfortunes of the early part of Heraclius' reign.

[128] *Chronicon Paschale*, 729.

[129] Evagrius, *HE* V.24.

[130] Thus I would not accept the notion of a "strong eastern tradition of church history" (Croke and Emmett, "Historiography", 9).

[131] E.g. Sozomen, *HE* I.1.

is represented in the *Anecdota Cramer*,[132] and instead returned to his Theodosian predecessors to continue their narratives from *ca.* 440 to his own time. This provided Evagrius with an opportunity that could be exploited to praise and defend the actions of his employer, Gregory of Antioch, whose death marks the conclusion of the whole work.[133]

Church affairs were the primary concern of ecclesiastical historiography, and in the aftermath of Constantine's establishment of Christianity this principally meant the progressive elimination of pagans and the struggle to establish "orthodoxy" (depending upon the author's definition of orthodoxy), coupled with edifying stories about Christian heroes—mainly saints, now that martyrs were in short supply. The use and citation of documents was an accepted part of the tradition,[134] a facet of the concern for the accuracy of the account. Some church historians expressed a reluctance to include the personal opinions and commentary that are a hallmark of their secular contemporaries,[135] an example of the fear that individual views might distort the truth of the whole. As the narrative approached the writer's own day, there was a tendency for the proportion of secular material to increase and for contentious aspects of religious affairs to be omitted or avoided. It seems to have been difficult to compose a good ecclesiastical history devoted to contemporary events.

This pattern is applicable to Evagrius. His early narrative is based on a variety of sources—conciliar acts, imperial religious proclamations, but also the Monophysite church historian Zachariah of Mitylene, and the chronicler Malalas.[136] The first three books are dominated by the Council of Chalcedon (451) and the subsequent efforts of Zeno and Anastasius to cope with its doctrinal decisions. In Book IV, which covers the reigns of Justin I and Justinian, there are indications of a change: the narrative still covers major ecclesiastical matters—the deposition of Monophysite bishops who resisted Justinian's patronage of Chalcedon and the Fifth Ecumenical Council—but more attention is

[132] Though he was familiar with the sixth-century Monophysite church history by Zachariah: see Allen, *Evagrius*, 8–9.

[133] Evagrius, *HE* VI.24.

[134] Cf. Sozomen, *HE* I.8.14, on laws.

[135] Sozomen, *HE* III.15.

[136] Allen, *Evagrius*, 6–11.

paid to military affairs which could be summarized from the narratives of Procopius.[137]

Two aspects of the book stand out. First, it reflects a dislike for Justinian on both religious and secular issues—the honesty of his support for Chalcedon is doubted,[138] his lapse into the aphthartodocete heresy leads to confrontation with Anastasius, the popular patriarch of Antioch,[139] and his greed and favoritism towards the Blue circus faction are criticized.[140] Second, there are numerous stories of holy men and miracles, which are perhaps intended to prove that a wicked emperor did not necessarily entail a godless reign. Not only are there stories or miracles concerning Barsanuphius, Simeon the Fool, Thomas, and the patriarch Menas,[141] but also Evagrius' summary of events described by Procopius is itself dominated by religious incidents, the pious Moor Cabaon, Cyprian's prediction of the overthrow of the Arian Vandals, the conversion of various foreign tribes, the piety of Narses, and the successful resistance to the Persians at Edessa.[142] Evagrius also introduces certain religious "improvements" to Procopius' narrative. At Edessa the divine aspect of the city's escape is increased by the addition of the story about the divinely made icon being responsible for the successful firing of the Persian siege mound, and by the omission of the ransom payment that eventually secured Khusrō's withdrawal.[143] With regard to Sergiopolis,[144] Evagrius attributes the retreat of Khusrō's army to a divine apparition on the city's walls, whereas Procopius states more prosaically that the besiegers ran short of water.[145] Evagrius' description of events at Apamaea[146] combines Procopius' account of the fire miracle associated with the display of the True Cross[147] with his personal experience, since his parents had

[137] Cf. Sozomen's use of Olympiodorus at the end of his history (*HE* IX.11–15).
[138] *HE* IV.10.
[139] *Ibid.*, IV.39–40.
[140] *Ibid.*, IV.30, 32.
[141] *Ibid.*, IV.33–36.
[142] *Ibid.*, IV.15–16, 20–24, 27.
[143] *Ibid.*, IV.27.
[144] *Ibid.*, IV.28.
[145] *Wars* II.20.15.
[146] *HE* IV.26.
[147] *Wars* II.11.16–20.

brought him to the city to see the revelation, but he glosses over the fact that, notwithstanding the miracle, Khusrō entered the city and extracted a heavy ransom.

Evagrius' last two books, devoted to the events of his adulthood, are dominated by narrative of the Persian wars of 572–91. For an orthodox writer there was relatively little to report in terms of general church history in the eastern Empire after the religious edict of Justin II in 570–71,[148] apart from the succession of bishops. In the Monophysite church there were important developments and debates in the 570s and 580s, as narrated by John of Ephesus, but it was not the business of an orthodox historian to exalt a schismatic group by recounting its affairs. Events in Italy and the western Mediterranean, where the Three Chapters controversy of Justinian's reign continued to reverberate, were beyond Evagrius' horizons. Two individuals are prominent, both patrons or benefactors of Evagrius: the patriarch Gregory, who is defended against the various accusations levelled against him,[149] credited with helping to resolve the mutiny of 588–89,[150] and involved in Khusrō II's dealings with the Romans in 590–92;[151] and Maurice, from whose parents Evagrius obtained information about the prodigies that foreshadowed his imperial elevation,[152] to add to the accounts of his military campaigns and his glorious marriage.[153]

Nevertheless, however secular this last part of Evagrius' *History* may seem, its balance and presentation are quite different from those of a secular historian. The great triumph over Persia that was facilitated by the flight and restoration of Khusrō II is passed over in three short chapters,[154] while more attention is focused on the Roman mutiny that Gregory helped to conclude, and on the offerings that the restored Khusrō dedicated to S. Sergius.[155] The treatment of the mili-

---

[148] Evagrius, *HE* V.4.
[149] *Ibid.*, V.18, VI.7.
[150] *Ibid.*, VI.11–12.
[151] *Ibid.*, VI.18, 21–22.
[152] *Ibid.*, V.21.
[153] *Ibid.*, V.19–20, VI.1.
[154] *Ibid.*, VI.17–19.
[155] *Ibid.*, VI.21.

tary achievements of Maurice's brother-in-law Philippicus is notoriously partisan, praising his limited successes, condemning other accounts of his activities, and introducing a serious distortion of his attempts to besiege Martyropolis.[156]

In all, Evagrius provides a personal view of contemporary historical events, a view centered on friends and acquaintances in those eastern provinces most closely tied to Antioch, partisan in its selectivity, and through its omissions suggesting that the mobility of historical information was increasingly restricted. This could be supported by the comment in his review of predecessors[157] that the work of Agathias, generally believed to have been terminated before 582, was not yet published by about 590—presumably meaning that a complete written version was not yet available in Antioch, whereas Evagrius might have heard public recitations of selections on his occasional visits to Constantinople. In terms of style, Evagrius has much in common with the secular historians: an elaborate speech is composed for the patriarch Gregory when addressing the mutinous Roman troops in 589,[158] the account of the Council of Chalcedon is preceded by an *ekphrasis* that describes the shrine of S. Euphemia where the bishops met,[159] and analysis of his language has revealed modest pretensions to a classical style.[160] His work must have been directed at the same educated audience as that of his classicizing contemporaries, who included his cousin and colleague John of Epiphania; this was an audience that appreciated stories of saints and miracles at least as much as narratives of military affairs, even of great victories.[161]

---

156 *Ibid.*, VI.3, 14; see Whitby, *Maurice*, 245, 289.

157 *Ibid.*, V.24.

158 *Ibid.*, VI.12.

159 *Ibid.*, II.3.

160 See Valerie A. Caires, "Evagrius Scholasticus: a Literary Analysis", *BF* 8 (1982), 29–50.

161 Although this survey is devoted to Greek writers, the existence of Part III of the Syriac *Ecclesiastical History* of John of Ephesus, which was written at Constantinople, should not be overlooked: *Iohannis Ephesini Historiae Ecclesiasticae pars tertia*, ed. and Latin trans. by E.W. Brooks (Leuven and Paris, 1935–36; *CSCO* 105–106, *Scr. Syri* 54–55; English trans. (less accurate) in R. Payne-Smith, *The Third Part of the Ecclesiastical History of John, Bishop of Ephesus* (Oxford, 1860).

Chronicles

The third type of historical work to be considered is the chronicle. The function of a chronicle is encapsulated in the title to the *Chronicon Paschale*: "Summary of the years from Adam the first-fashioned man, until the year 20 of the reign of Heraclius the most pious...",[162] i.e. an account of human history from the Creation to the present day. The preface to Malalas' *Chronicle* reveals a bit more about the method of composition:

> A report of John, descended from the time of Constantine the Great, beginning from the time of the creation of the world. I thought it right, after abbreviating some material from the Hebrew books written by Moses...in the narratives of the chroniclers Africanus, Eusebius of Pamphilia, Pausanias, Didymus...and many other industrious chroniclers and poets and learned historians, and to relate as truthfully as possible a summary account of events of my own lifetime which came to my hearing, I mean indeed from Adam to the reign of Zeno and those who came afterwards. My successors must complete the story relying on their own ability. Thus the majority of writers on world history have given an account of the following.

Basically the chronicler reworked, abbreviated, and combined existing historical accounts (probably not as many as listed in Malalas' preface) until he reached his own life, when the author began to compose a more personal narrative of events experienced by himself and his informants.

There are clear distinctions between chroniclers and secular and ecclesiastical historians in terms of content, scope, narrative balance,

---

Books I-V narrate the internal disputes and other troubles of the Monophysites from 565 to the 580s, interspersed with some chapters on secular events; the arrangement is somewhat haphazard, with some events being reported twice and chronological order disregarded. The final book constitutes a virtual appendix, entirely devoted to warfare between 571–72 and the late 580s, which John added since he took these manifold disasters as a sure sign that the end of the world was imminent.

[162] *Chronicon Paschale*, 32.

stylistic pretensions, literary adornment, and explicit authorial intervention, but the differences should not be pressed so far as to create a rigid dichotomy between the different branches of historiography. Chronicles were written by men of reasonable education for their peers, and many of their attitudes to secular and ecclesiastical matters can be parallelled in the other forms of history. The interrelationship is illustrated by Evagrius' explicit use of John the Rhetor, i.e. Malalas, as a source,[163] the division by the absence of John from Evagrius' review of the historiographical succession.[164]

The *Chronicle* of the Antiochene John Malalas, whose first version was completed in the early years of Justinian's reign, was the fundamental work for later Byzantine chronography.[165] His account naturally reveals a particular interest in the affairs of his native city, in that imperial buildings in Antioch and natural disasters which affected it are recorded in detail, the latter more especially after the mid-fifth century when there are long accounts of earthquakes and local riots.[166] Furthermore, Antioch was an important administrative center for the eastern provinces, and the *Chronicle* contains a detailed narrative of the Persian war of 527–32, reflecting the fact that much of this military action would have been coordinated through Antioch. Overall, the *Chronicle* reveals a geographical range that is not dissimilar to that of Evagrius: western events (anything west of Constantinople) might be recorded if the author had access, directly or indirectly, to a good source such as Priscus of Panium, but such accounts were liable to be distorted by errors of chronology and geography.

This "original" Malalas was then extended to cover the whole of Justinian's reign. It is by no means certain that this extension was by the same author since, apart from the disappearance of the type of cross-reference that has been noted as a feature of the first version,[167] there is a very marked reduction of interest in the affairs of Antioch

---

[163] Evagrius, *HE* IV.5.

[164] *Ibid.*, V.24.

[165] For more detailed discussion of all aspects of Malalas, see Elizabeth Jeffreys *et al.*, *Studies in John Malalas* (Melbourne, 1990).

[166] This is the point at which Malalas ceased to rely on the works of historical predecessors and began to collect his own information.

[167] For the cross-references, see Brian Croke, *Studies in John Malalas*, 20–21.

and the eastern provinces: thus an earthquake at Antioch, and even the disastrous sack of the city by the Persians in 540, are passed over very briefly,[168] and the Persian war of 540–61 is scarcely mentioned. Instead, Constantinople and its environs are the focus of attention: apart from the usual natural disasters, imperial affairs, and disputes between pope and patriarch, the Cotrigur attack of 559 is reported at greater length than any eastern military action, the arrival at Constantinople of news of events elsewhere is recorded rather than the events themselves,[169] and public disturbances in the capital are the category of event recorded most regularly and at length.

Assessment of Malalas, both the original text and its extension, is made difficult by the fact that only an abbreviated version survives, even though this can be supplemented by derivative accounts in other chronicles such as the *Chronicon Paschale* and Theophanes. However, the continuation of Malalas does reveal the type of information that an author working in Constantinople thought important or interesting, and this was presented to a readership,[170] which in itself presupposes individuals of some level of education, quite possibly officials in secular or ecclesiastical administration. It is clear that the range of interest and knowledge on the part of both author and audience was not particularly wide.

After 565 it appears that a Constantinopolitan writer continued the account of Malalas still further, since the ninth-century chronicler Theophanes had a source that provided him with the same type of information centered on the capital and a similar account was also available to Theophylact when he composed his classicizing narrative in the 620s.[171] How many phases of extension this account underwent cannot be determined, but its narrative must have continued beyond Phocas to some point in Heraclius' reign. Such piecemeal continuation of a major chronicle has been regarded as a feature of fifth-century Western chroniclers, who extended Jerome's translation of Eusebius'

---

[168] Ed. Dindorf, 478.16–17, 479:23–480:5.

[169] *Ibid.*, 486:14–18, 492:17–20, both Roman victories in Italy.

[170] It is difficult to imagine a chronicler reading out his work to an invited audience in the manner of a classicizing author.

[171] On this see Whitby, "Theophanes", and on the terminal date of Malalas, Brian Croke, *Studies in John Malalas*, 23–25.

Chronicle down to their own time,[172] but it appears that a similar development also occurred in the east after Malalas. The localized vision of the eastern chroniclers is also comparable to the narrow focus of their western counterparts.

One version of this extended chronicle (though not that available to Theophanes) may be equated with the fragments preserved in the Constantinian *Excerpta* under the name of John of Antioch. This appears to have been a fairly ambitious work which exploited Malalas, or information from the same tradition, for parts of its early narrative, especially of the Greek mythological period. But it reveals an interest in Roman affairs, which resulted in the use of somewhat more detailed information, including a Greek translation of the *Breviarium* of Eutropius (a fourth-century summary of Roman history), Cassius Dio, some of Plutarch's biographies, Priscus, and the church historian Socrates.[173] Unfortunately, nothing survives from John's account after the accession of Heraclius, but he recorded in some detail the overthrow of Maurice by Phocas in 602, and of Phocas by Heraclius in 610; his accounts are different from those in Theophylact and Theophanes, but his version of events in 610 has similarities with the narrative in the eighth-century *Breviarium* of the patriarch Nicephorus.[174]

With the *Chronicon Paschale* we are on safer ground, since the majority of the text is extant (although both beginning and end are lost). This work terminated in 630 and, like the original Malalas, attempted to provide a chronological narrative from Adam to the present day. The most striking concern of the anonymous author is with precise chronology: the beginning of the reign of each emperor is accompanied by a running total of the years since the Creation; the cycle of Olympiads, irrelevant long before the seventh century, is maintained right down to the end of the text; and each year of Roman history has a heading

---

[172] Croke and Emmett, "Historiography", 3–4.

[173] See P. Sotiroudis, *Untersuchungen zum Geschichtswerk des Johannes von Antiocheia* (Thessalonica, 1989), 85–147; Sotiroudis' assertion that the "real" John of Antioch was an early sixth-century writer, whose work was extended by an unknown seventh-century continuator, is unconvincing.

[174] This raises the intriguing question as to whether Nicephorus' account of the years 602–41 was derived from John: it seems to have originated in a well-informed contemporary source, but certainty is impossible.

that contains indiction and regnal years as well as consuls. One of the purposes of the work seems to have been to publicize a new date for the Creation, (5509 BC, nine years earlier than the previous consensus), and the last section of the text has several complex computations that were carried out by the author to verify the accuracy of his chronology: the end in 562 of the first great Easter cycle of 532 years from the Crucifixion has to be confirmed, the start of the narrative of Heraclius' revolt against Phocas (*s.a.* 609) is also placed in its long-term position, and there is a further calculation *s.a.* 616.[175] All contribute to an attempt to connect contemporary events with the progression of Christian history.

Like Malalas' *Chronicle*, the *Chronicon Paschale* is a combination of existing source material for the earlier parts and personal contributions for more recent times. Down to the Nika Riot in Justinian's reign (532), its account was based on a variety of sources that included a fifth-century Constantinopolitan chronicle and the original Malalas. Thereafter the unknown author, whose ecclesiastical interests suggest membership of the Constantinopolitan clergy under the patriarch Sergius, had to find his own historical material, and his varied achievement is another illustration of the limits of historical awareness in the early seventh century. After 533 the *Chronicon Paschale* records the succession of emperors, but otherwise contains little information on sixth-century events except for ecclesiastical affairs, and even these are presented selectively in order to highlight attempts to redefine Chalcedonian doctrine: two long doctrinal edicts of Justinian are transcribed verbatim (*s.aa.* 533, 552). With Maurice's accession there is a little more information, and it is likely that the author had access to some form of official record from this point: not only are precise dates and places recorded in the notice of the death of Tiberius in 582, but there are specific references to the way in which the consular year was recorded in 583 and 602 and to the coronation of Maurice's son Theodosius in 590 as an event whose formal significance was limited.

However, the chronicle really recommences as a continuous narrative with the coup of Phocas in 602, and from then on it seems to be based on a combination of official record and personal experience.

---

[175] See Michael and Mary Whitby, *Chronicon Paschale*, xxii–xxiv.

A detailed account of imperial affairs is provided—coups, plots, appointments, births, deaths, and marriages,[176] riots and other popular demonstrations, and ecclesiastical affairs, including not only the appointment of patriarchs but changes in the liturgy and the arrival in Constantinople of new relics. There are numerous references to the nicknames, official titles, or ranks of people mentioned (e.g. the plotters against Phocas, *s.a.* 605); the former positions held by the sequence of Constantinopolitan patriarchs are also noted—Cyriacus had been presbyter and *oikonomos*; Thomas a deacon, *sacellarius*, and in charge of appointments; Sergius a deacon, in charge of poor relief, and guardian of the harbor; Zachariah, a member of the Constantinopolitan clergy sent to Jerusalem to be patriarch there, is described as former presbyter and *skeuophylax*. The author was clearly interested in such matters, and expected his readers to be so as well.[177]

On the other hand, the *Chronicon Paschale*'s treatment of the great military events of the period is remarkably limited. Military action that affected Constantinople is reported—the coup of Heraclius (but only from the point when his ships have reached the Sea of Marmara), the Avar attempt to surprise Heraclius in 623, and the siege of the city in 626—but more distant action tends to be reported in terms of the arrival of the news in Constantinople: this is most clear in the treatment of Heraclius' victory over the Persians in 628, which is presented through the imperial victory dispatch that was read out in S. Sophia, but the death of Anastasius II of Antioch in 609 is also narrated as an event announced in Constantinople (in 610), and the incorrect dating of the Persian capture of Jerusalem in 614 probably also represents the occasion when the news of this disaster reached the capital. A lack of interest in military affairs is also evident in the earlier parts of the chronicle: virtually nothing is transcribed from the long account in Malalas of the Persian war of 527–32, and the only extended description of a military event is the narrative of the siege of Nisibis in 350, probably related because it offered an analogue for the divine deliverance of Constantinople in 626. It is possible to identify a contraction of inter-

[176]But with the significant omission of Heraclius' incestuous marriage to his niece Martina.

[177]The author also liked stories about the downfall of the high and mighty: e.g. Rhodanus the *praepositus* (*s.a.* 369) or Menas, prefect of the watch (465).

est in Malalas, if the original version is compared with the continuation of 565; likewise the *Chronicon Paschale*, although it is distinguished by extensive ecclesiastical information, had overall a limited range of interests and vision which is comparable to that in the continuation of Malalas.

Nevertheless, people were still interested in historical narratives in Heraclius' reign. The defeat of the Avar attack on Constantinople in 626, and the recovery both of Jerusalem and of the relic of the True Cross from the Persians, prompted the composition by Theodore Syncellus and Antiochus Strategius of celebratory homilies which included accounts of these events and their antecedents. The dispatches which Heraclius sent back from the eastern frontier recording the progress of his campaign against the Persians were read out from the ambo of S. Sophia. Furthermore, the chronological aspects of the *Chronicon Paschale* find a parallel, though a very brief one, in the list of Roman consuls compiled in the 620s.[178] The cause of this flurry of interest in chronology is unclear, although it may be connected with the eschatological propaganda that accompanied Heraclius' crusade against the Persians in the 620s: attention to future time might also stimulate people to think about the past.

In addition to the *Chronicon Paschale*, there were other chroniclers recording historical events in some detail, since Nicephorus and Theophanes had access to independent information. Nicephorus' treatment of the early seventh century is a literary reworking that does not entirely disguise the chronographic origin of the information, particularly towards the end of Heraclius' reign where entries are regularly introduced with variants of "At this time..."[179] If Nicephorus' stylistic improvements are discounted, the narrative may be seen to combine anecdotes about the imperial family (the trapping of Priscus, Eudocia's funeral, and the injustice of Voutilenos)[180] with events at the capital, and a military narrative in which Roman victories are much more prominent than defeats: thus Roman successes against Persians and Avars in the 620s occupy six pages of text (15–21), whereas the

[178] *Fasti Heracliani*, ed. Hermann Usener in *MGH*, *Auct. Ant.*, XIII: *Chronica minora saec. IV. V. VI. VII.*, III (Berlin, 1898), 386–410.

[179] Nicephorus, XXIV.3, 9, XXV.9.

[180] *Ibid.*, VI–VIII.

confused account of Arab victories in the 630s passes over these events in less than two pages (23–25). Investigation of the sources underlying Theophanes' account is a matter of extreme complexity, since information from a Byzantine chronicle is combined with extracts from George of Pisidia's poems and a Syriac chronicle,[181] but it substantiates the view that there was a certain amount of historical activity during Heraclius' reign, and that the victorious Persian campaigns of the 620s were treated at some length. However, the Arab expansion of the 630s, for which Theophanes was dependent on his Syriac source, was largely ignored by Greek writers.

The End of Traditional Historiography

After the reign of Heraclius it becomes difficult to make informed judgments about Greek historiography during the next 150 years, until the patriarch Nicephorus composed his *Breviarium* or *Short History* and George Syncellus, a monk aware of the continuing tradition of Syriac historiography, produced a new chronicle of world history from Adam to Diocletian's accession, a work which he persuaded Theophanes to continue down to the early ninth century.[182] Some people did compose historical accounts, for example the shadowy Traianus Patricius and the extremely fragmentary Great Chronographer (or whoever else was the joint source used by Nicephorus and Theophanes for their eighth-century narratives),[183] but there was so little historiographical activity

[181]See Ann S. Proudfoot, "The Sources of Theophanes for the Heraclian Dynasty", *Byzantion* 44 (1974), 367–439; Conrad, in this volume, also his "Theophanes and the Arabic Historical Tradition: Some Indications of Intercultural Transmission", *BF* 15 (1990), 1–44.

[182]In his "Who Wrote the Chronicle of Theophanes?", *ZRVI* 18 (1978), 9–17, Cyril Mango has argued that George was in fact responsible for much of the work for which Theophanes receives credit. The argument depends in part on accepting at face value evidence about Theophanes' poor health and his ill treatment by iconoclasts, but this material was designed to uphold Theophanes' reputation as an iconophile confessor and so may not be trustworthy.

[183]See L.M. Whitby, "The Great Chronographer and Theophanes", *BMGS* 8 (1982–83), 1–20; Cyril Mango, "The *Breviarium* of the Patriarch Nicephorus", in Nia A. Stratos, ed., Βυζάντιον: Αφιέρωμα στὸν Ανδρέα Ν. Στράτο (Athens, 1986), II, 545–48; with Michael and Mary Whitby, *Chronicon Paschale*, Appendix 2.

that it is reasonable to ask why there is a hiatus—or to put the question the other way, why there is no good record by a Greek historian of the Arab invasions. Authors, audience, and events are all possible factors, and any plausible explanation is likely to incorporate all three elements, since they interlock. But the starting point must be the comparative vitality of Greek historiography through the late sixth century and, at a slightly lesser level, into the early seventh century.

Greek historians in this period of late antiquity are marked by the diversity of their approaches to the task of producing a historical account. Agathias with his extended digressions is distinct from Menander with his detailed descriptions of diplomacy, and both are different from Theophylact; there is no comparison in Greek for Evagrius, the sole extant ecclesiastical historian. Among chroniclers, although the urban and especially Constantinopolitan focus creates a sense of uniformity, John of Antioch is apparently distinguished by his use of earlier secular historians, the *Chronicon Paschale* by its attempts at chronological precision and attention to contemporary doctrinal and liturgical interests. There is a common desire to create and relate a historical narrative, but the end product depends on the preferences of the individual author. The variety of these texts suggests that explanations of the demise of historiography in terms of a failure of nerve in the composition of critical history, or of the constraining influence of specific historiographical genres,[184] are not entirely adequate: authors had various possible explanatory methods, and to condemn an author's particular preference as a failure of nerve might be to impose modern standards of historical "usefulness" as the criteria for assessing ancient texts; the variety of late Roman historiography suggests that alleged generic constraints were not of great importance for these writers.

Personal factors that may be of greater relevance are the origin and education of the historians. Of the authors on whom we have specific information, only Menander was certainly of Constantinopolitan origin; although it is possible that the authors of the continuation of Malalas and of the *Chronicon Paschale* also came from the capital, the majority of writers were provincial—Agathias from Myrina in Asia Minor, John Malalas, John of Antioch, Evagrius, and John of Epiphania all from

[184] E.g. Allen, *Evagrius*, 69–70.

Syria, Theophylact from Egypt. Constantinople, like Rome before it, fed on the talents of provincials who used literature as a means of establishing or improving their position at the center.[185] These outsiders probably acquired their education in the provinces, in Alexandria, Antioch, or perhaps Gaza, before they moved to the capital: this is clear in the case of Agathias who, though Constantinople was the closer city, travelled from Myrina to Alexandria for his "literary" education prior to studying law in the capital, and the same progression can be suggested for Theophylact.

Thus the composition of literary works at Constantinople was likely to be seriously affected first by the destruction of provincial wealth in the Persian wars of 602–28, and then by the loss of Syria and Egypt to the Arabs. For generations, many of the provincial cities had been in a decline which could only have been sharply accentuated by the Justinianic plague,[186] but by constantly drawing the best literary talents to itself Constantinople had avoided the full cultural impact of these changes. Indeed, economic changes in the provinces could even have acted as a stimulus to literary production by prompting more potential writers to move to Constantinople in search of employment and wealth. Now, however, the capital was deprived of these reservoirs of potential talent. Furthermore, the acquisition of a good education became physically harder, as well as less affordable, since Constantinople itself could not generate the necessary teachers: Heraclius seems to have had to transfer the philosopher Stephen from Alexandria to provide advanced education at Constantinople, and the autobiography of Ananias of Shirak, even if somewhat mythical, presents a plausible pic-

---

[185] Other sixth-century examples are John the Lydian and Corippus (from Africa), and in the seventh century, George of Pisidia; for the fourth and fifth centuries, see Alan Cameron, "Wandering Poets: a Literary Movement in Byzantine Egypt", *Historia* 14 (1965), 470–509.

[186] For recent discussion of the fate of cities in late antiquity, see S.J.B. Barnish, "The Transformation of Classical Cities and the Pirenne Debate", *Journal of Roman Archaeology* 2 (1989), 385–400, who stresses the wide variations in urban prosperity between different parts of the Empire and former empire (with Asia Minor and Syria among the most prosperous in the sixth century). Cf. also Lawrence I. Conrad, "The Plague in Bilād al-Shām in Pre-Islamic Times", in Muḥammad 'Adnān al-Bakhīt and Muḥammad 'Aṣfūr, eds., *Proceedings of the Symposium on Bilād al-Shām During the Byzantine Period* (Amman, 1986), II, 143–62.

ture of students travelling from Constantinople to Trebizond to learn from Tychicus, who had declined invitations to move to the capital.[187]

Such developments will have meant that there were fewer people able to compose histories, or indeed any literary work, so that the shrinkage of historiography must to a certain extent be seen in the context of the demise of a broader range of categories of secular literature—panegyrics, epigrams, letters, philosophical works, legislation. But at the same time, other types of literature, essentially ecclesiastical, continued to be produced, and many of these demanded a high level of intellectual creativity and education: the Monothelete controversy generated doctrinal literature, bishops composed sermons and learned theological tracts (e.g. Germanus of Constantinople, *On Predestined Terms of Life*), saints' lives were also written, for example by Leontius of Neapolis. The absence of the secular literary superstructure in the seventh century requires that more attention be devoted to these ecclesiastical works,[188] but at the same time the degree of continuity with sixth-century production should not be overlooked: for example, Eustratius is a sixth-century precursor of Leontius in hagiography, the Three Chapters dispute of the Monothelete controversy, John the Faster of Germanus for sermons, Stobaeus of Maximus Confessor for florilegia. In the seventh century, the novelty is not so much the emergence of this literature as the disappearance of the secular literature whose existence in the sixth century has distracted our attention. Thus it is as important to consider why specific categories of literature disappeared as why other categories continued to develop during the seventh century—the questions are interrelated.

As a result, although it is not incorrect to present literary developments in the sixth to seventh centuries in terms of social and economic changes, an explanation that operates at such a generalized level may not highlight particular factors relevant to individual cases, such as the virtual cessation of Greek historiography in the 630s. Quite apart from the continued production of learned ecclesiastical literature during the seventh century, imperial administration and diplo-

[187]See Wanda Wolska-Conus, "Stéphanos d'Athènes et Stéphanos d'Alexandrie: essai d'identification et de biographie", *RÉB* 47 (1989), 5–89.

[188]As urged by Averil Cameron in this volume.

macy also still demanded the composition or interpretation of documents and the preservation of intellectual skills among the group which in the sixth century had constituted the clientele for historiography. But from the mid-seventh century, the literary talent available was not prompted towards historiography as it had been previously.

One factor affecting historiography was perhaps a general contraction in interests and awareness. Signs of this can already be detected in sixth-century Greek historians: a writer at Antioch focused primarily on local events and on actions on the eastern frontier that would be reported via Antioch to Constantinople, whereas the Balkans are a blurred and remote area; an author at Constantinople had a comparably narrow field of vision, centered on the capital. The collective historical memory had also contracted. John Malalas, working in about 530, seems to have been able to collect a substantial amount of evidence from the mid-fifth century onwards, i.e. about 80 years before the period of composition. Even if this information only becomes chronologically precise towards the end of Anastasius' reign (510s), it reflects the existence of a society with a reasonable awareness of its past. By contrast, in the seventh century, the collective memory does not extend more than about a generation into the past: the author of the *Chronicon Paschale* was content to record no information about most of the years between 534 and 601, as if the only significant events were the Fifth Ecumenical Council, the end of the first great Easter cycle, and the progression of emperors—the rest could be skipped.[189] Theophylact, composing his *History* at roughly the same time, the late 620s, also seems to have had little access to people who remembered sixth-century events, so that his narrative had to be based on a compilation of written sources.

An anecdote in Theophylact can perhaps be pressed to illustrate the limits of memory.[190] A young Gepid accused in the 590s of murdering an imperial bodyguard on the basis of his possession of a distinguished gold belt explained his acquisition of this unusual item as

[189] John of Antioch may also have recorded very little information about the period between 527 and 601–602.

[190] *Hist*. VI.10.4–18.

being his share of the booty from the victory of the Gepid king Cunimund over the Lombards (which had occurred *ca.* 566). This excuse was believed, and the Gepid released, until one of the attendants in the court "intelligently examined the story and attempted to ascertain the time of the events narrated by the Gepid"; as a result, the impossibility of the defense was recognized. Though the anecdote is fabulous, it presupposes a society in which accurate chronological knowledge of an event 25 years in the past is a rarity. This historical disjunction, or divorce from the past, that is hinted at in the works of the 620s can perhaps be taken as a foreshadowing of the more complete break that is evident in the early eighth-century *Parastaseis syntomai chronikai*.[191] In this investigation of Constantinopolitan monuments, the researcher(s), though attempting to produce an authoritative account and on occasion extracting from sources good information about specific statues, does not seem aware of the 400-year span of Constantinopolitan history that is being surveyed, so that the founder Constantine emerges as a symbolic rather than a historical figure,[192] and there is some uncertainty about the distinction between the fifth-century Leo the Great and the eighth-century Leo III.[193]

If there was a growing loss of contact with the past on the part of authors or audience, a significant factor which might increase this tendency is likely to have been the nature of events to be related. Military

[191]Ed. Th. Preger, *Scriptores rerum Constantinopolitanarum*, I (Leipzig, 1901); English trans. and comm. by Averil Cameron, Judith Herrin, *et al.*, *Constantinople in the Early Eighth Century: the Parastaseis Syntomoi Chronikai* (Leiden, 1984).

[192]See Cameron and Herrin, *Parastaseis*, 37.

[193]The identification of the reference to "Leo the Great and pious" (Chap. 3) with Leo III is argued by Cameron and Herrin (*Parastaseis*, 170–31); however, all other references in the text to Leo the Great denote Leo I (Chaps. 14, 29, 45, 61, 64, 67, 88), the epithet "pious" is perhaps more easily applied to Leo I than to the iconoclast Leo III, while the religious procession to the western (land) walls is analogous to those which followed an earthquake of 447 and a rain of ash in 472. On the latter see Brian Croke, "Two Byzantine Earthquakes and their Liturgical Commemoration", *Byzantion* 51 (1981), 122–47; also Michael and Mary Whitby, *Chronicon Paschale*, notes 256, 262, 295. For the present, the important point is that the author was not concerned about the chronological distinction between the two Leos.

success tended to generate historical narratives: Procopius had begun to collect historical information as the secretary of a victorious general, while triumphs in Africa and initially in Italy provided further stimulus that tended to weaken as troubles emerged for the reconquering armies in the 540s; Agathias was prompted to his continuation after the outcome of conflicts in Italy and Lazica was known; Menander was aware at least of Maurice's successes in the east, even if the situation in the Balkans was still desperate; John of Epiphania was inspired specifically by the successful conclusion of the Persian war in 591; and the only certain chronological indications in Theophylact point to the period of Roman successes in the late 620s as the time of composition.[194] But Theophylact, describing the events of the previous generation, was already operating at the limits of historical memory for the period and was dependent on earlier written sources for most of his evidence; after he had failed to extend his *History* into Heraclius' reign, the gap between events and author became too great for the classicizing writer to bridge, especially granted the limited incentive to compose.

The restricted horizons of Constantinopolitan authors probably reinforced the tendency to concentrate on military victories. Just as the author of the *Chronicon Paschale* was able largely to ignore the sequence of Persian successes in the years 602–20, so the source used by Nicephorus appears not to have dwelt on the Arab victories in the 630s—after all, for a contemporary observer there was no guarantee that they would be any more permanent or significant than the Persian triumphs of the previous generations, and they were certainly not likely to stimulate enthusiasm comparable to John of Epiphania's reaction to Roman victory in 591. Under Heraclius, the author of the *Chronicon Paschale* recorded at length the defeat of the Avar siege of Constantinople in 626 and the final victory over the Persians in 628; the impression that emerges of other lost chronicles suggests a similar concentration on Roman successes, though probably with a rather more extended coverage of the Persian campaigns of the 620s than in the *Chronicon Paschale*. Thereafter military victories were rare, and

[194]The sermons of Theodore Syncellus and Antiochus Strategius which contain narratives of historical events were similarly prompted by successes: the repulse of the Avar siege in 626 and the recovery of Jerusalem and the relic of the Cross in 630.

no urban chronicler would have been attracted by the litany of military failures on the contracting eastern frontier. And as the years passed, notions of a historiographical tradition waned: patrons were not interested in commissioning embarrassing narratives of defeats, and the potential audience of imperial officials neither demanded nor generated such accounts—in sum, the atmosphere conducive to historiography, especially to the laborious and elitist classicizing historiography, was missing.

The lack of incentive for historical composition may have been reinforced by a change of attitude towards historical events. In the 620s, as part of his attempts to revive Roman morale, Heraclius had introduced explicit religious overtones into his campaign against Persia: Khusrō was the enemy of God, whereas the Roman army, purified by participation in Christian festivals, was under God's protection—for example, when saved from the snowbound Zagros passes in February 628.[195] The Romans' reward for their divinely ordained victory was to be a golden age of world rule, a promise that is contained in three contemporary works: George of Pisidia's *Hexaemeron*,[196] the revised version of the Syriac *Romance of Alexander*, and an astrological prediction attributed to Khusrō II and preserved in Theophylact.[197] Triumph over the Persians and the death of Khusrō in 628, the accession of the Christian Shahrvarāz to the Persian throne in 629, and the restoration of the True Cross to Jerusalem in 630 all seemed to provide corroboration. The actions of Heraclius were translated into eschatological terms, and influenced the formulation in apocalyptic works of the legend of the last Roman emperor.

But the period of euphoria was brief. Victory in a world struggle may well be followed by anticlimax, but for the Romans there was catastrophe in the form of the Arab conquest of all the territories that had so recently been retrieved from the Persians: imperial armies were destroyed by opponents who had previously been despised, and the emperor himself could be seen to have abandoned the struggle and to have withdrawn into isolation at the suburban palace of Hieria outside

---

[195] *Chronicon Paschale*, 732.

[196] *Hexaemeron* 1845–1910; *PG* 92, cols. 1575–78.

[197] *Hist.* V.15; see Whitby, *Maurice*, 333.

Constantinople. It was easy to present the Arabs as an apocalyptic scourge, and the doctrinal innovations of Heraclius were regarded by many as rank heresy that must inevitably bring divine retribution upon the Roman world. For the first time in over 300 years, since the renascent Zoroastrian enthusiasm of the new Sasanian dynasty in the third century, the Romans were faced by an enemy fired by religious zeal. However, on this occasion the new religion was close to Christianity and the continued success of its adherents prompted a search among defeated Christians for correct doctrine rather than experience derived from historical narratives as the key to military victory. The eschatological propaganda of the 620s had encouraged the tendency, evident already in the classicizing authors of the late sixth century, to apply religious categories of explanation to historical events, with the result that it was difficult for writers who agreed with the emperor's religious doctrines to analyze the apocalyptic catastrophe of the 630s. These developments would not have contributed to the continuation of traditional forms of historiography in Greek.

In sum, while long-term social and economic changes led to a contraction of the literary élite, the surviving educated minority abandoned the impedimenta of historiography, whether by default or choice. A reduced level of interest and knowledge about historical matters was reinforced by a shortage of suitable events, combined with rapidly changing and inexplicable historical circumstances. A consequence was an interruption in Greek historiography; writers in Syriac and Coptic found it possible to compose histories because their perceptions, audiences, and traditions were different.[198]

The Pre-Islamic Arabs in Greek Historiography

This lack of Greek historiography is a serious blow to our understanding of the Arab invasions, since, whatever the shortcomings of individual authors or texts, the classicizing historians in particular could provide

[198] Thus in the later sixth century John of Ephesus regarded a detailed narrative of warfare as useful in so far as it demonstrated the imminence of the end of the world, an approach that does not seem to be found in Greek historians. Monophysites in the seventh century, such as the Coptic author John of Nikiu, could present Roman defeats as the direct result of the emperor's adherence to Chalcedonian doctrine.

an informed account of military and diplomatic events and of reactions in the capital to these. Ideally, of course, histories should be supplemented by a wider variety of other types of literature—saints' lives, laws, letters, inscriptions, philosophical treatises, conciliar records, doctrinal tracts, panegyrics—but for a military event such as the Arab takeover the historical tradition would have provided the basic information. The classicizing historians were, in general, good at presenting Roman interaction with foreigners, and the scope of these authors was capable of adapting to focus on new powers that emerged as important contacts for the Romans: on the eastern frontier, the Persians were a recurring preoccupation for all classicizing authors, but elsewhere the interest of Agathias in the Franks is succeeded by Menander's concern with the Turks and Avars, while Theophylact pays attention to Slavs as well as to Avars. There is no reason why the Arabs should not have replaced the Persians as the topic of learned digressions and diplomatic analysis; the Arabs were better known to Greek writers than the Turks, and attitudes had already been formed that could be used in presenting Arab successes.

In the sixth century, Roman knowledge of the Arabs came mainly from their dealings with the Ghassānids, the tribal federate grouping whose function was to defend the borders of Syria and Palestine, although diplomatic contacts with Ethiopia and the Ḥimyarites in south Arabia broadened this view.[199] The relationship between Romans and the federate allies was certainly dynamic, probably often tense. The easiest method of defending the desert section of the frontier between the Euphrates and the Sinai peninsula was to enlist the help of Arab tribes capable of patrolling the steppeland fringes between settled inhabitation and the transhumant landscape beyond, but a delicate bal-

[199] For exhaustive discussion of Arab relations with Rome, see Irfan Shahid, *Byzantium and the Arabs in the Fourth Century* (Washington, D.C., 1984), and *Byzantium and the Arabs in the Fifth Century* (Washington, D.C., 1988), to be continued by a volume devoted to the sixth and seventh centuries. Although it is likely that many aspects of my brief analysis of Roman–Arab relations in the sixth century will not be in accord with Shahid's, I fully share his belief—as set forth, for example, in *Speculum* 58 (1983), 454, reviewing Fred M. Donner, *The Early Islamic Conquests* (Princeton, 1981)—in the importance of the events of the sixth century for understanding the course of subsequent Islamic–Byzantine relations.

ance had to be maintained—the federates had to be sufficiently strong to protect Roman possessions, but not so over-mighty as to pose a threat to the Romans themselves—and this process was bound to be affected by Roman perceptions of the external threats that had to be repelled.

There is little evidence that the Romans had great confidence in their Ghassānid clients—they were one of the necessary mechanisms of frontier defense, but when appropriate the Romans tried to reduce the significance of their rôle by establishing contacts with the main Arab threat beyond, the Persian client federation of the Lakhmids. It would be simplistic to present the Ghassānids as loyal vassals, or to be surprised when they appear insubordinate: an individual leader might fight bravely for the Romans, like al-Ḥārith ibn Jabala at Callinicum in 531, but this was probably because Justinian had recently granted him the title of King and his new-found superiority vis-à-vis other Arab chiefs obliged him to remain when they fled.[200] When it was advantageous, al-Ḥārith would try to exploit his relationship with the Romans, as when he responded to an attempt by his great rival, the Lakhmid al-Mundhir, to take over the disputed border territory of the *strata* by claiming that it was Roman,[201] but on other occasions his personal conflicts with al-Mundhir would proceed without reference to the interests of his supposed masters. In the same way as the Lakhmids maintained intermittent links with the Romans, so too the Ghassānids were probably always open to approaches from the Persians, and it is likely that Khusrō I's victorious campaign in 573 and the capture of Dara owed much to a deal reached with al-Ḥārith's son al-Mundhir the Ghassānid.[202]

Procopius' treatment of the Ghassānids, and in particular his attitude towards their leader al-Ḥārith, has been criticized, but the arguments sustaining this critique are based ultimately on the conviction

[200] Correctly noted by Irfan Shahid, "Procopius and Arethas", *BZ* 50 (1957), 55.

[201] Procopius, *Wars* II.1.6–7. Shahid ("Procopius and Arethas", 52) regards this as a sign of Arethas' loyalty to his Roman masters, but an element of self-interest seems more probable: on the basis of past experience, Arethas was unlikely to succeed by himself in a dispute with al-Mundhir, so that it was essential to try to involve the Romans.

[202] See Whitby, *Maurice*, 257–58.

that faithlessness is impossible in a Christian Arab.[203] His account of the Roman defeat at Callinicum in 531 is certainly intended to exculpate Belisarius,[204] and he fails to specify that al-Ḥārith stood his ground when other Arabs fled; but the identification of the flight of the Arab federates as the decisive moment in the battle is corroborated by Malalas, who also refers to stories about the treachery of the Arab phylarchs.[205] When choosing between Procopius' two divergent accounts about the termination of Belisarius' Persian offensive in 542, it is by no means certain that the explanation in the scurrilous *Secret History* in terms of Belisarius' matrimonial concerns should be preferred to that in the *Wars*, where the deceptive conduct of the Ghassānid al-Ḥârith in command of a ravaging expedition is blamed. Procopius may at times distort the truth, but his serious reservations about the Ghassānids should be accepted as a reflection of contemporary attitudes and not dismissed as the product of personal historiographical biases.[206] The fifth-century historian Malchus believed that even Christian Arabs were shifty allies who should be kept firmly in their place as subordinates and overawed by a distant perception of Roman imperial might.[207]

Agathias did not find occasion to mention Arabs, but there is much material in Menander, both in his citation of the Fifty Years' Peace treaty and in his accounts of subsequent diplomacy. The specific inclusion of the Arabs in two clauses of the 561 treaty testifies to their nuisance value to Romans and Persians alike.[208] Earlier treaties appear

---

[203] Shahid, "Procopius and Arethas", esp. 53–54, for the argument that it would be incredible for an Arab king to be faithless.

[204] *Wars* I.18.

[205] Ed. Dindorf, 464.

[206] The contrary is argued by Shahid, "Procopius and Arethas"; also in *BZ* 50 (1957), 362–82, and 52 (1959), 321–43. Both articles are conveniently reprinted in Irfan Shahid, *Byzantium and the Semitic Orient before the Rise of Islam* (London, 1988).

[207] Ed. and trans. R.C. Blockley, *The Fragmentary Classicizing Historians of the Later Roman Empire*, II (Liverpool, 1983), frag. 1, where Leo I is criticized for treating the phylarch Amorkesos as an equal.

[208] Irfan Shahid, "The Arabs in the Peace Treaty of AD 561", *Arabica* 3 (1956), 212 (included in Shahid, *Byzantium and the Semitic Orient*), regards this as indicative of the Arabs' increasing importance.

not to have mentioned Saracens, an omission that was in part responsible for the breakdown of the Endless Peace in 540,[209] so that this failure had to be rectified: the second clause stipulates that Saracen allies must abide by the treaty and not attack each other, while the fifth clause attempts to ensure that Saracens and other foreign merchants engage in trade in accordance with official regulations and do not avoid payment of customs dues.[210] The mobility of the Saracens on the fringes of the two great empires was an obvious source of difficulty that had to be curtailed.

The Saracens were also a factor in the diplomatic wrangling that accompanied the negotiations which continued into the early years of Justin II's reign. The Romans were keen to gain control of the sub-Caucasian region of Suania, and as one means of diverting these requests the Persians seem to have advanced a demand by their clients, the Lakhmids, for the resumption of the payments which Justinian had made to guarantee peace.[211] When the Romans found themselves upstaged with regard to Suania, the Saracen issue was an opportunity to reassert themselves.[212] The payments which Justinian had made to the Lakhmid al-Mundhir in the 530s were an irrelevancy now that the behavior of the Saracens was regulated by a treaty. The Saracens were no more than an irritant, and both Romans and Persians resorted to abuse when discussing them: the Roman ambassador Comentiolus in 566 says, "Whenever I mention Saracens, consider, Persians, the outlandishness and untrustworthiness of the nation",[213] and when Māhbōdh leads a return embassy to Justin II he is reduced to cursing his Saracen allies whose interests he is supposed to be championing, the one aspect of his mission on which Justin could agree.[214] Justin's rejection of Lakhmid demands provoked them to attack the Ghassānids, but even though this seems to have been a breach of the 561 treaty, the incident was not sufficiently serious to involve the great powers or to be cited by Justin as a reason for breaking the peace in 572.

---

[209] Procopius, *Wars* II.1.4–5.

[210] Menander, frag. 6.1.320–22, 332–40.

[211] Frags. 6.1.288–303, 515–44;9.1.29–93.

[212] Frag. 9.3.43–123.

[213] Frag. 9.1.67–69.

[214] Frag. 9.3.99–104.

In the war of 572–91, Greek sources have little to say about the contribution of the Arab allies, and what they say is not over-favorable.[215] Menander might have been more explicit, but his military account is lost and most information is provided by the Syriac historian John of Ephesus. John was particularly well-disposed to the Ghassānid leader al-Mundhir as a champion of Monophysite doctrine and a man who attempted to reconcile the Monophysite factions whose feuds caused John such grief; the probable bias of John's evidence must not be forgotten.[216] Al-Mundhir's behavior on two occasions, in 573 and 581, was sufficiently suspect to require an apologia from John—the truth about his actions cannot be determined, but he may well have been attempting to achieve some degree of independence by maintaining good relations with Persians as well as Romans. The result was a reputation for treachery, with historians repeating traditional complaints: "The Saracen tribe is known to be most unreliable and fickle, their mind is not steadfast".[217] When the opportunity presented itself, the Ghassānid federation was dissolved after the arrest of its leader al-Mundhir and the capture of his son al-Nuʿmān, who had begun to harry the Romans.[218] The Ghassānids had become a liability rather than an asset, and the replacement of their united tribal group by fifteen independent princedoms reduced the Arabs once more to the position of usable allies. They might serve the Romans as scouts,[219] but the contribution of Armenian allies to the eventual Roman victory was much more significant, and it is not surprising that the Arabs are rarely mentioned by Greek writers. In the *Strategicon* of Maurice, a contemporary analysis of Roman military matters and of potential Roman enemies, the author did not consider it necessary to refer to the Arabs.

The Roman–Persian peace of 591 ensured that the Arabs remained marginalized. Patriarch Gregory of Antioch may have had some success with converting the pagan Lakhmids, thereby creating a new link

[215]Irfan Shahid, "Procopius on the Ghassānids", *JAOS* 77 (1957), 82, describes this silence as "a huge lacuna in the Byzantine sources", but this is to assume that there were significant events that should have been narrated.

[216]See Whitby, *Maurice*, 257, 272–73.

[217]Theophylact, *Hist.* III.17.7.

[218]John of Ephesus, *HE* VI.41–2, III.42; Evagrius, *HE* VI.2.

[219]Theophylact, *Hist.* II.2.5–6.

for the Romans with the pro-Persian Arabs,[220] and this may have contributed to Khusrō II's suspicions towards their leader al-Nu'mān that had begun with the Arab's refusal to accompany the king on his flight to the Romans in 590. The Arabs continued to lead their own existence outside the reach of the great powers; one dispute between rival groups might have been exploited as a pretext for war by Khusrō,[221] but the matter was defused. In the wars of the early seventh century, the Arabs remained peripheral: Khusrō attacked the Romans through upper Mesopotamia, north of the area protected by the Arab federates, and the irrelevance of the Arabs is revealed by his subsequent arrest of the Lakhmid leader al-Nu'mān and the reduction of that tribe's power.[222] Whether the Ghassānid tribes participated in the Roman opposition to Khusrō is unknown, and though there is one reference to their involvement in Heraclius' campaign of 628,[223] the recruitment of allies among Armenians, sub-Caucasian principalities, and trans-Caucasian Turks was a much more important factor.

The lack of detailed information in Greek historians about Arab affairs in the late sixth and seventh centuries accurately reflects their lack of importance in contemporary wars and diplomacy. Once the Arabs had emerged as the major eastern neighbor, attention could have been switched to them, but by then the stimulus for historiography in Greek was lacking. As a result, we are dependent on Syriac, Coptic, Armenian, and Arabic writers for our knowledge of the Islamic conquests.

---

[220] Evagrius, *HE* VI.22.

[221] Theophylact, *Hist.* VIII.1.

[222] *Chronicon anonymum de ultimis regibus Persarum*, ed. and Latin trans. by Ignazio Guidi (Paris, 1903; *CSCO* 1–2, *Scr. Syri* 1–2), 19–20 (text), 18 (trans.).

[223] *Chronicon Paschale*, 730.

2

New Themes and Styles in Greek Literature: Seventh–Eighth Centuries

Averil Cameron
(King's College London)

THE SEVENTH CENTURY, which saw the life of Muḥammad and the Arab victories which deprived the Byzantine Empire of such a high proportion of its territories, is traditionally regarded by Byzantinists as a dark age.[1] It was certainly marked by the profoundest social, economic, and administrative changes which had taken place in the eastern Empire since the third century AD, or even since its very beginning. These changes had many causes, of which the coming of Islam

[1]See, e.g., Michael G. Hendy, *Studies in the Byzantine Monetary Economy c. 300–1450* (Cambridge, 1985), 619–61; Cyril Mango, *Byzantium: the Empire of New Rome* (London, 1980), 45; A.P. Kazhdan and Ann Wharton Epstein, *Change in Byzantine Culture in the Eleventh and Twelfth Centuries* (Berkeley and Los Angeles, 1985), 1–10, esp. 4: "to condemn the seventh and eighth centuries as a Dark Age of decline and collapse would be misleadingly simplistic", with 10: "Byzantium emerged from the crises of the 'Dark Ages' more rapidly than did the western part of the ancient Roman Empire". Cf. Judith Herrin, *The Formation of Christendom* (Oxford, 1987), 133: "The seventh century is justifiably regarded as a 'dark age'". It is not very different in the visual arts: cf., for example, James Trilling, "Sinai Icons: Another Look", *Byzantion* 53 (1983), 300: "The period between the death of the emperor Justinian in AD 565 and the temporary triumph of the Iconoclast movement from 726 to 843 is, with the exception of the Iconoclast period itself, the most resistant to study of any in the long history of Byzantine art".

was only one, even if one of the most dynamic; but their impact was indeed felt very forcibly in the eastern provinces of the Byzantine Empire, where contact with Muslims had been preceded by a century of heightened religious tension and rivalry, intensified by an increasing dissatisfaction in many quarters with rule from Constantinople.[2] We are also gradually obtaining archaeological evidence from a broad range of sites which with increasing clarity indicates substantial changes in the traditional urban culture of classical antiquity, even before the Arab conquests;[3] and while this evidence is often difficult to interpret, the overall message is clear enough. In the papers by both John Haldon and Michael Whitby in this volume, the particular characteristics of Byzantine writing in the seventh century are rightly connected with these general developments.[4] I shall be making the same connection in mine, while at the same time arguing that the Arab invasions and subsequent contacts with the new rival faith of Islam provided special and additional stimuli.

Without going into detail, it might be helpful to mention briefly the factors which were already bringing about social change in the Byzantine Empire at the time of the Arab conquests. One such factor was certainly the demographic effects of the great epidemic of bubonic plague which swept Constantinople and the eastern provinces in 542, and which returned in successive waves throughout the sixth and sev-

---

[2]For the division of the churches in the eastern provinces from the sixth century onwards, see Susan Ashbrook Harvey, "Remembering Pain: Syriac Historiography and the Separation of the Churches", *Byzantion* 58 (1988), 295–308.

[3]The subject of urban continuity or discontinuity in the seventh century remains highly controversial. For brief remarks see Kazhdan and Epstein, *Change in Byzantine Culture*, 1–10; Mango, *Byzantium*, 60–73; recent comment—Josiah C. Russell, "Transformations in Early Byzantine Urban Life: the Contribution and Limitations of Archaeological Evidence", in *17th International Byzantine Congress, Major Papers* (New Rochelle, 1986), 137–54; S. Barnish, "The Transformation of Classical Cities and the Pirenne Debate", *Journal of Roman Archaeology* 2 (1989), 385–400. Recent archaeological work suggests urban change over a wide area by the late sixth or early seventh centuries: for a survey, see Richard Hodges and David Whitehouse, *Mohammed, Charlemagne and the Origins of Europe* (London, 1983); and on Syria, see Hugh Kennedy "From Polis to Madina: Urban Change in Late Antique and Early Islamic Syria", *Past and Present* 106 (1985), 3–27.

[4]See also in detail John Haldon, *Byzantium in the Seventh Century: the Transformation of a Culture* (Cambridge, 1990).

enth centuries and midway into the eighth.[5] Impossible though it is to quantify the mortality, since we only have the impressionistic accounts of literary sources, the effect on the population must have been great; in Constantinople itself plague mortality and long-term population effects must lie behind the catastrophic drop in population which took place between the sixth century and the eighth.[6] In addition, Justinian's wars, still going on when the plague first struck, proved a very serious drain on manpower and finance.[7] His successors managed to continue the war effort to some extent at least on the Persian front, but Heraclius' campaigns required intensive and difficult recruitment and fund-raising; it was then that the fundamental restructuring of the Byzantine military system seems to have begun.[8] As the new system was closely tied to land tenure its replacement had implications for the survival of the old landowning, provincial aristocracy, which had hitherto maintained secular culture; moreover, hand in hand with the military changes went basic alterations to the administrative structure of the Empire—again with profound implications for the educational system and the transmission of traditional secular culture.

---

[5]Described by Procopius, *BP* II.22–24 (Constantinople); Evagrius, *HE* IV.29 (Antioch); John of Ephesus, *HE*, trans. W.J. Van Douwen and J.P.N. Land in *Verhandelingen der koninklijke Akademie van Wetenschappen Afd. Letterkunde*, 18 (1899), 227–40 (Asia Minor); see P. Allen, "The Justinianic Plague", *Byzantion* 49 (1979), 5–20; Lawrence I. Conrad, "The Plague in Bilād al-Shām in Pre-Islamic Times", in Muḥammad 'Adnān al-Bakhīt and Muḥammad 'Aṣfūr, eds., *Proceedings of the Symposium on Bilād al-Shām During the Byzantine Period* (Amman, 1986), II, 143–63.

[6]See Mango, *Byzantium*, 77–81.

[7]See Hendy, *Studies in the Byzantine Monetary Economy*, 164–71, for an attempt to compute the cost.

[8]There is an enormous literature on the questions of "themes" and "Byzantine feudalism". See for instance F. Winkelmann, H. Köpstein, H. Ditten, I. Rochow, *Byzanz im 7. Jahrhundert. Untersuchungen zur Herausbildung des Feudalismus* (Berlin, 1978; *BBA* 48); also John Haldon, "Ideology and Social Change in the Seventh Century: Military Discontent as a Social Barometer", *Klio* 68 (1986), 139–90: *idem*, *Byzantium in the Seventh Century*. On the emergent new ruling class, see F. Winkelmann, *Byzantinische Rang- und Ämterstruktur im 8. und 9. Jahrhundert. Faktoren und Tendenzen ihrer Entwicklung* (Berlin, 1985; *BBA* 53); *idem*, *Quellenstudien zur herrschenden Klasse von Byzanz im 8. und 9. Jahrhundert* (Berlin, 1987; *BBA* 54).

But while these developments were taking place, it seems that the urban setting of traditional public life had itself undergone something of a transformation; as the open public spaces of classical cities were built over and fell into disuse, streets narrowed, grand houses were subdivided, and churches proliferated. And again at the same time the population of many cities (we might rather call them small towns or even large villages by modern standards) was divided both within itself and against the government in Constantinople by religious conflict, which the Fifth Ecumenical Council in 553 served only to intensify.[9]

This sketch of changes occurring in Byzantium at the beginning of the seventh century will suffice to illustrate the fact that the rise of Islam took place against an existing context of rapid social and economic change. How prosperous or how insecure the villages of Syria and Palestine actually were at the time of the conquests remains controversial. Nevertheless, in these general circumstances we might expect to find some new directions in cultural responses, perhaps a cessation or hiatus in some old forms, and overall a greater variety than before. In such a context, the advent of a new and disturbing phenomenon in the shape of Islam was likely to act as a major catalyst.

In what sense, then, were the seventh and eighth centuries really a Byzantine "dark age"?[10] This idea is partly the result of the blinkers through which we look at our evidence. Certainly, as Michael Whitby shows, historical writing in the traditional sense seems to have suffered a hiatus: classical historiography did not seem relevant any more. No Byzantine historian in the tradition of Procopius or Theophylact took the rise of Islam as his theme, or even wrote of the wars of Heraclius, let alone the Arab campaigns. The latter did not, of course, provide a congenial subject—such a history would have been a catalogue of Byzantine disaster and loss, followed, as the first victories were, by a series of terrible sieges of Constantinople at the end of the seventh and beginning of the eighth century. Thus, while the earlier and successful campaigns of Heraclius provided a subject for imperial panegyric, the later disasters were more likely to feature in Christian

[9]See Herrin, *Formation of Christendom*, 119–25.

[10]The notion recurs in Peter Brown, "A Dark-Age Crisis: Aspects of the Iconoclastic Controversy", *EHR* 88 (1973), 1–34.

theological works, where they were given a moral or religious explanation.

It was also a matter of the changed milieu from which writers might now come, and of the melting away of the audience they once enjoyed. Even in the capital, it seems, secular history in the traditional form was as little read as it was written, while much of the provincial territory whose cities had previously provided historians was now under Arab control. One might suppose that there was consequently all the more need to record the history of the conquests; but traditional secular history had been closely associated, both in its practitioners and its audience, with the Byzantine educational apparatus, which in turn served the administrative structure. When both of these ceased to exist, or in some cases adapted themselves to the conditions of Arab rule, the bottom fell out of the market for the secular history which had up until then flourished with such vigor. It was no longer secular institutions, but the Church which now gave support and patronage to Greek literature, above all in the Arab-ruled provinces. In our surviving sources it is only with the chronicle of Theophanes at the beginning of the ninth century that we find the rise of Islam receiving actual historical treatment in Greek.

Yet an enormous amount of writing *was* going on in the seventh and eighth centuries. Its very bulk tends to be obscured for us by the fact that so little of it had been edited in modern editions—so unappreciated is the work and so few the scholars capable of doing it. We simply do not "see" it unless we look harder than most historians are used to doing, and in different directions. For another reason why we do not see it is that so much of it is inherently theological in character, or at the very least written by monks or clergy; historians attuned to political history are not used to taking such literature seriously. But just as John Haldon shows in relation to the question-and-answer literature exemplified by the *Quaestiones* of Anastasius of Sinai,[11] until we can come to terms with homiletic, theological tracts, disputations, and polemic we shall not begin to understand the Greek contribution to the cultural ferment which coincided with the Arab conquests and the rise of Islam. The familiar distinction between "high" and "popular" writing is no

[11] Below, 129–47.

longer very helpful in relation to the actual situation in this period, when there was little secular writing of any description, and when the "theological" works range over an enormously broad spectrum, from the most "popular", in saints' lives or miracle stories, to the most sophisticated. Moreover, even here caution is probably needed before we too easily transfer these critical terms to deduce the supposed audience of the works in question.

We must consider at this point exactly what we mean by "the Greek contribution", for literature written in Greek is not necessarily the same as Byzantine literature. To take only examples near to hand, the papers on Syriac apocalyptic in this volume raise the same issue, if implicitly; further, while Anastasius, the author of *quaestiones*, may have had a connection with the Egyptian monastery at Sinai, as the manuscript attestations suggest, the internal evidence of the works themselves makes him very hard to place. The interplay of language and culture in the Near East in this period is extremely complex. Indeed, one of the most important problems for Byzantines in the pre-Islamic period was precisely, I would say, this question of identity—to what society did a monk of Sinai or Jerusalem, or an official in Alexandria actually owe his loyalty? Or seen from the other side, how far did a Byzantine in Constantinople think that the culture of Byzantium still stretched?[12] One can argue that the striking increase in consciousness of the Jews by Greek writers of this period is itself an indicator of identity problems.[13] When Arabs were added to the mix in a rôle distinct from that played to date, for instance, by the Ghassānid allies of the Byzantines, the problem gained a wholly new dimension. Even so, use of the Greek language is not in itself a guarantee of Byzantine loyalties, any more than use of Syriac is proof of immunity to them.[14] In Syria, in particular, we are in a world in which translation is the norm (ps.-Methodius' *Apocalypse*, for instance, was translated very quickly from Syriac to Greek), and

[12]See my paper "The Eastern Provinces in the Seventh Century AD: Hellenism and the Emergence of Islam", in S. Said, ed. *Hellenismos: Quelques jalons pour une histoire de l'identité grecque* (Leiden, 1991), 287–313.

[13]See notes 56–57 below; also G.G. Stroumsa, "Religious Contacts in Byzantine Palestine", *Numen* 36 (1989), 16–42, especially 34–36.

[14]On the continuance of classical influences, see G.W. Bowersock, *Hellenism in Late Antiquity* (Cambridge, 1990).

where loyalties do not always move along linguistic frontiers. I would like to see as a priority for the study of this period a comprehensive list of known translations, and of the many Greek works which survive only, or additionally, in Syriac or other versions. This may sound simple and obvious, but in fact it is not; we do not know as much as we sometimes tend to think about the readership and diffusion of much of this literature, whether in the Syrian context or elsewhere.

The question of the nature of the linguistic mix between Greek and Syriac in the eastern provinces is thus by no means as straightforward as it perhaps once seemed; establishing what it actually was seems to me a real priority.[15] As a parallel example, we may cite the question of the impact in the sixth and seventh centuries of a Greek-speaking Byzantine administration on North Africa, a province with centuries of Latin culture behind it. The famous debate of Maximus Confessor with the exiled patriarch Pyrrhus of Constantinople which took place in Carthage in the late 640s was held in Greek, and Maximus wrote in Greek to the Byzantine governor of Africa; yet we have little or nothing to suggest the local context in which that debate took place, or how the Latin-speaking African Church received it.[16] Neither Constantinople itself nor its few writers of the period (or even later) were interested enough to bother. As we know, Greek stubbornly persisted in Syria and Palestine after the Arab conquests; and while John of Damascus is sometimes represented as isolated from mainstream Byzantine culture, it is hard to square that view with the fact that he was able to produce the most powerful defense of images ever written, or with the alarm with which the strength of his arguments was recognized by iconoclast advocates in Constantinople.[17] For the

---

[15] For a general guide, see Rüdinger Schmitt, *Die Sprachen im römischen Reich der Kaiserzeit* (Bonn, 1980; *Beihefte der Bonner Jahrbucher* 40), 187–214.

[16] Debate with Pyrrhus: *PG* 91, 288–353; the point is made in Averil Cameron, "Byzantine Africa: the Literary Evidence", in John H. Humphrey, ed., *University of Michigan, Excavations at Carthage*, VIII (Ann Arbor, 1982), 29–62.

[17] Persistence of Greek up to and after the mid-eighth century: Robert Blake, "La littérature grecque en Palestine au VIIIe siècle", *Le Muséon* 78 (1965), 27–43; Sidney H. Griffith, "Greek into Arabic: Life and Letters in the Monasteries of Palestine in the Ninth Century: the Example of the Summa Theologiae Arabica", *Byzantion* 56 (1986), 117–38. Contacts between Constantinople and the Arab-ruled provinces in the eighth century: Robert Schick, *The Christian Communities of Palestine from*

time being, therefore, it is better to keep an open mind about inferences to be drawn from the use of Greek in the literature which comes from the eastern provinces in our period. By the same token, the term "Byzantine" is a very blunt instrument. It will serve well enough as a blanket description of the situation and the literature up to the time of the conquests—if a work was written in a Byzantine province, we might as well call it Byzantine, even if it was written in Syriac, though even that begs the question of local loyalty and culture. But what about later writers? Is John of Damascus, for instance, "Byzantine"? One can hardly deny that he was one of the foremost of all Byzantine theologians. In general, it is even more difficult to classify the texts and authors of the immediately post-conquest period.

These problems of terminology can and do stand in the way of historical understanding, especially in an interdisciplinary context such as this, in which, to take just one further example, Islamic archeologists are wont to call "late Byzantine" what Byzantine historians would themselves regard as extremely early. Just to confuse the issue still further, the terms "Hellenic", "Hellenism", and so on, tend to be used by our Christian sources writing in Greek in a highly pejorative sense, to refer not simply to what can be seen as classical, but to pagans and paganism; "Hellenic deceit" is a typical formulation, as are references to "Hellenes and Jews" in implied contrast to Chalcedonian Christians. I propose at least that for now we use the term "Greek" without prejudice to these problems of definition, and treat the nature of Greek literature in our period separately from ideas of Byzantium as a state or a national identity.

As Michael Whitby shows, history in the old secular form suffered a severe break during our period, and we must conclude that other sorts of writing took its place. All the same, historical works in the broader sense continued to be written, especially in those areas most affected by the conquests; again, North Africa is the complete exception, for apparently no one there recorded the story of its fortunes in the later seventh century until the Arab chroniclers of two or more

---

Byzantine to Islamic Rule: an Historical and Archaeological Assessment (Princeton, forthcoming), Chap. V.

centuries later.[18] We simply do not know from any literary account how the prosperous province which Heraclius left to overthrow Phocas and become emperor in 609–10 came to be so forgotten. Similarly, the fate of the cities of Asia Minor which were overrun by the Persians in 612 onwards is rarely recoverable, except from the archaeological record.[19] But the later sections of the *Chronicon Paschale*,[20] and Antiochus (Strategius)'s account of the taking of Jerusalem by the Persians in 614, preserved in complete versions only in Georgian and Arabic,[21] are indications of continued and rigorous historical writing in Greek, even if diverted into different forms. We also have to look for historical content in other genres. The panegyrical poems of George of Pisidia contain much of the historical information we possess on the campaigns of Heraclius against the Persians,[22] and there is more in the polemical tract against the Jews known as the *Doctrina Jacobi*, written in Palestine but set in Carthage in 634, a time when Africa still belonged within Byzantine consciousness.[23] In the same way, the main account of the momentous Avar-Persian siege of Constantinople in 626 outside the *Chronicon Paschale* comes from an extended homily.[24] By comparison

[18] Cameron, "Byzantine Africa", 29–62.

[19] See especially Clive Foss, "The Persians in Asia Minor and the End of Antiquity", *EHR* 90 (1975), 721–47; "Archaeology and the 'Twenty Cities' of Byzantine Asia", *AJA* 81 (1977), 469–86; the example of Aphrodisias: Charlotte M. Roueché, *Aphrodisias in Late Antiquity* (London, 1989), especially 123–46.

[20] See the annoted translation by Michael Whitby and Mary Whitby, *Chronicon Paschale 284–628* AD (Liverpool, 1989).

[21] See Gérard Garitte, ed., *La prise de Jérusalem par les Perses en 614* (Leuven, 1960; *CSCO* 202–203, *Scr. Iberici* 11–12); *idem*, *Expugnationis Hierosolymae a.d. 614 recensiones arabicae* (Leuven, 1973–74; *CSCO* 340–41, 347–48, *Scr. Arabici*, 26–29), 340–41, 347–48; English trans. in F.C. Conybeare, "Antiochus Strategius' Account of the Sack of Jerusalem in AD 614", *EHR* 25 (1910), 515–17; Greek frags.: *PG* 86.2, 3228–68.

[22] Ed. A. Pertusi, *Giorgio di Pisidia. Poemi I. Panegirici epici* (Ettal, 1960); see Joseph Frendo, "The Poetic Achievement of George of Pisidia: a Literary and Historical Study", in Ann Moffat, ed., *Maistor: Classical, Byzantine and Renaissance Studies for Robert Browning* (Canberra, 1985), 159–88.

[23] Ed. N. Bonwetsch in *Abhandlungen der königlichen Gesellschaft der Wissenschaften zu Göttingen*, Neue Folge, XII.3 (Berlin, 1910); rev. François Nau, *PO* 8 (1912), 711–80. A new edition is forthcoming in *TM*.

[24] Theodore Syncellus' homily: ed. Leo Sternbach, *Analecta Avarica* (Cracow, 1900); Ferenc Makk, "Traduction et commentaire de l'homélie écrite probable-

with the Syriac chronicle tradition, that in Greek in this period is hard to trace except indirectly from later works, and even then it is faint indeed;[25] there are some indications in the eighth-century *Parastaseis* of written sources for recent history in the capital, even though so many of its elaborate "citations" are quite misleading.[26] And a certain Theophanios wrote a chronological treatise in the early eighth century in which he predicted the date of the end of the world as 880.[27] All the same, it is clear that even in Constantinople energies were being directed elsewhere.

Seen from the perspective of the high valuation usually placed on reliable, critical history writing of the old school ("high" style), it is rather too easy to see what seems to have been happening in terms of a sad decline in standards. Michael Whitby writes of a shrinking of historical horizons,[28] and Dagron's provocative study of the growth of patriographic literature, only semi-historical, if that, shows how little, by the end of the seventh century, even educated people in the capital knew in any critical sense about their own past history.[29] Partly, it would seem, they no longer had access to the necessary materials; but it is also that they no longer cared much for what we think they should have been concerned about. Their view of the past was rapidly becoming a field peopled by legendary heroes like the now saintly emperor Constantine, and in which the most important single thread was the continued Christian existence of the city of Constantinople.[30] There

---

ment par Théodore le Syncelle sur le siège de Constantinople en 626", in Samuel Szádeczky-Kardoss, *Acta antiqua et archaeologica*, 19 (Szeged, 1975); see F. Barišić, "Le siège de Constantinople par les Avares et les Slaves en 626", *Byzantion* 24 (1954), 371–95; Paul Speck *et al.*, *Zufälliges zum Bellum Avaricum des Georgios Pisides* (Munich, 1980).

[25]See Hunger, I, 331.; see further Whitby, above, 66–74. For the problem of the (meager) sources of Nicephorus for the seventh century, see Cyril Mango, *Nikephoros, Patriarch of Constantinople. Short History* (Washington, D.C., 1990), Introduction, 12–18.

[26]See Averil Cameron, Judith Herrin, *et al.*, *Constantinople in the Eighth Century: the Parastaseis Syntomoi Chronikai* (Leiden, 1984), Introduction; G. Dagron, *Constantinople imaginaire* (Paris, 1984).

[27]Ernst von Dobschütz, "Coislinianus 296", *BZ* 12 (1903), 550–51; Beck, 473.

[28]See above, 70–74.

[29]Dagron, *Constantinople imaginaire*.

[30]See Averil Cameron, "Models of the Past in the Late Sixth Century: the Life

were few secular books available even to Theophanes in the early ninth century, and the situation at the end of the seventh was evidently not much better.[31] In any case, those were not the books that people would have been reading.

For these and other reasons, to construct our own history of the period from the Greek sources alone is quite misleading; even leaving aside the vast corpus of works in the Arab-Islamic historical tradition, surviving historical works in Armenian and Syriac are as important as those in Greek, not to mention the lost Coptic original of the *Chronicle* of John of Nikiu.[32] This represents a necessary broadening of the historian's perspective which makes the task of writing about the seventh and eighth centuries quite different from that of pursuing research on earlier periods.

The same broadening of perspective concerns the growing importance of the oral element to which John Haldon draws attention in relation to the question-and-answer literature represented by the works of Anastasius of Sinai. This mundane quality, hardly characteristic of formal literature, can be seen in many types of seventh-century writing—for example, saints' lives and other hagiographic literature, such as the *Pratum Spirituale* of John Moschus,[33] and especially in the characteristic collections of miracle stories associated with pilgrim

---

of the Patriarch Eutychius", in Graeme Clarke, ed., *Reading the Past in Late Antiquity* (Sydney, 1990), 205–23; F. Winkelmann, "Die älteste erhaltene griechische hagiographische Vita Konstantins und Helenas (BHG Nr. 365z, 366, 366a)", in Jürgen Dümmer, ed., *Text und Textkritik. Eine Aufsatzsammlung* (Berlin, 1987; *TU* 133), 623–38.

[31] A classic discussion is Cyril Mango, "The Availability of Books in the Byzantine Empire, AD 750–850", in *Byzantine Books and Bookmen* (Washington, D.C., 1975), 29–45 (36–37 on Theophanes).

[32] Among them in particular the history by the Armenian writer Sebēos, French trans. by Frédéric Macler, *Histoire d'Héraclius par l'évêque Sébéos* (Paris, 1904); on Syriac historical sources, see S.P. Brock, "Syriac Sources For the Seventh Century", *BMGS* 2 (1976), 17–36; *idem*, "Syriac Historical Writing: a Survey of the Main Sources", *Journal of the Iraqi Academy (Syriac Corporation)* 5 (1979–80), 1–30; John of Nikiu (preserved in Ethiopic): ed. and French trans. by H. Zotenberg, *Chronique de Jean, évêque de Nikiou* (Paris, 1883); English by Robert H. Charles, *The Chronicle of John (c. 690 AD) Coptic Bishop of Nikiu* (London, 1916).

[33] *PG* 87.3, 2847–3116; for bibliography see Philip Pattendon, art. "Johannes Moschus" in *TRE*, XVIII (Berlin, 1988), 140–44.

shrines. Orality is an equally prominent feature in the development of patriographic literature, though in its often wildly unhistorical extravagance the term mundane hardly applies.[34] And it plays an undoubted rôle, hard though it is to be precise about its exact extent or limits, in the mass of Greek polemical literature directed again Jews, heretics, and (later) Muslims.[35] Finally, one of the most important genres of the period in terms of sheer quantity, as it is also in terms of its contemporary impact, is that of the homily, and here too, while much has been written on the rhetorical origins and supposed Syriac influences on Greek homiletic,[36] I think we should pay more attention than hitherto to its close connection with the spoken word; while many homilies were composed in the study, and even may never have been delivered, in general the most important single influence forming their very distinctive style came from the penetration of the consciousness of the writers by hearing and practicing oral exposition of the Scriptures.

The lesson of this increased oral element in contemporary writing is twofold. On the one hand, we cannot apply the same criteria to these works as we would to formal histories; but on the other, we cannot afford not to take them seriously either as indicative of contemporary attitudes or, in many cases, as sources of historical information.

The papers in this volume focus in particular on historical records for the Arab conquests and early Islam, of which there are fewer in Greek than we would have liked. But if we are to try to trace the mutual effects of Arab on Greek and Greek on Arab culture, we must also be clear both about the changes which were already taking place, and about the other contemporary influences which affected their relations. In the rest of this paper I should like first to suggest (against the usual judgment) that the continuing Christian doctrinal controversies, especially Monophysitism and Monotheletism, actually had a stimulating and energizing effect on contemporary literary output, and then to discuss two particular ways in which this effect can be seen. When it reached the Byzantine provinces, Islam took root in a culture not only

---

[34] See especially Dagron, *Constantinople imaginaire*.

[35] See Averil Cameron, "Disputations, Polemical Literature and the Formation of Opinion in the Early Byzantine Period", in G.J. Reinink *et al.*, eds., *Dispute Poems and Dialogues in the Ancient and Mediaeval Near East* (Leuven, forthcoming).

[36] See *ibid.* for bibliography.

divided and tense, hardly recovered from the Persian invasions, but also one that was in a ferment of excited discussion. Naturally this atmosphere would also in due course affect writings addressed to or about Muslims.

Far from achieving the hoped-for peace of the Church, Justinian's Council of 553 intensified existing discontents and drove a larger wedge between East and West;[37] the seventh and eighth centuries saw renewed and ultimately ill-fated imperial religious initiatives in the shape of Monotheletism and the much-discussed iconoclastic measures of Leo III and Constantine V.[38] It was a great age for councils—the Lateran Synod in Rome in 649, the Sixth in 680–81, the Quinisext (in Trullo) in 691–92, the Council of Hieria in 754, and the Seventh (Nicaea II) in 787. We should not underestimate their power to stimulate and excite as well as to divide and disturb. Even while the Arab forces were outside Jerusalem the patriarch Sophronius was attacking Heraclius' Monothelite pronouncements,[39] while his friend Maximus, who went from Carthage to Rome at the time of the Lateran Synod, only to be mutilated and exiled to Bithynia, wrote voluminous works himself and inspired others to do the same. Germanus, patriarch of Constantinople, deposed at the orders of Leo III,[40] was one of the most eloquent writers of treatises and letters in defense of images. The issues were endlessly debated in literary works of all kinds and at all levels, and the councils themselves called forth an enormous volume of supplementary material, especially collections of arguments and citations from earlier authorities (see below). As is well known, this turned into such an industry that it provoked a lively trade in forged citations and neces-

[37]See Herrin, *Formation of Christendom*, 119–25; generally Ashbrook Harvey, "Remembering Pain".

[38]Herrin, *Formation of Christendom*, provides a useful narrative of these events; see also Jan-Louis van Dieten, *Geschichte der Patriarchen von Sergios I bis Johannes VI* (Amsterdam, 1972).

[39]The sources for the Monothelite controversy are very usefully listed with bibliography in F. Winkelmann, "Die Quellen zur Erforschung des monoergetisch-monothelitischen Streites", *Klio* 69 (1987), 515–59.

[40]Herrin, *Formation of Christendom*, 340–41; Lucian Lamza, *Patriarch Germanos I. von Konstantinopel (715–30)* (Würzburg, 1975); see Stephen Gero, *Byzantine Iconoclasm During the Reign of Leo III* (Leuven, 1973; *CSCO* 346, *Subsidia* 41).

sitated special procedures for the verification of such materials.[41] It is almost as though the critical methods of secular historiography had, paradoxically, passed over to the theological enquiries which were the real issues of the day.

It has often been argued that the religious divisions between Constantinople and the eastern provinces from the mid-sixth century on were a major factor in making the east more receptive to Islam. This is, I think, a rather simplistic view which requires much closer examination. But they certainly deeply influenced the Christian literary output in the eastern provinces and elsewhere in the Byzantine Empire, and this in turn affected the ways in which Greek authors approached the topic of Islam.

It is less often realized that these divisions actually served as a stimulus to writing. Far from being abstruse and irrelevant, as most historians tend to imply, the Greek theological literature of the period was eminently practical. We shall certainly understand it best if we set it against the real-life context in which the issues were discussed. We might start by looking at the range of writings of one or two representative figures.

Maximus Confessor is not exactly typical, for he is probably the single most important Greek writer of the seventh century; moreover, he is a highly intellectual writer. However, his colorful career and the range of his works make him a good starting point.[42] Maximus' own works were extensive and varied: they include the famous disputation with Pyrrhus, two sets of *quaestiones*, letters to friends and connections, including secular officials, a range of theological works, an orthodox florilegium,[43] and a commentary on the writings of the early sixth-

[41]Cf. Herrin, *Formation of Christendom*, 277–79, 421–22; Mango, "Availability of Books", 29–32, 35.

[42]In general, see P. Sherwood, *An Annotated Date-List of the Works of Maximus the Confessor* (Rome, 1982); Beck, 436–42.

[43]Dispute with Pyrrhus: above, n. 16, Winkelmann, "Quellen", no. 92; *Quaestiones ad Thalassium*: ed. Karl Laga and Carlos Steel (Turnhout and Leuven, 1980; *CCSG* 7); *Questiones et dubia*: ed. Jóse H. Declerck (Turnhout and Leuven, 1982; *CCSG* 10); see also *Solutiones*, *PG* 91, 217–28 (Winkelmann, no. 86); letters, etc.: *PG* 91; florilegium: *PG* 91, 280–85 (= Winkelmann, no. 89), cf. also *PG* 91, 153–84 (Winkelmann, no. 105).

century ps.-Dionysius the Areopagite.[44] In addition, we have several associated documents, including the report of his trials and a dialogue between Maximus and Theodosius of Caesarea in Bithynia during his first exile composed by his supporter Anastasius the *apocrisiarius*, as well as two lives, a later Greek one and an earlier Syriac one.[45] A friend of Anastasius, the monk Theodore of the Spoudaios monastery in Jerusalem, composed accounts of the arrest and subsequent exile of Pope Martin, the other chief opponent of Monotheletism at the Lateran Council.[46]

The amount of contact between East and West in these matters at this period is very striking. Eastern monks were prominent in Rome at the Synod of 649, as also was a bishop from Dora in Palestine.[47] Opposition to Monotheletism in Palestine in the circles around Sophronius was very strong. Bishop Stephen of Dora had been sent to Rome by Sophronius after swearing an oath on the site of Calvary that he would maintain orthodoxy, and the aged patriarch had himself composed a florilegium of 600 anti-Monothelite citations.[48] During the first exile in Trebizond of Anastasius, the supporter of Maximus, he was in touch with the Spoudaios monastery at Jerusalem and the clergy of the church of the Anastasis in Constantinople.[49] It is striking to see how even after

---

[44] *PG* 4, 15–432, 527–76.

[45] Trial (AD 655): *PG* 90, 109–29, cf. Robert Devreesse, "La vie de S. Maxime le Confesseur et ses recensions", *AB* 46 (1928), 23–34 (Winkelmann, no. 132); dialogue with Theodosius (AD 656): *PG* 90, 136–72, cf. C.N. Trypanis, "Acta S. Maximi", *Theologia* 43 (1972), 106–24 (Winkelmann, no. 145). Greek *Life*: *PG* 90, 68–109, (Winkelmann, no. 171; only one of the three recensions has so far been published); Syriac *Life*: ed. S.P. Brock, "An Early Syriac Life of Maximus the Confessor", *AB* 91 (1973), 299–346 (Winkelmann, no. 172).

[46] See Robert Devreesse, "Le texte grec de l'Hypomnesticum de Théodore Spoudée", *AB* 53 (1935), 49–80 (Winkelmann, no. 154); Latin trans. in *PL* 129, 681–90.

[47] Documents relating to the Lateran Synod: see Winkelmann, no. 110; Acts (originally in Greek): ed. Rudolf Riedinger, *ACO*, ser. II.10 (Berlin and New York, 1984); easterners: see Jean-Marie Sansterre, *Les moines grecs et orientaux à Rome aux époques byzantine et carolingienne* (Brussels, 1983), I, 117–21; Stephen of Dora: Mansi, X, 892–901.

[48] Mansi, *loc. cit.*, mentioning Sophronius' florilegium (Winkelmann, no. 46; cf. also no. 105, florilegium by Maximus.

[49] Cf. Herrin, *Formation of Christendom*, 278.

the surrender of Jerusalem to the advancing Arabs by Sophronius in 638, the issue of Monotheletism continued to play a rôle as a powerful influence on Palestinian monks and clergy, and how in this issue easterners and westerners could still be united. In the next decade many eastern clergy and monks fled to the west, to Italy and Sicily—so many indeed as to bring about a noticeable increase in the use of Greek and in the influence of Greek culture in general, including Greek and Syrian cult practice.[50] The effects of this exodus on Greek–Arab relations in the eastern provinces from which the refugees had come is less often considered than their impact on Italy and Sicily. But in the first two decades or so after the conquests there still seems to have been plenty of contact on religious issues between easterners and westerners. The conquest of Syria and Egypt did not immediately cut off East and West—in fact, the exodus of Christians from the conquered provinces did much to promote Greek in the West. In addition, it is a matter of great interest to see how much of the literary oeuvre of the leading theologians of the day—men like Maximus and Sophronius—was shaped by doctrinal and political concerns which had repercussions throughout the Mediterranean world, especially where eastern exiles congregated. Along with our list of translations and classification of known works, a geographical breakdown of Greek writing known from the period would be extremely helpful, and might produce interesting results.

Maximus himself displays in his writings the characteristic seventh-century forms of *quaestiones*, the florilegium, and the disputation. A century or so later, in the works of John of Damascus (even allowing for the formidable problems of authenticity), the dialogue or disputation has assumed an even greater significance, while the so-called *Sacra Parallela* attributed to John was the florilegium to end florilegia.[51] In

[50]See in particular Cyril Mango, "La culture grecque et l'Occident au VIII siècle", in *I problemi dell'Occidente nel secolo VIII* (Spoleto, 1974; *Settimane di Spoleto* 20), 683–70; Jean Irigoin, "La culture grecque dans l'Occident latin du VIIe au IXe siècle", in *La culture antica nell'Occidente latino dal VII all'XI secolo* (Spoleto, 1975; *Settimane di Spoleto* 22), 425–46; Sicily: Lellia Cracco Ruggini, *La Sicilia fra Roma e Bisanzio, Storia di Sicilia*, III (Naples, 1980), 1–96; "Christianisation in Sicily (IIIrd–VIIth Century)", *Gerion* 1 (1983), 219–34.

[51]*PG* 95–96; *CPG*, III, 8056.

the period between the two writers, there had been feverish activity in the collection of citations and the search for texts as the rival groups, especially at the Council of 680–81, vied with each other to produce more and yet more texts in support of their own position.[52] It is clear that this growing practice also had a secondary benefit, in that it stimulated a renewed interest in the preservation and accurate copying of texts—again a somewhat paradoxical side effect of the taste for "potted" theology. While the practice of reading earlier authors primarily in collections of excerpts already made by others meant that, for example, the compiler(s) of the *Parastaseis* had little if any access to or knowledge of complete texts (for instance, of the church historians), and were consequently prone to naive historical mistakes, more narrowly doctrinal and theological florilegia were now subjected to a rigorous process of source criticism.

But this quick glance at the range of writings associated with Maximus also illustrates how closely connected they were with the circumstances and needs of the day. The letter form, for instance, acquired a new urgency in the context of these religious disputes: not only Maximus and his supporters, the two Anastasii, wrote letters to their allies in these matters, but also Pope Martin I (to Theodore Spoudaios in Jerusalem), the patriarchs Zachariah of Jerusalem, and Sergius, Paul II, Peter, and Germanus of Constantinople; many more letters, official and otherwise, were sent before each council.[53] Monotheletism produced theoretical discussions from both sides, such as the *aporiai* of the Monothelite deacon Theodore of Constantinople,[54] or in the form of dialogues, real or imaginary, such as that between Maximus and Theodosius of Caesarea.[55]

The dialogue or disputation is itself a commonly chosen form in this period, from dialogues between orthodox and Monophysites to disputes between Christians and Jews or (at the end of the period) Christians and Muslims.[56] The range goes from the literary dialogue, descen-

[52] Well brought out by Herrin, *Formation of Christendom*, 278.

[53] See the many items listed by Winkelmann, "Quellen"; also John Climacus, letters to John of Rhaitu, *PG* 88, 624–28.

[54] *PG* 91, 215–16; answered by Maximus, *ibid.*, 217–28.

[55] Above, n. 45.

[56] General introduction: Cameron, "Disputations"; for the anti-Muslim literature,

dant of the classical dialogue form which had been taken over early by Christian apologetic[57] to out and out polemic, or to the reporting of real debates. But even the most literary examples also belong in a context of actual formal and informal debate.

Formal public debates on religious issues were not a new phenomenon in late antiquity; but from the sixth century on they do seem to have become almost regular occurrences, from the elaborate occasions organized by the emperor Justinian in the early 530s to the conferences held with Nestorians and Monophysites in the east in the 560s.[58] In the capital itself, continual debate was going on at informal levels between Chalcedonians and Monophysites, especially with the many Monophysites who were sheltered in the imperial palace by the empress Theodora.

Extraordinarily large numbers of monks—as many as 90 or 100 at a time—were sometimes involved on the more formal occasions.[59] Although both now and later the records are often preserved by Syriac writers rather than Greek (as Monophysites, they had more reason to preserve them), we must not allow ourselves to be misled by this into supposing that it was not also a Greek phenomenon; the debates held in the capital and those involving official spokesmen would of course necessarily have used Greek, if necessary with interpreters. When we come to the seventh and eighth-century Near East there is naturally

see especially Adel-Théodore Khoury, *Les théologiens byzantins et l'Islam* (Leuven and Paris, 1969).

[57]Earlier history: Gustav Bardy, art. "Dialog" in *RAC*, III (Stuttgart, 1957), 949–55; Manfred Hoffman, *Der Dialog bei den christlichen Schriftstellern der ersten vier Jahrhundert* (Berlin, 1966; *TU* 96). The literary dialogue is most apparent in relation to Jews, where it had already had a long tradition: see Arthur L. Williams, *Adversus Iudaeos: A Bird's-Eye View of Christian Apologiae until the Renaissance* (Cambridge, 1935); Heinz Schreckenberg, *Die christliche Adversus-Judaeos Texte und ihr literarisches Umfeld* (Frankfurt and Bern, 1982–88).

[58]See for the former, S.P. Brock, "The Conversations with the Syrian Orthodox under Justinian (532)", *OCP* 47 (1981), 87–121; for the latter, Antoine Guillaumont, "Justinien et l'église de Perse", *DOP* 23–24 (1969–70), 41–66; "La colloque entre orthodoxes et théologiens nestoriens de Perse sous Justinien", *CRAI*, 1970, 201–207.

[59]Letters signed by 97 and 139 monks respectively at Council of 536: Eduard Schwartz, *ACO*, III, 33–38, 44–52; see Ernest Stein, *Histoire du Bas-Empire*, II (Paris, 1949), 383–84.

increasing evidence for the use of Syriac, and later still for Arabic, and Greek very gradually begins to recede. But again it was the minority which preserved the records, just as the earliest surviving reports of controversies with Muslims are edited by Christians.

In this way, therefore, the composition of literary disputes between Christians and Jews, Chalcedonians and Monophysites, or Christians and Muslims (to name only the chief categories) went hand in hand with real contemporary practice. We have a vast body of such material, which remains to be studied as a whole, and of which many individual examples remain without proper modern editions.[60] How common the dispute was as a form can be seen, for example, from its appearance in the oeuvres of almost all the major writers, Anastasius of Sinai and John of Damascus included, not to mention the minor ones. I hope to work more on this difficult subject; meanwhile, one can make a few general points. First, it is obvious that Christian–Muslim dialogues, when they began, owed a great deal to the long preexisting tradition of using the dialogue form for Christian apologetic and polemic purposes, and particularly so in relation to anti-Jewish literature. Here again the seventh century saw a great increase in the amount of such literature in Greek—the *Doctrina Jacobi nuper baptizati*, the *Trophies of Damascus*, the *Apology* of Leontius of Neapolis, to name only the most obvious[61]—and it was natural to continue in this form when Muslims rather than Jews became the subject.[62] It is very difficult among this material to sort out the real and the fictitious, or should we just say the literary, elements. Certainly a good deal of the contents are extremely stereotyped and do not neccessarily reflect real knowledge on the part of the writer.[63] A different yet related problem presents

[60] Cameron, "Disputations".

[61] On the latter, and for much guidance, see the very useful article by V. Déroche, "L'authenticité de l'"Apologie contre les Juifs' de Léontios de Néopolis", *BCH* 110 (1986), 655–69.

[62] Besides Khoury, *Théologiens byzantins et l'Islam*, see also Alain Ducellier, *Le miroir de l'Islam* (Paris, 1971).

[63] For discussion of the purpose of this polemical literature, see Stroumsa, "Religous Contacts", 34–36; S. Stroumsa and G.G. Stroumsa, "Aspects of Anti-Manichaean Polemics in Late Antiquity and under Early Islam", *HThR* 81 (1988), 27–58. For "real" debate: Sidney H. Griffith, "The Prophet Muḥammad, His Scripture and His Message According to the Christian Apologies in Arabic and Syriac

itself in relation to the later Greek disputes directed against Muslims, when it is a matter of trying to distinguish whether the writer actually knew much about Islam at firsthand, and how much (if any) access he had to Qur'ānic knowledge.

Yet overall, the intensity of production that we now see devoted to such disputes must be related to a real context of argument in contemporary society. It cannot be mere accident that the Qur'ān is so concerned to give instructions to believers as to how they should or should not conduct debate with unbelievers.[64] Several obvious reasons explain why such an intensity of sectarian argument should have come about at this time. Firstly, there was the chronic division between Monophysites, Chalcedonians, and Nestorians, which gained renewed intensity in the period after the Fifth Ecumenical Council of 553; then the Persian campaigns of the early seventh century and Heraclius' triumphant restoration of the True Cross to Jerusalem made the status of Jerusalem as a holy city, and with it the threat which Christians in Palestine saw in the Jews, into a major issue, heightened still further by Heraclius' aggressively anti-Jewish policies.[65] When the Arab conquerors arrived in Palestine and Syria only a few years after these stirring events, they found already in existence a level of polemic, argument, and religious rivalry to which little comparable can have existed previously. Naturally, those who were at the center of the religious issues turned even more enthusiastically to the dispute form which was already serving them so well.

In the case of hagiography, by contrast, its relation to a real context, and the extent of variation to be found in terms of literary elements versus historical reliability, do not need any new emphasis. But two other types of writing characteristic of this period also have to be seen against a day-to-day context. The first of these is homiletic, again not of course new, but represented now by a large quantity of material, again mostly still to be studied in any detail.[66] Now the writers of

from the First 'Abbāsid Century", in Toufic Fahd, ed., *La vie du prophète Mahomet* (Paris, 1983), 99–146, especially 117.

[64]See Khoury, *Theologiens byzantins et l'Islam*, 15–30.

[65]On all these issues, see further Cameron, "Eastern Provinces in the Seventh Century".

[66]In general: Albert Ehrhardt, *Überlieferung und Bestand der hagiographischen*

disputations were usually also the writers of homilies, some of which contained very similar material, and some of which also related to contemporary themes or events, like the homilies of Sophronius on the themes of Christmas, baptism, and the Cross, or the long homily of Theodore Syncellus on the siege of Constantinople in 626.[67] A study of the themes and styles favored by the authors of homilies in this period would be extremely useful, beginning with those which are securely attributed (there are many which are not). We might find that there are certain favorite themes—the feasts of the Virgin, especially the Koimesis (Dormition), the *myrophori*—and some others relating to contemporary topics like the Cross.[68] We would certainly also observe the closeness of the relation between Greek and writing in Syriac, the use of dialogue, and the continuity of both topic and arguments over long periods.

The second notable genre is that of collections of miracle stories associated with saints and their shrines, like the *Miracula S. Artemii*, of the shrine of John the Baptist at Oxeia in Constantinople, the *Miracles* of S. Demetrios at Thessaloniki, or the *Miracles* of S. Therapon, whose relics were moved from Cyprus to Constantinople under Justinian II;[69] these might be semi-popular in character, or they might be published by such a major literary figure as Sophronius, who edited the *Miracles of Cyrus and John*, which centered on the famous shrine at Menouthis near Alexandria.[70] The miracles clearly follow the locations of the pilgrim shrines, and in our period the majority of extant collections belong to Constantinople or to Egypt; but it was Sophronius of Jerusalem who collected the miracles of SS. Cyrus and John, whose shrine was in

und homiletischen Literatur der griechischen Kirche (Leipzig and Berlin, 1937–52); Beck, 454–49.

[67]Sophronius: *PG* 87, 3201–3364; Christmas sermon, ed. Hermann Usener, *RM*, Ser. 3, 41 (1886), 500–16; Theodore Syncellus: above, n. 24.

[68]For a very interesting attempt to link popular themes in visual art and in written sources in this period, see Anna Kartsonis, *Anastasis* (Princeton, 1986), Chaps. II and III.

[69]See Beck, 466; Pierre Maraval, *Lieux saints et pèlerinages d'Orient: Histoire et géographie des origines à la conquête arabe* (Paris, 1985), 394–96, 405, and see further, Haldon's paper in this volume.

[70]Ed. N. Fernandez Marcos, *Los Thaumata de Sofronio* (Madrid, 1975); Maraval, *Lieux saints et pèlerinages d'Orient*, 318–19.

Egypt, and we should see this genre as a widespread side product of pilgrimage centers, wherever they happened to be. The orality of which John Haldon writes in relation to question-and-answer literature is to be found here too.

But side by side with these developments went an incipient scholasticism, on whose evolution the councils of the seventh and eighth centuries had a great impact. We have seen already that the supporters and opponents of Monotheletism marshalled arrays of Biblical and patristic citations in support of their case, and in fact this is the golden age of florilegia—collections of extracts from earlier writings, chosen with some specific purpose in mind and frequently used to practical effect in ecclesiastical debate. The practice had begun at least as early as the fifth century;[71] nevertheless, it became more and more important from the late sixth century on, especially under the influence of an increased pressure of christological controversy, until, with the debates on Monotheletism in the seventh century, it acquired, as it were, a scientific method all its own. As their purpose was usually polemical or apologetic, florilegia and the citations they contained were soon themselves scrutinized for lack any of rigor, or even for actual falsification.[72] After this, it was inevitable that the practice should continue to be employed in the course of the debate on images, and indeed it was particularly important at the Second Council of Nicaea in 787, when citations brought forward in defense of images by Pope Hadrian were subjected to verification from eastern copies.[73] As we have seen, Maximus, Sophronius, and John of Damascus were all associated with such collections, and it has been suggested that this activity represents a kind of eastern scholasticism in the making.[74] At any rate, doctrine

[71]See in the first instance Henry Chadwick, art. "Florilegium" in *RAC*, VII (Stuttgart, 1969), cols. 1131–60; Marcel Richard, "Les florilèges diphysites du Ve et VIe siècle", in Aloys Grillmeier and Heinrich Bacht, eds., *Das Konzil von Chalkedon* (Würzburg, 1951), 721–48.

[72]Further (for the late sixth century), in my article "Eustratius' Life of the Patriarch Eutychius and the Fifth Ecumenical Council", in Julian Chrysostomides, ed., *Kathegetria: Essays Presented to Joan Hussey for her 80th Birthday* (Camberley, 1988), 225–47, and see above.

[73]See Paul Van den Ven, "La patristique et l'hagiographie au concile de Nicée de 787", *Byzantion* 25–27 (1957), 325–62; Mango, "Availability of Books", 30–31.

[74]See Patrick Gray, "Neochalcedonianism and the Tradition: From Patristic to

was felt to be sound only if it could be defended by reference to past authority; but the canon of the great Fathers belonged to the past, and the task of the new generation was to uphold it and interpret it, not to change it. The many councils in the period surely speeded this process, by constantly going over the same ground with yet greater refinement of argument and citation. A striking example comes from the preliminaries to the Fifth Council in 553; when the allegedly obscure Eutychius produced a new argument from Scripture in support of imperial policy against Origenism, he was universally acclaimed and made patriarch at once.[75]

It seems to me that the growth of florilegia for use in doctrinal argument tended, like the increasing composition of literary disputes between religious groups, often along repetitive lines, to crystallize lines of thought along preset tracks. It can hardly have helped Christians writing in either Syriac or Greek to keep calm in the face of Muslim argument, especially when, for instance as at the end of the seventh century, Christians were confronted by a desire on the Muslim side to assert its own identity over against Christianity. The literary disputes between Christians and Muslims, as between Christians and Jews, tended to remain just that—stereotyped exercises rehearsing familiar arguments. On what ground were the two sides to meet in such a situation? The Syriac apocalyptic works discussed by Gerrit Reinink and Han Drijvers in this volume do not give one much confidence in their authors' knowledge of or sympathy for the Muslims, and the situation of writers using Greek is not likely to have been so different. If we knew how often the ordinary Christian and the ordinary Muslim talked to each other, instead of how they are presented in the confrontational dialogues, we might have a much more realistic impression. Even so, it is fair to conclude that the religious controversies which divided Christians themselves had served to harden their various positions and ways of thinking and arguing, and that this in turn may have made it harder for them to approach Islam.

Byzantine Theology", *BF* 8 (1982), 61–70.

[75] Evagrius remembered the argument a generation later: *HE* IV.38; see Cameron, "Eustratius' Life of the Patriarch Eutychius", 228.

Nothing happened with the beginning of official Byzantine iconoclasm under Leo III to change the situation outlined above. Greek literature continued in the same forms, though with a new dimension of polemic. Logically, of course, one may think that Byzantine iconoclasm ought to have made rapprochement easier, both officially and for individuals. In fact, and ironically, the greatest Greek writer under Arab rule in the eighth century was also the greatest defender of images. Not simply Monophysitism and Dyophisitism, but also the issue of Monotheletism and the imperial support it enjoyed, had divided Christians fiercely in the seventh century, and acted as a catalyst in many of the literary developments which I have traced. Now Christians were divided again, and again imperial policy was a major factor. Ever more ingenious scholastic arguments and citations had to be mobilized, and now both sides felt equally threatened by Islam—especially in view of recent hostilities and recent Umayyad policy towards Christians. This new split between Christians was not likely to help understanding between Christians and Muslims; nor is it a coincidence that our main source for the history of Byzantine–Islamic relations in the early period, the *Chronographia* of Theophanes, was completed only when Iconoclasm had been defeated, nor that a return to some degree of secular learning after the very low ebb reached in the eighth century, was also possible only after this diversion.[76]

The literature written in Greek during our period, both generally and specifically in relation to or proximity with Islam, is full of problems. On the other hand, there is a great deal of it, and it offers far more possibilities for historical analysis than have as yet been realized. I think that the main point that has emerged from this paper is that in order to use this literature in relation to early Islam, or even the immediately pre-Islamic period, we must first recognize the extent to which it was conditioned by what was happening in the Byzantine world, and formed by such apparently distant influences as conciliar argument. Even after the loss of the eastern provinces, these influences continued to be strongly felt, and the legacy of earlier ones remained.

---

[76]See Michael Whitby's paper in this volume (above, 66–74) for further suggestions as to why we have almost no serious writing by contemporary Byzantines about the Arab invasions.

The inhabitants of the Arab-ruled provinces had had a severe identity problem even before the conquests, and the impact of Islam inevitably worsened it. This is what we have to bear in mind when trying to use their Greek writings as source material. Surprisingly little has been done in any general way as yet to evaluate it from this point of view, despite the interest and importance which it has both in itself for the cultural and literary historian, and as source material for history. Most of the work that has been undertaken to date has been done, perhaps predictably, from the points of view either of theological content or of the history of texts. When this literature is finally studied in a broader context, one of our main tasks will be to identify and distinguish the differing degrees of influence in each individual case; only then will it be possible to see how they may affect the work in question as a source for the historian, and to go on to make better use of the Greek sources in the context of the history of the Near East in this period.

3

The Works of Anastasius of Sinai: A Key Source for the History of Seventh-Century East Mediterranean Society and Belief*

John Haldon
(University of Birmingham)

Introduction

I HAVE ARGUED ELSEWHERE that the seventh century marks a moment of cultural transformation for the East Roman or Byzantine world, not just in terms of the obvious political changes which took place, nor simply with respect to the changes in social, economic, and administrative patterns of life within the Empire or outside it, in those territories which were firmly in Muslim hands by the late 640s, but also in respect of patterns of belief and, more significantly, the ways in which people perceived their world and expressed their attitudes to what had happened. This process was not sudden, of course, nor was it simply "caused" by the Muslim conquests: much of it represented the last stages of a series of longer-term developments which reflect the evolution of late Roman

*I should like to express my thanks to Dr. Joseph Munitiz, currently completing a new edition of the *Quaestiones et Responsiones* of Anastasius for the *CCSG*, for much valuable discussion on the textual tradition of the works ascribed to Anastasius and on Anastasius himself.

Christian society and culture from the third century on. In the Monophysite East, change was clearly perceived by contemporaries in the sixth century. But it was the Muslim conquests which set the seal on these developments and made them irrevocable. Henceforth, Christian society in the East Mediterranean region, whether within the Empire or not, had to come to terms with the existence of a new and intellectually dynamic religious system and new political forms, within which new modes of domination and subordination were particularly significant. This is all well known, of course; the ways in which Christian culture responded to the arrival of the Arabs have been discussed, albeit usually very partially and from an understandably limited perspective (given the nature of the sources), by several scholars.[1] In particular, the emphasis that apocalyptic writings received in the second half of the seventh century has been highlighted—quite rightly—as a significant indication of a change in Christian attitudes, which were obliged to begin to reconcile the probable permanence of the new state of affairs with traditional political ideologies and millenarian assumptions.[2] I should like here to consider some of the writings attributed to one seventh-century Christian thinker and ascetic, Anastasius of Sinai. In doing so, I wish not only to relate these writings to the context in which they were compiled, both in respect of literary and theological antecedents and of specific historical events, but also to illustrate several features

[1]See, for example, Walter E. Kaegi, Jr., "Initial Byzantine Reactions to the Arab Conquest", *Church History* 38 (1969), 139–49; S.P. Brock, "Syriac Views of Emergent Islam", in G.H.A. Juynboll, ed., *Studies on the First Century of Islamic Society* (Carbondale, 1982), 9–21; and for a survey of later Syriac/Monophysite views, see Susan Ashbrook Harvey, "Remembering Pain: Syriac Historiography and the Separation of the Churches", *Byzantion* 58 (1988), 295–308, esp. 298–302.

[2]See my remarks in "Ideology and Social Change in the Seventh Century: Military Discontent as a Barometer", *Klio* 68 (1986), 139–90, esp. 167–69; and more particularly G.J. Reinink, "Pseudo-Methodius und die Legende vom römischen Endkaiser", in W. Verbeke, D. Verhelst, and A. Welkenhuysen, eds., *The Use and Abuse of Eschatology in the Middle Ages* (Leuven, 1988), 82–111. On apocalyptic in general, see Wolfram Brandes, "Die apokalyptische Literatur", in F. Winkelmann, ed., *Quellen zur Geschichte der frühen Byzanz* (Berlin, 1989; *BAA* 57), 305–22; and note Francisco Javier Martinez, *Eastern Christian Apocalyptic in the Early Muslim Period: Pseudo-Methodius and Pseudo-Athanasius*, Ph.D. dissertation: Catholic University of America, 1985; and especially the contributions of Drijvers and Reinink in this volume.

of this period of transformation common to all the cultures of the East Mediterranean zone, both in its Christian and its Muslim aspects.

Anastasius and His Cultural Milieu

I must begin by making it clear that I approach the works of Anastasius from the perspective of a cultural historian. I am not particularly concerned that the attribution to Anastasius of some of the *narrationes* I shall mention remains uncertain, nor that there is still some lingering doubt concerning the *Questions and Answers* usually ascribed to him. I am concerned that the material I use belongs with little or no doubt to the seventh century, primarily the second half of that century. Nor am I overly concerned by the possibility that there may in fact have been at least two figures in the East at this period, both seemingly well known in their own lands, with the name Anastasius: Anastasius of Sinai, and Anastasius the humble monk—the textual tradition makes it almost impossible in certain cases to distinguish which texts belong to which author. My own preference is to see no distinction, and to regard them as being one and the same individual; but this is difficult to prove, and such an endeavor would require a much more exacting philological and textual analysis of the key texts than space permits here. In addition, there remains some debate as to whether the Anastasius to whom a number of texts are traditionally ascribed is actually Anastasius of Sinai, or Anastasius, patriarch of Antioch (559–70, 593–99), although it is reasonably clear, both on the basis of internal coherence and style, and on that of internal historical references, that the texts with which we are concerned here do belong to the last 50 or so years of the seventh century, and not earlier.

The situation is further complicated, potentially more seriously for our concerns, by the fact that the corpus of stories and *apophthegmata* of the eastern monastic world has a continuous tradition, both in narrative style and subject matter as well as in geographical extent, from the fifth century to the later seventh. A number of themes were regularly borrowed or reused, and sometimes whole stories were simply taken from earlier collections by later writers. It is therefore difficult in many instances to provide a date for a particular tale, or to tie it to any specific historical moment. Some stories in the *Pratum Spirituale* of John

Moschus, for example, appear also in the *narrationes* ascribed to Anastasius; and it is not always possible to say whether we are dealing with an Anastasian borrowing from an earlier collection, or a later interpolation from the Anastasian collection into the *Pratum*. Other stories, in contrast, were already firmly ascribed to Anastasius by the middle of the eighth century: John of Damascus refers to a story concerning an icon of S. Theodore, for example, which belongs to the so-called "second collection" of tales more or less firmly ascribed to Anastasius. Similarly, a number of themes taken up in the *Questions and Answers* of Anastasius pursue topics dealt with in the sayings of the desert fathers, the *Pratum Spirituale* of John Moschus or, indeed, the *Ladder of Divine Ascent* of John Climacus—among them the whole question of the rôle of tears as a symbol of repentance and as an expression of the transformation of the sensual fluids of the body into cleansing spirituality. Finally, key issues relating to the universal problem of divine foresight and foreknowledge, on the one hand, and the determinist or fatalist roots of predestinarianism, on the other, occur in Anastasius as well as in much earlier collections, and represent aspects of the typical content of Christian apologetic and exegetical literature.[3]

[3]See the remarks of François Nau, "Le texte grec des récits utiles à l'âme d'Anastase (le Sinaïte)", *OC* 3 (1903), 56–75, at 59–60. For Anastasius of Antioch, see Beck, 380–81; *CPG*, III, nos. 6944–69; Günter Weiss, *Studia Anastasiana I. Studien zum Leben, zu den Schriften und zur Theologie des Patriarchen Anastasius I. von Antiochien* (Munich, 1965); and the review by Weiss in *BZ* 60 (1967), 339–42, of S.N. Sakkos, Περὶ Ἀναστασίων Σιναϊτῶν (Thessaloniki, 1964), who believes he can distinguish seven different Anastasii ranging from Anastasius I of Antioch (second half of the sixth century) to an otherwise unknown Anastasius of the ninth-tenth centuries. See also the critical remarks of Evangelos Chrysos, "Νεώτεραι ἔρευναι περὶ Ἀναστασίων Σιναϊτῶν", Κληρονομία 1 (1969), 121–44.

Moschus' collection is especially important, representing some 50 years of personal eyewitness experience of the monastic and ascetic world, ranging across Syria, Palestine, and Egypt to the Aegean isles and Italy. For a brief survey, see Elpidio Mioni, art. "Jean Moschus" in *Dict. spirit.*, VIII (Paris, 1972), 632–40; and on the *apophthegmata*, Th. Klauser and P. de Labriolle, art. "Apophthegma" in *RAC*, I (Stuttgart, 1950), 545–50. For the story of the Saracens and the icon of S. Theodore, see Nau, "Récits utiles à l'âme", no. 44, 64–65; John of Damascus, *De imaginibus*, III, *PG* 94, 1393; and Paul Canart, "Une nouvelle anthologie monastique: le vaticanus graecus 2592", *Le Muséon* 75 (1962), 109–29. Note also the story of the monk and the icon of the Virgin in Jerusalem, incorporated into the ps.-Athanasius

A second point concerns the textual history and tradition of this material. The works of Anastasius have only recently begun to appear in modern editions: the *Hodēgos* or *Viae dux*, the two *Sermones in constitutionem hominis secundum imaginem Dei*, a third *Sermo adversus Monotheletas*, the florilegium *adversus Monotheletas*, and five *Capita adversus Monotheletas* have now been critically edited, with a detailed analysis of their textual history, by Karl-Heinz Uthemann.[4] This extremely important work has gone a long way towards solving some of the problems associated with Anastasius' writings. In addition, the work of Paul Canart has contributed to the resolution of many of the difficulties and contradictions connected with the various collections of *narrationes* associated with the name of Anastasius of Sinai. It is now possible to reconstruct a reasonably homogeneous corpus of such tales dated to the middle and later seventh century, although it must be emphasized that this corpus is still far from complete. There is still a substantial body of such material in Arabic and Ethiopic, for example, which needs to be studied and made accessible before the real scale of any corpus of stories by Anastasius can be appreciated.[5]

---

as part of Qu. 39, but present also in the *Pratum Spirituale*, *cap*. 45 (*PG* 87, 2900B); and see Wolfgang Lackner, "Zwei Membra disiecta aus dem *Pratum Spirituale* des Ioannes Moschos", *AB* 100 (1982), 341–50; J.A. Munitiz, "The Link Between some Membra Disiecta of John Moschus", *AB* 101 (1983), 295–96; and especially Robert J. Penella, "An Overlooked Story about Apollonius of Tyana in Anastasius Sinaita", *Traditio* 34 (1978), 414–15.

Questions of predestination and determinism had been addressed by earlier Christian thinkers, such as the (probably) fifth-century bishop Nemesius of Emesa (see n. 62 below) and even the historian Theophylact Simocatta in the early seventh century. On the latter, see Leendert G. Westerink, "Theophylactus Simocattes on Predestination", in *Studi in onore di Vittorio de Falco* (Naples, 1971), 535–51; cf. also now Theophylact, *On Predestined Terms of Life*, ed. and trans. Charles Garton and Leendert G. Westerlink (Buffalo, 1978). On the nature of the debate and its development into the seventh century, see esp. David Amand, *Fatalisme et liberté dans l'antiquité grecque* (Leuven, 1945).

[4]Anastasius of Sinai, *Viae Dux*, ed. K.-H. Uthemann (Leuven, 1981; *CCSG* 8); *idem*, *Sermones duo in constitutionem hominis secundum imaginem Dei necnon opuscula adversus Monotheletas*, ed. K.-H. Uthemann (Brepols, 1985; *CCSG* 12). See *CPG*, III, nos. 7745, 7747–49, 7756.

[5]Canart, "Nouvelle anthologie monastique"; *idem*, "Nouveaux récits du moine Anastase", in *Actes du XIIe Congrès International d'Études Byzantines* (Belgrade, 1964), II, 263–71. The *Narrationes* have been partially published by Nau: "Récits

Anastasius of Sinai was a prolific writer. Apart from the works to which reference has already been made above, he apparently also wrote a two-volume treatise against the Jews and an apologetic tract for lay people (neither of these has survived),[6] a short tract on heresies and synods,[7] a confession of faith comprising also an anti-heretical defense of neo-Chalcedonian orthodoxy,[8] a series of sermons on diverse themes,[9] a series of homilies,[10] and a dogmatic *tomos* of patristic extracts intended as an intellectual tool in his life-long struggle against Monophysitism.[11] In addition, he has traditionally been credited with the authorship of a number of other much later texts—the inevitable fate of many writers whose works were widely disseminated during or after their lifetimes.[12] Finally, and for our purposes most importantly, he has been credited with the compilation of one of the most important medieval collections of *Questions and Answers*—*erōtapokriseis*—written down some time

utiles à l'âme d'Anastase"; "Le texte grec des récits du moine Anastase sur les saints Pères du Sinai", *OC* 2 (1902), 58–87; and *Les récits inédits du moine Anastase* (Paris, 1902), which includes a number of tales not included in the *OC* articles. See also G. Levi della Vida, "Sulla versione araba di Giovanni Mosco e di Pseudo-Anastasio Sinaita secondo alcuni codici Vaticani", *Miscellanea G. Mercati* (Rome, 1946), 104–15; and Victor Arras, trans., *Quadraginta historiae monachorum* (Leuven, 1988; *CSCO* 506, *Scr. Aethiopici* 86), 138–51., for tales attributed to an Anastasius relating to Egypt and Sinai. For a list of the *Narrationes* and bibliography, see *CPG*, III, no. 7758 (pp. 458–62).

[6]See *PG* 89, 933; and for the τόμος δογματικὸς πρὸς τὸν λαόν, *ibid.*, 97, 124.

[7]In J.B. Pitra, *Iuris ecclesiastici Graecorum historia et monumenta*, II (Rome, 1868), 257–71 (although its ascription to Anastasius is not certain). See Sakkos, Περὶ 'Αναστασίων Σιναϊτῶν, 171–74; K.-H. Uthemann, "Die dem Anastasios Sinaites zugeschriebene Synopsis de haeresibus et synodis", *Annuarium historiae conciliorum*, 14 (1982), 58–95.

[8]In Pitra, *Iuris ecclesiastici graecorum*, 271–74, also of uncertain authorship. Sakkos (Περὶ 'Αναστασίων Σιναϊτῶν, 174) ascribes it to Anastasius of Sinai.

[9]See *CPG*, III, nos. 7752 (on the deceased), 7753 (on the transfiguration); and Beck, 443.

[10]*CPG*, III, nos. 7750–51, 7754–55.

[11]*CPG*, III, no. 7771. See Ferdinand Cavallera, "Les fragments de S. Amphiloque dans l'Hodegos et le tome dogmatique d'Anastase le Sinaite", *RHE* 8 (1907), 473–97.

[12]Including, for example, a treatise on the Creation, the *Hexaemeron*: see Beck, 444; *CPG*, III, no. 7770; and Uthemann, introduction to his edition of the *Sermones duo*, cxxxix, where he dates it to the eleventh or twelfth centuries. For other dubia, see *CPG*, III, nos. 7771–81, with literature cited.

during the later seventh century.[13] I will discuss this collection in detail in a moment.

In many ways, Anastasius is a most appropriate figure for those interested in the seventh century, since his life coincided almost exactly with it. Born probably in the early years of the century, he was still writing in about the year 700–701. Thanks to the work of Marcel Richard and Karl-Heinz Uthemann in particular, it is possible to date some of his most important works: the *Hodēgos* to the period after 641–42 and before 680–81 (and probably well before, although both dates are approximate), with a revised version equipped with scholia by Anastasius himself, and produced *ca.* 686–89;[14] the tract on heresies and synods to the years 692–95; the *Sermo adversus Monotheletas* to about 701; and the *Oratio de sacra synaxi* to approximately the same period as the *Quaestiones et responsiones*, the last few years of the seventh century.[15]

In spite of his wide-ranging theological interests, his actual knowledge of and access to the secular and ecclesiastical history of his own time seems to have been very limited. It was colored by his travels in Egypt, the Sinai area, and Palestine, but reflects little of the turbulent history of the East Roman state at this time. He may have travelled to or come from Cyprus, although this is uncertain. But when he recounts the history of the beginnings of Monotheletism, he seems to be basing his account on garbled and inaccurate oral traditions and his

---

[13]See *CPG*, III, no. 7746; and below.

[14]Uthemann, *Viae Dux*, ccvi-ccxvii, ccxviii n. 72; Marcel Richard, "Anastase le Sinaite, l'Hodegos et le Monothélisme", *REB* 16 (1958), 29–42, reprinted in Richard's *Opera Minora*, III (Leuven, 1976–77), 29–34, no. 63.

[15]Uthemann, *Viae Dux*, ccxviii n. 72; Richard, "Anastase le Sinaite". The *Quaestiones et responsiones* refer to a period of 700 years as having elapsed since the time of Christ (*PG* 89, 769B14–C1, Qu. 117/*69); the *Oratio de sacra synaxi* refers in detail to two issues in particular which occur in the *Quaestiones*: the cleansing and purifying value of tears, and the virtue of not judging one's fellow men. The former was an old subject: see the relevant entry in G.W.H. Lampe, *A Patristic Greek Lexicon* (Oxford, 1961), s.v. δάκρυον, 331–32, for the long list of Christian authorities from the third century on who deal with this matter; and note in particular John Climacus, *Scala Paradisi*, *PG* 88, 805C–808D. On the latter, see *Quaestiones et responsiones*, *PG* 89, 757C4–760A8 (Qu. 105/*49), and 432A5–B12 (Qu. 10/*73); together with 832D1–833A14, 837A3–11, 848B8–849A2, where both of these issues are developed.

own memory, rather than on any written records. As one commentator has noted, he makes no mention of either Maximus Confessor or the patriarch Sophronius, two of the key protagonists in the opening stages of Monothelite discussion; he makes Athanasius of Antioch, a Monophysite, responsible for suggesting Monotheletism to Heraclius, who then proposes it to the patriarch Sergius of Constantinople and Pope Martin. The Lateran Synod of 649 is presented as the response to Heraclius' *Ekthesis* of 638 (rather than to the *Typos* of Constans II); and Pope Martin's exile occurs before the Muslim conquest of Palestine, Syria, and Egypt. On the other hand, one of the *narrationes* ascribed to Anastasius mentions Thalassius, friend and correspondent of Maximus and abbot of a monastery in Libya, for the time of Niketas, *augustalis* of Egypt.[16] It is perhaps indicative of the time in which Anastasius did most of his writing—the 630s and after—that he appears to have no accurate records at his disposal: even a deliberate falsification of some of the history of the origins of Monotheletism, undertaken in order to demonstrate the culpability of Sergius or Heraclius, would not require quite such a distortion of the chain of events. It may also reflect the fact that after the death of Sophronius in 638 there was an interregnum in Jerusalem of some 29 years, a result partly of the Monothelite politics of the Constantinopolitan church and the state, and partly of the Muslim conquests and their consolidation, the neo-Chalcedonian communities of Palestine and Arabia being fiercely hostile to the new doctrine. Only in northern Syria does there seem to have been any real support for the imperial policy, as demonstrated by the case of the patriarch of Antioch, Makarios, and his followers during and after the Sixth Ecumenical Council of 680–81, held in Constantinople. All this may well suggest that Alexandria is the most likely base from which Anastasius conducted much of his business and where his numerous writings were set down. Since there is, indeed, little real evidence to connect him with Sinai apart from the ascription in the manuscript tradition, his ignorance of imperial politics might the more readily be understood. But his overriding concern with defending Chalcedonian

[16] *Sermones duo*, iii, i.18–112. See Richard, "Anastase le Sinaite", 33–34, 41–42. For Thalassius, see Nau's edition of the *Narrationes* in *OC* 2 (1902), 84:10–15, 87:4. He was one of the leading theologians of his time and can be ranked alongside Maximus and Sophronius; see Beck, 450–51.

orthodoxy against heresy (from which I think it reasonable to infer an overriding concern to protect the interests and further existence of a minority community among the Christian populations of the Near East) seems to me an adequate justification for his lack of interest in imperial affairs. His concern was the Christian community of Egypt and Syria and its struggle against the majority Monophysite tradition.[17]

Apart from what can be gleaned from his own writings, little else is known of Anastasius.[18] As we have said, as a neo-Chalcedonian living in an area in which the Church to which he belonged was, from the 640s on, only one of several competing congregations, he devoted much of his life to polemicizing against Monophysitism in particular. In the *Hodēgos* he invoked his knowledge of Islamic writings to demonstrate that Muslim christology evolved as a reaction to the Monophysite dogma of the followers of Severus of Antioch, rather than as a development from it.[19] Like others of his generation, he accepted the popular assumption that the Muslim invasions were a punishment visited upon the Chosen People—the Romans—by God for their sins, specifically,

[17] See Julius Assfalg, ed., *Kleines Wörterbuch des christlichen Orients* (Wiesbaden, 1975), 255–56; John F. Haldon, *Byzantium in the Seventh Century: the Transformation of a Culture* (Cambridge, 1990), 286–89, 299–313. See also the useful survey by Hugh Kennedy, "The Melkite Church from the Islamic Conquest to the Crusades: Continuity and Adaptation in the Byzantine Legacy", in *Seventeenth International Byzantine Congress, Major Papers* (New York, 1986), 325–42.

[18] For further discussion on Anastasius, see J.-B. Kumpfmüller, *De Anastasio Sinaita* (Würzburg, 1865); and Nau, "Récits utiles à l'âme", 57; Sakkos, Περὶ Ἀναστασίων Σιναϊτῶν; Canart, "Nouveaux récits", 267–71.

[19] If, as Nau has argued, he is also the author of the *Narrationes*, he seems to have travelled as far afield as Cyprus, and moved frequently between Damascus, Jerusalem, Sinai, and Alexandria/lower Egypt. See Nau, "Récits utiles à l'âme", 57–58; Canart, "Nouveaux récits", 265–67; and Marcel Richard, art. "Anastase le Sinaite" in *Dict. spirit.*, I (Paris, 1937), 546–47. Note also K.-H. Uthemann, "Antimonophysitische Aporien des Anastasios Sinaites", *BZ* 74 (1981), 11–26. On Anastasius' view of Islam, see Sidney H. Griffith and Robin Darling, "Anastasius of Sinai, the Monophysites and the Qur'ān", *Eighth Annual Byzantine Studies Conference, Abstracts of Papers* (Chicago, 1982), 13. At *Viae Dux* (ed. Uthemann), I.1.44–49 and X.2.4.1–3, he refers explicitly to the views of the "Arabs" and the "Saracens" on christological issues. This seems to be among the earliest Christian references to Islamic theology. For the tradition which develops from the eighth century on, see Adel-Théodore Khoury, "Apologétique byzantine contre l'Islam (VIIIe-XIIIe siècles)", *POC* 29 (1979), 242–300; 30 (1980), 132–74; 32 (1982), 14–49.

the heresy of Monotheletism. He represented also, however, the ordinary people, as is clear from many of the answers ascribed to him in the collection of *Questions and Answers*: he demonstrates a sympathy and understanding for the humdrum, day-to-day existence of ordinary folk which was no doubt common to many holy men and churchmen, but which is—as one might expect—not so readily found in the theological works of a Maximus or the polemical writings of a Sophronius. And it is in this context that the collection of *Questions and Answers* is so important.

The Textual Tradition and Genre

Collections of questions and answers originated in classical antiquity, and were generally the form through which specific questions in both the secular and the religious spheres were expressed as an educational and didactic exercise.[20] In the Christian tradition, this classical model was adapted to the purpose of Biblical exegesis and, more particularly, the clarification of key concepts in Christian dogma. Beginning in the later third and fourth centuries with compilations attributed to Eusebius of Caesarea, the best-known of these early collections is that of the so-called Ambrosiaster, spuriously attributed to Augustine, and compiled in Rome *ca*. 370–75. It deals with Biblical exegesis (both Old and New Testaments), Arianism and pagan beliefs, and questions of dogma and of Christian morality. Similar compilations followed: an exegetical series ascribed to Jerome, a series of questions and answers on dogma ascribed to Augustine, and others by Eucherius of Lyons and Salonius (son of the latter), which deal in addition with matters such as the origins of ethnic names, the months of the year, Hebrew technical terms and names in the Old Testament, and so on, dating to the fifth century. Similar collections exist for the sixth century, ascribed to a certain Junilius, an official in Justinian's bureaucracy who wrote in about 542,

[20]Hermann Dörries, art. "Erotapokriseis" in *RAC*, VI (Stuttgart, 1966), 342–70. For a less analytic but still valuable descriptive account, see Gustave Bardy, "La littérature patristique des *Quaestiones et responsiones* sur l'Ecriture Sainte", *RB* 41 (1932), 210–36, 341–69, 515–37; 42 (1933), 14–30, 211–29, 328–52; and for a less detailed account, Otto Bardenhewer, *Geschichte der altkirchlichen Literatur* (Freiburg, 1913–32), IV, 12–13.

and to Isidore of Seville. All these collections can be related to classical *zētēmata*-forms; but other classical forms were also developed in a Christian guise, most importantly the *eisagōgai*, intended, as the name suggests, to introduce a field of learning or knowledge to a beginner, and therefore covering all the key principles of knowledge in the field in question. This was the form adopted by the earliest monastic *apophthegmata*, intended to provide confessional guidance and advice from those who were credited with the appropriate experience and divine inspiration.

Very quickly, however, the two forms were intermixed, so that from the original confessional compilations a hybrid form developed. The *Regulae brevis tractatae*, or *Askētikon*, of Basil, and a similarly constructed text of Symeon, dated to the fourth century, are followed by the ascetic *conlationes* of John Cassianus, in which the confessional aspect is widened to incorporate a more expansive and detailed series of questions on the eremitic life and its purpose and function within Christian society. The literary character of these last compilations contrasts with the originally oral character of the *apophthegmata*. But the compilation known as the *Four Dialogues* of ps.-Caesarius widens its scope to produce a version of both traditions, and is the first real hybrid. Its ascription to the brother of Gregory of Nazianzus may be doubted, although it contains material which may derive from several sources over a considerable period. In its final form it seems to belong to about the mid-sixth century.[21] Two similar compilations are to be ascribed to Theodoret, one certainly, one possibly—the former a polemical collection of *Quaestiones ad Judaeos*, the latter known as the ps.-Justin.[22]

[21] *Caesarii sapientissimi viri fratris Gregorii theologi Dialogi quattuor*, in *PG* 38, 852–1189. Bardy, "Littérature patristique", *RB* 42 (1933), 343, notes that this collection includes references to Maximus Confessor, and concludes that this consequently dates it to the eighth century or later. But the references seem clearly to be a later interpolation—similar instances can be found in the ps.-Anastasian collection of 88 questions (see below) and in the ps.-Athanasian *Quaestiones ad Antiochum ducem*. For a full analysis of this text, see Rudolf Riedinger, *Pseudo-Kaisarios. Überlieferungsgeschichte und Verfasserfrage* (Munich, 1969).

[22] The genuine text is fragmentary: *Quaestiones in loca difficilia scripturae sacrae*, in *PG* 80, 77–858. For the ps.-Justin, *Quaestiones et responsiones ad orthodoxos*, see *PG* 6, 1249–1400; and cf. Dörries, "Erotapokriseis", 356–58; Marcel Richard, art. "Florilèges spirituels grecs" in *Dict. spirit.*, V (Paris, 1964), 475–510.

And finally, if we leave to one side the *Quaestiones ad Thalassium* and the 79 *Questions and Answers* on various problems of Maximus Confessor, which are restricted to the purely theological and exegetical field,[23] we come to the two collections with which I am most concerned here: the so-called ps.-Athanasius, *Quaestiones ad Antiochum ducem*, and the *Quaestiones et responsiones* of Anastasius of Sinai.

These two collections, and especially that of Anastasius, are important for several reasons. They have a strongly oral element, although there is little doubt that both were originally compiled as more or less finished collections. Like some earlier collections (especially the ps.-Caesarius and the ps.-Justin), both reflect contemporary concerns and anxieties within an established exegetical-confessional framework. Both, but especially that of Anastasius, contain a great deal of contemporary material, in contrast to most earlier compilations. The ps.-Athanasian collection is clearly based in many respects on the Anastasian. But at the same time, both collections pose a number of difficulties for the historian, for the textual tradition of the Anastasian collection in particular has been heavily interpolated; and their widespread dissemination in medieval times has meant a proliferation of manuscript witnesses which poses particularly difficult problems for any editor. It will be best briefly to summarize these difficulties before looking at the *Questions and Answers* and their value as sources for the society, culture, and beliefs of the seventh-century East Roman world.

First, then, the *Questions and Answers* of Anastasius. Briefly, these were first edited in the early seventeenth century by Johann Gretser; and Richard has shown that he in fact edited a text which was already the result of a combination of two earlier collections at some point during the eleventh or twelfth centuries. The older of the two collections, which the eleventh-century redactor emended and altered in many places, consisted of 103 questions attributed to the abbot Anastasius, with no florilegia. The original form of this collection is fortunately preserved in two ninth/tenth-century codices in Moscow and Wolfenbüttel. These two manuscripts complement each other in several

[23]Now edited by Karl Laga and Carlos Steel, *Maximi confessoris Quaestiones ad Thalassium I: Quaestiones I-LV* (Turnhout and Leuven, 1980; *CCSG* 7); Jóse H. Declerck, *Maximi confessoris Quaestiones et dubia* (Turnhout and Leuven, 1982; *CCSG* 10).

ways, and have permitted Richard both to reestablish the original text of the seventh-century *Questions and Answers*, and to fill one or two important gaps.

The second collection which the eleventh-century redactor employed is an exegetical and spiritual florilegium of the later ninth or tenth century, and comprises 88 questions and answers. The author of this work used the Anastasian collection for some 29 of his questions; and the eleventh-century redactor then put the two collections together, using the second and later collection as his base. He thus uses only 66 of the original *Questions and Answers* of Anastasius, so that the final collection of 154 questions represents only very partially the Anastasian corpus. This is the text edited by Gretser, as mentioned above. In addition, Gretser took a further 15 questions attributed to Anastasius in an appendix to one of the recensions of the florilegium of 88 questions, which are the *Quaestiones extra ordinem* of the Migne edition.

Most of the detective work on the Anastasian collection is the result of the research of Marcel Richard, who unfortunately died before he was able to produce an edition. This task has now been taken up by Father Joseph Munitiz, who has nearly finished the project (with some emendations to Richard's original conclusions) and intends to publish the text in the *Corpus Christianorum* series.[24] Richard gives a complete concordance of the relationship between a) the florilegium of 88 questions and answers, and the original 103 questions and answers of Anastasius; and b) between the Gretser edition republished in *PG* 89, and the original collection; together with the text of questions and answers omitted from the edition but belonging to the original Anastasian corpus.[25]

---

[24] Marcel Richard, "Les véritables 'Questions et réponses' d'Anastase le Sinäite", *Bulletin de l'Institut de recherches et d'histoire des textes* 15 (1967–68), 39–56; = his *Opera Minora*, III, no. 64, with App. IV-V; *idem*, "Les textes hagiographiques du Codex Athos Philotheou 52", *AB* 93 (1975), 147–56. His views are summarized in "Les fragments du commentaire de S. Hippolyte sur les proverbes de Salomon", *Le Muséon* 79 (1966), 61–94, see 61–62. The two key manuscript witnesses to the original Anastasian corpus are from the Historical Museum, Synodal Library, Ms. Mosqu. graec. 265 (Vlad. 197), fols. 241–298v; and Ms. Wolfenbüttel, Bibl. Herzog-August 4240 (Guden graec. 53), the former of the ninth-tenth centuries, the latter of the tenth.

[25] Richard, "Les véritables 'Questions et réponses'", 42–50, 55–56.

The exact date at which these various questions and answers were first written down is not clear. But there is enough internal historical evidence to suggest a date some time in the second half of the seventh century, perhaps around the year 700, certainly after the Muslim conquest of Palestine, Egypt, and Syria. I will discuss this evidence in a moment.

Less can be said about the ps.-Athanasian *Quaestiones ad Antiochum ducem*. The text is still in need of a critical edition and detailed analysis, and it is consequently difficult to reach any firm conclusions. There is no reference to the Arabs or Muslims, or to any of the traumatic developments of the later 630s and after. But this is in itself no evidence of an earlier date. The text of one of the answers refers to the fact that the Arians had held Palestine and the Holy Places for only a short time before they had been driven out, and that "barbarians" had often invaded the region in the past. This might refer to the Persian invasion and occupation of the period 614 to 626–27.[26] The collection is concluded by a long answer to Qu. 137 on how the Jews can be persuaded to accept the fact that Jesus was the Messiah and not simply another prophet.[27] This section is remarkable for two reasons. In the first place, it is not a polemic *adversus Judaeos* in the traditional sense, but an attempt to persuade by fairly rational argument, although it is not lacking entirely in the polemical and sometimes vituperative language of the genre. Second, although it is very much more concise and rigorously ordered, in its disposition it is not unlike the better-known *Doctrina Jacobi nuper baptizati*, a text which purports to be the argument of a Jewish forced convert, intended to persuade his fellows of the need to embrace Christianity.[28] The *Doctrina* appears to have been written down in the middle years of the 630s, perhaps shortly after 634;[29] and it is a tempting possibility that the ps.-Athanasian text of

[26] Dörries, "Erotapokriseis", 358, thought this reference to Arians might apply rather to the "barbarians", and hence the Persians; *Quaestiones ad Antiochum ducem*, in *PG* 28, Qu. 44 (625B1-C16), see 625C7–16. See the description of the collection by Bardy, "Littérature patristique", *RB* 42 (1933), 328–32.

[27] *PG* 28, 684C6–700C5 (*CPG*, III, no. 7795).

[28] *Doctrina Iacobi nuper baptizati*, ed. N. Bonwetsch in *Abhandlungen der königlichen Gesellschaft der Wissenschaften zu Göttingen, philologisch-historische Klasse*, Neue Folge, 12.8 (Berlin, 1910).

[29] See the comments of Bonwetsch, *Doctrina Jacobi*, xv-xvi; and the text at v.20;

the answer to Qu. 137, which is subdivided into thirteen carefully argued paragraphs (and which seems to have circulated independently of the rest of the ps.-Athanasius, at least after the seventh century, as the evidence of the manuscript tradition would suggest), was written at a time when the emperor Heraclius' edict ordering the compulsory baptism of Jews in the Empire was being carried out. Like the *Doctrina*, it provided a valuable weapon in the theological armory of those interested in winning over the Jews.[30] But the inexactness of the other historical references and the possibilities of interpolation and contamination in a manuscript tradition still in need of analysis, make dating this text to either the seventh century (where it might at first sight appear to belong) or a later period very hazardous. Richard always thought that the Anastasian collection was the source of the ps.-Athanasius; and Munitiz has found that in editing the text of Anastasius, this is a much more likely explanation for the abbreviations and omissions of the ps.-Athanasius. Until a critical edition has been prepared, therefore, the exact relationship of these two collections must remain unclear.[31]

The original form of the *Questions and Answers* of Anastasius and that presented in the Felckmann edition of the *Questions* to Antiochus *dux* in *PG* 28 have much in common, both in their presentation and their content. These shared elements give them a particular character which sets them apart both from earlier collections and from the later, derivative collections of Photius and after. Both, it seems to me, demonstrate elements of great originality, although it is also clear that both draw very extensively on earlier collections or, at the very least, on the preexisting tradition. The original Anastasian collection, for example, shows a closeness to the ps.-Caesarius in at least seven questions, the ps.-Justin in two; the ps.-Athanasius has some 21 such

ed. Bonwetsch, 91:9.

[30]On these events, see the documents listed in Franz Dölger, *Regesten der Kaiserurkunden des oströmischen Reiches von 565–1453* (Munich and Berlin, 1924–32), nos. 196, 197, and esp. 206; Beck, 447; Robert Devreesse, "La fin inédite d'une lettre de S. Maxime: un baptême forcé de Juifs et de Samaritains à Carthage en 632", *RSR* 17 (1937), 25–35 (see *CPG*, III, no. 7699 [Ep. 8]).

[31]The problem of interpolations in the text of ps.-Athanasius has not yet received any detailed treatment. For Richard's views on the matter, see "Les véritables 'Questions et Réponses'", 55 n. 1; "Les fragments du commentaire de S. Hippolyte", 61 n. 1.

instances altogether; and both draw extensively on the writings of the Church Fathers of the third to the fifth centuries, with whom a wide range of themes and interests are shared.[32]

More importantly, the Anastasian collection and the ps.-Athanasius demonstrate a great number of mutual borrowings, although whether the ps.-Athanasius borrows from Anastasius, as Richard and Munitiz have argued, or whether Anastasius borrowed from an older ps.-Athanasius, remains unclear: I have identified at least 47 cases where there is a clear borrowing by the ps.-Anastasian text from other compilations, and many others where an indirect borrowing has occurred. This can be seen more easily in tabular form (where asterisked numbers denote the original order of the Anastasian collection of 103 questions):

Anastasius	*ps.-Athanasius*
5/*47	92
8/*25	95, 96, 107
10/*73	105 (?)
12/*83	76 (parts)
13/*55	90
14/*58	86
16/*65	121
18/*29–*30	71 (cf. ps.-Caes. Qu. 188)
20/*62	111, 124, 125 (cf. ps.-Justin Qu. 5, 100)
21/*17	36
23/*23	47–50 (cf. ps.-Caes. Qu. 141–48)
75/*2	2

[32]See ps.-Athanasius, Qu. 1, 3–9, 12, 47–50, 53, 56, 69–71 (PG 28); and compare with the ps.-Caesarius, Qu. 2, 44–48, 49, 61–62, 86, 90, 119, 140, 149–53, 171, 188. Note also similarities between Anastasius, Qu. 1/*1, 18/*29–30, 23/*23, 60/*96, 87/*15, 96/*28, 109/*59 and ps.-Caesarius, Qu. 171, 188, 141–48, 190, 61–62, 86, 188, 189 respectively (where unmarked numbers = those in the *PG* edition, asterisked numbers represent the original order of the Anastasian collection of 103 questions and answers). For the patristic and other sources used by both the ps.-Athanasius and by Anastasius, see Bardy, "Littérature patristique", *RB* 42 (1933), 328–32, 339–43; Dörries, "Erotapokriseis", 362–64.

Anastasius	*ps.-Athanasius*
79/*7	101
81/*9	5
83/*11	84, 72–73, 94
87/*15	53 (cf. ps.-Caes. Qu. 61–62)
88/*16	113
89/*19	(cf. Qu. 16–26, 32–35)
90/*20	" "
91/*21	17, 20, 21, 22
92/*22	114, 135
95/*27	119
96/*28	69, 105 (cf. ps.-Caes. Qu. 86, 188)
98/*34	15
99/*37	98
100ter/*42	34
100quater/*47	92
101/*43	129
102/*44	87
105/*49	80
106/*50	78, 122
107/*56	122, 131–32
113/*64	112
114/*66	103, 104
116/*68	44, 137
117/*69	44
118/*70	42, 43
119/*71	11
120/*72	99, 100
124/*77	95
125/*79	100
126/*80	10
127/*81 (part)	119, 47 (part)
129/*83	76
135/*91	93
136/*92	88
139/*100	97

The Anastasian collection seldom merely copies an exemplar. On the contrary, it often expands the original question and its answer to fit the context or the audience or (monastic) readership for which the work was intended. Thus Qu. 14/*58 on whether one should give alms to the Church or the poor, 16/*15 on the divine sanctioning of leaders, 75/*2 on how one knows whether Christ has truly won one's soul, 96/*28 on why God permits some good men to die early and evil men to prosper, 113/*64 on whether and how one can take communion among the non-orthodox, 127/*81 (although only indirectly related to its ps.-Athanasian equivalent) on the character differences among human beings, 126/*80 on the reasons for Satan's being cast down from heaven, and 105/*49 on the purifying function of tears—all these questions produce somewhat different answers to questions which are essentially concerned with the same theme. It is these differences, together with the topical references to contemporary mores and anxieties, and the originality of the Anastasian collection, which impart to this work, as well as to other writings attributed to Anastasius, their particular interest and importance.

One could argue, of course, that the validity of this assumption is questionable—that Anastasius' collection represents merely a wide range of topoi, and that no "real" situation is described. But we must then ask two questions: what was the purpose of the collection, and what was the relevance of the questions themselves?

In answer to the first question, there seems little doubt, given the lack of literary pretensions, the sometimes confused order in which certain subjects are raised and then dropped, only to reappear under a slightly different guise later on, and the nature of the later florilegia to the collection (clearly intended to clarify some of Anastasius' more obscure positions and explanations), that the collection was no mere literary exercise, such as that compiled in the ninth century by the patriarch Photius. It would have been used by Christians in positions of authority—whether within the secular Church (i.e. external to the monastic establishment) or not—to elucidate and explain, to provide advice and suggest codes of conduct. That it had a practical function is clear enough from the insistence on maintaining a clearly neo-Chalcedonian position on a number of issues which must have affected the minority community which Anastasius represented. And it is quite different from that other source of advice and rhetorical support, the "logical compendium", a genre which, while owing its origins and raison d'être to the late antique context of the years from the second half of the sixth century to the middle of the eighth century (and the need to set out clearly the basic terms of the debate between the different Christian churches), nevertheless represented a more learned and philosophically informed level of debate.[33]

In answer to the second question, the proportion of questions specific to the situation of neo-Chalcedonian Christians in the Egypt-Palestine-Syria region after the Muslim conquests makes it eminently clear that this was a collection which reflected both real conditions and problems as well as the experiences of many years travelling and advising members of these congregations. Of course, all the standard questions on cosmogony, the nature of the soul, and so forth, are present. But the topical element impresses the reader in its directness and its relevance to the situation as described in the historical record. And it seems highly unlikely that so many topical points of reference would have been falsified or invented. To what end? For the collection must have reflected an experienced reality to have had any value as a source of advice. And that is clearly what it was.

The Historical Context

Having looked at the tradition in which the collections of *Questions and Answers* of the ps.-Athanasius and of Anastasius of Sinai are to be understood, I would like at this point to comment briefly on the historical context through which these collections and related texts can be interpreted and which they serve to illuminate. Since I have discussed this aspect of the evolution of late Roman society in greater detail elsewhere, where the justification for my general analysis is to be found, I will confine myself to a brief summary here.[34]

In the first place, I want to emphasize the significance of the collapse of antique municipal culture and civilization. Since at least the

[33]For the logical compendia, see Mossman Roueché, "Byzantine Philosophical Texts of the Seventh Century", *JÖB* 23 (1974), 61–76, esp. 61–67.

[34]See my "Ideology and Social Change in the Seventh Century", esp. 161–73; and *Byzantium in the Seventh Century*, 348–75, 425–35.

third century, the classical form of civic society had been evolving in a direction contradictory to that taken by the forms of state power and authority and the administrative (especially fiscal) apparatuses which dominated it. That is to say, and put somewhat crudely, civic autonomy, especially in the sphere of fiscal supervision of municipal resources, was no longer able to guarantee the state the income it needed. The result was increasingly central supervision of and intervention in municipal affairs, and a concomitant shift in patterns of investment by local élites away from their own cities to the sources of power: Constantinople in the East, senatorial latifundia in the West.[35] The Arab invasions and raids in Asia Minor, Slav, Avar, and later Bulgar occupation or devastation of much of the Balkan area, and the actual conquest and occupation of the Near East and North Africa, with the resulting replacement of the traditional élites from key loci of economic and political power—these were the events which sealed the fate of an already declining and weakened institution. Both inside and outside the eastern Empire, the literary and political culture of municipal life as it had existed was transformed. Within the Empire, and with the exception of Constantinople, it all but vanished entirely. Outside the Empire, the old élite certainly survived, up to a point, but in conditions which made the nurturing of traditional forms of literary culture more difficult. In both areas, however, the Church survived, and it was the Church which preserved and maintained its own version of the traditional culture.

This is particularly evident when one considers the sorts of literature which continued to be produced during the seventh century and into the eighth. For the second point that I would like to emphasize is the fact that there is, after the late 620s and early 630s, and up until the later eighth or early ninth century, a more or less complete disappearance of secular literary forms within the Empire, a phenomenon that has provoked much discussion. After the works of Theophylact Simocatta, for example, or the anonymous *Paschal Chronicle*, or that of John of Antioch; and with the exception of the supposed (and probably quite legendary) lost history of a certain Trajan *patricius* and a

[35] For the West, see C.J. Wickham, "The Other Transition: From the Ancient World to Feudalism", *Past and Present* 103 (1984), 3–36; for the East, John F. Haldon, "Some Considerations on Byzantine Society and Economy in the Seventh Century", *BF* 10 (1985), 75–112, esp. 78–94.

hypothetical "great chronographer" on whom both Theophanes and the patriarch Nicephorus supposedly drew in the later eighth and early ninth centuries, there is a lacuna of almost 200 years until the next surviving historical work. Similarly, this period provides no examples of geographical, philosophical, or philological literature; there is no epic poetry after George of Pisidia, and only a trickle of legal literature and secular rhetoric. Apart from the letters of a few powerful persons and churchmen and the surviving documents of state and Church as institutions, the literary output of the seventh century appears to have been almost entirely theological in nature, or at the least, very closely related to such—matters of dogma, devotion, various aspects of liturgical practice, problems of day-to-day piety and observance, and so forth. Only outside the Empire, in particular in northern Syria and Iraq, does a secular tradition linger on into the eighth century, particularly in the case of the history or chronicle of Theophilus of Edessa.[36]

Some historiographical or annalistic activity may have continued in Constantinople, of course, just as we know that other forms of literature (such as a limited legal literary activity) continued. But the latter was at least relevant to the state and its survival, as well as to Constantinopolitan perceptions of state and imperial power and tradition. Other literary forms were less tied in to such "needs". Indeed, attitudes to even the immediately local environment and its past reflect a real caesura in the metropolitan cultural assumptions of the sixth century and before, as the so-called "Short Historical Notes" (*Parastaseis syntomai chronikai*) would suggest. And any literary activity which did take place had been quite forgotten by the time of Photius, whose *Bibliotheca* makes no reference to them. Even if we allow for some loss or destruction, the disappearance of the old forms of cultural organization seem to have had clear repercussions in the forms of literature and literary concerns which survived. And this lack of literature in the fields I have described—which cannot possibly be a reflection of some supposed (and remarkably selective!) failure of the secular literary out-

[36]See the relevant surveys in Hunger, on the secular literature referred to. On historiography, see the article of Whitby in this volume; and on Theophilus of Edessa, that of Conrad. Note most recently the comments of Cyril Mango, "The Tradition of Byzantine Chronography", *Harvard Ukrainian Studies* 12–13 (1988–89), 360–72, esp. 364.

put of the seventh and eighth centuries to survive—along with the fact that theological writings, in the broadest sense, not only survive but flourish, is particularly important. For the Church was able to maintain its traditional organization and administration within the Empire and, to a great extent also, its sources of revenue. It needed to be able to educate its clergy, and it needed literate and cultured men for its highest offices. Even here, however, it was topical questions of the day, matters of ecclesiastical politics, the study of the writings of the Church Fathers, and the records of the general councils, along with scripture and Biblical exegesis, that provided the main fields of concern. Interest in the secular, pre-Constantinian, much less the pre-Christian, culture of the past was, for a century or so, a rarity.[37] It is difficult to generalize from the experience of the lands which remained within the Empire to those outside it. But the evidence with which I am familiar suggests that a pattern not dissimilar from that described above applied here also. Of course, there may well be exceptions to any general development; and the conflict of interests within the Christian community in the East, especially between neo-Chalcedonians and Monophysites, left more room for cultural maneuver among the educated clergy and monastic circles and within the secular élite, than was the case within the Empire. In particular, and as mentioned already, there seems to have flourished in the North Syrian cities of Edessa and Emesa (Ḥimṣ) in the last years of the seventh and first half of the eighth centuries both a Christian chronographical or historiographical tradition, represented by the lost work of Theophilus of Edessa, for example, and the sources underlying later Syriac annalistic writings; as well as the apocalyptic tradition represented in the ps.-Methodius *Apocalypse* and that of the Twelve Apostles. The cultural context—especially the survival of urban life, and indeed the importance of both Edessa and Emesa in the Umayyad military and civil administration of these regions—may partly account for this.

Nevertheless, Islam had to be confronted outside the Empire directly, both intellectually and spiritually, and at the level of community

[37]See Beck, 430–32. On the *Parastaseis*, see Averil Cameron, Judith Herrin, *et al*, *Constantinople in the Eighth Century: the Parastaseis Syntomoi Chronikai* (Leiden, 1984); and esp. Gilbert Dagron, *Constantinople imaginaire: études sur le recueil des Patria* (Paris, 1984).

politics. The dangers of apostasy were always present, even though—remarkably—the final Islamization of Syria and Palestine does not seem to have had a great deal of success before the later ninth and tenth centuries.

The sources available for elucidating the ways in which East Mediterranean Christian society and culture changed, therefore, are limited, both for the imperial territories and for the areas which were conquered and which did not necessarily suffer the same fate as the Empire in respect of warfare and disruption of economic and social life. From the historiographical point of view, there are a number of Syriac sources, some near-contemporary Arab histories, the Armenian account of Sebēos, and the Coptic history of John of Nikiu. But the majority of these were themselves the products of either a Christian and monastic context, or of the ethos and perspective of the Muslim conquerors. As general accounts, they usually tell us little or nothing about ordinary, day-to-day attitudes and beliefs.[38] In the context of the seventh century, in which the cultural pluralism of the late ancient past was replaced by an introversion within Christian society, both within and without the Empire, the attitudes and practices revealed in the writings of Anastasius of Sinai, among others, are especially important.[39]

Anastasius and the Concerns of Seventh-Century Society

The *Questions and Answers* of Anastasius of Sinai cover a wide range of concerns. In the following, I will single out those where a clearly context-bound response from Anastasius either substantially emends an answer given in the older collection of ps.-Athanasius, or where the Anastasian Question and Answer is not found in any other collection

[38]For the Syriac tradition, see S.P. Brock, "From Antagonism to Assimilation: Syriac Attitudes to Greek Learning", in Nina G. Garsoian, Thomas F. Mathews, Robert W. Thomson, eds., *East of Byzantium: Syria and Armenia in the Formative Period* (Washington D.C., 1982), 17–34; *idem*, "Syriac Sources for Seventh-Century History", *BMGS* 2 (1976), 17–36; and Reinink, "Pseudo-Methodius und die Legende vom römischen Endkaiser". For the North Syrian tradition, see in particular the contributions of Reinink, Drijvers, and Conrad in this volume.

[39]See Haldon, "Ideology and Social Change", 165–70.

in the form in which it is presented in his collection.[40]

Dagron has already noted the originality of many of the questions in the Anastasian collection, and has pointed in particular to the ambiguous position occupied in both the ps.-Athanasius and the Anastasian collection by quasi-occultic concerns, predictions, astrology, and the pre-Christian medical and physiological tradition.[41] These, and several other themes, represent central elements in the text. Most important seem to me to be those that deal with matters of day-to-day observance; with the implicit relationships between Christian ideas and traditional practices; current understandings of the relationship between God and mankind, on the one hand, and the political situation of Christians, especially those outside the Empire; the difficulties experienced by the latter; the rôle and function of monks and holy men (often compared with that of ordinary people); and the problem of the redemption of sins.

Within these themes are to be found a great diversity of important sub-themes—medicine, the body, sexuality, the relationship between wonders wrought by divine power and those wrought by Satan, and so on. Noticeable throughout is an element of uncertainty, perhaps not out of place in a collection of questions and answers. But there is a difference in tone between Anastasius' collection and earlier, usually more formalistic collections. This is especially true where the questions concern what is clearly a novel situation—Christians under Muslim rule, Christian slaves of Muslims, and Christians outside the Empire, whatever their creed. Perhaps most interesting of all, however, is the fact that the daily observances of belief and Christian ritual can be shown to be much less rigorously and uniformly observed within the neo-Chalcedonian community than the "official line" represented in the canons of the Quinisext, for example, would suggest. So much

[40]The wide range of topics covered by the collection has been summarized by Dörries, "Erotapokriseis", 362–64, and by Richard, "Florilèges spirituels grecs", 500–501.

[41]Gilbert Dagron, "Le saint, le savant, l'astrologue: étude de thèmes hagiographiques à travers quelques recueils de 'Questions et réponses' des Ve-VIIe siècles", in *Hagiographie, cultures et sociétés (IVe-VIIe siècles): études augustiniennes* (Paris, 1981), 143–55, reprinted in G. Dagron, *La romanité chrétienne en Orient* (London, 1984), IV.

is clear, of course, both from the references to popular and traditional practices in the latter, as well as from the commentary to those canons of later writers such as Balsamon, whose remarks illustrate the continuous existence of these pre-Christian (but not necessarily un-Christian) customs.[42] But the *Questions and Answers* of Anastasius provide valuable corroborative evidence for the pluralism of practice within neo-Chalcedonian Christianity, as well as the lack of any clear directives on many matters touching upon everyday life. They also demonstrate the divergences in practice which may have developed as the Imperial Church within the Empire lost its more immediate hold on the affairs of the churches henceforth under Muslim rule.

Such day-to-day matters of Christian life under Muslim rule are expressed in many ways. In Qu. 132/*87[43] the questioner asks how he can redeem his sins if, having been reduced to servitude or captured in war, he can no longer go to church when he so wishes, or fast, or observe a vigil. The answer points out that it is not necessarily in physical acts that true faith is to be shown; keeping one's faith with God and showing true humility of spirit are just as important, the more so in the conditions described by the questioner, which represent also a form of redemption of sins, since these trials and tribulations were sent as a test of faith. Qu. *88 follows this up with a request for advice on how to obtain forgiveness for one's sins if one lives in the "world" and possesses adequate wealth and property (perhaps also being married and with children). The answer, which is quite extensive and detailed, is interesting: nearly all those who have shown themselves pleasing and acceptable to God in Scripture—Abraham, Joseph and others, Moses, David, and many tens of thousands of others (!)—were also men of the world, possessing both wealth and families. Indeed, it is one of Satan's tricks to convince men that it is impossible to obtain redemption unless one gives up the secular world and becomes a monk or hermit, dwelling in the wilderness. For many have been thus deceived and, carrying on with their sinful ways, confidently assume that they will eventually be able to drop their secular life-style and redeem their

[42]See Haldon, *Byzantium in the Seventh Century*, 371–75.

[43]For the text of the question, see PG 89, 784C1–5; the answer is in Richard, "Les véritables 'Questions et Réponses'", 48, with n. 5 (a reference to a story concerning S. Antony).

sins. But in the end they find the ascetic life too hard, and thus face eternal damnation.

Equally interesting is Qu. 5 (with 100)/*47, on how one can be saved if one is unable to pursue the monastic vocation. The answer is straightforward and honest: God did not ordain celibacy or *anachoresis* as the only means of salvation—true humility and faith are just as important.[44]

Such answers throw an interesting light on attitudes both to the monastic and eremitic life and to the degree to which the popular piety of the official prescriptions on Christian practice were or were not observed. It is important to note that Anastasius is keen to present the Christian way of life as not incompatible with an ordinary secular existence. Implicit also is a reflection of a popular assumption that only the monks and holy men can attain salvation, a viewpoint which may represent the over-successful propaganda of such men and women since the fourth century,[45] and which surely must have presented a threat to the solidarity of Christian communities in the face of the new religious force of Islam. In the context of the second part of his answer, he notes that the "present generation" finds itself in a period of spiritual crisis, not dissimilar to that experienced by the Children of Israel during the Babylonian captivity.[46]

Many other questions deal with matters of everyday concern which were clearly relevant to Christians everywhere. Can one go straight

[44]Qu. *88 is to be found in Richard, "Les véritables 'Questions et Réponses'", 48; the answer = resp. 132 and 133 of the *PG* text (*PG* 89, 784C7–785C13). Qu. 5 + 100/*47 appears also in the ps.-Athanasian collection, but is less specific and makes no mention of the monastic life as such. See *PG* 89, 361B6–C1, C5–10; *PG* 28, 653C–D6. Cf. also Anastasius, Qu. 93/*23 on the same theme. For a closer parallel to Anastasius' text, see, for example, John Climacus, *Scala Paradisi*, 1, 636B.

[45]The gulf separating the "ordinary" Christian from the holy man and ascetic, perhaps more clearly discernible in Syria than elsewhere, but nevertheless a common element of Christian culture from the fourth and fifth centuries in the East in particular, has been well described by Peter Brown, *The Body and Society: Men, Women and Sexual Renunciation in Early Christianity* (London and Boston, 1988), see 305–38; also Norman H. Baynes, "The Thought-World of East Rome", in his *Byzantine Studies and Other Essays* (London, 1960), 24–46, esp. 26–27, with Brown's discussion in *The Body and Society*, 205–207.

[46]*PG* 89, 785B1–5.

from the marital bed or from a dream into church after having bathed (Qu. 98bis/*38)? Can one take communion in the same state (Qu. 98ter/*39)? Can one take communion having accidentally swallowed bathwater (Qu. 100/*40)? How often should one take communion—daily, at intervals, on Sundays only (Qu. 100bis/*41)? Many of these are, of course, ancient subjects closely related to the Judaic traditions of physical and spiritual purity (to which I will return), and form a continuous thread of concern from the earliest Christian times. And even though many of the taboos of which they are symptomatic had been reformulated and modified by centuries of Christian debate, Anastasius' *Questions and Answers* suggest that they still provoked some degree of confusion and uncertainty.[47]

The answers provide the faithful with several options, depending upon one's commitments; but no firm denial of access is pronounced—physical purity does not interest God, only spiritual purity. The answer to Qu. *41 is interesting. Anastasius divides up those who take communion into several groups: there are those who should take communion daily, those for whom this is unsuitable, and those who should not take communion at all. Then again, there are those who have distanced themselves from the holy mysteries and have fallen into sinful ways, such as the race of the Armenians; others partake hypocritically as a means of insuring themselves against sin; others again partake frivolously and without due thought, thereby opening their souls to Satan; while others still merely intend at some time to take communion, and carry on in their sinful ways; and so on. These concerns are very similar to those expressed by Anastasius in a brief sermon on the liturgy, in which he bewails the sloppy, ignorant, and disrespectful way in which many of his contemporaries behave during church services. Such matters were clearly dear to his heart.[48]

---

[47]The printed edition contains only a fraction of a much longer text: see *PG* 89, 753B13–C7; with Richard, "Les véritables 'Questions et Réponses'", 44–45, for the bulk of the answer. The question of the polluting nature of the sexual and the consequent trajectory of development of relations between men and women in the Christian world is discussed at length by Brown, *The Body and Society*; see esp. 140–42, 230–32.

[48]See *S. Anastasii Sinaitae oratio de sacra synaxi*, in *PG* 89, 825A–849C. Note especially 829A–832A9 for a damning description of how congregations treat the

The difficulties posed by life in a heterodox world were also problems of concern to Anastasius and his questioners. Should you carry the Eucharist with you in a *skevophorion* while travelling away from home, or take communion wherever you find it? The answer is yes, take the Eucharist with you, for you should never take communion with heretics—a reflection of Anastasius' fierce opposition to Monophysitism.[49] How it is that even heretics can work miracles (an old concern, appearing in the ps.-Justin, Qu. 5 and 100, and ps.-Athanasius, Qu. 111) is the subject of Qu. 20/*62. Why are heretics who return to the fold of orthodoxy not rebaptized (Qu. 86/*14)? This is again an older question, but one reflected also in the canons of the Quinisext.[50] Is it good to confess

liturgy and service cynically, yawning and falling asleep when the priest preaches too long, rushing from the church and fleeing prayer "as though from the courthouse" (an interesting metaphor for legal historians!). Some leave before the service is finished; others go only when their friends tell them that communion is about to take place, whereupon they rush into church "like dogs" and, grabbing the sacred bread, rush out again; others gather to chatter and gossip, ignoring the service entirely; while others, having taken communion, cannot wait to get back to the pleasures of the flesh. Anastasius adds that many stand around in the church ogling the women in the congregation, while others discuss matters of business and money. No doubt the picture is exaggerated; but it gives us again some idea of the concerns of this seventh-century monk and holy man, and of the attitudes of ordinary people to the formal elements of faith.

[49] *PG* 89, 765A–B (Qu. 113/*64). The same question is found in ps.-Athanasius, Qu. 112 (*PG* 28, 665C–668A). But whereas in the latter the question revolves around whether one should forego communion altogether as an alternative to taking it with heretics, in the former one is permitted to carry the Eucharist with one—suggestive, perhaps, of the isolation of some neo-Chalcedonian communities in the areas with which Anastasius was familiar. Monophysitism and the struggle against heresy figure prominently in the collection: Qu. 116/*68 asks for advice on what to do when a heretic asks for an exposition of orthodox dogma; Qu. 117/*69 provides a complex historico-theological apologia for the orthodox in such situations; both questions are also echoed in ps.-Athanasius, Qu. 44 and 137, but the Anastasian versions reflect their own times (e.g. the comment that the barbarians currently hold the Holy Places, and that 700 years have elapsed since the birth of Christ): see *PG* 89, 768B2–769C2; *PG* 28, 625A13–C16. Similarly, Qu. 118/*70 wonders why Satan did not cause divisions and schisms in other faiths such as those he has caused to erupt among the Christians—again, echoed in ps.-Athanasius, Qu. 42 & 43 (*PG* 89, 769C3–772A4; *PG* 28, 624B8–625A12).

[50] On Qu. 20/*62 see also Dagron, "Le saint, le savant, l'astrologue", 146–47; for Qu. 86/*14: *PG* 89, 712B13–C8; Richard, "Les véritables 'Questions et Réponses'",

one's sins (Qu. 105bis/*52, repeated in Qu. 6/*52)? The answer is, of course, in the affirmative—but only to a recognized and tried *anēr pneumatikos*: the assumption implicit in the reply is that there are a number of less competent "holy men" about, dubious figures by whom the believer might unknowingly be misled or deceived. This is again a concern reflected in other texts—in both the canons of the Quinisext, and in the probably (in parts) late-seventh-century fictional *Life* of S. Andrew Salos.[51]

Questions which reflect more directly the new political and religious order represent an important innovation in the genre. Thus Qu. 110/*60 wonders whether one should pray for political leaders if they are pagans, Jews, or heretics; Qu. 16/*65 asks whether every leader, or king, or bishop is appointed by God (the answer to both questions is "yes");[52] Qu. 17/*101 asks whether all the evils which the Arabs have

43; but cf. ps.-Justin, Qu. 14. For the Quinisext, see Canon 95 in Mansi, XI, 984B–E. This is itself based on Canon 7 of Constantinople I (AD 381); see Mansi, II, 676–77; Karl Hefele and Henri Leclerq, *Histoire des conciles* (Paris, 1907–52), II, 1.

[51] *PG* 89, 369D–372A7, 760A9–B2. Quinisext: Canons 41 and 42—Mansi, XI, 964A–C, 964D. For a warning tale of a woman who was taken in by a "false" holy man, *Vita Andreae Sali* (*PG* 111, 621–888), 777C–781A; and cf. François Halkin, *Bibliotheca hagiographica graeca* (Brussels, 1957), no. 117. The *Life* is fictional, but may be of late seventh-century date: see Cyril Mango, "The Life of St. Andrew the Fool Reconsidered", *Rivista di studi bizantini e slavi* (Bologna, 1982; *Miscellanea A. Pertusi*), II, 297–313, reprinted in his *Byzantium and its Image* (London 1984), VIII. Against this, and arguing a later ninth or tenth-century date, see Lennart Rydén, "The *Life* of St. Basil the Younger and the *Life* of St. Andrew Salos", in *Okeanos: Essays Presented to Ihor Ševčenko on his Sixtieth Birthday by his Colleagues and Students* (Cambridge, Mass., 1983; *Harvard Ukrainian Studies* 7), 568–86. In fact, the *Life* seems to be of seventh-century origin, but with numerous ninth-century interpolations (similar, therefore, to the *Miracula S. Artemii*, also set in Constantinople, albeit with fewer obviously interpolated passages).

[52] *PG* 89, 476B–477A15, with a previously unpublished section, in Richard, "Les véritables 'Questions et Réponses'", 47. The answer is interesting. Anastasius relates two tales (and the similarity of style with the *Narrationes* is clear), one concerning God's reason for inflicting the wicked tyrant Phocas upon the Christian world ("I could find no one worse"), the other concerning a wicked town in the Thebaid. The final section of the answer remarks that even when Man has received the leaders and rulers he has deserved for his sins, still in the midst of his afflictions he continues in his wickedness; and Anastasius continues: "Believe me when I say

perpetrated on the lands and peoples of the Christians are invariably a result of God's will.[53] Qu. 121/*74 deals with the possibility of a Christian taking a pagan or barbarian wife; and Qu. 123/*76 concerns the problem of Christian women who, as slaves and captives, commit certain transgressions.[54]

Two questions in particular seem to relate to persecution and oppression: Qu. 122/*75 asks whether the person who flees in time of persecution commits a sin, to which the answer is (as with so many of Anastasius' replies): it depends. If persecution will lead to the extinction of a Christian soul, flight is in order. If, on the other hand, mere physical chastisement and suffering are all that is at stake, then it is not (and there is an echo, here also, of Canon 37 of the Quinisext dealing with the provincial clergy's abandonment of their congregations in devastated or threatened areas.[55] Qu. 134/*89, in contrast, wonders why it is that so many can be seen "nowadays" rushing to their death on account of their faith, but upon reaching the very threshhold of death, are suddenly set free, either by the prayers of men or by the change of

today that even if the race of the Saracens were to depart from us, straightway tomorrow the Blues and Greens would rise up again and the East, and Arabia, and Palestine, and many other lands would bring slaughter upon themselves". Not only the Arabs, but also the Blues and Greens, were seen as elements in this picture of heavenly punishment. Note that this question occurs in the ps.-Athanasius (Qu. 121, *PG* 28, 676A), but with a very much shorter answer and without the contemporary detail furnished by Anastasius.

[53]Fragments of the text: *PG* 89, 484B4–13; for the question, see Richard, "Les véritables 'Questions et Réponses'", 50.

[54]*PG* 89, 773A10–C1. Again, the answer is interesting, and deals with the relative merits of those who are forced into sin through sheer need—hunger, for example—and those who sin through wantonness and love of pleasure. The latter are to be condemned; and the example given picks out the Christian courtesans of the cities who gain wealth and jewels through betraying their own sisters, whom they see in chains.

[55]*PG* 89, 773A1–9; and see Mansi, XI, 960C–E. Note also Qu. 114/*66 (*PG* 89, 765A–B, extended by ps.-Athanasius, Qu. 112, *PG* 28, 665C–668A) on whether it is possible to flee the plague—a topical question given the terrible epidemic which struck Syria and the surrounding districts in the 680s. See Theophanes, *Chronographia*, ed. Karl de Boor (Leipzig, 1883–85), 364:3–4; S.P. Brock, "North Mesopotamia in the late Seventh Century. Book XV of John Bar Penkāyē's *Rīš Mellē*", *JSAI* 9 (1987), 51–75, see 68, *s.a.* 686–87. Note also *Narratio* 40 (ed. Nau, *OC* 2, 83:17–26) on the problem of sinners vainly attempting to escape the plague.

mind of tyrants. The answer is noncommittal; essentially, God works in mysterious ways. But the question then begs itself, to what events is this text referring? Is this a faint echo of the vagaries in the policy of the various Islamic authorities to Christian resentment of their rule, or does it perhaps refer to the question of conversion?[56]

Other questions relate the fate that has befallen the Empire and the Christian communities to the traditional explanation of punishment for transgressions. But Anastasius gives them an unusual twist. For example, in Qu. 94/*26 he is asked why there are more people suffering from various physical afflictions— maimed, arthritic, gouty, leprous, epileptic—among the Christians than among the infidels. His answer produces an interesting and significant compromise: on the one hand, there is an explanation which relates such afflictions to the fact that God has sent them as a trial of the Christians' faith and love for Him. On the other hand, certain persons believe that it is a question of climate, habitat, racial character, and diet, so that the Jews, for example, who are given to excessive eating and drinking, nevertheless escape the illnesses they should thereby contract by virtue of living in a dry climate and having the corresponding racial characteristics. Anastasius gives an interesting example: in Cyprus, shortly before 647, a *philosophos* and *iatrosophos* observed a crowd of people suffering from a variety of afflictions at the sanctuary of S. Epiphanius, hoping for a miraculous cure. The *philosophos* suggested that they might be helped by the application of a certain dietary régime, purgatives, and bleeding; undertaking to effect this on the orders of the bishop, he succeeded in curing many.[57]

This text has been commented upon by Dagron, as have Qu. 95/*27 and 96/*28 on the differences between the variety of human personality types, and on the reasons why certain virtuous Christians die young, whereas many evil men enjoy long and successful lives. Dagron has noted in particular the strong antithesis which emerges in these questions between the simple notion of divine will, on the one hand, and more complex ideas rooted in ancient medical and astrological theory on the nature of man. The key question for Anastasius was how to

[56] *PG* 89, 785D1–788A10.

[57] *PG* 89, 732B9–733A7.

reconcile these divergent approaches within a Christian framework of divine providence; for by admitting that a natural mediation of the divine *pronoia* could play a fundamental rôle, he implicitly challenged the more reductionist interpretations of divine order upon which the hagiographic tradition, for example, was based.[58] I will not repeat Dagron's analysis and conclusions here, since this particular problem is not my concern; but I would like to emphasize this decidedly pre-Christian tradition—the more so, since Anastasius himself remarks that it may no longer be acceptable.

In Qu. 127/*81 the same theme is taken up once more, and presents a very different explanation. The questioner asks why, given that there is a physiological explanation for the differences between men and women, some women cannot bear children, while others bear many and yet others only a few?[59] The answer once again returns to a pre-Christian medical and physiological tradition, while in the process casting some light on attitudes to poverty and deprivation. For Anastasius notes that the causes of childlessness are many and varied, depending equally on climatic and physiological traits: prostitutes, for example, who are wont to cast aside the seed, conceive with difficulty. Similarly, many wealthy persons who live lives of affluence and who desire children are unable to have them; whereas the poor often have very many. Their bodies are parched through need, like thirsting soil, and immediately seize upon the moisture of the seed which

[58]See Dagron, "Le saint, le savant, l'astrologue", 144–46. For Qu. 95/*27: *PG* 89, 733A9–736A3; Qu. 96/*28: *PG* 89, 736A5–749D2. Both questions are repeated in the ps.-Athanasius, however, unlike the previous one: see *PG* 28, 673B6–C14 (Qu. 119), and 636B1–637A9 (Qu. 69) with 661D2–664A8; but in the case of Anastasius' Qu. 96/*28, he offers a much extended discussion, referring, incidentally, to settlements of Cypriot prisoners on the shores of the Dead Sea at Zoera and Tetrapyr(g)ia who, once again because of their "dry" homeland, can withstand the rigors of their new habitat (*PG* 89, 745A6–B4). There appear to have been mines (for salt?) in this district, for Eusebius refers to the fact that Christians used to be condemned to serve out their sentences there under the pagan emperors. See Eusebius' *Liber de martyribus palaestinae* (*Die palaestinischen Maertyres des Eusebius*), ed. Bruno Violet (Leipzig, 1896; *TU* 14.4), 105–106, 118. The climate does not appear to have affected them fatally. I thank Avshalom Laniado for this reference.

[59]Anastasius: *PG* 89, 776C10–780C8.

enters them—just like those "among us" who are destitute, poor, mendicant, or like the Arabs, who can scarcely afford bread, yet have many children.[60]

But Anastasius goes on to note that the physiological explanations are all part of the natural and physical worlds, and therefore a part of God's divine creation. And he continues with a discussion of the daily changes in the human physiology, which he likewise relates to natural-biological factors which are all part of the divine plan. What is particularly interesting, however, is his recognition that such arguments are no longer really acceptable. At one point, he notes that an antagonist might accuse one who gave such an explanation as casting doubt on God's creation of the universe.[61] And at the beginning of his answer, he makes an important remark: "If we wish to explain these and similar matters in detail, it will be necessary to go into certain medical enquiries into natural phenomena, not altogether in accordance with what is usually read out in church; but since the explanation given was vague (referring to a previous answer), I will try to clarify".[62] I will return to this theme at the end of the paper.

Anastasius' *Questions and Answers* take up many other subjects of interest. I will end this brief survey by looking at the problem of

[60] *PG* 89, 776D8–777A11. Compare John Climacus, *Scala Paradisi*, 15, 889A.

[61] In spite of Anastasius' argument, there of course remains the problem of how to relate direct divine intervention on the hagiographical model to these longer-term, naturalistic-physiological explanations, as Dagron notes in connection with Qu. 94/*26, 95/*27 and 96/*28.

[62] *PG* 89, 777A15–B2, and especially 776D2–6. Munitiz notes that the Gretser text is incorrect: τῇ κοινῇ ἐκκλησίᾳ και ἀκροάσει should read, according to the Mss.: τῇ κοινῇ ἐν ἐκκλησίᾳ ἀκροάσει. Contrary to what might be expected, Anastasius rarely appears to invoke a classic text in connection with such matters, Nemesius of Emesa's *De natura hominis*. John of Damascus, on the other hand, draws on Nemesius very frequently, as do many later commentators. See K. Burkhard, "Iohannes' Damascenus Auszüge aus Nemesius", in *Wiener Eranos zur 50. Versammlung deutscher Philologen* (Vienna, 1909), 89–101. Although the later florilegia on the Anastasian text contain two specific extracts from Nemesius, only a short section seems to have been used by Anastasius in his original compilation. See 100ter/*42 (*PG* 89, 545C11–D5). On the other hand, Anastasius' account of the theory of the four elements—for example, at Qu. 96/*28 (*PG* 89, 736A5-749D2)—is very explicit and may well draw on an account such as that of Nemesius. See Nemesius' *De natura hominis*, IV, V; ed. Moreno Morani (Leipzig, 1987), 44:22–55:7.

prediction and soothsaying. While this has also been examined briefly by Dagron, one aspect which he did not take up is worthy of attention here. In Qu. 108/*57, Anastasius is asked whether Christians are permitted to seek an answer to their questions through *lachnistērion*, that is to say, by the random opening of the Scriptures and the interpretation of the text thus revealed. His answer is, once more, equivocal: the Fathers make no mention of permitting it, but imply that it is to be counted among the practices of soothsayers and sorcerers. If one does wish to employ this device, one should first pray to God and ask permission, and then, upon opening (the Bible), ask Him if He calls the supplicant to open with reference to the matter in hand. If God permits this, then the Scriptures should be opened, but *only* if God permits it.[63]

While there is a tradition of the invocation of (apparent) "chance" in the Acts of the Apostles, this is not a particularly satisfactory answer in the context of the seventh century; and so in Qu. 109bis/*97 the question is raised again: "In what way should we understand: 'if two or three of you should agree on every request which is made [to God], it will be granted them'"? The answer explains that God wishes us to trust not in ourselves alone, unless we lead an especially virtuous and holy life, but rather to obtain the agreement and advice of fellow Christians in prayer in respect of our questions. He who makes such requests alone often falls into vanity, whereas many praying together retain humility. Anastasius himself had often prayed thus with others, he says, and had success. He therefore recommends the practice to his questioner. For frequently, if two or three pray or fast together, their prayer is answered. Once more, this is a motif familiar from the *apophthegmata* and from Moschus.

So much for the first part of his reply. But he then goes on to suggest using the *lachnistērion* method in order to obtain a true answer; and he suggests further that on account of this the Christian should have a spiritual *ephod*, that is, the Holy Spirit should shine upon him and show him what is fitting and what is not. "For those who possess this have told us that, when they make a request to God concerning any matter, if the request is pleasing to Him, the grace of the Holy Spirit covers

[63] *PG* 89, 761A5–B1.

them".[64] Here we have once again recourse to methods of which the Church undoubtedly disapproved, at least at the formal level: witness the relevant canons of the Quinisext condemning and prohibiting a variety of methods of prediction and soothsaying.[65] But Anastasius' value as a reflection of ordinary people's beliefs and attitudes and of the practices of day-to-day life is borne out by later hagiography, among other sources, and provides also an important check on the weight often given to the formal and official sources, such as the canons.[66]

The quasi-magical efficacy of the original Biblical *ephod* is explained in Qu. 40/*98, where a somewhat garbled description of this garment (described in detail in Exodus 28:6–13, 39:1–26) is given, together with how it functioned. Its scriptural pedigree was impeccable, of course, but it nevertheless represented a tradition with which the Church was clearly not happy, as the prohibition (however ineffectual it might ac-

[64] For the Scriptural tradition, see Acts 1:26, Colossians 1:12. The Church seems never to have reached a formal ruling on *lachnistērion*. This and related practices were condemned by Augustine, by several Western synods in the fifth and sixth centuries, and by Gregory the Great. Thomas Aquinas regarded the example of Matthew in Acts 1:23–26 as an exception and was otherwise suspicious of the use of lots and chance selection by Christians. See A. Michel, art. "Sort" in Alfred Vacant, Eugène Mangenot, and Émile Amann, eds., *Dictionnaire de théologie catholique*, XIV.2 (Paris, 1941), 2420–21; Ernst von Dobschütz, art. "Sortes apostolorum or sanctorum" in Samuel Macauley Jackson *et al.*, eds., *The New Schaff-Herzog Encyclopaedia of Religious Knowledge* (London and New York, 1911), XI, 9. The way in which Anastasius formulates his answer reflects this situation, partly induced also by the fact that the use of lots and chance had an ancient and decidedly pre-Christian aspect to it. On the other hand, some Byzantines at least had no qualms about employing *lachnistērion*, as indicated by the examples of the emperor Heraclius (who reportedly took advice in this way while on campaign against the Persians) and the emperor Leo VI, to whom is attributed (although doubtfully) a short tract on the subject. See Phédon Koukoulès, Βυζαντινῶν Βίος καὶ Πολιτισμός, A/II (Athens, 1948), 158. It is still in use in the Orthodox world today. Only part of this question is published at *PG* 89, 761C1–764A9; the omitted section on the ephod is published by Richard, "Les véritables 'Questions et Réponses'", 49.

[65] See Canon 61, proscribing soothsayers, diviners, fortune-tellers, and others who deceive the ordinary people, for example; Mansi, XI, 969E–972A.

[66] See Balsamon's commentary to the relevant canons, in K. Rhalles and M. Potles, Σύνταγμα τῶν θείων καὶ ἱερῶν κανόνων (Athens, 1852–59), II, 442–47, for the continued survival of these traditions; and see the examples of popular faith cited in Haldon, *Byzantium in the Seventh Century*, 333–37.

tually have been) on various forms of fortune-telling in Canon 61 of the Quinisext makes clear.[67] The metaphorical *ephod* which Anastasius mentions represents a state of mind, of course, perhaps the practice of "discernment of spirits", which was an accepted tradition; but it may equally imply the possibility that what was meant was an induced, trancelike state in those who pray—again, a feature of popular faith with which the ecclesiastical authorities were less than comfortable.[68]

In the end, the point is that there is no clearly delineated line to be drawn in the answers of Anastasius between the purely Christian (surely always a hypothetical level of praxis) and the pre- or sub-Christian. Anastasius is quite clear on heresy; he is also clear on the marginal status of some forms of knowledge and explanation he has to offer. He is clear that simple astrology and the belief in fate or chance are not Christian and endanger the soul.[69] His collection of *Questions and Answers*—like the *narrationes* also ascribed to his name—reflects the same world of malevolent demons, humans manipulated by the Devil, and good souls saved by true faith, which is mirrored in the stories of the Desert Fathers and the hagiography of the fifth and sixth centuries. But his answers also reflect the uncertainty and insecurity of the age, I believe, and it is this which has most drawn my attention in reading the works attributed to him. Collections of *Questions and Answers* are, by their very nature, bound to represent uncertainties. But this collection seems to represent a particular moment in East Mediterranean Christian cultural history, a moment of massive change in popular conceptions of the experienced, day-to-day world, as well as in relations of political power and authority. It also hints at a narrowing and limiting of horizons, at a closing in of perspectives on the relationship between the divine and the mortal, and at the closing off of discourses which

---

[67] *PG* 89, 585A6–B14; and cf. Richard, "Les véritables 'Questions et Réponses' ", 49.

[68] See Canon 60 of the Quinisext; Mansi, XI, 969D. For *diakrisis*, or discernment of spirit, see the art. "Discernement des ésprits" in *Dict. spirit.*, VII, 1222–91, esp. 1252–54; and Joseph T. Lienhard, "On 'Discernment of Spirits' in the Early Church", *Theological Studies* 41 (1980), 505–29.

[69] As, for example, Qu. 19/*85 on Fate (and cf. Richard, "Les véritables 'Questions et Réponses' ", 48).

had been part of the common cultural heritage of the Hellenistic and Roman world. I am not suggesting that Anastasius was himself an exponent of this closing off. On the contrary, his breadth of vision and his intellectual pluralism make such a notion untenable. But his *Questions and Answers* represent the wider cultural context as well, and it is this with which I am concerned. Even outside the political boundaries and the reach of the Empire and the imperial Church which was finally consolidated during this period, the cultural introversion of eastern Christianity and imperial ideology had their effects upon the thinkable and the ways in which the world was to be understood. And those effects mark the real establishment of the medieval world.

This cultural and intellectual introversion, which was particularly marked within the Empire, also had consequences in the Christian world under Muslim rule. However, I would like to end this paper by stressing one or two elements of cultural continuity which existed between the Islamic and Christian worlds. The conflict between Hellenistic rationalism, if it can be called that, and Christian views on direct divine intervention—a conflict represented in the work of Anastasius, for example, by the juxtaposition of answers on natural-physiological causation, on the one hand, and by divine and miraculous intervention through icons and amulets, on the other—remains implicit in Christian culture throughout the following centuries. As Dagron has clearly noted, the pre-Christian tradition incorporated into Anastasius' work implies a physical influence which is not predetermined, in which doctors can manipulate the laws of nature, so to speak, and in which divine intervention is exceptional.[70] It contrasts with the sort of miraculous intervention brought about through prayer and faith alone,[71] and constitutes in effect its antithesis. Anastasius' efforts at compromise were theologically not entirely convincing, at least in respect of popular piety and belief. But in the history of Christian thinking thereafter,

[70]See esp. Qu. 94/*26, 95/*27, 96/*28, 98/*34, the last three all based on questions in the ps.-Athanasius (119, 69 and 105, and 15 respectively; see also ps.-Caesarius, Qu. 86 and 188 in respect of Anastasius' Qu. 96/*28). Note also Qu. 114/*66 (= ps.-Athanasius, Qu. 103, 104) on the causes of plagues.

[71]As exemplified in near-contemporary works of hagiography—e.g. the miracles of Artemius and of Therapon or those recounted in the *Life of Andrew the Fool*; or in the *Narrationes* ascribed to Anastasius himself.

the compromise was not forgotten. Indeed, the later textual history of his collection, the addition of lengthy florilegia detailing received opinion (or that favored by the Church authorities) which served to conceal his originality and his open-minded pragmatism, make it clear that Anastasius could not be ignored. Both the "rationalist" tradition of the Hellenistic world and the divinely ordained world order of heavenly *pronoia* coexisted at different social and intellectual levels and in different literary genres throughout the medieval period, occasionally brought together more explicitly in the writings of such men as John of Damascus, Photius, and Michael Psellus.

But it is worth recalling that the Christian tradition to which I have been referring was also heavily influenced by Judaic thought. This is especially so in the case of ideas about the body, attitudes to illness and its causes, and the remedies that apply thereto. Hellenistic medicine asserted that the essential condition for good health was internal bodily equilibrium, and that its remedies therefore involved the application of measures designed to alter the internal balance of the body's elements. Jewish medicine, in contrast, was designed to expel evil which polluted the sufferer from the outside. Illness was, in effect, the consequence of a healthy body being invaded by some external force.[72] And it is precisely the Christian version of this, also reflected, for example, in notions of demonic possession, which comes to dominate attitudes of people in the late Roman and Byzantine worlds—ideas which, importantly, are also paralleled in attitudes to political and cultural identity. The exclusivity expressed in the anti-pluralist and anti-heterodox tendencies of late Roman culture during the late sixth and especially the seventh century seems to represent a further aspect of this.

Internal purity thus became the hallmark of orthodoxy and of the imperial state; and however it may have worked in practice, it was certainly a leitmotif of the political orthodoxy of the later seventh century and afterwards. External pollution, however introduced, was perceived as the main threat. Chastisement from heaven was the remedy, de-

[72]See John Wilkinson, *Health and Healing: Studies in New Testament Principles and Practice* (Edinburgh, 1980); Darrel W. Amundsen, "Medicine and Faith in Early Christianity", *Bulletin of the History of Medicine* 56 (1982), 326–50; Vivian Nutton, "From Galen to Alexander: Aspects of Medicine and Medical Practice in Late Antiquity", *DOP* 38 (1984), 1–14.

signed to drive out the evils afflicting the body politic. As long as such evil could be held at bay, orthodoxy, and therefore God's support and approval, were assured—these are the fundamental premises of Byzantine political-religious ideology throughout its history, and are crucial to later debates on both heresy as well as, in the twelfth century and after, the relationship between eastern and western Churches. I would argue that it is in the seventh century that the two traditions, Judeo-Christian and Hellenistic, confronted each other most obviously, and when the Judeo-Christian model was the victor. The establishment of boundaries, the exclusion of groups perceived as marginal to the health of the state and society—groups which could henceforth be regarded as polluting evils and dealt with accordingly, just as evil spirits had to be driven out from the sick body—these are the obvious features of medieval popular political orthodoxy.[73] Hence also the regular use of epithets evoking precisely these external, and polluting, influences to designate and also explain the actions of those perceived as enemies of the orthodox order: "Saracen-minded", "Jewish-thinking", and so forth.

The parallel goes further. Pain and suffering as a means of cleansing and purifying applied as much to the physical body as to the "state".[74] Attitudes to punishment for sins and to remedies for malaise, real or metaphorical, are the same, and by the sixth century they had become part of the standard ideological vocabulary of Christian culture and political thinking. But the fact that Anastasius explicitly attempted a compromise is important. And although it failed—as the continued parallel existence of both traditions attests—it demonstrates the nature of the cultural changes which were taking place.

What is perhaps most important in this respect is the wider context within which the *Questions and Answers* of Anastasius are to be

---

[73]See Haldon, *Byzantium in the Seventh Century*, 348–75, 425–35; and especially Martin D. Goodman, *The Ruling Class of Judaea: the Origins of the Jewish Revolt against Rome* AD *66–70* (Cambridge, 1987), 99–106, where the model of the body in notions about the structure and workings of society, on the one hand, and of the opposition between the poles of purity–pollution, purity–danger as developed in anthropology is usefully employed. See, for example, Mary Douglas, *Natural Symbols* (Harmondsworth, 1978), 93–112, based ultimately on Durkheim.

[74]See Nutton, "From Galen to Alexander", 8, arguing from, e.g., Cyprian, *De mortalitate* 9.

understood. For the key question of the nature and degree of human free will, and its relationship to divine providence and foresight, was of central importance to Christian thinkers throughout the Roman and late Roman periods, and was one of the major sources of debate among Muslim theologians in the eighth and ninth centuries. Just as Anastasius presents a middle road between determinism, whereby God's foreknowledge is equated effectively with the foreordained nature of human existence, and free will, so his contemporary, the Monophysite Jacob of Edessa, confronts and argues much the same position, albeit from a Monophysite perspective.[75] And it is clear from both Anastasius and Jacob that the views of those who defended the argument for free will were set in a context in which determinist attitudes dominated the agenda. This certainly fits with many of Anastasius' questions and the answers which he gives to them. And, as Michael Cook has suggested, it provides at least to a degree the background to the development of early Islamic dogma, however evolved and distanced a stage its first literary witnesses may represent from this original period of dialogue and confrontation. For it seems clear that the first generation of Islamic apologists and dialecticians had to contend on the basis of certain common features with both Christian and Zoroastrian or dualist philosophical challenges, as well as the internal debates between the different sects of early Islam which developed from the 660s in particular.[76]

[75] On Jacob of Edessa, see Baumstark, 248–56, esp. 249–50 on his letters: with the discussion on the letters and their content in Michael Cook, *Early Muslim Dogma: a Source-Critical Study* (Cambridge, 1981), 145–58.

[76] Cook, *Early Muslim Dogma*, 150–52, 153–58; C.H. Becker, "Christliche Polemik und islamische Dogmenbildung", in his *Islamstudien* (Leipzig, 1924–32), I, 432–49. See also George F. Hourani, "Islamic and Non-Islamic Origins of Mu'tazilite Ethical Rationalism", *IJMES* 7 (1976), 59–87. Hourani searches in vain for clear evidence of contacts between individual Christian and Zoroastrian thinkers, on the one hand, and Muslim thinkers or *mutakallimūn*, on the other. The latter are neatly described by Cook (*Early Muslim Dogma*, 157), as "the dialectical militias of the warring sects"; see also Cook's, "The Origins of *Kalām*", *BSOAS* 43 (1980), 32–43. Hourani argues for the influence of other pre-Islamic traditions on the first Muslim thinkers (72–75). Cook is more sceptical, but does not deny the original and formative context within which Islamic dogma evolved (see esp. *Early Muslim Dogma*, 153–58). On the other hand, Hourani looks to John of Damascus as a possible early intellectual stimulus which, as Cook has argued, is really rather too late. Thinkers such as Jacob of Edessa and Anastasius of Sinai, among others of

The point here, of course, is not a new one. The Hellenistic heritage of both seventh-century Christianity, split by internal conflicts over christological issues and confronted by a new and dynamic religious system, and of Islam itself, presented both religions with the same, or very similar, fundamental theological and political problems, drawn from familiar cultural contexts. Each dealt with this in different ways. The writings of Anastasius provide a fascinating insight into the attitudes and problems which confronted one side of this new political and religious equation during a period of major social and cultural transformation.

their generation, might well be much more representative (even if there existed no direct contact between them, or others like them, and their Muslim counterparts) of the bearers of that non-Islamic cultural context and tradition. Anastasius certainly seems to have been familiar with some aspects of Muslim thought, as we have seen, as was Jacob of Edessa: see François Nau, "Lettre de Jacques d'Edesse sur la généalogie de la sainte Vierge", *ROC* 6 (1901), 522.

4

Ps.-Methodius: A Concept of History in Response to the Rise of Islam

G.J. Reinink

(Rijksuniversiteit Groningen)

In Chapter XIII.6–15 of his text, the author of the ps.-Methodius *Apocalypse*[1] expresses his hopes for the end of Muslim domination:

And after these calamities and chastisements of the sons of

[1]The division into chapters and sections is that of the edition of the Greek texts by Anastasios Lolos, *Die Apokalypse des Ps.- Methodius* (Meisenheim am Glan, 1976); *idem*, *Die dritte und vierte Redaktion des Ps.-Methodius* (Meisenheim am Glan, 1978). Of the ps.-Methodius *Apocalypse*, originally written in Syriac, only four Mss. are known today: Vat. syr. 58 and three Mardin Mss., all belonging to the West Syrian tradition. On the Mss. and their transmission, see n. 54 below. The text of Vat. syr 58 (AD 1584–86) has been published by Harald Suermann, *Die geschichtstheologische Reaktion auf die einfallenden Muslime in der edessenischen Apokalyptik des 7. Jahrhunderts* (Frankfurt am Main, 1985), 34–85, and in a much better edition by Francisco Javier Martinez, *Eastern Christian Apocalyptic in the Early Muslim Period: Pseudo-Methodius and Pseudo-Athanasius* (Ph.D dissertation: Catholic University of America, 1985), 58–92. References here will be to the Martinez edition, but the translations are based on my forthcoming new *CSCO* edition of the Syriac text, incorporating all manuscript evidence. For English translations of the Vat. syr. 58 text, see Martinez, *Eastern Christian Apocalyptic*, 122–201; also Paul J. Alexander, *The Byzantine Apocalyptic Tradition* (Berkeley, Los Angeles, and London, 1985), 36–51.

Ishmael, at the end of that week,[2] when men will be lying in the peril of chastisement[3] and will have no hope that they may be saved from that hard servitude, being persecuted and oppressed and suffering indignities, hunger, and thirst, and being tormented by the hard chastisement, whereas these barbarian tyrants[4] will delight themselves with food and drink and rest and will boast of their victory, how they

---

[2]The ps.-Methodius *Apocalypse* divides world history into seven millennia, elaborating the chronology of the *Cave of Treasures*; cf. Albrecht Götze, "Die Nachwirkung der Schatzhöhle", *ZS* 2 (1923), 52–56; G. J. Reinink, "Der Verfassername 'Modios' der syrischen Schatzhöhle und die Apokalypse des Pseudo-Methodios", *OC* 67 (1983), 46–64. This in turn is dependent on the chronology of Julius Africanus; see Albrecht Götze, *Die Schatzhöhle. Überlieferung und Quellen* (Heidelberg, 1922), 80–85; cf. also Su-Min Ri, "La caverne des trésors: problèmes d'analyse littéraire", in H.J.W. Drijvers, R. Lavenant, C. Molenberg, and G.J. Reinink, eds., *IV Symposium Syriacum 1984* (Rome, 1987), 190. Ps.-Methodius places the Arab conquests in the seventh and last millennium (XI.1; ed. Martinez, 77:1–3) and confines the time of Muslim domination to ten "weeks of years", or 70 years (V.9, X.6, XIII.2, 4; ed. Martinez, 66:54–55, 76:47, 85:5–6, 17–18). The beginning of these 70 years probably coincides with the year 622 and "the end of that week" (i.e. the last and tenth "week of years") with 692. See 178 below and n. 125.

[3]The word "chastisement" (Syriac, *mardūtā*) has a pregnant meaning in ps.-Methodius. In explaining the word *mardūtā* in II Thessalonians 2:3 as "chastisement" (XI.17; ed. Martinez, 80:92–95), ps.-Methodius describes the Muslim domination as the time of "chastisement" preceding the appearance of the Antichrist. See F.J. Martinez, "The Apocalyptic Genre in Syriac: the World of Pseudo-Methodius", in *IV Symposium Syriacum 1984*, 344; G.J. Reinink, "Pseudo-Methodius und die Legende vom römischen Endkaiser", in Werner Verbeke, Daniel Verhelst, and Andries Welkenhuysen, eds., *The Use and Abuse of Eschatology in the Middle Ages* (Leuven, 1988), 95–97.

[4]The term "tyrants", which ps.-Methodius repeatedly applies to the Arabs, also has a pregnant meaning in the *Apocalypse*. It has both a metaphorical function, indicating the cruelty and barbarism of Muslim domination, and a Biblical, symbolic meaning rooted in the Syriac exegesis of Matthew 16:18, in which the "bars of hell" are explained as the "tyrants of hell", i.e. Death and Satan, who were shattered by the Cross of Christ. See the *Apocalypse* XI.8–9; ed. Martinez, 74:53–63; and especially G.J. Reinink, "Tyrannen und Muslime. Die Gestaltung einer symbolischen Metapher bei Pseudo-Methodius", in H.L.J. Vanstiphout, K. Jongeling, F. Leemhuis, and G.J. Reinink, eds., *Scripta Signa Vocis: Studies about Scripts, Scriptures, Scribes and Languages in the Near East, Presented to J. H. Hospers by his Pupils, Colleagues and Friends* (Groningen, 1986), 163–75. See further below, 154.

had laid waste and destroyed Persia and Armenia and Cilicia and Isauria and Cappadocia and Africa and Sicily and Hellas and the inhabited parts of the country of the Romans and all the islands of the seas[5] and will be dressed like bridegrooms and will be adorned like brides and blaspheme by saying: "The Christians have no savior",[6] then suddenly the pangs of affliction as [those] of a woman in travail will be awakened against them and the king of the Greeks will go out against them in great wrath and "awake like a man who has shaken off his wine",[7] who was considered by them as dead. He will go out against them from the sea of the Ethiopians and will cast desolation and destruction in the desert of Yathrib and in the habitation of their fathers. And the sons of the king of the Greeks[8] will descend from the western regions and will destroy by the sword the remnant that is left of them in the land of promise. And fear will fall upon them from all sides. And they and their wives and their sons and their leaders and all their camps in the land of the desert of their fathers will be delivered into the power of

[5]For a synopsis of the lists in ps.-Methodius of regions conquered by the Muslims, see Martinez, *Eastern Christian Apocalyptic*, 202–205; Alexander, *The Byzantine Apocalyptic Tradition*, 34–36. I do not agree with Alexander's opinion (25) that the *Apocalypse* must have been composed before 678, since it does not mention the unsuccessful Arab siege of Constantinople (in 674–78). Nor does the fact that most Greek Mss. (all of a late date) bear an interpolation at XIII.7–10, with an allusion to the siege of Constantinople, lend any support to the supposition that the original Syriac text was written before these events, *pace* Lolos, *Die Apokalypse des Ps.-Methodius*, 22.

[6]See n. 14 below. The word *pārūqā*, "savior", which is used here, also refers to Christ, the Savior. The king of the Greeks, who will suddenly rise to defeat the Muslims, will act as Christ's deputy on earth (see below, 153)

[7]Psalms 78:65.

[8]The term "sons of the king of the Greeks" does not refer to the sons of the Byzantine emperor in the literal sense, but to the Byzantines in general, just as the Arabs are called the "sons of Ishmael". It has nothing to do with Jewish messianic ideas. See G.J. Reinink, "Die syrischen Wurzeln der mittelalterlichen Legende von römischen Endkaiser", in Martin Gosman and Jaap van Os, eds., *Non nova, sed nove: mélanges de civilisation médiévale dédiés à Willem Noomen* (Groningen, 1984), 198–99; *pace* P.J. Alexander, "The Medieval Legend of the Last Roman Emperor and Its Messianic Origin", *JWCI* 41 (1978), 7.

> the king of the Greeks. And they will be surrendered to the sword and to destruction and to captivity and to slaughter. And the yoke of their servitude will be seven times more severe than their own yoke. And they will be in a hard affliction from hunger and from exhaustion. And they will be slaves, they and their wives and their sons. And they will serve as slaves to those who were serving them. And their servitude will be a hundred times more bitter than theirs. And the land which was desolated of its inhabitants will find peace. And the remnant that is left will return, everyone to his land and to the inheritance of his fathers: Cappadocia and Armenia and Cilicia and Isauria and Africa and Hellas and Sicily. And the entire remnant that is left over from the captives and which was in the servitude of the captivity, everyone will return to his country and to the house of his father. And man will multiply like locusts on the land which had been laid waste. And Egypt will be laid waste and Arabia will burn and the land of Hebron will be laid waste and the tongue of the sea will be pacified. And all the wrath and anger of the king of the Greeks will be vented upon those who had denied Christ.[9]

With these words the author expresses his hope that at the end of ten "weeks of years" of Muslim domination the Byzantine emperor will suddenly and unexpectedly, by a large-scale military operation, put an end to the rôle of the "sons of Ishmael" on the stage of world history.[10]

In referring to the words of Psalm 78:65, the author does not merely use a Biblical metaphor to show that the appearance of the Byzantine emperor will occur at a time when the Arabs feel safe and strong, without any fear of a genuinely threatening Byzantine attack. He was well aware too of the christological connotations of the words of the Psalmist. In the *Cave of Treasures*, one of his main sources, the words:

[9]Ed. Martinez, 86:35–88:78 (the few deviations in my translation from the Martinez text are due to the better readings in the Mardin Mss.). The problem of apostasy plays a prominent part in the *Apocalypse*: cf., for example, XII.1–8; ed. Martinez, 83:1–84:42.

[10]See n. 2 above.

"And the Lord awoke like a sleeper and like a man who shakes off his wine", were associated with the sleep and awakening of Noah from his wine[11] as a symbol of the crucifixion, death, and resurrection of Christ.[12] It is very probable that ps.-Methodius seeks to suggest to his readers that just as Christ was as if dead, but rose from the dead and defeated Satan, the Enemy, so also the emperor "who was considered by them (i.e. by the Arabs) as dead" will arise and defeat the Muslims, the enemies of the Christian religion.[13] The immediate cause of the sudden intervention of the emperor is the blasphemy uttered by the Muslims according to which "the Christians have no savior". With these words it is not only a political savior that is meant; the thought is also implied that the military successes of the Muslims could be regarded as a proof for the superiority of Islam over Christianity.[14]

These observations highlight the important fact that for a proper understanding of this apocalypse we must constantly bear in mind that the author uses the typical Syriac method of typological and symbolic exegesis to explain and describe historical phenomena.[15] Very often his words refer at the same time to a historical and a Biblical or theological reality, using typological models and Biblical symbolic speech to link both levels. If we disregard this double function of the language used by ps.-Methodius, we shall run the risk of seeking solutions to the many problems posed by this difficult work in the wrong direction.[16]

---

[11] Genesis 9:24.

[12] *Cave of Treasures* XXI.18–22; ed. Su-Min Ri, *La caverne des trésors: les deux recensions syriaques* (Leuven, 1987; *CSCO* 486–87, *Scr. Syri* 207–208), 162–65 (text); 62–63 (trans.).

[13] The symbolic exegesis lies behind ps.-Methodius' use of the expression "tyrants" for the Muslims (see n. 4 above).

[14] See n. 6 above; also Reinink, "Die syrischen Wurzeln", 198; *idem*, "Pseudo-Methodius und die Legende vom römischen Endkaiser", 105.

[15] It is the same line of thought as one encounters, for example, in Ephraem's *Hymns Against Julian*; cf. Sidney H. Griffith, "Ephraem the Syrian's Hymns 'Against Julian': Meditations on History and Imperial Power", *VC* 41 (1987), 245–46.

[16] For examples of ps.-Methodius' typological and symbolical interpretation of history, see G.J. Reinink, "Ismael, der Wildesel in der Wüste. Zur Typologie der Apokalypse des Pseudo-Methodius", *BZ* 75 (1982), 336–44; *idem*, "Die syrischen Wurzeln", 195–205; *idem*, "Tyrannen und Muslime," 163–71.

In applying Biblical passages with a christological interpretation to the emperor of Byzantium, ps.-Methodius' *mēmrā* "On the Succession of the Kingdoms and the End of the Times" manifests one of its most striking and remarkable features.[17] In one of the key passages in the text the words of Paul at I Corinthians 15:24 referring to Christ, who at the End will hand over the kingdom to God the Father, are applied to "the king of the Greeks", who after the appearance of the Antichrist will hand over his kingdom—the last and only empire to remain on earth in the final days of mankind—to God the Father.[18]

Who was the author of this *Apocalypse*? More properly, we might seek to clarify the historical circumstances in which he felt obliged to develop a concept of history in which the traditional view of the continued existence of the Roman/Byzantine Empire until the coming of the Antichrist[19] was extended to ascribe an eschatological rôle to the Byzantine emperor, who, as the savior of the whole Christian world and the defender of the Christian religion, would destroy the Muslim "tyranny",[20] punish the apostates,[21] and establish the final world dominion of the Christian empire.[22] This question confronts us with one of the most difficult and controversial problems of this Syriac apocalypse, which may be considered as the first attempt by a Christian writer to explain the rise of Muslim power within the framework of a "political" history of the succession of the kingdoms from the beginning of mankind to the end of the world.[23] We should also note that after

[17]See below, 156–57.

[18]XIV.3–6; ed. Martinez, 90:12–91:28. By connecting Psalm 68:31 (see below, 162–63) with I Corinthians 15:24, ps.-Methodius relates the Son who will hand over the kingdom of the Christians to God the Father (X.3; ed. Martinez, 75:15–16) to the "son of Kūshyat" who is the king of the Greeks. Cf. Reinink, "Pseudo-Methodius und die Legende vom römischen Endkaiser", 101.

[19]Cf., for example, Gerhard Podskalsky, *Byzantinische Reichseschatologie* (Munich, 1972), 55. Ps.-Methodius (X.1; ed. Martinez, 75:4–6) develops the traditional patristic "Rome exegesis" of II Thessalonians 2:7, which is also common in Syrian Monophysite exegetical sources. See Reinink, "Pseudo-Methodius und die Legende vom römischen Endkaiser", 102–103, and especially notes 90–91; also see below, notes 119 and 145.

[20]See n. 4 above.

[21]See n. 9 above.

[22]See below, 159.

[23]Alexander, *The Byzantine Apocalyptic Tradition*, 16 n. 10, very properly ob-

being translated into Greek,[24] and then from Greek into Latin,[25] this work was to become one of the most influential apocalyptic texts in both the East and the West.[26]

---

serves that in presenting world history as a "succession of kingdoms", ps.-Methodius follows the model of the *Cave of Treasures*, which describes the "succession of the generations" from Adam to Christ.

[24]The Greek translation must have taken place very soon after the composition of ps.-Methodius, perhaps already before the end of the seventh century, since the oldest known Latin Ms. (*cod.* Bern, Burgerbibliothek, no. 611) probably already dates from the late 720s. However, the oldest Greek manuscript was written in 1332–33, whereas the remaining 28 Mss. date from the fifteenth to seventeenth centuries. At least four recensions can be distinguished in the Greek textual tradition, but already the first recension shows traces of a later revision. The new edition of the Greek recensions by Lolos (see n. 1) has been criticized by Martinez, *Eastern Christian Apocalyptic*, 21; and Thomas Frenz, "Textkritische Untersuchungen zu 'Pseudo-Methodius'. Das Verhältnis der griechischen zur ältesten lateinischen Fassung", *BZ* 80 (1987), 50–58.

[25]There is an edition of the Latin text based on four old Mss. in Ernst Sackur, *Sibyllinische Texte und Forschungen. Pseudomethodius, Adso und die tiburtinische Sibylle* (Halle, 1898), 59–96; also an edition of a later recension of the Latin text by Otto Prinz, "Eine frühe abendländische Aktualisierung der lateinischen Übersetzung des Pseudo-Methodius", *Deutsches Archiv für Erforschung des Mittelalters* 41 (1985), 1–23. For a general view of the Latin manuscript evidence, see now Marc Laureys and Daniel Verhelst, "Pseudo-Methodius, *Revelationes*: Textgeschichte und kritische Edition. Ein Leuven-Groninger Forschungsprojekt", in *The Use and Abuse of Eschatology in the Middle Ages*, 112–36. For the old Slavonic translations from the Greek, see now F.J. Thompson, "The Slavonic Translations of Pseudo-Methodius of Olympus' Apocalypsis", in *Kulturno razvitie na Bălgarskata dăržava. Krajăt na XII-XIV vek. Četvărti meždunaroden simpozium, Veliko Tărnovo, 16–18 oktomvri 1985 g.* (Sofia, 1985), 143–73.

[26]For the influence of ps.-Methodius in the East, see, e.g., Martinez, *Eastern Christian Apocalyptic*, 11–16; Cyril Mango, *Byzantium: the Empire of New Rome* (London, 1980), 201–17; Hans Schmoldt, *Die Schrift "vom jungen Daniel" und "Daniels letzte Vision". Herausgabe und Interpretation zweier apokalyptischer Texte* (Ph.D dissertation: Universität Hamburg, 1972), *passim*; Alexander, *The Byzantine Apocalyptic Tradition*, *passim*. For the influence of ps.-Methodius in the West, see, e.g., P.J. Alexander, "Byzantium and the Migration of Literary Works and Motifs: the Legend of the Last Roman Emperor", *Medievalia et Humanistica*, New Series, 2 (1971), 47–68; reprinted in Alexander's *Religious and Political History and Thought in the Byzantine Empire* (London, 1978); *idem*, "The Diffusion of Byzantine Apocalypses in the Medieval West and the Beginnings of Joachimism", in Ann Williams, ed., *Prophecy and Millenarianism: Essays in Honour of Marjorie Reeves* (London, 1980), 62–71; Bernard McGinn, *Visions of the*

Sebastian Brock sets forth the problem very clearly when, in his article on Syriac views of emergent Islam, he states that "Pseudo-Methodios is in fact much more in line with what seems to have been the Chalcedonian attitude in Syria, where in the early eighth century John of Damascus was writing hymns which pray for deliverance, at the hands of the Byzantine emperor, from the enemies of Christ, the Ishmaelites".[27] He goes on to wonder "whether Pseudo-Methodios may not in reality have been a Chalcedonian, whose work (unobjectionable Christologically to the Monophysites) happens to have been transmitted in Syriac by Monophysite scribes".[28] F.J. Martinez too does not exclude the possibility of a Melkite origin of the *Apocalypse*, in view of the consideration that such a hypothesis would better explain some features of the work,[29] although he admits that none of the arguments is conclusive and that a Melkite origin of the text remains only a probability.[30]

Upon initial reflection the hypothesis of a Chalcedonian origin for the work of ps.-Methodius seems to give the best explanation for the fact that he appears to be, to quote Michael Kmosko, "ein warmer, soger fanatischer Anhänger der byzantinischen Kaiseridee".[31] On the other hand, the proposition of a Byzantine emperor rescuing the Chris-

End: Apocalyptic Traditions in the Middle Ages (New York, 1979), 70–76 and *passim*.

[27]Sebastian Brock, "Syriac Views of Emergent Islam", in G.H.A. Juynboll, ed., *Studies on the First Century of Islamic Society* (Carbondale and Edwardsville, 1982), 19; reprinted in Brock's *Syriac Perspectives on Late Antiquity* (London, 1984).

[28]*Ibid.*, 19–20.

[29]Martinez mentions ps.-Methodius' dependence on the Syriac *Alexander Legend* (for this work, see n. 73 below), his silence about christological issues, and his "ecumenical" attempt to show that Byzantines and Ethiopians are brothers. Martinez's conclusion that ps.-Methodius intentionally avoids discussing christological issues is surely correct; however, the most important question is why he does so. Although I earlier rejected the hypothesis of a Monophysite origin of ps.-Methodius (cf. my "Der Verfassername", 60; "Ismael", 344; and Suermann's proper criticism of my argument based upon Nestorian exegetical sources in *Die geschichtstheologische Reaktion*, 161), I have more recently revised my opinion. Cf. my "Pseudo-Methodius und die Legende vom römischen Endkaiser", 108–11.

[30]Martinez, *Eastern Christian Apocalyptic*, 28.

[31]Michael Kmosko, "Das Rätsel des Pseudomethodius", *Byzantion* 6 (1931), 291.

tians from the oppressive Ishmaelite yoke does not seem to fit very well into the general pattern of reactions to the Arab conquests as known from the reports of some Monophysite and Nestorian authors.[32] Certainly, Chalcedonian authors could also at first put the blame for the Arab successes on the ecclesiastical policy of the emperor;[33] however, it is conceivable that in the course of time, as people became more and more aware that the Arab conquests must be more than a *temporary* punishment because of Christian sins,[34] the Chalcedonian communities in the countries now ruled by the Arabs found themselves in a particularly awkward situation.[35] Is it not possible, therefore, to look on the *Apocalypse* as an attempt by a Chalcedonian writer to find a solution for his community's dilemma?[36] At the end of the seventh century the Armenian Monophysite historian Sebēos substituted the Ishmaelites

---

[32]Some Monophysite chroniclers expressed the view that the Arabs delivered the Monophysites from the oppressive yoke of the Byzantines. See Michael I Qīndasī, *Chronique de Michel le Syrien*, ed. and trans. J.-B. Chabot (Paris, 1899–1924), II, 413 (trans.); IV, 410 (text); *Chronicon ad annum Christi 1234 pertinens*, I, ed. and trans. J.-B. Chabot (Paris and Leuven, 1916–37; *CSCO* 81, *Scr. Syri* 36), 237 (text), 185 (trans.); and on this material, Brock, "Syriac Views", 10–11; Harald Suermann, "Orientalische Christen und der Islam. Christliche Texte aus der Zeit von 632–750", *Zeitschrift für Missionswissenschaft und Religionswissenschaft* 67 (1983), 122.

For the view of the Nestorian monk Jōḥannān bar Penkāyē, writing shortly before ps.-Methodius, see Alfonse Mingana, *Sources syriaques*, I (Mosul and Leipzig, 1908), 143*–45*; cf. also Reinink, "Pseudo-Methodius und die Legende vom römischen Endkaiser", 86.

We should beware of applying these incidental statements too simply to a precisely dated work such as the ps.-Methodius *Apocalypse*. However, one point is perfectly clear: ps.-Methodius was well aware of the bad reputation of Byzantine emperors who had persecuted Monophysites in the past. It is for this reason that he portrays the coming Greek emperor who would liberate the Christians from the Muslim yoke as a second Alexander, Constantine, and Jovian, types of the good Christian emperor protecting Christendom as a whole.

[33]See Walter E. Kaegi, "Initial Byzantine Reactions to the Arab Conquest", *Church History* 38 (1969), 142–43; Brock, "Syriac Views", 11.

[34]Kaegi, "Initial Byzantine Reactions", 139–40; Brock, "Syriac Views", 9.

[35]Brock, "Syriac Views", 20.

[36]Cf. *ibid.*, 20–21: "It is thus probably the Chalcedonian community's dilemma, as well as the worsening conditions for Christians during the Second Civil War, and fears aroused by the census, that led to the rise of the apocalyptic literature, around 690, which found a ready audience in all three religious communities".

for Rome as the fourth beast in Daniel's prophecy.[37] This reinterpretation of the traditional identification of Daniel's fourth world empire with Rome[38] shows that at the end of the seventh century the opinion had taken shape that an Islamic empire, in terms of an enduring political entity, had come into existence.[39] Ps.-Methodius, on the other hand, also writing at the end of the seventh century, defends the traditional pattern of four kingdoms—Babylonians, Medes, Persians, and Greeks/Romans—and simply denies the existence of anything like an Arab kingdom.[40] In fact, his "Revelation on the Succession of the Kingdoms" can be considered as representing, from beginning to end, a plea for the view that the Greek/Roman/Byzantine kingdom, founded by the conquests of Alexander the Great, is the fourth kingdom of Daniel and the last empire in the history of mankind.[41] The rôle of the "sons of

[37]Sebēos, *History of Heraclius* XXXII; trans. Frédéric Macler, *Histoire d'Héraclius par l'évêque Sebêos* (Paris, 1904), 104–105. Cf. Kaegi, "Initial Byzantine Reactions", 146–47. Sebēos gives a new interpretation to the four kingdoms of Daniel by connecting them with the four quarters of the earth: 1. the kingdom of the Greeks in the West; 2. the kingdom of the Sasanians in the East; 3. the kingdom of Gog and Magog in the North; and 4. the kingdom of Ishmael in the South. For the much-discussed question of Sebēos' authorship and the literary problems of the *History of Heraclius*, see, e.g., the contributions of Mesrob K. Krikorian, "Sebēos, Historian of the Seventh Century", and Zaven Arzoumanian, "A Critique of Sebēos and his History of Heraclius, a Seventh-Century Armenian Document", in Thomas J. Samuelian, ed., *Classical Armenian Culture: Influences and Creativity* (Philadelphia, 1982), 52–67, 68–78. See also Robert W. Thomson, *Moses Khorenats'i. History of the Armenians* (Cambridge, Mass., 1978), 53.

[38]For the earlier Syriac tradition, see Harald Suermann, "Einige Bemerkungen zu syrischen Apokalypsen des 7. Jhds.", in *IV Symposium Syriacum 1984*, 331–32; cf. also Martinez, "The Apocalyptical Genre", 345–46.

[39]Kaegi, "Initial Byzantine Reactions", 147; Brock, "Syriac Views", 9–10. Although in Syriac sources dealing with the seventh century the Arab domination is regularly described as a "kingdom" (see Brock, "Syriac Views", 14), Sebēos is the first author who clearly places the Arabs as a world empire on a line with the Greeks (Byzantines) and the Persians within the Daniel scheme of the four world empires in the history of mankind.

[40]Ps.-Methodius never applies the word *malkūtā*, "kingdom", to the Arab domination (cf. also Martinez, "The Apocalyptic Genre", 342). This is certainly for polemical reasons (see above, n. 39). The common designation in ps.-Methodius of the "sons of Ishmael" in relation to their political rôle is "tyrants", also used in a highly polemical way (see n. 4 above).

[41]Cf. also Martinez, "The Apocalyptic Genre", 346.

Ishmael" is confined to that of a temporary "chastisement",[42] a scourge in the hand of God to destroy the "fatlings of the Greeks",[43] to punish the Christians because of their sins (especially sexual ones),[44] and to separate the true believers from the unbelievers, viz. apostates.[45] The Arabs are portrayed as "barbarian tyrants",[46] the uncivilized descendants of "Ishmael, the wild ass of the desert",[47] devastating the civilized world and desecrating the holy places of the Christians.[48]

This is all highly polemical. Must we accept, however, that a Chalcedonian author is here polemicizing against Monophysites who, in their hatred against the Chalcedonians, cooperate with the Muslim "tyrants" at the expense of the Chalcedonian communities in Syria and North Mesopotamia?[49] This question must be answered in the negative. The main problem for ps.-Methodius is in fact the danger of voluntary apostasy by members of his own Church.[50] Walter E. Kaegi arrives at the right conclusion when he states that "the author of the Pseudo-Methodius apocalypse foresaw a subsequent period in which many Christians would convert to Islam".[51] Is ps.-Methodius, however, "a loyal Byzantine Christian" who "confidently predicted and joyously looked forward to the ultimate triumph of the Byzantine emperor and the eradication of the Arabs and Islam"?[52] A loyal Byzantine

---

[42] Above, n. 3.

[43] XI.3; ed. Martinez, 77:9–10.

[44] XI.6–7; ed. Martinez, 78:26–39.

[45] XIII.4–5; ed. Martinez, 85:20–86:36.

[46] See above, n. 4.

[47] See Reinink, "Ismael", 342–44.

[48] XI.3–4, 8–18; ed. Martinez, 77:11–18, 78:43–82:125.

[49] Cf. also Jōḥannān bar Penkāyē, who suggests that the Monophysites, taking advantage of the favorable political conditions during Mu'āwiya's reign (661–80) "turned almost all the churches of the Romans (i.e. Byzantines) to their own impious opinion" (ed. Mingana, 147*); cf. Reinink, "Pseudo-Methodius und die Legende vom römischen Endkaiser", 87, 108. However, ps.-Methodius does not polemicize against Monophysites converting Chalcedonians to Monophysitism; he is more concerned to combat the expected apostasy of co-religionists to Islam.

[50] See also Reinink, "Der Verfassername", 63; *idem*, "Die syrischen Wurzeln", 198; *idem*, "Pseudo-Methodius und die Legende vom römischen Endkaiser", 104. Cf. also Martinez, *Eastern Christian Apocalyptic*, 32.

[51] Kaegi, "Initial Byzantine Reactions", 145.

[52] *Ibid.*

Christian means a Melkite. However, it is difficult to assume that ps.-Methodius was a Melkite who tried to prevent apostasy by warning his co-religionists that soon the emperor of Byzantium would appear to destroy the Arabs and punish the apostates. Not only did the author live in all probability in the region of Sinjār (about 100 kilometers southeast of Nisibis), which in the seventh century had become a strong center of Monophysitism;[53] in addition, new Syriac manuscript evidence for this work points to a long and complicated history of textual transmission in the West Syrian tradition.[54] But the most important argument in

[53]It is generally accepted that the mention of the mount of Sinjār as the place of revelation of the *Apocalypse* in the preamble to ps.-Methodius can be considered as an indication that the work was composed in the town of Sinjār itself or in its vicinity, Mount Sinjār; e.g. Alexander, *The Byzantine Apocalyptic Tradition*, 28; Sebastian Brock, "Syriac Sources for Seventh-Century History", *BMGS* 2 (1976), 34; *idem*, "Syriac Views", 18; Martinez, "The Apocalyptic Genre", 340; *idem*, *Eastern Christian Apocalyptic*, 26. Suermann (*Die geschichtstheologische Reaktion*, 160), on the other hand, is more inclined to favor an origin for the work in Edessa or the vicinity of Edessa.

For a general history of Sinjār, see David Oates, *Studies in the Ancient History of Northern Iraq* (London, 1968), 97–106. For a survey of the history of Christianity (especially East Syrian) in this region, see Jean-Maurice Fiey, *Nisibe, métropole syriaque oriental et ses suffragants des origines à nos jours* (Leuven, 1977; *CSCO* 388, *Subsidia* 54), 269–73. For the expansion of Monophysitism in this region, see Jérôme Labourt, *Le Christianisme dans l'empire perse sous la dynastie sassanide (224–632)* (Paris, 1904), 217–31, esp. 220; Paul Peeters, "La passion arabe de S. 'Abd al-Masīḥ", *AB* 44 (1926), 278–87; Ernst Honigmann, *Le couvent de Barṣaumā et le patriarcat jacobite d'Antioche et de Syrie* (Leuven, 1954; *CSCO* 146, *Subsidia* 7), 95–97; Jean-Maurice Fiey, *Jalons pour une histoire de l'église en Iraq* (Leuven, 1970; *CSCO* 310, *Subsidia* 36), 141; cf. also Alexander, *The Byzantine Apocalyptic Tradition*, 28–29. There seems not to be much evidence for Chalcedonian communities in this region; cf. Jean-Maurice Fiey, "'Rūm' à l'est de l'Euphrate", *Le Muséon* 90 (1977), 365–420.

[54]The Syriac text in Vat. syr. 58 (copied AD 1584–86) was rediscovered by Kmosko; on this exemplar see his "Das Rätsel des Pseudomethodius", 273–96. Arthur Vööbus discovered three further Mss. which are now in the library of the Syrian Orthodox episcopal residence in Mardin, Turkey: Mardon Orth. 368 (AD 1365), Mardin Orth. 891, written in a modern West Syrian hand, but certainly older than Mardon Orth. A. (AD 1956); see Vööbus' "Discovery of an Unknown Syrian Author, Methodios of Peṭrā", *Abr-Nahrain* 17 (1976–77), 1–4. Vat. syr. 58 and the three Mardin Mss. represent two different text recensions, each of which has its own value for the reconstruction of the Syriac text upon which the original Greek translation depended. It should also be observed that the interrelations between the

favor of a Monophysite background can be taken from the contents of the *Apocalypse* itself. It is in fact the very peculiar, not to say enigmatic rôle of Ethiopia (Kūsh) in the work which compels us to look for a connection between the author and Monophysitism.

Paul J. Alexander was the first scholar who surmised a polemical aim related to Monophysitism[55] behind ps.-Methodius' interpretation of the words of Psalm 68:31 (Peshiṭtā): "Ethiopia (Kūsh) will hand over the power (lit. "hand") to God".[56] According to ps.-Methodius, David actually spoke these words concerning the kingdom of the Greeks, which descends from the offspring of Kūshyat,[57] daughter of Pīl, king

---

three Mardin Mss. point to a long history of text transmission within one and the same recension (for further details, see the introduction to my forthcoming edition in the *CSCO*). The fact that the manuscript evidence of ps.-Methodius shows a long history in the West Syrian tradition is not decisive for a Monophysite origin of the work, but may in combination with other arguments be a further indication for such an origin.

[55] Already Kmosko ("Das Rätsel des Pseudomethodius", 290) surmised a polemical intention behind ps.-Methodius' use of Psalm 68:31. But his suggestion that ps.-Methodius combined this verse with a political "Schmähwort augenscheinlich persischen Ursprungs" (the mother of Alexander would have been a Kūshite slave) to demonstrate that the Roman emperors would reign until the end of the world has found little support.

[56] P.J. Alexander, "The Syriac Original of Pseudo-Methodius' Apocalypse", in Denis Sinor, ed., *Proceedings of the 27th International Congress of Orientalists* (Wiesbaden, 1971), 107; similarly, cf. the same author's studies "Medieval Apocalypses as Historical Sources", *AHR* 73 (1968), 1006 (reprinted in Alexander, *Religious and Political History*, XIII); "Byzantium", 58–59; "Psevdo-Mefodij i Efiopija", *Antichnaja Drevnost i Srednie Veka*, 10 (1973), 21–27 (reprinted in Alexander, *Religion and Political History*, XI); *The Byzantine Apocalyptic Tradition*, 29.

[57] The spelling of the name *kwšyt* (Mardin Mss.) is no doubt to be preferred over the form *kwšt* in Vat. syr. 58, as it is a derivation from the *gentilicum kūšāytā*, "Ethiopian (wife)". Perhaps ps.-Methodius knew the exegetical tradition by which Kūsh in Psalm 68:31 was connected with the "Queen of Kūsh and Sheba" as well as the legendary traditions by which the Queen of Sheba was connected with Alexander the Great; cf. Reinink, "Pseudo-Methodius und die Legende vom römischen Endkaiser", 100 n. 84.

Ps.-Methodius makes Kūshyat the mother of Alexander the Great, who after Alexander's death married Byzas, the legendary founder of Byzantium. From this marriage was born a daughter Byzantia, who married Romulus, king of the Romans. They had three children: Romulus, who reigned in Rome, Urbanus, who reigned

of the Ethiopians (Kūshites).[58] David's prophecy will be fulfilled when the Last Emperor of the Greeks, after the appearance of the Antichrist, will go to Golgotha, place his crown on top of the Cross, and "hand over the kingdom to God the Father".[59]

Alexander concluded from these passages that ps.-Methodius "argued explicitly against anonymous opponents who interpreted Psalm

---

in Byzantium, and Claudius, who reigned in Alexandria (IX.1–7; ed. Martinez, 72:1–73:39). The genealogy demonstrates the unity of Daniel's fourth kingdom: Macedonians, Greeks, Romans, Byzantines (cf. also Martinez, "The Apocalyptic Genre", 346) and connects the Christian kingdom of Ethiopia with the Byzantine Empire for typological and idealogical reasons: there will be one world dominion of the Christian empire ruled by the Last World Emperor, protecting all Churches after his victory over the Arabs.

[58]IX.7–9; ed. Martinez, 73:36–74:56. When ps.-Methodius remarks in this context too that many "brethren of the clergy" were wrong in thinking that David made this statement about the kingdom of the Kūshites ("many brethren of the clergy supposed that David spoke of the kingdom of the Kūshites, but those who thought so have been in error"), he seems simply to defend his own exegesis, deviating from the traditional exegesis of Psalm 68:31 by which Kūsh was connected with Ethiopia and its future conversion; see Reinink, "Pseudo-Methodius und die Legende vom römischen Endkaiser", 100 n. 85. At any rate, it is impossible to gather from this passage that ps.-Methodius is confuting the opinion of contemporary members of his Church who use this verse to demonstrate that a politico-religious savior from Ethiopia would deliver the Christians from the Muslim yoke. Ps.-Methodius himself, by connecting Psalm 68:31 with I Corinthians 15:24 (see above, n. 18, and below, n. 59), gives a new eschatological meaning to the Psalm verse (cf. Reinink, *ibid.*, 100–103); in so doing he is of course obliged to discuss the "brethren of the clergy" who represented the normal interpretation of Psalm 68:31. Ps.-Methodius is well aware of his innovation. However, as appears also from the following words (IX.9; ed. Martinez, 74:56–63), by introducing this new exegesis he seeks to strengthen his view that the Arabs will never take the place of the Roman Christian Empire in the succession of the kingdoms: already David had prophesied that the Christian empire and not the "pagan tyrants" (the Arabs) would be the last empire in world history. For a more detailed discussion of the issues and questions raised by IX.9, see my "Tyrannen und Muslime", 166–67.

[59]XIV.3–6; ed. Martinez, 90:12–91:28. Using the correspondence of the words in I Corinthians 15:24 and Psalm 68:31 in the Syriac Bible, ps.-Methodius identifies the subject of the clause I Corinthians 15:24: "when he will hand over the kingdom to God the Father"—he (Christ) = the Byzantine emperor as Christ's deputy—with the subject of the sentence in Psalm 68:31 (Kūsh = the son of Kūshyat, i.e. *Alexander redivivus* or the Last World Emperor).

68:31 ('Ethiopia shall haste to stretch out her hands unto God') as indicating that liberation from the Muslim yoke would come from the ruler of Ethiopia".[60] Although Alexander later corrected his view that the author was a Monophysite polemicizing against *contemporary* members of his Church who placed their hope on the Monophysite ruler of Ethiopia,[61] most scholars have followed his suggestion that ps.-Methodius is refuting the opinion of contemporaries who understood Psalm 68:31 to mean that a savior would appear from Ethiopia.[62] Even Brock, who gives serious consideration to a Chalcedonian origin of the *Apocalypse*, holds the view that its author refutes such an interpretation of the verse by providing an elaborate genealogy for the Greek kingdom, going back to the Kūshite mother of Alexander the Great.[63]

However, it is difficult to assume that if ps.-Methodius was a Chalcedonian, he would have made the refutation of an unreal and obscure expectation of a coming Ethiopian savior[64] the focus of his work. As

---

[60] Alexander, "Medieval Apocalypses", 1006.

[61] In his "Additional Remarks" to his article "Byzantium" in his collected articles in *Religious and Political History*, 68–68a, Alexander rightly observes that ps.-Methodius is refuting a past interpretation of Psalm 68:31. However, Alexander believed that the verse was used by Monophysites who placed their hope on the Ethiopian king: "The author, therefore, means not that contemporary members of the Mesopotamian clergy placed their hope on the Ethiopian ruler, but that members of the Mesopotamian clergy had done so in the past". Moreover, he concludes that this passage "neither requires nor allows any inference as to ps.-Methodius' christological orientation or ecclesiastical affiliation"; cf. also Dorothy de F. Abrahamse's remarks in Alexander, *The Byzantine Apocalyptic Tradition*, 29 n. 49. See, however, n. 58 above, on reservations to the hypothesis of expectations that such a savior would come from Ethiopia.

[62] Cf. Martinez, *Eastern Christian Apocalyptic*, 27; Suermann, *Die geschichtstheologische Reaktion*, 161; also Irfan Shahīd, "The *Kebra Nagast* in the Light of Recent Research", *Le Muséon* 89 (1976), 174–76. Shahīd even suggests that ps.-Methodius knew the *Kebra Nagast* and polemicized against its ideas in this work. But as Martinez argues (*Eastern Christian Apocalyptic*, 15–16), it is much more probable that the relations between ps.-Methodius and the *Kebra Nagast* are to be explained in the opposite way and that it is the *Kebra Nagast* which polemicizes against the concept of history set forth by ps.-Methodius. See also n. 64 below.

[63] Brock, "Syriac Views", 18.

[64] Such an expectation was unreal considering the political circumstances in the Near East, in which Ethiopia no longer played any rôle as a military power; cf.

has been observed above, his main concern is to neutralize the danger of apostasy within his own community by developing a concept of history with the purpose of demonstrating that Daniel's fourth and last empire is still the Greek/Christian kingdom, and that this will never be replaced by an Arab empire. He is troubled not by an Ethiopian, but by an Arab problem, not by a milieu in which a King-Savior from Ethiopia is the better alternative to a King-Savior from Byzantium, but by the conviction that Islam had become a serious and dangerous threat to Christianity and that the only one who would be able, and even had the holy duty, to face this threat was the emperor of Byzantium. Alexander was correct in postulating that the rôle of Ethiopia must have something to do with the Monophysite milieu of the author. But for the explanation of this we may have to look in another direction.

Now the *mēmrā* of ps.-Methodius is a very carefully composed work in which the first historical part has a typological relation to the second prophetic part.[65] Just as in exegetical tradition history before

Alexander, "Byzantium", 58; *The Byzantine Apocalyptic Tradition*, 29. In his article "Psevdo-Mefodij", Alexander, discussing the relations between the *Kebra Nagast* and ps.-Methodius, suggests that the latter, knowing an older eschatological "Ethiopian interpretation" of Psalm 68:31, wrote his apocalypse as a response to this interpretation, since "by his time political and military reliance on the ruler of Ethiopia had become futile and he thus transferred his hopes for deliverance from the Arab yoke to the powerful emperor on the Bosporus" (English summary in Alexander's *Religious and Political History*, 27a). However, we do not possess any witness for such an eschatological interpretation in Syriac-speaking Christian circles before ps.-Methodius, and the ps.-Methodian passage in question does not support the interpretation (see above, notes 58 and 61).

It is interesting to note that there are some early Muslim traditions in which an invasion of Arabia by the Ethiopians is predicted; see Wilferd Madelung, "Apocalyptic Prophecies in Ḥimṣ in the Umayyad Age", *JSS* 31 (1986), 177–78. But it would have to be established that such traditions, being connected with the figure of *dhū l-suwayqatayn* ("the one with the two thin legs"), were known in circles of Syriac-speaking Christianity in North Mesopotamia; cf. also D.S. Attema, *De Mohammedaansche Opvattingen omtrent het Tijdstip van den Jongsten Dag en zijn Voortekenen* (Amsterdam, 1942), 132–43.

[65] Ps.-Methodius develops three main typologies: 1) Midianites—Gideon, Israelites (Judges 6–8): Arabs—emperor of Byzantium, Christians; 2) Alexander the Great, foundation of the Greek empire: Last World Emperor, end of the Christian empire; 3) Julian the Apostate (pagan tyrant)—Jovian (the restorer of the Chris-

Christ, as reflected in the writings of the Old Testament, foreshadows the realization of God's plan of salvation in the New Testament, so ps.-Methodius outlines a concept of history in which the future (including the *vaticinia ex eventu*[66]) could be understood through consideration of the events of the past. He reinforces this "typological description" of history by mixing events of the recent past and the present with themes and motifs derived from Biblical history and vice versa.[67] By doing so he attempts to strengthen his view that no new and lasting Arab kingdom has arisen, for Biblical history informs us that already in the past God saved the Israelites and the whole civilized world from these "sons of Ishmael". He thus implies that the recent second invasion by the Arabs from the desert of Yathrib is nothing more than a repetition of their former attempt at conquest, and that this too would result in their ruin, this time effected by the initiative of the Byzantine emperor.[68]

For a correct understanding of the connection between the Last World Emperor and Ethiopia, we must bear in mind that ps.-Methodius uses the same typological method here, so as to connect the events of the past with those of the future. Some scholars have wondered how he could create a dynastic succession of Roman emperors from Alexander the Great to the end of the world, and have sought the solution to this in his dependence on Persian ideas about kingship.[69] The latter suggestion may be true; however, ps.-Methodius' primary concern is to create a typological relation between Alexander, the first king of the Greeks, and the last king of the Greeks.

Ps.-Methodius' genealogy, in which the kingdoms of Macedonia, Greece, and Rome are joined with one another by the common ancestress Kūshyat, an Ethiopian princess, serves to stress the unity of

---

tian kingship): Arabs (pagan tyrants)—the Byzantine emperor restoring the peace for the Churches and punishing the apostates (see below).

[66]The historical part of the *Apocalypse* concludes at the end of Chap. X, when the struggle between the Romans and the Ishmaelites for "ten weeks of years" is prophesied.

[67]For examples, see my "Ishmael", 339 n. 21, 342 n. 33.

[68]*Ibid.*, 341–42.

[69]See, for example, Kmosko, "Das Rätsel des Pseudomethodius", 288; cf. also Martinez, *Eastern Christian Apocalyptic*, 6, 26; Suermann, *Die geschichtstheologische Reaktion*, 136.

Daniel's fourth empire and to create the possibility of a typological pattern in which its first ruler could be compared with its last ruler, its beginning to its end.[70] Alexander the Great, the pious king, son of Kūshyat, founded the Greek empire, marched to the East, defeated the Persians, conquered large parts of the world, and confined the unclean, eschatological peoples of Ezekiel (Gog and Magog) behind the gates of the North.[71] The last king of the Greeks, the pious defender of the Christian religion, will march to the southern and eastern countries, defeat the Muslims, punish the apostates, and establish the world dominion of the Greek empire, after which the gates of the North will be opened and the eschatological peoples of Ezekiel will go out to destroy the earth. Then, at the final stage of the eschatological drama, when the Antichrist is born, this "son of Kūshyat" will bring the Greek kingdom to an end by giving his kingdom to God the Father, thus fulfilling the prophecy of Psalm 68:31.[72] Using motifs from the Syriac *Alexander*

---

[70]See above, n. 57.

[71]VIII.2–10; ed. Martinez, 69:7–71:59. Here ps.-Methodius relies heavily upon the Syriac *Alexander Legend* (below, n. 73).

[72]XIII.11–12, XIV.2–6; ed. Martinez, 87:49–89:115, 90: 9–91:28; cf. above, notes 18, 58–59. It is important to note that the idea of the eschatological world dominion of Alexander's empire connected with the idea that the "kingdom of the house of Alexander" would conquer the world at the end of time and hand over the kingdom of earth to Jesus Christ is also derived from the Syriac *Alexander Legend*, ed. Budge (see below, n. 73), 270:11–14, 275:9–12. But in using these motifs ps.-Methodius had to solve one basic problem. How could it be expected that the "kingdom of the house of Alexander" would obtain eschatological world dominion, if Alexander died childless and history taught that different kingdoms succeeded one other after Alexander, while even the present historical situation showed at least two Christian kingdoms (Byzantium and Ethiopia), not one? In the Syriac *Alexander Legend* (275:10–12) ps.-Methodius read the prophecy that the kingdom of the Romans would reign until the end of time and deliver the kingdom (*tašlem malkūtā*) to Christ. As usual, ps.-Methodius sought a Biblical foundation for this and found it in I Corinthians 15:24, where he read the same expression (*mašlem malkūtā*) in an eschatological context (for the exegetical background, see Reinink, "Pseudo-Methodius und die Legende vom römischen Endkaiser", 101 n. 87), and in the prophecy in Psalm 68:31 speaking of Kūsh who would deliver (*tašlem[y]*) power to God. With the help of these Biblical materials, ps.-Methodius built up a brilliant construction: by creating a Kūshite mother of Alexander from Psalm 68:31 (see above, notes 57 and 59) ps.-Methodius could create not only a genealogical relation between Macedonia, Greece, and Rome by

Legend,[73] ps.-Methodius creates an idealized image of the last emperor as an *Alexander redivivus* with the purpose of demonstrating again that no lasting Arab empire had come into being. The "sons of Ishmael", Daniel's "arm of the South",[74] will be contending with the Greek kingdom for only ten "weeks of years", because with their appearance the last period of world history has begun and "there is no space of time in between".[75]

Likewise, through his invention of an Ethiopian mother for Alexander, the author could associate the Monophysite Christian kingdom of

---

which the "kingdom of the house of Alexander" could be considered as a "historical" unity, even including the Christian kingdom of Ethiopia, but also a typological pattern—the Last World Emperor not acting as a Chalcedonian persecutor, but as an *Alexander redivivus*—more acceptable to his Monophysite audience (see below).

[73]This work, bearing the title of *Neṣḥānā d-'Aleksandrōs*, was edited and translated by E.A. Wallis Budge, *The History of Alexander the Great* (Cambridge, 1889), 255–75 (text), 144–58 (trans.). It is a Christian legend, composed in North Mesopotamia shortly after Heraclius' victory over the Persians, presumably in 629–30, by a Syrian author who defended the emperor's policy of political and ecclesiastical reunion of the Empire by creating an Alexander-Heraclius typology; see G.J. Reinink, "Die Entstehung der syrischen Alexanderlegende als politisch-religiöse Propagandaschrift für Herakleios' Kirchenpolitik", in C. Laga, J.A. Munitiz, and L. van Rompay, eds., *After Chalcedon: Studies in Theology and Church History, Offered to Professor Albert van Roey for his Seventieth Birthday* (Leuven, 1985), 263–81. This *Alexander Legend* not only influenced the *mēmrā* on Alexander the Great, attributed to Jacob of Sārūj, but was actually composed by an anonymous Monophysite author before the Arab-Islamic conquests; see G.J. Reinink, *Das syrische Alexanderlied. Die drei Rezensionen* (Leuven, 1983; *CSCO* 454–55, *Scr. Syri* 195–96). It was also one of ps.-Methodius' main sources; cf. also Martinez, "The Apocalyptic Genre", 342. The reinterpretation by ps.-Methodius of the motifs taken from this source very probably relates to the renewed repression of the Monophysites by the Byzantine authorities after Heraclius' reconquest of the eastern provinces. See Brock, "Syriac Views", 10–11; J.B. Segal, *Edessa, "The Blessed City"* (Oxford, 1970), 99–100; W.H.C. Frend, *The Rise of the Monophysite Movement: Chapters in the History of the Church in the Fifth and Sixth Centuries* (Cambridge, 1979), 347. Also see n. 32 above.

[74]Daniel 11:15. Cf. also *The Gospel of the Twelve Apostles*, in which the struggle between the "South" and the "Man of the North" has its roots in Daniel 11; see J. Rendel Harris, *The Gospel of the Twelve Apostles Together with the Apocalypses of Each of Them* (Cambridge, 1900), 21; also the paper by Drijvers in this volume.

[75]X.6; ed. Martinez, 76:44–48.

Ethiopia[76] with Byzantium and its Chalcedonian church of the Empire by pointing at their common roots.[77] By creating a typological relation between the first Greek king, Alexander, and the last Greek king, he could portray an idealized image of the coming "king of the Greeks" which would be more acceptable to his Monophysite audience. This emperor would not act as a defender and restorer of the Chalcedonian church of the Empire and as a persecutor of the Monophysites,[78] but rather as a protector of all Churches, establishing the final world dominion of the Christian empire.[79] This Last Emperor would be the defender of Christianity, as such, against the Muslims and against all those Christians who might put their trust in a new and lasting Arab empire and defect to Islam.

It does not require a Melkite, even at the end of the seventh century, to tell us what a true Christian emperor should be like. The idea that the Church was meant to live under the protection of the kings of Rome until the second coming of Christ was, as Sidney Griffith has shown, deeply rooted in Syriac-speaking Christianity.[80] In his hymns *Against Julian* Ephraem Syrus (*ca.* 306–73) defines the rôle of the emperor as "shepherding mankind, caring for cities, and driving away wild animals".[81] For Ephraem, Constantine and Constantius,

[76] For the relations between Byzantium and Ethiopia in the sixth century, see, e.g., A.A. Vasiliev, *Justin the First: an Introduction to the Epoch of Justinian the Great* (Cambridge, Mass., 1950), 283–302. For a general view of Christianity in Ethiopia, see, e.g., Frend, *The Rise of the Monophysite Movement*, 304–308.

[77] See above, n. 57. Martinez ("The Apocalyptic Genre", 348) states that ps.-Methodius' "Ethiopian story" indicates his desire for an alliance between the two Christian kingdoms. I can agree with this conclusion on the understanding that ps.-Methodius' desire for an alliance between Ethiopia and Byzantium was not motivated so much by strategic as by politico-religious considerations aimed at bringing his Monophysite co-religionists to rely on the Byzantine emperor.

[78] See above, notes 32 and 73; also Reinink, "Pseudo-Methodius und die Legende vom römischen Endkaiser", 107–108.

[79] Reinink, "Pseudo-Methodius und die Legende vom römischen Endkaiser", 111.

[80] Sidney H. Griffith, "Ephraem, the Deacon of Edessa, and the Church of the Empire", in Thomas Halton and Joseph P. Williman, eds., *Diakonia: Studies in Honor of Robert T. Meyer* (Washington, D.C., 1986), 48.

[81] Ephraem, *Contra Julianum* I.1; ed. Edmund Beck, *Des heiligen Ephraem des Syrers Hymnen de Paradiso und Contra Julianum* (Leuven, 1957; *CSCO* 174–75, *Scr. Syri* 78–79), 71:6–7 (text), 65 (trans.). For the polemical background of these

predecessors of the mad tyrant Julian, are the "truth-loving kings" who "cultivated, adorned the earth",[82] and the true archetypes of the Christian emperor.[83] Jovian, too, the restorer of Christian rule after the pagan Julian, is portrayed as "the believing king, the associate of the Victorious [kings]", i.e. Constantine and Constantius.[84] In his *Carmina Nisibena*, XXI, written on Jovian's accession in 363, Ephraem expresses in the following words his hopes to Bishop Abraham that peace will reign again in the churches under the reign of the pious God-loving Jovian:

> May the earth be at peace in your days,
> which saw you being full of peace;
> May the churches be rebuilt under you,
> and be clothed in their ornaments;
> and may their books be opened in them,
> and their tables be set in array;
> and may their servants be shining,
> that praise ascends from them,
> as a first-fruit for the Lord of peace;
> blessed is he who will raise to life our churches![85]

Similarly, ps.-Methodius describes the period following the victory of the Greek emperor over the Arabs and the subsequent punishment of the apostates as a period of peace and restoration:

> And there will be peace on earth the like of which there has not been before, because it is the last peace of the end

words, see Griffith, "Ephraem, the Deacon of Edessa", 33.

[82]Ephraem, *Contra Julianum* I.12; ed. Beck, 73:19–24 (text), 67 (trans.).

[83]Cf. Griffith, "Ephraem, the Deacon of Edessa", 251–52; *idem*, "Ephraem the Syrian's Hymns 'Against Julian'", 32–33.

[84]Ephraem, *Contra Julianum* III.8; ed. Beck, 83:10 (text), 78 (trans).

[85]Ephraem, *Carmina Nisibena* XXI.19; ed. Edmund Beck, *Des heiligen Ephraem des Syrers Carmena Nisibena I*, (Leuven, 1961; *CSCO* 218–19, *Scr. Syri* 92–93), 58:13–17 (text), 72:9–16 (trans.). From XXI.14 on, Ephraem expresses his hopes for a new era for the Church under Jovian; see Robert Murray, *Symbols of Church and Kingdom: a Study in Early Syriac Tradition* (Cambridge, 1975), 30. For the peace restored by Jovian after Julian's pagan rule, see also Ephraem, *Contra Julianum* III.8; ed. Beck, 83:5–10 (text), 78 (trans).

> of the world. And there will be joy on the whole earth, and men will dwell in great peace, and the churches will be restored, and the cities will be rebuilt, and the priests will be freed from tax, and priests and men will recover at that time from labor and weariness and exhaustion, because this is that peace of which He said in His Gospel: "There will be a great peace the like of which there had not been before, and men will live at rest and will eat and drink and rejoice in the joy of [their] heart, and men will take wives and wives will be given to men" (Matthew 24:38), and they will build edifices and will plant vineyards (cf. Ezekiel 28:26).[86]

Here he is not inspired by the Jewish concept of a messianic *Zwischenreich* founded by a Last Roman Emperor modelled on the figure of the late Jewish Messiah, as Alexander and after him Harald Suermann believed.[87] Rather, behind these words lies the concept of peace and restoration by a Christian emperor protecting the Church and Christianity after a period of pagan rule. The concept of restoration is given a new function in the *Apocalypse* by being connected with the eschatological world dominion of Alexander's empire. It is the "last peace of the end of the world" before "the coming of the Son of man"[88] and "the day of the Lord",[89] which will last until the destroying incursion of the terrible eschatological peoples from the North.

The suggestion that ps.-Methodius' Last World Emperor is modelled on the concept of the Roman emperor as an idealized protector of Christianity is corroborated by the fact that he also applies to this figure motifs borrowed from the Syriac *Romance of Julian the Apostate*, especially those related to the highly idealized image of Jovian presented in this work.[90] The author compares Jovian, "the man who burned with love of God with all his heart and with all his soul", with

[86] XIII.15–18; ed. Martinez, 88:79–90.

[87] Alexander, "The Medieval Legend", 7–8; Suermann, *Die geschichtstheologische Reaktion*, 157. See also n. 116 below.

[88] Cf. I Matthew 24:38–39.

[89] Cf. Thessalonians 5:2–3.

[90] *Iulianos der Abtruennige. Syrische Erzaehlungen*, ed. Johann Georg Ernst Hoffmann (Leiden, 1880), 3–342. An English translation (not always reliable) was published by Hermann Gollancz, *Julian the Apostate* (Oxford and London, 1928). On

Constantine,[91] and the peace that "reigned in the churches during his days" with the peace in the days of Constantine.[92] After the paganism of the "mad tyrant" Julian, the truly Christian king Jovian restores Christian Roman kingship, fulfilling the holy duty of the Christian emperor to protect Christianity in the whole world and to combat paganism:

> And he (i.e. Jovian) exalted and did honor to the churches and restored to them the treasures which Julian, the wicked, had taken from them. And he freed from tax the holy covenant of God, and he wrote letters of peace, of reconciliation and pardon, of honor and exaltation, to all the churches of his realm. He wrote letters even to the other governments concerning the peace of the churches and the rest of the Christians. And he purified the kingdom of the Romans from the stink of the sacrifices of paganism, and he overthrew their tables and destroyed their altars, he banished their erroneous doctrines, destroyed their houses of assembly, and removed their treasures to the treasures of the Church.[93]

The most telling part of the *Romance of Julian* in respect of the figure of the Last Greek Emperor in ps.-Methodius is, however, the episode relating Jovian's assumption of the crown of royalty after Julian's death in Persia. When Julian's armies wish to make Jovian their emperor, he finally assents to their wish on condition that they return from paganism and give a demonstration of their conversion "by adoring the Cross which is the sign of salvation for all who believe in Him":[94]

---

this work, see Theodor Nöldeke, "Ueber den syrischen Roman von Kaiser Julian", *ZDMG* 28 (1874), 263–92 and now also Michael van Esbroeck, "Le soi-disant roman de Julien l'Apostat", in *IV Symposium Syriacum 1984*, 191–202. In my opinion there are reasonable grounds for the assumption that the work originated in Edessa in the fifth century.

[91] *Iulianos der Abtruennige*, 239:22–26.

[92] *Ibid.*, 240:20–21.

[93] *Ibid.*, 239:26–240:6.

[94] *Ibid.*, 199:7–8: *nīšā d-purqānā l-kulhūn da-mhaymnīn bēh*. So also ps.-

> And let Christ be king over you first, secretly as God, and then will I also be king over you as man, publicly.[95]

Seeing their willingness to comply, Jovian takes the Cross, which as a standard, "the sign of victory of our kingdom", went in front of the army,[96] and fixes it upon a high place in front of the troops. Then he orders them to place the crown on top of the Cross:

> Let it not be that the crown of a pagan with which he adored idols should be set on my head before it is placed on top of the Cross. And when Christ has become king over you by His Cross and the crown of our kingdom has been blessed and sanctified by it, then also I will accept it fittingly and rightly from the blessed right hand filled with holiness, by which the unclean were sanctified and the sins were remitted. Approach then, and put the crown that is in your hands on top of the Cross, and come, let us implore Christ by the worship of His Cross for peace and the sustenance of your kingdom.[97]

His command having been executed, Jovian prays before the Cross "for the peace of the churches, for the salvation of their children, for the victory of the Romans, and for the sustenance of their kingdom",[98] and beseeches the Lord that he may receive the royal crown from His right hand, as it is His will that he will be the leader and the king "to the guilty who have taken refuge to Thy Cross and look for Thy salvation".[99] Then a miracle takes place:

Methodius (XIV.4; ed. Martinez, 90:17–19) calls the Cross the "sign" (*nīšā*) of salvation, as the Savior was crucified "for the salvation of all men who believe in Him" (*ḥlāp purqānā d-kulhūn bnaynāšā da-mhaymnīn bēh*). Here too ps.-Methodius deliberately takes a non-sectarian position, stressing the unity of Christendom against the Muslims.

[95] *Iulianos der Abtruennige*, 199:9–11.

[96] *Ibid.*, 199:14, 18–27. For the Cross as the "sign of victory" of the Christian empire in ps.-Methodius, see Reinink, "Ismael", 340–41 n. 25; *idem*, "Die syrischen Wurzeln", 200–201. See also n. 150 below.

[97] *Iulianos der Abtruennige*, 200:5–12.

[98] *Ibid.*, 200:17–19.

[99] *Ibid.*, 200:26. This motif, which repeatedly occurs in the *Romance of Julian*

> And when Jovian had finished the words of his prayer, he inclined and bowed himself before all his troops, and he made the sign of the Cross on his breast and on his forehead, and he approached with the ardor of his faith and inclined his head before the Cross. And the royal crown descended, and placed itself on his head, the hand of man not having approached it. And all the people of the Romans were stupefied and marvelled at this great miracle which was wrought, and they cried out, and said: "Henceforth, Christ is King over us in heaven, and Jovian is king over us on earth".[100]

It is Jovian's crown, sanctified by the Cross and received directly from the hands of the Lord, the symbol of Christian emperorship representing on earth the heavenly kingship of Christ, which ps.-Methodius' Last World Emperor hands over to God at the end of time:

> And as soon as the Son of Perdition[101] is revealed, then the king of the Greeks will go up and stand on Golgotha. And the Holy Cross will be set in that place in which it was fixed when it bore Christ. And the king of the Greeks will place his crown on top of the Cross and stretch his two hands towards heaven and the king of the Christians will hand over the kingdom to God the Father.[102] And the Holy Cross will be raised up to heaven and the royal crown with it, because the Cross on which Christ was crucified for the salvation of all men who believe in Him is the sign that will appear before the Coming of Our Lord[103] to put to shame the apostates.[104] And the prophecy of David concerning

(*ibid.*, 202:10, 15, 18) is taken over by ps.-Methodius and transferred to the Byzantine Empire.

[100] *Ibid.*, 201:8–15.

[101] I.e. the Antichrist; cf. II Thessalonians 2:3.

[102] I Corinthians 15:24.

[103] Cf. Matthew 24:30.

[104] Ps.-Methodius here uses the word *kāpūrē*. Ps.-Methodius is using the same root when he describes the Muslims and the conduct of the apostates who defect to Islam and will be punished by the Last World Emperor (XII.3, 7, XIII.15; ed.

> the end of times will be fulfilled, which says: "Ethiopia (Kūsh) will hand over the power (lit. "hand") to God",[105] because it is the son of Kūshyat, daughter of Pīl, king of the Ethiopians (Kūshites), who will hand over the power (lit. "hand") to God. And as soon as the Cross is raised up to heaven, the king of the Greeks will deliver his soul to his Creator. Then all sovereignty and all power will come to an end.[106]

Just as Jovian received the sanctified crown by its descent from the top of the Cross unto his head, so the Last Emperor will place his crown on top of the Cross and restore the Christian kingdom to God by the ascension of the Cross bearing the imperial crown. In exactly the same words as the *Romance of Julian*, ps.-Methodius defines the Cross as the sign of salvation of all men who believe in Christ, thus stressing the unity of Christendom against a non-Christian world—in fact, the world ruled by the Muslims.[107] The eschatological rôle of the Cross, identified with the "sign of the Son of Man in heaven",[108] seems to betray our author's acquaintance with the *Letter of Cyril of Jerusalem on the Vision of the Cross*.[109] In this letter to Constantius II, the bishop of Jerusalem informs the emperor of the miraculous appearance in Jerusalem on "a Cross splendid in size and fashioned as if of light" which "appeared in heaven above the place of our Lord's crucifixion, which is Golgotha, extending as far as the holy place which is called the Mount of Olives",[110] with the purpose "that when you (i.e. the emperor) learn this you may be convinced that the inheritance of the

Martinez, 83:14–17, 84:37, 88:78). Cf. also Reinink, "Die syrischen Wurzeln", 198; *idem*, "Pseudo-Methodius und die Legende vom römischen Endkaiser", 106 n. 106.

[105] Psalms 68:31.

[106] XIV.2–6; ed. Martinez, 90:9–91:28. The final sentence again derives from I Corinthians 15:24.

[107] See notes 94 and 96 above.

[108] Matthew 24:30.

[109] On this letter, see the bibliography in *CPG*, II, 291, no. 3587. The Syriac version cited below is edited and translated by J.F. Coakley, "A Syriac Version of the Letter of Cyril of Jerusalem on the Vision of the Cross", *AB* 102 (1984), 77–84. In the Syriac letter the addressee is called Constantine Augustus (cf. Coakley, 81 n. 27).

[110] II.4; ed. Coakley, 78 (text), 82 (trans.).

crown, the throne, and the honor of your fathers has been given to you by God".[111] Cyril connects the miraculous appearance of the Cross in his days with the appearance of the Cross at the end of times, referring to Matthew 24:30:

> About this sign, Christ-loving victorious emperor, the prophets testify. And without variation, according to the sense of those things said by Christ in his Gospel it has now been performed—and indeed will be performed hereafter at the time of the End—marvellously. For in the Gospel of Matthew he teaches us thus. When our Savior was speaking with the blessed Apostles, his disciples, about the things to come, and they in turn were asking him about them, Christ himself cried out in a plain voice and said to them: "And then shall appear the sign of the Son of Man in heaven".[112]

Again ps.-Methodius gives a polemical turn to his words by the addition that the Cross, "the sign of the Son of Man", will put to shame the apostates. In the first place, the apostasy caused by the actions of the Antichrist is meant,[113] but it is also implied that the action of the Last World Emperor in persecuting the apostates can be compared to Christ's final victory over the Antichrist and those who followed the "Son of Perdition".[114]

Thus ps.-Methodius' last Greek king does not represent the figure of a messianic warrior-king[115] borrowed from or competing with the late Jewish idea of a Messiah-Savior;[116] rather, he represents the figure of

---

[111]II.3; ed. Coakley, 77 (text), 81 (trans.).

[112]II.6; ed. Coakley, 79 (text), 83 (trans.).

[113]Cf. II Thessalonians 2:3. Although ps.-Methodius interprets the *apostasia* (Syr. *mardūtā*, root *mrd*) in this verse as "chastisement" (root *rd'*; see n. 3 above), he describes the actions of the Antichrist in accordance with tradition (XIV.7; ed. Martinez, 91:33–41).

[114]See n. 104 above.

[115]This is the expression used by J. Wortley, "The Literature of Catastrophe", *BS* 4 (1977), 10.

[116]Thus Alexander, "The Medieval Legend", 8–9, defends the thesis that ps.-Methodius' Last World Emperor reflects Jewish traditions of the Anointed King who would redeem his people, and suggests that either ps.-Methodius or one of his

the idealized Christian emperor in conformity with the image of Constantine, Constantius, and especially Jovian, as known from tradition. Our author's reinterpretation of this tradition mainly bears upon the eschatological rôle of the idealized emperor, adapted to the exigencies of the changed historical circumstances and to a Biblical-typological way of arguing. In doing so, he uses and elaborates the typology of the *Alexander Legend* to convince his co-religionists that they must put their trust in this emperor, since he would establish *one* Christian world dominion protecting all Churches within his empire. He is, like Jovian before him, the representative of Christ on earth; and in fighting against "pagan" Arabs[117] and apostates he is merely acting according to his holy task. The application of scriptural passages connected with Christ to the acts of the Last Greek Emperor serves to emphasize strongly his function as the deputy of Christ on earth and his task as protector of the Churches.[118] In locating the abdication of

---

sources infused Judaic elements into the Christian tradition or belonged to a Christian community with strong links with late Judaism. Alexander's thesis has been adopted by Suermann, *Die geschichtstheologische Reaktion*, 157, 160. In my article "Die syrischen Wurzeln", I argued that the range of ideas in ps.-Methodius which Alexander attributed to the influence of late Jewish messianism are to be explained rather by ps.-Methodius' Syriac sources, his typological and symbolical exegesis, and the specific historical circumstances under which he developed his concept of history. In a response to this study Suermann attempted in his article "Der byzantinische Endkaiser bei Ps.-Methodius", *OC* 71 (1987), 140–55, to reconcile both views (p. 155): "Konnte Alexander die Ähnlichkeit der spätjüdischen Messiasideen mit den Vorstellungen des Pseudo-Methodius über den Endkaiser feststellen und so den Blick auf das Judentum lenken, so hat Reinink die syrischen Wurzeln der Motive gezeigt, die die Voraussetzung für die Akzeptanz der Ideen bei den Christen sind". However, it remains unnecessary to assume any influence of late Jewish messianism so long as all the motifs used by ps.-Methodius to develop his concept of history are rooted in the traditions of Syriac-speaking Christianity.

[117] According to Martinez, "The Apocalyptic Genre", 342, ps.-Methodius "does not seem to know any specific Muslim tenets or beliefs". However, we should not conclude too quickly from ps.-Methodius' silence in this respect that he is not familiar with at least some religious conceptions of nascent Islam. It is for polemical reasons that ps.-Methodius presents the Muslims as "pagan tyrants" (IX.9; ed. Martinez, 74:57), wishing to demonstrate that Christians who defect to Islam in fact belong to the *kāpūrē*, i.e. those who deny the true Christian belief, the Holy Cross, and the Sacraments (see n. 167 below). Cf. Reinink, "Tyrannen und Muslime", 165.

[118] The idea that the Christian emperor also protects Christians who live under a

the Last Emperor on Golgotha, ps.-Methodius depends on traditions related to the Cross and Golgotha in the *Cave of Treasures*, which he applied to II Thessalonians 2:7,[119] and in particular on the typology of the *Alexander Legend* by which the Last Emperor, after the example of Alexander the Great, transfers the symbol of his royal power to Jerusalem,[120] the place where the Savior was crucified and where the Cross was found by Helena, the mother of Constantine.[121] But above all, Jerusalem and its holy places represent the unique religious center of all Christians.[122] The important place that ps.-Methodius gives to Jerusalem and the Holy Land in his *mēmrā* does not simply have a traditional anti-Jewish tenor;[123] it is also, as will be shown below, an

---

non-Christian domination, applied to Jovian in the Syriac *Romance of Julian the Apostate*, already finds expression in Eusebius' *Life of Constantine*; see Sebastian Brock, "Christians in the Sasanian Empire: a Case of Divided Loyalties", *Studies in Church History* 18 (1982), 1–2.

[119]Ps.-Methodius explains the word *mṣa'tā*, "middle", in II Thessalonians 2:7 as the "center of the world" (IX.8–9, X.1–2; ed. Martinez, 73:48–74:63, 75:1–9), i.e. Golgotha and Jerusalem. See *Cave of Treasures* XLIX.1–10; ed. Su-Min Ri, 406–409 (text), 156–57 (trans.); also Reinink, "Die syrischen Wurzeln", 201; Martinez, "The Apocalyptic Genre", 351.

[120]Ed. Budge, 258:1–4, 275:17–18. Cf. Martinez, "The Apocalyptic Genre", 349; Reinink, "Pseudo-Methodius und die Legende vom römischen Endkaiser", 110 n. 123. Behind the connection between Alexander and Jerusalem in the *Alexander Legend* lies the Alexander-Heraclius typology which refers to the relic of the Cross which was restored to Jerusalem by Heraclius. Cf. Reinink, "Die Entstehung der syrischen Alexanderlegende", 279–80.

[121]An explicit reference to the *Cyriacus Legend* occurs in the *Apocalypse* which is an Edessan adaptation of ps.-Methodius. The text was edited with French translation by François Nau, "Révélations et légendes: Méthodius - Clément - Andronicus", *JA* 11.9 (1917), 425–46 (here 427:4–13); it was republished from Nau and translated into English by Martinez, *Eastern Christian Apocalyptic*, 222–46, and into German by Suermann, *Die geschichtstheologische Reaktion*, 86–97. Although Martinez (p. 219) suggested that his work was composed shortly before AD 1284, there are reasonable grounds for the assumption that it belongs to the seventh century and that it should be considered as an Edessene revision of ps.-Methodius made shortly after the composition of ps.-Methodius in Sinjār.

[122]Cf. Reinink, "Die Entstehung der syrischen Alexanderlegende", 279.

[123]As it has, for example, in the *Cave of Treasures* and in the Syriac *Cyriacus Legend of the Finding of the True Cross*. On the latter, see Eberhard Nestle, *De Sancta Cruce. Ein Beitrag zur christlichen Legendengeschichte* (Berlin, 1889), 25–36.

essential component in his polemic against the idea of an Arab empire with a lasting politico-religious place in world history.[124]

To reduce the problem of ps.-Methodius to the question of whether a Monophysite could or could not be a fervent supporter of the "byzantinische Kaiseridee" may therefore be too simple an approach to the enigma. Much more important seems to be the question of under what specific historical circumstances he felt compelled to develop a concept of history by which the political situation was described in a highly polemical way, as if it were a temporary pagan rule—comparable to the reign of Julian the Apostate—which would be ended by a good Christian Roman emperor—comparable to Jovian—as the protector of all Christendom.

Brock has convincingly argued that the *Apocalypse* must have been written in the tenth and last "week of years", i.e. between 685 and 692,[125] and probably at the end of this period (690 or 691), when rumors of 'Abd al-Malik's tax reforms reached Mesopotamia.[126] Indeed, it seems very probable that ps.-Methodius' fear of a voluntary apostasy of his co-religionists had something to do with the census of 'Abd al-Malik.[127] But there is yet another argument for the suggestion that the work was written shortly after this caliph's restoration of Umayyad authority in Mesopotamia.[128]

---

[124]Below, 181–86.

[125]Brock, "Syriac Sources", 34; *idem*, "Syriac Views", 19. Also see n. 2 above.

[126]Brock, "Syriac Sources", 34; *idem*, "Syriac Views", 19. Cf. the chronicle of Ps.-Dionysios mentioning AG 1003 = AD 691–92 as the year of 'Abd al-Malik's tax reform: *Incerti auctoris chronicon pseudo-Dionysianum vulgo dictum*, ed. J.-B. Chabot (Paris, 1927–33; *CSCO* 91, 104, *Scr. Syri* 43, 53), II, 154:17–28; French trans. by J.-B. Chabot, *Chronique de Denys de Tell-Maḥré, quatrième partie* (Paris, 1895), 10. On this passage, see Daniel C. Dennett, *Conversion and the Poll Tax in Early Islam* (Cambridge, Mass, 1950), 45–47.

[127]As the convert would be freed of his poll tax. See Dennett, *Conversion and the Poll Tax*, 48; also notes 9 and 50 above.

[128]For the political turbulences during the Second Civil War, see in general 'Abd al-Ameer 'Abd Dixon, *The Umayyad Caliphate 65–86/684–705 (A Political Study)* (London, 1971), 121–42; Gernot Rotter, *Die Umayyaden und der zweite Bürgerkrieg (680–692)* (Wiesbaden, 1982; *AKM* 45.3); G.R. Hawting, *The First Dynasty of Islam: the Umayyad Caliphate AD 661–750* (London, 1986), 46–57; Hugh Kennedy, *The Prophet and the Age of the Caliphates: the Islamic Near East from the Sixth to the Eleventh Century* (London, 1986), 89–98.

The chaotic political situation born of the Second Civil War, and especially the revolt of the Shī'ite leader al-Mukhtār ibn Abī 'Ubayd al-Thaqafī in al-Kūfa (685–87), together with the outbreak of a devastating plague and famine in 686–87, had given rise to strong apocalyptic feelings in some circles of Mesopotamian Christianity. It was expected that very soon the Arab empire would collapse definitively and that the subsequent power vacuum would not be filled again, either by a revived Persian régime or by the Roman Empire, since the end of time was imminent.[129] Ps.-Methodius is still an exponent of

[129]At the end of the last book (XV) of his *Ktābā d-rīš mellē*, a short "theological" world history from the time of Creation until his own days, composed in or shortly after 687, Jōḥannān bar Penkāyē describes the devastating plague of the year AH 67 (= AD 686–87) as one of the signs of the End. He expects that the *šurṭē* of al-Mukhtār (al-Mukhtār's troops mainly drawn from the *mawālī* in al-Kūfa who after al-Mukhtār's death in 687 joined the *šurṭē* in Nisibis) will fulfill the prophecy in Genesis 16:12, as they are "the hand of all" destroying the "Ishmaelites" and terminating the Arab kingdom. However, these *šurṭē* will not establish a lasting political power, since they will be mingled in with other kingdoms and another people will come, the one whose activities are predicted by the prophets (i.e. the eschatological peoples of the North, the Gog-Magog motif), who will strive to undo also the Byzantine kingdom. Finally "the evil hidden in good, like poison in honey" (i.e. the Antichrist) will appear, after which the kingdom of the Lord will come. See *Ktābā d-rīš mellē* XV; ed. Mingana, 160*:4–168*:7; an English translation is now available in Sebastian Brock, "North Mesopotamia in the Late Seventh Century: Book XV of John Bar Penkāyē's *Rīš Mellē*", *JSAI* 9 (1989), 57–74. For a comparison between Jōḥannān and the Arab sources see Rotter, *Die Umayyaden*, 214–16. For a detailed comparison between Jōḥannān and ps.-Methodius, who lived in the same time and in the same region, see especially Reinink "Pseudo-Methodius und die Legende vom römischen Endkaiser". Notwithstanding some differences in outlook, both Jōḥannān and ps.-Methodius can be considered as representatives of different circles of Syriac-speaking Christianity in North Mesopotamia who expected the imminent end of the world. Very soon after the composition of ps.-Methodius the apocalyptic tension seems to have been diminished considerably, as appears from two apocalypses which are dependent on ps.-Methodius. In the Edessan revision of ps.-Methodius (see n. 121 above) the Byzantine emperor who will put an end to the Arab domination, after which the Greek kingdom will last for 208 years, and the Last World Emperor, who will be from the race of Kūshyat, are no longer one and the same person. Nor does the *Gospel of the Twelve Apostles* (see n. 74 above) identify explicitly the emperor from the race of Constantine, during whose days the earth shall be ruled in peace (predicted in the Revelation of James) with the "Man of the North" who will destroy the Ishmaelites (predicted in the Revelation of John the Less). Moreover, the essential elements of the eschatological drama (Gog-

these apocalyptic feelings. Within a few years, however, the political scene had changed drastically, and he was faced with a completely new dilemma.

The expectation that al-Mukhtār's revolt would usher in the fall of the Arab empire had already been frustrated in 687, when the Shī'ite leader was defeated and killed by Muṣ'ab ibn al-Zubayr, brother of the anti-caliph 'Abd Allāh ibn al-Zubayr.[130] But still more embarrassing must have been the peace treaty between the emperor Justinian II and 'Abd al-Malik in about 688,[131] which enabled the fifth Umayyad caliph to focus all his attention on the restoration of the unity of the Arab empire under Umayyad authority.[132] After two unsuccessful campaigns in 689 and 690, 'Abd al-Malik was able to reestablish Umayyad control over Mesopotamia in 691.[133] In the same year the caliph introduced tax reforms in Mesopotamia by which the tax burden was considerably increased.[134]

It is against this historical background that we should view ps.-Methodius' concept of history. His problem was not the idea of a Jewish Messiah or that of an Ethiopian King-Savior, but how the expectation of the imminent end of world history could be reconciled with changing political circumstances which seemed to point to a wholly different future: the recovery of the unity of the Arab empire under Umayyad rule.[135] Holding fast to the opinion that the Arab-Islamic conquests

---

Magog, the Antichrist, the second coming of Christ) are absent from the *Gospel of the Twelve Apostles*.

[130]H.A.R. Gibb, art. "'Abd al-Malik b. Marwān" in *EI*², I (Leiden, 1960), 76; cf. also Kennedy, *The Prophet and the Age of the Caliphates*, 96; Rotter, *Die Umayyaden*, 218.

[131]Cf. Georg Ostrogorsky, *Geschichte des byzantinischen Staates*, 3rd ed. (Munich, 1963), 108. For the question of the date of this peace treaty, see A.N. Stratos, *Byzantium in the Seventh Century*, trans. Marc Ogilvie Grant and Harry T. Hionides (Amsterdam, 1968–75), V, 20–24; cf. also Dixon, *The Umayyad Caliphate*, 122–23; Rotter, *Die Umayyaden*, 180.

[132]See Stratos, *Byzantium in the Seventh Century*, V, 28–30.

[133]Gibb, "'Abd al-Malik ibn Marwān", 76; Kennedy, *The Prophet and the Age of the Caliphates*, 98; Dixon, *The Umayyad Caliphate*, 124, 128, 131, 134; Rotter, *Die Umayyaden*, 226–37.

[134]See above, n. 126.

[135]In my opinion there is a connection between ps.-Methodius' stresses on the unity of the Christian empire and the restoration of the unity of the Arab empire

belonged to the political disturbances ushering in the last period of world history meant that there could be no room for the idea that a lasting Arab empire had come into existence. But how could it be imagined that this temporary "chastisement"[136] would soon come to an end, if it could no longer be expected that the internal Arab struggles of the Second Civil War would lead to the dissolution of Muslim domination? The only remaining possibility lay in the assumption that the Byzantine emperor would fulfill the eschatological task of ending Arab domination, thus introducing the ultimate stage of world history. The expectation that the "sleeping emperor"[137] would soon arise to defeat the Muslims was not so strange, as in the same year, 691, many signs seemed to indicate that the peace treaty between Justinian II and 'Abd al-Malik would come to a speedy end.[138]

But what really made the author take up his pen to prophesy the imminent destruction of Arab power by the Christian emperor was his fear of a subsequent period in which many of his co-religionists would plunge into a voluntary apostasy to Islam.[139] Undoubtedly this fear was rooted in the awareness that the recovery of Islamic power, going hand in hand with the frustration of apocalyptic hopes and greatly increased taxation of Christians, created circumstances highly favorable to conversion to Islam.[140] But it may be that in fact another event in 691 induced him to describe the Muslim domination as a time under "pagan tyranny" which would lead to "apostasy" among the Christians and which could only be terminated and set right by a true God-loving Christian emperor, protecting Church and Christianity.

In 691 'Abd al-Malik constructed what Christel Kessler has called the "first monumental building of Islam, planted in the heart of the supreme Christian city, modelled after Christian churches and intended

by 'Abd al-Malik.

[136]See n. 3 above.

[137]Above, 153.

[138]Theophanes mentions 691 as the year in which Justinian dissolved the peace treaty with 'Abd al-Malik, whereas some Arab sources and Syrian chroniclers mention 692 as the year in which the Arabs invaded Byzantine territory; see Stratos, *Byzantium in the Seventh Century*, V, 30–40, discussing the source material; also Gibb, "'Abd al-Malik ibn Marwān", 77.

[139]See notes 9 and 50 above.

[140]See n. 127 above.

to surpass them in splendour", a monument which "provided the old and new believers and also the possible converts with impressive physical evidence of the power of the new faith..."[141] The best explanation for the foundation of the Qubbat al-Ṣakhra, the Dome of the Rock, built in the Temple area in Jerusalem is, as Oleg Grabar has suggested, that the caliph sought to erect "a monument proclaiming the new faith and empire in the city of the older two religions" as a "missionary monument of victory, built at a time when 'Abd al-Malik was concerned with Christian enmity, but especially when he sought to proclaim Islamic uniqueness within a common religious tradition, as, for instance, in his coinage".[142]

Not only 'Abd al-Malik's restoration of the political unity of the Arab empire, but in particular the accompanying religious propaganda, proclaiming the superiority of Islam over Christianity,[143] may have compelled ps.-Methodius to compose his *mēmrā* demonstrating the unity of the Greek/Roman/Byzantine Empire, which, "as long as it takes refuge in the life-giving Cross which has been set up in the center of the earth (i.e. Jerusalem)",[144] he claims, is the only heir of the "priesthood and kingship" until the second coming of Christ.[145] The report of the building of the Dome of the Rock, located on the site of the Jewish Temple, must have spread like wildfire and must have reached Christian communities in Mesopotamia very soon. And even if the anti-Christian polemics of 'Abd al-Malik's mosaic inscription inside the Dome were

[141] Christel Kessler, "'Abd al-Malik's Inscription in the Dome of the Rock: a Reconsideration", *JRAS*, 1970, 12.

[142] Oleg Grabar, art. "Ḳubbat al-Ṣakhra" in *EI*², V (Leiden, 1986), 298; cf. also *idem*, "The Umayyad Dome of the Rock", *Ars Orientalis* 3 (1959), 33–62; Michel Écochard, "A propos du Dôme du Rocher et d'un article de M. Oleg Grabar", *BEO* 25 (1972), 37–45. Cf. also Rotter, *Die Umayyaden*, 227–30, who argues that 'Abd al-Malik began building the Dome of the Rock shortly after his successful Iraq campaign in 691; but cf. Hawting, *The First Dynasty of Islam*, 59: "In spite of a recent attempt to argue that this date (i.e. the year 72 AH of the inscription inside the Dome) refers to the beginning of the building, it is more likely, and is generally accepted, that it is the date of its completion".

[143] Cf. Kessler, "'Abd al-Malik's Inscription", 11–12; Rotter, *Die Umayyaden*, 230.

[144] IX.9; ed. Martinez, 74:54–55; see also notes 99 and 119 above.

[145] X.1–2; ed. Martinez, 75:4–16. For this passage in ps.-Methodius, cf. also Reinink, "Pseudo-Methodius und die Legende vom römischen Endkaiser", 102–103 n. 90.

not known immediately,[146] the very fact that the Arabs had built a sanctuary on the site of the Jewish Temple could be considered not only as an act comparable with the rebuilding of the Temple,[147] a deed by which the most ancient holy place of the world and the symbol of the unity of Christendom was adopted by the new religion, but also as an event by which Islam could claim to be the successor of the other two monotheistic religions of the Near East[148] and the only true heir of the "priesthood and kingship" connected with Jerusalem, the "center" of the world.[149]

Ps.-Methodius is indeed very much concerned to show that the "pagan tyrants" (i.e. the Arabs) can never take the place of the Greek empire, provided that this empire clings to the Cross, the sign of victory that was set up in the Holy City.[150] The "excellent gifts" of Judaism—the priesthood, prophecy, and kingship—were lost by the Jews when Vespasian and Titus destroyed the Holy City;[151] after that the priesthood, the kingship, and the Holy Cross are "in the center",[152] and only the Christian empire "standing in the center", taking refuge in the Cross,[153] will be victorious and exist until the appearance of the

[146] For the text of this inscription, see especially Kessler, "'Abd al-Malik's Inscription", 4–7.

[147] Thus some chronicles connect 'Umar's alleged building of the Dome of the Rock with the idea of rebuilding the Temple; cf. Brock, "Syriac Views", 12, who points to Michael the Syrian, II, 431 (trans.); IV, 421 (text); *Chronicle of 1234*, I, 260–61 (text), 204 (trans.); Sebēos XXXI; trans. Macler, 102–103. For the Jewish reactions see Patricia Crone and Michael Cook, *Hagarism: the Making of the Islamic World* (Cambridge, 1977), 161 (n. 1 to Chap. 2). Cf. also Hawting, *The First Dynasty of Islam*, 60: "Whatever specifically Muslim associations came to be attached to the rock over which the Dome was built, at the time it was generally held, by Muslims, Jews and Christians, to be part of the ancient Jewish Temple of Jerusalem. As such it had great cosmological significance and was regarded as the centre of the world...".

[148] Cf. also G.R.D. King, "Islam, Iconoclasm, and the Declaration of Doctrine", *BSOAS* 48 (1985), 274–75.

[149] See notes 119 and 145 above.

[150] IX.8–9; ed. Martinez, 74:52–63.

[151] X.4; ed. Martinez, 76:26–35. For the background of this tradition, cf. *Cave of Treasures* L.13–16, LI.17, LII.17–18; ed. Su-Min Ri, 418–19, 428–31, 442–43 (text); 160–61, 164–65, 172–73 (trans.).

[152] X.2; ed. Martinez, 75:6–7.

[153] XI.1–2; ed. Martinez, 75:4–9.

Antichrist.[154] Again, the fact that ps.-Methodius makes the Last Greek Emperor reside in Jerusalem after the period of the devastating invasions of the eschatological peoples, and that he makes him abdicate on Golgotha after the appearance of the Antichrist,[155] is not to be explained by his dependence on late Jewish traditions about a Messiah whose activities were centered on Mount Zion,[156] but is meant rather to demonstrate that Jerusalem had become and will always remain the City of Christendom.[157]

There was one event in the history of Jerusalem after the destruction of the Second Temple that was naturally compared with the foundation of the Muslim sanctuary on the site of the Jewish Temple, viz. the attempted rebuilding of the Temple under Julian the Apostate.[158] Ordered by Julian early in 363, this project was regarded by Christian writers as an act directed against the Christian religion, and one which, by miraculous divine intervention, was thwarted before it could be carried out.[159] The author of the *Romance of Julian the Apostate* portrays the Jews as collaborators, prepared even to offer pagan sacrifices to the idols in order to gain Julian's permission for the rebuilding of the Temple,[160] and proclaiming in a public letter that the emperor was the expected King-Messiah who would deliver them from their enemies (i.e. the Christians).[161] Already Ephraem, in his hymns *Against Julian*, put the attempted rebuilding of the Temple on a level with the

---

[154]See n. 19 above.

[155]XIII.21, XIV.2; ed. Martinez, 89:115–18, 90:9–12.

[156]So Alexander, "The Medieval Legend", 7.

[157]Cf. Reinink, "Die syrischen Wurzeln", 200–202, and notes 120 and 122 above.

[158]See, in general, Josef Vogt, *Kaiser Julian und das Judentum. Studien zum Weltanschauungskampf der Spätantike* (Leipzig, 1939), 46–59; M. Adler, "The Emperor Julian and the Jews", *JQR* 5 (1893), 591–661; reprinted in German translation in Richard Klein, ed., *Julian Apostata* (Darmstadt, 1978), 48–111; Robert Browning, *The Emperor Julian* (London, 1975), 176; Glen W. Bowersock, *Julian the Apostate* (London, 1978), 88–90; Günter Stemberger, *Juden und Christen im Heiligen Land. Palästina unter Konstantin und Theodosius* (Munich, 1987), 163–74.

[159]For an English translation of the main accounts in Syriac sources, see the Appendix in Sebastian Brock, "A Letter Attributed to Cyril of Jerusalem on the Rebuilding of the Temple", *BSOAS* 40 (1977), 283–86.

[160]*Iulianos der Abtruennige*, 108:9–116:12.

[161]*Ibid.*, 114:28–115:8.

introduction of paganism in Jerusalem.[162] But ps.-Methodius may also have known traditions such as those preserved in the Syriac *Letter on the Rebuilding of the Temple*, attributed to Cyril of Jerusalem,[163] according to which Julian, who in his hatred against Christ had ordered the rebuilding of the Temple, was punished for this by his death in Persia. By this "the sign of the power of the Cross was shown, as he (i.e. Julian) had denied Him who had been hung upon it for the salvation and life of all".[164]

The hypothesis that the *Apocalypse* of ps.-Methodius was composed in reaction to 'Abd al-Malik's foundation of the Dome of the Rock on the site of the Jewish Temple is very attractive. It throws new light on the way in which this author describes Muslim domination as a time of Christian suffering under "pagan tyrants",[165] comparable to the time of the "pagan tyrant" Julian.[166] It explains how he compares the voluntary conversion to Islam of his co-religionists who "deny the true belief of the Christians, the Holy Cross, and the Glorious Sacraments"[167] with a return to pagan idolatry and the "doctrine of the demons".[168] It can also explain how, being a Monophysite, he could look for a Christian emperor who, being Christ's deputy on earth, would put an end to "pagan" rule, punish the apostates, and restore peace for the Churches, just as Jovian had done in earlier times, uniting all Christian churches in one final world dominion of the Christian empire.

Is it merely coincidental that the emperor Justinian II, who was the likely candidate to fulfill this task, was the first Byzantine emperor to issue a coinage that carried on the one side the image of Christ with the Cross behind his head and on the other the emperor wearing

---

[162] Cf. Ephraem, *Contra Julianum* IV.22; ed. Beck, 89:25–90:2 (text), 85 (trans.); cf. Griffith, "Ephraem the Syrian's Hymns 'Against Julian'", 258–60.

[163] See Sebastian Brock, "The Rebuilding of the Temple under Julian: a New Source", *PEQ* 108 (1976), 102–107. The letter was composed, according to Brock, at the beginning of the fifth century; ed. and trans. in Brock, "A Letter Attributed to Cyril", 269–76.

[164] "Letter", xii; ed. Brock, 272; see also n. 94 above.

[165] See notes 4 and 117 above.

[166] "Tyrant" is also the usual denomination of Julian in ps.-Methodius' source, the Syriac *Romance of Julian the Apostate*.

[167] XII.3; ed. Martinez, 83:13–15.

[168] XII.4; ed. Martinez, 83:20.

a crown with a cross and carrying a Cross in his hand?[169] It is very tempting to assume that ps.-Methodius, who relates the figure of the Last World Emperor closely to Christ, was aware of the implication of this iconography representing the emperor as the *servus Christi*.[170] If so, we must assume that the *Apocalypse* was composed at the earliest in 692, in the very last year of the apocalyptic tenth "week of years".[171] This is not impossible, since the *mēmrā* shows all the signs of being a *Gelegenheitsschrift*, written in a short time under the pressure of very specific historical circumstances and meant to provide his religious community with a ready answer to acute problems.[172]

By giving some examples of his typological and symbolic way of describing history, and by pointing out the historical circumstances under which ps.-Methodius' view of history could develop, I have tried to put forward some arguments for the thesis that it is not necessary to regard his concept of history as a response to a specific dilemma of the Chalcedonian community or as a response to supposedly polemical politico-religious discussions between Chalcedonian and Monophysite communities in Mesopotamia. Nor are there compelling reasons to follow the suggestion that ps.-Methodius developed his concept of history "in der Konfrontation mit der jüdischen Geschichtsdeutung".[173] On the contrary, his concept of history seems to be primarily a response to the rise of Islam which, during the caliphate of ʿAbd al-Malik, was manifesting itself again as a lasting politico-religious power, openly asserting its claims to being not only the political successor of the Byzantine Empire, but also the religious successor of Christendom in the Near East.

The real problem for ps.-Methodius was thus the fear that rapidly changing political and social circumstances would encourage many of his co-religionists to convert to Islam. Against the idea that conversion to Islam meant the adoption of a new religion which was the true heir to the "priesthood and kingship", he expressed the opinion that in

---

[169] Stratos, *Byzantium in the Seventh Century*, V, 65.

[170] As the inscription on the coins minted between 692 and 695 reads; cf. Stratos, *loc. cit.*; Ostrogorsky, *Geschichte*, 116.

[171] See n. 2 above.

[172] See n. 129 above.

[173] Suermann, "Der byzantinische Endkaiser", 155; cf. *idem*, "Einige Bemerkungen", 334; also n. 116 above.

reality conversion meant nothing less than apostasy to paganism, comparable with the situation in the days of the "pagan tyrant" Julian, who—just as the Muslims now did—denied the belief in the redeeming power of the Cross, the sign of victory of the Christian world and the Christian empire.[174] Holding fast to the opinion that he was living in the last days of world history, he explains this apostasy as belonging to the eschatological trials by which the true believers are separated from the unbelievers,[175] a temporary "chastisement" which would be put to an end by the Christian emperor, restoring the time of peace for the Churches as Jovian had done. However, this peace would be the eschatological peace of the world and its restorer the Last World Emperor representing the good and true God-loving Christian emperor—not a persecutor of the Monophysites, but he who would unite all Christians in one final world dominion of the Christian empire and conclude the succession of earthly kingdoms by handing over the kingdom to God the Father.

[174]For the suppression of the Cross by the Muslims in the Umayyad period, cf. King, "Islam, Iconoclasm, and the Declaration of Doctrine", especially 269–75. For the rôle of the Cross in ps.-Methodius, see n. 96 above.

[175]XII.2; XIII.4; ed. Martinez, 83:7–9, 85:20–86:24. See also n. 3 above.

5

The Gospel of the Twelve Apostles: A Syriac Apocalypse from the Early Islamic Period

Han J.W. Drijvers

(Rijksuniversiteit Groningen)

AS WITH SO MANY other Syriac texts, the *Gospel of the Twelve Apostles*, published by J. Rendel Harris in 1900, has not received the attention it deserves.[1] Apart from Harris' short introduction to his edition, only Harald Suermann has studied the work, and then only in a rather superficial and unsatisfying manner.[2] But since this Syriac apocalyptic text, short though it is, reflects the thought of Syrian Christians in northern Mesopotamia in the early Islamic period, it merits more detailed study, the more so since the ideas it contains were not restricted to northern Mesopotamia.

The *Gospel of the Twelve Apostles* occupies folios 47r to 58r of Syriac Ms. 85 of the Rendel Harris collection, now in the Harvard College

[1] J. Rendel Harris, *The Gospel of the Twelve Apostles Together with the Apocalypses of Each of Them* (Cambridge, 1900). Cf. Friedrich Haase, *Literarkritische Untersuchungen zur orientalische-apokryphen Evangelienliteratur* (Leipzig, 1913), 30–35; Baumstark, 70.

[2] Harald Suermann, *Die geschichtstheologische Reaktion auf die einfallenden Muslime in der edessenischen Apokalyptik des 7. Jahrhunderts* (Frankfurt am Main, 1985). Cf. the reviews by Sebastian Brock in *BO* 44 (1987), 813–16, and G.J. Reinink in *Le Muséon* 104 (1991), forthcoming.

Library.[3] The manuscript, very incompletely preserved, also contains a series of questions on canonical matters put to Jacob of Edessa by the priests Addai and Thomas and John the Stylite, together with Jacob's answers and a series of short chapters containing the replies of the holy fathers to questions sent to them by the Christians in the Orient (the *madnḥayē*).[4]

This material precedes the *Gospel of the Twelve Apostles*, which is followed by an extract from the *Doctrina Addai*, part of the farewell address of the apostle to his flock before his death. The passage, evidently meant as some sort of consolation, deals with the immortality of souls as they depart from human bodies, arguing that the thoughts and knowledge of the soul are the image of the immortal God.[5] Then follows an extract from the 38th discourse of Severus of Antioch against Grammaticus on the origin of the Nestorian heresy, and a series of apostolic canons and canons of synods—Nicaea, Ancyra, Neocaesarea, Gangra, Antioch *in encaeniis*, Laodicaea, Ephesus, and Chalcedon—followed by a *libellus* for those recanting from heresy.[6]

Though the codex is mutilated, its main contents are clear enough: the *Gospel of the Twelve Apostles*, preceded and followed by canonical material, mainly from Jacob of Edessa and from the synods. The inclusion of a passage from the *Doctrina Addai*, located in the city of Edessa, also points to an Edessan origin for the collection. It stems from Monophysite circles, and may well have been put together to bring

[3]Moshe H. Goshen-Gottstein, *Syriac Manuscripts in the Harvard College Library: a Catalogue* (Missoula, 1979), 75–76, Syr. 93.

[4]See Harris, *Gospel of the Twelve Apostles*, 8; Baumstark, 82–83. For literature on Jacob's work in ecclesiastical law, see H.J.W. Drijvers, art. "Jakob von Edessa" in *TRE*, XVI (Berlin, 1987), 468–70.

[5]Ms. fol. 58r. The text can be found in George Howard, *The Teaching of Addai* (Chico, Ca., 1981), 92–95; and more literally in William Cureton, *Ancient Syriac Documents Relative to the Earliest Establishment of Christianity in Edessa* (London and Edinburgh, 1864), 108.

[6]Ms. fols. 58r–9lv; cf. Harris, *Gospel of the Twelve Apostles*, 10–11. For the discourses of Severus of Antioch against Grammaticus, see the former's *Liber contra impium Grammaticum*, ed. Joseph Lebon (Leuven, 1929–38; *CSCO* 93–94, 101–102, 111–112, *Scr. Syri* 45–46, 50–51, 58–59). A *libellus poenitentiae* (or *recantatiae*) was a formula of abjuration or renunciation which was to be recited by those recanting from heresy.

apostates back to the true faith and teach them discipline and church order. In other words, the selection and order of the different elements preserved in this unique manuscript are not coincidental, but rather a matter of deliberate choice. Harris dates the origin of the *Gospel of the Twelve Apostles* and possibly of the manuscript itself to the middle of the eighth century, but we shall see that an earlier date is much more likely.

The full title of the treatise forming the nucleus of the Ms. is given as "The Gospel of the Twelve Apostles together with the revelations of each one of them". The *Gospel* itself is written in such a way as to provide the introduction to the following three apocalypses. It begins as follows:

> The beginning of the Gospel of Jesus Christ, the son of the living God, according to the words of the Holy Spirit: "I send an angel before his face, who shall prepare his way". It came to pass in the 309th year of Alexander, the son of Philip the Macedonian, in the reign of Tiberius Caesar, in the government of Herod, the ruler of the Jews, that the angel Gabriel, the chief of the angels, by the command of God went down to Nazareth to a virgin called Mariam of the tribe of Judah....

The birth of Jesus in the 309th year of the Seleucid era is an Edessan tradition attested in the acts of the martyr Barsamyā, bishop of Edessa, in the so-called *Doctrine of the Apostles*, itself an Edessan writing, and in the works of Jacob of Edessa, one of whose letters is on the subject of this chronology.[7]

In Gabriel's annunciation to the Virgin it is said: "They who do not confess the Savior shall perish, for his authority is in the lofty heights and his kingdom does not pass away". The *Gospel* thus constitutes a serious warning and a call to faith. It summarizes Jesus' appearance to the world "as it is written by the four truthful Evangelists", and

[7]François Nau, "Lettre de Jacques d'Edesse à Jean le Stylite sur la chronologie biblique et la date de la naissance du messie", *ROC* 5 (1900), 581–96; cf. Cureton, *Ancient Syriac Documents*, 24 (the *Doctrine of the Apostles*), 72 (martyrdom of Barsamyā).

emphasizes the choice of the twelve Apostles from the twelve tribes of Israel, "to whom he promised twelve thrones that they may judge Israel".[8] After the crucifixion and resurrection, Jesus appeared to his disciples and ordered them to go out into the four quarters of the world and preach the Gospel and baptize, saying: "The Kingdom of Heaven is come nigh unto you".[9] But here the well-known text is extended with the addition of the apocalyptic claim of the imminence of the kingdom.

In Jesus' presence the Apostles utter a long prayer in which the dominant theme is that of the end of the world:

> Yea! our Lord, enrich us according to thy promises, that we may speak with new tongues by the Spirit that is from thee; and let us know what is the end of the world, because we stand in the midst of the offenses and scandals of the world. Reveal and interpret to us, our Lord, what is the manner of thy coming and what is the End, and what offenses exist in the world.

Jesus rebukes them and says:

> It is not as with other evangelists who talk of what they have seen and repeat what they have heard, but you shall speak by the Spirit of my Father of those things that are and of those that are to come. And those who believe and do shall see new life in the kingdom of my Father in Heaven.

After Jesus' departure from the world the twelve Apostles speak to the people in different languages, preaching repentance and inviting them to the kingdom of God. Then they gather in the upper room and pray to God for a revelation concerning the End:

> ...grant us, Lord, and count us worthy, that all of us with one soul and with one mind may see thy revelation, that great and marvellous revelation by which thou art to reveal to us concerning things created, and that we may understand

[8] Luke 22:30.
[9] Mark 16:14.

> the times before thy coming again, and how they pass away and are no more, and who are the rulers of those [times], and their lives; and what men are to see the End; and who is he that is to come as thy adversary and to contend with the truth; and whether all men stray from thee and cleave to error....

When the Apostles finish their prayer, a great light appears to them from heaven and a voice speaks from it:

> Go forth to the mountain to the place in which Moses and Elias appeared unto you; and there it shall be spoken to you in spirit concerning the world and the End and concerning the Kingdom of God, and all of you shall speak of it in the tongues of the Holy Fathers.

The Apostles subsequently went to the mountain of the Transfiguration, where they fasted and prayed for seven days, were miraculously fed with all good things, and received the Spirit of God and revelations of the End.

Clearly the *Gospel of the Twelve Apostles* summarizes the Gospel story as told by the four Evangelists and the beginning of Acts, while casting it into an apocalyptic perspective. It functions as an introduction to the subsequent three revelations, and thereby enhances their claims to truth. The offenses and scandals of the world, the things that are to come, the rulers of the world and their lives, who is to come as Jesus' adversary, the errors of men—these are the subjects of the following apocalypses. There is no doubt that the *Gospel of the Twelve Apostles* and the three apocalypses that follow it form a whole, artfully constructed to function in a particular historical situation. The three apocalypses claim to be true apostolic writings, buttressed by the authority of the Twelve and their Lord.

The Apocalypse of Simeon Kepha

The first is the revelation of Simeon Kepha, and deals with Christianity. It describes the miserable state of the church and of true belief:

> I saw the time that is to be after us, full of offenses and evils and sins and lying; and the men in that time will be crafty, perverse, and depraved, men who know not God and understand not the truth; but a few of them shall understand their God because of his works which they behold daily, those which are established in Heaven and those which are brought forth on earth; and they know the Lord, as if they did not discern him; for this name is called upon them that are believers.

The few believers speak the truth, know God and understand his beloved Son and do not deny the Spirit, and perform signs and great works of power; but they will be killed by bribed judges and deniers of the true faith.

> And after these things shall have happened, the faith shall fail from the earth and orthodoxy shall come to an end: and those who are named as being baptized in our Lord and as confessing his name shall be more miserable than all men; and they shall trample on the faith and talk perversely and they shall divide our Lord; and in that time there shall be reckoned many teachers, as the Spirit of the Father does not speak in them, and they shall divide our Lord.

The text is clearly of Monophysite origin. The Monophysites, who "do not divide our Lord", had a long history of enmity and conflicts with their Chalcedonian Byzantine rulers in northern Mesopotamia. It is the Chalcedonians, here (as commonly elsewhere) described as Dyophysites, who "divide our Lord", and are therefore the evildoers and the causers of all misery, so that no one can find the Lord. According to the revelation of Simeon Kepha, the Chalcedonians will be delivered to evils, misery, pillage, and tribute, until they ask for death for themselves, when they will not find a savior. The text mirrors all the misery, pillage, and tribute which the Monophysite population of northern Mesopotamia felt that they had suffered from the Byzantines, and in particular from their armies when they went to war against the Sasanians.

> But the few who shall be scattered in the countries, who confess the Son in the way that is right for them to do, of these the Lord shall supply their needs.

Apparently the Monophysites form a minority, or they feel like a minority. The Chalcedonians, on the other hand, are compared to the heathen, their Church in a state of complete disorder and moral perversion:

> But those who do not believe in him, and who are called baptized people, shall felicitate the heathen, and they shall envy them and say: "Why are these things so, and why has it been given to us on this wise?" And even those who preach among them, on whom the name of the Lord was called, in the headship over their brethren and in the offices of the Church will be disturbers and self-exalting persons and haters of one another: lovers of money and destroyers of order, and who do not keep the commandments: but they will not love their flocks, and in their days men will appear as sheep who are ravening wolves, and they will eat up the labor of the orphans and the sustenance of the widows, and every ruler shall pervert justice and their eyes shall be blinded by bribery, and they shall love vainglory, and because of all these evils that are performed by them, they shall call upon the Lord, and there will be none to answer them, and there will be no Savior for them...men shall see their sons and their daughters and their wives and their revenues made a prey by their enemies.

This misery will last until the Chalcedonians return and:

> shall confess our Lord according as we received from him, and according as we believed in the Son, the Life-Giver and Savior of the world; and after this there will be one flock and one Church and one baptism, true and one; and it will come to pass in that day that every one that shall call upon the name of the Lord shall be saved, and whosoever worships the Paraclete shall be delivered.

Simeon Kepha does not describe the history of Christian belief in the Roman Empire; he rather concentrates on schism in the Church. Only when the Chalcedonians return to the true Monophysite belief will there be a state of peace and grace in which Christians can be saved. Simeon's description of the miserable state of church affairs is, at the same time, partly based on the picture given by the *Apocalypse* of ps.-Methodius of the evils which befall Christians as a result of Islam. It also reminds us of Jōḥannān bar Penkāyē's account (to which I shall return later) of the corrupt state of his own Nestorian church after so long a period of peace.[10]

The Apocalypse of James

The second revelation, from James the Apostle, son of Zebedee, deals with Judaism and Jerusalem. The subject is appropriate for James, just as that of the church is appropriate for Simeon Kepha—was not James, the brother of the Lord, known as the first bishop of Jerusalem? However, there seems to be a conflation here of James, the son of Zebedee, and the James who had special relations with Jerusalem.[11] James describes the destruction of the Temple:

> Alas, our Lord Jesus, for the desolation that I see in this holy city! for lo! after a certain time the Temple will be laid waste, the house of the Lord, the great and renowned; and the city of Jerusalem shall be laid waste; and it shall be disturbed and become a place of pollution; and it shall be delivered up to a people that knoweth not God and doth not understand the truth, because of the wickedness of them that dwell therein; in that they have blasphemed the name of our Lord Jesus and have crucified and killed him.

James next reveals the coming of a man "renowned in name and fearsome in appearance", who will banish and destroy those who dwell in

---

[10] Alphonse Mingana, *Sources syriaques*, I (Leipzig, 1908), 177*–181*; cf. S.P. Brock, "North Mesopotamia in the Late Seventh Century: Book xv of John Bar Penkāyē's *Rīš Mellē*", *JSAI* 9 (1987), 51–75.

[11] Acts 12:17, 15:13, 21:18; cf. Eusebius, *HE* II.23. Cf. Friedrich Haase, *Apostel und Evangelisten in der orientalischen Überlieferungen* (Münster, 1922).

Jerusalem. The reference must be to Hadrian, who expelled the Jews from Jerusalem after the suppression of the second Jewish revolt in AD 135.[12] The next reference in James' revelation is probably to Licinius:

> and after all these things have happened to the city of the Lord, there shall come forth a man who oppresses them by war against his enemies, and in that war he shall die.

In all probability the revelation hints at the final war between Constantine and Licinius in AD 324, which ended with the murder of Licinius.[13] The central figure of James' apocalypse is, however, Constantine the Great, who built the Church of the Holy Sepulcher and made Jerusalem a Christian city:

> and there shall be in authority over her another man, and he shall set up edicts and shall settle her, and there shall be built in her sanctuaries to the Lord, consecrated and renowned, and they shall come from the ends of the earth and from its bounds.

It is clear that James' revelation refers (however inaccurately) to the so-called "Edict of Milan", and to Constantine's great basilica, to which pilgrims travelled from the whole *oikoumene*.[14] James describes the church at Jerusalem at some length, and then continues:

> The Lord shall set up therein a sign that overcomes the evil of the wicked, and no man shall grudge thereat, nor be evilly affected: for there will be therein another house of worship, because peace is decreed to her by the Holy One of

[12]See Emil Schürer, *The History of the Jewish People in the Age of Jesus Christ (175 BC–AD 135)*, rev. and ed. Geza Vermes and Fergus Millar (Edinburgh, 1973–87), I, 553–57.

[13]See Timothy D. Barnes, *Constantine and Eusebius* (Cambridge, Mass., 1981), 214; A.H.M. Jones, *The Later Roman Empire 284–602* (Oxford, 1964), I, 82–83.

[14]On the "Edict of Milan", see Andreas Alföldi, *The Conversion of Constantine and Pagan Rome*, trans. Harold Mattingly (Oxford, 1948), 37; the reference may be more general, however. On Constantine's basilica, see Erik Wistrand, *Konstantins Kirche am heiligen Grab in Jerusalem nach den ältesten literarischen Zeugnissen* (Göteborg, 1952).

> Israel; and a great and renowned house shall be built in her at great cost, with gold of Ophir and beryls of Havilah, and its name shall go forth and be renowned, more than all the houses in the earth: and they shall say that never before it [was there such], and never after it will it be so. And that king who began to build it shall die on the completion of his building.

The sign which overcomes the evil of the wicked refers of course to the True Cross, highly venerated in Jerusalem and supposedly discovered by Constantine's mother Helena. It was preeminently seen as a sign of victory.[15] The description of the Church of the Holy Sepulcher, with its gold and beryls, recalls Eusebius' description of its interior as shining with gold and jewels.[16] It was dedicated in September 335 as part of the celebrations in honor of Constantine's 30th year as emperor, and Constantine himself died soon after, in May 337; the apocalypse is thus not far off the mark when it predicts that the emperor would die on completion of his building.[17]

The last sentences of the second apocalypse are, however, enigmatic. Immediately after the mention of the death of Constantine, James continues:

> And one from his seed shall rise up in his place and shall burden the chief men with many ills; and he shall have great and vigorous rule, and the earth shall be governed in his days in great peace; because from God it has been so spoken concerning him and concerning his people by the mouth of the prophet Daniel: and it shall come to pass that whosoever shall call upon the name of the Lord he will save.

[15] See H.A. Drake, "Eusebius on the True Cross", *JEH* 36 (1985), 1–22; J.W. Drijvers, *Helena Augusta: Waarheid en Legende*, Ph.D. dissertation: Rijksuniversiteit Groningen, 1989; Erich Dinkler, "Das Kreuz als Siegeszeichen", in his *Signum Crucis* (Tübingen, 1967), 55–76.

[16] Eusebius, *Vita Constantini* III.33–40; ed. F. Winkelmann (Berlin, 1975; *Eusebius Werke* I.1), 99–101.

[17] Barnes, *Constantine and Eusebius*, 248–53. See Eusebius, *Vita Constantini* IV.43, ed. Winkelmann, 138.

Harris thought that the reference to Constantine's seed could not take us beyond Constantius II or perhaps Julian. But it is striking that the last sentence of James' apocalypse is almost identical with that of Simeon Kepha's revelation. Simeon predicts a future of peace after God's judgment on the hated Chalcedonians, when there will be one Church, as in Constantine's reign. In that time, "everyone who calls on the name of the Lord will be saved". The second apocalypse refers to the same situation, but claims that it is a ruler from the house of Constantine who will govern the earth in great peace. The passage does not refer to a historical emperor, but to an "Endkaiser" for whom Constantine serves as model. Daniel's prophecy concerning this last Roman emperor and his people is probably contained in Daniel 7:27: "And the kingdom and dominion and the greatness of the kingdom under the whole heaven shall be given to the people of the saints of the most High, whose kingdom is an everlasting kingdom, and all dominions shall serve and obey it".

The Apocalypse of John the Little

The first two apocalypses thus deal, respectively, with Christianity and Judaism. Their main focus is on Church unity as a necessary condition for the restoration of Christian belief and peace, and on the coming of a last emperor from the seed of Constantine who will reign over the earth in great peace. The last apocalypse, however, takes us to the time of Islam. This is the revelation of John the Little, brother of James and son of Zebedee. He is identified with John the Evangelist and author of the Book of Revelation, as is clear from the opening sentence:

> And there was suddenly a great earthquake and John, brother of James and the initiate of our Lord, fell on his face on the earth and with a great trembling he worshipped God the Lord of all; and our Lord sent to him a man in white raiment and mounted on a horse of fire, and his appearance was like the flashing of fire.[18]

The scene is constructed on the basis of Revelation:

[18] Cf. Daniel 7:9; Revelation 4:4, 6:11, 7:13–14.

> And I beheld and an angel approached me, one of those that are near to him; and he brought me scrolls written with the finger of truth[19] and inscribed in them times and generations and the iniquities and sins of men, and the miseries that are to come on the earth.

John the Little is invited to reveal the contents of the scrolls:

> And I beheld that there was written on the scrolls what men are to suffer in the last times.... Woe, woe to the sons of men who are left to the generations [and] to the times that are to come! For there shall rise up the kings of the North and they shall become strong and shall shake the whole world, and there shall be among them a man who subdues all the peoples by the marvellous sign which appeared to him in Heaven, and he shall be prosperous and it shall go well with him. And after him shall rise up kings of the Romans, insolent, evil, idol-worshipping, godless.

Constantine again enters the apocalyptic vision as the ideal Roman emperor, a king of the North who conquers the whole world with the victorious cross which appeared to him in Heaven.[20] But after him serious moral and religious decay manifests itself, for which the Lord sends punishment:

> The Lord shall send wrath upon them from Heaven, and Persia shall become strong against them, and shall drive away and expel this kingdom from the world, because it hath done exceeding evil, and kings shall rise up among them great and renowned, and lovers of money, and they shall take away government from the earth: and there shall be one of them who because of his love of money shall destroy many men, until commerce and trade shall perish from

[19] Cf. Revelation 5–6.

[20] Eusebius, *Vita Constantini* I.40; ed. Winkelmann, 36–37. Cf. Andreas Alföldi, "Hoc signo victor eris", in *Pisciculi. Studien zur Religion und Kultur der Altertums* (Munich, 1939; Dölger Festschrift), 1–5; Dinkler, *Signum Crucis*, 63–65.

> off the whole earth, and by the son of his own body he shall die. And all the silver and gold that he has collected shall not save him; and after this Persia shall rule for a little time, and it too shall be delivered over to Media; because of their evil sins the God of heaven shall abolish their rule, and shall destroy their kingdom; and they shall perish and cease to be.

The reference is to the Sasanians under Khusrō II Parvīz (591–628), who used his military strength to extort major concessions from the Byzantine emperors.[21] Khusrō conquered a large part of the Byzantine Empire in the years from 603 on, Constantinople itself being saved only with great difficulty, until Heraclius' counterattack proved successful and Khusrō was murdered by his own son and ministers.[22]

It is noteworthy that the emperor Heraclius is totally absent in this apocalypse, and that Media is mentioned as Persia's successor. It would seem, however, that the concept of the four empires in the book of Daniel is responsible for the introduction here of the Median empire, which has no place at this period. The author of the Daniel apocalypse describes the succession of four world empires: the Babylonian, the Median, the Persian, and the Greek empire of Alexander the Great and his successors. Ps.-Methodius took this historical scheme in an almost unchanged form from the Book of Daniel. He considers the Greco-Roman-Byzantine empire as the last one, and consequently introduces the Byzantine emperor as the Endkaiser. Like ps.-Methodius, but in a different way, our author is interested in the succession of four empires—the Roman, the Sasanian, the Median, and the Arabian—after which there will be a Christian and unified empire without ecclesiastical controversy, under an ideal Roman emperor, Constantine *redivivus*. The ideal state of the Roman Empire under Constantine will return at the end of days, when the Muslim reign will have come to an end through internal conflicts.

[21] Georg Ostrogorsky, *History of the Byzantine State*, trans. Joan M. Hussey, 2nd ed. (Oxford, 1968), 85, 94–95, 102–104.

[22] John Haldon, *Byzantium in the Seventh Century: the Transformation of a Culture* (Cambridge, 1990), 42–46.

The successive fall of these empires is caused by their sins, for which they are punished by God's judgments:

> But there will be deniers of the truth and men that know not God and do corruptly in their lasciviousness, those who provoke God, and then suddenly shall be fulfilled the prophecy of Daniel, the pure and the desired, which he spake, that God shall send forth a mighty wind, the southern one; and there shall come from it a people of deformed aspect, and their appearance and manners like those of women; and there shall rise up from among them a warrior, and one whom they call a prophet, and they shall be brought into his hands...those like to whom there has not been any in the world, neither do there exist their like; and everyone that hears shall shake his head and shall deride him and say: "Why doth he speak thus? And God seeth it and regardeth it not".

The appearance of Muḥammad, warrior and prophet,[23] is seen as the fulfillment of Daniel's prophecy in Chapter 11 on the war between the king of the South and the king of the North. The mighty southern wind refers to Daniel 7:2: "Daniel spake and said, I saw in my vision by night, and behold, the four winds of the heaven strove upon the great sea". This text is linked with Daniel 11:5: "And the king of the South shall be strong". The deformed, "female" appearance of the Arabs from the desert is a borrowing from ps.-Methodius, who gives a vivid picture of the perverted morals of the Christians in his time: men dress like harlots and wear jewellery like young girls and behave in a lascivious and shameful way.[24] Another passage in ps.-Methodius describes the triumphant Muslims as being dressed like bridegrooms and adorned like

[23] See Sidney H. Griffith, "The Prophet Muḥammad, His Scripture and His Message According to the Christian Apologies in Arabic and Syriac from the First 'Abbāsid Century", in Toufic Fahd, ed., *La vie du prophète Mahomet* (Paris, 1983), 131–43.

[24] Ps.-Methodius, *Apocalypse*, Vatican Ms. Syr. 58, fol. 128v.; Suermann, *Die geschichtstheologische Reaktion*, 62:340–45.

brides.[25] Such references to men dressing and behaving like women, a clear sign of moral perversity, may comprise the background for John the Little's portrait of the Muslims.

The Muslims, the people from the South, have subdued Persia and Rome as was ordained by the Holy One of Heaven. John the Little prophesies that:

> Twelve renowned kings shall rise up from that people, according as it is written in the law when God talked with Abraham and said to him: "Lo! concerning Ishmael thy son I have heard thee, and twelve princes shall he beget along with many other princesses"; and he, even he, is the people of the land of the South.

The reference is to Genesis 17:20: "And as for Ishmael I have heard thee: behold I have blessed him, and will make him fruitful and will multiply him exceedingly; twelve princes shall he beget, and I will make him a great nation".[26] Harris supposed that the twelve princes referred to twelve caliphs, bringing the date of the apocalypse and consequently of the entire work to the mid-eighth century.[27] But it is more in accord with the tenor of the treatise to consider the meaning as symbolic: as the first apocalypse emphasizes, Christianity had twelve Apostles to judge the twelve tribes of Israel, and Islam consequently had twelve princes. In the Bible, the appearance of groups or things in terms of "twelves" is a sign that the hand of God is involved.[28] It is therefore important to keep the number to twelve. When the Levites are excluded from the twelve tribes of Israel, Joseph's sons Ephraim and Manassah become "tribes" in order to keep the twelve complete.[29] Similarly, in the New Testament we find that the Apostles choose Matthias to

---

[25] Vat. Ms. Syr. 58, fol. 133r; Suermann, *Die geschichtstheologische Reaktion*, 74:497–98.

[26] Cf. Genesis 25:16.

[27] Harris, *Gospel of the Twelve Apostles*, 21. According to a well-known *ḥadīth* of the Prophet, twelve caliphs were to rule after him; see Wilfred Madelung, "Apocalyptic Prophecies in Ḥimṣ in the Umayyad Age", *JSS* 31 (1986), 150.

[28] See, for example, Genesis 35:22–26, Matthew 14:20, 26:53.

[29] Cf. Numbers 1:1–54.

replace Judas, again maintaining the twelve.[30] In Islam this symbolism is carried over, where the idea of the twelve is that of an élite chosen by God, or a force sent forth according to some divinely ordained plan.[31]

As for the identification of Ishmael with the Muslims, the people of the land of the South, that too occurs in ps.-Methodius.[32] The Muslims subdue almost the whole world and oppress its inhabitants with heavy tribute:

> He (i.e. Ishmael) shall lead captive a great captivity among all the people of the earth, and they shall spoil a great spoiling, and all the ends of the earth shall do service and there shall be made subject to him many lordships; and his hand shall be over all, and also those that are under his hand he shall oppress with much tribute; and he shall oppress and kill and destroy the rulers of the ends [of the earth]. And he shall impose a tribute on the earth, such as was never heard of; until a man shall come out from his house and shall find four collectors who collect tribute; and men shall sell their sons and daughters because of their need: and they shall hate their lives and shall wail and weep, and there is no voice or discourse except Woe, Woe! and they shall be covetous with a hateful cupidity: and they shall be converted like bridegrooms and like brides...and there shall prosper with them all those who take refuge with them, and they shall enslave to them men renowned in race, and there shall be among them hypocrites, and men who know not God and regard not men except for prodigals, fornicators, and men wicked and vengeful.

[30] Acts 1:12–26.

[31] See Nu'aym ibn Ḥammād, *Kitāb al-fitan*, ed. Lawrence I. Conrad (Wiesbaden, forthcoming), nos. 104, 221–29, 250, 269, 331, 535, and frequently elsewhere (index, *s.v.* "12"). I would like to thank Dr. Conrad for drawing this dimension of the symbolism of twelve to my attention and providing me with the relevant Biblical and Arabic references.

[32] Vat. Syr. 58, fol. 127v; Suermann, *Die geschichtstheologische Reaktion*, 60:315–17. Cf. G.J. Reinink, "Ismael, Der Wildesel in der Wüste. Zur Typologie der Apokalypse des Pseudo-Methodios", *BZ* 75 (1982), 336–44.

The heavy tribute, "never heard of before", is the tax laid upon Christians by the Muslims, specifically by means of the tax reforms and census of 'Abd al-Malik. Suermann related the number of tax collectors to the four traditional Muslim law schools, but this is impossible, since in the eighth century these law schools (*madhāhib*) did not yet exist. The proposition that Sunnī Islam has specifically four schools of law would not have been true until after about the twelfth century AD. Before that time there were numerous other regional schools, which were not in place until the eighth-ninth centuries AD.[33] Again ps.-Methodius provides the clue: the number four is used to indicate the four chiefs or heads of the chastisements (*rīšā d-mardūtā*) which fall on Christians under Muslim rule, which is in turn sent by God to chastise his people for their sins.[34] Heavy tribute is also described by ps.-Methodius—so heavy indeed that, as with John the Little, men are said to sell their sons and daughters.[35] Like ps.-Methodius, John foresees a massive apostasy among his co-religionists: they will be converted like bridegrooms and brides (cf. ps.-Methodius' picture of the triumphant Muslims as bridegrooms and brides). John calls them hypocrites, prodigals, fornicators, etc., and ps.-Methodius again does the same.[36]

The lamentable state of Christians under Muslim supremacy is a sign of the End that is at hand, and which will come after "one great week and the half of a great week", i.e. after ten and a half years:

> But woe! woe! to the children of men in that time; and they (i.e. the Muslims) shall rule over the world[37] for one

[33]See Joseph Schacht, *An Introduction to Islamic Law* (Oxford, 1964), 57–68.

[34]Suermann, *Die geschichtstheologische Reaktion*, 18–81; Vat. Syr. 58, fol. 128r; Suermann, 62:331–34.

[35]Vat. Syr. 58, fol. 132v. Suermann, *Der geschichtstheologische Reaktion*, 72:475. 'Abd al-Malik's tax reform is described by the chronicle of ps.-Dionysius. See J.-B. Chabot, *Chronique de Denys de Tell-Maḥré* (Paris, 1895), 10; cf. G.J. Reinink, "Pseudo-Methodius und die Legende vom römischen Endkaiser", in W. Verbeke, D. Verhelst, A. Welkenhuysen, eds., *The Use and Abuse of Eschatology in the Middle Ages* (Leuven, 1988), 104.

[36]Vat. Syr. 58, fol. 128v; Suermann, *Die geschichtstheologische Reaktion*, 62:340–46; see in particular fol. 131v.; Suermann, 70:440–55.

[37]The manuscript contains a scribal error here: read *'amarta* "habitable world", instead of *ma'rta* = "cave".

> great week and the half of a great week; and every king who shall arise from among them shall strengthen and be made strong, and shall be more vigorous than his fellow; and they shall gather together the gold of the earth....and it shall come to pass after the week and the half of a week that the earth shall be moved concerning them, and God shall require the sins of men from their hands.[38] And the South wind shall subside and God shall bring to naught their covenant with them.

John the Little takes the period of one great week and the half of a great week from ps.-Methodius, who wrote at the end of ten "great weeks" of Muslim rule, i.e. in 692.[39]

Ps.-Methodius prophesies that then the last Byzantine emperor will come and will stay in Jerusalem for one and a half weeks, i.e. for ten and a half years; after this period the son of perdition (the destroyer) and the Antichrist will manifest themselves. Ps.-Methodius thus applies the Danielic scheme of one and a half weeks[40] to the events of his own day, and the author of the *Gospel of the Twelve Apostles* takes over the mention of the same period of time, after which the Muslims will split into two rival parties and make war with each other because they hate the name of the Lord and love sin:

> But so much the more will they (i.e. the Muslims) afflict all those who confess our Lord Christ; because they shall hate to the very end the name of the Lord and shall bring to naught his Covenant; and truth shall not be found among them, but only villainy shall they love and sin shall they have an affection for. And whatever is hateful in the eyes of the Lord that will they do: and they shall be called a

[38] The Ms. reads *ḥetaha d-berīta*, which Harris translates as "the sins of creation"; it seems better, however, to interpret *bryt'* as *brīta*, "creature", and to translate "the sins of men".

[39] Vat. Syr. 58, fol. 123v; Suermann, 72:474–75; fols. 133r: 2–133v:13; Suermann, 74. Cf. Reinink, "Pseudo-Methodius und die Legende vom römischen Endkaiser", 106.

[40] Cf. Daniel 7:25, 9:27.

> corrupt people; and after these things the Lord shall be angered against them, as he was against Rome, and against Media and Persia; and straightaway there will come upon them the End, and suddenly the time [will come]; and at last in the completion of the week and a half God shall stir up against them desolation; and an angel of wrath shall descend and shall kindle evil among them...and they shall be lifted up one against the other, and they shall make and become two parties and each party shall seek to call himself king, and there shall be war between them, and there shall be many murders by them and among them, and much blood shall be shed among them at the fountain of waters which is in the place which was spoken of beforetime in the *Book of the Sibyl*.

At the time of writing, then, the author of the *Gospel of the Twelve Apostles* expected the end of Muslim rule after one and a half great weeks, through internal conflicts between two rival factions. At that time there were perhaps already signs of this conflict, even actual battles. But while the author seems to have known a Sibylline oracle about a battle near a fountain, no such oracle is attested in extant collections.[41] The battle at the fountain of waters most likely denotes the bloody conflict between the caliph ʿAbd al-Malik and his rival Ibn al-Zubayr. In the autumn of 73/692 the latter was finally defeated at Mecca, the place of the fountain Zamzam that played an important rôle in the ceremonies of the *ḥajj*, the Islamic pilgrimage.[42]

The final battle between the two Muslim parties will bring the Byzantine emperor back onto the scene of world history. He will besiege the Muslim armies and drive them back from whence they came:

---

[41] See Sebastian Brock, "A Syriac Collection of Prophecies of the Pagan Philosophers", *OLP* 14 (1983), 203–46; *idem*, "Some Syriac Excerpts from Greek Collections of Pagan Prophecies", *VC* 38 (1984), 77–90, concluding that there were other collections of pagan prophecies, among them Sibylline oracles, which no longer survive.

[42] See Hugh Kennedy, *The Prophet and the Age of the Caliphates: the Islamic Near East From the Sixth to the Eleventh Century* (London, 1986), 98; G.R. Hawting, *The First Dynasty of Islam: the Umayyad Caliphate* AD *661–750* (London, 1986), 49.

> And when the man of the North shall hear this report, he shall not boast and say:[43] "By my might and by my arm have I overcome". Then shall he associate with him all the peoples of the earth, and he will go forth against him, and they shall destroy and devastate his armies and lead captive their sons and daughters and their wives, and there shall fall upon them a bitter wedlock and misery; and the Lord shall cause the wind of the South to return to his place from whence he came forth, and shall bring to naught his name and his fame; and it shall come to pass that when they shall enter again the place from whence they came out, the enemy shall not pursue them thither, and they shall not fear hunger and they shall not tremble, and it shall come to pass in that day that their reliance [shall be] upon silver which they have got by wrong and by plunder which they have hidden in the place named Diglath,[44] and they shall return and settle in the land from whence they came out; and God shall stir up for them there evil times and times of plagues, and without war they will be laid waste, and unto all generations of the world there shall not be among them any who holds a weapon and stands up in battle....

Here the apocalypse of John the Little ends. The angel Michael leaves him and a voice orders John to go to his companions, Simeon and James, so that they may talk with him.

---

[43] Harris' translation is not correct here: he translates "he shall not be affrighted and he shall say", but *nštbhr* means "to glorify oneself, to boast". See Jessie Payne Smith, *A Compendious Syriac Dictionary* (Oxford, 1903), 36, s.v. *bhr*.

[44] The Syriac here is the exact equivalent to the Arabic *Dijla*, the Tigris River, and may therefore allude to the founding of the city of Wāsiṭ on the Tigris in 702–705 by al-Ḥajjāj. See Jean Périer, *Vie d'al-Ḥadjdjādj ibn Yousof* (Paris, 1904), 205–13. This establishment of a permanent garrison of Syrian troops had enormous economic consequences for the local population. If this reference to "the place called Diglath" does in fact betray knowledge of the existence of Wāsiṭ, it would imply that the *Gospel* cannot have assumed its present form until shortly after 702. I am grateful to Dr. Conrad for drawing my attention to this point.

The Social and Cultural Context

The *Gospel of the Twelve Apostles* is a literary unity, consisting of a prologue and three apocalypses, of which the first two function as a preparation for the third and last. It is anti-Chalcedonian and anti-Jewish, sees Constantine as the ideal Christian emperor, and proclaims a Constantine *redivivus* as the last Byzantine emperor who will subdue the Muslims with all other peoples, just as Constantine subdued all peoples by the sign of the Cross. When and in what historical circumstances was this apocalyptic treatise written?

The author used several sources, or at least, his treatise manifests an awareness of the thought of certain writings circulating in his milieu. The prologue displays influence from the so-called *Testamentum domini nostri Jesu Christi*, an apocalyptic writing, supposedly from the fifth century, which forms the introduction to a collection of ecclesiastical laws, apostolic constitutions, and apostolic canons.[45] Its message is that only believers who strictly keep the commandments of God and the Church will be saved at the end of time, when the son of perdition, the Antichrist, will appear. Jesus instructs his disciples about the signs of the End, when the son of perdition will come, and it is noteworthy that these signs are virtually the same as those given in the *Gospel of the Twelve Apostles*. Moreover, the *Testamentum* urges its readers to return to the true Church, as the *Gospel* urges its readers back to true belief. Both writings emphasize the aid of the Holy Spirit in understanding the signs of the End and finding the strength to keep the commandments.[46] According to the colophon of the only surviving Ms. of the *Testamentum*, it was translated from Greek into Syriac by a monk Jacob, in all likelihood the famous translator Jacob of Edessa, in 687.[47] This is the very year in which Jōḥannān bar Penkāyē wrote

---

[45] *Testamentum domini nostri Jesu Christ*, ed. Ignatius Ephraem II Rahmani (Mainz, 1899); see Anton Baumstark, "Überlieferung und Bezeugung des Testamentum Domini Nostri Jesu Christi", *Römische Quartalschrift* 14 (1900), 1–45; Franz Xavier von Funk, *Das Testament unseres Herrn und die verwandten Schriften* (Mainz, 1901).

[46] See already Harris, *Gospel of the Twelve Apostles*, 16–17.

[47] *Testamentum*, 149. On Jacob of Edessa as a translator, see Ignatius Ortiz de Urbina, *Patrologia Syriaca* (Vatican City, 1965), 181–82; Drijvers, "Jakob von Edessa", 468–70.

his *Ktābā d-rīš mellē*, of which Book XV describes the sufferings of northern Mesopotamia, afflicted by famine, plague, and heavy tribute, which made Jōḥannān expect the end of times and of Muslim rule.[48] We may surmise that the same situation provided a stimulus for Jacob of Edessa to translate the *Testamentum domini nostri* into Syriac. Jacob of Edessa was a strong-minded advocate of the strict maintenance of ecclesiastical canons against the pressure of Islam; and indeed, this brought him into such conflict with his clerics at Edessa that he left his bishopric in 688.[49] Even if the apocalyptic prologue of the *Testamentum* already existed (so far no Greek text has been discovered), Jacob may have updated it in the process of translation so as to bring it into line with existing conditions,[50] when the political and social situation evidently aroused apocalyptic expectations among Nestorians and Jacobites alike. The arrangement of the manuscript of which the *Gospel of the Twelve Apostles* forms a part also manifests the same tendencies that urged Jacob of Edessa to emphasize the strict maintenance of ecclesiastical law as a weapon against apostasy. The *Gospel* functions as an apocalyptic sermon to the readers, urging them to keep the canons, while for possible converts from heresy, i.e. Christians who had apostatized and embraced Islam, an additional *libellus* is added.

A second source for the *Gospel* is the *Apocalypse* of ps.-Methodius, written in 692 as a reaction to the heavy tribute imposed by ʻAbd al-Malik, and the subsequent mass conversions to Islam.[51] The *Gospel* gives a similar account of the tribute and conversions and knows the same periodization of history: the Muslims will reign for another one and a half great weeks, and then the man from the North, the Christian emperor, will come and destroy them; as a result also of their internal conflicts, Muslim rule will end. The two Muslim parties, each of which

---

[48]Cf. Brock, "North Mesopotamia in the Late Seventh Century", 52; Reinink, "Pseudo-Methodius und die Legende von römischen Endkaiser", 84–86.

[49]See Baumstark, 248; Drijvers, "Jakob von Edessa", 468.

[50]See François Nau, "Fragment inédit d'une traduction syriaque jusqu'ici inconnue du Testamentum D.N. Jesu Christi", *JA*, 9ème Série, 17 (1901), 233–56; J.P. Arendzen, "A New Syriac Text of the Apocalyptic Part of the Testament of the Lord", *JThS* 2 (1901), 401–16; Funk, *Das Testament unseres Herrn*, 83–85.

[51]Reinink, "Pseudo-Methodius und die Legende vom römischen Endkaiser", is the basic study; also see his study in this volume.

wants to rule, probably denote ʿAbd al-Malik and the rival caliph ʿAbd Allāh ibn al-Zubayr at Mecca. Even after the defeat of Muṣʿab, Ibn al-Zubayr's brother, at Dayr al-Jathālīq in 691 and Ibn al-Zubayr's final overthrow and death in autumn 692 at Mecca, the conflicts were still not yet over. In northern Mesopotamia in particular, in the Jazīra and in the Palmyrena, there were continuous feuds between the Yamanīs and the Qaysīs, who represented rival factional interests.[52] The *Gospel* was therefore written in the years following 692, when the memory of the struggle between ʿAbd al-Malik and Ibn al-Zubayr was still fresh and the conflicts still continued, while the burden of ʿAbd al-Malik's tribute was still heavily felt and conversion to Islam posed a threat to the Monophysite community.[53] Its place of origin was probably Edessa, where even after bishop Jacob's departure his influence was still considerable.

There is, however, a major difference between the *Apocalypse* of ps.-Methodius and the *Gospel of the Twelve Apostles*, one which manifests itself most clearly in their view of the four world empires. Ps.-Methodius sees the Byzantine Empire as the last one; he dismisses the Muslims as wild asses from the desert whose power will not long endure—they will soon disappear from the world scene. The author of the *Gospel*, however, considers the Umayyad caliphate as the last world empire and does not see it as a temporary phenomenon. He must have lived when ʿAbd al-Malik had firmly consolidated his rule and expectations of the end of Muslim power had considerably diminished. It is in accordance with all the sources and with the socio-political situation to assume that the *Gospel of the Twelve Apostles* was written at the end of ʿAbd al-Malik's reign (he died in 705), when expectations of an imminent end to Muslim rule had disappeared and no one could reasonably expect the Byzantine emperor to repel the Muslims and reconquer his lost territories. This is why, in contrast with ps.-Methodius, the author of the *Gospel of the Twelve Apostles* did not expect the coming of the last Byzantine emperor, a Monophysite descendant of Alexander the Great. Our writer forecast the coming of the man of the North, who

[52]See Kennedy, *The Prophet and the Age of the Caliphates*, 90–100; Hawting, *The First Dynasty of Islam*, 59.

[53]As noted above (n. 44), it may be that the text reached its present form some time shortly after 702.

would not overcome the Muslims by his own power, his might and arm. He is a shadowy figure, a man from the seed of Constantine, if we combine the information from the second apocalypse with what John the Little prophesies of the man of the North. The schism between Chalcedonians and Monophysites, the source of so much trouble, would then come to an end and all would return to one undivided Church, which once existed under the rule of Constantine the Great in the distant past.

The seventh century, when real historical knowledge of the Roman past was quickly fading, was notable for the emergence of a semi-legendary, saintly Constantine.[54] It is especially noticeable that our author avoids mentioning the last emperor actually known to the Orient, namely Heraclius, despite his active rôle in defeating the Persians and restoring the Cross to Jerusalem, instead preferring to recall the now almost mythical origins of the Christian empire and its first emperor. Heraclius' victories had given way to defeat by the Muslims, and memories of recent Byzantine rule were too painful and expectations too faint to allow our author to evoke a last Byzantine emperor with the expectation that such a figure could really bring salvation and deliverance from Muslim rule. Nor does the *Gospel* mention the Cross in relation to the last emperor, only referring to it in the context of Constantine's victories and building activity at Jerusalem. For while the Cross had come to the forefront of attention as a result of Heraclius' campaigns, it had more recently become a major bone of contention between Muslims and Christians; that may be why it was thought better to omit it here.[55] Again, our author differs from ps.-Methodius. The latter wrote in a time of severe crisis, when the danger of apostasy was very threatening to the Church; on the other hand, the second Muslim civil war made the coming of the Byzantine emperor seem a real possibility in an apocalyptic climate. The author of the *Gospel of the*

[54]See F. Winkelmann, "Die älteste erhaltene griechische hagiographische Vita Konstantins und Helenas (BHG Nr. 365z, 366, 366a)", in Jürgen Dümmer, ed., *Texte und Textkritik. Eine Aufsatzammlung* (Berlin, 1987; *TU* 133), 623–38; cf. A. Khazdan, "'Constantine imaginaire': Byzantine Legends of the Ninth Century about Constantine the Great", *Byzantion* 57 (1987), 196–250.

[55]See G.R.D. King, "Islam, Iconoclasm and the Declaration of Doctrine", *BSOAS* 48 (1985), 267–77.

Twelve Apostles did not live under such conditions. Muslim rule was firmly established, and he was therefore more interested in drawing the boundaries of his Monophysite community against the Chalcedonians and the Jews. His apocalyptic expectations had consequently faded somewhat and were now focussed on the man of the North as pictured in Chapter 11 of the Book of Daniel.

The *Gospel of the Twelve Apostles* was thus written after 692, when ps.-Methodius wrote, and before 705, when ʻAbd al-Malik's reign ended. A date shortly after the end of the seventh century is the most plausible, as this was a time when, on the one hand, Muslim rule was firmly established, but when, on the other, the continuous fighting between rival Muslim factions could encourage expectations that the hegemony of Islam would end one day in the future. A unified Christian empire would then rule again over the whole world under the scepter of the man of the North, a shadowy and ill-defined Constantine *redivivus*. The *Gospel* gives us a fascinating insight into the thoughts and hopes current in Edessa in the last decade of the seventh century and the beginning of the eighth, when the Muslims threatened the very existence of the Christian Monophysite population, who considered themselves the true heirs of Constantine's orthodoxy. There were signs in recent events which Christians could interpret as indicating that there might at some time be an end to their sufferings. Meanwhile, they had to come to terms with Muslim rule and preserve their identity against both the hated Chalcedonians and the Jews.

6

Early Islamic State Letters: The Question of Authenticity

Wadād al-Qāḍī
(University of Chicago)

Introduction

MUCH ARABIC PROSE material has come down to us from the early Islamic period up until the fall of the Umayyad dynasty in 132/750. This prose consists of several genres, including orations, sermons, epistles, treatises, historical accounts, traditions (*ḥadīth*) of the Prophet Muḥammad, and wisdom sayings. Each of these genres must be handled separately, not only because of the immense quantity of each that has been preserved in the sources, but also because each genre poses for the researcher different sets of problems which must be addressed through recourse to methodologically different tools and techniques. This does not mean that the various genres share no common problems; but assigning first priority to the establishment of basic criteria for work within each genre is the only way by which research can reach reliable results, which may then be assessed for their more general relevance and utility.

At the outset, then, I should say that the present paper will not deal with any orally transmitted material. This immediately eliminates genres which were oral by their very nature, such as orations, sermons, wisdom sayings and, albeit for different considerations, the traditions of the Prophet, as well as genres which were oral at least in their earliest stages of transmission before they came to be recorded in writing, such as historical accounts. Nor will it consider written materials which have no literary or artistic purpose, in other words, material the sole aim of which was "communicative", whether polemical or otherwise. This eliminates all treatises, be they theological, exegetical, or legal. What remains then, are the epistles, and these, unlike many treatises, have seldom been studied for the purpose of addressing the question of their authenticity.

A great deal can be said about the Arabic literary epistles of this period, but for present purposes only a few observations are required. The first is that almost all of these epistles (in Arabic, *rasā'il*) were letters written by one person and addressed to one person or a group of people, rather than essays written for a general audience.[1] The second is that although these letters are of varying content—official, personal, or a combination of both—it is noteworthy that the majority of them are of a "public" nature, most dealing with official matters and some comprising testaments, proclamations, letters of instruction, and so forth. This means that the relation between the letters and the various symbols of political authority (caliphs, governors, notables, and military leaders, as well as their contestants: rebels and critics) is a very close one indeed. This observation finds further confirmation when one examines the names of the individuals who wrote these letters (or those on whose behalf they were written) and those of the persons addressed: they are mainly either members of the actual ruling groups (the state) or those who entered into dialogue with them, more often than not in order to disavow or overthrow them (e.g. enemies and rebels).[2]

This conclusion may not be be representative of the character of the total corpus of literary letters written during this period; it may rather reflect only the interests of the later chroniclers and litterateurs, as well as the political historians and the historians of literature, who preserved those letters for us. That is, the message of these later trans-

[1]The Arabic word *risāla*, pl. *rasā'il*, allows for both of these meanings.

[2]The most comprehensive available collection of early Arab-Islamic letters and epistles to the end of Umayyad times is to be found in the first two volumes of Aḥmad Zakī Ṣafwat, *Jamharat rasā'il al-'arab* (Cairo, 1356/1937). For the Umayyad period in particular, see also the collection of Muḥammad Māhir Ḥamāda, *Al-Wathā'iq al-siyāsīya wa-l-idārīya li-l-'aṣr al-umawī* (Beirut, 1405/1985).

mitters might be: "We are interested in recording only those letters of public figures who played significant rôles in public life"—and almost no one else's. This certainly poses a problem for the researcher, but it is a problem with which one has to live: one can take into account, but not "solve", the difficulty posed by the selectivity of our sources. This having been said, however, it remains striking that the bulk of the extant early Arab-Islamic letters are centered around the affairs of the state, too much so to suppose that this focus represents the mere product of chance, rigorous selectivity, speculation, or invention.

The socio-administrative history of this period strengthens the postulate about the close association between the state and letter-writing. First, while we have little verifiable information about the early stages of the Islamic state as a coherently articulated political entity, we do know that it had become well established by 73/692. From that time onward it began to take major steps towards administrative sophistication, especially after the famous and far-reaching reforms of the Umayyad caliph ʻAbd al-Malik ibn Marwān (65–86/684–705), particularly his arabization of the *dīwāns* (departments of the state) and the official mints. The degree of this sophistication, particularly in the realm of taxation, is attested by the papyri, some dating back to 91/709 and 92/710, which have been discovered in Egypt.[3] Second, the *dīwān al-rasā'il*, the State Chancery, is reported to have existed as early as the reign of the first Umayyad caliph, Muʻāwiya ibn Abī Sufyān (41–60/661–80), if not earlier, and our sources have actually preserved for us the name of at least one of its scribes, or secretaries.[4] Further research of my own has proven almost conclusively that by the last years of the caliphate of ʻAbd al-Malik, the Chancery had already become a complex institution in which there were numerous scribes, both apprentices and established secretaries. Indeed, it had evolved into something like

[3]For a good study of the early Islamic state, see Fred M. Donner, "The Formation of the Islamic State", *JAOS* 106 (1986), 283–96. Donner makes extensive use of the papyri.

[4]See al-Ṭabarī, *Ta'rīkh al-rusul wa-l-mulūk*, ed. M.J. de Goeje *et al.* (Leiden, 1879–1901), II, 837; Ibn ʻAbd Rabbih, *Al-ʻIqd al-farīd*, ed. Aḥmad Amīn, Aḥmad al-Zayn, and Ibrāhīm al-Ibyārī (Cairo, 1368–84/1949–65), IV, 164; al-Jahshiyārī, *Al-Wuzarā' wa-l-kuttāb*, ed. Muṣṭafā al-Saqqā, Ibrāhīm al-Ibyārī, and ʻAbd al-Ḥafīẓ Shalabī (Cairo, 1357/1938), 124.

a training center for prospective official letter-writers, a place where young aspiring scribes underwent extensive training, prepared for and passed exams, received promotions, and became accomplished professional secretaries whose task it was to produce good solid pieces of prose written in a literary style that elevated these epistles above the level of the simple communication of one or more basic ideas. The highest possible position in the Chancery that a scribe could achieve was head of the Chancery (*ṣāḥib dīwān al-rasāʾil*), a post which made him the secretary to the highest authority in the Islamic state, the caliph.[5]

A third factor bearing on the close connection between the state and letter-writing was the spread of literacy. It is true that literacy in Arabic increased dramatically, mainly for religious and practical reasons, after the rise of Islam; one might particularly note its rapid spread following the conquests in the first/seventh and second/eighth centuries. However, it is also true that the Islamic state was an active participant in the spread of literacy, and played a rôle of increasing importance as time went on. As the major employer in the empire, and as one that eventually required knowledge of Arabic from its employees, especially after the reforms of ʿAbd al-Malik, it must also, whether knowingly or not, have encouraged literacy in Arabic. Indeed, it is quite probable that sometime during this movement the state was the major reformer of the Arabic script, adding to it diacritics and vowel signs and thus rendering the reasonable mastery of the language more feasible, especially for the vast non-Arab majority of the population.[6]

This increase in literacy in Arabic rendered more people living under the domain of the Islamic state—both Muslims and non-Muslims—capable of writing letters in Arabic. The state, however, must have remained far ahead of any individual in sponsoring this kind of writing. Not only were its needs far greater, but its resources, financial and otherwise, also made it possible for it to bring into its service

[5]This is discussed in the first chapter of my forthcoming book, *State and Statecraft in Early Islam*.

[6]My remarks here are derived from a general reading of the sources. As far as I know, no one has studied the question of literacy in early Islam, particularly with regard to the rôle played by the state in this. Although the material on the subject in the sources is scanty, it is worthy of study.

trained, professional writers, scribes who could produce more elaborate and sophisticated letters. As a result, the letters emanating from the various departments of the state were not only more numerous but also of a higher literary standard than the letters produced by individuals; indeed, when one examines the letters written by (or on behalf of) the opponents of the state (the rebels), one notes that they were produced most frequently when those rebels had established something like a "mini-state" of their own in whatever domain they had conquered.[7]

It is this situation that explains, at least partially, what I have termed the preponderantly "public" nature of the letters preserved in the later historical and literary sources. The authors of these sources had a much larger corpus of letters from which to choose than the corpus which had been written by politically uninvolved individuals, and the quality of much of this corpus was characterized by strict adherence to prevailing linguistic conventions, elaborate stylistics, and general professionalism; such epistles often represent the result of long training, and not merely the fruits of an individual's mysterious artistic "gift". In addition, one must note that the later authors citing these letters lived mainly from the third/ninth century onwards (as will be discussed below): that is, they were writing at a time when the state had become—in administrative terms—far more complex than it had been under the Umayyads, and when earlier official letters were being sought to serve as models, in particular for the secretaries of the Chancery. In this connection it must be noted that although literary taste did change rather rapidly with the passage of time, official (public) letters could maintain a great deal of their attractiveness for

[7]There are several examples of this. It is related in one source that in 81/700, when the famous rebel Ibn al-Ash'ath wanted to declare the crucial withdrawal of his allegiance to al-Ḥajjāj ibn Yūsuf, the domineering governor of the East, he asked a man known for his eloquence, Ibn al-Qirrīya, to write a letter to al-Ḥajjāj on his behalf; see (ps.-)Ibn Qutayba, *Al-Imāma wa-l-siyāsa*, ed. Muḥammad Ṭāhā al-Zaynī (Cairo, n.d.), II, 30. Also, when the leader of the 'Abbāsid underground movement, Abū Muslim al-Khurāsānī, went public with his revolt in 129/746, he set up departments similar to the departments of the state and appointed a secretary to the "chancery"; see al-Jahshiyārī, *Al-Wuzarā' wa-l-kuttāb*, 85. Although the Zubayrids can hardly be called rebels in the strict sense of the word, they too had their secretaries; *ibid.*, 44, for the secretary of Muṣ'ab ibn al-Zubayr, for example.

litterateurs, not only due to their historical importance and literary elegance, but also because they demonstrated the continuation of the ancient venerable tradition of loyalty to the state and highlighted an awed sense of extreme distance between the mundane world of the populace and the august domain of the caliphate and its apparatus—as symbolized by the extreme stylistic and literary distance between ordinary prose and speech, and the ornate and complex style of the imperial Chancery.

This leads to the third point I would like to make about these letters, namely that of their authenticity. As I have already alluded to above, all of the extant early Arabic letters up to the middle of the second/eighth century have been recorded by authors who flourished, at the earliest, in the third/ninth century, with the possible exception of a few whose recording dates back almost half a century or so earlier.[8] What this means is that the letters cannot be shown to be genuine from contemporary evidence, so that their authenticity must be established before any fully reliable work can be done on them. But while this "authenticity problem" is a very important one, one should perhaps not exaggerate its difficulty, lest one fall into the abyss of nihilism and the barrenness of self-serving skepticism. The fact that we do not now possess earlier sources does not necessarily mean that such sources did not once exist. Indeed, Ibn al-Nadīm's *Fihrist*, a bibliography of Arabic works in the various fields of scholarship until the end of the fourth/tenth century,[9] makes clear two points apropos of such matters. First, it tells us that scores of books and treatises were compiled by authors who flourished in the late first/seventh and early second/eighth centuries, and these works could very well have served as sources for

[8]For an example of letters recorded in sources dating to the latter half of the second/eighth century, see al-Madā'inī, *Kitāb al-ta'āzī*, ed. Ibtisām Marhūn al-Ṣifār and Badrī Muḥammad Fahd (Najaf, 1391/1971), 32. Al-Madā'inī was born in 135/752 and died at the earliest in 215/830 and at the latest in 228/843; on this important historian, see Ursula Sezgin, art. "al-Madā'inī" in EI^2, V (Leiden, 1986), 946.

[9]The best edition of this book is that of Riḍā Tajaddud (Tehran, 1391/1971), which will be cited here. Also still frequently used by scholars is that of Gustav Flügel (Leiden, 1871–72). An English translation is available in two volumes in *The Fihrist of al-Nadīm: a Tenth-Century Survey of Muslim Culture*, ed. and trans. Bayard Dodge (New York, 1970).

the later, third/ninth century authors.[10] Second, the vast majority of these early compilations have been lost and are now known to us only by their titles. Among those probably early compilations are some collections of letters of early prose writers, some of whom were secretaries to the Umayyad state.[11]

Returning to the authenticity question, I should add that to judge from the painstaking efforts of scholars to authenticate early Arab-Islamic materials,[12] it would seem quite impossible for one individual to embark on a project to pass judgment on the authenticity (or the lack thereof) of all the letters which have come down to us in the later sources; the sheer quantity—several hundred survive[13]— is overwhelming, and their varying states of preservation pose difficulties of vexing complexity. Such a project will, I believe, require cooperation among many scholars and a great deal of time, perhaps spanning decades. I myself have experienced the difficulties and the immense amount of work required to assess the authenticity of a single letter, a testament attributed in some late sources to the fourth caliph and the first imam of the Shīʿites, ʿAlī ibn Abī Ṭālib (d. 40/660); in this case, research has shown that this document is a later forgery not written before the end of the third/ninth century.[14] In the present paper, I shall make a similar attempt, though on a much wider scale, to examine the corpus of letters attributed in the later sources to ʿAbd al-Ḥamīd ibn Yaḥyā al-Kātib (d. 132/750), who was, among other things, the secretary to the last Umayyad caliph, Marwān ibn Muḥammad (also d. 132/750).

---

[10] I am of course aware that there is a difference between admitting that a certain text existed at some early point, and assuming that this early text is reproduced, fully and unaltered, in some version that was transmitted later. But here I am speaking about a principle which has not received the attention it deserves from modern scholars. Textual authentication remains a must in my opinion.

[11] See Ibn al-Nadīm, *Fihrist*, 131. We shall return to the subject of Umayyad secretaries below.

[12] A good example of this is Josef van Ess' *Anfänge muslimischer Theologie* (Wiesbaden and Beirut, 1977), in which van Ess defends the authenticity and early dating of two first-century treatises against the Qadarīya.

[13] Cf. the letters collected in the works cited above in n. 2. As many new historical and literary sources have been published since the appearance of the standard anthologies, the number of early letters has grown even larger.

[14] Wadād al-Qāḍī, "An Early Fāṭimid Political Document", *SI* 48 (1978), 71–108.

'Abd al-Ḥamīd al-Kātib

'Abd al-Ḥamīd was a Muslim of non-Arab (probably Persian) descent, and was born in Iraq around 66/686.[15] He worked first as a teacher and then as a private tutor. Later, shortly before 86/705, he came to Damascus and in the capital of the caliphate began his formal training as a scribe at the Chancery, where he met Sālim Abū l-'Alā', an established secretary who became his teacher and father-in-law (or brother-in-law). Eventually 'Abd al-Ḥamīd was promoted, and by 106/725 at the latest he was already writing official letters on behalf of the Umayyad caliph Hishām ibn 'Abd al-Malik (105–25/723–42). In 114/732, he was appointed secretary to the Umayyad governor of Armenia and Ādharbayjān and the commander-in-chief of the Muslim army there, Marwān ibn Muḥammad, who was also a member of the Umayyad ruling family. He remained in the service of Marwān until 126/743, when Marwān hurried back to Syria after the outbreak of discord among members of the caliphal house. There Marwān was eventually given the allegiance of most men of influence and was declared caliph. 'Abd

[15]The best study published thus far on 'Abd al-Ḥamīd is that of Iḥsān 'Abbās in his *'Abd al-Ḥamīd ibn Yaḥyā al-kātib wa-mā tabaqqā min rasā'ilihi wa-rasā'il Sālim Abī l-'Alā'* (Amman, 1988), 25–60; also good is the study of Derek Latham, "'Abd al-Ḥamīd al-Kātib", in A.F.L. Beeston *et al.*, eds., *The Cambridge History of Arabic Literature: Arabic Literature to the End of the Umayyad Period* (Cambridge, 1983), 164–79. Other studies include, in chronological order, Muḥammad Kurd 'Alī, "'Abd al-Ḥamīd al-Kātib", *RAAD* 9 (1929), 513–31, 557–600; *idem*, "'Abd al-Ḥamīd al-Kātib", in his *Umarā' al-bayān*, I (Cairo, 1355/1937), 38–98; *GAL*, SI, 105; 'Umar Farrūkh, "'Abd al-Ḥamīd ibn Yaḥyā al-Kātib", in his *Al-Rasā'il wa-l-maqāmāt* (Beirut, 1361/1942), 6–17; Francesco Gabrieli, "Il kātib 'Abd al-Ḥamīd Ibn Yaḥyā e i primordi della epistolografia araba", *RANL* 8 (1957), 320–38; Shawqī Ḍayf, *Al-Fann wa-madhāhibuhu fī l-nathr al-'arabī*, 3rd ed. (Cairo, 1960), 113–21; H.A.R. Gibb, art. "'Abd al-Ḥamīd ibn Yaḥyā al-Kātib" in *EI*^{2}, I (Leiden, 1960), 65–66; *GAS*, I, 595; Muḥammad Nabīh Ḥijāb, *Balāghat al-kuttāb fī l-'aṣr al-'abbāsī* (Cairo, 1965), 65–68 and *passim*; 'Umar Farrūkh, *Ta'rīkh al-adab al-'arabī* (Beirut, 1965–72), I, 723–31; Anīs al-Maqdisī, *Taṭawwur al-asālīb al-nathrīya fī l-adab al-'arabī*, 5th ed. (Beirut, 1974), 146–67; Ghānim Jawād Riḍā, *Al-Rasā'il al-fannīya fī l-'aṣr al-islāmī ḥattā nihāyat al-'aṣr al-umawī* (Baghdad, 1978), *passim*; Hannelore Schönig, *Das Sendschreiben des 'Abdalḥamīd b. Yaḥyā (gest. 132/750) an den Kronprinzen 'Abdallāh b. Marwān II* (Stuttgart, 1985), pp. 1–3. In all the controversial points in the life of 'Abd al-Ḥamīd, as stated above, I follow the conclusions reached in the first chapter of my forthcoming *State and Statecraft in Early Islam*.

al-Ḥamīd went with him and became the head of the Chancery during his caliphate. This reign ended in 132/750 with the overthrow of Marwān, and with him, of the Umayyad dynasty itself. Both the caliph and his chief secretary were killed by the agents of the victorious new régime, that of the ʿAbbāsids.

Less than two centuries after his death ʿAbd al-Ḥamīd was already being declared the founder of Arabic prose,[16] and from that time until today this judgment has been accepted by literary historians.[17] ʿAbd al-Ḥamīd's style seems to have exerted a great influence on later prose writers in general, and on the secretaries of the Chancery under the ʿAbbāsids in particular, so much indeed that one of the greatest Arabic prose writers of the era, al-Jāḥiẓ (d. 255/869), counted ʿAbd al-Ḥamīd's letters among the few "textbooks" which the secretaries studied in al-Jāḥiẓ's time, about a century after ʿAbd al-Ḥamīd had died, in order to round out their professional secretarial education.[18] At that time the extant letters must have been quite numerous. ʿAbd al-Ḥamīd had spent at least a quarter of a century writing letters on behalf of Umayyad rulers, in addition to other personal letters which we know

[16]The first recorded and certifiable statement to this effect comes from Ibn ʿAbd Rabbih, who died in 328/949; see his *Al-ʿIqd al-farīd*, IV, 165.

[17]For early authorities who recognized ʿAbd al-Ḥamīd's founding rôle in Arabic prose, see Ibn al-Faqīh, *Mukhtaṣar kitāb al-buldān*, ed. M.J. de Goeje (Leiden, 1885), 194, quoting Jaʿfar ibn Yaḥyā al-Barmakī (d. 187/803); Ibn al-Nadīm, *Fihrist*, 131; al-Thaʿālibī, *Yatīmat al-dahr* (Cairo, AH 1375–77), III, 154–55, copied by Ibn Khallikān in his *Wafayāt al-aʿyān*, ed. Iḥsān ʿAbbās (Beirut, 1972–75), V, 104; al-Ḥusayn ibn ʿAlī al-Wazīr al-Maghribī, *Adab al-khawaṣṣ fī l-mukhtār min balāghat qabāʾil al-ʿarab*, I, ed. Ḥamad al-Jāsir (Riyadh, 1400/1980), 80; Ibn Khīra al-Mawāʿīnī, *Al-Rayḥān wa-l-rayʿān*, Fatih Camii Kütüphanesi (Istanbul), Ms. 3909, I, fol. 102 (quoted in ʿAbbās, *ʿAbd al-Ḥamīd*, 57 n. 3); also quoted in al-Qalqashandī, *Ṣubḥ al-aʿshā fī ṣināʿat al-inshā* (Cairo, 1331–38/1913–19), I, 282. Soon thereafter ʿAbd al-Ḥamīd's name became proverbial; see a number of lines of verse referring to him, cited in ʿAbbās, *ʿAbd al-Ḥamīd*, 19. Almost all modern historians of Arabic literature consider him the founder of Arabic prose; cf. the studies cited in n. 15 above.

[18]See al-Jāḥiẓ, "Risāla fī dhamm akhlāq al-kuttāb", in *Rasāʾil al-Jāḥiẓ*, ed. ʿAbd al-Salām Muḥammad Hārūn (Cairo, 1384–99/1964–79), II, 191–92. A century later, al-Masʿūdī described ʿAbd al-Ḥamīd's epistles as "collected and widely circulated letters which were taken as a model and emulated" (*lahu rasāʾilu majmūʿatun mutanāqalatun yuqtadā bihā wa-yuʿmalu ʿalayhā*); see his *Al-Tanbīh wa-l-ishrāf*, ed. ʿAbd Allāh Ismāʿīl al-Ṣāwī (Cairo, 1357/1938), 284.

he wrote. He had become very close to the Umayyads, especially to the caliph Marwān, and his loyalty to him in particular and to the Umayyad cause in general was beyond doubt. In the fourth/tenth century, these letters, or at least some of them, were available to the author of our above-mentioned bibliography, Ibn al-Nadīm; according to him, they ran to 1000 folios.[19] Not unexpectedly, most of them have now been lost; the latest estimate of the surviving corpus is that it amounts to about 50 folios only.[20]

'Abd al-Ḥamīd's Letters

Many of the extant letters have been in print in a Cairene collection of Arabic prose for almost a century now.[21] A widely circulated anthology of Arabic epistles published in Cairo in 1913 made them more readily available for researchers,[22] as did two subsequent Cairene anthologies published almost simultaneously in 1355/1937[23] and 1356/1937.[24] The letters were thus being increasingly discussed by modern Arab literary historians by the second decade of this century, though only a few Western scholars have made them the subject of their studies in the past four decades. It must be noted, however, that none of these publications has presented 'Abd al-Ḥamīd's (or other prose writers') epistles in a critically edited form: the published letters have been almost mechanical reproductions of the texts as they appear in manuscripts or printed sources, with no critical apparatus, or only a minimal one. One had to wait until 1988 for 'Abd al-Ḥamīd's letters to be published in a reliable edition by the pre-eminent scholar of Arabic literature, Iḥsān 'Abbās.[25]

[19] *Fihrist*, 131. This statement was copied by Ibn Kathīr in his *Al-Bidāya wa-l-nihāya* (Cairo, 1351–58/1932–39), X, 55. Al-Dhahabī, in his *Ta'rīkh al-islām* (Cairo, 1367/1947–48), V, 270, says that 'Abd al-Ḥamīd's letters fill 100 notebooks (*kurrāsa*). Such a notebook normally consisted of about ten folios; see 'Abbās, *'Abd al-Ḥamīd*, 63. Cf. also al-Mas'ūdī's statement, cited in the previous note.

[20] See 'Abbās, *'Abd al-Ḥamīd*, 64.

[21] Aḥmad Miftāḥ, *Miftāḥ al-afkār fī l-nathr al-mukhtār* (Cairo, AH 1316), 230–69.

[22] Muḥammad Kurd 'Alī, *Rasā'il al-bulaghā'* (Cairo, 1913), 173–226. I shall be using the third edition of 1365/1946.

[23] Kurd 'Alī, *Umarā' al-bayān*, I, 52–97.

[24] Ṣafwat, *Jamharat rasā'il al-'arab*, 432–38, 473–556, 568, 569–71.

[25] See above, n. 15.

The contribution of Iḥsān 'Abbās consists not only of a critical edition of 'Abd al-Ḥamīd's letters (and those of his teacher, Sālim), but also includes the addition of 17 new letters to our répertoire of 'Abd al-Ḥamīd's epistles, letters which 'Abbās discovered in manuscripts that no other scholar had previously consulted.[26] To this most valuable collection he has added the texts of three letters which he regards as probably from 'Abd al-Ḥamīd's hand, although not attributed to him in the sources (nos. 61–63), and the texts of short fragments and wise sayings—many of them brought to light for the first time—which the sources explicitly assign to the authorship of 'Abd al-Ḥamīd (nos. 39–60). He introduces this corpus with a lengthy essay offering innumerable insights into a variety of topics that go beyond the actual texts, not the least important of which touch on early Arabic prose in general. What he has not addressed, however, is the "authenticity problem" of 'Abd al-Ḥamīd's letters. In addressing this question here, I do so by way of complementing his work.

Perhaps the best starting point for pursuing this problem is provided by a general overview of the letters to be examined.[27] Setting aside the letters not explicitly attributed to 'Abd al-Ḥamīd in the sources, they consist of 60 pieces, to which two others can be added,[28] and amount to over 100 printed pages. Of these 62 pieces, two are definitely oral sayings (nos. 61 and 62), with the probable addition of a third one (no. 52), and these must be excluded from consideration here. Also excluded will be nos. 20, 40, 43, 48, and 59, for authentication reasons to which I shall return below in the section on problems of attribution. The remaining 54 pieces include two which are explicitly referred to in the sources as *tawqī'*, written signatory comments (nos. 41 and 60); they are hence not "letters" strictly speaking, although—like letters—

[26] These are the *Al-'Aṭā' al-jazīl fī kashf ghaṭā' al-tarsīl* by Abū l-Qāsim Aḥmad ibn Muḥammad al-Quḍā'ī al-Ishbīlī, known as al-Balawī (nos. 1–15), and the *Al-Tadhkira l-ḥamdūnīya* by Abū l-Ma'ālī Muḥammad ibn al-Ḥasan Ibn Ḥamdūn (nos. 16 and 17).

[27] For a list of these letters, see the Appendix to this paper.

[28] I came upon these two pieces during my own work on 'Abd al-Ḥamīd. The first letter is to be found in al-Balādhurī, *Ansāb al-ashrāf*, III, ed. 'Abd al-'Azīz al-Dūrī (Wiesbaden and Beirut, 1978), 164; and the second is in Ibn Nubāta, *Sarḥ al-'uyūn sharḥ risālat Ibn Zaydūn*, ed. Muḥammad Abū l-Faḍl Ibrāhīm (Cairo, 1383/1964), 239.

they are addressed to specific individuals. Again, these will not be considered here.

From the viewpoint of completeness (or lack thereof), the remaining documents fall into three categories: complete letters, fragments of letters, and short extracts. The complete letters are considered as such either because their completeness is textually attested at the beginnings and ends of the letters,[29] or because their style at beginning and end, as well as the development of the subject matter, points to this conclusion.[30] The fragmentary letters either bear textual testimony to

[29]All these letters begin with the same standard formula *ammā ba'd*, meaning "hereafter", i.e. "after thanking God, praising His Prophet, and greeting the addressee". They end in either one of two formulae: *wa-l-salām*, "and peace", a short form of "and the peace, mercy, and blessings of God be upon you", as stated in full at the end of no. 35; or *wa-kataba sanata*..., "and he (i.e. the secretary) wrote [this letter] in the year...", followed by the date. The former ending is used in nos. 2–5, 7, 9–15, and 22, and the latter appears in no. 8. Letter no. 21 bears both *wa-l-salām*... and *wa-kataba*... at its end.

[30]Some of these letters bear textual evidence at their beginnings through the formula *ammā ba'd* (as in the previous note), but their endings are inferred through the usage of concluding invocations, admonitions, or religious citations, as in nos. 1, 17, 19, and 38. Other letters manifest textual evidence at their ends through the usage of the formula *wa-l-salām*, but their beginnings are inferred from their emphatically introductory statements of purpose, as in no. 29, in which the letter begins with: "Verily the Commander of the Faithful has written to you..." (*fa-inna amīra l-mu'minīna kataba ilayka*), clearly indicating the beginning of a letter; and no. 31, where the letter begins with: "Verily the first matter which the people of fidelity took up..." (*fa-inna awlā mā i'tazama 'alayhi dhawū l-ikhā'*...). The completeness of the remaining complete letters may be inferred from a variety of stylistic considerations. No. 6 begins with a sentence which clearly indicates that it is the beginning of a letter, since it speaks of the arrival of the addressee's letter which the author is now going to answer (*wāfā kitābuka*...) and ends with the citation of a tradition of the Prophet, "There is no power or strength save in God, Most-High, Almighty" (*wa-lā ḥawla wa-lā quwwata illā bi-llāhi l-'alīyi l-'aẓīm*—cf. the end of no. 8). No. 23 begins with an invocation to God that He should long keep the Commander of the Faithful well (*aṭāla llāhu baqā'a amīri l-mu'minīna*...) and ends with a formulaic religious expression of thanks (*wa-l-ḥamdu li-llāhi 'alā kulli ḥāl*). No. 30 opens with an emphatic statement of purpose (*inna llāha bi-ni'matihi 'alayya*...) and ends with a concluding explanatory sentence (*fa-innī innamā ataqallabu fī ni'amihi*...). No. 33 begins with an emphatic statement of purpose (*inna llāha amta'a amīra l-mu'minīn*...) and ends with two successive concluding citations from the Qur'ān: Sūrat al-Fātiḥa (1), v. 2, "Praise be to God, Lord of the Worlds" ([*f*]*a-l-ḥamdu li-llāhi rabbi l-'ālamīn*), and Sūrat al-Baqara (2), v. 156, "We are God's and unto

their fragmentary nature,[31] or suggest this in that their texts do not constitute a meaningful whole—in most cases there is no indication that their beginnings are the beginnings of the original letters from which they were copied, and in most cases their ends are not necessarily the ends of the original letters.[32] The category of short extracts comprises

him we shall return" (*innā li-llāhi wa-innā ilayhi rāji'ūn*). No. 36 is a brief straightforward letter of recommendation; and no. 37 opens with a statement of purpose (*naẓartu fī l-amri lladhī u'ātibuka fīhi 'alayhi*...) and ends with a gentle admonition (*fa-mā awlāka bi-l-ta'ahhudi li-ma'ūnatin*...).

[31]There is only one letter, no. 32, which explicitly concedes that it is fragmentary. It has a clear beginning with *ammā ba'd* and an inferred end with a long invocation. However, in the middle of its most complete version, the source preserving the epistle interrupts its text with this statement: "and he said in another section of it" (*wa-qāla fī faṣlin ākhara minhā*), meaning that there has been an omission.

[32]The clearest set of letters of this kind is comprised of the *taḥmīd*, or *te deum*, genre: nos. 24 (two cycles), 25 (one cycle), 26 (five cycles), and 27 (one cycle). It is reasonably certain that the fragments we have represent the beginnings of these letters, and in the cases of nos. 26 and 27 this is conclusively established by the fact that they begin with the formula *ammā ba'd*. Due to the nature of this genre, however, it is almost impossible to tell whether we have a complete letter or not; each consists of one or a series of cycles, with no definitive conclusion whatsoever. One never knows when the cycles originally ended, or indeed how they could have ended. Nos. 16, 18, and 34 bear a different kind of evidence for their fragmentariness: these all begin with sentences introduced by particles the referents of which must have been given earlier. In the first two, the letters begin with causal sentences (*fa-fī ṭā'ati l-a'immati fī l-islāmi...muhimmu kulli ni'ma*..., and *fa-inna l-fitnata tastashrifu bi-ahlihā*...). These sentences are in effect nothing but "proofs" advanced by the author in defense of "propositions" which he must have postulated earlier in the letters; one may thus conclude that at least the beginnings of these two letters are missing (it is difficult to tell whether their preserved ends are the actual ends of the original letters). In fact, no. 16 is introduced by the author of the only source to preserve the letter, Ibn Ḥamdūn, with the following sentence: "And *from* (*wa-min*) a letter of his (i.e. 'Abd al-Ḥamīd's) about civil discord". Such a sentence normally means that the author of the source has "selected" a part of a letter. This is not, however, a conclusive proof of its fragmentary state, for Ibn Ḥamdūn uses a similar expression to introduce a complete letter (no. 17), the beginning of which is clearly preserved since it opens with *ammā ba'd*. Similarly, no. 34 begins with an adverb, "until" (*ḥattā*), and the first verb to appear thereafter carries a pronoun with an unknown referent (*a'naqū*). This clearly means that in the original letter there was some material preceding the beginning of the passage that survives today. This fragment is most probably its last part, since it ends

short sentences of a gnomic nature: wisdom sayings on ethics, professional secretaryship, and literary criticism, as well as admonitions, long similes, and metaphorical images. They are mere "selections" from some written material of 'Abd al-Ḥamīd's, almost certainly letters.[33]

The pieces vary greatly in length. The short extracts range between a few words and two and a half lines; the fragmentary letters are generally not long, as short as three and a half lines (no. 28) and at any rate not longer than one page and a half (no. 16); a few of the complete letters are short (no. 36 is in one and a half lines, no. 33 in five and a half lines), but most are longer (no. 23 is in three pages, no. 35 in five pages, and no. 21 in forty).

The subjects with which these letters deal vary, although one prominent feature is that most of them have something to do with Umayyad caliphs, other Umayyad figures, or with state matters. Setting aside the short extracts, for which the nature of the original letter-sources cannot be identified, only four of the other 37 pieces are of a purely personal nature and mention nothing pertaining to public office or matters of the state and its personalities: no. 2, written to a close friend of 'Abd al-Ḥamīd's and wondering about the change in this friend's attitude towards him; no. 9, also written to a friend, on the occasion of the birth of 'Abd al-Ḥamīd's first-born son; no. 31, written to a friend and depicting the characteristics of fraternity; and no. 37, in which 'Abd al-Ḥamīd gently rebukes a friend of his.

To be sure, there are other letters which are also personal, in the sense that 'Abd al-Ḥamīd wrote them in his own name and not on behalf of any official of the state, but they invariably reflect some connection with his office or his sovereigns in the state. No. 5, for example, is a

with a citation from the Qur'ān. By contrast, no. 15 (in the version printed in the text, not in the footnote; see below) represents the first part of a letter, as it begins with the formula *ammā ba'd*. Its preserved end, however, is almost certainly not its original end, for after enumerating a string of fifteen other qualities, it stops at one of the qualities required in a prospective good slave woman. Furthermore, when one compares the end of this version with that of the other (i.e. the one in the footnote), it will be observed that in the latter there is an additional sentence which rounds the letter up, contrary to the version at hand. An even clearer indication of fragmentariness is found in no. 28, neither the beginning nor the end of which may be discerned.

[33]These cases, nos. 39, 42, 44–47, 49–51, and 53–58, are self-explanatory.

letter of condolence to an unidentified addressee, but its place in the source where it appears, al-Balawī's *Al-'Aṭā' al-jazīl*, indicates that the addressee was a member of the Umayyad house. No. 10, written from Armenia to a friend of 'Abd al-Ḥamīd's, talks about the advantages of private life and the disadvantages of being in public office, but goes on to describe the actual living conditions of its author in Armenia with the commander of the army, the military, the bureaucracy, and so forth. No. 14 is addressed to a certain person who had provoked the anger of the caliph (Marwān ibn Muḥammad) and had thus repeatedly been pestering 'Abd al-Ḥamīd with letters requesting the latter's assistance for a reconciliation with the caliph. No. 30 is a letter addressed to the caliph Marwān in which the author reveals that he has become needy. No. 32 is a farewell letter written by 'Abd al-Ḥamīd to his family shortly before his death. Although it is a highly personal letter, one can still detect echoes of public life in its hints of the dangers threatening him and the possibility of his capture by the enemy (i.e. the 'Abbāsids). No. 36, a short letter of recommendation, could not have been written unless its author was an influential public figure. As for no. 35, this is his famous "Letter to the Secretaries," in which 'Abd al-Ḥamīd advises the secretaries what to study and tells them how to behave in public, especially with their sovereigns. It draws its great power from the fact that its author was himself a secretary in the state, a civil servant.

In a similar way, two other "personal" letters of 'Abd al-Ḥamīd which should have had nothing to do with public affairs, since they are descriptive in nature, still receive their (genuine or affected) public touch. These are no. 6, in which 'Abd al-Ḥamīd describes the flooding of the Euphrates, and no. 23, in which he describes a hunting trip. Both letters are addressed to the "Commander of the Faithful".

The remaining 24 letters are all official letters: 'Abd al-Ḥamīd wrote them either on behalf of the "Commander of the Faithful", without indicating which caliph is meant, or on behalf of the caliph Hishām, or on behalf of Marwān, first in his capacity as the governor of Armenia and Ādharbayjān, then in his capacity as caliph. There are two letters of unspecified caliphal authority: no. 7, in which the caliph instructs 'Abd al-'Azīz ibn 'Umar ibn Hubayra, possibly an aid of his,[34] to buy a slave

[34]I have not been able to identify this man. His father, 'Umar ibn Hubayra,

woman for him—I believe this letter was written on behalf of Hishām;[35] and no. 22, in which the caliph instructs a governor of his (or all the governors in the empire, in which case the letter would be a public proclamation) to prohibit the playing of chess in his/their domain(s)—I estimate that this letter was written on behalf of Marwān.[36]

There are four letters written on behalf of Hishām. No. 11 is a proclamation from the caliph to his governors upon his performance of the pilgrimage in 106/725,[37] and no. 12 is a proclamation on the occasion of the beginning of the month of Ramaḍān.[38] In no. 29, which is addressed to the governor of Yemen, Yūsuf ibn 'Umar al-Thaqafī,[39] the caliph reports the good tidings that he is well (perhaps after an illness, or after a plague epidemic?[40]) and asks the governor to read

---

however, was a well-known governor for the Umayyads. When Hishām became caliph in 105/723, he was governor of Iraq. Hishām replaced him with Khālid al-Qasrī, who imprisoned him; but 'Umar was able to flee from jail and make his peace with Hishām through the mediation of a member of the Umayyad house. He died around 110/728. See Khayr al-Dīn al-Ziriklī, *Al-A'lām*, 4th ed. (Beirut, 1979), V, 68–69.

[35]This agrees with the conclusion of 'Abbās (*'Abd al-Ḥamīd*, 67). Hishām was particularly known for his interest in and acquisition of slave women; see 'Abd al-Majīd Muḥammad Ṣāliḥ al-Kabīsī, *'Aṣr Hishām ibn 'Abd al-Malik* (Baghdad, 1975), 81.

[36]Here I would differ with 'Abbās' conclusion (*'Abd al-Ḥamīd*, 70) for reasons which are too complicated to be raised here, but which I hope to discuss on another occasion.

[37]Hishām's pilgrimage in 106/725 was the last by an Umayyad caliph; see Khalīfa ibn Khayyāṭ, *Ta'rīkh*, ed. Akram Ḍiyā' al-'Umarī (Beirut and Damascus, 1397/1977), 336, 360 (AH 106); al-Ṭabarī, *Ta'rīkh*, II, 1482; al-Maqrīzī, *Al-Tibr al-masbūk fī man ḥajja min al-mulūk* (Cairo, n.d.), 35–36. Cf. 'Abbās, *'Abd al-Ḥamīd*, 67.

[38]This may be inferred from the nature of the letter, which is comparable to other letters of this genre that go back to the time of Hishām. See 'Abbās, *'Abd al-Ḥamīd*, 67.

[39]Yūsuf was Hishām's governor of Yemen from 106/724 until 121/738; see al-Ziriklī, *A'lām*, VIII, 243.

[40]It is not impossible that the "well-being" of the caliph should have been advertized following one of the plagues which ravaged Syria during Hishām's caliphate. We know from several sources that he used to flee to the *bādiya* at such times: see, for example, al-Balādhurī, *Ansāb al-ashrāf*, Süleymaniye Kütüphanesi (Istanbul), Ms. Reisülküttap no. 598, fols. 123v, 128r; al-Ṭabarī, *Ta'rīkh*, II, 1737–38; Yāqūt, *Mu'jam al-buldān* (Beirut, 1374–76/1955–57), II, 47a; Ṣalāḥ al-Dīn al-Munajjid,

his letter aloud to the people so that they will rejoice at the news. One imagines that the two aforementioned proclamations (nos. 11 and 12) were also read to the public in all parts of the empire. Then there is no. 15, in which the addressee is asked to buy Berber or Maghribī slave women for the caliph. One version of this letter specifies neither the sender nor the addressee, but the other (more complex) version specifies the sender as the caliph Hishām and the addressee as the governor of Ifrīqiya (i.e. modern Tunisia and eastern Algeria).

The letters written by ʿAbd al-Ḥamīd on behalf of Marwān are the most numerous. Seven belong certainly to the "Armenian period". Three of these are addressed to Hishām: a letter of condolence on the occasion of the death of one of Hishām's infants (no. 28), another upon the death of Hishām's favorite concubine (no. 33), and a letter about the spread of the Qadarīya politico-theological group in the army and their successful proselytizing in Armenia (no. 13). The other epistles from this period are *taḥmīd*, or *te deum*, letters, written presumably on the various occasions of the conquests achieved by the Muslims against non-Muslims (nos. 24–27).[41] It is probable that these letters were also proclamations meant to be read publicly in the various parts of the empire, since no specific addressees are mentioned in them.

The letters which belong to the "caliphal period" of Marwān's career are of varying character. It is clear that all the letters on obedience (no. 17), civil discord in general (nos. 16 and 18), the civil disobedience of

---

Muʿjam Banī Umayya (Beirut, 1970), 185. His welfare during these disappearances must have been a matter of concern, especially in light of the unsettled affairs of the empire in those days. The date of the letter must fall sometime between 106/724 (the year of Yūsuf ibn ʿUmar's appointment as governor of Yemen) and the end of 113/731 (the last year ʿAbd al-Ḥamīd was in the service of Hishām before departing for Armenia). Within this range there were two plagues in Syria, in 106/734–35 and in 108–109/726–727. The second of these plagues is recorded by Theophanes, *The Chronicle of Theophanes*, trans. Harry Turtledove (Philadelphia, 1982), 96. As for the first, a German pilgrim's account speaks of the devastation of Syria and specifically states that he could not see "Murmumni" (i.e. the caliph Hishām, the *Amīr al-muʾminīn*, "Commander of the Faithful") because the latter had fled to the desert; see Willibald, *Hodoeporicon* I.10; ed. Titus Tobler in his *Itinera Hierosolymitana et descriptiones Terrae Sanctae*, I (Geneva, 1879), 268–69. I am grateful to Dr. Lawrence Conrad for drawing my attention to the possible connection between this letter and the plague.

[41] See ʿAbbās, *ʿAbd al-Ḥamīd*, 68.

particular rebels, whether identified by name or not (nos. 19 and 34), and the major rebellion in Khurāsān which was to culminate with the death of Marwān and the demise of the Umayyad caliphate, i.e. the 'Abbāsid underground movement (nos. 8 and 38), belong to this period. To this period also belongs no. 1, a letter in which the caliph gently rebukes his governor of Iraq, Ibn Hubayra, for mistreating a relative of his. Of a more intimate nature are 'Abd al-Ḥamīd's letter on behalf of Marwān to a brother of Marwān's informing this relative of the death of another member of the family, possibly Marwān's uncle or son (no. 4), and his letter to Marwān's son and crown prince, 'Ubayd Allāh (or 'Abd Allāh) ibn Marwān, on the occasion of his marital problems with his wife, 'Ā'isha, the daughter of the late caliph Hishām. The crowning letter of this period is 'Abd al-Ḥamīd's longest known epistle: the testament he wrote to the same crown prince in 129/747, advising him on all matters of state—ethical, political, religious, and above all military—when 'Ubayd Allāh was heading to fight a rebel from the Khārijites (no. 21).[42]

The Authenticity Question

Like all surviving early Arabic letters, 'Abd al-Ḥamīd's letters have been preserved not in contemporary works, but rather in later sources, the earliest of which was compiled by an author who died in 280/893. These sources—in chronological order and excluding those which reproduce only some of his short extracts, which cannot be examined as letters—can be listed as follows:

1. *Al-Manẓūm wa-l-manthūr* by Aḥmad Ibn Abī Ṭāhir Ṭayfūr (d. 280/893). This author has preserved twelve letters by 'Abd al-Ḥamīd, both complete and fragmentary, official and personal (nos. 9, 21–31).

2. *Kitāb al-wuzarā' wa-l-kuttāb* by Muḥammad ibn 'Abdūs al-Jahshiyārī (d. 331/942). Two letters are preserved in this work, one complete (no. 35) and one with an omission in the middle (no. 32).

[42] *Ibid*, 68–69.

3. The anonymous *Ta'rīkh al-khulafā'* of the fifth/eleventh century. This work reproduces a part of no. 32.

4. *Al-Tadhkira al-ḥamdūnīya* by Abū l-Ma'ālī Muḥammad ibn al-Ḥasan Ibn Ḥamdūn (d. 562/1166). This text has preserved five letters of 'Abd al-Ḥamīd's, both complete and fragmentary, all of which, with the exception of his "Letter to the Secretaries", are official (nos. 16–18, 34, 35). It is to be noted that two of these letters (nos. 16 and 17) appear solely in this book, and another (no. 34) appears here for the first time.

5. *Akhbār al-nisā'* by Abū l-Faraj Ibn al-Jawzī (d. 597/1200). The book itself is lost, but one of 'Abd al-Ḥamīd's letters (no. 15) has been copied from it by Muḥammad ibn Aḥmad al-Tijānī in his *Riḥla* (*Tuḥfat al-'arūs wa-nuzhat al-nufūs*).

6. The *Al-'Aṭā' al-jazīl fī kashf ghaṭā' al-tarsīl* by Abū l-Qāsim Aḥmad ibn Muḥammad al-Quḍā'ī al-Ishbīlī, known as al-Balawī (d. 657/1258). He has preserved the largest number of 'Abd al-Ḥamīd's letters to be found in one source so far: fifteen letters, both personal and official, all but two of which are complete (nos. 1–15). It is also to be noted that only one of the letters recorded here is preserved elsewhere (no. 9), and that another (no. 15), though preserved elsewhere, appears in a different version here.

7. *Wafayāt al-a'yān* by Ibn Khallikān (d. 681/1282), preserving one short but complete letter (no. 36).

8. The *'Unwān al-murqiṣāt wa-l-muṭribāt* and the *Al-Muqtaṭaf min azāhir al-ṭuraf*, both by Ibn Sa'īd al-Maghribī al-Andalusī (d. 685/1286), reproduce the first and longest version we have of no. 38.

9. The *Ghurar al-khaṣā'iṣ* by Muḥammad ibn Ibrāhīm al-Waṭwāṭ (d. 718/1318) copied the same short letter found in the *Wafayāt*, no. 36.

10. The same letter (no. 36) is also to be found in the *Nihāyat al-arab* by al-Nuwayrī (d. 733/1332).

11. Jamāl al-Dīn Ibn Nubāta al-Miṣrī (d. 768/1366) recorded in his *Sarḥ al-'uyūn sharḥ risālat Ibn Zaydūn* five letters, both complete and fragmentary, official and personal (nos. 32–34, 36, 38). Again it is to be noted here that one of the letters appears solely in this book (no. 33).

12. The *Al-Bidāya wa-l-nihāya fī l-ta'rīkh* by Abū l-Fidā Ibn Kathīr (d. 774/1372) has preserved the same short letter already mentioned several times (no. 36).

13. The well-known *Muqaddima* (Prolegomena) of Ibn Khaldūn (d. 808/1406) has preserved the text of the "Letter to the Secretaries" (no. 35).

14. *Ṣubḥ al-a'shā fī ṣinā'at al-inshā* by Abū l-'Abbās al-Qalqashandī (d. 821/1418) has preserved four letters by 'Abd al-Ḥamīd (nos. 18, 19, 21, and 35), in addition to another, problematic letter (no. 20) to be discussed below, since it appears in an earlier source with a different attribution.

In considering this list, four problems arise for one's attention almost immediately. The first is that, as mentioned above, the oldest source recording any of 'Abd al-Ḥamīd's letters dates back only to the latter half of the third/ninth century. As we know that 'Abd al-Ḥamīd wrote his letters roughly between 106/725 (at the latest) and 732/750, this means that there is well over a century between 'Abd al-Ḥamīd's death and the time at which we have exact record of his letters (the short extracts excluded). The second problem is that more than half his letters surfaced only much later, in the fifth/eleventh century, with Ibn Ḥamdūn and Ibn al-Jawzī (authors nos. 4 and 5 in the above list), in the seventh/fourteenth century with al-Balawī and Ibn Sa'īd al-Maghribī (nos. 6 and 8 in the list), and even in the following century with Ibn Nubāta (no. 11 in the list). The third is that there is more than one version for some of these letters (nos. 5 and 6 in the list), and the fourth is that there is at least one problematic letter attributed to a hand other than that of 'Abd al-Ḥamīd (no. 14 in the list). For purposes of clarity, I shall handle each of these problems separately.

The Problem of Unattested Early Transmission

The first problem strikes directly to the heart of the authenticity question: it requires that we account for a long period of silence—over a century, and in the case of some letters longer—with no direct attestation of 'Abd al-Ḥamīd's letters, and that we eventually come to grips with the question of possible forgery. While it is true that no actual texts of 'Abd al-Ḥamīd's letters have come down to us from this period, this could in principle be explained by arguing that there is no earlier attestation because the early works in which these letters were recorded have not survived. The weakness of this argument, however, is that it bears upon general possibilities rather than specific cases and fails to address the possibility of forgery. That is, we need not only to determine that genuine letters by 'Abd al-Ḥamīd were in circulation in the years immediately following his death, but also to adduce evidence showing that these documents specifically included the texts that survive today. Though this is no easy task, given the limitations imposed by the nature and extent of the materials in hand, one can still find ample evidence that 'Abd al-Ḥamīd's letters are authentic.

During the first crucial century, and some decades between 'Abd al-Ḥamīd's death in 132/750 and the time when Ibn Ṭayfūr compiled his *Manẓūm*, let us say around 250/864, one does in fact find comments and anecdotes which are extremely informative and important for their bearing on the authenticity problem. Setting aside those reports which are difficult or impossible to verify (and these are quite numerous), what we have are some hard facts.

The first is that at least three of the most influential first secretaries and viziers who worked for the nascent 'Abbāsid state had been connected professionally with 'Abd al-Ḥamīd, in that they were trained by him, or by his "administration" of the Chancery, under the Umayyads. He was in a sense their teacher, and at least one of them expressed a great deal of admiration for him.[43] The second is that

[43]These are the famous Khālid ibn Barmak (d. 163/780), Ya'qūb ibn Dāwūd (d. 187/803), who was the secretary and vizier of the caliph al-Mahdī, and Aḥmad ibn Yūsuf (d. 213/828), the secretary and vizier of the caliph al-Ma'mūn. See 'Abbās, *'Abd al-Ḥamīd*, 57.

eight of 'Abd al-Ḥamīd's sons were "drafting letters" (*yuḥarrirūna l-kutub*) in the Chancery during 'Abd al-Ḥamīd's lifetime, which means that they were being trained as secretaries there.[44] One of them at least, Ismā'īl, actually did become a famous secretary in the 'Abbāsid state, and was very proud of his father's achievement; indeed, he was a source of information about his father for the secretaries in early 'Abbāsid times.[45] The third is that one of 'Abd al-Ḥamīd's (presumably youngest) sons, Dāwūd, lived a very long life which must have extended to the end of the second/eighth century, if not later, since he survived long enough to meet al-Balādhurī, the renowned Muslim historian who died in 279/892.[46] The fourth is that two of 'Abd al-Ḥamīd's great-great-grandsons were recruited from al-Raqqa, in the province of al-Jazīra, where his family had settled, to work as secretaries in Egypt for the founder of the Ṭūlūnid dynasty (a local vassal dynasty to the 'Abbāsids) in the middle of the third/ninth century; one of these two descendants, Ḥasan ibn (al-)Muhājir, rose to join a small élite of influential state employees in the Ṭūlūnid régime and is reported to have been a staunch defender of his great-great-grandfather's achievement.[47]

---

[44] This information appears in what is probably the earliest extant book on secretaries, the *Kitāb al-kuttāb* of 'Abd Allāh ibn 'Abd al-'Azīz al-Baghdādī (d. after 255/869), published with a study by Dominique Sourdel, "Le 'Livre des Secretaires' de 'Abdallāh al-Baghdādī", *BEO* 14 (1952–54), 148. In the case of this particular sentence, one may note the impact that a faulty reading (or what seems to have been a slight oversight) can have on the meaning of a statement and hence the conclusions that may be drawn from it. Sourdel's edition has it that 'Abd al-Ḥamīd went to the Chancery one day, *fa-ra'ā fīhi thamāniyata awlādin yuḥarrirūna l-kutub*, i.e. "and saw in it (that is, in the Chancery) eight youths drafting letters". But upon checking this sentence in the Istanbul Ms. of the work (Fatih Camii Kütüphanesi, no. 5036), I found the manuscript crystal clear in its reading *fa-ra'ā lahu*.... This small difference in the preposition and pronoun changes the whole meaning, for what al-Baghdādī actually wrote was: "and he saw eight children *of his* drafting letters"!

[45] On 'Abd al-Ḥamīd's son Ismā'īl, see al-Baghdādī, *Kitāb al-kuttāb*, 149; Ibn Khallikān, *Wafayāt al-a'yān*, III, 231.

[46] See al-Balādhurī, *Ansāb al-ashrāf*, III, 54, 123; cf. also 164.

[47] For the "Banū (l-)Muhājir" or "Banū Abī (l-)Muhājir", see al-Jahshiyārī, *Al-Wuzarā' wa-l-kuttāb*, 82–83; al-Mas'ūdī, *Al-Tanbīh wa-l-ishrāf*, 284; al-Balawī, *Sīrat Aḥmad ibn Ṭūlūn*, ed. Muḥammad Kurd 'Alī (Damascus, 1356/1937), *passim*; Ibn Sa'īd al-Maghribī, *Al-Mughrib fī ḥilā l-maghrib: Sīrat Aḥmad ibn Ṭūlūn* (*Fragmente aus dem Muġrib des Ibn Sa'īd*), ed. Karl Vollers (Berlin, 1894), *passim*.

The fifth is that at some moment in time under the early 'Abbāsids, the secretaries in the state administration in the capital, who had developed a strong sense of group solidarity, were highly respectful of 'Abd al-Ḥamīd and his work and, as a result, cared for one of his younger sons.[48] The sixth is al-Jāḥiẓ's statement, already mentioned above, that in the latter half of the second/eighth century or the first half of the following century, the secretaries in the 'Abbāsid state were using 'Abd al-Ḥamīd's letters as a kind of textbook, a pedagogical model, in order to become good secretaries. The seventh is to be drawn from the sentence with which a late second/eighth or early third/ninth century author introduced the text of 'Abd al-Ḥamīd's famous "Letter to the Secretaries" (no. 35). It reads as follows: "I have found, in the hand of Maymūn ibn Hārūn, a letter he (i.e. 'Abd al-Ḥamīd) wrote to the secretaries...."[49] Although I have not been able to identify this "Maymūn ibn Hārūn", it is clear from the context that he was a copyist, scribe, or perhaps even a secretary, who was neither a contemporary of nor a person known in any remote way to the author who mentioned him, but was active at some earlier, distant time; one could estimate that he lived, at the very latest, in the first half of the third/ninth century, if not earlier.

But perhaps the most important report we have is one indicating that already in the lifetime of 'Abd al-Ḥamīd's son, Ismā'īl, in early 'Abbāsid times, at least one person possessed a copy of 'Abd al-Ḥamīd's letters (or some of them) written in a large notebook (*daftar kabīr*). This unique piece of information appears in a story related in al-Baghdadī's *Kuttāb*, which states that when Yaḥyā ibn Khālid ibn Barmak (d. 190/805), the secretary and vizier to the caliph al-Manṣūr (136–58/753–74), heard about Ismā'īl's comments concerning his father, he called for him. He showed Ismā'īl a large notebook and asked him whether he knew what it was. Ismā'īl thought it was a copy of the Qur'ān. Yaḥyā answered: "No, they are the letters of your father. We never seek an argument in support of sovereignty without finding that your father had preceded us in adducing it".[50] Now, this report

[48]See al-Baghdādī, *Kitāb al-kuttāb*, 149.
[49]Al-Jahshiyārī, *Al-Wuzarā' wa-l-kuttāb*, 73.
[50]Al-Baghdādī, *Kitāb al-kuttāb*, 149

is certainly not beyond doubt, especially in view of the "theatricality" in which its last part is cast. On the other hand, it cannot be simply ignored in its totality, and hence what one should ask is whether it is nothing but a forgery. Such a forgery must serve a motive. What can this motive be? It could be asserted that the report is meant to elevate the image of 'Abd al-Ḥamīd as a skillful stylist-propagandist; as he was probably of Persian origin, or so the argument would go, the persophile secretaries of the day would benefit from this elevated image. But the secretaries stood in no need of engaging in such an exercise. They were mainly Persian by origin, and they believed they were competent civil servants; but above all, they were powerful government figures who were quite secure in their positions. Indeed, the persophile secretaries were perhaps never as mighty as they were in the first decades of 'Abbāsid rule—until the fall of the Barmakids in 188/803. As for the claim that the report insinuates Sasanian administrative superiority, as part of the Shu'ūbīya movement in which state secretaries under the 'Abbāsids were sometimes active participants, it is to be noted that the Shu'ūbīya at the time of al-Manṣūr was not yet a ripe movement—strictly speaking, one could not speak of it as a movement at this early stage. Furthermore, looking at the report from the Umayyad vs. 'Abbāsid angle, it would be quite strange—indeed, astonishing—to find praise directed at the bitter enemies of the ruling régime. It is true that 'Abd al-Ḥamīd was the writer of his public, propagandist letters, but it was the Umayyads who ordered him to write what was appropriate from their viewpoint. He wrote it; they signed it; it became their "image" for their subjects, and for posterity too. And this does not serve the nascent 'Abbāsid cause, nor does it, perhaps, help them justify some of the failings of the dynasty they overthrew, since their propaganda ("arguments in support of sovereignty") had been exhausted by that dynasty, according to the report.

There is another point in this report which requires some reflection, namely the fact that 'Abd al-Ḥamīd's collection of letters is taken for a *muṣḥaf*, a word which is normally used for a copy of the Qur'ān. Now, the only thing that the text explicitly states about this collection is that it is of large size (*daftar kabīr*). This size must then be the basic reason for the ensuing confusion about it: it is as big as a copy of the Qur'ān. To draw other conclusions from this assumed comparison between 'Abd al-Ḥamīd's collection of letters and the Qur'ān would be, in my opinion, risky and textually unjustifiable (e.g. suggesting that 'Abd al-Ḥamīd's words were as good as those of the Qur'ān). In spite of that, I am tempted to believe that we do not stretch the text too far when we see in the juxtaposition of the two an indication of the visual status of both "notebooks": that they were well-bound—but this too is speculative. If it is true, however, it may indicate a high degree of care in preserving 'Abd al-Ḥamīd's letters. In view of the above, this report, if taken to be a later creation, strikes me as one devoid of motive and serving no particular purpose. It appears rather naive, with a simple, even crude ring to it; and for these reasons I tend to believe that it is not forged. Assuming that it is in fact genuine, we can conclude that at least some of 'Abd al-Ḥamīd's letters did physically exist shortly after his death. The fact that the person who possessed a copy of them is reported to have been Yaḥyā ibn Khālid ibn Barmak in particular makes the story all the more plausible, since Yaḥyā was the son of one of 'Abd al-Ḥamīd's students,[51] which brings us back to the consideration with which I opened this section—the continuation of 'Abd al-Ḥamīd's memory as a distinguished prose writer among his pupils.

All this is highly informative apropos of the survival of 'Abd al-Ḥamīd's letters in the period between his death and the time when his letters are first textually attested. The main point illustrated by these facts is that the physical preservation of the "'Abd al-Ḥamīd legacy", in terms of his professional literacy work, was not adversely affected by his death, but rather was carried on shortly after his death and continued up until the time of the third/ninth century (and later) scholars who copied parts of it into their own books and hence made it available to us. For one thing, this legacy was in the hands of individuals who were extremely loyal to 'Abd al-Ḥamīd (his numerous sons, grandsons, and great-great-grandsons[52]), persons who appreciated and identified with him (early 'Abbāsid secretaries), or those who acknowledged the value of his work without necessarily promoting it, possibly for political

---

[51] See above, n. 43.

[52] For a genealogical table of 'Abd al-Ḥamīd's family, see the first chapter of my forthcoming *State and Statecraft in Early Islam*.

reasons (the influential first ʿAbbāsid secretaries and viziers, ʿAbd al-Ḥamīd's former pupils). Secondly, as some of ʿAbd al-Ḥamīd's progeny lived long enough to be contemporaries of the early authors who included his letters in their compilations, such documents were readily available to later authors. It is particularly interesting to observe that the first author known to have recorded ʿAbd al-Ḥamīd's letters, Ibn Abī Ṭāhir Ṭayfūr, was a contemporary of the historian al-Balādhurī, who met one of ʿAbd al-Ḥamīd's sons—indeed, Ibn Abī Ṭāhir died only a year after al-Balādhurī. Thirdly, the fact that some of ʿAbd al-Ḥamīd's sons and great-great-grandsons were themselves professional secretaries means that when they boasted about their father/great-great-grandfather in front of professional secretaries or other educated people, as some of them indeed did, they must have had something tangible to substantiate their claims—the proof without which their boasting would have been criticized and dismissed as filial bombast. This in itself should mean that the secretaries in front of whom such boasting took place must themselves have been familiar with at least some of ʿAbd al-Ḥamīd's work.[53] Fourthly, the fact that a scribe or a secretary of the first half of the third/ninth century or earlier copied ʿAbd al-Ḥamīd's "Letter to the Secretaries" means that at least some of his letters were sufficiently admired to be copied as single literary pieces, a practice customary in the early stages of early Arabic recording, as attested by some of the titles cited in Ibn al-Nadīm's *Fihrist*. Then there is the unique piece of information that ʿAbd al-Ḥamīd's letters were studied by the secretaries in the ʿAbbāsid state in the late second/eighth or early third/ninth century. Now, if we remember that the litterateur who reported this information, al-Jāḥiẓ, was not at all sympathetic either to ʿAbd al-Ḥamīd personally or to the professional

[53]A case in point here is the report recorded by al-Baghdādī (*Kitāb al-kuttāb*, 149) that a group of secretaries (in early ʿAbbāsid times) reacted immediately to the mention of ʿAbd al-Ḥamīd's name, and then asked his son Ismāʿīl, the secretary, to explain to them the exact nature of ʿAbd al-Ḥamīd's eloquence, which he proceeded to do in a fairly long speech (i.e. fifteen lines of text). This speech demonstrates Ismāʿīl's great admiration for his father's contribution to letter writing on the one hand, and on the other, the secretaries' familiarity, at least in general, with ʿAbd al-Ḥamīd's distinction in eloquence. For another case of boasting on the part of one of ʿAbd al-Ḥamīd's descendants in front of a highly educated man, Ibrāhīm ibn al-Mahdī, in Ṭūlūnid times, see al-Jahshiyārī, *Al-Wuzarāʾ wa-l-kuttāb*, 83.

secretaries as a group, and that he was in fact disdainful of the secretaries for deriving their education solely from recent (modern) prose writers,[54] the value of his testimony increases. Indeed, it poses a decisively pertinent question: if the secretaries of the 'Abbāsid state at the turn of the third/ninth century had access to 'Abd al-Ḥamīd's letters, then where were these letters previously? Or to reverse the question, can we, having adduced positive arguments for the authenticity of 'Abd al-Ḥamīd's letters, also show that a counter-claim for non-authenticity should be dismissed, for entirely different reasons, as weak and unlikely?

Let us first note that some of 'Abd al-Ḥamīd's letters were very long by any standard, so long indeed that in the light not only of the higher copying costs, but also of the increased risk of exposure in forging such epistles, we can hardly credit the suggestion that someone would have taken the trouble to "compile" such lengthy letters, as opposed to shorter ones, and attribute them to someone else in the hope that they would be "marketed" by scribes. It is true that writing a piece of literature and attributing it to a famous writer, rather than to oneself, was not an unknown phenomenon at the time. Al-Jāḥiẓ himself is reported to have indulged in this practice as a young man. But once a writer became well-known in his own right—i.e. when his work came to be circulated, through professional scribes—he "reclaimed" his work, or at least "uncovered" his earlier tactics. But nothing of the sort happened with 'Abd al-Ḥamīd's long letters: no one else "reclaimed" them after they had become well-circulated, though a forger would hardly be expected to confine himself to anonymity once these works had become a source of literary glory to anyone who could prove himself their author. It is true that only one of 'Abd al-Ḥamīd's long letters has survived, namely his "Testament to the Crown Prince" (no. 21), written on behalf of Marwān to his son. But we know that he did write

[54]The mere title of al-Jāḥiẓ's treatise, "An Essay in Rebuke of the Secretaries' Demeanor", is sufficient to illustrate this point. The entire treatise (in al-Jāḥiẓ, *Rasā'il*, II, 183–209) abounds with "proofs" of the meanness of the secretaries and their profession throughout Islamic history until the author's time. Al-Jāḥiẓ considers 'Abd al-Ḥamīd, as a secretary, responsible for the downfall of the Umayyads because he disliked the governor of Khurāsān and gave his sovereign, the Umayyad Marwān, bad advice as to how to handle the 'Abbāsid rebels there. See *Rasā'il*, II, 202; also cf. 191–92.

another very long letter on behalf of Marwān, an epistle to the leader of the underground 'Abbāsid movement, Abū Muslim al-Khurāsānī, which the latter refused to read and possibly destroyed.[55] In addition, all the sources agree that 'Abd al-Ḥamīd was the first prose writer in Arabic to have introduced prolixity into Arabic prose as a literary value,[56] and this feature is precisely what one finds in the extant letters ascribed to him.

But even 'Abd al-Ḥamīd's shorter letters are unlikely to have been forged. A careful examination of their content, I think, quite clearly establishes this. Setting aside, again, the short extracts, one can view the remaining pieces as falling into several categories, from the angle of possible forgery. The first is that of the "'Abbāsid letters" (nos. 8 and 38). From a political point of view it is utterly inconceivable that any later author should have forged these epistles. All the litterateurs who lived after 'Abd al-Ḥamīd flourished under the 'Abbāsids, and in some cases they were closely associated with their court; 'Abd al-Ḥamīd's "'Abbāsid letters", on the other hand, accuse the followers of the 'Abbāsids of gravely un-Islamic or anti-Islamic behavior, stating that they had only recently been fire-worshippers, that they had nothing to do with Islam, and that they were Persian fanatics rising against the Arab state. It might be argued, of course, that enemies of the 'Abbāsids fabricated these letters in order to disqualify them from the caliphate. But again, this is extremely unlikely, for we know from political and religious history that prior to the textual attestation of the 'Abd al-Ḥamīd letters in the third/ninth century, the 'Abbāsids had no such enemies who had the willingness or ability to launch this sort of sophisticated literary propaganda against them. Indeed, the very fact that such letters were recorded indicates that they were taken to be historically genuine: they were written early, at a time when the 'Abbāsids were still the leaders of a revolutionary movement, not the rulers of a state.

Similar arguments can be used to establish the authenticity of the "conquest letters" (nos. 25–27) and the "civil discord/obedience letters"

---

[55] This is reported in a multitude of sources; see 'Abbās, *'Abd al-Ḥamīd*, 39–40 and the relevant note.

[56] *Ibid.*, 145.

(nos. 16–19, 24, and 34), which were the product of certain turbulent historical circumstances that comprised matters of no relevance during 'Abbāsid times and were thus not commonly addressed in official prose. Also not addressed by official prose under the 'Abbāsids were the specific occasions raised in some of 'Abd al-Ḥamīd's letters at the command of the caliph Hishām, namely those caliphal proclamations about the caliph having performed the pilgrimage, having been well, or remembering the beginning of the month of Ramaḍān (nos. 11, 12, and 29); indeed, they seem to have become obsolete already by the time of Marwān. To this category should be added no. 22, the "letter on chess". In an 'Abbāsid context this letter would have been a crass anachronism, for in spite of opposition from some religious leaders, by 'Abbāsid times chess had become quite widespread, and an official state prohibition of it would have verged on the ridiculous. Indeed, one of the close secretaries to three 'Abbāsid caliphs (al-Rāḍī, al-Muktafī, and al-Muqtadir) towards the end of the third/ninth century, Abū Bakr Muḥammad ibn Yaḥyā al-Ṣūlī (d. 335/946), was nicknamed al-Shiṭranjī, the "man of chess", because he was such an expert on chess and in fact was an author about it.[57]

Next there is the unique letter on the spread of the Qadarīya group among the military and the population in Armenia (no. 13). This letter is so important that it deserves a separate study. Here it will suffice to say that its authenticity lies on historical grounds (the connection of the Qadarite religious thinker Ghaylān al-Dimashqī with Armenia at this time, and the governorship of Marwān on Armenia during the same period) as well as politico-theological considerations (the political program of the Qadarīya and their sharp criticism of the Umayyad régime).[58]

[57]See al-Ziriklī, *A'lām*, VII, 136. His book on chess, together with that of al-'Adlī, has been published as *Book on Chess (Kitāb al-Shaṭranj), Selected Texts from al-'Adlī, Abū Bakr al-Ṣūlī* (Frankfurt am Main, 1986). See also the introduction in Félix M. Pareja Casañas, *Libero del ajedrez, de sus problemas y sutilezas de autor árabe desconocido*, I (Madrid and Granada, 1935). For the playing of chess in Islam, see Reinhard Wieber, *Das Schachspiel in der arabischen Litteratur von den Anfängen bis zur zweiten Hälfte des 16. Jahrhunderts* (Waldorf-Hessen, 1972); see also Franz Rosenthal, *Gambling in Islam* (Leiden, 1975), *passim*.

[58]The best study on Ghaylān and his Qadarism is van Ess' "Exkursus" in his *Anfänge muslimischer Theologie*, 177–245; see esp. 234–35, 238–41.

The rest of ‘Abd al-Ḥamīd's letters are unlikely to have been fabricated simply because, to start with, there could have been no motive for such fabrication. To this category belong all ‘Abd al-Ḥamīd's personal letters, regardless of whether or not they include a reference to state affairs (nos. 2, 5, 9, 10, 14, 30–32, 35–37), in addition to his two descriptive letters (nos. 6 and 23). Again, these letters would have been reclaimed later had they been forged by aspiring young prose writers. The lack of motive is also to be argued apropos of the letters which have to do with the Umayyad house (nos. 1, 3, 4, 7, 15, 28, and 33). Who, for example, would have forged a letter of condolence on the occasion of the death of a favorite concubine of the caliph? Who would have undertaken the curious and pointless task of forging a letter about the marital problems of the crown prince, claiming that the letter had been written on behalf of the caliph, and addressing it to his neglectful son?

But there is an additional feature in ‘Abd al-Ḥamīd's letters which strengthens the case made here for their authenticity. This is the fact that several are addressed to or speak about persons who are historically unknown. Letter no. 4 offers condolences to Marwān's brother (unidentified by name) on the occasion of the death of a certain al-Ḥakam ibn Marwān. Judging by his name, one could assume that this person was, in all probability, an Umayyad, perhaps a son of Marwān's or an uncle of his. Yet this person appears in not even the genealogical sources, be they general or particularly confined to the tribe of Quraysh. Letter no. 7 is addressed to a certain ‘Abd al-‘Azīz ibn ‘Umar ibn Hubayra, who is unknown in the sources in spite of the fact that his father was one of the pillars of the late Umayyad régime.[59] Similarly, letter no. 14 is addressed to a certain Ibn al-Buḫturī (?), who is completely unknown in the historical and biographical works. And the same applies to letter no. 24, which is addressed to a Khārijite rebel by the name of Abū l-‘Alā’ al-Ḥarūrī. Now, had these letters been forged, they would have been associated with known persons in order to place the texts within a more "credible" context of familiar names. But this does not occur. Nor, in the same vein, are most of ‘Abd al-Ḥamīd's other letters assigned specific names of senders (nos. 7, 11, 12, 16, and 24), or of

[59]See above, n. 34.

addressees (nos. 2, 6, 9, 10, 23, 31, 36, 37, and 41), or indeed of either (nos. 16–19, 22, 25–27, 34, and 38).

If we add to all this what I have called the "continuous 'Abd al-Ḥamīd legacy", the fact that a number of the preserved letters are introduced in the sources each by a sentence, either identifying the occasion on which they were written, or stating to whom they were addressed, or on behalf of whom they were written, and if we note the harmony of style premeating all of them, then on the theoretical level at least, we can rest assured that they came from the hand of 'Abd al-Ḥamīd.

The Problem of Late Attestation

The second problem, the fact that over half of 'Abd al-Ḥamīd's letters surface only quite late, not earlier than the fifth/eleventh century, belongs also to the theoretical realm, and has been partially answered in the discussion above. However, there is more to be said on this matter.

Let us consider the nature of several key sources which have recorded 'Abd al-Ḥamīd's letters. The best starting point is the earliest one, Ibn Abī Ṭāhir's *Manẓūm*. This book is possibly the largest anthology of Arabic prose and poetry ever compiled, for we know with certainty that it consisted of at least thirteen volumes (since Volume 13 has survived), and that each volume was probably quite substantial in size.[60] Of all these, only Volumes 11, 12, and 13 have survived,[61] which means that more than three quarters of the book has been lost. Is it not

[60]The three surviving volumes (see the following note) comprise a total of over 500 packed, large-format pages.

[61]All three volumes are available in two manuscripts which were copied from the same original at the Egyptian National Library (Dār al-Kutub) in Cairo. Volume 11, which is mainly on the eloquent sayings of women, has been printed under the title *Kitāb balāghāt al-nisā'* (Najaf, 1361/1942). Volume 12, mainly on the unique poems and epistles/letters, is still largely in manuscript form; only some pieces have been selected from it by compilers of modern literary anthologies. The same applies to Volume 13, which is on selections from literary pieces of various genres (*fuṣūl mukhtāra fī kulli fann*). I am grateful to Iḥsān 'Abbās for permitting me to use his microfilm of the manuscript.

possible that some additional letters of ʿAbd al-Ḥamīd's should have been included in the lost parts of the book? Not only is this possible, it is also probable, since the structure of the book is very chaotic: its arrangement is certainly not by genre, since poetry and prose are mixed in all the extant volumes, nor is it chronological, in which case ʿAbd al-Ḥamīd's letters would have come in a much earlier volume, since in fact selections in this work extend right to the time of Ibn Abī Ṭāhir himself. What the structure of the *Manẓūm* was is difficult to tell. Having had the opportunity to work with what has survived of it several times, I at first thought that its structure was "thematic" or "topical", a possibility sometimes attested in the surviving parts. Upon further examination, however, I discovered that this criterion is only approximate, in the sense that it is often ignored for no apparent reason. Indeed, the very title of Volume 13—"Pieces Selected from Every Genre"—attests to this fact.[62]

There is another related matter to consider with respect to Ibn Abī Ṭāhir's *Manẓūm*. This book was compiled by a litterateur who was very close to the state and its secretaries, and who had an almost endless répertoire of official and personal letters and treatises from which to select.[63] For this reason, his book, judging by what has survived of it, is filled almost to overflowing with letters written by various secretaries of the state across the centuries. What is more, especially when the "thematic criterion" is adhered to, the author produces "model" letters for possible "occasions" that the secretaries were likely to address, possibly from his own hand. The book was meant, then, not only to record the corpus of the literary material which the Arabs and the Muslims produced over time, but also to instruct the secretaries of the Chancery at any place or time in Islamic lands. Is it then likely that such an author, with such a background and such a purpose, should exclude from his multi-volume book ʿAbd al-Ḥamīd's "Letter to the Secretaries", the very first and the most important letter about them in Arabic literature, and one which first defined them as a separate class, gave them a sense of identity, and raised their profession high

[62]See n. 61 above.

[63]For the biography of Ibn Abī Ṭāhir and his works, see Franz Rosenthal, art. "Ibn Abī Ṭāhir Ṭayfūr in *EI*[2], III (Leiden, 1971), 692–93.

above most others? And yet this letter of ʻAbd al-Ḥamīd's does not appear in the *Manẓūm*. In view of the above, I would maintain that Ibn Abī Ṭāhir Ṭayfūr did indeed include ʻAbd al-Ḥamīd's "Letter to the Secretaries" in his book; its place, however, was in the part of the text which has been lost. And if this is the case of one of ʻAbd al-Ḥamīd's letters, it very well may be the case of some of his other letters.

Discussion of the *Manẓūm* may here be concluded with the observation that in all probability, many of the writers after Ibn Abī Ṭāhir took texts of ʻAbd al-Ḥamīd's letters from him, for his huge anthology, if not fully available to us today, was nevertheless available to them. The delay in the surfacing of some letters thus does not speak against the conclusion that they existed in earlier times, very possibly already from the second half of the third/ninth century, and certainly since there are such telling objections to the proposition that the letters are later fabrications.

One final point bearing on the nature of the Arabic literary sources must be mentioned. Arabic literature abounds with anthologies and, to a lesser extent, with manuals containing material deemed useful to the secretaries of the Chancery (styles of handwriting, sharpening of the pen, use of the ink-bottle, etc.).[64] This much may be conceded as obvious. But it is also true that most anthologies and books meant for the secretaries (as well as those about viziers) had constraints of space or intentionally set selective criteria for inclusion, such as the desire to be entertaining. These works thus tended to select short pieces (anecdotes, sayings, instructions, and so forth) in their books, and this applied also to selections from earlier prose writers which were intended to serve as enjoyable pieces of literature (in the literary anthologies) or as good, effective models for emulation—possibly in order to be memorized—by the secretaries (in the secretaries' manuals). This holds true for the method applied by Ibn ʻAbd Rabbih (d. 328/939) in his *Al-ʻIqd al-farīd*, Abū Ḥayyān al-Tawḥīdī (d. 414/1023) in his *Al-Baṣāʼir wa-l-dhakhāʼir*, Abū Manṣūr al-Thaʻālibī (d. 429/1037) in several works, such as his *Khāṣṣ al-khāṣṣ*, Jār Allāh al-Zamakhsharī (d. 538/1143) in his *Rabīʻ al-abrār*, al-Waṭwāṭ (d. 718/1318) in his *Ghurar al-khaṣāʼiṣ*,

[64]See Rudolf Sellheim and Dominique Sourdel, art. "Kātib" in EI^2, IV (Leiden, 1978), 756.

and other literary anthologies. Among authors of books on secretaries and viziers, we find a similar selective trend in practice by Abū Bakr al-Ṣūlī (d. 335/946) in his *Adab al-kuttāb*, al-Tha'ālibī in his *Tuḥfat al-wuzarā'*, and al-Māwardī (d. 450/1058) in his *Qawānīn al-wizāra*. In fact, it is for this reason that these and similar kinds of books have preserved for us many of 'Abd al-Ḥamīd's short extracts, but none of his letters. To this general observation there are, of course, some exceptions, but they are very few: Ibn Abī Ṭāhir Ṭayfūr's *Manẓūm* abounds with long letters, as do, to a lesser extent, Ibn Ḥamdūn's *Al-Tadhkira al-ḥamdūnīya*, al-Balawī's *Al-'Aṭā' al-jazīl*, and al-Qalqashandī's *Ṣubḥ al-a'shā*, the four major sources for 'Abd al-Ḥamīd's letters proper. As for al-Jahshiyārī's *Al-Wuzarā' wa-l-kuttāb* and Ibn Khaldūn's *Muqaddima*, they single out 'Abd al-Ḥamīd's "Letter to the Secretaries" (no. 35), quoting its entire text because of its unique importance in the literature on the secretaries, as they both state in their introduction to it. Indeed, al-Jahshiyārī considers it overly long (supposedly in view of the kind of book he was writing), but says that he will reproduce it in full, without omitting any part of it, "because a secretary cannot dispense with the likes of it (*li-anna l-kātiba lā yastaghnī 'an mithlihi*)".[65] It must be noted, though, that al-Jahshiyārī, sensitive and committed secretary that he was, did preserve a relatively long fragment (one page) of one other letter by 'Abd al-Ḥamīd (his farewell letter to his family, no. 32), presumably because of its unique personal, historical, and literary value.

The Problem of Multiple Versions

'Abd al-Ḥamīd's "Letter to the Secretaries" brings us to another problem in the preservation of 'Abd al-Ḥamīd's epistles, namely the fact that some of his letters survive in more than one version. This applies not only to this particular letter (no. 35), but also to letter no. 15.[66]

[65] Al-Jahshiyārī, *Al-Wuzarā' wa-l-kuttāb*, 73.

[66] I shall not discuss letter no. 15 here, since it poses fewer problems than the "Letter to the Secretaries", and those it does present are all addressed in the course of the following assessment of the multiple versions of the latter.

A close examination of the versions of the "Letter to the Secretaries" reveals the following conclusions: 1) that the letter has been preserved in four sources which will be referred to here, for purposes of convenience, as J (al-Jahshiyārī), IḤ (Ibn Ḥamdūn), IK (Ibn Khaldūn), and Q (al-Qalqashandī); 2) that there are extensive differences between the versions of the letter in these sources; 3) that the text of the letter as edited by Iḥsān 'Abbās is essentially that of al-Jahshiyārī—the critical apparatus attached to this edition is extensive but not exhaustive; thus, for a minute examination of the variant readings of its versions the letter must be re-edited, as I hope to do elsewhere; and 4) that, without going into the individual details of each and every one of these variant readings, these variants fall into two main categories: those differences of no or little importance to the provenance of the letter, and significant variants which pose questions about the history of the text's transmission.

Among the variants of the first category, the following groups of readings can be cited:

a. Readings among which the differences are of no significance whatsoever, these being ones which have to do with pious phraseformulae. These can easily be discarded, for they may very well be the work of scribes across the centuries rather than the work of the author himself. An example of this would be the expression *'azza wa-jalla*, "may He be glorified and exalted" as opposed to *ta'ālā*, "Almighty", after God's name is mentioned.

b. Readings among which the differences are of very little significance, since they are orthographic; they have to do with the nature of the Arabic script. There are several letters so similar in form that they can be easily mistaken one for the other; other letters are identical in form and are distinguished one from the other only by the number of dots (one, two or three) they bear and the position of these dots (above or below) on the letter. Also, this dotting (*tanqīṭ*) was often dropped by scribes while copying manuscripts. To this category belong differences such as the usage of the *ya* or *ta* at the beginning of the imperfect, of the *wa/fa* and *wa/aw* as conjunctions, and words such as *al-ḥilm wa-l-rawīya* vs. *al-'ilm wa-l-razāna* and *al-'ilm wa-l-riwāya*, *istiqṣā'* vs. *istiqḍā'*, *ṣabrihi* vs. *khayrihi*. Other peculiarities of the Arabic script are responsible for other differences in readings, such as insertion or omission of the long *alif mamdūda* (e.g. *muḥjiman* vs. *miḥjāman*, *ṣan'a* vs. *ṣinā'a*), or when the definite article *al-* is mistaken for the preposition *li-* attached to the definite article (i.e. *li-l-*), e.g. *wa-l-umūr* vs. *wa-li-l-umūr*. I believe that another difference which occurs once (*wa-tawāṣalū*/*wa-tawāṣaw*) is the result of the same phenomenon: the first form is simply a mistake for the second, the *lām* having been mistakenly read for the hook of the letter *ṣād* (this could even be a printing error).

c. Readings among which the differences are negligible, as in the cases where prepositions are not the same in all versions. This kind of difference is unimportant because most of its forms occur in the case of *fī* vs. *min* (also when attached to a pronoun—*fīhā* vs. *minhā*, etc.), and the two words are easily mistaken one for the other due to the nature of the Arabic script and the proximity in meaning between them. Only in certain cases is it of some significance, such as replacing *lahā* with *'alayhā*, and still more significant, since it affects the meaning, when *'alā infādh* bears a positive meaning, whereas *'an infādh* has a negative sense. At any rate, the same applies to the exchange of one particle for another, particularly *in* for *idhā*, and one conjunction for another dissimilar to it in orthographic form: *wa*/*bal* and *wa*/*thumma*.

d. Also unimportant are the readings the differences among which are no more than the presence/absence of the conjunction *wa* ("and") at the beginnings of successive clauses within the same sentence. Classical Arabic tends to drop this conjunction, but it is not unusual to keep it. The same applies to differences which result from the presence or absence of the vocative particle *yā* ("oh") before the vocative noun, and of the prepositions *min* or *bi-* before the nouns *dūn* or *ghayr* ("without").

e. There are differences among readings which are of some significance, although these differences ought not to be exaggerated due to the nature of the Arabic language in addition to the Arabic script. In particular, Arabic, like other Semitic languages, is a language of derivation, with the verbal root being the basis for a variety of both nominal and verbal formations, and similiarly, nouns and adjectives quite often can be used interchangeably and verbal nouns can sometimes have the same meaning in the singular and the plural, in all cases the syntax permitting of course. Thus, the fact that we get *ṣunʿ* in place of *ṣanīʿ*, *luṭf* in place of *laṭīf*, or *murūʾa* instead of *murūʾāt*, is really of less significance than at first sight appears. This same phenomenon also occurs with respect to verbs, where multiple verb forms have the same meaning and can be used interchangeably (thus form VIII *ittaqāhā* vs. form V *tawaqqāhā*), and in places where the usage of either the singular or the plural makes no difference (thus *yadihā* vs. *yadayhā*, *ṭarīqihā* vs. *ṭuruqihā*).

f. Another peculiarity of Arabic is at the root of some differences in readings, namely that the past tense can have the sense of the continuous tense, which is more frequently expressed by the imperfect. We thus discover a difference of no great importance when we find *li-man wusima* in one version and *li-man yūsamu* in another. Similarly, the *nomen generis* can be expressed by either the indefinite or definite singular (thus *rajulan* or *al-rajul*, meaning the same thing), and the verb, when preceded by a relative pronoun, can either stand on its own or include an accusative pronominal referent (thus *ʿammā yahwā* or *ʿammā yahwāhu*).

g. There are variants of slightly greater significance, namely when a word in one version is substituted in another by a different word identical to it in *meaning*. In many cases, the two words are orthographically identical or almost identical if one disregards the dots, and in these cases the differences are not important (e.g. *yubṣirūna* vs. *yanẓurūna*, *khadamun* vs. *khadamatun*, *wāsūhu* vs. *āsūhu*). In other cases, however, the two words are, in their contexts, simple synonyms whose written forms are quite dissimilar, in which case the differences between them become somewhat significant (e.g. *akhīhi* vs. *murāfiqihi*, *ʿujb* vs. *ightirār*, *tammamtuhu* vs. *khatamtuhu*, *ṣinf/ṣunūf* vs. *fann/funūn*). This phenomenon occurs also in phrases, not only in individual words (e.g. *kāna muta'arriḍan* vs. *fa-qad ta'arraḍa*, *min nāhiyati* vs. *min qibali*).

h. Another kind of difference has to do with syntax, where the words in a sentence are the same but their order varies in different versions. A good example of this would be the reading *wa-mu'āmalatihi li-man yuḥāwiruhu wa-yunāẓiruhu mina l-nās* vs. *wa-mu'āmalatihi mina l-nāsi li-man yuḥāwiruhu wa-yunāẓiruhu*, and vs. yet a third reading *wa-mu'āmalatihi li-man yuḥāwiruhu mina l-nāsi wa-yunāẓiruhu*. But here again, one should bear in mind the tremendous flexiblity of the Arabic sentence syntactically. Actually, the essential difference between the three readings is not much more than a matter of emphasis and style. And, in fact, some differences of this kind occur sometimes in phrases made up of a string of words connected by conjunctions, so that it really does not make much difference which words come first and which second, e. g. *gharībahā wa-ma'āniyahā* vs. *ma'āniyahā wa-gharībahā*, *al-danā'a wa-l-jahāla* vs. *al-jahāla wa-l-danā'a*.

i. In a similar vein, there are some cases in which corresponding sentences in various versions have practically the same meaning and employ essentially the same words; however, the structure of the sentences varies in the different versions, leading to some differences of minor significance, mainly grammatical, e.g. *wa-lā yaḍī'anna naẓrukum fī l-ḥisāb* vs. *wa-lā tuḍayyi'ū l-naẓara fī l-ḥisāb*, or *'alā mā tasmūna ilayhi bi-himamikum* vs. *'alā mā tasmū ilayhi himamukum*. The grammatical significance is also the only one distinguishing between the two readings *wa-lā yaqul* vs. *wa-lā yaqūlu*, depending on whether one considers the *lā* as the negative imperative particle or merely the negative particle.

j. Finally, there is one strange phenomenon: there are two cases in which the meanings of two expressions mentioned in one version are turned into their opposites in another. Thus, instead of *'alā mā sabaqa bihi l-kitāb* we have *'alā mā ya'tī fī hādhā l-kitāb*, and in place of *fī ghayri ḥīni l-ḥājati ilā dhālika minhu* one finds *'inda l-ḥājati ilayhi.* In both cases, the phrases are, paradoxically, premissible in context. I have no explanation for this difference, nor can I assess its significance.

But there are other differences which are clearly of much greater significance, in that they raise questions about the original provenance of the letter and the history of its transmission. In this connection, the most important point is that despite the apparently wide range of variant readings among the four versions of the "Letter to the Secretaries", there are actually only *two distinct versions* of it. Close examination of all the variants indicates that when mainly significant differences are scrutinized, the J and IḤ versions follow each other closely, while IK and Q are, setting aside printing errors, almost identical. Taking the first version as a working text and considering what the second does with it, we find that these differences fall into three categories: changes, additions, and deletions. In addition, there are some instances in which the two versions present widely differing readings.

THE CHANGES

The changes that the IK-Q version makes to the J-IḤ one are extensive. The significant ones among them manifest two tendencies. The first and perhaps more interesting one is the tendency to exchange rather difficult, uncommon words for simpler, more familiar ones. Thus one finds changes such as these:

sirbāl al-ni'ma	to	*mā aḍfāhu mina l-ni'ma*
bi-mā ya'tī wa-yadharu	to	*bi-mā ya'tī mina l-nawāzil*
shadā minhu shadwan	to	*akhadha minhu bi-miqdāri mā*
masāffi/masāwi'i l-umūr	to	*safsāfi l-umūr*
al-'amal	to	*al-shughl*
bi-mā huwa harīyun an yuḥaqqiqahu	to	*jazā'an li-ḥaqqihi*
fa-l-yastashiffa	to	*fa-l-yakhtabir*
ḥādhiqan	to	*baṣīran*
lam yulāḥihā wa-tatabba'a hawāhā	to	*qama'a bi-rifqin hawāhā*

Such changes have no particular bearing on the original written by 'Abd al-Ḥamīd. They do mean, however, that, at some stage in the copying of the letter, before the time of Ibn Khaldūn, the letter was copied by a copyist who was not sufficiently well-versed in Arabic to understand some its terminology, and so exchanged unfamiliar terms for other, more current words which maintained the meaning more or less intact.

This is further confirmed, perhaps, by the second tendency evident in these changes, namely a tendency towards clarification. In one case, a noun replaces an original pronoun, thus making its referent crystal clear (*fa-mawqi'ukum minhum* becomes *fa-mawqi'ukum mina l-mulūk*), and in another expression the clarifying "and that" or "i.e." (*wa-dhālika*) is added at the beginning of an explanatory phrase. In a third case, an elliptic but elegant expression is amplified, apparently in order to avoid confusion: *wa-lākin qad yalzamu l-rajula* thus becomes *wa-'alā kulli wāḥidin mina l-farīqayni*. In still a fourth, the word "secretaries" towards the end of the letter is changed in order to indicate the wider range of "scribes" (*al-kuttāb* becomes *al-kataba*), and another word is added to include the apprentices among the scribes as well (*al-ṭalabati*). This last change is no small alteration, given its particular place in the letter and its bearing on its overall message. Thus again here I suspect a not-too-learned copyist's (scribe's!) intervention.

THE ADDITIONS

The additions of the IK-Q version to the J-IḤ version are numerous and must be assessed carefully. In some instances, they betray a kind of "innocent" zeal to add emphasis to the purport of the letter. This occurs particularly in cases where the first version lists a series of qualities (linked by conjunctions) which the author wants the secretaries to adopt or avoid; the second version inserts one (or more) compatible qualities in the middle of the string. Thus we get phrases like (the additions/insertions being indicated by square brackets) *wa-iyyākum wa-l-kibra* [*wa-l-sukhfa*/*wa-l-ṣalafa*] *wa-l-'aẓamata fa-innahā shiyamu ahli l-faḍli* [*wa-l-'adli*] *wa-l-nubli*.... In other instances, the additions seem to aspire to further clarification and elaboration, as one sees in the addition *wa-ra'ā anna ṣāḥibahu a'qalu minhu wa-aḥmadu fī ṭarīqatihi* in the context of advising secretaries not to claim that they are better than their colleagues. Another example confirms this tendency and betrays a new one: *wa-li-l-ra'īyati muta'allifan* [*wa-'an adhāhum/īdhā'ihim mutakhallifan*] *bi-alṭafi ḥīla* [*wa-ajmali wasīla*]. Here, not only is the sense elaborated upon, but the addition serves to effect a change in style, making the individual phrases rhyme at their ends (*muta'allifan*/[*mutakhallifan*], *ḥīla*/[*wasīla*]), thus introducing rhymed prose (*saj'*) into the style. Since this style is not unknown in 'Abd al-Ḥamīd's writings, the additions seem to fit perfectly well. Hence, they confuse us as to which of the two sentences represents the original that 'Abd al-Ḥamīd wrote, for it is clear that if such words and phrases were indeed additions to the original, then they were introduced by someone quite familiar with 'Abd al-Ḥamīd's style. And such stylistic additions are indeed more frequent in the area of parallelism (*izdiwāj*), a much more outstanding characteristic of 'Abd al-Ḥamīd's style all through. These additions may come in the form of one word paired in the next phrase by another one—*fa-yu'iddu li-kulli amrin 'uddatahu* [*wa-'atādahu*], *wa-yuhayyi'u li-kulli amrin uhbatahu* [*wa-'ādatahu*], or in the form of a phrase—*ḥattā tarji'a ilayhi ḥāluhu* [*wa-yathūba ilayhi amruhu*]. In several cases they serve the stylistic purposes of both parallelism and rhyme: *ṣurūf al-ṣinā'āt* [*wa-ḍurūb al-muḥāwalāt*]. One final stylistic addition which I have noted goes well with what has been described above, namely the addition of the word *alā* at the beginning of the concluding paragraph of the letter. This word, which means "lo", fits its context perfectly and does not appear at all unusual for 'Abd al-Ḥamīd's style.

There are, however, four additions/changes which are quite different in nature from the additions/changes mentioned so far and thus deserve separate consideration. It is noteworthy that they all occur in the first paragraph of the letter.

The first addition occurs in the context of defining the hierarchies of human beings. The text of J-IḤ has it that God made the people, after the prophets, messengers, and kings, as "commoners" (*suwaqan*). After this word, however, IK-Q adds: "albeit they are in reality of equal status" (*wa-in kānū fī l-ḥaqīqati sawā'*). This clause is clearly an "Islamic" addition.

The second occurs in the context of the usage of the term *mulk* ("kingship" or "sovereignty"). The text of J-IḤ states that the secretaries are the means by which kingship becomes systematized (*bikum yantaẓimu l-mulk*), i.e. it takes shape. IK-Q, however, has the reading *bikum yantaẓimu/tantaẓimu li-l-khilāfati maḥāsinuhā*, i.e. through the secretaries, the merits of the *caliphate* become systematized. In other words, "kingship" becomes "the caliphate". This again appears to be a simple "Islamic" transformation which has required an addition besides the change. But the situation here is more complicated. The term "kingship" might be thought of as a neutral, general term; however, in the Umayyad context in particular, it carried specific, derogatory significations, for the opponents of the Umayyads denied the legitimacy of their régime by referring to them as "kings" rather than "caliphs", the implicit charge being that they were worldly rather than religious rulers. Now, since 'Abd al-Ḥamīd was a staunch defender of the Umayyad cause, one might surmise that the "caliphate" version was the one he originally wrote. Upon further examination of the text, however, one notes that the word "kings" (*mulūk*) occurs in other places, indeed in the next phrase, in *both* versions of the letter, and that the "caliphate" change was made only this once. This means that whatever the original version was, it did contain references to "kings" as the masters the secretaries serve. The addition/change, then, represents a successful "Islamization" of the text and a failing "Umayyadization" of it.

The third addition is rather more subtle. While discussing the rôle of the secretaries with the kings, the author says, in J-IḤ, that due to the secretaries' administration and policy-making, "God makes good for the kings their sovereignty" (*yuṣliḥu llāhu sulṭānahum*), i.e. the kings' sovereignty. In IK-Q, however, the text reads: *yuṣliḥu llāhu li-l-khalqi sulṭānahum*, i.e. God makes good for mankind *their rulers*. Thus, by the addition of one word (*li-l-khalqi*) the entire meaning has changed, this by virtue of the fact that the word *sulṭān* in Arabic can be both an abstract noun (a verbal noun, "sovereignty") or a common noun ("ruler"). The addition is clearly an "Islamic" one; the mere appearance of the word *khalq*, i.e. "created beings", in the sense of "mankind", confirms this.

This is further reinforced by the continuation of the sentence, which comprises our fourth case of the different additions. J-IḤ goes on to say that, as a result, "their taxes are collected and their lands are cultivated", *wa-yajtami'u fay'uhum wa-ta'muru bilāduhum*. IK-Q makes a few subtle changes in terminology, but by these the entire meaning of the sentence is changed. It has *wa-yajma'u fay'ahum wa-ya'muru bilādahum*, i.e. "[*He*] collects their taxes and makes their lands cultivated". What has happened is that one reflexive and hence intransitive verb (*yajtami'u*) has been replaced by the transitive form of the same root of the verb (*yajma'u*), and the other verb (*ya'muru*), which permits of both transitive and intransitive interpretations, has been changed in usage from intransitive to transitive. The primary result of this shift is to permit the activities mentioned (collecting taxes, cultivating lands) to be construed in an "active" sense rather than in the passive sense conveyed in the first version. Now an active action requires an actor, a subject for the verb. This is God. Thus we have another case of "Islamization".

THE DELETIONS

Although the deletions of the IK-Q version from the J-IḤ version are far fewer than its additions (no more than about fifteen), these are more confusing for the researcher. The purposes or tendencies of some of them, in fact, contradict the additions/changes in the areas of elaboration (or explanation) and style. Thus the explanatory phrase *idh kāna l-āfatu l-'uẓmā min āfāti 'aqlihi...* is dropped out, and phrases which lead to further elaboration are also deleted, for example: *wa-annahumā lā yajtami'āni fī aḥadin abadan*, *wa-l-yaqṣid fī kalāmihi*, *wa-majammatun li-dhihnihi*; and a number of words in a string of qualities is once dropped out: after *ahla l-adabi wa-l-murū'ati wa-l-ḥilmi wa-l-rawīyati* the following is deleted: *wa-dhawī l-akhṭāri wa-l-himmati/l-himami wa-sa'ati l-dhar'i fī l-ifḍāli wa-l-ṣilati*. In a similar vein, one elaborating simile is dropped: *wa-idhā ṣaḥiba aḥadukum al-rajula fa-l-yastashiffa khalā'iqahu [kamā yastashiffu l-thawba yashtarīhi li-nafsihi]*. With regard to style, a phrase which achieves perfect antithetical pairing is again dropped: *shadīdan fī mawḍi'i l-shidda* after *layyinan fī mawḍi'i l-līn*. And yet there is another deletion which works to opposite effect, just like the additions above, causing the two phrases of one sentence not only to pair well but also to rhyme: the word *layyinan* is dropped from the following sentence: *wa-l-yakun fī majlisihi ḥalīman layyinan, wa-fī istijlābi/sijillāti kharājihi wa-istiqṣā'i ḥuqūqihi rafīqan*! A concluding sentence about the good qualities of the secretaries is also dropped: *fa-ni'ma l-'awnu 'awnukum 'alā ṣiyānati dīnikum wa-ḥifẓi amānatikum wa-ṣalāḥi ma'āshikum*.

Two other deletions seem strange, since they result in the absence of full ideas from the letter, each not being elaborated upon by other sentences. The first is that the kings take the secretaries, and not their own blood relatives and their advisors, as their sole confidants when it comes to important matters. One cannot imagine how such an important, perhaps even central, idea should have been skipped. And the second is that prolixity is sometimes premissible. In this last context, only the preceding idea about the necessity of brevity is mentioned in the IK-Q version. One might venture to suggest that this could have been an addition that 'Abd al-Ḥamīd did not write; but actually it probably was in the original, since, as mentioned above, 'Abd al-Ḥamīd was famous as the writer who introduced long-windedness into Arabic literature.

THE WIDELY DIFFERING READINGS

There are two instances in the letter where the two versions present widely differing readings. In the first, the meaning in both versions is actually the same and the diction is also close; only the syntax and the length differ, the IK-Q version being longer. Thus J-IḤ has *fa-qad 'alimtum anna l-rajula minkum qad yuṣfī l-rajula idhā ṣaḥibahu fī bad'i amrihi min wafā'ihi wa-shukrihi*..., while IK-Q expands this to *fa-qad 'alimtum anna l-rajula minkum idhā ṣaḥibahu man yabdhulu lahu min nafsihi mā yajibu 'alayhi min ḥaqqihi fa-wājibun 'alayhi an ya'taqida lahu min wafā'ihi wa-shukrihi*.... The difference could thus be considered in line with the additions/changes which aim at elaboration. The second case is rather more complex, and, so far as I can judge, bears on the question of manuscript copying and textual transmission. After the section on brevity and prolixity in the J-IḤ version, a new paragraph begins by advising the secretary not to allow the grace God has bestowed upon him, i.e. by making him successful, to become something which leads him to arrogance, for arrogance is harmful to one's religion, mind, and demeanor: *wa-lā yad'uwanna l-rajula minkum ṣun'u llāhi ta'ālā dhikruhu fī amrihi wa-ta'yīduhu iyyāhu bi-tawfīqihi ilā l-'ujbi l-muḍirri bi-dīnihi wa-'aqlihi wa-adabihi.* The version then goes on to talk about success being the work of God rather than the secretary. The IK-Q version, however, takes a different line. Immediately following the discussion of brevity (and there is nothing on prolixity), this version advises the secretary to plead to God to make him successful, lest he should fall into error, an eventuality which is harmful to one's body (orthographical change from *dīn*, "religion", to *badan*, "body"), mind, and demeanor: *wa-l-yaḍra' ilā llāhi fī ṣilati tawfīqihi wa-imdādihi bi-tasdīdihi makhāfata wuqū'ihi fī l-ghalaṭi l-muḍirri bi-badanihi wa-'aqlihi wa-adabihi....* The text then goes on, like its counterpart, to speak of success being the work of God rather than the secretary.

This departure of the IK-Q version from the J-IḤ text is certainly disturbing. However, upon closer scrutiny, it may prove to be less of a problem than might at first appear. The basic idea in the J-IḤ version is admonition against arrogance, and the flow of the reading in question prepares the way for a smooth transition to the next idea, which is that accomplishment is not the making of man but of God. In the IK-Q version, on the other hand, the basic idea centers on "error" rather than arrogance, and thus the following reference to accomplishment as the work of God rather than man comes rather unexpectedly. In other words, with the central idea of arrogance dropped out, the flow of the text in question in this version does not prepare the way for the next idea as its natural consequent. How, then, did this shift occur? To pursue this we must re-examine the similarities and differences between the reading in question in the two versions:

a. Both readings have two ideas in common: success and God as the source of success; they actually have some similarities in diction in this area: *tawfīq*, *Allāh*, and for *ta'yīd* in one version we have the rhyming synonym *tasdīd* in the other.

b. Both readings cite verbatim, with one orthographical change, the negative consequences of arrogance/error.

c. The word for arrogance (*'ujb*) is not readily interchangeable orthographically with the word for error (*ghalaṭ*). However, judging by other changes which the IK-Q version makes to the J-IḤ version, such a shift would not be totally unexpected. In fact, I would not rule out the possibility that this change was indeed an orthographical one which occurred through repeated copying over the centuries.

d. Thus, the main difference between the two readings is the flow which itself occasioned the change in meaning.

As an explanation for this divergence in the two versions, I would suggest, firstly, that the reading in the J-IḤ version must have been the original reading, for it accords with 'Abd al-Ḥamīd's usual style of argumentation by degrees, offering a slow but logically smooth flow of ideas. Secondly, I would argue that whoever copied the sentence in question in the IK-Q version from the J-IḤ one at some point in time had in front of him an unclear, disturbed exemplar. Thus, while he did his best to render his own text as closely as possible to the original at his disposal, his effort fell wide of the mark on this score and resulted in a serious change in a key idea and in the flow of argumentation.

The general conclusion, then, about the two version of the "Letter to the Secretaries" is that the J-IḤ text represents a form much closer to the original as written by 'Abd al-Ḥamīd, and that the IK-Q version is a later, corrupted rendering of this original.

The Problem of Attribution

Out of the twenty or so "wisdom sayings" which the sources attribute to 'Abd al-Ḥamīd, there are four which some, but not all, sources attribute to someone else: no. 40 to Ḥammād al-Rāwiya, no. 43 to Abū 'Ubayd Allāh Kātib al-Mahdī, no. 48 to "a philosopher", no. 59 to al-Rashīd, and one cited without any particular attribution (*wa-qīla*, "it was said"). This perennial problem in Arabic literature is of little significance in general,[67] and for present purposes it is of no significance at

[67] See the Introduction to my edition of Abū Ḥayyān al-Tawḥīdī, *Al-Baṣā'ir wa-l-dhakhā'ir*, VII (Tunis, 1978), 61.

all, since we are here concerned only with 'Abd al-Ḥamīd's *letters*. Of these, there are two attributed to someone other than 'Abd al-Ḥamīd.

The first, no. 2, is a letter in which the writer addresses a friend of his, telling him that he is perplexed by his behavior: at first the recipient of the letter had been courteous to him, but then suddenly and inexplicably changed and turned his back on him. The writer thus asks his friend to clarify how he wishes their relationship to proceed.

The letter has been recorded as 'Abd al-Ḥamīd's in al-Balawī's *Al-'Aṭā' al-jazīl*, i.e. it has survived in a late source (seventh/thirteenth century). In a much earlier source, al-Jāḥiẓ's *Al-Bayān wa-l-tabyīn*, which dates back to the third/ninth century, it is attributed to 'Abd Allāh ibn Mu'āwiya (d. *ca.* 131/749), who was a contemporary of 'Abd al-Ḥamīd's.[68] And there is a further complication: the two sources present different versions of the letter in the last three and a half of its six lines. The message, or meaning, in the two versions of the latter part is essentially the same, and the style is also quite similar, although the 'Abd al-Ḥamīd version is somewhat more subtle and sophisticated. Both versions of the letter are complete: they begin with *ammā ba'd* and end with *wa-l-salām*.

The first problem that comes to mind is that the attribution of the letter to 'Abd Allāh ibn Mu'āwiya is rather peculiar. This 'Abd Allāh was a Qurashite Hāshimite Arab and a brave, harsh, generous, and ambitious man.[69] Rather like the Hāshimite leaders of the underground 'Abbāsid movement, he seized the opportunity posed by Shī'ite potential and disarray, together with the more widespread social malaise and anti-government (anti-Umayyad) feelings in his time, and in 127/744 provoked a "Shī'ite" revolt, allegedly with gnostic extremist dogma, in Iraq, western Iran, and then Khurāsān. Less than two years later, his interests came to clash with those of the much more powerful 'Abbāsid rebels, and he was forced to make his peace

[68] Al-Jāḥiẓ, *Al-Bayān wa-l-tabyīn*, ed. 'Abd al-Salām Muḥammad Hārūn (Cairo, 1367–70/1948–50), II, 84–85. For further sources, see 'Abbās, *'Abd al-Ḥamīd*, 192 and n. 2.

[69] On him, see K.V. Zettersteen, art. "'Abd Allāh ibn Mu'āwiya" in *EI*², I (Leiden, 1960), 48–49; Marshall G.S. Hodgson and Marius Canard, art. "Djanāḥīya" in *EI*², II (Leiden, 1965), 441; Wadād al-Qāḍī, *Al-Kaysānīya fī l-ta'rīkh wa-l-adab* (Beirut, 1974), 240–43 and *passim* (see index).

with their leader, Abū Muslim al-Khurāsānī. In 129/746, however, Abū Muslim, wishing to take no chances, had him imprisoned and then killed.

Besides being known for his historical and theological rôle, ʻAbd Allāh ibn Muʻāwiya is cited in the sources as a good poet and an outstanding orator; some pieces of his poems and speeches have been preserved.[70] The situation is different with regard to his image as a "prose writer", however, for none of the sources speak of him in this regard. Now it would be naive, of course, to think that he never wrote letters: as a political leader, he certainly did. But that does not make him, strictly speaking, a writer of literary prose. In fact, there is textual evidence in at least one source that he actually employed a secretary to write on his behalf.[71] On the other hand, al-Jāḥiẓ attributes to him not only the letter we are studying, but also what al-Jāḥiẓ calls "his famous letter"—a longer (20 lines) epistle which he says ʻAbd Allāh wrote to Abū Muslim from jail.[72] Bearing in mind al-Jāḥiẓ's early date and the fact that he recorded the two letters attributed to ʻAbd Allāh ibn Muʻāwiya one immediately following the other, we may conclude that ʻAbd Allāh ibn Muʻāwiya did in fact write some literary letters. Only one of these epistles became well-known, however, and ʻAbd Allāh's reputation in prose writing never reached the same level as that of his reputation in poetry and orations. Could the letter attributed to ʻAbd al-Ḥamīd by al-Balawī thus actually be the work of ʻAbd Allāh ibn Muʻāwiya?

This difficult question may be addressed by first analyzing the style of ʻAbd Allāh ibn Muʻāwiya's "famous letter", the attribution of which is apparently not in doubt. Here one notes three outstanding features: parallelism, very short phrases, and rhymed prose, all conven-

[70] See al-Jāḥiẓ, *Al-Bayān wa-l-tabyīn*, I, 312, 353; also I, 59, 278; II, 84; al-Mubarrad, *Al-Kāmil fī l-adab wa-l-lugha*, ed. Muḥammad Abū l-Faḍl Ibrāhīm and al-Sayyid Shiḥāta (Cairo, 1956), I, 163, 212, 214; Abū l-Faraj al-Iṣfahānī, *Kitāb al-aghānī* (Beirut, 1974), XII, 231–38.

[71] See Abū l-Faraj al-Iṣfahānī, *Aghānī*, XII, 230. His name was Ḥamza ibn ʻUmāra, on whom see Marshall G.S. Hodgson, "How Did the Early Shīʻa Become Sectarian?", *JAOS* 57 (1955), 6; al-Qāḍī, *Kaysānīya*, 205–208 and *passim* (see index).

[72] See al-Jāḥiẓ, *Al-Bayān wa-l-tabyīn*, II, 82–83; there is also a fragment of it in Abū l-Faraj al-Iṣfahānī, *Aghānī*, XII, 229.

tions to which the author strictly adheres. Thus, the beginning of the letter reads: *innaka mustawada'u wadā'i', wa-mūlī ṣanā'i'; wa-inna l-wadā'i'a mar'īya, wa-inna l-ṣanā'i'a 'ārīya; fa-udhkuri l-qaṣāṣ, wa-uṭlubi l-khalāṣ; wa-nabbih li-l-fikri qalbaka, wa-ittaqi llāha rabbaka....* Now, if we compare this style with that of the letter we are studying, the difference between them is clearly immense. Except for parallelism, which is typical of the styles of both 'Abd al-Ḥamīd and 'Abd Allāh ibn Mu'āwiya, there is nothing else in common. This applies not only to the first part of the letter which is attributed to both writers, but also to its latter, divergent part, in both versions. For how can the sentences cited above be stylistically comparable with the beginning of our letter, which reads: *fa-qad 'āqanī l-shakku fī amrika 'an 'azmati l-ra'yi fīka, ibtada'tanī bi-l-luṭfi 'an ghayri khibratin, thumma a'qabahu jafā'un bi-ghayri dhanbin, fa-aṭma'anī awwaluka fī ikhā'ika, wa-ay'asanī ākhiruka min wafā'ika*? And how can it be comparable to the 'Abd al-Ḥamīd version, where one reads: *fa-a'tib min kathabin fa-dhū l-i'tābi min dhanbin ka-man lam yudhnib; waqānā llāhu wa-iyyāka fitnata l-khallati, wa-'aṣamanā wa-iyyāka bi-wafā'i ahli l-dīn*, or even with the 'Abd Allāh ibn Mu'āwiya version, where one reads: *fa-subḥāna man law shā'a kashafa bi-īḍāḥi l-ra'yi fī amrika 'an 'azīmati l-shakki fīka, fa-aqamnā 'alā i'tilāfin aw iftaraqnā 'alā ikhtilāfin*? The style of the letter we are studying is most certainly *not* that of 'Abd Allāh ibn Mu'āwiya. It is, furthermore, so typical of 'Abd al-Ḥamīd's style that there can be hardly any doubt that the letter has come from 'Abd al-Ḥamīd's hand.

As to how this epistle came to be attributed in a different version to 'Abd Allāh ibn Mu'āwiya, so little information can be brought to bear on this question that all one can suggest is that the faulty attribution took place before the time al-Jāḥiẓ wrote his *Al-Bayān wa-l-tabyīn*. This much would seem clear from the fact that this tremendous stylistic difference could not have escaped the discerning eye of a towering stylist—and an early one for that matter—such as al-Jāḥiẓ.

The second letter raising the problem of attribution is no. 20, which is attributed to 'Abd al-Ḥamīd in al-Qalqashandī's *Ṣubḥ al-a'shā*, a very late source of the ninth/fifteenth century. Two earlier authors, al-Zubayr ibn Bakkār (d. 256/870) and al-Mubarrad (d. 276/889), attribute it to Sālim, 'Abd al-Ḥamīd's teacher and father/brother in-law, or to Sālim's son 'Abd Allāh.[73] Like the letter just discussed, this one survives in two versions: there is a short beginning which is common to both versions (10 lines), followed by a long, additional part (51 lines) which occurs only in the Sālim version. The 'Abd al-Ḥamīd version is clearly an incomplete segment of a letter, with a clear beginning (*ammā ba'd*) but no end, while the Sālim version has a clear beginning and a clear end stating that the epistle was written in 119/737 (*wa-kataba* [*'Abd Allāh ibn*] *Sālim*). The first version is cited by al-Qalqashandī without any identification besides the statement that 'Abd al-Ḥamīd wrote it; the second, attributed to Sālim or his son, follows a long introduction within a *khabar* transmitted on the authority of al-Madā'inī (d. 228/843), explicating the circumstances that occasioned its composition.[74] It was written by Sālim or his son on behalf of the caliph Hishām, and was addressed to Hishām's governor of Iraq, Khālid al-Qasrī (d. 126/743).[75] The caliph, having been angry for some time at Khālid for a variety of reasons, both official and personal, seized the opportunity to write him this letter upon learning that Khālid had harshly mistreated a subject of his. The letter angrily cites Khālid's failings, past and present, and warns him that his continuation in office is completely dependent on the caliph's pleasure.

In order to solve this attribution problem, it is useful to begin by examining the common, first part of the letter, then to go on to compare this part with the longer part found only in the Sālim/'Abd Allāh version. Two points about the first part are striking:

a. Although there are some differences in readings between the two versions, these are all insignificant. Some are orthographical (*al-*

---

[73] See al-Zubayr ibn Bakkār, *Al-Akhbār al-muwaffaqīyāt*, ed. Sāmī Makkī al-'Ānī (Baghdad, 1392/1972), 290–95 (attributed to Sālim, though "corrected" by the editor, on the basis of al-Mubarrad's text, to read "'Abd Allāh ibn Sālim"); al-Mubarrad, *Kāmil*, IV, 121–25 (attributed to 'Abd Allāh ibn Sālim).

[74] I am grateful to Stefan Leder for drawing my attention to the fact that the Sālim/'Abd Allāh version occurs within a *khabar*; see his "Features of the Novel in Early Historiography: The Downfall of Xālid al-Qasrī", *Oriens* 32 (1990), 72–96. Dr. Leder kindly sent me the proofs of his article prior to publication.

[75] For Khālid, see G.R. Hawting, art. "Khālid ibn 'Abd Allāh al-Ḳasrī" in *EI*², IV (Leiden, 1978), 925–27. For a more detailed study on Khālid's political career, see Harald Cornelius, *Ḫālid b. 'Abdallāh al-Qasrī, Statthalter vom Iraq unter den Omayyaden (724–738 n. Ch.)* (Ph.D. dissertation: Frankfurt, 1958).

'ashā vs. *al-ghiyār*, *wa-istathqala* vs. *wa-istaqalla*); some involve changing a preposition (*ilayka* vs. *'indaka*, *'alayka* vs. *ilayka*) or a particle (*fa-inna* vs. *inna*, *jama'a* vs. *la-jama'a*); others involve changing words, deleting some or adding others, without seriously altering the meaning, and hence are transmission-related (*la-raddaka ilā mā kunta 'alayhi* vs. *wa-raddaka ilā manzilatin anta ahluhā*, or *wa-law arāda amīru l-mu'minīna mukāfa'ataka bi-lafẓika wa-ma'ājalata fasādika* vs. *wa-law arāda amīru l-mu'minīna ifsādaka*).

b. The 'Abd al-Ḥamīd version drops about six lines from the part common to both versions, almost three lines before its end. A careful examination of this omission indicates that it makes clear, personal reference to Khālid: his lowly tribe of Bajīla, a sentence he is reported to have said in public, and a sly reference to another statement in which he made a mistake in a speech in 119/737—all of which are historically attested.[76] What this interesting omission means is that the 'Abd al-Ḥamīd version has been "neutralized"; all one can extract from it historically is that it was written on behalf of a caliph (the "Commander of the Faithful") to a subject of his who is probably in some high office, since he has gained several tokens of grace from the caliph. It has now been reported to the caliph that there has occurred an incident in which his "high official" has arrogantly misbehaved toward a particular person. But such are things: when a man receives many graces and succeeds, he thinks that he has gained what he has through his own assets; however, when misfortune befalls him, he becomes meek, repentant, and weak, and then easily falls prey to his enemy. Should the Commander of the Faithful wish to recompense the official in line with his misconduct, he would confront him with the person whom he has wronged; but should he wish really to give him his due, he would cast him down to the (lowly) position he has always deserved.

At this point, it becomes possible for the researcher to clarify the transmission of this letter. One point is certain, and that is that the

[76] Cf. the studies cited in the previous note.

long Sālim/'Abd Allāh version must represent the original text. At some time before al-Qalqashandī, someone extracted a part from it. He "neutralized" this selection by deleting from it all material that could trace it to a particular time and to particular circumstances; hence the omission noted above and the partial transmission of the letter, since the latter long part all deals with Khālid and his misconduct. But why should anyone do such a thing? I think the answer is fairly easy: he wanted to present a "model letter", one that other secretaries should emulate when they themselves need to write a letter on the same subject on behalf of their superiors. If this is true, then this "process of selection" could have occurred at any time between the late second/eighth and the late eighth/fourteenth centuries. I am inclined to think, however, that it was done earlier rather than later, simply because the style of the letter was in vogue—and was hence useful for the secretaries—not too long after the death of 'Abd al-Ḥamīd. Already by the middle of the fourth/tenth century the secretaries were writing in a different style, one much more ornate and yet less imposing and tortuous than that of 'Abd al-Ḥamīd; and when later anthologists included in their books the texts of letters by 'Abd al-Ḥamīd, they did this either for literary/historical purposes or because of their individual tastes. In fact, as Iḥsān 'Abbās has suggested, one of the main reasons why the vast majority of 'Abd al-Ḥamīd's letters were lost was the relatively rapid change in literary taste.[77] In the case of this particular letter, it could overcome the obstacle of change in taste, and hence survive as a model, because of its stylistic imperiousness, power, directness, and (now, after reduction) brevity. Such characteristics made it perennially useful for secretaries of the Chancery at all times, since through them it could, as I have mentioned earlier, evoked an awed sense of the extreme distance between the mundane world of the populace (including in this case a high-ranking official) and the august domain of the caliph, the latter being portrayed here as a towering figure who alone holds sway over all his subjects and is in complete control of all the affairs of his realm.

It remains to consider why the text of this letter was attributed to Sālim or his son 'Abd Allāh in the long version and to 'Abd al-Ḥamīd in the short one. To begin with, the letter was undoubtedly written by

[77] See 'Abbās, *'Abd al-Ḥamīd*, 65–67.

Sālim or his son for a very simple reason, namely that 'Abd al-Ḥamīd was not in Hishām's service in Syria in 119/736, when this epistle was written, but rather in the service of Marwān ibn Muḥammad in Armenia. At that time, Sālim was the chief of the Chancery, and the friction between Hishām and his governor Khālid, which is historically well attested, was already far advanced: Hishām had Khālid expelled from office in the following year. Khālid was imprisoned, next put under what amounts to house arrest, and then was killed shortly after Hishām's death.[78] Thus it is only natural that Sālim should have written this letter to Khālid on behalf of Hishām, just as he wrote many of the caliph's other letters, some of which have been preserved.[79]

Whether it was Sālim himself who wrote this letter, or his son 'Abd Allāh, is a more difficult question. The two sources citing this letter in its "Sālim form" both mark the end of the letter with the formula *wa-kataba...*, "and ... wrote"; however, one source has it *wa-kataba Sālim* and the other *wa-kataba 'Abd Allāh ibn Sālim*, a difficulty which compounds the problem rather than helps to solve it.[80] One must therefore seek criteria other than textual ones to find a plausible answer. If one were to take style as a criterion, then one would say that the letter portrays a style which could certainly be that of Sālim. But we can state this simply because we have other samples of Sālim's epistles against which we can compare other letters of disputed attribution. The same does not apply to 'Abd Allāh ibn Sālim, none of whose letters have survived (other than this one, if it is indeed from his hand), and about whom we know next to nothing aside from the fact that he was a secretary, like his father—not to Hishām, though, but to his successor in the caliphate, al-Walīd ibn Yazīd (125–26/743–44).[81] In fact, there is nothing that dictates against 'Abd Allāh's authorship of this letter, since we know that not only the chief of Hishām's Chancery, Sālim, wrote on behalf of the caliph, but also others did as well, such as

[78] See Hawting, "Khālid ibn 'Abd Allāh al-Ḳasrī", 926–27.

[79] For Sālim's letters, see 'Abbās, *'Abd al-Ḥamīd*, 305–19; also 28–31 for the best study published so far on him.

[80] See n. 73 above.

[81] See al-Jahshiyārī, *Al-Wuzarā' wa-l-kuttāb*, 68. It is interesting to note that al-Ṭabarī does not mention his name among the secretaries of al-Walīd ibn Yazīd; see his *Ta'rīkh*, II, 839–40.

'Abd al-Ḥamīd. And if we return to the criterion of style, we could easily presume that 'Abd Allāh, who, like 'Abd al-Ḥamīd, must have been trained by Sālim in the Chancery, learned his father's style and emulated it in his own writing. This is further confirmed by the fact that there is a fair degree of similarity in style between 'Abd al-Ḥamīd's prose and that of Sālim. And it is precisely this that caused the plurality of attribution in the letter at hand. Dated and historically set into context, it was of necessity cited as coming—as it really did—from the hand of Sālim or his son; without date and historical content, it could pass as the work of 'Abd al-Ḥamīd.

Here another criterion comes into play for historians of literature, namely that of fame. Although all three prose writers write in similar styles, 'Abd al-Ḥamīd is by far, and of old, the most famous and most prolific stylist of them all. Now let us suppose that an anthologist is compiling a book that would benefit the secretaries, one which would include "model letters" which they could emulate. He finds a dated, documented letter from the hand of Sālim (or his son). He likes the letter and wishes to include it in his anthology. But he has no historical motives and no particular taste; besides, he does not want to record a long letter, only a part which could be useful for the secretaries. He thus "selects" a part which suits his purpose; and as this selection must be "neutral", so as to allow for extensive usage, he omits the "historically revealing" passages. The remaining "selection" then stands on its own. At this point he has two choices: either to attribute it to someone or to omit the mention of an author. He decides to mention the author, perhaps for authentication. But upon looking carefully at the letter, and being of necessity familiar with styles and the history of Arabic prose, he finds that the letter, though actually from the hand of Sālim or his son, could easily pass as 'Abd al-Ḥamīd's stylistically, now that it is short and "neutral". And as 'Abd al-Ḥamīd is so much more famous and authoritative than his mentor or the latter's son, the secretaries are likely to emulate him rather than the other two. The short form of the letter thus comes to be attributed, for quite "innocent" motives, to 'Abd al-Ḥamīd.

There is one last argument I would like to put forward in connection with the "fame issue". It is this very criterion that inclines me to believe that the original full letter was written by 'Abd Allāh ibn Sālim rather than by Sālim. For fame is a relative matter, and when ʿAbd al-Ḥamīd is dropped out of the picture, Sālim, of the remaining two prose writers, is certainly the more famous one: not only was he ʿAbd al-Ḥamīd's tutor, but his work was deemed worthy of being collected, like ʿAbd al-Ḥamīd's, into a book.[82] A letter from the hand of Sālim's son could thus easily be attributed to him. This could also have happened either as a simple oversight ("ʿAbd Allāh ibn Sālim" could be read without the first three words), or by perplexity upon encountering an unknown name, in which case the familiar replaces the unfamiliar, and the original comes to be regarded as an error. The reverse process, it is to be noted, could not have happened: that is, a scribe or anthologist making use of a letter by the famous Sālim would not have ascribed it in his own copy or collection to the almost unknown ʿAbd Allāh ibn Sālim.

Conclusion

In this study I have tried to examine the problems one encounters at a very early period in the history of Arabic literary prose when dealing with the question of the authenticity of ʿAbd al-Ḥamīd's letters. As I have shown, these letters, like most of the literature that has been preserved for us in the sources, are closely connected with the Umayyad state. The main theoretical problem about them is that none of them has been recorded in a contemporary source; rather, they all survive only in later sources at least a century removed from his time, for reasons that have more to do with the pace of the recording movement in Islamic civilization than with the letters per se. A related problem is that some of the epistles have been preserved in sources that date from several centuries after the death of ʿAbd al-Ḥamīd. In the preceding pages, I have discussed these two problems at length and have shown that they do not pose a serious challenge to the authenticity of the letters, mainly because of a physical, continuous, and living "Abd al-Ḥamīd literary legacy", and because of the nature and degree of preservation and selection in the Arabic literary sources. The other two problems—practical considerations—have to do with the questions

[82] Ibn al-Nadīm, *Fihrist*, 131.

of some letters surviving in more than one version, and others being attributed in certain sources to prose writers other than 'Abd al-Ḥamīd. In dealing with the first issue, I have considered the most striking example of a letter transmitted in more than one version—'Abd al-Ḥamīd's "Letter to the Secretaries"—and have examined the patterns of variant readings that may be discerned in the two distinct versions of this text. This examination has shown that of the two, one (J-IḤ) represents 'Abd al-Ḥamīd's original letter, while the other (IK-Q) suffers from serious transmission, scribal, and Islamic-prejudice problems. The first of the two versions, I have concluded, should be be considered closest to the authentic text. With regard to the attribution problem, I have examined the two letters in which this issue occurs. In the case of one letter I have tried to establish authenticity on transmission grounds, and in the second authenticity has been disproved on similar though slightly wider grounds, in which case the letter should be deleted from the available 'Abd al-Ḥamīd literary corpus.

What the examination of all these problems shows on a more general level is that the transmission issues related to the theoretical problems may be deemed resolved, while those related to the practical ones admit of only provisional solutions. Thus, should we in the future, by some stroke of luck, happen upon new letters by 'Abd al-Ḥamīd, or upon new versions of extant letters by him, these will each have to be examined separately before their attribution and textual reliability may be fully established.

APPENDIX
‘Abd al-Ḥamīd’s Letters
(According to the ‘Abbās Edition)

No.	*Subject*	*Degree of Preservation*	*Length (lines)*	*Pg.*
1	From Marwān to Ibn Hubayra, rebuking him for mistreatment of the caliph’s kinsman	complete	23	191
2	From ‘Abd al-Ḥamīd to a friend, inquiring about a change in his attitude towards him	complete	7	192
3	From Marwān to his son ‘Ubayd Allāh, concerning the latter’s problems with his wife	complete	29	193
4	From Marwān to his brother, about the death of al-Ḥakam ibn Marwān	complete	11	194
5	From ‘Abd al-Ḥamīd, in condolence to a member of the Umayyad family	complete	14	195
6	From ‘Abd al-Ḥamīd to the Commander of the Faithful, describing the flooding of the Euphrates	complete	19	196
7	From the Commander of the Faithful to ‘Abd al-‘Azīz ibn ‘Umar ibn Hubayra, concerning the purchase of a slave woman	complete	20	197

No.	*Subject*	*Degree of Preservation*	*Length (lines)*	*Pg.*
8	From the Commander of the Faithful to Naṣr ibn Sayyār, on seditious activities in Khurāsān	complete	56	198
9	From ʻAbd al-Ḥamīd to a friend concerning his first-born child	complete	23	201
10	From ʻAbd al-Ḥamīd to a friend concerning private v. public life	complete	42	203
11	From the Commander of the Faithful to his governors, concerning the caliph's pilgrimage in 106/725	complete	32	205
12	From the Commander of the Faithful, concerning Ramaḍān	complete	8	206
13	From Marwān to Hishām, concerning the spread of the Qadarīya in the army and in Armenia	complete	13	207
14	From ʻAbd al-Ḥamīd to Ibn al-Buḥturī concerning the latter's request for assistance for reconciliation with the caliph	complete	9	207
15	From the Commander of the Faithful, concerning the purchase of Berber or Maghribī slave women	complete	7	208

No.	*Subject*	*Degree of Preservation*	*Length (Lines)*	*Pg.*
16	On civil discord (*fitna*)	partial	31	209
17	From the Commander of the Faithful, concerning obedience	complete	57	210
18	On civil discord (*fitna*)	partial	8	213
19	To a rebel	complete	20	214
20	From the Commander of the Faithful, to an official (attribution to ʻAbd al-Ḥamīd unlikely)	partial	10	215
21	From Marwān to the crown prince ʻUbayd Allāh, advising him on matters of state, especially military topics	complete	846	215
22	From the Commander of the Faithful, a prohibition of the playing of chess	complete	58	265
23	From ʻAbd al-Ḥamīd to the Commander of the Faithful, describing a hunting trip	complete	60	268
24	A *taḥmīd* about Abū l-ʻAlāʼ al-Ḥarūrī	partial	11	271
25	A *taḥmīd* about a conquest	partial	10	272
26	A *taḥmīd* about a conquest	partial	22	273

No.	*Subject*	*Degree of Preservation*	*Length (Lines)*	*Pg.*
27	A *taḥmīd*	partial	9	274
28	From Marwān to Hishām, in condolence for the death of the caliph's son	partial	6	274
29	From Hishām to Yūsuf ibn 'Umar, announcing that the caliph is well	complete	14	275
30	From 'Abd al-Ḥamīd to Marwān requesting something	complete	6	276
31	On fraternity (*ikhā'*)	complete	41	276
32	From 'Abd al-Ḥamīd to his family (farewell letter written shortly before his death)	partial	19	278
33	From Marwān to Hishām, in condolence for the death of the latter's favorite concubine	complete	5	280
34	On the rebellion of an official	partial	7	280
35	From 'Abd al-Ḥamīd, his "Letter to the Secretaries"	complete	110	281
36	From 'Abd al-Ḥamīd, recommending someone	complete	2	288
37	From 'Abd al-Ḥamīd, rebuking a friend	complete	3	288

No.	*Subject*	*Degree of Preservation*	*Length (Lines)*	*Pg.*
38	On the Khurāsānian rebels	complete	8	289
40	From Marwān to a governor, concerning a gift (attributed to another author)	fragment	1	290

7

The Literary Use of the *Khabar*: A Basic Form of Historical Writing*

Stefan Leder
(Frankfurt am Main)

THE EARLY PERIOD of Islamic history, dating from the appearance of the Prophet in the second decade of the seventh century to the establishment and dynastic consolidation of Arab-Islamic rule, is of paramount significance. Its importance for Islamic culture is also reflected in numerical proportions in al-Ṭabarī's *Annals*, completed in AD 915,[1] which cover Biblical history, the ancient history of Persia, and the first three centuries of Islamic history in about 7800 pages.[2] A third of this work is devoted to the eight decades which cover the mission of the Prophet, the conquests, and the first fundamental conflicts within the Muslim community. Early Islamic history is dealt with in several fields of Arabic literature: Prophetic tradition (*ḥadīth*), which contains countless reports about sayings and deeds of Muḥammad; Qur'ānic commentaries (*tafsīr*), where the revelation is related to the life of the

---

*I am indebted to Dr. Hilary Kilpatrick, Lausanne, for her stylistic revision of this text.

[1]Franz-Christoph Muth, *Die Annalen von aṭ-Ṭabarī im Spiegel der europäischen Bearbeitungen* (Frankfurt am Main, 1983), ii. The publication history and existence of several recensions of this work are discussed by Franz Rosenthal, *The History of al-Ṭabarī*, XXVIII: *The Return of the Caliphate to Baghdad* (New York, 1985), xiv–xxi; cf. vol. I (as n. 11 below), 133.

[2]Al-Ṭabarī, *Ta'rīkh al-rusul wa-l-mulūk*, ed. M.J. de Goeje *et al.* (Leiden, 1879–1901).

Prophet; historiography, and finally *adab* literature, which displays the ideal of refinement and unites entertaining and didactic tendencies.

Historiographical literature about early Islamic times is divided mainly according to historical periods. Material on the life of the Prophet (*sīra*), the military campaigns directed by the Prophet or his Companions (*maghāzī*), and the conquests (*futūḥ*), as well as particular cases (*waq'a, maqtal*) are kept distinct, although not entirely separate. Biographically organized works (*ṭabaqāt*) and collections of *ḥadīth* may include all of these materials. Narratives about the pre-Islamic battle-days (*ayyām al-'arab*) are often considered to be the predecessors of and model for Arabic historiographical narration;[3] this seems questionable, however, since the extant textual evidence cannot claim an origin prior to other branches of literature about early Islamic times.

The historiographical and biographical compilations, works on poets and poetry, and those which treat linguistic matters, are to a great extent compilations of short texts. These include simple statements, utterances of authoritative scholars, saints, or statesmen, reports of events, and—sometimes rather complex—stories about historical events and personalities. These texts, which may vary in length from one line to several pages are designated by the term *khabar* (pl. *akhbār*).

Historiographical tradition also contains speeches and such documents as treaties or letters, as well as chronological and onomastical data. Materials of this kind may appear as traditions independent from *akhbār* narration and will be excluded from our analysis here. Further investigation is needed to elucidate whether they are more entitled to claim historicity than *akhbār*, and less affected by distortion in transmission.

In any case, *akhbār* may also convey historical facts. The discussion of this form of historical writing, however, must concentrate on the difficulties raised by this assertion. *Akhbār* in general are characterized by an intense and complex process of "reactive transmission", includ-

[3]Franz Rosenthal, *A History of Muslim Historiography* (Leiden, 1952), 67; Ursula Sezgin, *Abū Miḫnaf. Ein Beitrag zur Historiographie der umaiyadischen Zeit* (Leiden, 1971), 90f.; Geo Widengren, "Oral Tradition and Written Literature among the Hebrews in the Light of Arabic Evidence, with Special Regard to Prose Narratives", *Acta Orientalia* 23 (1959), 238; Claude Cahen, "L'Historiographie arabe: des origines au VIIe s.H.", *Arabica* 33 (1986), 136.

ing unadmitted authorship and fundamental reshaping of the "original" narrations. This process is at work even before *akhbār* appear in our earliest sources, and often continues in textual transmission. Analytical consideration of a synopsis of all the relevant sources, however, allows the authorial contributions made in the course of transmission to be identified (as we shall see below), and permits one to assess the narrative elaboration and interpretation of events in early tradition, which, for historiographical purposes, is later reduced to seemingly factual reports. Storytelling, a mode of discourse far removed from historiographical intentions, thus appears to be one root of the *akhbār* tradition. These observations will be discussed, in conclusion, in the light of different types of narration manifest in *akhbār* literature.

The basic meaning of *khabar* denotes "a piece of information", as reflected also by the verbal use of this root.[4] In a literary context, however, the notion applies to narration in a more general sense. The use of the term, as well as the nature of some *akhbār*, indicates that they do not fully correspond to the concept of factual information. Yet the presumption that *akhbār* possess factual validity is widespread and dominates the medieval understanding of these texts.[5] Moreover, the style of *akhbār*[6] and the general features of narrative form give rise to the impression that *akhbār* are reports truthfully handed down from prior witnesses.

The *khabar* constitutes a self-contained narrative unit which depicts an incident or a limited sequence of occurrences or conveys sayings. In most cases it does not make any reference to the historical situation, nor does it hint at the context in which it arose. In our sources these texts "are not explicitly linked to one another in any way; they are simply juxtaposed end to end...."[7] As a result, *akhbār* literature basically consists of compilations[8] which gather and arrange traditions according

---

[4]*khabura*, "to possess knowledge"; *akhbara*, "to inform".

[5]For a more detailed discussion, see Stefan Leder, "Features of the Novel in Early Historiography—the Downfall of Xālid al-Qasrī", *Oriens* 32 (1990), 72–96.

[6]See the masterly description in Widengren, "Oral Tradition", 232–33.

[7]R. Stephen Humphreys, *Islamic History: a Framework for Inquiry* (Minneapolis, 1987), 71.

[8]Humphreys (*ibid.*, 70) distinguishes the "digest" from the "compilation". The "digests" he mentions, such as the *Al-Akhbār al-ṭiwāl* of Abū Bakr al-Dīnawarī (d.

to various concepts, and their depiction of history is characterized by an "atomistic" character.[9] In some instances, and rather exceptionally, *akhbār* may be components of extended narratives.[10]

Authors of compilations are, of course, not supposed to have produced the texts they present. Consequently, in most of our sources we find quotations—mostly without any indication of the written sources used—from scholars who were themselves occupied with the collection and transmission of *akhbār*. Since these scholars quite often refer to earlier authorities, we find chains of transmitters (*asānīd*, sing. *isnād*) which connect the author of the compilation with the person whose words are quoted, or with an eyewitness.

The compilers, e.g. al-Ṭabarī, made use of earlier collections.[11] In most cases, the oldest collections that we know of from medieval bio-bibliographical sources, or that may be inferred from internal evidence, have survived only in the scattered quotations of our sources. There are only a few exceptions: for example, the collection of materials on the life of the Prophet composed by Ibn Isḥāq (d. 150/767) in the middle of the eighth century and preserved in the redaction of Ibn Hishām (d. 218/833).[12] The oldest preserved collections of *akhbār* date from the end of the eighth and the beginning of the ninth century. The chains of transmitters given in our sources enable us to identify the early collectors as those authorities quoted, who refer in turn to various informants.[13] But in most cases the identification of *authors* among the

282/895, see n. 85 below), go back to the same sources as the "compilations" or directly draw on these works. They condense the *akhbār*, try to integrate them in a more continuous narration, and omit the chains of authorities (*asānīd*).

[9]The concept of "molecular" structure was developed by Tadeusz Kowalski [1935]; see Bertold Spuler, *Iran in frühislamischer Zeit* (Wiesbaden, 1952), xvi. Cf. Patricia Crone's "Historiographical Introduction" to her *Slaves on Horses: the Evolution of the Islamic Polity* (Cambridge, 1980), 15, and 5.

[10]As is the case in the narrative on the downfall of Khālid al-Qasrī (see n. 5); cf. Crone, *Slaves on Horses*.

[11] *The History of al-Ṭabarī*, I: *General Introduction and From the Creation to the Flood*, trans. Franz Rosenthal (New York, 1989), 53, 56.

[12]Ibn Hishām, *Al-Sīra al-nabawīya*, ed. Muṣṭafā al-Saqqā *et al.*, 2nd ed. (Cairo, 1375/1955); trans. Alfred Guillaume, *The Life of Muhammad* (Oxford, 1955).

[13]Gregor Schoeler, "Die Frage der mündlichen und schriftlichen Überlieferung der Wissenschaften im Islam", *Der Islam* 62 (1985), 216. The information given in the *Geschichte des arabischen Schrifttums* by Fuat Sezgin is in many instances based

authorities quoted remains questionable and demands thorough study. This problem cannot be considered here in detail. But certainly, the study of the origin, transmission, and narrative form of the *akhbār* associated with the most important early collectors will long yield results which can contribute to our understanding of the development, particularities, and meaning of these texts.

The Historian's Evaluation of Akhbār

Historical evaluation has to construe the isolated tradition within a context that must be inferred from other relevant traditions gathered from several sources. In most cases the *akhbār* include many variants and contradictory statements. Disregarding the epistemological aspects of the problem, the historian may accomplish his task by evaluating *akhbār* on the grounds of chronology and the logical course of events. This approach proves especially successful when the information gained from *akhbār* can be related to Qur'ānic passages.[14] However, the filiation of sources and the evaluation of information that cannot be judged in the light of other evidence remain questions crucial to our understanding of the early development of this literature. For this reason, the evolution of historical tradition during the 150 to 200 years which extend from the occurrence of actual events and the compilation of *akhbār* about them has long been a subject of inquiry.

Indications given by the *isnāds* and data on the lives and reputations of the transmitters[15] still offer guidance to modern research, and have naturally been used in the past. Joseph Horovitz, for example, based his survey of early biographies of Muḥammad on them.[16] Some 70 years

on this approach. Vol. I (Leiden, 1967) owes much to quotations in the *Al-Iṣāba fī tamyīz al-ṣaḥāba* by Ibn Ḥajar al-'Asqalānī (d. 852/1449), and vol. II (Leiden, 1975) draws on the *isnāds* given in the *Kitāb al-aghānī* of Abū l-Faraj al-Iṣfahānī (d. 356/967).

[14] Cf. Uri Rubin, "The 'Constitution of Medina'—Some Notes", *SI* 62 (1985), 5–23.

[15] The oldest extant collections of these materials were composed at about the same time—and sometimes by the same authors (e.g. Khalīfa ibn Khayyāṭ, d. 240/854) as our early sources on history.

[16] Joseph Horovitz, "The Earliest Biographies of the Prophet and Their Authors", *IC* 2 (1927), 535–59; 3 (1928), 22–54, 164–82, 495–526.

earlier, Alois Sprenger had already traced the beginnings of historical writing according to the information which he found in biographical literature and works on methods of transmission and teaching (*'ilm al-taḥammul*).[17] Studies of this kind, however, neglect criteria which may be established from the study of the text itself; and in this respect they share the insufficiency of medieval Islamic criticism, which is based on the evaluation of the formal correctness of the *isnād*.

Concern with the substance of traditions quite naturally engendered a method of textual criticism which was established in Arabic philology at the end of the nineteenth century. The consideration that traditions on religious doctrine and juridical matters (*ḥadīth*) were impregnated with dogmatical and political tendencies suggested conclusions as to the time and milieu of their origin.[18] But this approach cannot always be applied to early historiography. Even in the case of a narration which is obviously biased, it often remains difficult to relate the underlying tendency to the evolution of dogmatic thought, so that any conclusion as to chronology will remain somewhat hazardous. However, the comprehension of historiographical traditions within the context of historical development and doctrinal evolution may sharpen awareness of elements that have originated *post eventum*. We may still agree in general with Julius Wellhausen's observation that reports about early Islamic and Umayyad history may reveal the views and attitudes of authors who cannot have been contemporary to the events.[19]

Wellhausen further assumed that the historiographical value of early collections could be assessed on the basis of their conceptual character.[20] His presumption has been challenged by the discovery that these collections, i.e. the materials quoted in our sources from some authorities of the first half of the eighth century, do not represent any homogeneous

[17] "On the Origin and Progress of Writing down Historical Facts among the Musulmans", *Journal of the Asiatic Society of Bengal* 25 (1856–57), 303–29, 375–81. Cf. *idem*, "Das Traditionswesen bei den Arabern" *ZDMG* 10 (1856), 1–17.

[18] Ignaz Goldziher, *Muhammedanische Studien* (Halle, 1889–90), II, 88–130.

[19] Julius Wellhausen, "Prolegomena zur ältesten Geschichte des Islams", in his *Skizzen und Vorarbeiten*, VI (Berlin, 1899), 4–5.

[20] Earling Ladewig Petersen's assumption that "letters" and "speeches" are "expressive of the historian's own conception of characters of the past" thus also seems committed to the idea that "authors" molded their weltanschauung into *akhbār*; see his *'Alī and Mu'āwiya in Early Arabic Tradition* (Copenhagen, 1964), 17.

historical view, but themselves encompass various tendencies.[21] The materials attributed to any particular *akhbārī* (pl. *akhbārīyūn*), the collector and/or compiler of *akhbār*, do not display ideological uniformity.

In contrast, influences of local traditions and tribal interests can be discerned. Such factors asserted themselves in the formation of predominant themes as expressed by narrations,[22] and were also reflected in certain compilations.[23]

The interrelatedness of the source material has become clear through the study of elements of form, and this has proved the value of a "literary" analytical effort—an approach upon which our contribution too is based. Even *akhbār* of seemingly independent origins and reports on different events often show common motifs.[24] If they hold key positions in the context, i.e. if they give shape to essential parts of the plot, the factual validity of the narrative is of course affected in that it has thereby been shown to have been constructed out of disparate narrative material.

Common elements of presumedly independent narrations not only are traceable in motifs, but also emerge from the comparison of parallel *akhbār*. Descriptions of one and the same event which converge in significant respects, but while purporting to be of different origins, are likely to be connected by a non-explicit relationship. Here, as in the case of common motifs, evaluation must be based on the analysis of narrative structure. Conformity evident in elaborated elements of narrative composition, whether they concern details of narrative technique

---

[21] Albrecht Noth, "Der Charakter der ersten grossen Sammlungen von Nachrichten zur Kalifenzeit", *Der Islam* 47 (1971), 197. Cf. also the observations in Crone, *Slaves on Horses*, 10, 13 n.77.

[22] A.A. Duri, *The Rise of Historical Writing among the Arabs*, trans. Lawrence I. Conrad (Princeton, 1983), 22–23 and *passim*.

[23] Lawrence I. Conrad, "Al-Azdī's History of the Arab Conquests in Bilād al-Shām: Some Historiographical Observations", in Muḥammad 'Adnān al-Bakhīt and Iḥsān 'Abbās, eds., *Proceedings of the Second Symposium on the History of Bilād al-Shām during the Early Islamic Period up to 40 A.H./640 A.D.* (Amman, 1987), I, 48–55.

[24] Albrecht Noth, "Iṣfahān–Nihāwand. Eine quellenkritische Studie zur frühislamischen Historiographie", *ZDMG* 118 (1968), 244–96; Lawrence I. Conrad, "Narrative Elaboration in the Early Arabic *Futūḥ* Tradition", unpublished contribution for the Colloquium on Ḥadīth and Historiography (Oxford, 1988).

or a complex structure of the plot, cannot be ascribed to polygenesis or explained by the course of events.[25] The analytical consideration of relevant source material should therefore include the entire narrative appearance of *akhbār* and should not be confined, as is often the case in historical research, to informative details.

Comparisons of parallel narratives have demonstrated the proportions of divergence and shown that the editing of *akhbār* implies operations similar to authorship. Different versions are produced by the authors of our sources, especially when old compilations—those of Ibn Isḥāq, al-Wāqidī (d. 207/822), and Ibn Sa'd (d. 230/844)—are concerned.[26] Careful reading of variant texts permits the identification of the material which was supplied by the compilers and editors of historical traditions.[27] When more recent works like the *Annals* of al-Ṭabarī are considered, it is more likely that *akhbār* were given their final shape by the authors of their sources.[28] As will be demonstrated below, comparative study of the sources may also reveal how traditions can grow through false attribution.

Unavowed Authorship

Reproductions of *akhbār* quoted from the same authorities may differ in wording, narrative structure, or even content. Fundamental reshaping can be regarded as a form of unavowed authorship, because the ascription to an early authority is maintained while no hints as to the author of the adaptation are given. Moreover, the practice of compilation favors the transmission of falsely ascribed texts. The very nature

---

[25] See Stefan Leder, *Das Korpus al-Haiṯam ibn 'Adī (st. 207/822). Herkunft, Überlieferung, Gestalt früher Texte der Aḫbār Literatur* (Frankfurt, 1991), 127–39.

[26] Ella Landau-Tasseron, "Processes of Redaction: the Case of the Tamīmite Delegation to the Prophet Muḥammad", *BSOAS* 49 (1986), 253–70; John Mattock, "History and Fiction", *Occasional Papers of the School of Abbasid Studies* 1 (1986), 85–97.

[27] G.R. Hawting, "Ḥudaybiyya and the Conquest of Mecca: a Reconsideration of the Tradition About the Muslim Takeover of the Sanctuary", *JSAI* 8 (1986), 8, also 2, 16–17.

[28] Leder, "Features of the Novel", 76–83. In this light, Widengren's conclusions ("Oral Tradition", 244–53) concerning al-Ṭabarī's adaptation must be reassessed.

of *akhbār* literature implies that their transmission is not tied to a certain work, since they may have been successively detached from and introduced into a series of works before they appear in the source under consideration. In most cases, our sources draw their material from earlier collections, so that the ascription to an early authority will be cited and reproduced without any original writing of this quoted authority being consulted or any other confirmation being taken into consideration.

As for the assessment of religious and juridical tradition (*ḥadīth*), the reliability of the *isnāds* is also a major issue in the study of *akhbār*. When some texts extant in several renderings manifest specific characteristics which correspond to their transmission as attested by the *isnāds*, we find confirmation of *isnād* through textual proof. The *isnāds* are falsified, on the other hand, when texts which are allegedly transmitted independently, or seem to have different origins, are in fact related by specific features. Although the example given here belongs to the *akhbār al-shu'arā'* ("accounts of the lives of poets"), it is quoted on the authority of collectors who are ubiquitous in historical tradition. A comparison of the fourteen versions of the story which I have encountered so far allows for both an assessment of the degree to which the *akhbārīyūn* are responsible for its formation and an observation of the growth of tradition.[29]

The story tells of the death of the poet 'Urwa ibn Ḥizām, one of the 'Udhrī love heroes of the early Islamic period.[30] His tragic love for his cousin 'Afrā' and his love poetry are famous and familiar to every student of Arabic literature. We shall leave out the biographical background to our story and only deal with the different versions of an eyewitness account about the poet's sad end.

The collation of the texts provides us with some insight into their transmission; textual proof here does not confirm all of the indications

[29] For a detailed discussion of these texts, see Leder, *Korpus al-Haiṯam*, 103–10.

[30] 'Urwa died before 61/680; *GAS*, II, 264–65. The tribe of 'Udhra lived to the north of Medina in the regions of the Ḥijāz and northwest Najd; see Werner Caskel, *Ǧamharat an-nasab. Das genealogische Werk des Hišām b. Muḥammad al-Kalbī* (Leiden, 1966), II, 565–66. It became famous for its poet Jamīl, who sings of his (unhappy) love; see Francesco Gabrieli, art. "al-Djamīl" in *EI*², II (Leiden, 1965), 427–28.

given in the *isnāds*. The renderings quoted from al-Haytham ibn ʻAdī (d. 207/822) and Ibn al-Kalbī (d. 204/819 or 206/821) show, despite the various instances of difference, specific characteristics of two distinct versions reflecting the contribution of the Kūfan *akhbārīyūn* in the formation of this tradition. The existence of several contradictory accounts finally demonstrates the production of "new" narratives.

The renderings of Thaʻlab (d. 291/904), al-Masʻūdī (345/956), Abū l-Faraj al-Iṣfahānī (d. 356/967), and Ibn al-Jawzī (d. 597/1201) manifest a homogeneous plot.[31] Al-Nuʻmān ibn Bashīr (d. 65/684), a champion of early Umayyad politics and one of the heads of the Medinan Anṣār,[32] relates (in the first person) how he witnessed the death of ʻUrwa. He is sent by the caliph to collect the tribute (*ṣadaqāt*) among the tribesmen of the Banū ʻUdhra. On his way back he passes by an isolated encampment. He turns towards it and, coming close, recognizes a young man asleep in front of the tent; behind him, at the entrance, an old woman is sitting. The wording of this description already reveals a relation between the texts (A) of Thaʻlab and Abū l-Faraj, as well as between the renderings (B) of al-Masʻūdī and Ibn al-Jawzī.[33]

The existence of two distinct versions among the texts quoted from al-Haytham is confirmed in the subsequent part of the story. In response to the greetings of al-Nuʻmān the young man pronounces some verses, at the end of which he sobs as if his heart would break. Subsequently, al-Nuʻmān realizes that the young man has died. In the versions (B) of al-Masʻūdī and Ibn al-Jawzī, al-Nuʻmān draws the woman's attention to what has happened, and she goes to see with her own eyes that the young man is dead. Al-Nuʻmān then asks her who he was. The renderings (A) of Thaʻlab and Abū l-Faraj show a somewhat dif-

---

[31] Aḥmad ibn Yaḥyā Thaʻlab, *Al-Majālis*, ed. ʻAbd al-Salām Muḥammad Hārūn (Cairo, 1948–49), I, 291–93; Abū l-Faraj al-Iṣfahānī, *Kitāb al-aghānī* (Cairo, 1345–94/1927–74), XXIV, 162–63; al-Masʻūdī, *Murūj al-dhahab wa-maʻādin al-jawhar*, ed. Charles Pellat (Beirut, 1966–1979), V, 70–71; Ibn al-Jawzī, *Dhamm al-hawā*, ed. Muṣṭafā ʻAbd al-Wāḥid (Cairo, 1381/1962), 415–16.

[32] K.V. Zetterstéen, art. "al-Nuʻmān b. Bashīr" in *EI*[1], III, 952–53.

[33] In Thaʻlab's version Nuʻmān says: *fa-idhā anā bi-shābbin rāqidin bi-fināʼi l-bayti fa-idhā anā bi-ʻajūzin min warāʼihi fī kisri l-bayti.* The *Kitāb al-aghānī* has the same wording. In al-Masʻūdī's text, however, we read: ...*bi-shābbin nāʼimin fī ẓilli l-bayti wa-idhā ʻajūzun jālisa fī kisri l-bayti.* The same words are used in Ibn al-Jawzī's rendering.

ferent order of events. After having witnessed the young man's death, al-Nuʿmān directly asks who it is who has just died. From his question, the woman understands what has happened. In all of the texts, she then explains in a few words that he was her son ʿUrwa, who had been afflicted by love. Al-Nuʿmān stays with her until the dead body has been washed and buried.

The differences between the two groups of renderings are insignificant and do not occasion any change in the plot or meaning. However, we can hardly believe that identical expressions are completely coincidental, brought about by changes introduced independently into the text. But this is what the *isnāds* of the four versions suggest. All of them claim to have been transmitted independently from al-Haytham ibn ʿAdī.[34] We can ignore here the names of the transmitters given in the *isnāds* connecting the authors of our sources with al-Haytham. Important in our context is the fact that, as far as we know from biographical sources, there was no contact between them. As the specific convergences deduced here must be due to certain interrelations in the transmission, it follows that the *isnāds* do not reveal the real transmission of the texts. The preponderant common traits of all four reproductions may, so far, formally be regarded as going back to the report of the eyewitness al-Nuʿmān.

We have not yet presented all the story. There is an end to it which is common only to the versions quoted from al-Haytham. Asked why he attended the burial of the young man, al-Nuʿmān answers that God will reward this noble deed. This appendix is curious for two reasons. First, its narrative construction is defective. The dialogue shows al-Nuʿmān involved in a conversation with a character who has not previously been introduced into the story. Obviously the authors who reproduced the story also felt this was a weak point, and they tried to solve the problem in different manners. Thaʿlab and Ibn al-Jawzī—Abū l-Faraj does not reproduce this part of the story—interrupt the account of

[34] A well-known *akhbārī*; cf., e.g., al-Khaṭīb al-Baghdādī (d. 463/1071), *Taʾrīkh Baghdād* (Cairo 1349/1931), XIV, 50–54; Charles Pellat, art. "al-Haytham b. ʿAdī" in *EI*[2], III (Leiden, 1971), 328. All of these texts agree on al-Haytham's sources. He appears quoting the Medinan traditionist Hishām ibn ʿUrwa (d. 146/763; see *GAS*, I, 88–89), who refers to his father (i.e. ʿUrwa ibn al-Zubayr, d. 94/712–13), who in turn quotes al-Nuʿmān.

al-Nu'mān, who has told the story in the first person, and introduce another unidentified voice that begins an account in the first person: "I asked al-Nu'mān". In the *isnād*, though not within the story, this speaker may be represented by al-Nu'mān's transmitter, Hishām ibn 'Urwa (d. 146/763). More skill is displayed in al-Mas'ūdī's version. Al-Nu'mān continues his account, mentioning that the caliph 'Uthmān asked him this question. Thus, 'Uthmān is belatedly introduced as a listener to the story al-Nu'mān was telling.

The content of this final part of the story is also unusual. It serves to comment on the events which have just transpired, since al-Nu'mān's answer implies an appraisal of the young man's fate. Death caused by love appears to be devoid of any moral reproach, otherwise al-Nu'mān, an authority of weight, would not have prayed at the victim's graveside. This addition by al-Haytham emphasizes the esteem in which heroes of love stories were held with a sort of ironic simplicity, and gives proof of the respectability of this genre of narratives.

The story about al-Nu'mān witnessing 'Urwa's death is also known from other texts. Ibn al-Jawzī provides another version also quoted—through another *isnād*—from al-Haytham.[35] The first part is identical with what we have just seen. In the second part, al-Nu'mān brings the tidings to the family of 'Afrā', 'Urwa's beloved, and then witnesses her death from grief. Although the tragic death of pairs of lovers is a motif familiar to Ibn al-Jawzī, the far-fetched character of this story induces him to point out its fictitious character: he remarks that he does not accept this version as a reliable reproduction of what al-Haytham ibn 'Adī had taught.

Close to the above-mentioned versions is a narrative preserved by al-Kharā'iṭī (d. 327/938).[36] It shows some resemblance to the accounts (B) of al-Mas'ūdī and Ibn al-Jawzī, especially in those parts which diverge from group A. One element, however, links al-Kharā'iṭī's rendering with other texts: al-Nu'mān describes the morbid thinness of the young man who lay stretched out on the ground.[37] This description has

[35] *Dhamm al-hawā*, 413–14.

[36] *I'tilāl al-qulūb*, Ulu Camı (Bursa), Ms. no. 1535, fols. 53r–v.

[37] Extreme emaciation was a common symptom in the pathology of love. The text reads: *fa-idhā bi-finā'ihi shābbun mustalqin 'alā qafāhu lam yabqa minhu illā jildun 'alā 'aẓamin.*

no equivalent in the versions quoted from al-Haytham, but it also occurs, word for word, in a text rendered by Ibn Qutayba (d. 276/890).[38] This latter authority cites as his source Hishām ibn Muḥammad al-Kalbī (= Ibn al-Kalbī), a contemporary of al-Haytham and a compatriot of his from al-Kūfa.[39] Ibn al-Kalbī in turn also refers—through Abū l-Sā'ib al-Makhzūmī[40]—to Hishām ibn 'Urwa.[41] Another version, again from Ibn al-Kalbī, which has almost no word in common with Ibn Qutayba's text, is preserved in the literary anthology of al-Qālī (d. 356/965).[42] However, both texts agree on the motif of 'Urwa's thinness and the tiny detail that he lies stretched out on the ground. These elements can be recognized as components of a version by Ibn al-Kalbī.

The motif of thinness is found again in another version reproduced by al-Sarrāj (d. 500/1106).[43] Here it is expressed in very different wording and rather bluntly: al-Nu'mān mentions that all that was left of the poor 'Urwa was his head (*lā yurā illā ra'suhu*). Al-Sarrāj quotes al-'Utbī (d. 228/842),[44] who refers to Hishām ibn 'Urwa. Hence, besides al-Haytham ibn 'Adī and Ibn al-Kalbī, we have a third *akhbārī* who spread a tradition of Hishām. Al-'Utbī's version differs greatly from those of the authorities from al-Kūfa and his relation to Hishām is obscure, though it is probable that his rendering is related to the version of Ibn al-Kalbī. The *isnād* is rather unclear about this: "al-'Utbī, from his father, from [some] man (*'an rajulin*), from Hishām". Al-Sarrāj also

[38] *Al-Shi'r wa-l-shu'arā'* (Beirut, 1964), 522–23; Ibn Qutayba's account also includes the death of 'Afrā'.

[39] See W. Atallah,, art "al-Kalbī" in *EI*², IV (Leiden, 1978), 495–96.

[40] Al-Mas'ūdī mentions this authority among his "sources" in his *Murūj al-dhahab*, I, 13:8; for further references, see Pellat's comments in his index to the *Murūj al-dhahab*, VI, 107.

[41] Hishām refers, as in the traditions above, through his father 'Urwa ibn al-Zubayr to al-Nu'mān.

[42] See Abū 'Alī l-Qālī, *Kitāb al-amālī wa-dhayl al-amālī wa-l-nawādir* (Cairo, 1344/1926), III, 157. Again Abū l-Sā'ib al-Makhzūmī, who refers to Hishām ibn 'Urwa, etc., is Ibn al-Kalbī's informant.

[43] *Maṣāri' al-'ushshāq* (Beirut, 1378/1958), I, 30.

[44] *GAS*, I, 371; see also the discussion in Régis Blachère, "Un auteur d'*adab* oublié: al-'Utbī, mort en 228", in *Mélanges d'orientalisme offerts à Henri Massé* (Tehran, 1963), 38–47.

quotes an identical text from al-Mubarrad (d. 285/898), who refers to another eyewitness.[45] So we have two seemingly independent reports which converge in every single word. Probably al-Mubarrad or some later authority has fabricated this *isnād.*

In the case of al-Haytham and Ibn al-Kalbī, it is impossible to determine whether the tradition was in fact spread by Hishām, or whether the name of the Medinan traditionist was simply commandeered—possibly by one of the Kūfan transmitters,[46] who was later imitated by his colleague—in order to do justice to the geographical setting of the events. In any case, we can clearly perceive that a consistent account, differentiated by certain details into two distinct versions, was spread by the Kūfan authorities.

Against the story reproduced on the authority of Hishām can be set other narrations about 'Urwa's death. The renowned Meccan *élégant* Ibn Abī 'Atīq[47] witnesses the tragedy under quite different circumstances, according to the account reproduced by al-Washshā' (d. 325/936),[48] and Tha'lab and Abū l-Faraj refer to Ibn Abī 'Atīq for yet another depiction of the incident.[49] And finally, we find a third witness in 'Urwa ibn al-Zubayr (d. 94/712–13 or 99/718), Hishām's father and his informant according to the versions above, who is quoted by al-Zubayr ibn Bakkār (d. 256/870).[50] His account is irreconcilable with all the other versions.

---

[45] *Maṣāri' al-'ushshāq*, II, 118.

[46] Note that al-Haytham refers directly to Hishām, whereas Ibn al-Kalbī quotes al-Makhzūmī.

[47] 'Abd Allāh ibn Muḥammad (= Abū 'Atīq) ibn 'Abd al-Raḥmān ibn Abī Bakr, great-grandson of the first caliph; see Charles Pellat, art. "Ibn Abī 'Atīḳ" in EI^2, III (Leiden, 1971), 682; Ibn al-Kalbī, *Jamharat al-nasab: Riwāyat Muḥammad ibn Ḥabīb 'anhu*, ed. Maḥmūd Firdaws al-'Aẓm (Damascus, 1406/1986), I, 96–99.

[48] *Al-Muwashshā aw al-ẓarf wa-l-ẓurafā'*, ed. Kamāl Muṣṭafā (Cairo, 1372/1953), 72–73.

[49] Abū l-Faraj, *Aghānī*, XXIV, 161–62, refers to al-Zubayr ibn Bakkār who quotes, through 'Abd al-Malik ibn 'Abd al-'Azīz, the above-mentioned Abū l-Sā'ib. The same text is reproduced by Tha'lab (*Majālis*, I, 290–91), who also quotes, independently from Abū l-Faraj, al-Zubayr ibn Bakkār with the corresponding *isnād.* Al-Zubayr (d. 256/870; *GAS*, I, 317–18) seems to be the author of this version.

[50] Al-Sarrāj, *Maṣāri' al-'ushshāq*, I, 316; here Ibn al-Marzubān (d. 309/921; see 'Umar Riḍā Kaḥḥāla, *Mu'jam al-mu'allifīn*, Damascus, 1376–81/1957–61, IX, 285–86), a well-known compiler of *akhbār* of this type, refers to al-Zubayr.

These narratives are certainly only a part of what once existed. The story about the death of the famous love poet was well known and often told, and thus underwent several adaptations. In view of the literary character of the topic, we abstain from a discussion of the historicity of these stories; we may be satisfied here with the conclusion that the versions of the Kūfan authorities are more consistent than the other narratives, although they probably do not both originate entirely from Hishām ibn 'Urwa. In this respect, the example may illustrate a common phenomenon. Here, as in many instances, a variety of narratives are attributed to a rather limited number of authorities. Certain authorities may of course have passed on more than one version and thus have contributed to a proliferation of narratives. In our case, however, we see that experts—al-Haytham and Ibn al-Kalbī—come up with unmistakable adaptations and at the same time maintain the reference to an appropriate and established authority. This procedure seems also to be involved in the implausible ascriptions of two different accounts to Ibn Abī 'Atīq[51] and al-Zubayr ibn Bakkār respectively.[52]

From Lore to Historiography

A minute element of historiographical tradition about the first Islamic schism invites a study of the gradual formation of narrative material into a plausible and cohesive narration, one in which, again, comparison of several renderings allows us to perceive the interrelationship of versions quoted from different sources. However, it is not our purpose here to probe the authorial contributions of transmitters and the concealment of authors behind *isnāds*; the object of the study is to assess the point of departure and chronological order of various adaptations.

Historical Context

The schism between the Sunnī and Shī'ī branches of Islam dates back to a conflict in which 'Alī ibn Abī Ṭālib (d. 40/661), the cousin and son-in-law of the Prophet, confronted the governor of Syria, Mu'āwiya

[51] See nn. 48 and 49 above.
[52] See nn. 49 and 50 above.

ibn Abī Sufyān (d. 60/680), in the years 35–40/656–61. The latter did not consent to 'Alī's nomination as the fourth caliph in succession to 'Uthmān ibn 'Affān (d. 35/656), who had been murdered by rebelling Muslims.[53] Mu'āwiya still refused to pay homage even when 'Alī had overcome his opponents from Mecca and Medina at the "Battle of the Camel" (*al-jamal*) in 36/656.[54] Both sides gathered armies and set out to fight; they met at Ṣiffīn, but the decision was not reached in battle. At the request of the Syrian side a truce was accepted, and 'Alī, constrained by rivalry among his partisans,[55] was compelled to agree to arbitration. A document meant to define the principles on which arbitration should be based seems to have been decisive to the outcome of the negotiations. Among the points of controversy, one may have been that 'Alī's title "Commander of the Faithful" did not appear in the document, in which he was mentioned only by his name.[56] In our sources this is considered a ruse by the Syrians, since they were able to claim that 'Alī had himself renounced his rank of caliph and thus was no more than Mu'āwiya's equal. As a matter of fact, the disintegration of the alliance on 'Alī's side began after this first arbitration meeting. Quarrelling and dissension soon deprived 'Alī of his military power. When Mu'āwiya became caliph after 'Alī's death (in 40/661), he was able to contain the various forces and lead them to a new wave of expansion. Yet his attempt to establish dynastic rule met with resistance. 'Alī's partisans, precursors of the later Shī'a, considered his descendants as legitimate rulers who could ensure guidance for the Muslims.

In general, our sources present Mu'āwiya as a shrewd and moderate personality gifted for political leadership, whereas 'Alī appears as an example of piety, virtue, and sagacity. Mu'āwiya owed much of the arrangement and ingenious execution of the arbitration to his ally 'Amr ibn al-'Āṣ (d. *ca.* 43/663), who had led the conquest of Egypt and had administered this province as its governor until removed by 'Uthmān,

[53] For details on 'Alī's life, as well as his position in Islamic tradition, see I.K. Poonawala and Etan Kohlberg, art. "'Alī ibn Abī Ṭālib" in *Encyclopaedia Iranica*, I (London and New York, 1982), 838–48.

[54] See Laura Veccia Vaglieri, art. "al-Djamal" in *EI*², II (Leiden, 1965), 414–16.

[55] Martin Hinds, "Kûfan Political Alignments and Their Background in the Mid-Seventh Century A.D.", *IJMES* 2 (1971), 361–65.

[56] Cf. Martin Hinds, "The Ṣiffīn Arbitration Agreement", *JSS* 17 (1971), 100–101.

'Alī's predecessor. Loyalty to the murdered 'Uthmān, whose case was advocated by Mu'āwiya,[57] could hardly have induced 'Amr to ally with the ruler of Syria, nor could enmity toward 'Alī have been the cause. His choice is explained in the sources by the advantages he derived by making common cause with Mu'āwiya.

Literature testifies to 'Amr's judgment through his aphorisms and illustrates his masterly conduct of political affairs. Anecdotal *akhbār* also show 'Amr and Mu'āwiya as a pair well matched in acumen and political skill, but not always in agreement.[58] A particularly impressive depiction of 'Amr's policy is part of an apparently rather old account of the alliance between 'Amr and Mu'āwiya.

In contrast to 'Alī, who proves to be an upright advocate of the legacy of the Prophet, 'Amr and Mu'āwiya embark on an alliance based exclusively on mutual self-interest. In the negotiations for this deal, they appear—in quite natural terms—as opponents. Both of them apply trickery very similar to the ruse displayed at the Ṣiffīn agreement. The motif of trickery as an instrument of their struggle already reveals the anecdotal character of this narration.[59] Whereas the narrative form and the process of reshaping may be regarded as typical of *akhbār* literature, the severe characterization of 'Amr and Mu'āwiya in terms of a paradigm of simplistic moralizing relates these narratives to a more popular form of tale.

The Alliance of 'Amr and Mu'āwiya

The earliest source for this narration is the work *Waq'at Ṣiffīn* compiled by Naṣr ibn Muzāḥim (d. 221/827). For his account of the beginnings of the alliance, Naṣr refers mainly to two informants: Muḥammad ibn 'Ubayd Allāh al-Qurashī, who is quoted citing al-Jurjānī,[60] and

[57] See below, 300.

[58] E.g. al-Bayhaqī, *Al-Maḥāsin wa-l-masāwī*, ed. Friedrich Schwally (Giessen, 1902), 294; Ibn 'Abd al-Barr, *Bahjat al-majālis wa-uns al-mujālis*, ed. Muḥammad Mursī al-Khūlī (Cairo, n.d. [*ca.* 1968–74]), 320–21, 760.

[59] As described below, 310–12.

[60] Occasionally called 'Uthmān ibn 'Ubayd Allāh; he might be identified with his namesake al-A'raj, d. 169/776–77. See Khalīfa ibn Khayyāṭ, *Kitāb al-ṭabaqāt*, ed. Akram Ḍiyā' al-'Umarī (Baghdad, 1387/1967), 273.

'Umar ibn Sa'd,[61] known as a transmitter of Abū Mikhnaf (d. 157/775) and a collector of *akhbār* on Ṣiffīn.[62] The narration in *Waq'at Ṣiffīn* is the most detailed version and will therefore be summarized here. We have divided the plot into several sections in order to facilitate comparison with other versions.

1. *The Invitation.*[63] The extract begins with a letter in which Mu'āwiya asks 'Amr to come to Damascus. In view of the preceding narration, this letter appears to function more as an elegant transition between two narrative parts than as a prelude to the subsequent account. The letter sums up events which have already been reported in detail, and if genuine, the document would hardly have contained any news for 'Amr.

Communication by letters often occurs in Naṣr's narration about the conflict between 'Alī and Mu'āwiya. Arabic historiography has certainly preserved some authentic documents.[64] Here, however, the letters often carry little weight, and in the course of the narration they obviously perform a connecting function and sometimes provide rhetorical embellishment. They may have been composed, as has been proposed, in accordance with a narrative pattern adopted from the novels of late antiquity.[65]

2. *The Counsel.*[66] Having received the invitation, 'Amr seeks the advice of his sons, who reflect the dilemma of his situation by making contradictory recommendations. 'Abd Allāh advises 'Amr to content himself with the recognition he has received from the Prophet and the first two caliphs; he should keep away from the quarrel and should not, for the sake of petty temporal gains (*'alā dunyā qalīlatin*), become a retainer (*ḥāshiya*) of Mu'āwiya. The second piece of advice mentions

---

[61] Ibn Abī Ḥātim (d. 327/938), *Al-Jarḥ wa-l-ta'dīl* (Hyderabad, 1371–72/1952–1953), III.1, 112.

[62] Cf. Sezgin, *Abū Miḥnaf*, 137–44.

[63] *Waq'at Ṣiffīn*, ed. 'Abd al-Salām Muḥammad Hārūn (Cairo, AH 1382), 34.

[64] See Rubin, "The 'Constitution of Medina'", 5–23; also R.B. Serjeant, "The Caliph 'Umar's Letters to Abū Mūsā al-Ash'arī and Mu'āwiya", *JSS* 29 (1984), 65–79.

[65] Carl Brockelmann, "Naṣr ibn Muzāḥim, der älteste Geschichtschreiber der Schia", *ZS* 4 (1926), 15.

[66] *Waq'at Ṣiffīn*, 34–35.

that 'Amr's position would certainly be undermined were the conflict to be settled without his participation; he should ally with the Syrians and demand revenge for the murder of 'Uthmān.[67] In his answer, 'Amr expresses the controversial character of their views; whereas the first recommendation was appropriate in view of the demands of religion (*dīn*), the second had in mind what was best in terms of worldly interests (*dunyā*). 'Amr then retires and expresses his conflicting feelings in verses introduced by a recurrent motif that functions as a transition between narration and poetry: 'Amr recites the verses when darkness surrounds him (*fa-lammā jannahu l-layl*). The verses also contain a message: his son 'Abd Allāh listens to them and predicts 'Amr's deplorable alliance with Mu'āwiya.

By their careful mode of expression and their fundamental character, the recommendations prove a skillful and meaningful composition. Subsequently, the alternative choice between temporal advantage and the obligations of religion, by which 'Amr, according to his own words, is confronted, alludes to a fundamental judgment on his politics, which is stated more clearly below.

3. *The Rapprochement.*[68] 'Amr proceeds to Damascus to meet with Mu'āwiya. After keeping him waiting some time, Mu'āwiya receives him and expounds upon the three main perils he is facing. 'Amr proposes measures, but as far as Mu'āwiya's resistance to 'Alī is concerned he reminds him only of the latter's reputation and prominence as a warrior.[69] He endorses this point by noting that 'Alī could only be removed through an act of injustice.[70]

4. *The Demand.*[71] The account up to this point is quoted from both of the informants mentioned above.[72] Naṣr refers to 'Umar ibn Sa'd alone for the subsequent section,[73] which again has 'Amr extolling 'Alī's su-

---

[67] See below, 300–301.

[68] *Ibid.*, 37.

[69] *lā tusawwī l-'Arab baynaka wa-baynahu fī shay'in min al-ashyā' wa-inna lahu fī l-ḥarbi laḥẓan mā huwa li-aḥadin min Quraysh.*

[70] *fa-innahu la-ṣāḥiba mā huwa fīhi illā taẓlimahu.*

[71] *Ibid.*, 37–38.

[72] *Ibid.*, 34: *Naṣr 'an 'Umar ibn Sa'd wa-Muḥammad ibn 'Ubayd Allāh qālā.*

[73] *Ibid.*, 37:13: *Naṣr: 'Umar ibn Sa'd bi-isnādihi.* The *isnād* may refer to Naṣr's quotation (*Waq'at Ṣiffīn*, 27, cf. 51): *'Umar ibn Sa'd 'an Numayr ibn Wa'la*—for

periority. When Mu'āwiya asks him to join in the religious warfare (*al-jihād*) against 'Alī, 'Amr mentions 'Alī's religious seniority (*mā laka hijratuhu wa-lā sābiqatuhu wa-lā ṣuḥbatuhu wa-lā jihāduhu*) and his knowledge of Islam (*wa-lā fiqhuhu wa-lā 'ilmuhu*) in his reply. This admission, which is obviously polemical, serves to denounce any resistance to 'Alī as a wicked and godless act. The emphatic intensity of the argument here stands out in some contrast to other parts of the narrative, although the same judgment, in more moderate terms, underlies the account there too.

Immediately after 'Amr's confession of 'Alī's superiority, the conversation turns to business matters. 'Amr points out the hazard involved in a war against 'Alī—an argument which accords with the evaluation of 'Alī's position (Section 3 above)—and demands a reward for his engagement. When he finally asks for the governorship of Egypt as a means of subsistence (*ṭu'ma*), Mu'āwiya hesitates to consent.

Naṣr here adds a farcical tale quoted from an anonymous source.[74] Mu'āwiya pretends to worry about the effect on 'Amr's reputation were it to become known that he had fought on Mu'āwiya's side only for the sake of worldly advantage. When 'Amr rejects this objection,[75] Mu'āwiya argues that were he so inclined, he could deceive 'Amr with false promises. 'Amr does not take this warning seriously, and Mu'āwiya thereupon asks him to come close since he wants to confide something to him. He then bites 'Amr's ear as proof of the latter's credulity: 'Amr should have been able to identify the ruse, Mu'āwiya explains, for as the two were in complete privacy he had no reason to whisper. The witty scene is also reproduced by Ibn Abī l-Ḥadīd (d. 656/1258), who owes much of his material on the conflict between 'Alī and Mu'āwiya to Naṣr. An adjoining comment[76] rebukes Mu'āwiya for his lack of dignity. Disgust at the ungodly alliance against 'Alī, it seems, has induced the author to take this tale more seriously than it was meant.

the latter see al-Dhahabī, *Mīzān al-i'tidāl fī 'ilm al-rijāl*, ed. 'Alī Muḥammad al-Bijāwī (Cairo and Aleppo, 1382/1963), IV, 273—*'an 'Āmir al-Sha'bī* (d. 103/721; *GAS*, I, 277).

[74] *Waq'at Ṣiffīn*, 38: *qāla Naṣr wa-fī ḥadīth ghayr 'Umar.*

[75] *Ibid.*, 38:7: *da'nī 'anhu.*

[76] By Abū l-Qāsim al-Balkhī; see Ibn Abī l-Ḥadīd, *Sharḥ nahj al-balāgha*, ed. Muḥammad Abū l-Faḍl Ibrāhīm (Cairo, 1959–64), II, 65.

5. *The Deal.*[77] After this burlesque Naṣr returns to 'Umar's account[78] and presents, rather abruptly, verses recited by 'Amr. They refer to the importance of Egypt and what 'Amr would gain, and this then becomes the subject of a dispute between 'Amr and Mu'āwiya. 'Utba, Mu'āwiya's brother, thereupon enters the scene and succeeds in settling the dispute by advancing the clever argument that Mu'āwiya would buy 'Amr with a prize to be handed over to him only if they were victorious against 'Alī (and only in this case would Mu'āwiya assign Egypt to 'Amr). Mu'āwiya asks 'Utba to stay overnight, and when he listens—again at night (*lammā janna 'alā 'Utbata l-laylu*), according to the motif already mentioned[79]—to some verses of his brother 'Utba, he finally adopts this proposal, calls for 'Amr, and promises him the governorship of Egypt.

Afterwards, Mu'āwiya wants to evade his promise and resorts to a ruse. In Naṣr's account, this segment is added rather awkwardly and is introduced by the quotation of an unnamed narrator (*qāla*, "he said").[80] A document is drawn up, and Mu'āwiya signs with the words: "The setting of a condition (i.e. 'Amr's reward) must not impair obedience" (*'alā an lā yanquḍa sharṭun ṭā'atan*). Realizing that this formula would bind him to unconditional allegiance, 'Amr avoids his defeat and the recrudescence of their dispute by inverting the wording, so that it reads: "The [demand of] obedience must not impair a condition" (*'alā an lā tanquḍa ṭā'atun sharṭan*).

6. *Allied Forces.*[81] Referring again to Muḥammad ibn 'Ubayd Allāh as his source,[82] Naṣr subsequently gives an account of their first political moves. These correspond to 'Amr's previous recommendations (Section 3 above); moreover, the grant of Egypt is here repeated. It thus becomes clear from Naṣr's quotations that he has combined two coherent accounts.

[77] *Waq'at Ṣiffīn*, 38–44.

[78] *Ibid.*, 38: *thumma raja'a ilā ḥadīth 'Umar.*

[79] Cf. above, 295.

[80] *Ibid.*, 40:13–41:1: *qāla* marks the beginning of a new section. The preceding lines (40:8–12) contain Mu'āwiya's oath and a short dispute between 'Amr and his sons, who do not share their father's satisfaction with this deal.

[81] *Ibid.*, 44(–51).

[82] *Ibid.*, 44:4: *Naṣr: Muḥammad ibn 'Ubayd Allāh 'an al-Jurjānī.*

The narratives show the succinctness and terseness of early Arabic prose.[83] The composition unfolds a detailed representation of the actors scene by scene and, as the extract demonstrates, features the significance of the situation. Its intrinsic meaning aims at a moral evaluation of the events—pronounced, as usual in the narrative form of *akhbār*, in the characters' own words. In this vein, the characters are vividly represented in a context of social thinking and acting; the attention is thus drawn towards circumstantial aspects, the historical setting being more of a background against which they unfold.

Adoption and Adaptation

A. As we may conclude from the way Naṣr is quoted, the work *Waq'at Ṣiffīn*, in its preserved form, is most probably a copy of a redaction made by a student of Naṣr.[84] The earliest source known to depend on *Waq'at Ṣiffīn* is the *Al-Akhbār al-ṭiwāl* of al-Dīnawarī. Although Naṣr is not quoted, many accounts agree with the *akhbār* of *Waq'at Ṣiffīn* in their sequence and contents, and even some of the wording is identical in both texts.[85] However, comparison reveals many differences in phrasing, mostly due to al-Dīnawarī's inclination to summarize.[86] Some of his expressions reappear in the rendering of Ibn A'tham al-Kūfī (d. 314/926?).[87] Ibn A'tham also used *Waq'at Ṣiffīn* as a source;[88] in the corresponding collective *isnād*[89] he quotes al-Ḥasan, son of Naṣr, as the transmitter from his father. This may indicate that al-Dīnawarī also made use of the same redaction (by al-Ḥasan) which probably was not identical with the version of al-Khazzāz, who transmitted the *Waq'at Ṣiffīn* as we have it.

---

[83] Cf. Brockelmann, "Naṣr ibn Muzāḥim", 1–2.

[84] See, e.g., nn. 72, 73, 74, 82.

[85] *Al-Akhbār al-ṭiwāl*, ed. 'Abd al-Mun'im 'Āmir and Jamāl al-Dīn al-Shayyāl (Cairo, 1960), 156ff. (cf. *Waq'at Ṣiffīn*, 15ff.); for the extract presented here, see 157:14—158:11.

[86] E.g. *Al-Akhbār al-ṭiwāl*, 156:8–10, and *Waq'at Ṣiffīn*, 15:6–16:7.

[87] Ibn A'tham al-Kūfī, *Kitāb al-futūḥ*, ed. Muḥammad 'Abd al-Mu'īd Khān (Hyderabad, 1388–95/1968–75), II, 352:11–13, 374:11–14, 374:16–375:3, as compared to al-Dīnawarī, *Al-Akhbār al-ṭiwāl*, 157:2–4, 157:4–7, 157:9–11.

[88] See below, n. 106.

[89] *Kitāb al-futūḥ*, II, 345.

B. Naṣr ibn Muzāḥim's quotations refer, for Sections 1–3 (*Invitation, Counsel, Rapprochement*), to 'Umar ibn Sa'd and Muḥammad ibn 'Ubayd Allāh, for Sections 4 and 5 (*Demand, Deal*), with the exception of a short comic interlude, only to 'Umar ibn Sa'd, and finally, for Section 6 (*Allied Forces*), to Muḥammad ibn 'Ubayd Allāh again. More insight into the origin of these narratives and Naṣr's arrangement of them can be gained from accounts given in other sources. The compilation ascribed to Ibn Qutayba under the title *Al-Imāma wa-l-siyāsa*, which has been identified as the work of an anonymous contemporary,[90] contains two accounts of 'Amr's demand for a reward. The first one includes a reproduction of Sections 4 and 5 (*Demand* and *Deal* above) and seems to derive from the narrative which Naṣr had received from 'Umar ibn Sa'd.[91] The first part of Section 3 (*Rapprochment*, Mu'āwiya keeps 'Amr waiting) also appears in ps.-Ibn Qutayba's account[92] and should also be related to 'Umar ibn Sa'd's narration.

However, the essential scene of Section 3 which Naṣr quotes from two authorities ('Amr's advice to Mu'āwiya) can be identified as belonging to an account of Muḥammad ibn 'Ubayd Allāh, because Section 6 (*Allied Forces*), which Naṣr quotes from him, perfectly corresponds to it, as we have noted above, and seems to be its continuation. Ps.-Ibn Qutayba's account of 'Amr's advice is roughly in accordance with this part of Section 3 in *Waq'at Ṣiffīn*, but then, in its account of Mu'āwiya's request for 'Amr's support against 'Alī, diverges markedly from Section 4, and finally from Section 5, the agreement on Egypt, both of which

---

[90] Maḥmūd Makkī, "Egipto y los origenes de la historiografía árabe–española", *Revista del Instituto de Estudios Islámicos en Madrid* 5 (1957), 210–20. The author of the *Al-Imāma wa-l-siyāsa* is also discussed by Muḥammad Yūsuf Najm in "Kitāb al-imāma wa-l-siyāsa al-mansūb li-Ibn Qutayba—man huwa mu'allifuhu?", *Al-Abḥāth* 14 (1961), 122–32, and again by Jibrā'īl Jabbūr, "Kitāb al-imāma wa-l-siyāsa al-mansūb li-Ibn Qutayba—man huwa mu'allifuhu?: radd 'alā naqd", *Al-Abḥāth* 14 (1961), 326–41.

[91] Ps.-Ibn Qutayba, *Al-Imāma wa-l-siyāsa*, ed. Ṭāhā Muḥammad al-Zaynī (Cairo, n.d.), I, 87:20f., 87:21, 87:23–88:7, and the corresponding passages in *Waq'at Ṣiffīn*, 37:1, 38:3f., 39:7–10, 40:8, 40:18–41:7, 42:13–16.

[92] *Al-Imāma wa-l-siyāsa*: *lammā qadama ilā Mu'āwiya wa-'arifa ḥājatahu ilayhi bā'adahu wa-kāyada kullu wāḥidin minhumā ṣāḥibahu*, as compared to *Waq'at Ṣiffīn*: *fa-sāra ḥattā qadama ilā Mu'āwiya wa-'arifa ḥājata Mu'āwiya ilayhi*... (etc., as *Al-Imāma*).

Naṣr quotes from ʻUmar ibn Saʻd. This account, which will further be designated as the B version, thus is obviously related to material that Naṣr received from Muḥammad ibn ʻUbayd Allāh.[93] It can be recognized in a contemporary work by al-Balādhurī (d. 279/892), his *Ansāb al-ashrāf*, where it appears as part of a comprehensive narration on the alliance between ʻAmr and Muʻāwiya.[94] A summary of al-Balādhurī's rendering will explain the characteristics of this version.

Al-Balādhurī gives a concise depiction of the alliance. Its first part, the "Counsel" of ʻAmr's sons,[95] already contains this version's leitmotif, which seems to elaborate on a theme inherent in the narrative as presented by Naṣr. ʻAmr is warned by his son not to spoil his religion (*dīn*) through trivial enjoyment of the present world (*ʻalā dunyā yasīratin*). The image of a transaction in the course of which *dīn* is exchanged for *dunyā* is characteristic of this narrative; it is used repeatedly, without significant alteration in meaning,[96] and at the expense of a more subtle and diversified significance in the tale as Naṣr has preserved it.

In contrast to this sort of overstatement, which occurs quite frequently where moral convictions are advocated, the negotiations between ʻAmr and Muʻāwiya keep to a consistent and logical course and are related to the historical background. ʻAmr's advice—as given in *Al-Imāma wa-l-siyāsa*—is omitted by al-Balādhurī, who begins the scene with ʻAmr's praise of ʻAlī, which corresponds to the end of this part in *Waqʻat Ṣiffīn*.[97] In his response we find Muʻāwiya, instead of calling for *jihād*,[98] proposing that ʻAlī should be called to account for the murder of ʻUthmān.

---

[93] *Al-Imāma wa-l-siyāsa*, I, 88:10–16, 88:16–21 (not in *Waqʻat Ṣiffīn*), 88:21f., as compared to *Waqʻat Ṣiffīn*, 37:2–11, 42:16–18. The last passage, which tells about Marwān's anger, is contained in the narrative (in Section 5, not mentioned in our summary) quoted by Naṣr from ʻUmar ibn Saʻd. It is added there incoherently and does not seem to be an original part of ʻUmar's narration. It therefore does not jeopardize our assumption that this second narrative must be seen in relation to material attributed by Naṣr to Muḥammad ibn ʻUbayd Allāh.

[94] Al-Balādhurī, *Ansāb al-ashrāf*, II.1, ed. Muḥammad Bāqir al-Maḥmūdī (Beirut, 1394/1974), 284–88.

[95] Cf. Section 2 of *Waqʻat Ṣiffīn*.

[96] Al-Balādhurī, *Ansāb al-ashrāf*, II.1, 285:12, 288:1, 288:11.

[97] *Ibid.*, II.1, 287:2: *fa-lā tusawwī. . .Quraysh*. Cf. n. 69 above.

[98] See Section 4 above.

Mu'āwiya's claim to sponsor the vengeance sought for the injustice done to 'Uthmān appears in one form or another in all the historical sources, including *Waq'at Ṣiffīn*, at different points,[99] and became one of the principal arguments legitimating Mu'āwiya's refusal to pay homage to 'Alī. Here, however, it gives rise to a scathing and historically very unlikely reply by 'Amr, who declares that neither he himself nor Mu'āwiya had been willing to give any help to 'Uthmān when he was besieged. Mu'āwiya simply ignores this invalidation of his argument and requests 'Amr's homage.[100]

After Mu'āwiya's unscrupulousness has thus been proved, 'Amr declares that if he is to give up his *dīn* he should be recompensed by a share of Mu'āwiya's worldly gains (*dunyā*); he now finally asks to be granted Egypt. Here too, Mu'āwiya hesitates and is still unsure when, at night, he listens to the verses of 'Amr, who is his guest.[101] Only on the next morning, when he receives the advice of his brother 'Utba, is he willing to give in. In contrast to the version which Naṣr cites from 'Umar ibn Sa'd, 'Utba here suggests to Mu'āwiya that he should buy 'Amr's *dīn* with the grant of Egypt.

The agreement on Egypt, as depicted in al-Balādhurī's version, corresponds with the beginning of the Section 6 account (*Allied Forces*) which Naṣr quotes from Muḥammad ibn 'Ubayd Allāh; there, as in the *Ansāb al-ashrāf*, Mu'āwiya grants Egypt to 'Amr the morning after 'Amr has spent the night in his house.[102] Since we attribute 'Amr's advice (Section 3 in *Waq'at Ṣiffīn*) to Muḥammad ibn 'Ubayd Allāh, the B version is not only rendered by al-Balādhurī and in *Al-Imāma wa-l-siyāsa*,[103] but has also been incorporated into *Waq'at Ṣiffīn* among

[99] *Waq'at Ṣiffīn*, 32:10, 34:13, 44.

[100] Al-Balādhurī, *Ansāb al-ashrāf*, II.1, 287ult: *da' dhā wa-hāt fa-bāyi'nī.*

[101] These verses appear in Section 5 of *Waq'at Ṣiffīn*. As mentioned above, Naṣr's arrangement shows a striking lack of coherence between 'Amr's verses and the foregoing narration. Al-Balādhurī's account also mentions Mu'āwiya listening at night to 'Utba's verses, as told in *Waq'at Ṣiffīn*; in al-Balādhurī's arrangement (*Ansāb al-ashrāf*, II.1, 288:6–9), 'Utba's verses are placed after the narration about the agreement.

[102] *Waq'at Ṣiffīn*, 44; Mu'āwiya's ruse (Section 5 of *Waq'at Ṣiffīn*) is also placed here in al-Balādhurī's version.

[103] The condensed account of al-Ya'qūbī (d. 284/897) shows particular convergence with the material rendered in *Ansāb al-ashrāf*. Cf. his *Ta'rīkh*, ed. M.Th. Houtsma

the materials quoted from Muḥammad ibn ʿUbayd Allāh. Naṣr's rendering of the account, however, is not identical with the version in al-Balādhurī's work and probably derives from an older stage in the development of the text. On the basis of the extracts reproduced by Naṣr ibn Muzāḥim, we may refer to it as the proto-B version.

Peculiar to the B version, in contrast to the narration of ʿUmar ibn Saʿd, are ʿAmr's advice from Section 3 and all of Section 6 in *Waqʿat Ṣiffīn*. The counsel of ʿAmr's sons, the negotiations between Muʿāwiya and ʿAmr, and their agreement differ in arrangement and contents from the corresponding sections in *Waqʿat Ṣiffīn*. Although both versions have some parts in common, the features of the B version are clearly distinct.

C. A detailed report on the alliance between ʿAmr and Muʿāwiya is also given by Ibn Aʿtham,[104] who has molded accounts from different sources into an uninterrupted narrative.[105] He obviously draws, among other sources, on *Waqʿat Ṣiffīn*;[106] the B version is also discernible as part of his account.[107] For this material, however, Ibn Aʿtham does not depend on al-Balādhurī, because he includes parts not contained in *Ansāb al-ashrāf* (namely the *Rapprochement* section) and diverges also with respect to the sequence of events;[108] he further mentions the document that assures the grant of Egypt, but has completely spoiled the point of Muʿāwiya's ruse.[109] Some elements of his account can be identified as hyperbolic embellishments for which Ibn Aʿtham may himself be responsible.[110] At any rate, disregarding the differences

(Leiden, 1883), II, 214–18, as compared to *Waqʿat Ṣiffīn*, 27–28, and al-Balādhurī, *Ansāb al-ashrāf*, II.1, 288.

[104] *Kitāb al-futūḥ*, II, 382–389.

[105] As he explains himself, *ibid.*, II, 345:8.

[106] E.g. the burlesque in which Muʿāwiya bites ʿAmr's ear (Section 4 above): *Waqʿat Ṣiffīn*, 38:5–10, and *Kitāb al-futūḥ*, II, 387:1–5. Cf. also n. 88 above.

[107] *Kitāb al-futūḥ*, II, 385:5–386:7; ps.-Ibn Qutayba, *Al-Imāma wa-l-siyāsa*, 88:10–16; also *Kitāb al-futūḥ*, II, 386:14–18, 387:5–8, 388:1–5, as compared to al-Balādhurī, *Ansāb al-ashrāf*, II.1, 287:4–7, 287:6–288:2, 288:10–18.

[108] *Kitāb al-futūḥ*, II, 388:1–5, as compared to *Ansāb al-ashrāf*, II.1, 288:10–18.

[109] Al-Balādhurī has it correctly, *Ansāb al-ashrāf*, II.1, 288:12.

[110] Extension of the dialogue and addition of arguments in praise of ʿAlī in *Kitāb al-futūḥ*, II, 386:7–11; cf. al-Balādhurī, *Ansāb al-ashrāf*, II.1, 288:2–4. Noteworthy here is the mention of *sābiqa*, *ṣahāra*, and *qarāba*. Muʿāwiya's sending of spies who

between Ibn A'tham's and al-Balādhurī's texts, their convergence in the B version points to a common source which both of them and the author of *Al-Imāma wa-l-siyāsa* have adopted.

Ibn A'tham does not refer to the same authorities as al-Balādhurī, but names a number of other sources in his collective *isnād*;[111] it is, however, impossible to determine whom among the transmitters mentioned is his source for the B version. Al-Balādhurī refers through al-Madā'inī (d. 228/843) to Ibn Da'b (d. 171/787).[112] Al-Balādhurī's reference to al-Madā'inī as his immediate source is confirmed by a quotation from al-Madā'inī elsewhere;[113] that account exactly borders on al-Madā'inī's narrative rendered in the *Ansāb al-ashrāf*. The indications given in the *isnāds* are sparse, but invite some speculation. One could presume that the narration originated (at the latest) around the middle of the eighth century with an unknown informant of Ibn Da'b, who could also have functioned as the informant of one of the *akhbārīyūn* mentioned by Ibn A'tham. Since this tradition is related to the proto-B version in *Waq'at Ṣiffīn*, one could think of al-Jurjānī (Muḥammad ibn 'Ubayd Allāh's source) or his entourage as the missing link. However, this conclusion has no firm basis because in contrast to the case of narrations on the poet 'Urwa ibn Ḥizām, where we encounter an irritating number of (false) ascriptions, the lack of attributions here prevents us from identifying the common link of these renderings.

The *isnāds* do not indicate that the B version and the account of 'Umar ibn Sa'd go back to a common origin which may be regarded as the archaic narrative material adapted in our *akhbār*. Both versions concord in elements of the plot, namely the counsel of 'Amr and his sons,[114] 'Amr's verses, his demand for Egypt as a means of subsistence (*ṭu'ma*),[115] 'Utba's intervention and—although introduced differently—

listen at night to 'Amr's verses is also a peculiar element (*Kitāb al-futūḥ*, II, 387:11). Here again we find the motif of *lamma janna 'alayhi l-layl* (above, 295); Ibn A'tham seems to have preferred the account of *Waq'at Ṣiffīn* (Section 4, on the authority of 'Umar) at this point.

[111] *Kitāb al-futūḥ*, II, 344–45.

[112] Cf. Charles Pellat, art. "Ibn Da'b" in *EI*², III (Leiden, 1971), 742.

[113] Al-Ṭabarī, *Ta'rīkh*, I, 3254–55.

[114] If it really belongs to both versions; in any case, this section was very widespread (see below, 304–305).

[115] *Waq'at Ṣiffīn*, 38:3; ps.-Ibn Qutayba, *Al-Imāma wa-l-siyāsa*, I, 88:21; al-

his verses, and finally Mu'āwiya's ruse when he sets the "condition" in opposition to "obedience".[116] This narrative material was probably considered common property by those who dealt with historiographical tradition; it does not show much consideration for historical reality, but rather seems designed to entertain, while reflecting the preoccupation of storytellers (*quṣṣāṣ*) with this topic.[117]

The study of the narratives involved provides us with an approximate chronological frame. The B version, as it stands in al-Balādhurī's text and in the extracts of Ibn A'tham and *Al-Imāma wa-l-siyāsa*, is characterized by the elaboration of a motif already inherent in Naṣr's compilation. In *Waq'at Ṣiffīn* (Section 2),[118] 'Amr's choice between religious obligation and worldly interests expresses a more general view of the moral aspects of 'Amr's politics, whereas the B version features the vicious and consciously arranged exchange of *dīn* for *dunyā*. This theme is not to be found in the account which Naṣr reproduced from Muḥammad ibn 'Ubayd Allāh (proto-B version), nor is 'Umar ibn Sa'd, who is known for his Shī'ite convictions and probably responsible for the essential features of his account (Sections 4 and 5), influenced by the narrative of the B version. The author of the B version thus could not have lived before the time of Muḥammad ibn 'Ubayd Allāh and 'Umar ibn Sa'd; in terms of chronology, this would mean that it took shape in the early 'Abbāsid period. Only one of the *akhbārīyūn* of that time, i.e. the third quarter of the eighth century, can be regarded as the common source of the renderings of the B version.

D. It is obvious that the transmission of narrative material implies the reshaping and gradual elaboration of *akhbār*. One expression of this process is the differentiation of versions, another is the refinement of historical perspective. Some of the narrative units which form the narration in *Waq'at Ṣiffīn* were widely known; the counsel of 'Amr and

---

Balādhurī, *Ansāb al-ashrāf*, II.1, 288:2; the expression reappears in Naṣr's proto-B version, 44:5.

[116]This last element, which is awkwardly annexed to the narration quoted from 'Umar ibn Sa'd (see Section 5 above), may have been introduced by Naṣr from another source.

[117]See below, 311–12.

[118]The counsel of 'Amr's sons (Section 2) is quoted by Naṣr from both 'Umar and Ibn 'Ubayd Allāh.

his sons in particular is rendered in several instances independently from the narratives presented so far. It is presented by Ibn 'Asākir (d. 571/1176) as a self-contained *khabar* identical to that in *Waq'at Ṣiffīn.*[119] His *isnād* refers through Ibrāhīm ibn al-Ḥusayn ibn 'Alī (d. 281/894)[120] to al-Walīd al-Balkhī; again, the *isnād* does not reveal the origin of the narrative. Among other proofs for the dissemination of the material,[121] accounts that adhere to a more genuine historical tradition are most interesting, because they allow us to see how historiographical *akhbār* took shape.

Al-Ṭabarī's *Ta'rīkh* also includes a *khabar* about the alliance of 'Amr and Mu'āwiya which is quoted from al-Wāqidī.[122] The "Counsel" has been adapted here so as to harmonize into a comprehensive explanation of 'Amr's attitude in the affair. 'Amr is shown expressing his bias against 'Alī already when he is informed about the murder of 'Uthmān. Subsequently, he communicates this opinion to his sons when he asks for their advice. In spite of these differences, it is evident from the sons' recommendations and 'Amr's reply that this depiction must share the same origin as the tale given in *Waq'at Ṣiffīn.*[123] The view that 'Amr was the driving force behind the plan is supported by the rest of al-Wāqidī's narrative. 'Amr is not invited by Mu'āwiya, but rather is obliged to persuade him to take action against 'Alī. To do so, he bluntly admits that they must seek worldly gains.[124] The coherent account of al-Wāqidī shows the design of a historical survey, which gives way to

[119] Ibn 'Asākir, *Ta'rīkh madīnat Dimashq* (Medina, AH 1407), XIII, 519:20–520:14.

[120] Cf. *GAS*, I, 321.

[121] The "Counsel" is also part of another version about the alliance in *Ta'rīkh madīnat Dimashq*, XIII, 519:1–19. Mu'āwiya's ruse is contained in al-Mubarrad (d. 285/898), *Al-Kāmil fī l-lugha wa-l-adab*, ed. Muḥammad Abū l-Faḍl Ibrāhīm and al-Sayyid Shaḥāta (Cairo, n.d.), I, 325.

[122] *Ta'rīkh*, I, 3252–54; reproduced by al-Nuwayrī (d. 733/1333) in his *Nihāyat al-arab fī funūn al-adab*, XX, ed. Muḥammad Rif'at Fatḥ Allāh (Cairo, 1395/1975), 240. Here again the *isnād* does not indicate any connection to the transmitters mentioned so far: al-Wāqidī refers to Mūsā ibn Ya'qūb, who quotes his uncle. For Mūsā, who is also quoted by al-Wāqidī in Ibn Sa'd, *Ṭabaqāt* (as n. 132 below), III.1, 116, see Ibn Ḥajar al-'Asqalānī, *Tahdhīb al-tahdhīb* (Hyderabad, 1325–27/1907–1909), X, 372–73.

[123] Al-Ṭabarī, *Ta'rīkh*, I, 3253:3–10. The author has emphasized the antithesis in 'Amr's reply through parallelism.

[124] *Ibid.*, I, 3254:1: *wa-lākinnā innamā aradnā hādhihī l-dunyā.*

an analytical point of view; 'Amr's alliance is proved—indeed, through his own words!—to be based on his fundamental disapproval of 'Alī. If considered self-evident, the narrative does not disclose that it is based on old narrative material of a rather popular character.

A similar example is given by Ibn 'Abd Rabbih (d. 328/940) in his *Al-'Iqd al-farīd*,[125] where a variation is introduced in the theme of "Choice between the Present World and the Hereafter". 'Amr demands Egypt as a reward, because he considers it impossible that by taking sides with Mu'āwiya he could gain anything for the life to come. The narrative here also includes Mu'āwiya's ruse, 'Utba's conciliatory proposal, and 'Amr's verses. Although this adaptation is introduced by an *isnād* which refers to contemporary authorities, evidence for a rather late origin comes from the fact that the narrative centers on the characters' motivation, the explication of which does not emerge from the dramatic setting, but rather is given quite artificially. Mu'āwiya "knows" that he will not succeed without having won over 'Amr, and 'Amr's demand to compensation for his loss of *al-ākhira* with the grant of Egypt is an elaboration and embellishment of the polemical charge that he gave up *dīn* for *dunyā*.

The assessment of fictitious elements in historiographical *akhbār* may draw attention to their literary quality, but it does not necessarily invalidate them as historical sources. A comparative analysis, however, is indispensable for their evaluation, because it may provide insights into the formation of the narratives and help to assess their origin. In general, a given *khabar* may not be attributed to one single author, but is subjected to successive modifications; in spite of this seemingly impenetrable "collective composition", the gradual evolution of historical tradition can be studied if the entire form of the narratives is taken into consideration. Moreover, when narrative form is assessed, it proves to match the highly developed literary character of the *akhbār* themselves.

---

[125]Ibn 'Abd Rabbih, *Al-'Iqd al-farīd*, ed. Aḥmad Amīn *et al.* (Cairo, 1359–72/1940–53), IV, 345: *Sufyān ibn 'Uyayna* (d. 196/811) *qāla akhbaranī Abū Mūsā al-Ash'arī* (d. *ca.* 42/662) *qāla akhbaranī l-Ḥasan*. On the question of this defective *isnād*, see Walter Werkmeister, *Quellenuntersuchungen zum Kitāb al-'Iqd al-farīd des Andalusiers Ibn 'Abdrabbih (246/860–328/940)* (Berlin, 1983), 455.

Features of the Khabar

When we attempt to assess the impact of *akhbār* on historical writing, we must explain their realistic appearance as created by narrative structure. Notwithstanding this general effect, we may discern various literary traditions which relate this literature to a more specifically historiographical attitude, on the one hand, and to legendary tales on the other.

Narrative Structure

The German author Georg Büchner (d. 1837) constructed his famous novella *Lenz* using the records of the pastor Friedrich Wilhelm Oberlin, who cared for the mentally disturbed poet Lenz. No reader will regard Büchner's novel as the account of an earlier eyewitness. The convention of literary communication and the literary form of the text itself preclude any such interpretation. The novella is certainly perceived as a literary artistic expression of the author's views. In contrast to this example, *akhbār* do not denote any involvement on the author's part. On the contrary, they are presented mostly as renderings of reports by somebody who witnessed the events. The alleged realism of these texts is due to two important elements: first, the chain of transmitters, which supports the reliability of the narration; and second, narrative technique, which enables the narrator to remain in the background and even to hide behind the characters of the narrative.

The narrator is absent from the narration and does not serve as a focus for the reader's perception. He does not convey insight into the characters by describing their plans and thoughts: his vision is entirely external. In this vein, *akhbār* present narratives that seem to be objective in character; the narrator functions like a machine that records every movement and every spoken word.[126]

Two modes of representation may be distinguished: the narrator's voice and the words of the characters, which are given in direct speech. Some sources contain only a very few *akhbār* that employ dialogues,[127]

[126] Cf. Leder, "Features of the Novel", 91–93.

[127] E.g. *Naqā'iḍ Jarīr wa-l-Farazdaq*, ed. Anthony Ashley Bevan (Leiden, 1905–1912).

and others show the use of direct speech as a predominant feature.[128] Yet it seems difficult to turn this distinction into a typology of *akhbār*; comparison of parallel *akhbār* has proved that the narrator's voice may originate through the adaptation of older source material which includes dialogues.[129]

Direct speech, a dramatic or mimetic technique of representation, is used to reduce the narrator's account and avoid any comment or interpretation.[130] The narrator not only abstains from any explanation by merely introducing these words with the stereotyped formula: "he (or she) said" (*qāla*); he also resorts as often as possible to words which are attributed to the characters.[131] This technique's deeper sense becomes clear when employed to shorten the narrator's account. It is used in order to avoid a certain perspective that seems to be felt inappropriate and may even undermine the foundations of *akhbār* narration. A phrase like: "Aḥmad wanted to marry the daughter of his paternal uncle and asked his father to give him support" would be very unusual. Instead we find something like: "Aḥmad liked the daughter of his paternal uncle. He said to his father: 'Will you ask your brother to give me his daughter in marriage'". In other words, the intentions of the characters tend to be expressed in their own words. The narrator neither explains nor interferes, and thus does not indicate that he is the omniscient creator of the narrative.

It is evident that the apparent objectivity of *akhbār* contributes to the illusion of reality. This form of narration reinforces the impression that these texts are narrative representations of events, not subject to the literary creativity of an author. The difference between a well-told story and one of lesser quality seems to be due to the degree of abilities and narrative mastery of an original reporter. Only when we encounter two or more irreconcilable accounts of the same event, possibly quoted from the same eyewitness, do we become aware that *akhbār* are fabricated. When we understand the apparently objective presentation of these texts as a narrative technique we shall be able to

---

[128] E.g. Naṣr ibn Muzāḥim, *Waq'at Ṣiffīn*.

[129] Cf. Leder, "Features of the Novel", 89–90.

[130] Cf. Widengren, "Oral Tradition", 233.

[131] Stefan Leder, "Prosa-Dichtung in der aḫbār Überlieferung", *Der Islam* 64 (1987), 26–27.

discern the underlying rules of literary composition. The combination of both analytical methods—comparative analysis and study of the narrative form—may prove the fictional character of *akhbār* and may help to understand their intrinsic meaning.

Factual Material and Fictitious Matters

Along with the names of actors and occasionally dates of events, the collectors of historiographical *akhbār* were also concerned with lists of names. The listing of names is manifest in the material of Mūsā ibn ʻUqba (d. 143/758), as reflected in the quotations from him by Ibn Saʻd,[132] and is quite common in the *Sīra* material of Ibn Isḥāq. Such lists may be linked to a narrative context,[133] but more often they appear as independent sections.[134] Lists are given of various topics; they enumerate the participants in the raids of the Prophet, or, in later literature, name the members of professional groups or persons afflicted by a certain disease.[135] This type of text, although not to be regarded as *akhbār* when it lacks a narrative context, may be considered part of *akhbār* literature. The extension of this term must also be applied to the genealogical tradition. The detailed knowledge of genealogy evident in our sources reflects the tribal background of the Arabs and, for this reason, the concern with lists of names is considered to stand at the very beginning of historical tradition.[136] Along with geographical and

[132] *Kitāb al-ṭabaqāt al-kabīr*, ed. Eduard Sachau *et al.* (Leiden, 1904–40), e.g. III.2, 120.

[133] Eg., Ibn Hishām, *Sīra*, II, 492–93, 530.

[134] *Ibid.*, II, 122, etc.; cf. Rudolf Sellheim, "Prophet, Chalif und Geschichte. Die Muḥammed Biographie des Ibn Isḥāq", *Oriens* 18–19 (1967), 74.

[135] See the lists of names in the work of Muḥammad ibn Ḥabīb (d. 245/860), *Kitāb al-muḥabbar*, ed. Ilse Lichtenstädter (Hyderabad, 1361/1942); *idem*, *Al-Munammaq fī akhbār Quraysh*, ed. Khurshīd Aḥmad Fāriq (Hyderabad, 1384/1964).

[136] W. Montgomery Watt, "The Materials Used by Ibn Isḥāq", in Bernard Lewis and P.M. Holt, eds., *Historians of the Middle East* (London, 1962), 26; Sellheim, "Prophet, Chalif und Geschichte", 73; Joseph Schacht, "On Mūsā b. ʻUqba's Kitāb al-Maghāzī", *Acta Orientalia* 21 (1953), 299; *idem*, "The *Kitāb al-Tārīkh* of Khalīfa ibn Khayyāṭ", *Arabica* 16 (1969), 79–81; M.J. Kister, "The *Sīrah* Literature", in A.F.L. Beeston *et al.*, eds., *The Cambridge History of Arabic Literature*, I: *Arabic Literature to the End of the Umayyad Period* (Cambridge, 1983), 353.

topographical data,[137] names form the backbone of factual information in historical tradition.

Akhbār often appear in combination with poetry,[138] which may or may not be incorporated into the composition by some narrative device.[139] Apart from the technical aspects of the composition, the structural relationship between verses and narrative also varies. Verses are often connected with a narrative in a rather associative manner, but they may also illustrate an aspect of the given incident and even form its core. *Akhbār* may also explicate the situation which is said to have led to the composition of certain verses.[140] In this context, *akhbār* may be of etiological origin; accounts of the lives of poets in particular tend to include such *akhbār*.[141] Like poetry, proverbs (*amthāl*) too have inspired etiological narratives,[142] which are, as a rule, distinct from historiographical *akhbār* in that they do not center on the well-known personalities of Islamic history.

The most widespread type of *akhbār* narration may be called anecdotal insofar as it concerns "stories about particular incidents".[143] This definition, of course, denotes a very general feature of *khabar*. A more precise application of the term may be proposed here. The anecdotal type of narration aims less to furnish evidence about an incident than to delineate the characters. This is a frequent phenomenon in *akhbār*, since the personalities we meet are often known for certain traits of character, especially in the case of prominent personalities of early Islamic history; through innumerable repetitive representations in various

---

137 Evaluated in an exemplary manner in Fred McGraw Donner, *The Early Islamic Conquests* (Princeton, 1981).

138 Joseph Horovitz, "Die poetischen Einlagen der Sīra", *Islamica* 2 (1926), 308–13; James T. Monroe, "The Poetry of the *Sīrah* Literature", in *Cambridge History of Arabic Literature*, I, 368–73. See also Nabia Abbott, *Studies in Arabic Literary Papyri* (Chicago, 1957–72), I, 15.

139 E.g. above, 297.

140 Abū l-Faraj, *Aghānī*, I, 21:1–2.

141 The etiological character of biographical material has been demonstrated by Tilman Seidensticker, *Die Gedichte des Šamardal ibn Šarīk. Neuedition, Übersetzung, Kommentar* (Wiesbaden, 1983), 4–9.

142 Werner Caskel, "Einheimische Quellen zur Geschichte Nord-Arabiens", *Islamica* 3 (1922), 331–41, 332–33.

143 Watt, "The Materials Used by Ibn Isḥāq", 29.

situations, they have come to personify certain attributes. This penchant for the depiction of characteristics may be due to the connection of *akhbār* with a conventional or "public" art of storytelling. Related to this important orientation of *akhbār* narration is its characteristic edifying, moralizing impulse.

Anecdotal narrations are not, however, determined with respect to their narrative tone. They may be committed to the unobtrusive, restrained form of the report, or indulge in dramatic effects and colorful descriptions.[144] Elements of skillful illustration and glorification seem to be folkloric in nature, and appear to derive from the style of popular storytellers (*quṣṣāṣ*). For this reason, the meaning of the term *qiṣaṣ*, which denotes particularly the genre of tales and myth relating to the prophets of the Qur'ān or the Old Testament,[145] may be extended to include other stories that manifest this kind of "popular" imprint. Thanks to this terminology, *qiṣaṣ* in the sense of popular tales are sometimes regarded as distinct from supposedly more reliable *akhbār* material.[146] True enough, *elements* of *qiṣaṣ* are to be discovered in the materials of Ibn Isḥāq, al-Wāqidī and, as our example has shown, Naṣr ibn Muzāḥim.[147] But while it is possible to single out the early authorities known as *quṣṣāṣ* who were engaged in preaching and explaining the issues of Islam,[148] it would seem that the distinction between *qiṣaṣ* and *akhbār* cannot be established from our texts. Instead, it is expedient to accept that historiographical narratives quoted from collectors of *akhbār* may include *qiṣaṣ* material. In light of these considerations, it cannot be concluded that the terminology implies any distinction as to the origins of these texts, nor does it offer any basis for the pursuit of arguments on the question of their factual validity.

---

[144] See Wellhausen on the style of Sayf ibn 'Umar (d. 180/796) in his "Prolegomena", 74–75, and on Abū Mikhnaf in his *Die religiös-politischen Oppositionsparteien im alten Islam* (Berlin, 1901), 68.

[145] Régis Blachère, "Regards sur la littérature narrative en arabe au 1er siècle de l'Hégire (= VIIe S.J.-C.)", *Semitica* 5 (1955), 86.

[146] Duri, *Rise of Historical Writing*, 42, 52, and *passim*.

[147] *Ibid.*, 33, 34, 47.

[148] G.H.A. Juynboll, "On the Origins of Arabic Prose: Reflections on Authenticity", in G.H.A. Juynboll, ed., *Studies in the First Century of Islamic Society* (Carbondale and Edwardsville, 1982), 166; Jamāl Muḥammad Dāwūd Jūda, "Al-Qiṣaṣ wa-l-quṣṣāṣ fī ṣadr al-Islām", *Dirāsāt ta'rīkhīya* 33–34 (1989), 105–39.

Akhbār narratives, just like *qiṣaṣ*, have their roots in the oral tradition of social gatherings.[149] Moreover, *qiṣaṣ* may also contain authentic historical information, and anecdotal *akhbār* may of course be sheer inventions, or may have been modified or distorted in the interest of certain parties.[150]

Legendary embellishment, which is characterized by plainly hyperbolic descriptions, can easily be singled out as a fictitious element. Narratives of early Islamic military expeditions which are distinguished by the extensive use of miraculous and fantastic tales constitute a literature *sui generis*.[151] Although the use of the *isnād*—here a purely fantastic element[152]—and the basic narrative techniques resemble those found in *akhbār*, these tales have their own idiosyncracy, the glorification of the main characters' virtues. In this respect, they come close to the epic genre.[153] Details of transmission, rhetorical embellishment by rhyming prose (*saj'*), and anti-Christian tendencies suggest a relatively late origin for some of these narratives.[154] The material, as well as a conception that is reminiscent of the *chanson de geste*,[155] may be much older.[156] Narratives of a miraculous nature are widespread also in *akhbār* on early Islamic history, apart from the material on the life of the Prophet. It has rightly been argued, therefore, that legendary elements do not allow any conclusions to be drawn as to the age and origin of the texts.[157] For this reason, again, narratives of legendary

[149] See, for example, Duri, *Rise of Historical Writing*, 138: "Narratives were related primarily in tribal social gatherings (*majālis*)".

[150] Watt, "The Materials Used by Ibn Isḥāq", 29.

[151] Cf. Ferdinand Wüstenfeld, *Der Tod des Ḥusein ibn 'Alí und die Rache. Ein historischer Roman aus dem Arabischen* (Göttingen, 1883); Rudi Paret, *Die legendäre Maghāzi-Literatur. Arabische Dichtungen über die muslimischen Kriegszüge zu Mohammeds Zeit* (Tübingen, 1930). See also Rosenthal, *History of Muslim Historiography*, 186–93.

[152] Rudi Paret, "Die legendäre Futūḥ-Literatur. Ein arabisches Volksepos?", *Atti del convegno internazionale sul tema: La poesia epica e la sua formazione* (Rome, 1970), 740–41.

[153] *Ibid.*, 746–47.

[154] *Ibid.*, 745.

[155] M.ª Jesús Rubiera, "Estructura de 'Cantar de Gesta'", *Revista del Instituto Egipcio* 23 (1985–86), 63–78.

[156] Paret, "Die legendäre Futūḥ-Literatur", 746.

[157] Sezgin, *Abū Miḫnaf*, 117–18.

nature must not be kept separate from the *akhbār* tradition, but must be considered part of it.[158]

The Emergence of Akhbārīyūn

Some of the authorities known to us from our sources as important early collectors of *akhbār*, such as Ibn Shihāb al-Zuhrī (d. 124/742)[159] or 'Urwa ibn al-Zubayr, were also renowned for their expertise in juridical and dogmatic tradition and may have been prominent authorities of *ḥadīth*.[160] Their care for historiographical narration was part of a more general concern with Islamic tradition.[161] However, other authorities in the field of history, such as Sayf ibn 'Umar[162] or Abū Mikhnaf,[163] were not held in esteem as *muḥaddithūn* and probably neither associated with the circle of traditionists nor gained their acceptance. Those authorities mentioned in biographical literature who lived before the second half of the ninth century were conventionally treated as transmitters of *ḥadīth* material and judged according to the standards of traditionists. Authorities of *akhbār* were quite often judged disapprovingly in these works; this is particularly conspicuous in the case of authorities who are not quoted in the collections of *ḥadīth*, but seem to have been exclusively devoted to the transmission of *akhbār*.[164]

A change is noticeable in the treatment of *akhbār* collectors who died in the first decades of the ninth century. Even those who are considered unreliable authorities on *ḥadīth*, for instance al-Wāqidī and al-Haytham

---

[158] Maḥmūd 'Alī Makkī, "Al-Asāṭīr wa-l-ḥikāyāt al-sha'bīya al-muta'allaqa bi-fatḥ al-Andalus", *Majallat al-ma'had al-miṣrī* 23 (1985–86), 27–50, discusses parallels in *akhbār* literature to legendary elements in the Arab-Islamic accounts on the conquest of Spain.

[159] *GAS*, I, 280–83.

[160] *Ibid.*, 278–79.

[161] This is also confirmed by a remark of Mālik ibn Anas (d. 179/795) on the *Maghāzī* of Mūsā ibn 'Uqba, as given by Ibn Abī Ḥātim, *Al-Jarḥ wa-l-ta'dīl*, IV.1, 154.

[162] *Ibid.*, II.1, 278.

[163] *Ibid.*, III.2, 182

[164] E.g. al-Khaṭīb al-Baghdādī, *Ta'rīkh Baghdād*, IX, 272–73; cf. Leder, *Korpus al-Haiṯam*, 308–13.

ibn ʿAdī, are recognized in their capacity as experts on *akhbār*. Others, namely Hishām ibn Muḥammad al-Kalbī and al-Madāʾinī, are primarily considered as scholars of historiographical tradition. It seems that in the second half of the eighth century the transmission of *akhbār* reached a professional standard and won the recognition of scholarly circles. During this period, working on *akhbār* became a discipline of its own, the practitioners of which may be termed *akhbārīyūn*.[165] These *akhbārīyūn* were not specialized in the transmission of historical traditions, but collected narratives in all fields of *akhbār* literature. As demonstrated above, their activity comprised the transmission and arrangement, adoption (by the attachment of new *isnād*s to *akhbār*), reshaping, and creation of narrative material.

They also participated in the development of written literature, which came about in a process characterized by the interplay of oral and written forms of transmission.[166] Notebooks of scholars played an important rôle in the evolution from single sheets to complete books.[167]

In many instances our sources present contradictory accounts. Obviously, the compiler did not feel obliged to point out conflicting elements in his materials, or do more than occasionally comment on the credibility of a narrative.

This attitude must not be interpreted as a result of incompetence or lack of critical discernment. Any assessment of the compiler's work must take into account the consideration that discussion of the materials to hand was probably not regarded as a very important task. The compiler confined himself primarily to the collection and adaptation of texts, because all reports quoted from accepted authorities were considered to be equally valid. Consequently, the truth of a statement or the veracity of a report do not constitute issues that the compiler felt obligated to discuss. He merely preserved testimonies of different origins and collected accounts reflecting various tendencies, thus creating a multivoiced chorus. In doing so he introduced dissent into his collec-

[165]The term appears first in the bibliography of Ibn al-Nadīm (d. 380/990), *Al-Fihrist*, ed. Riḍā Tajaddud (Tehran, 1391/1971), 101.

[166]See Schoeler, "Die Frage der mündlichen und schriftlichen Überlieferung".

[167]Rosenthal, *History of Muslim Historiography*, 69; cf. *idem*, "Introduction" to *The History of al-Ṭabarī*, I, 52; Johannes Pedersen, *The Arabic Book*, trans. Geoffrey French, ed. and intro. Robert Hillenbrand (Princeton, 1984), 23ff.

tion, but at the same time he avoided controversy by disregarding the dogmatic background of the different narratives.

The compiler of *akhbār* gathered the material or opinions that contributed to the process of forming a consensus on accepted tradition. Every opinion, every voice which could be added to his collection reinforced the community of believers by the weight of authority as a witness of the Islamic past and a part of it.

This discourse established by the compilers accords with the concealment of authorship. Personal views are not discussed, either in *akhbār* or on the level of the compilation. The absence of an author marks the absence of individual perception and reasoning as the focus of literary communication.

8

The Conquest of Arwād: A Source-Critical Study in the Historiography of the Early Medieval Near East*

Lawrence I. Conrad

(Wellcome Institute)

TWO KILOMETERS off the Syrian coast near Ṭarṭūs lies the island of Arwād (classical Arados, now known as Ruwād), a rocky shelf 800 meters long (north to south) and about 500 meters wide. A site that for millennia has attracted settlement, it enjoys a strategic and easily defended location and, along a coastline otherwise generally devoid of good harbors, two protected anchorages along its eastern side now known as the Marbaṭ Jeanne d'Arc and the Marbaṭ Sidnūs (Cydnus). These features endowed it—like Tyre further south—with considerable importance and enabled it to make its mark in the course of ancient history. As continues to be the case today, Arwād seems to have been a place entirely dominated by seamen and maritime power

*I would like to thank the participants in the LAEI Workshop, and in particular Hugh Kennedy, for their valuable discussion of this paper. I am also grateful to Sebastian Brock, Michael Cook, and Andrew Palmer for their comments and suggestions.

politics and trade.[1] It was an independent state already in the second millennium BC, and in the diplomatic correspondence of the Amarna tablets it figures as a naval power of considerable authority in the eastern Mediterranean.[2] Israelite lore makes the Aradians descendants of Canaan,[3] and by the sixth century BC the island was tributary to Tyre and provided the latter with troops and seamen.[4] It was active in the maneuvering among the great powers of antiquity, and was at various times under Egyptian, Assyrian, Babylonian, and Persian suzerainty. Its fleet fought with the Persians at Salamis (480 BC), and in the era prior to its conquest by Alexander the Great (333 BC) it ranked with Byblos, Sidon, and Tyre as one of the four great coastal cities of Syria. Seleucid times comprised an era of efflorescence for the island: Arwād initiated its own era in 259 BC, enjoyed complete autonomy, issued its own coinage, and in this period developed into a flourishing and powerful city. The great walls surrounding the island on all but the harbor side were at least ten meters high in places and were built of tremendous blocks up to six meters long and two meters high, and the city was the capital for a régime that controlled mainland territories extending from Jabala, 70 km. north of Arwād, to the district of Eleutheros, 40 km. to the south of the island. Under Hasmonean rule, and especially during the reign of Simon Maccabeus (141–135 BC), it continued to be a center of both political and military significance.[5]

[1]When this writer visited Arwād in 1974, the approximately 3000 Sunnī Muslim Rwaydīs, as they call themselves (there were no Shī'īs, 'Alawīs, Christians, or Jews, I was told), almost all earned their livelihood as sailors, ferrymen, fishermen, shipwrights, or craftsmen and laborers involved in trades supporting the island's maritime concerns. On the island in modern times, see Carl Ritter, *Die Erdkunde im Verhältnis zur Natur und zur Geschichte des Menschen* (Berlin, 1822–59), XVII.A, 53–55; Ernest Renan, *Mission de Phénicie* (Paris, 1864), 22–25; R. Savignac, "Une visite à l'île d'Rouad", *RB* 13 (1916), 574; Albert Trabaud, "Un marin gouverneur de l'île de Rouad", in *En patrouille à la mer* (Paris, 1929), 97–135; 'Abd el-Majyd Solaymân and Henri Charles, *Le parler arabe de la voile et la vie maritime dans l'île d'Arwâd et sur la côte syro-libanaise* (Beirut, 1972), 54, 97–101.

[2]See J.A. Knudtzon, *Die El-Amarna-Tafeln* (Leipzig, 1915), I, 453–55 (no. 101:11–18), 465–67 (no. 105:11–21), 469–71 (no. 105:85–87), 619 (no. 149:57–63); II ("Anmerkungen"), 1199, 1202–1203, 1248.

[3]Genesis 10:18, I Chronicles 1:16.

[4]Ezekiel 27:8, 11.

[5]I Maccabees 15:23.

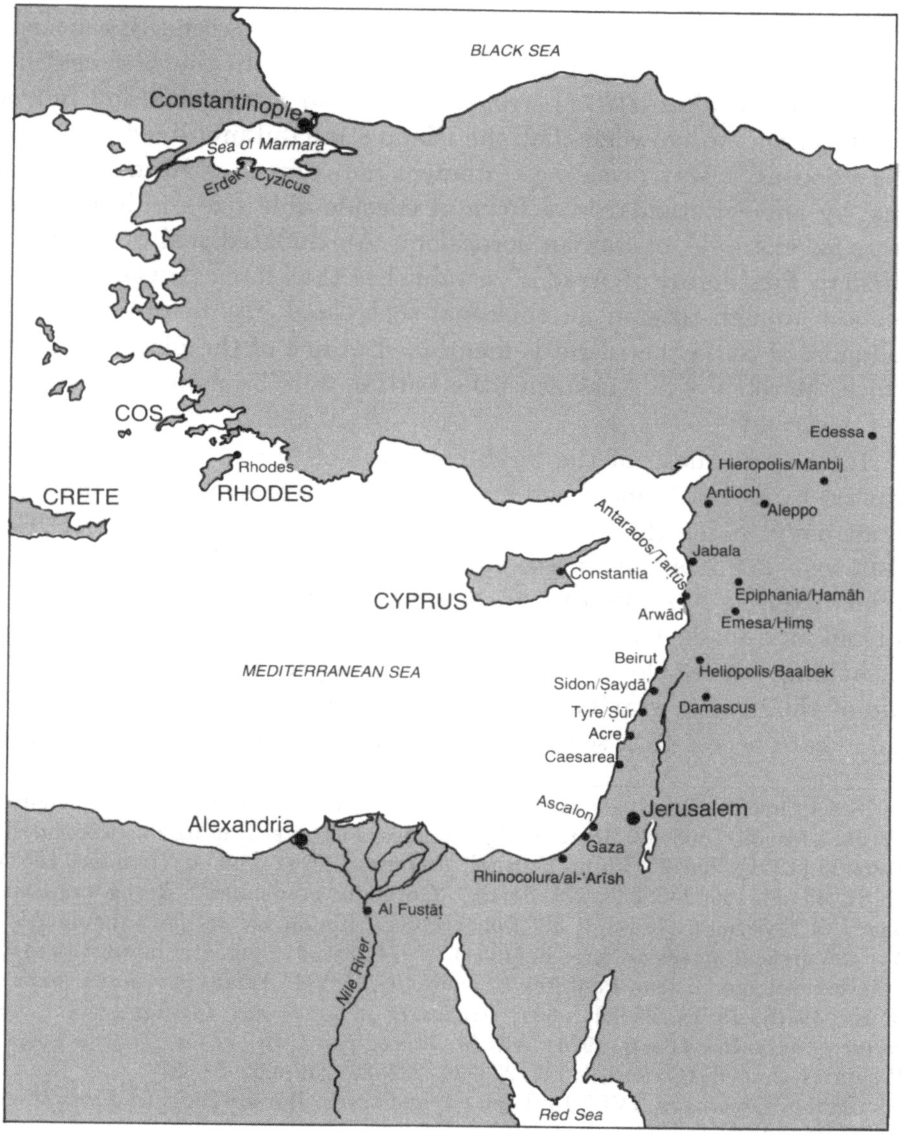

Map of Eastern Mediterranean

Though it was not as important under the Romans and Byzantines, Arwād remained an urban center of some note.[6] In the first century AD Strabo (d. after AD 21) wrote that Arwād was in his day full of dwellings and so crowded that the island's inhabitants lived in multistory houses.[7] This revealing statement indicates that Roman Arwād was, by ancient standards, a town of considerable size—fully half the area, for example, of Roman Jerusalem. An undated seal of a certain "Bishop Pantherius of Arados" establishes that later Arwād was important enough to gain an episcopal seat,[8] and just before the Arab conquest of Syria the island is mentioned as one of the places through which the relics of S. Anastasius the Persian were brought on their way to Caesarea.[9]

In the aftermath of the Arab conquest of Syria, Arwād was confronted by a hostile mainland and the rapid expansion of the nascent Arab navy under the able direction of the Arab governor of Syria, Muʿāwiya ibn Abī Sufyān (d. 60/680). Although Muʿāwiya was not immediately in a position to storm a place as well endowed with natural and man-made defenses as Arwād, Byzantium's long-term prospects for holding it were bleak. The very likely prospect of total blockade was one of the utmost gravity, for on Arwād itself the population had no immediate access to a source of fresh water. This could be obtained

---

[6]See Immanuel Benzinger, art. "Arados" in P/W, *RE*, II.1, 371–72; Savignac, "Visite à Rouad", 565–92; Henri Seyrig, "Aradus et sa pérée sous les rois séleucides", *Syria* 28 (1951), 206–20; Philip K. Hitti, *History of Syria*, 2nd ed. (London, 1957), 71, 82, 83, 84, 130, 232, 238, 271; Seyrig, "Questions aradiennes", *Revue numismatique*, VIme Série, 6 (1964), 9–50; Honor Frost, "Rouad, ses récifs et mouillages", *Annales archéologiques de Syrie* 14 (1964), 67–74 (a study of greater interest than its title would suggest); Jean-Paul Rey-Coquais, *IGLS*, VII: *Arados et régions voisines* (Paris, 1970), 15–18, 25–50; *idem*, *Arados et sa pérée aux époques grecque, romaine et byzantine* (Paris, 1974); A.H.M. Jones, *The Cities of the Eastern Roman Provinces*, 2nd ed. (Oxford, 1971), 233–34, 238–39, 256, 260–62, 267.

[7]Strabo, *Geography* XVI.2.13; Loeb ed. and trans. Horace Leonard Jones (London, 1916–32), VII, 257.

[8]See Costas P. Kyrris, *History of Cyprus* (Nicosia, 1985), 187. The seal was found on Cyprus and is now in the Cyprus Museum in Nicosia. Though attempts have been made to link this seal with the Arab conquest of Arwād, the artifact is in fact undated and Bishop Pantherius is an otherwise entirely unknown figure. Cf. n. 86 below.

[9]*Acta martyris Anastasii Persae*, ed. Hermann Usener (Bonn, 1894), 13b:37–38.

only by collecting rainwater in cisterns, carrying water across from the mainland, or taking advantage of a spring that gushed fresh water up from the sea bottom in the shallows a short distance from the island.[10] The first of these options was unreliable, the second no longer possible, and the third increasingly doubtful as Arab naval power increased.

The fall of the island was thus simply a matter of time, and most Arabists and Byzantinists have taken little interest in the accounts of its capitulation in 29/650. Several scholars have commented upon the importance of Byzantine Arwād,[11] and Stratos has given a summary (and rather credulous) account of the Arab siege.[12] But otherwise the events in question are briefly dismissed or ignored, even in contexts in which they would seem to be of particular relevance and importance,[13] and the

[10] A detailed account of the means used by the ancient Aradians to secure fresh water is given in Strabo, *Geography* XVI.2.13; ed. Jones, VII, 257. Later in medieval times, this spring gushed fresh water with such force that the turbulence on the sea surface above was brisk enough to prevent the approach of small boats; see al-Dimashqī (wr. *ca.* 700/1300), *Nukhabat al-dahr fī ʿajāʾib al-barr wa-l-baḥr*, ed. A. Mehren (Leipzig, 1923), 120:11–12. Cf. also Lucretius (d. 55 BC), *De rerum natura* VI.890–91; ed. Joseph Martin (Leipzig, 1953), 265; Pliny the Elder (d. AD 78), *Natural History* II.227; ed. Ludwig Jan and Karl Mayhoff (Leipzig, 1897–1909), I, 217:12–16; Hitti, *History of Syria*, 83; Rey-Coquais, *Arados et sa pérée*, 60.

[11] See, for example, Ekkehard Eickhoff, *Seekrieg und Seepolitik zwischen Islam und Abendland. Das Mittelmeer unter byzantinischer und arabischer Hegemonie (650–1040)* (Berlin, 1966), 14–15; Romilly Jenkins, *Byzantium: the Imperial Centuries, AD 610–1071* (London, 1966), 38; Robert Browning, "Byzantium and Islam in Cyprus in the Early Middle Ages", Ἐπετηρὶς Κέντρου Ἐπιστημονικῶν Ἐρευνῶν 9 (1977–79), 102; Vassilios Christides, "The Naval Engagement of Dhāt aṣ-Ṣawārī, AH 34/AD 655–56: a Classical Example of Naval Warfare Incompetence", *Byzantina* 13.2 (1985), 1334.

[12] Andreas N. Stratos, *Byzantium in the Seventh Century*, trans. Marc Ogilvie and Harry T. Hionides (Amsterdam, 1968–75), III, 40–42.

[13] See, for example, Julius Wellhausen, "Die Kämpfe der Araber mit den Romäern in der Zeit der Umaijiden", *Nachrichten von der Königliche Gesellschaft der Wissenschaften zu Göttingen, Philologisch-historische Klasse*, 1901, 419; Savignac, "Visite à Rouad", 569; George Fadlo Hourani, *Arab Seafaring in the Indian Ocean in Ancient and Early Medieval Times* (Princeton, 1951), 56; Archibald R. Lewis, *Naval Power and Trade in the Mediterranean, AD 500–1100* (Princeton, 1951), 55–56; A. Papageorgiou, "Les premières incursions arabes à Chypre et leurs conséquences", in Ἀφιέρωμα εἰς Κωνσταντῖνον Σπυριδάκιν (Nicosia, 1964), 2 of the offprint; Aḥmad Mukhtār al-ʿAbbādī and al-Sayyid ʿAbd al-ʿAzīz Sālim, *Taʾrīkh al-baḥrīya al-islāmīya fī Miṣr wa-l-Shām* (Beirut, 1981), 18.

especially valuable historiographical aspects have been considered only in the discussion of Caetani, which predates the publication of some of the key eastern Christian sources and, oddly enough, omits the Arabic material.[14]

More thus remains to be said about the events themselves, and in this respect it is worth noting that the Cyprus–Arwād expedition marked the first stage of a long naval campaign that step by step brought Mu‘āwiya closer to his ultimate objective—Constantinople.[15] Viewed in this light, the events at Arwād must be seen as more significant than has previously been the case. Here, however, my remarks will not primarily concern matters of historical reconstruction, which, as we shall see, the extant information allows only to a severely limited extent. Of far greater importance are the broader historical observations and historiographical points that come to light if one analyzes and compares what the Islamic and the various eastern Christian traditions have to offer concerning the siege and surrender of Arwād. Such an approach allows one to achieve some illuminating insights into the mutual perceptions of the local Syrian Christian communities and their new Arab rulers, and also to reach some important conclusions concerning the treatment and transmission of historical narratives and reports in the various historical traditions of the early medieval Near East.

Theophilus of Edessa and the Eastern Christian Tradition

The end of Byzantine rule on Arwād came soon after the invasion of Cyprus by Mu‘āwiya in 28/649. Shortly thereafter a Byzantine fleet appeared in the eastern Mediterranean, thus posing a major threat to the now far-extended Arab position in the region. Mu‘āwiya ordered his naval forces to fall back to the Syrian coast, and anxious to deprive the Greeks of a base so far advanced in waters now contested by the caliphate, he turned his attention to Arwād. The fullest account of the campaign for the island is in the anonymous Syriac *Chronicle of*

[14] Leone Caetani, *Annali dell'Islam* (Milan, 1905–26), VII, 227–31, proceeding on the basis of the accounts in Theophanes and Michael.

[15] Georg Ostrogorsky seems to have been the first scholar to notice (in 1940) the overall purpose of Mu‘āwiya's naval campaigns. See his *History of the Byzantine State*, trans. Joan Hussey, 2nd ed. (New Brunswick, 1969), 116, 124.

1234. Immediately after discussing the invasion of Cyprus, this work continues as follows:

> *On how Ardw, a fortified city in the sea, was conquered*
>
> The city of Ardw, which is called Arad Qōsṭ, is an island which is in the sea and is located opposite Antarados at a distance of three [Roman] miles therefrom. When Mu'awyā was unable to subdue it by force, he sent to them a certain bishop named Tōmā to demand that they abandon the city and they themselves might depart in peace. But when the bishop arrived among them they seized him and did not allow him to return, nor did they submit to Mu'awyā. When this happened, Mu'awyā went back to Damascus, because winter had begun and they were not able to approach the city in time of winter.[16] But when spring arrived, Mu'awyā again besieged Ardw with forces much more numerous and better equipped than previously. When the people of Ardw saw the dire straits they were in and the mighty forces that Mu'awyā had brought to bear against their city, they requested terms for their lives, according to which some of them would settle in Byzantine territory (*bēth Rōmāyē*) and some would make their homes in Syria, wherever they wished to dwell. When the inhabitants of the island's town departed, Mu'awyā gave orders, its walls were razed, and the city was put to the torch and destroyed. They made the city into [a state in which] it could never again be rebuilt and inhabited.[17]

The author of this report gives a cogent account of events without resorting to stereotyped narrative topoi to fill gaps and explain motives: the cavalier treatment of the governor's ecclesiastical envoy, for example, could easily have provided a starting point for a tale of how Arwād

[16] I.e. the Arabs could not maintain the siege because the stormy weather of the east Mediterranean winter made the seas too dangerous for the continual presence of the naval units obviously essential for a campaign against an island fortress. See n. 141 below.

[17] *Chronicon ad annum Christi 1234 pertinens*, ed. J.-B. Chabot (Paris, 1916–20; *CSCO* 81–82, *Scr. Syri* 36–37), I, 273:1–22.

was razed to avenge this insult, or an opening for introduction of an elegant speech demonstrating the author's (or transmitter's) rhetorical skills. Our informant also avoids the temptation to engage in polemical or tendentious arguments—e.g. by attributing the capture of Arwād to divine wrath at the sins or injustices of a rival Christian sect, or belaboring acts of violence or cruelty associated with the Arab conquest. He makes no effort to conceal the fact that a Christian bishop had agreed to cross over to Arwād, back in Christian territory, to encourage fellow Christians to capitulate, and he does not hesitate to report that after the surrender the islanders were allowed to resettle wherever else they wished. It is also worth noting that the account reveals awareness of points that only a well-informed north Syrian authority might have been expected to know. It gives the precise location of Arwād off the coast from Antarados (modern Ṭarṭūs), and specifies its distance from the mainland town.[18] In particular it refers to Arwād as Arad Qōsṭ, which seems to be an abbreviated or mutilated form of Arad Qōsṭanṭīyā.[19] Antarados, a former colony of Arados, was detached and renamed Constantia by Constantine in the fourth century.[20] It gradually came to outstrip Arados in prosperity and importance; and just as Antarados had earlier owed its name to the fact that it was "across from Arados", the island of Arwād now seems to have been referred to as Arados Constantiae, "the Arados of Constantia", probably to distinguish it from other places called Arados.[21] Indeed, Arados was

[18]Arwād is about 2.5 km. from the closest mainland point, but about 4 km. from Ṭarṭūs, which is slightly further up the coast to the north of that point.

[19]Cf. *Chronicle of 1234*, I, 43pu, where a cryptic reference in Jubilees 8:22 to the "Sea of Aṭēl" (Atlantic Ocean?) is likewise taken up without comment or clarification.

[20]*Chronicon ad annum Domini 724 pertinens*, ed. E.W. Brooks in *Chronica minora*, II (Paris, 1904; *CSCO* 3, *Scr. Syri* 3), 131:2–4; Theophanes (d. 818), *Chronographia*, ed. Karl de Boor (Leipzig, 1883–85), 38:8–9; and perhaps copying from Theophanes, Cedrenus (wr. after 1057), *Historia*, ed. Immanuel Bekker (Bonn, 1838–39; *CSHB* 24), I, 523:13–16. Jones proposes that Constantine had detached Antarados from its former master because the Aradians were stubborn pagans: see his *Cities of the Eastern Roman Provinces*, 267; *idem*, *The Greek City from Alexander to Justinian* (Oxford, 1940), 92.

[21]For the toponomy of "Arados" in the period just prior to the Arab conquests, see Stephanus of Byzantium (fl. mid-6th c.), *Ethnica*, ed. August Meineke (Berlin, 1849), 108:10–12.

so closely associated with Antarados/Constantia that one pilgrim who visited the area in the later sixth century referred to Arados as "the island of Antarados".[22]

Thus, while one must obviously raise the question of the origins of this account and how faithfully it was transmitted to the thirteenth century, it does not, on initial assessment, betray signs of forgery, recasting, or later elaboration. On the contrary, it seems to represent an account most of which was simply transcribed and transmitted from one work to the next, regardless of whether or not everything it said was still understood. The curious phrase "Arad Qōsṭ", for example, is unlikely to have been clear to Syriac copyists of manuscripts and transmitters of reports in later medieval times.

The provenance of the account can fortunately be traced with considerable precision, as represented on the transmission chart on the following page. Chabot argued that the *Chronicle of 1234* owes its Edessan emphasis to reliance on the now-lost *History of Edessa* by Abū l-Faraj Basileius bar Shūmmānā, metropolitan of Edessa (d. 1171), and that the author of the *Chronicle of 1234* itself was a monk at the patriarchal monastery of Mār Barṣawm.[23] While Chabot's argument raises several important points, it does not take note of the fact that the *Chronicle of 1234* is a "layered" chronicle of a type frequently encountered in Syriac historical writing. In its present form, the text represents an extension of an earlier Edessan Syriac chronicle completed early in 1204,[24] which in turn was an updated version of another Edessan chronicle written about 1150. This earliest redaction of the text is at numerous points identical to quotations cited elsewhere from Bar Shūmmānā, though it must be noted that this earliest level also contains much that would seem to be irrelevant to the history of Edessa,

[22] See the account of ps.-Antoninus Placentius (wr. *ca.* 570), *Itinerarium* I.3; ed. and trans. Celestina Milani, *Un viaggio in Terra Santa del 560–570 d.C.* (Milan, 1977), 88–89.

[23] See J.-B. Chabot, "Un épisode de l'histoire des Croisades", in *Mélanges offerts à M. Gustave Schlumberger* (Paris, 1924), I, 169–70; also his preface to his edition of the *Chronicle of 1234*, II, i-ii.

[24] The colophons for this level of the work have been preserved in the present text. See *Chronicle of 1234*, II, 213ult–214:1 (end of the civil history: AG 1514, or AD 1203), 340:11–24 (end of the ecclesiastical history: beginning of Shebāṭ 1515, or February 1204).

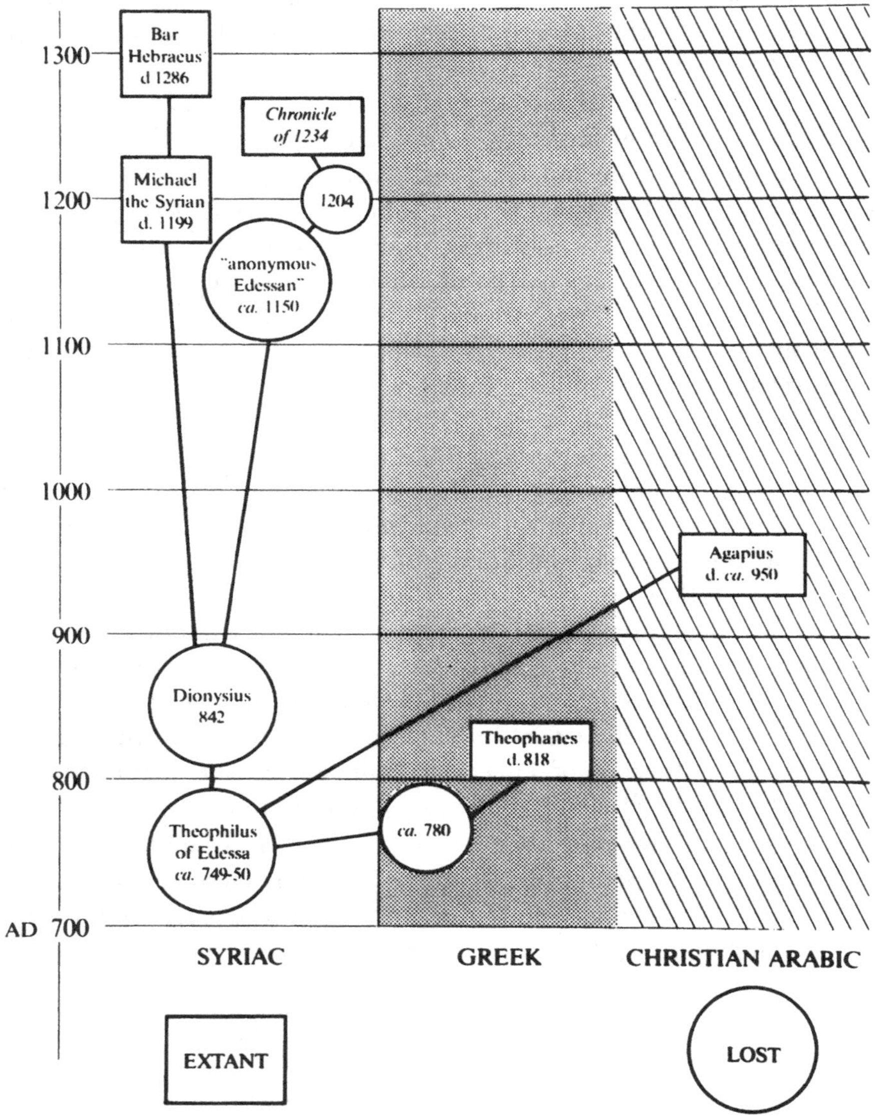

TRANSMISSION OF THE CHRONICLE
OF
THEOPHILUS OF EDESSA

e.g. a long account of King Priam and the siege of Troy.[25] Whatever the truth of this matter proves to be, the point of primary importance here is that the earliest redaction of what was eventually to become the *Chronicle of 1234* may be assigned to twelfth-century Edessa. In this study the author will be referred to as the "anonymous Edessan".

For the early Islamic period, this author's main source was the history (covering events from 582 until 842) by the Jacobite patriarch Dionysius of Tell-Maḥrē (d. 845), another ecclesiastical writer of Edessan origin.[26] This important work was also the primary source for Michael I Qīndasī ("Michael the Syrian", d. 1199);[27] and in Michael's history, among events dated to AG 961 (AD 649), we find the following account of the struggle for Arwād:

> Proceeding next to the city of Arvad, which is an island, when Mu'awyā pressed a siege against it and was unable to achieve its capture, he sent the bishop Tōmā to tell [the inhabitants] to leave the city and depart in peace. When they did not agree [to do so], Mu'awyā went back to Damascus. Then when spring arrived Mu'awyā again came against it and besieged Ardw. All the populace then left, and Mu'awyā destroyed it so that it would not be inhabited again.[28]

This report is unquestionably a condensation and paraphrase of the same account that made its way into the *Chronicle of 1234*, and the two so clearly spring from a common source, repeating even the same Syriac words and phrases, that the underlying version may confidently be attributed to Dionysius of Tell-Maḥrē, the common source of the two chronicles in question.[29] Michael's omissions are revealing. The

[25] *Ibid.*, I, 66:8–78:24.

[26] See *ibid.*, I, 236:22–24; II, 13:13–16, 315ult–316:1, on the Edessan background of Dionysius.

[27] See Michael's references to Dionysius in *Chronique de Michel le Syrien*, ed. and trans. J.-B. Chabot (Paris, 1899–1924), II, 356–58; III, 112 (trans.); IV, 377:1–378:38, 544:20–545:5 (text).

[28] *Ibid.*, II, 442 (trans.); IV, 430:19–22 (text).

[29] The rôle of Dionysius as the common source of Michael and the anonymous Edessan enabled Rudolf Abramowski to discover much of importance concerning

topographical detail is dropped, as are most references to matters of motive and intent, e.g. why Mu'āwiya abandoned the siege and why the Aradians surrendered after standing firm the previous year. The fate of Bishop Thomas is no longer explained, and the diplomatic dimension practically disappears. While the anonymous Edessan preserves a sense of options, constraints, and maneuvering on both sides, Michael's version is simply the tale of a city laid waste by the Arabs.

One must consider, of course, the possibility that four centuries of transmission have witnessed elaborations to Dionysius' account in the version that eventually appeared in the *Chronicle of 1234*, as well as condensation of Dionysius at the hands of Michael. So how faithfully did the anonymous Edessan, insofar as the chronicler of 1234 allows us to discern his work, reproduce the account of Dionysius? Fortunately, this issue can be resolved by reference to the Arabic history by the Syrian Melkite author Agapius (d. *ca.* 950), who has this to say on the fall of Arwād:

> In the third year of [the reign of] 'Uthmān, Mu'āwiya sailed across the sea and proceeded to Cyprus and conquered it. He had with him 1700 ships full of heavily armed troops and equipment, and on [Cyprus] and the islands surrounding it he took many people prisoner. Then word reached him that the forces of the Greeks were making their way toward him, so he went back to Syria and descended upon Arwād. But though he exerted his utmost effort, he could not take it. So he sent a bishop called Tūmā, and [the latter] asked them to leave the island and to withdraw to Greek territory (*al-Rūm*) so that the Arabs could occupy it. But when the bishop arrived among them they detained him and neither allowed him to return to Mu'āwiya nor paid any heed to his message. Then Mu'āwiya went back to Damascus, since it was the beginning of winter and also because he was close to the sea. When this winter ended and spring began, Mu'āwiya went back to the island of Arwād

Dionysius' lost chronicle; see his *Dionysius von Tellmahre, jakobitischer Patriarch von 818–845. Zur Geschichte der Kirche unter dem Islam* (Leipzig, 1940; *AKM* 25.2). Abramowski does not, however, discuss the Arwād materials.

> with forces mightier and more copious than the earlier time, descended upon [the place], and pressed a very tight siege upon them. When the people of Arwād (*al-Rūd*) saw the dire straits they were in and the forces that loomed over them, they requested a guarantee of security according to which they would depart for Syria and settle wherever they wished. Mu'āwiya ibn Abī Sufyān agreed to their terms, and they departed from the island. When they departed, Mu'āwiya ordered that its walls be razed. So [Arwād] was razed, put to the torch, and burned.[30]

Agapius' text represents a translation from Syriac into Arabic that generally adheres to the fuller presentation in the *Chronicle of 1234* so closely that there can be no doubt that the two ultimately derive from the same source. At the same time, they confirm that Michael has drastically condensed the text of Dionysius, while the anonymous Edessan and his continuators have sought simply to copy rather than to abridge or elaborate. Of the variations in the Arabic version some reflect editorial changes. Agapius has a drastically abbreviated account of the attack on Cyprus; and as he seeks to proceed smoothly on to the account of the siege of Arwād, he had also dropped the topographical introduction concerning the island. Similarly, he has decided against keeping the concluding statement on why Arwād was destroyed.

Some passages, however, betray interesting anomalies. The third year of the reign of 'Uthmān fell in 646–47, not 649; and while the early Damascene authority Yazīd ibn 'Ubayda (d. 177/793) would seem to corroborate the earlier date,[31] it is more likely, in light of the general agreement of our sources on 649 as the date for the first attack on Cyprus, that this represents an error arising from Agapius' effort to convert dates in other dating systems into that of the regnal years for the caliphs. The claim that Mu'āwiya wanted the Aradians to leave

[30]Agapius, *Kitāb al-'unwān*, ed. Louis Cheikho (Paris, 1912; *CSCO* 65, *Scr. Arabici* 10), II, 346:4–15.

[31]See Abū Zur'a al-Dimashqī (d. 281/894), *Ta'rīkh*, ed. Shukr Allāh ibn Ni'mat Allāh al-Qūchānī (Damascus, 1400/1980), I, 184:10–15. In this report Yazīd ibn 'Ubayda states that there were two attacks on Cyprus, one in 25/646 and the next in the following year.

their island "so that the Arabs could occupy it" (*li-tanzilahā l-'arab*) is, as we shall see, entirely erroneous and probably represents a gloss insinuated into the Arabic text in the course of its later transmission. Elsewhere there are inconsistencies that may be assigned to problems that arose during the transition from Syriac to Arabic. The Syriac of the *Chronicle of 1234* states that the Aradians seized Bishop Thomas and did not allow him to return, "nor did they submit to Mu'awyā" (*wal-Mu'awyā lā ešta'badw*). Agapius, however, says that they detained him and neither allowed him to return to Mu'āwiya, "nor paid any heed to his message" (*wa-lā ltafatū ilā risālatihi*). This shift suggests not a rather exegetical translation, but more likely a damaged or unclear passage in the original, a place where the translator has had to guess at the intended sense. One line later a similar problem arises. The Syriac clearly states that Mu'āwiya had to abandon the siege of Arwād because winter had begun and "he was not able to approach the city in time of winter", but in the Arabic this phrase becomes "he was close to the sea" (*kāna bi-qurbi l-baḥr*). In a third case, the Syriac specifies that Mu'āwiya's second expedition was "much more numerous and better equipped than previously"; but Agapius says that the Arab force "was mightier and more copious". By "more copious" (*akthar*), any reader will immediately presume the sense of "more numerous", but this is already implicit in "mightier" (*a'ẓam*) and obscures the Syriac's clear sense that equipment and supplies are meant. In none of these cases is the Syriac text difficult or ambiguous, and again, one must surmise that the basis for these discrepancies is a mutilated or unclear exemplar of the original Syriac text.

In the case of Arwād, however, Agapius serves to confirm that what he found in his own source was not significantly different from what was eventually to appear in the *Chronicle of 1234*. This is, in fact, what one might in any case expect. As has been noted above, the *Chronicle of 1234* is largely based on Edessan sources; and Agapius was from Manbij, the ancient Hierapolis, a north Syrian town only about 100 km. from Edessa.

The question of Agapius' source leads us further back into the transmission process. At the end of his account of the Umayyads and the 'Abbāsid revolution in the mid-eighth century, Agapius suddenly volunteers the following important information:

> Theophilus the astrologer, from whom we have taken these narratives (*akhbār*), said: "I have myself been a continuous eyewitness to these conflicts,[32] and I set matters down in writing so that nothing pertaining to them should escape me". He wrote many books on such subjects, and from them we have condensed this book, adding what we knew could not be dispensed with, while avoiding prolixity.[33]

The authority cited here is Theophilus bar Tōmā of Edessa (d. 169/785), a Maronite historian who wrote a chronicle extending from Creation to the 'Abbāsid revolution and the collapse of the Umayyad caliphate. In 'Abbāsid times he seems to have abandoned historical writing in favor of other (perhaps less sensitive?) pursuits: he served as the chief astronomer/astrologer to the 'Abbāsid caliph al-Mahdī (158–69/775–85), and also composed a highly regarded Syriac translation of the *Iliad* and perhaps also the *Odyssey*.[34] His chronicle seems still to have been extant in the time of Bar Hebraeus (d. 1286), who praised it as "a fine work on chronology",[35] but since then it has been lost and is now known to us only through citations in later works. The link with Theophilus is, however, extremely important, since in the colophon of Dionysius' history, as copied by Michael, Dionysius names Theophilus as one of his sources.[36] Indeed, from this colophon one must conclude that for civil history through the Umayyad period (though not for ecclesiastical history, since, as a Maronite, he "made it his business to vilify the Orthodox folk") Theophilus was a key source for Dionysius, and probably his main source.[37] In other words, our account of the capture of Arwād, taken from Dionysius by both Michael and the anonymous

[32] I.e. the disturbances at the time of the 'Abbāsid revolution.

[33] Agapius, *Kitāb al-'unwān*, II, 369:2–6.

[34] See Baumstark, 341–42; Michel Breydy, *Geschichte der syro-arabischen Literatur der Maroniten vom 7. bis 16. Jahrhundert* (Opladen, 1985), 132–38, 240–41, 271; Lawrence I. Conrad, "Theophanes and the Arabic Historical Tradition: Some Indications of Intercultural Transmission", *BF* 15 (1990), 43.

[35] Bar Hebraeus, *Chronicon syriacum*, ed. Paul Bedjan (Paris, 1890), 127:1–2; *idem*, *Ta'rīkh mukhtaṣar al-duwal*, ed. Antoine Ṣāliḥānī (Beirut, 1890), 220:2.

[36] Michael, II, 358 (trans.); IV, 378:32–38 (text).

[37] For a translation of this important colophon, as well as discussion on Dionysius more generally, see Lawrence I. Conrad, "Syriac Perspectives on Bilād al-Shām during the 'Abbāsid Period", in Muḥammad 'Adnān al-Bakhīt and Robert Schick,

Edessan, was taken by Agapius from Dionysius' source, the chronicle of Theophilus of Edessa.[38] As Agapius bypasses Dionysius (in that he cites his own source not as Dionysius, but rather as Theophilus, who was also a source for Dionysius), his version may be taken as confirmation of the accuracy with which Dionysius rendered the account of Theophilus in his own history.

As I have suggested elsewhere, it is Theophilus, and not the obscure Yōḥannān bar Shemūēl favored by Brooks,[39] to whom we must assign the "Eastern Source", a Syriac work commonly found to underlie the various Syriac historical works for the early Islamic period and a Greek rendition of which was used by the Byzantine chronicler Theophanes (d. 818).[40] This hypothesis may now be checked by consulting Theophanes

eds., *Proceedings of the Fifth International Conference on Bilād al-Shām: Bilād al-Shām during the 'Abbāsid Period (132–451/750–1059)* (Amman, forthcoming).

[38]It is not possible at this point to address in detail the question of whether or not there was an intermediary between Theophilus and Agapius. Indications at present tentatively suggest that there was not, but further investigation of the transmission of Theophilus' accounts of other events to Agapius may well cast a different light on the matter.

[39]E.W. Brooks, "The Sources of Theophanes and the Syriac Chroniclers", *BZ* 14 (1906), 582–87. Cf. Baumstark, 273.

[40]Conrad, "Theophanes and the Arabic Historical Tradition", 43. For earlier research on the Eastern Source, see Krumbacher, I, 343; Karl de Boor, "Zur Chronographie des Theophanes", *Hermes* 25 (1890), 301–307; *Chronica minora saec. IV. V. VI. VII*, ed. Theodor Mommsen in *MGH*, *Auct. Ant.*, XI.2, 324; Theodor Nöldeke, "Epimetrum", in *Chronica minora*, 368–69; Brooks, "Theophanes and the Syriac Chroniclers"; Nina Pigulevskaja, "Theophanes' Chronographia and the Syrian Chronicles", *JÖBG* 16 (1967), 55–60; Ann S. Proudfoot, "The Sources of Theophanes for the Heraclian Dynasty", *Byzantion* 44 (1974), 405–26; Hunger, I, 336–37. Cyril Mango has argued that the *Chronographia* is to all intents and purposes the work of George Syncellus: it is well-known that George compiled the text to the reign of Diocletian (AD 284–305), but Mango proposes that George also assembled the materials for the subsequent period, and then just before his death (placed in 810–11 by most scholars, but pushed back past 813 by Mango) passed them on to Theophanes. Lacking the skill to write these up in polished form, Theophanes simply published them as George had left them, with only minor revisions and additions. See Cyril Mango, "Who Wrote the Chronicle of Theophanes?", *ZRVI* 18 (1978), 9–17. This thesis is controversial and has been attacked, e.g. by I.S. Čičurov in his "Feofan Ispovednik: Publikator, Redaktor, Avtor?", *VV*, New Series, 42 (1981), 78–86 (cf. also the reservations of Whitby, 66 n. 182 above), but still has much to recommend it. The issue is not of particular consequence here, however,

to see if he gives an account of the fall of Arwād that may be linked to the above reports, all of which are clearly variations of Theophilus' original version of the events in question. Theophanes provides the answer in two passages in his *Chronographia*. Under AM 6140 (AD 648–49) he tells us:

> [Mauia] heard that the *cubicularius* Kakorizos was also advancing against him with a large Greek force, and brought back his fleet to take up positions to attack Arados. He anchored before the citadel (πολίχνην) of the island, the Kastellos, and tried to take it with all sorts of engines of war (μηχαναῖς). Achieving nothing by force, he sent to them a bishop named Thomarichos, hoping to intimidate them into handing over the city, agreeing to terms of truce, and leaving the island. When the bishop betook himself to them they seized him as soon as he came in and did not yield to Mauia. The siege of Arados continued without a decision, and Mauia went back to Damascus when winter came.[41]

And in the following year, AM 6141 (AD 649–50), we read:

> In this year Mauia launched a mightily equipped expedition against Arados. He took it on his agreement that its inhabitants could go to resettle wherever they wished. He burned the town, razed its walls, and turned the island into an uninhabited waste, which is what it is up to the present day.[42]

The strictly chronological framework of his history has obliged Theophanes to break into two parts what is clearly yet another version of the account of Theophilus of Edessa. Reading the dates according to the

since in either case the final compilation must be seen as the product of work done in or near Constantinople, based on the same sources coming into the capital. For the sake of convenience I will continue to refer to the author of the *Chronographia* as "Theophanes", while conceding the possibility of a significantly greater authorial rôle for George than has traditionally been granted.

[41] Theophanes, *Chronographia*, 344:1–10.

[42] *Ibid.*, 344:12–15.

scheme worked out by Ostrogorsky,[43] this produces a chronology identical to that of Michael. For present purposes this account is very useful. At many points Theophanes offers further confirmation that the *Chronicle of 1234* bears a largely faithful rendering of the original account by Theophilus; and in particular, Theophanes confirms that in two of the above-noted cases of major discrepancy between the anonymous Edessan and Agapius, the Syriac version is to be preferred. What the Aradians refused to do was to submit to Mu'āwiya, not to allow Thomas to return to Mu'āwiya, and the Arab governor's second expedition was indeed "better equipped" rather than "more copious/numerous".

But while the Greek chronicler is clearly dependent upon Theophilus for much of his account, there remain important differences at the beginning and end of the account that cannot be written off to the errors and glosses involved in translation and later transmission. At the very beginning of the account, it may be noted that neither Agapius nor the anonymous Edessan, who repeat Theophilus in detail and agree for the most part on what the content of his account had been, mention the name of the *cubicularius* Kakorizos. In fact, the involvement of this officer is recorded in no other source.[44] Nor do our other authorities make any reference to the existence of the citadel on Arwād[45] or where

[43]Georg Ostrogorsky, "Die Chronologie des Theophanes im 7. und 8. Jahrhundert", *BNJ* 7 (1928–29), 1–56.

[44]On this personality several Byzantinists and historians of Cyprus cite, as confirmation of the testimony of Theophanes, a *Historia miscella* attributed to Paul the Deacon (d. *ca.* 799) and published in *PL* 95 (Paris, 1861), cols. 739–1144. One still encounters references to this work as an independent source, but in fact the attribution is false. The *PL* text gives a late version (from a Vatican Ms.) of the Latin translation of Theophanes' *Chronographia* made by the pontifical librarian Anastasius (wr. 873–75) for his *Historia tripertita*. See Karl de Boor's discussion of the Anastasius Mss. in *Chronographia*, II, 426–31.

[45]There are currently two fortifications, both of recent Arab origin, on Arwād. The larger one, which is in a more dominating position (see the photograph facing 352 below), is located approximately in the center of the island and has long been assumed to stand on the site of fortifications built earlier. Archaeology, however, can unfortunately tell us little about this. Ancient and medieval stonework has been repeatedly reused all over the island; and as the extant structures are almost everywhere erected directly on exposed bedrock, there are no underlying levels to investigate. Of the Crusader period, for example, a time when Arwād is known to have been a busy and heavily fortified town, there is now little trace. Parts of the

Mu'āwiya's fleet anchored, or say anything about Arab siege machinery. At the very end of the account, no other version of Theophilus volunteers the information that Arwād is still uninhabited.

The introduction of this new information is unlikely to have been the work of Theophanes, for several reasons. First, and most bluntly put, the synthesis is rather too well executed to be the work of Theophanes, who is notorious for the very careless way in which he combined material from different sources (or, following Mango, felt free to publish George Syncellus' rough materials "as is").[46] Second, Byzantine Constantinople in the early ninth century, when Theophanes was writing, was a place where information about the seventh-century history of the Near East was extremely scarce. The Constantinopolitan chronicle used by the patriarch Nicephorus (d. 828), for example, was written shortly after 641,[47] yet had access to so little accurate information about the Arab conquest of Byzantine lands that it telescoped the events in question into an extremely confused account of a single campaign, a state of affairs which Nicephorus himself could do nothing to correct.[48] Of the period from 641 until the accession of Constantine IV in 668 Nicephorus has absolutely nothing to say, and this gap would hardly have been allowed to stand had he found any source at all from which he could have taken material to fill it. Theophanes too had trouble with this period, but was able to do better because he had access to the Eastern Source, while Nicephorus did not and so had to leave an enormous gap in his history.[49] Finally, the information added to the

---

ancient walls (at least Seleucid, and in part probably earlier) have survived because of the enormous size of the stones used to build them.

[46]See the examples discussed in Conrad, "Theophanes and the Arabic Historical Tradition", 3, 25–26.

[47]See Cyril Mango, "The *Breviarium* of the Patriarch Nicephorus", in Nia A. Stratos, ed., Βυζάντιον: Αφιέρωμα στὸν Ανδρέα Ν. Στράτο (Athens, 1986), II, 543; also his Introduction to his edition and translation of the *Breviarium* (Washington, D.C., 1990), 12–14. I am much endebted to conversations with Professor Mango for my own understanding of this important text. The main points raised in Mango's studies are missed, however, by Harry Turtledove in his "The Date of Composition of the Historia Syntomos of the Patriarch Nikephoros", in *Byzantine Studies in Honor of Milton V. Anastos* (Malibu, 1985; *Byzantína kai metabyzantína* 4), 91–94.

[48]See Nicephorus, *Breviarium* XX; ed. and trans. Mango, 14–15, 68–69, 186–88.

[49]Mango, "The *Breviarium* of the Patriarch Nicephorus", 545. Cf. also Mango's

account of Theophilus reflects detailed knowledge of local conditions—the existence of a citadel on the island, the Arab use of siege engines, where the Arab fleet anchored—and of the continuing uninhabited status of the island up to "the present day". If Byzantine writers in the capital were so ill-informed on this period that they could find nothing about the entire reign of Constans II (641–68), it is unlikely that they disposed of minutiae about the fall of Arwād.[50]

If this additional detail was not introduced by Theophanes, then it must most reasonably be attributed to the individual who translated Theophilus from Syriac into Greek. That is, this step was not just one of translation and updating, but also of revision and additions to the old material. According to Brooks' analysis, this stage is represented by the rendering of an original Syriac text into Greek by a Palestinian Melkite monk working in about 780; this new Greek version came to Constantinople with monks fleeing the destruction of Palestinian monasteries in 813.[51] Brooks' case for a date of about 780 is a solid one: for the period up to 780 Theophanes clearly had access to a source providing him with highly detailed information on developments in Palestine and Syria, while after that date he seems to know nothing about the region aside from matters for which no written source would have been required (e.g. the succession of the caliphs). The argument for a Palestinian origin, however, is weak, resting on the repeated references to Palestine and Jerusalem made by Theophanes after 746, i.e. after Brooks' approximate date for the composition of the Eastern Source and so attributable to the Greek translator of the work rather than to its Syriac author. But any Christian monk could be expected to take great interest in developments in the Holy Land, and attacks on monasteries and churches in 813–15 were widespread in Syria, Sinai, and northern Mesopotamia,[52] not just in Palestine. Further, the post-746 parts of Theophanes in fact reveal greater interest

Introduction to his edition and translation of the *Breviarium*, 14–15.

[50]On the dearth of Greek historical writing in the seventh and eighth centuries, see the discussions above in the papers of Whitby (66–74), Cameron (84–85, 88–90), and Haldon (125–29).

[51]Brooks, "Theophanes and the Syriac Chroniclers", 586–87.

[52]See, for example, Theophanes, *Chronographia*, 499:15–30; *Chronicle of 1234*, II, 10:9–24.

in and more detailed knowledge of other parts of Syria, especially—as the following examples illustrate—the north:

AM 6246—the Syrians and the revolt of ʿAbd Allāh ibn ʿAlī in 754[53]
AM 6248—earthquake in Palestine and Syria in 757[54]
AM 6252—rebellion led by a Syrian named Theodore against Arab rule in villages around Heliopolis/Baalbek in 761[55]
AM 6252—rebellion of ʿAbbāsid elements at Dābiq, north of Aleppo, in 761[56]
AM 6255—iconoclasm and the anathematization of Cosmas Comanites, bishop of Epiphaneia/Ḥamāh, in 763[57]
AM 6258—the Khārijite rebellion in the Syrian desert near Palmyra in 766[58]
AM 6261—the great "reconciliation" in Syria in 769[59]
AM 6266—a procession of heads (*sic.*) from North Africa through Syria in 774[60]
AM 6270—the rebellion of Thumāma at Dābiq and resulting unrest in 778[61]
AM 6272—persecution of Christians from Dābiq south as far as Damascus in 780[62]

In particular, this material manifests a special interest in the affairs of Emesa/Ḥimṣ:

AM 6242—an anti-ʿAbbāsid rebellion in the mountains near Emesa in 750[63]

[53] Theophanes, *Chronographia*, 428:15–429:14.
[54] *Ibid.*, 430:2–3.
[55] *Ibid.*, 431:23–27.
[56] *Ibid.*, 431:28–34.
[57] *Ibid.*, 433:28–434:5.
[58] *Ibid.*, 439:12–15.
[59] *Ibid.*, 444:10–12.
[60] *Ibid.*, 447:28–29.
[61] *Ibid.*, 451:11–452:2.
[62] *Ibid.*, 452:20–453:4.
[63] *Ibid.*, 427:3–4.

AM 6246—capture of Emesa by the forces of ʿAbd Allāh ibn ʿAlī in 751[64]
AM 6252—the head of John the Baptist moved to Emesa in 761[65]
AM 6272—anti-Christian persecutions in Emesa in 780[66]

The Arwād account in Theophanes further suggests a north Syrian provenance, since it is surely there that we must expect to find the person who had access to further detailed information about the Arwād campaign, and, even more to the point, knew that the island was still uninhabited.

This last detail is of particular interest, for there can be little doubt that Arwād was indeed still uninhabited at the time the translator/continuator of Theophilus was writing. Arwād was razed because the Arabs had no need for such a base far from other harbors and naval facilities on the mainland, but at the same time could not simply allow the island to be occupied and leave it to its own devices. The perils posed by such a situation had only recently, in 645, been demonstrated in a most vivid way by the brief Byzantine reoccupation of Alexandria,[67] and later during Muʿāwiya's tenure as governor of Syria similar dangers would be highlighted by an uprising in Ascalon aided and abetted by the Byzantines.[68] In Umayyad times, and especially during the caliphate of ʿAbd al-Malik (65–86/685–705), the Greeks mounted raids on various cities along the Syrian coast, including Tyre, Acre, Caesarea, and Ascalon, encouraged Mardaite depredations within Syrian territory as far as Mount Lebanon and Palestine, and maintained pressure on the Umayyads along the frontier.[69] All this provoked extreme anxiety among the Muslims of northern Syria (still, we must recall, a small minority of the population), and it should come

[64] *Ibid.*, 429:3.

[65] *Ibid.*, 431:16–21.

[66] *Ibid.*, 452:25–453:2.

[67] See Alfred J. Butler, *The Arab Conquest of Egypt and the Last Thirty Years of the Roman Dominion*, 2nd ed. by P.M. Fraser (Oxford, 1978), 465–83.

[68] Al-Balādhurī (d. 279/892), *Futūḥ al-buldān*, ed. M.J. de Goeje (Leiden, 1866), 142ult–143:1.

[69] See Gernot Rotter, *Die Umayyaden und der zweite Bürgerkrieg (680–692)* (Wiesbaden, 1982; *AKM* 45.3), 169–80.

as no surprise that in late Umayyad times the possibility of yet another Byzantine seaborne attack was still a matter of considerable concern to them. The Ḥimṣī transmitter Khālid ibn Ma'dān (d. 103/721–22) and the Damascene Abū 'Āmir al-Ilhānī (d. *ca.* 118/736) predict that the Byzantines will attack Antarados itself, leading to the deaths of 300 Muslim troops in a battle which will spread the alarm as far as al-'Arīsh/Rhinocolura, and that the invaders will then proceed to occupy Ḥimṣ.[70] Other traditions assert that various estuaries and such coastal towns as Acre and Ascalon are also at risk, and local perceptions of the ubiquitous nature of the Byzantine threat are highlighted in a tradition of the Damascene Makḥūl (d. *ca.* 112/730). Here we find that among the Greeks there will be born a prince who will grow and mature at a miraculous rate, and who at the age of twelve will be crowned as emperor. He will then use shipyards "on the islands and on the mainland" to construct warships which he will load with troops and use to mount an attack on the Syrian coast—the landing will be "somewhere between Antioch and al-'Arīsh".[71] The grave implications of such an attack are explored in another Ḥimṣī tradition related by Yazīd ibn Khumayr, who was a security official during the caliphate of Hishām ibn 'Abd al-Malik (105–25/724–43).[72] Here it is suggested that there will be a Byzantine landing on the coast of the district of Ḥimṣ; the Muslims of the city will sally forth to confront the threat, but once they have left, leaving their wives and children behind, the Christians of Ḥimṣ will rise in rebellion and close the gates on the Muslim forces.[73] That such speculations represent not scholarly whimsies, but genuine fears which were generally felt among Syrian Muslims, especially in the north, is illustrated by an incident which occurred in mid-Umayyad times: according to the Damascene historian and traditionist al-Walīd ibn Muslim (d. 195/810), there was widespread panic in Syria shortly after Sulaymān ibn 'Abd al-Malik's accession to the caliphate (96/715), as reports spread of a Byzantine landing on the coast of the military

---

[70]See Nu'aym ibn Ḥammād (d. 228/844), *Kitāb al-fitan*, ed. Lawrence I. Conrad (Wiesbaden, forthcoming), nos. 1245, 1250, 1363.

[71]*Ibid.*, no. 1210.

[72]See Ibn Ḥajar al-'Asqalānī (d. 852/1449), *Tahdhīb al-tahdhīb* (Hyderabad, AH 1325–27), XI, 324:4–5, no. 622.

[73]Nu'aym ibn Ḥammād, *Kitāb al-fitan*, no. 1373.

district (*jund*) of Ḥimṣ (*sāḥil Ḥimṣ*).[74] The speculations on impending Byzantine attacks of apocalyptic proportions are surely linked in a fundamental way to such fears, and in this environment of anxiety it is unlikely that the Umayyad and early 'Abbāsid authorities in the area would have allowed the resettlement of Arwād. The continuator of Theophilus may thus be taken as confirming that this prohibition remained in force.

Aside from a brief and uninformative reference to the fall of Arwād in the chronicle of the ps.-Dionysius (wr. *ca*. 774)[75] and another brief account that Bar Hebraeus seems to have excerpted from Michael,[76] this exhausts the Eastern Christian evidence for the campaign. At this point we may pause to recapitulate what has thus far emerged. Historically, we have an account of events that, in terms of how reliably things are known for this period, is very reliable indeed. First, the date of 650 for the capture of Arwād is probably at least approximately correct. A place like Arwād could not have held out after the destruction of the Byzantine fleet at the battle of Phoenix/Dhāt al-Ṣawārī in *ca*. 34/655;[77] and had the island tried to do so, Mu'āwiya would have needed to do no more than blockade it with a few ships and allow the defenders to choose between surrender or dying of thirst and starvation. Before Dhāt al-Ṣawārī there was for some time little reason to bother with Arwād, but this changed with the intrusion of a Byzantine fleet into the area just after the invasion of Cyprus.[78] At this point, the reduction

[74]Ibn al-Murajjā (fl. 5th/11th c.), *Faḍā'il Bayt al-Maqdis wa-l-Khalīl wa-l-Shām*, Universität Tübingen, Ms. Ar. no. 27, fol. 82v:10–11.

[75]See *Chronicon anonymum pseudo-Dionysianum vulgo dicto*, ed. J.-B. Chabot (Paris, 1927–33; *CSCO* 91, 104, *Scr. Syri* 43, 53), II, 151:24–25: "In the year 960 (648–49) Mū'awyā invaded Cyprus, and in the same year Arvad (Ms. 'Advar') was conquered".

[76]Bar Hebraeus, *Chronicon syriacum*, 105:16–18: "After these events (i.e. operations in Cyprus) Mū'āwiyā besieged the city of Arvad, which is also an island; and when he captured it he obliged its inhabitants to leave and destroyed it so that it would not be inhabited again".

[77]On this battle, see Lewis, *Naval Power and Trade*, 57; Eickhoff, *Seekrieg und Seepolitik*, 18–21; Andreas N. Stratos, "The Naval Engagement at Phoenix", in Angeliki E. Laiou-Thomadakis, ed., *Charanis Studies: Essays in Honor of Peter Charanis* (New Brunswick, 1980), 229–47; al-'Abbādī and Sālim, *Ta'rīkh al-baḥrīya al-islāmīya*, 28–31; Christides, "Dhāt aṣ-Ṣawārī", 1329–45.

[78]On the campaign for Cyprus, see Wellhausen, "Kämpfe der Araber mit den

of Arwād became an urgent priority: with an advancing Byzantine fleet in the area, threatening a zone in which the Arabs were now very far extended, Mu'āwiya could not wait indefinitely for the island to be abandoned.

Secondly, Theophilus' account offers valuable insights into how the local Christian communities and the newly established Arab régime in Syria perceived each other and interacted, even in a wartime situation. As the siege began the outlook for the Aradians could hardly have been promising. Their island was blockaded and cut off from supplies of food and fresh water, and in the midst of the crisis precipitated by the invasion of Cyprus they could not have expected—assuming they even knew that a Byzantine fleet was at sea—that there would be any thought of coming to the assistance of a small outpost right on the Syrian coast. Further, a bishop came across from the mainland and advised them to accept Mu'āwiya's offer of safe passage if they would depart for Byzantine territory. The "Bishop Thomas" referred to by Theophilus is probably to be identified as the "Thomarichos, bishop of Apamaea" whose death in 665 Theophanes (probably citing Theophilus) also records.[79] In earlier times Arwād had been under the metropolitan see of Tyre,[80] and our extant information on the ecclesiastical geography of Syria after the region's reconquest from the Persians in 628 is too scanty to sustain the argument that Arwād had shifted to the see of Apamaea by the time of the Arab siege. It is significant, however, that when the Aradians were prevailed upon by such a distinguished ecclesiastical figure to surrender, they not only stood firm, but also incarcerated him and refused to discuss terms further.

Romäern", 418–19; Caetani, *Annali dell'Islam*, VII, 222–31; Sir George Hill, *A History of Cyprus* (Cambridge, 1940–52), I, 284–86, 326–29; A.I. Dikigoropoulos, "The Political Status of Cyprus, AD 648–695", *Report of the Department of Antiquities, Cyprus*, 1940–48, 94–98; Lewis, *Naval Power and Trade*, 55–56; Papageorgiou, "Premières incursions arabes"; Stratos, *Byzantium in the Seventh Century*, III, 39–41; Browning, "Byzantium and Islam in Cyprus", 102–104; Kyrris, *History of Cyprus*, 176–90, *passim*; A.H. de Groot, art. "Ḳubrus" in *EI*², V (Leiden, 1986), 302.

[79] Theophanes, *Chronographia*, 348:23–24.

[80] See Michel Le Quien, *Oriens christianus* (Paris, 1740), II, 827–28; Ernest Honigmann, *Evêques et évêchés monophysites d'Asie antérieure au VIe siècle* (Leuven, 1951; *CSCO* 127, *Subsidia* 2), 43.

In light of all this, what induced the Aradians to surrender when Mu'āwiya returned to the attack in the following spring? The second Arab expedition may have been larger and better-equipped, and a campaign beginning in the spring raised the prospect of a longer siege before the winter storms on the Mediterranean coast would renew water supplies on the island and force the departure of the Arab fleet. But Arwād was surely no less endowed with fortifications and defenders then than it had been the previous fall, and the island was peppered with tanks and cisterns carved out of the bedrock. The immediate prospects were thus no worse than before, and the long-term ones no better. The crucial difference rather seems to have been that while in 649 the proffered surrender terms specified that the Aradians would be guaranteed safe passage to Byzantine territory, in 650 Mu'āwiya was willing to allow those who desired to do so to *stay* in Syria and to relocate wherever they wished.

The islanders' reaction to this shift highlights some interesting perceptions and lines of conflicting loyalties. While in the best of all possible worlds the Aradians may have desired the continuation of both Christian rule and their own residence in their native land, when forced to choose between the two their primary attachment was to Syria. Departure to lands still under Byzantine control and the spiritual tutelage of the Church would have meant resettling nowhere closer than Cyprus or Asia Minor, and thus complete dislocation. Rather than face this, they preferred to stand against pressures they had no long-term chance of resisting, and even arrested the envoy Bishop Thomas, an act which, while impossible to assess in detail on the basis of the surviving evidence, must surely have been a rather extreme response to the situation.

Such desperate reactions are typical of the response of peoples in the early medieval Near East to the specter of displacement from their homelands. These were not adventuresome folk, for theirs was a precarious world in which one's only defense against a host of natural and man-made perils was the strength of the ties with one's kinsmen, fellows, and colleagues. Family, religious, occupational, and personal bonds were of great emotional and practical importance, and to venture beyond the domains of their protection was to expose oneself to great risk of harm with no commensurate assurance of any refuge or source of relief. People thus clung to these ties with a stubborn and fearful tenacity, and could react in extreme ways to any threats to these bonds. Theophanes reports, for example, that when Nicephorus I (802–11) ordered the mass deportation of Christians from all the provinces to repopulate parts of the Balkan peninsula, those forced to leave their homes wept over the graves of their ancestors and considered the dead more fortunate than the living; some hanged themselves rather than leave.[81] Similarly, we are told that when the leader of a pre-Islamic clan proposed to his people that they should relocate to a new region better able to accommodate their increased numbers, they refused, saying: "It is impossible for us to move away from our own land, the place where we were born, the place that witnessed the birthing of our forefathers. If we are separated from our kinsmen we will be despised by those others among whom we live."[82] In medieval Islam there was a copious literature of maxims, anecdotes, and poetry on the theme of *al-ḥanīn ilā l-awṭān*, "longing for the homelands", that captures the intensity of these attachments in a very immediate way,[83] and among the Jewish communities of the medieval Mediterranean world similar sentiments are to be found in the Geniza documents.[84]

---

[81] *Ibid.*, 486:10–23. Even allowing for the effects of Theophanes' well-known hostility to Nicephorus (see, for example, Hunger, I, 335) on his presentation of this story, it does seem to reflect the intensity of the popular reaction to such measures.

[82] See Iḥsān 'Abbās, "Naṣṣān jadīdān 'an al-dīn fī l-jāhilīya", *Al-Abḥāth* 26 (1973–77), 33.

[83] See, for example, al-Jāḥiẓ (d. 255/868), *Rasā'il*, ed. 'Abd al-Salām Muḥammad Hārūn (Cairo, 1384–99/1964–79), II, 379–412 (an early essay, but its ascription to al-Jāḥiẓ is erroneous); Ibn al-Marzubān (d. *ca.* 330/942), *Kitāb al-ḥanīn ilā l-awṭān*, ed. Jalīl 'Aṭīya (Beirut, 1407/1987); Abū l-Faraj al-Iṣfahānī (d. 356/967), *Adab al-ghurabā'*, ed. Ṣalāḥ al-Dīn al-Munajjid (Beirut, 1972); 'Ayn al-Quḍāt (d. 525/1131), *Shakwat al-gharīb 'an al-awṭān ilā 'ulamā' al-buldān*, ed. Mohammed ben Abd el-Jalil in *JA* 216 (1930), 1–76, 193–297. On this literature, see Hilary Kilpatrick-Waardenburg, "The *Kitāb adab al-ghurabā'* of Abu l-Faraj al-Iṣfahānī", in *La signification du bas moyen âge dans l'histoire et la culture du monde musulman, Actes du 8me congrès de l'Union européenne des arabisants et islamisants* (Aix-en-Provence, 1978), 127–35.

[84] See S.D. Goitein, *A Mediterranean Society: the Jewish Communities of the Arab World as Portrayed in the Documents of the Cairo Geniza* (Berkeley and Los Angeles, 1967–88), IV, 40–47. Cf. also Ron Barkai and Aviva Doron, "Mi corazón [está] en el Oriente y yo lejos de la tierra de las palmeras: La poesía de Sión de Yehudah ha-Leví", *Helmantica* 32 (1981), 239–51.

There were of course many—such as merchants, seamen, march warriors, pilgrims, ascetics and preachers, and itinerant scholars—who did venture forth, but this was made tolerable, and even possible, by networks of contacts that served to sustain them along the way. The Cairo Geniza merchants, for example, a rare case in which much about these networks can be known, depended upon a vast system of personal and professional contacts, friendships, and other bonds that provided them with extremely important assistance and support in their travels.[85] It is in this light that we should probably view the sudden radical change of attitude among the Aradians, when, in the spring of 650, Muʿāwiya agreed to allow them to resettle wherever else in Syria they wished. Nothing is known about the professional and family connections of the Aradians in this period, but with their long history of contacts and trade in the eastern Mediterranean, they too, like their later Jewish counterparts in Fāṭimid Egypt, probably had important connections at various ports and stations along the coast and within Syria. To relocate within the region to which Arwād belonged, then, if not the most desirable prospect, was to many of them at least a bearable one; and in view of Arwād's proximity to and dependence upon the mainland, the Aradians' conception of "home" may well have included lands along the coast as well on Arwād itself.[86]

It is illuminating to note that the Aradians seem to have anticipated no particular problem with resettling on the mainland after resisting two Arab expeditions and deliberately abusing the Arab governor's envoy. The north Syrian littoral seems not to have been the scene of serious fighting during the Arab conquests a decade earlier, and most

---

[85] See Goitein, *Mediterranean Society*, I, 164–86, and frequently elsewhere in this magisterial work; *idem*, "Formal Friendship in the Medieval Near East", *Proceedings of the American Philosophical Society* 115 (1971), 484–89; Avrom L. Udovitch, "Formalism and Informalism in the Social and Economic Institutions of the Medieval Islamic World", in Amin Banani and Speros Vryonis, eds., *Individualism and Conformity in Classical Islam* (Wiesbaden, 1977), 61–81.

[86] Kyrris (*History of Cyprus*, 187) regards the seal of Bishop Pantherius of Arados, found on Cyprus, as proof that the Aradians fled there in 650. But the seal is undated, Pantherius is an otherwise unknown figure (indeed, even the name he bears is unknown in later Roman and early Byzantine prosopography), and the mere presence of one Aradian ecclesiastical seal on Cyprus tells us nothing about how or why, much less when, the artifact came to be there in the first place.

places in the area probably surrendered without a struggle once it became clear that Byzantine arms would no longer be able to protect them. Most of the region had probably seen little of the large Arab armies that had operated in the interior, and Syria remained a land still almost entirely populated by Christian communities of long residence there.[87] For the Aradians their *bête noire* was clearly not Arab occupation or non-Christian rule, but rather the possibility of expulsion from their homeland or forced relocation in remote places unknown to them and where they had no kin or contacts upon whom they could rely for friendship and support.[88]

In like manner, Mu'āwiya too seems to have found nothing unusual about the arrangements for the evacuation of Arwād, the population of which was to be treated magnanimously while the city itself was to be laid waste. If Theophilus' view of the situation is correct, the Arab governor's attack was not aimed at the Aradians themselves, but at a potentially troublesome Byzantine outpost the continued presence of which he could no longer tolerate. Thus the Aradians themselves, on the one hand, could be granted generous terms for their relocation elsewhere in Syria in exchange for their capitulation and the evacuation

[87] There is no reliable data for the course of conversion to Islam in this period, but on the basis of some valuable indicators in naming patterns Richard W. Bulliet suggests that by the end of the Umayyad caliphate Muslims in Syria, the capital province of the régime, still comprised less than ten percent of the total population. See his *Conversion to Islam in the Medieval Period: an Essay in Quantitative History* (Cambridge, Mass., 1979), 104–113. The literary sources offer occasional glimpses of demographic realities which tend to confirm Bulliet's findings, at least in terms of general orders of magnitude. An illustrative example of this is the late Umayyad tradition already cited (above, 339) on a possible Christian uprising in Ḥimṣ, which clearly reflects Muslim anxieties over their position as a small ruling minority in the midst of a population which was still overwhelmingly Christian.

[88] Forced relocation was common to Byzantine and Umayyad imperial policy. For the Byzantine side, see Peter Charanis, "The Transfer of Population as a Policy in the Byzantine Empire", *Comparative Studies in Society and History* 3 (1961), 140–54; and for the Umayyad side, see the discussion and references in Christides, "Dhāt aṣ-Ṣawārī", 1333–34. Christides of course errs in saying that in such practices "the most conspicuous example of Mu'āwiyah's policy is shown in Aradus". As we have seen, it is simply untrue that the governor "removed all the local inhabitants sending them to Byzantium". Such is the impression left only by Theophanes and Michael, whose accounts are drastically abbreviated.

of their island; military considerations, on the other hand, as discussed above, dictated that the fortifications and city of Arwād be destroyed.

In historiographical terms the eastern Christian accounts of the fall of Arwād provide an illuminating example of the transmission of historical information about the early Islamic period through to the later eastern Christian sources, as shown in the transmission chart above. In northern Syria under the early Umayyads there were probably many, including church functionaries, who were well informed about what had happened at Arwād. From this base of potential informants an account of the island's fall was either transmitted to or composed by Theophilus bar Tōmā in later Umayyad times. This account then spread in versions recorded by later historians who used the chronicle of Theophilus. In about 780 a monk in northern Syria (most probably in the Emesa region) translated this work into Greek with his own revisions and additions: in his hands the account of Arwād was abbreviated, but also supplemented with details from another source (or informant) not known to other authors whose works have survived. This revised Greek version in turn passed to Constantinople, where it was extensively used by George Syncellus or Theophanes and so comprises a key source for the *Chronographia* associated with the latter's name. Independently of this line of transmission, the chronicle of Theophilus was also used by Agapius, whose Arabic version of Theophilus' account of Arwād reproduced most of the content of the original, but suffered from the intrusion of an erroneous gloss and important errors of translation suggesting that Agapius' Arabic was based on a damaged or unclear original Syriac text. Finally, Theophilus' chronicle was used by Dionysius of Tell-Maḥrē, who preserved an accurate transcription of the account of Arwād in his history. This work was then used by the anonymous Edessan and his continuators, with the Arwād narrative remaining intact through the course of textual transmission that culminated in the *Chronicle of 1234*. Dionysius was also used by Michael, in whose history the account of Arwād suffered major abridgment and the loss of important details.

This process of transmission brings to light a number of important points:

1) The Syriac, Greek, and Christian Arabic sources for this historical event, as well as for many others, owe their similarities not to their origins in independent observation of what had actually happened, but rather to their origins in a common source—the chronicle of Theophilus of Edessa. Therefore, citation of the various participants in this process of borrowing proves nothing in and of itself, since it begs the question of whether Theophilus himself is to be trusted for the information under consideration. Only by considering this issue can one proceed further; and as we shall see, Theophilus is not always a reliable source.[89]

2) Comparison of the various accounts indicates how the original account of Theophilus fared in the hands of its later transmitters and translators. While it would obviously require further studies to establish the extent to which these patterns apply more generally to the overall transmission of Theophilus' chronicle, the following may for the time being be taken as suggestive of the features that may prove to be of broader validity:

i) A particularly useful rendering of Theophilus' account is to be found in the *Chronicle of 1234*, which despite its late date thus proves to contain material that is extremely important not only for the unique insights it bears, but also for the fact that it is possible in many cases to determine whether this information came from Theophilus.

ii) Also important for determining the original text of Theophilus is the *Kitāb al-'unwān* of Agapius, although it already seems clear that in at least some places the text from which he worked was corrupt or physically damaged. It must also be noted that one can already see that while Agapius may preserve one account in detail (in this case, Arwād), he may sharply abridge his discussion of another (e.g. the invasion of Cyprus).

iii) Michael, though far more widely cited in modern scholarship than the *Chronicle of 1234* (since his work has long been available in the French translation of Chabot), bears in this particular case only an abbreviated version of Theophilus that destroys much of the sense and content of the original text. While it is sometimes Michael who has the better text from Theophilus, the fact remains that the appearance of a report in Michael immediately suggests the possibility of a parallel and potentially fuller and more accurate rendering in the *Chronicle of 1234*.

---

[89] See below, 399–400.

iv) Theophanes has long been recognized as a beneficiary of the Eastern Source, although, like Michael, he often gives only a drastically condensed version of the original, reflecting a process of abridgment that in the main should be attributed to the predecessor of his who rendered Theophilus from Syriac into Greek. Here too, the appearance of a report for Near Eastern events in the period up to 749–50 immediately imposes the requirement that one consider the possibility that a fuller and more accurate version may be had elsewhere—not only in Michael, the usual companion of Theophanes in modern scholarship, but also in Agapius and the *Chronicle of 1234*.

v) Theophanes proves to be the bearer of material that was added to Theophilus' work during the course of the work's translation into Greek. This material is extremely important, since—if indications from the Arwād account hold true more generally—it can be reliably separated from the original account of Theophilus, dated to the period between 749–50 and 780, and traced to northern Syria.

3) It has often been noted that Byzantine historiography for the period beginning with the Arab conquests is extremely sparse, and a similar picture now emerges in the Syriac and Christian Arabic traditions, in which the apparent wealth of material on the seventh-century Near East seems likely to consist in large part of extracts from a single source, the chronicle of Theophilus. For research into the history of this period, then, an item of very high priority must be to isolate all the materials that originate in this lost source, not only to allow for further work on Theophilus himself, but also to determine the quantity, origins, and historical value of the material that derives from seventh-, eighth-, and ninth-century Syriac, Greek, and Arabic sources and authorities *other* than Theophilus.

The Arab-Islamic Tradition: Ibn A'tham on Arwād

As the taking of a major Byzantine base so close to the Syrian mainland marked a significant victory for the Arab régime, and most particularly for the Syrian forces loyal to Mu'āwiya ibn Abī Sufyān, we would naturally expect to find the campaign fully described in the historical sources of the Arab-Islamic tradition. We do in fact find several accounts, but the content of these reports differs to an extraordinary extent from the version of events given by Theophilus of Edessa. In fact, the Arabic narratives are so utterly irreconcilable not only with Theophilus, but also with traditional views on the transmission of Arab-Islamic accounts pertaining to the conquests and early Islamic history, that they raise historiographical issues of no less importance than those that have emerged concerning the transmission of the chronicle of Theophilus of Edessa.

The fullest Arab-Islamic account of the capture of Arwād appears in the *Kitāb al-futūḥ* of Ibn Aʿtham al-Kūfī (wr. 254/858[90]). As this record of events also stands apart from other Arab-Islamic reports on

[90]The era to which Ibn Aʿtham belongs is disputed. The latest date proposed is 393/1003, suggested by Ferdinand Wüstenfeld, *Die Geschichtschreiber der Araber und ihre Werke* (Göttingen, 1882), 253, no. 541, but there is no evidence to support this surmise. The date usually cited is about 314/926–27; see *GAL*, I, 144; SI 220; *GAS*, I, 329; C.A. Storey, *Persian Literature: a Bio-Bibliographical Survey*, I.1 (London, 1927), 207, no. 261. There is, however, no authority whatsoever for this date either, and all citations of it can be traced back to C.M. Frähn's *Indications bibliographiques relatives pour la plupart à la littérature historico-géographique des Arabes, des Persans et des Turcs* (St. Petersburg, 1845), 16, no. 53. Frähn's work was a "wish list" of desirable historical and geographical texts prepared for the Russian Academy of Sciences and addressed to "our functionaries and travellers", based on the assumption that important manuscript treasures could be gained for the Academy by watchful officials and travellers in the wake of the Russian advance into Central Asia. Its inventory of (largely lost) texts is essentially derived from the *Kashf al-ẓunūn* of Ḥājjī Khalīfa (d. 1067/1657), and as would be expected in a work of this period, Frähn's list is full of mistakes and erroneous conjectures. Where Ibn Aʿtham is concerned, the date of 314/926–27 for his death is proposed as a guess and no evidence for it is cited. In fact, no such evidence exists. Yāqūt (d. 626/1229), the only medieval biographer who has original information on Ibn Aʿtham, knows nothing about his life or date of death and only discusses his historical works, the latest of which extended, he says, to the reign of the ʿAbbāsid caliph al-Muqtadir (295–320/908–32); see Yāqūt's *Irshād al-arīb ilā maʿrifat al-adīb*, ed. D.S. Margoliouth, 2nd ed. (Leiden, 1923–31), I, 379:1–8, no. 104. This last work is unlikely to be the history as Ibn Aʿtham left it, however, since when al-Mustawfī made a Persian translation from the book in 596/1199, he stated that he was working from an Arabic Ms. which gave a date of composition of 204/819; see ʿAbd Allāh Mukhliṣ, "Ibn Aʿtham al-Kūfī", *RAAD* 6 (1926), 142–43; M.A. Shaban, *The ʿAbbāsid Revolution* (Cambridge, 1970), xviii. But this date runs afoul of the fact that while al-Mustawfī translated the text only as far as the death of al-Ḥusayn ibn ʿAlī in 61/680, the Arabic version as we now have it continues to the deposition of the ʿAbbāsid caliph al-Mustaʿīn bi'llāh in 252/856. This raises the possibility that the date al-Mustawfī saw before him was not AH 204, but 254, which he misread

Arwād, it may here be considered first, before moving on to the other Arab-Islamic materials:

Account of the conquest of the island of Arwād

> What happened was that the Muslims captured a Greek in one of the coastal districts and asked him: "Where are you from?" "From Arwād", he replied. So they brought him to Muʿāwiya, and Muʿāwiya began to question him about Arwād and to seek information from him about where in the sea it was located. "Yes, O Amīr", he responded, "it is a vast island", and such and so forth concerning the situation of the place and its people. Muʿāwiya thereupon called for a man, one of the champions of the Syrians named Junāda ibn Abī Umayya, put him in command of 4000 men, and ordered him to mount a campaign against Arwād. Junāda thus marched forth until he reached the coast, then his companions set out in ships (there were twenty ships). With them was that Greek to guide them to the island, so that when they conquered it they would restore his kinsmen, property, and children to him. The ships sailed until, when they drew near to the island, the guide ordered them to drop anchor in the sea, on the surface of the water. They did so [and remained at anchor] until, when night fell, the guide ordered them to proceed. So they proceeded until they reached the island, the people of which were unaware [of their approach]. The Muslims anchored their ships at the shore of the island, debarked from them with their weapons, and proceeded onto the island. Forcing the gate of the citadel, the Muslims rushed through and attacked by surprise. The islanders fared no better than slaughtered sheep: some of their warriors were killed, and the others hid in their houses as though they were women. Junāda ibn Abī Umayya, in

because of the similarity between the 0 and 5 in Arabic orthography. The question of when this text was composed clearly merits further inquiry, but for present purposes it will suffice to suggest 254/858 as a tentative date, and place Ibn Aʿtham among the Arabic authors of the generation immediately before that of such great historians as al-Balādhurī and al-Ṭabarī.

> that citadel of theirs, then granted them a truce settlement (*ṣulḥ*) providing that he take a certain amount of money (*māl*, or "property") from them and impose the poll-tax (*jizya*) upon them. He took some booty from them and set out until he reached the Syrian coast safe and sound and brought the booty to Mu'āwiya. Mu'āwiya took the fifth from it and sent it to 'Uthmān, and what remained he divided among the Muslims.[91]

Aside from the very general point that Arwād was captured by an Arab fleet sent by Mu'āwiya while he was governor of Syria, there is little here that can be reconciled with the account of Theophilus. Theophilus has it that the Arab fleet pulled back to Arwād because its advanced position along the coast of Cyprus put it at risk of being cut off by an approaching Byzantine fleet. Here, however, Arwād is attacked after the fortuitous capture of an Aradian along the Syrian coast makes the Arab conquerors aware of the island's existence and situation; nothing is said of the threat posed by an advancing hostile fleet. The Syriac account has the Arabs sending Bishop Thomas to negotiate with the Aradians, while in the Arabic there is nothing of this and we read instead of the Aradian traitor. Theophilus speaks of an effort to negotiate Arwād's surrender, a first siege thwarted by the approach of winter, and a second siege that finally led to the island's surrender on terms; the version in Ibn A'tham, on the other hand, describes events solely in terms of a successful surprise attack. In the Syriac, and in the Greek additions to it, we are told that Arwād was destroyed and that the Aradians were obliged to move elsewhere, while in the Arabic there is mention of a truce and terms according to which the islanders were allowed to remain on Arwād.

As it has already been argued that the account of Theophilus is probably an accurate and reliable one, what are we to make of these discrepancies? In sum, this problem is resolved by numerous indications that the Arabic account is largely ahistorical. Firstly, as any visitor to the place today will confirm, Arwād is clearly visible from the

[91] Ibn A'tham al-Kūfī, *Kitāb al-futūḥ*, ed. Muḥammad 'Abd al-Mu'īd Khān (Hyderabad, 1388–95/1968–75), II, 145:9–146:11.

Syrian coast and can be reached easily by a good swimmer.[92] As a crowded island unable to produce its own foodstuffs and not even possessed of its own independent fresh water resources, it had no choice but to maintain continuous well-established relations with the mainland. There could hardly have been anyone in the area in the aftermath of the Syrian conquest who did not know of the existence of Arwād, and it is most certainly not to be believed that the Arab authorities were unaware that the Byzantines remained entrenched there. Mu'āwiya would not have required the good fortune of capturing an Aradian on the mainland in order to know of the island or its situation. All of the details concerning the capture of the Aradian, the interview with Mu'āwiya, and the ensuing rôle of the traitor as a guide may therefore be dismissed as literary creations with no historical basis beyond the observation that invaders often derive important intelligence from local informants. Indeed, it is precisely this important consideration that seems to have comprised the starting point for the utterly ahistorical varia on this theme that appear in Ibn A'tham's account of the fall of Arwād.[93]

Second, we may note that whereas Arwād is a small island right on the Syrian coast, the narrative in Ibn A'tham not only presumes it to be a "vast island" (*jazīra 'aẓīma*), but even more incredibly imagines that it is a very long distance from Syria. This is already implicit in the notion that Mu'āwiya was unaware of any such place and needed an Aradian informant to gain knowledge of the island's existence, and as the narrative proceeds this assumption looms very large indeed. The Muslims sail for the better part of a day, drop anchor to wait for nightfall (i.e. all of the sailing so far has still not brought them within sight of the place), and then after dark continue until they reach Arwād.[94]

---

[92]Cf. the photograph facing this page.

[93]That early Islamic society was much exercised by the problem of dealing with potential traitors and spies (again, reflecting the anxieties of a small Muslim ruling minority in the midst of a vastly Christian subject population; cf. above, 345 and n. 87) is evident from the legal literature of this period. See, for example, Majid Khadduri, *War and Peace in the Law of Islam* (Baltimore, 1955), 107–108, 162–69.

[94]Here it might be objected that the Arabs may have set out from a base along the coast (Acre, for example) that was some considerable distance from Arwād. But even were this the case, the Arabs' alleged ignorance of the existence of Arwād, coupled with the notion that a guide should be needed to find it, indicate that the

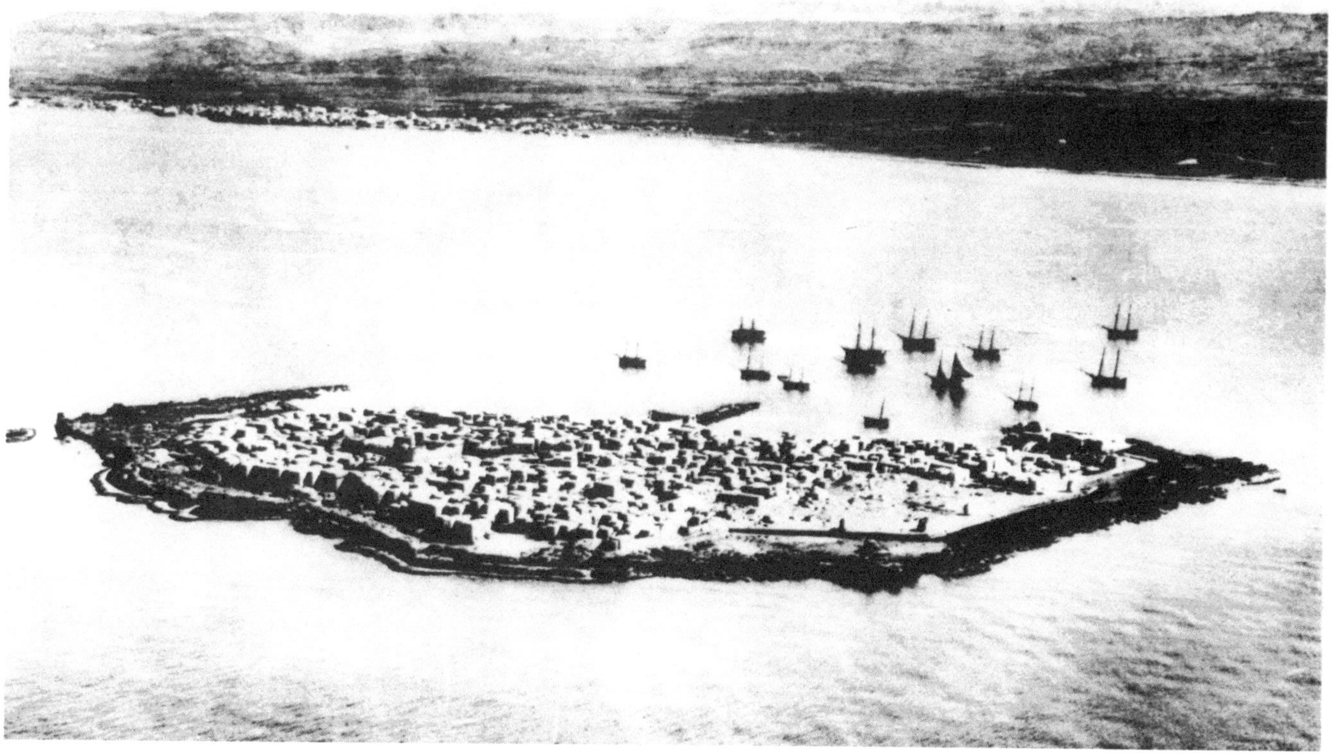

Arwād in 1935, view eastward to Ṭarṭūs on the mainland

(*By Permission of the British Library*)

Similarly, Ibn A'tham's account presupposes an island so far away from Syria that its garrison would not be prepared for, much less expecting, an Arab attack. Though the location of Arwād is never specified, Ibn A'tham's (or his sources') ill-informed conception of Mediterranean geography is sharply highlighted by the statement that the Arwād campaign occurred after the invasion of Sicily.[95]

Similarly baseless are all the details concerning the capitulation of the island. The claims that the traitorous guide was to be guaranteed the security of his family and property, and that Junāda ibn Abī Umayya granted the Aradians a truce settlement (*ṣulḥ*) and imposed the poll-tax (*jizya*) upon them, all imply that the people were allowed to stay on their island, something which Theophilus absolutely contradicts. Arwād was, for strategic considerations, immediately razed and abandoned. And as the Greek translator of Theophilus specifically states, Arwād had remained an abandoned waste from the time of its conquest up to this translator's own time, *ca.* 780. All of Ibn A'tham's details concerning fiscal matters thus represent the retrojection from later times of perceptions of how the great commanders of early Islam must have behaved, not because someone knew and reported what Junāda had actually done at Arwād, but rather because, among transmitters (in Arabic, *ruwāt*) and compilers in later times, this had come to be perceived as the proper Islamic course of action which such great commanders must surely have followed. Fighting takes place; the victorious Muslims agree to terms for a truce; the vanquished are obliged to pay the *jizya*; tribute and booty are taken; a fifth of the booty is sent on from the commander (in this case, Mu'āwiya) to the caliph in Medina (here, 'Uthmān ibn 'Affān).[96] In fact, there are signs that

---

assumption upon which the story rests is rather that suggested above.

[95]Ibn A'tham, *Kitāb al-futūḥ*, II, 145:7–8.

[96]The tendency for such features to be repeated through various accounts of different conquests has been discussed in several important studies by Albrecht Noth. See his "Der Charakter der ersten grossen Sammlungen von Nachrichten zur frühen Kalifenzeit", *Der Islam* 47 (1971), 168–99; *Quellenkritische Studien zu Themen, Formen und Tendenzen frühislamischer Geschichtsüberlieferung*, I. *Themen und Formen* (Bonn, 1973), 59–192; "Zum Verhältnis von kalifaler Zentralgewalt und Provinzen in umayyadischer Zeit. Die 'Ṣulḥ'–''Anwa'-Traditionen für Ägypten und den Iraq", *WI* 14 (1973), 150–62; "Die literarisch überlieferten Verträge der Eroberungszeit als historische Quellen für die Behandlung der unterworfenen Nicht-

the elaboration of the account was still in progress in the version set forth by Ibn A'tham. The specification that "there were twenty ships" abruptly interrupts the story with a detail that has been added recently, but not yet "smoothed" into the flow of the narrative; and it can hardly have been the original formulator of the tale who said that the raiders anchored *fī l-baḥr*, "in the sea", and then added the redundant ps.-clarification *'alā wajhi l-mā'*, "on the surface of the water".

A similarly ahistorical feature is the number used to specify the strength of the Muslim assault force—4000. The figure is not in itself unreasonable, but as I have sought to establish elsewhere, such numbers as 40, 400, 4000, 40,000, and so forth, are standard topoi of the narrative art in the medieval Near East and convey to us nothing more specific than the medieval author or transmitter's perception or claim that the army was "large", and perhaps also his effort to project the notion that the hand of God is to be seen at work in the events in question.[97] In Byzantine usage it was customary to use the figure of 10,000 (as in classical Greek historiography), and also 1000, as a topos for the idea of "many",[98] and among the early Arab tradents there was a similar tendency to enumerate large numbers of individuals in terms of arbitrary blocks of 1000. The *Futūḥ al-Shām* of al-Azdī (wr. *ca.* 190/805), for example, is a compendium of *futūḥ* reports by the "Yemenite" transmitters of Ḥimṣ;[99] and here one encounters practically

Muslime durch ihre neuen muslimischen Oberherren", in *Studien zum Minderheitenproblem im Islam* (Bonn, 1973), 282–314; "Abgrenzungsprobleme zwischen Muslimen und Nicht-Muslimen. Die 'Bedingungen 'Umars (*al-šurūṭ al-'umariyya*)' unter einem anderen Aspekt gelesen", *JSAI* 9 (1987), 290–315.

[97]See Lawrence I. Conrad, "Abraha and Muḥammad: Some Observations apropos of Chronology and Literary Topoi in the Early Arabic Historical Tradition", *BSOAS* 50 (1987), 230–32. Cf. also Ignaz Goldziher's introduction to his edition of Abū Ḥātim al-Sijistānī's *Kitāb al-mu'ammarīn*, published in his *Abhandlungen zur arabischen Philologie* (Leiden, 1896–99), II, 22–23; Oskar Rescher, "Einiges über die Zahl Vierzig", *ZDMG* 65 (1911), 517–20; *idem*, "Einige nachträgliche Bemerkungen zur Zahl 40 im Arabischen, Türkischen, und Persischen", *Der Islam* 4 (1913), 157–59; Caetani, *Annali dell'Islam*, IV, 175, 357.

[98]See Conrad, "Abraha and Muḥammad", 240 n. 99; also Noth, *Quellenkritische Studien*, 152, with reference to the Persian *hazārmard*, the man worth a thousand others.

[99]For an assessment of this text, see Lawrence I. Conrad, "Al-Azdī's History of the Arab Conquests in Bilād al-Shām: Some Historiographical Considerations",

interchangeable statements on troop numbers that refer sometimes to "a great number" (*'adad kathīr/kabīr*) or "a goodly number" (*'idda ḥasana*) of men, at other times to "many people" (*nās kathīr*), and on yet other occasions to 1000, 2000, 3000, or 5000 men, all of these amounting to nothing more precise than the idea of "many men".[100] The topos of "4000" is thus a special usage combining the metaphor of "four" with the arbitrary unit of "1000". As is stated in an Umayyad tradition of the Prophet in which the name of al-Zuhrī (d. 124/742) figures as the common link: "The best of the Companions are four, the best of the expeditions [of the Prophet] are 400, the best of the armies are 4000, and no army of 12,000 will ever be defeated by reason of its meager numbers (*min qillatin*)".[101]

This notion of a graded élite of righteous warriors for the cause of God, as symbolized in the number four and its multiples by ten, was an important concept in historical narrative. There must undoubtedly

---

in Muḥammad 'Adnān al-Bakhīt and Muḥammad 'Aṣfūr, eds., *Proceedings of the Second Symposium on the History of Bilād al-Shām during the Early Islamic Period up to 40 AH/640 AD* (Amman, 1987), I, 28–62. "Yemenite" has generally been taken to refer to Umayyad tribal factions claiming descent from "southern" Arabian tribes. However, Suliman Bashear has now demonstrated that to a certain extent this is a secondary development and that the notions of "Yaman" and "Yamānīya" originally had important messianic and other religious significations. See his "Yemen in Early Islam: an Examination of Non-Tribal Traditions", *Arabica* 36 (1989), 327–61.

[100] See al-Azdī, *Futūḥ al-Shām*, ed. William Nassau Lees (Calcutta, 1854), 11pu, ult, 12:2, 19:10, 20:9, 25:7–8, 28:4, 32:1–2, 43ult–44:2, 44:12, 68:11, 14, 70:2, 79ult, 83:1–4, 93:11–12, 95:13–14, 130:7, 159:5–6, 164:13–14, 166:5, 202:18–19, 214:11, 15, 257:4.

[101] 'Abd al-Razzāq al-Ṣan'ānī (d. 211/826), *Al-Muṣannaf*, ed. Ḥabīb al-Raḥmān al-A'ẓamī (Beirut, 1390–92/1970–72), V, 306:2–4, no. 9699; Aḥmad ibn Ḥanbal (d. 242/855), *Musnad* (Cairo, AH 1311), I, 294:9–11, 299:15–18; al-Dārimī (d. 255/869), *Sunan*, ed. Muḥammad Aḥmad Dahmān (Beirut, n.d.), II, 215:8–12, *Siyar* no. 4; Ibn Māja (d. 273/886), *Sunan*, ed. Muḥammad Fu'ād 'Abd al-Bāqī (Cairo, 1372–73/1952–53), II, 944:2–8, *Jihād* no. 25; Abū Da'ūd (d. 275/888), *Sunan*, ed. Muḥammad Muḥyī l-Dīn 'Abd al-Ḥamīd (Beirut, n.d.), III, 36:17–22, *Jihād* no. 82; al-Tirmidhī (d. 279/892), *Ṣaḥīḥ*, ed. with the commentary of Ibn al-'Arabī (d. 543/1148), *'Āriḍat al-aḥwadhī*, by 'Abd al-Wāḥid Muḥammad al-Tāzī (Cairo, 1350–51/1931–34), VII, 44:10–45:11, *Siyar* no. 7; Ibn Ḥibbān al-Bustī (d. 354/965), *Ṣaḥīḥ*, ed. in the recension of 'Alā' al-Dīn al-Fārisī (d. 739/1339), *Al-Iḥsān bi-tartīb Ṣaḥīḥ Ibn Ḥibbān*, by Kamāl Yūsuf al-Ḥūt (Beirut, 1407/1987), VII, 107:16–108:3, no. 4697.

have been some cases in which a group of 4 or 40, and perhaps even 400 or 4000, did something for which their numbers were noted and their deed passed on to posterity. But perusal of the Arabic *futūḥ* tradition will quickly demonstrate that even if one concedes the possibility of such genuine cases, the available accounts are so completely overwhelmed by the figurative usages, and pose such serious problems as to whether *any* figure can be accepted as even approximately correct, that the burden of proof seems more reasonably to lie upon those who would assert that a specific case does *not* represent a manifestation of the stereotyped literary paradigm to which most of the examples surely do belong. Thus, one finds that 4000 Greeks attacked Khālid ibn Sa'īd at Marj al-Ṣuffar;[102] that Abū 'Ubayd faced 4000 Persians at the Battle of the Bridge;[103] that Sa'd ibn Abī Waqqāṣ set out from Medina with 4000 men,[104] and then later selected 4000 men from the tribes of Tamīm and al-Ribāb for special duty prior to the battle of al-Qādisīya;[105] that al-Muthannā ibn Ḥāritha commanded 4000 men who had remained in Iraq after the departure of Khālid for Syria and 4000 survivors of the Battle of the Bridge;[106] that al-Qa'qa'a ibn 'Amr led 4000 men to reinforce Abū 'Ubayda in Syria;[107] that prior to the Battle of the Camel al-Aḥnaf ibn Qays had 4000 warriors at his command.[108] Much the same applies to the discussion of Alexandria, which upon its capture, we are told, proved to contain "4000 villas with 4000 baths, 40,000 Jews liable for the poll-tax, and 400 royal places of diversion".[109] In some cases one finds specific and unequivocal indications that "4000" is nothing more than a symbol for "many". Al-Wāqidī (d. 207/823),

[102] Al-Ṭabarī (wr. 303/915), *Ta'rīkh al-rusul wa-l-mulūk*, ed. Muḥammad Abū l-Faḍl Ibrāhīm, 2nd ed. (Cairo, 1968–69), III, 406:18–19, citing past authorities in general (*qālū*, "they said").

[103] Al-Dīnawarī (d. 282/891), *Al-Akhbār al-ṭiwāl*, ed. 'Abd al-Mun'im Muḥammad 'Āmir (Cairo, 1960), 113:11–12.

[104] Al-Ṭabarī, *Ta'rīkh*, III, 484:7, 485:3 (both accounts from Sayf ibn 'Umar, d. 180/796).

[105] *Ibid.*, III, 486:13 (from Sayf).

[106] *Ibid.*, III, 486:17–18 (from Sayf).

[107] *Ibid.*, IV, 51:1–6 (from Sayf).

[108] *Ibid.*, IV, 500pu–501:2 (from Qatāda ibn Di'āma, d. 118/736).

[109] Ibn 'Abd al-Ḥakam (d. 257/870), *Futūḥ Miṣr wa-akhbāruhā*, ed. Charles C. Torrey (New Haven, 1922), 82:1–4.

for example, has it that when Caesarea Maritima fell to Arab forces in the closing stages of the conquest of Syria, 4000 prisoners were taken and sent to Medina.[110] When al-Wāqidī elaborates on this, however, we find that Caesarea had a garrison of 700,000 Byzantine troops, including 100,000 night guards, that its population included 30,000 Samaritans and 20,000 Jews, and that there were 300 active markets in the city.[111] It has been observed by Noth that it is a common feature of early Arabic historiography for reports by one and the same compiler to disagree or even completely to contradict one another,[112] but in this case I would submit that no contradiction exists. Both of al-Wāqidī's reports use numbers as symbols conveying a perception of Byzantine Caesarea as a large and impressive place—a view sustained by archaeological work at the site,[113] but one that in the specific numerical terms of these reports must be rejected in its entirety. The situation is even clearer in al-Azdī's account of the battle of al-Yarmūk. Here he estimates that the Byzantine forces were "as numerous as the pebbles, as the grains of soil, as the specks of dust", and then proceeds to clarify this with the observation that they had "400,000 troops, along with their followers and servants".[114] In some cases the symbolic number obviously represents an ideal of completeness or culmination, a metaphor for the sake of which accounts were consciously shaped and manipulated. There

[110] Al-Balādhurī, *Futūḥ al-buldān*, 142:1–2.

[111] *Ibid.*, 141:11–142:1 (al-Wāqidī from ʿAbd Allāh ibn ʿĀmir al-Aslamī, d. *ca.* 150–51/767–68). Cf. Lawrence I. Conrad, "Seven and the *Tasbīʿ*: On the Implications of Numerical Symbolism for the Study of Medieval Islamic History", *JESHO* 31 (1988), 55–57.

[112] *Quellenkritische Studien*, 13–16. To this it may be added that this tendency is particularly prominent in *ḥadīth* collections, which routinely cite traditions which are contradicted elsewhere in the compendium in question. In fact, grave contradictions often arise not only within the same tradition, but also even within the same sentence: e.g. "There is no such thing as contagion, but do not mix the sick [camels] with the healthy ones"; or "There is no such thing as *ṣafar*, which is a malady of the stomach". See al-Bukhārī (d. 256/870), *Al-Jāmiʿ al-ṣaḥīḥ*, ed. Ludolf Krehl and T.W. Juynboll (Leiden, 1864–1908), IV, 57:6, 69ult–70:3, *Ṭibb* nos. 19, 53.

[113] See Antonio Frova *et. al.*, *Scavi di Caesarea Maritima* (Milan, 1965); Joseph Ringel, *Césarée de Palestine: étude historique et archéologique* (Paris, 1975); Lee I. Levine and Ehud Netzer, *Excavations at Caesarea Maritima: 1975, 1976, 1979—Final Report* (Jerusalem, 1986; *Qedem* 21).

[114] Al-Azdī, *Futūḥ al-Shām*, 155:5–7.

were 37,000 Muslim warriors ready for battle prior to al-Yarmūk, then another 3000 horsemen arrived to "complete" the 40,000.[115] A son of 'Abd Allāh ibn 'Umar spends 30 days on frontier duty (*ribāṭ*) and then returns home, only to be sent back by his father for another ten days' service so as to reach a "complete" total of 40 days.[116]

The figure "4000" for the strength of the force attacking Arwād is thus a symbol of no specifically numerical content. Aside from the notion of a "large" force, all it suggests is that Ibn A'tham's account is probably of Iraqi origin (as we would in any case expect). The symbolism of four and its multiples by ten was extensively used by the Kūfan and other Iraqi tradents when they wished to estimate the strength of military units; among the Syrians, on the other hand, as well as in the early *sīra* literature, this particular usage of such symbolism is encountered less frequently.

On one point, however, the account of Ibn A'tham does seem to add something with a basis in historical reality. The commander of the expedition against Arwād is named as Junāda ibn Abī Umayya, and as is usually the case with personalities from the early Islamic period there is much uncertainty and discrepancy concerning this man's career. The biographical literature of medieval Islam describes him as a member of the "southern" tribe of Azd, and the dispute over whether or not he was a Companion of the Prophet suggests that he was probably a young boy in the lifetime of Muḥammad. Some authorities claim that he participated in the conquest of Egypt; but of particular interest to us here is the information—cited on the authority of the Egyptians al-Layth ibn Sa'd (d. 175/791) and 'Abd al-Raḥmān ibn Aḥmad ibn Yūnus (d. 347/958) and the Syrian al-Walīd ibn Muslim (d. 195/810)—that "he directed the sea raiding (or 'sea raiding against the Byzantines') for Mu'āwiya". This lapsed, we are told, during the First Civil War (35–40/656–61); but reports to this effect probably imply no more than the fact that Mu'āwiya's preoccupation with the conflict with 'Alī ibn Abī Ṭālib left the former with no funds or forces to devote to naval operations against Byzantium. With the end of the war and

---

[115] Ibn A'tham, *Kitāb al-futūḥ*, I, 228:5–7.

[116] See, for example, Ibn Abī Shayba (d. 235/849), *Al-Kitāb al-muṣannaf fī l-aḥādīth wa-l-āthār*, ed. 'Abd al-Khāliq al-Afghānī *et al.* (Bombay, 1399–1403/1979–83), V, 328:6–9.

Mu'āwiya's accession to the caliphate in 40/661, Junāda resumed his former duties and continued to lead the maritime expeditions launched against Byzantium. He directed Syrian sea raiding on into the reign of Mu'āwiya's son Yazīd (60–64/680–83), and although the medieval authorities disagree on his date of death, the year 80/699 is usually preferred and may be at least approximately correct.[117]

None of these accounts mentions a word about the conquest of Arwād, but they do agree that it was Junāda who held overall command of Arab naval operations throughout the period of concern to us here. There is no reason to doubt that this was indeed the case, and some support for this—though indirect and highly circumstantial—arises from another quarter. There are numerous traditions extolling pursuit of the *jihād* by sea, e.g. asserting that "the recompense for a day on the sea is equal to that for a month on land", or that "the merit of the warrior by sea over the warrior by land is comparable to the merit of the warrior by land over the man who sits in his house".[118] Junāda does

[117]The best authorities on Junāda are authors with earlier Syrian and Egyptian informants: see Ibn 'Abd al-Barr (d. 463/1070), *Al-Istī'āb fī ma'rifat al-aṣḥāb*, ed. 'Alī Muḥammad al-Bijāwī (Cairo, n.d.), I, 249:8–251:5, no. 336; Ibn 'Asākir (d. 571/1175), *Ta'rīkh madīnat Dimashq*, Al-Maktaba al-ẓāhirīya (Damascus), Mss. *Ta'rīkh* nos. 1–18, 113, IV, fols. 15r:19–17v:1; = *Tahdhīb ta'rīkh Dimashq al-kabīr*, unfinished abridgment by 'Abd al-Qādir Badrān and Aḥmad 'Ubayd (Damascus, AH 1329–51), III, 411:5–412:24; al-Mizzī (d. 742/1341), *Tahdhīb al-kamāl fī asmā' al-rijāl*, ed. Bashshār 'Awwād Ma'rūf (Beirut, 1400/1980–proceeding), V, 133:4–135:8, no. 971; al-Dhahabī (d. 748/1348), *Siyar a'lām al-nubalā'*, ed. Shu'ayb al-Arna'ūṭ *et al.* (Beirut, 1401–1404/1981–84), IV, 62:7–63:10, no. 16; Ibn Kathīr (d. 774/1373), *Al-Bidāya wa-l-nihāya* (Cairo, 1351–58/1932–39), IX, 26:9–11; Ibn Ḥajar, *Al-Iṣāba fī tamyīz al-ṣaḥāba*, ed. 'Alī Muḥammad al-Bijāwī (Cairo, 1389–92/1970–72), I, 502:11–503pu, no. 1203; *idem*, *Tahdhīb al-tahdhīb*, II, 115ult–116:13, no. 184. For other accounts, see Ibn Sa'd (d. 230/844), *Kitāb al-ṭabaqāt al-kabīr*, ed. Eduard Sachau *et al.* (Leiden, 1904–40), VII.2, 151:10–12; Khalīfa ibn Khayyāṭ (d. 240/854–55), *Kitāb al-ṭabaqāt*, ed. Akram Ḍiyā' al-'Umarī (Baghdad, 1387/1967), 116:1–2, 305:8–9, 309:1; al-Bukhārī, *Al-Ta'rīkh al-kabīr* (Hyderabad, 1360–64/1940–44), I.2, 231:11–232:2, no. 2297; al-Balādhurī, *Futūḥ al-buldān*, 235:12–236:16; Ibn Abī Ḥātim (d. 327/938), *Al-Jarḥ wa-l-ta'dīl* (Hyderabad, 1371–72/1952–53), I.1, 515:4–8, no. 2129; Ibn al-Athīr (d. 630/1233), *Usd al-ghāba fī ma'rifat al-ṣaḥāba* (Cairo, AH 1280), I, 297:7–25.

[118]See, for example, 'Abd al-Razzāq, *Muṣannaf*, V, 284:9–287:2, nos. 9628–34; al-Ḥumaydī (d. 219/834), *Al-Musnad*, ed. Ḥabīb al-Raḥmān al-A'ẓamī (Beirut, AH 1381–82), I, 169:12–170:2, no. 349; Ibn Abī Shayba, *Muṣannaf*, V, 314:2–315ult,

not appear in any of these traditions, but his name is associated with a more general Egyptian tradition promoting continued *hijra* for the sake of *jihād*. According to this tradition, people were arguing over whether *hijra* would now cease (i.e. because Mecca had just been captured) and Junāda raised the issue with the Prophet, who replied: "The *hijra* will not cease so long as there is *jihād*".[119] There are other versions of this tradition in which Junāda plays no rôle;[120] and pursuing the observation already made above, he must have been only a boy at the time of Muḥammad's occupation of Mecca in 8/630, an event that occurred almost 70 years prior to Junāda's death (*ca.* 80/699). The tradition is certainly a later creation, the Egyptian transmitters of which betray its provenance,[121] but the association of its most prominent form with the name of Junāda may be due to recollection of his rôle in pursuing the *jihād* by sea against the Byzantines. At the time of the Cyprus-Arwād campaign he must still have been very young, perhaps only in his twenties; but there are numerous parallel cases in which other very young men attained high command in the military forces of early Islam,[122]

340:14–16; al-Dārimī, *Sunan*, II, 210:1–13, *Jihād* no. 28; Ibn Māja, *Sunan*, II, 927:8–928:11, *Jihād* no. 10; Ibn Ḥibbān, *Ṣaḥīḥ*, IX, 160:11–19, no. 7145.

[119] Aḥmad ibn Ḥanbal, *Musnad*, IV, 62:22–25; V, 375:18–22; Ibn 'Abd al-Barr, *Istī'āb*, I, 250:9–17; Ibn 'Asākir, *Ta'rīkh madīnat Dimashq*, IV, fol. 16v:2–10; = *Tahdhīb*, III, 411:15–18; Ibn al-Athīr, *Usd al-ghāba*, I, 297:17–22; Ibn Ḥajar, *Iṣāba*, I, 502:16–18.

[120] See Aḥmad ibn Ḥanbal, *Musnad*, V, 270:12–16, 363:24–26; al-Nasā'ī (d. 303/915), *Sunan*, (Beirut, n.d.), VII, 146:7–147:5, *Bay'a* no. 15; Ibn Hibbān, *Ṣaḥīḥ*, VII, 179:2–6, no. 4846.

[121] The various citations of this tradition all quote it from al-Layth ibn Sa'd (d. 175/791), from his teacher Yazīd ibn Abī Ḥabīb (d. 125/743), from Abū l-Khayr Marthad ibn 'Abd Allāh al-Yazanī (d. 90/709), a renowned scholar esteemed as the leading Egyptian authority of his time. Al-Layth is the common link, but he would have had far less motive for forging the tradition than either Yazīd ibn Abī Ḥabīb or Abū l-Khayr. The latter may have known Junāda, and Yazīd and Abū l-Khayr were both active in the era of the great Umayyad operations against Constantinople itself. Either one of these individuals could have set this tradition in circulation in Egypt.

[122] See, for example, al-Jāḥiẓ, *Rasā'il*, I, 91:9–92ult, 295:10–301:1 (a detailed discussion with many examples). The rise of very young men to high command was also of frequent occurrence in early modern Europe. See Philippe Ariès, *Centuries of Childhood: a Social History of Family Life*, trans. Robert Baldick (New York, 1962), 331.

and Junāda's youth does not make it unlikely that he was already an important commander at this time.

A more serious problem, however, is posed by the fact that the Eastern Christian sources state that the Arab commander of Arab forces on Cyprus in 28/649 was a certain Abū La'war/'Αβουλαούαρ, who also figures in these sources as the commander of Arab forces in attacks on Cos, Crete, and Rhodes and at the battle of Phoenix/Dhāt al-Ṣawārī.[123] This is supported by a brief report in which the Damascene Yazīd ibn 'Ubayda (d. 177/793) names Abū l-A'war al-Sulamī as the commander of an expedition sent against Cyprus by Mu'āwiya in 26/647.[124] This man is Abū l-A'war 'Amr ibn Sufyān al-Sulamī,[125] concerning whom the Arabic sources for the early Islamic period offer the following information. A tribesman of Sulaym during the career of the Prophet, he was a pagan (though his mother was a Christian) opposed to Islam and the rising power of Muḥammad in Mecca. He took part in negotiations with the Prophet on the side of the pagans of Mecca and fought against the Muslims at the battle of Ḥunayn (8/630); but his tribe was an influential one with connections with the powerful clan of 'Abd Shams, and the sources present him as an important property owner in Mecca. Within the next few years he seems to have been converted to Islam and rehabilitated. He commanded a squadron of cavalry at al-Yarmūk during the conquest of Syria, and was also reportedly consulted by the caliph 'Umar ibn al-Khaṭṭāb (13–23/634–44) on matters concerning the administration of this province. His later career, difficult to follow in detail, was a combination of administration—governing the province of al-Urdunn—and military command. In this latter capacity, he commanded the Syrian army in the expedition to Amorium/'Ammūrīya (23/644), held responsibility for the cavalry of

[123]See Theophanes, *Chronographia*, 345:27 (note De Boor's erroneous emendation to 'Αβουλαθάρ, following the reading in the Latin translation of Anastasius; read 'Αβουλαούαρ, with the Greek Mss.); Michael, II, 442–43 (trans.); IV, 430:14, 17, 22–23 (text); *Chronicle of 1234*, I, 271:9, 272:8, 274:24, 275:15. Here again, the confluence of these sources reveals that the account comes from the chronicle of Theophilus.

[124]Abū Zur'a, *Ta'rīkh*, I, 184:14–15.

[125]*Not* Abū l-Anwār, as in De Groot's *EI*^{2} art. "Ḳubrus", 302, and elsewhere. It is unclear how this error originated.

Mu'āwiya, and played a prominent rôle in the battle of Ṣiffīn and shortly thereafter led the contingent from al-Urdunn in the Umayyad occupation of Egypt (38/658). His later activities and date of death are unknown.[126]

The extent to which all this information is to be trusted is an important issue that cannot detain us here, and for present purposes it will suffice to note that none of the sources refers to Abū l-A'war in any military capacity other than an army commander. To the extent that he actually "commanded" the Arab forces attacking Cyprus, Crete, Cos, and Rhodes, or fighting at Dhāt al-Ṣawārī, it must be assumed that this refers to command of troops attached to the fleet, and not necessarily to the ships and actual naval operations as well. Medieval sources are not particularly discriminating on such matters and routinely refer, for example, to an attack by Mu'āwiya when we must obviously assume that actual command was delegated to an experienced field officer. The rôle of Abū l-A'war as a commander does not, then, comprise an obstacle preventing us from conceding that Junāda ibn Abī Umayya may well have held the position ascribed to him by our sources. If it is objected that Junāda's name may have been arbitrarily assigned by the *ruwāt* to numerous accounts for which no commander had hitherto been specified, one must observe that if later Muslim authorities have placed a "Junāda" at the helm of every Arab flagship, then at his side stands an "Abū l-A'war" provided by the eastern Christians.

As we have already seen, however, every other detail that appears in Ibn A'tham's account must be rejected. This narrative therefore cannot be one that was passed down—whether orally or in writing[127]—from the era of the conquerors until Ibn A'tham's own time, nor can the report be redeemed by the argument for a possibly accurate—or reasonably factual—account that later came to be distorted at the hands of Ibn A'tham (well-known for the dramatizing and popularizing tendencies of

[126]The Arabic materials on Abū l-A'war are collected and discussed in Michael Lecker, *The Banū Sulaym: a Contribution to the Study of Early Islam* (Jerusalem, 1989), 28, 76–77, 80, 109 n. 14, 131, 138–40, 141–42. To the sources consulted in this work there may be added the above-mentioned account in Abū Zur'a, and al-Kindī (d. 350/961), *Kitāb al-wulāt wa-kitāb al-quḍāt*, ed. Rhuvon Guest (Leiden, 1912), 29:6–18 (from Yazīd ibn Abī Ḥabīb).

[127]A controversial question in early Islamic studies. See above, 16–17 and n. 24.

his work[128]) or his immediate predecessors. Once the baseless material is removed, we are left not with a reduced but more reliable account, but rather with no account at all. And it is worth stressing that this conclusion is not reached by making the *a priori* assumption that Syriac sources—or non-Islamic sources in general—are more reliable than Arab-Islamic ones. Theophilus' version of events wins our confidence on the basis of 1) its lack of stereotyped formulae or polemical arguments or overtones, 2) its agreement with an independent Greek account from which the translator of *ca.* 780 added details to Theophilus' Syriac, and 3) its agreement with the geographical facts and historical remains of the island of Arwād. Ibn A'tham, on the other hand, offers a narrative that proves to consist almost entirely of arbitrarily imposed narrative motifs, topoi, and schematic features, which we identify not just by the way they contradict Theophilus, but also by the frequency with which they recur in accounts of the conquest of other places and by the way in which they are rendered absurd by the physical facts of geography.

The topos of the Aradian traitor is a vivid illustration of this. There is no such element in Theophilus' account; but while this silence certainly merits notice, in itself it proves nothing. On the other hand, the topos of the traitor who is promised security for the lives and possessions of his kin, and then guides the Arab conquerors to the weak spot in his city's defenses, is a common narrative motif—involving cases of both Christians and Jews—in the Arabic *futūḥ* tradition[129] and is probably related to the topos of the wily and treacherous Jewish *agent provocateur* that one encounters so frequently in the *sīra* tradition.[130] What is more, to accept the account of the Aradian traitor is to accept propositions that in purely topographical terms are sheer nonsense: that an island measuring 800 by 500 meters is "vast" in size; that the Arab conquerors, more than a decade after their occupation of

[128]Or those of his sources. Even before the publication of the original Arabic version of the text, this problem was already evident to Brockelmann; see *GAL*, SI, 220. In this regard, Shaban's enthusiastic evaluation in *The 'Abbāsid Revolution*, xvii–xix, and in his art. "Ibn A'tham al-Kūfī" in *EI*², III (London, 1971), 723, must be regarded with considerable caution.

[129]See Noth, *Quellenkritische Studien*, 24, 150–51. Cf. above, 352.

[130]See John Wansbrough, *The Sectarian Milieu: Content and Composition of Islamic Salvation History* (London, 1978), 18–21, 109.

Syria, remained ignorant of the existence of an island that can easily be seen—complete with anchorages, ships, citadel, and houses—from the mainland shore;[131] that an Aradian would have been needed in order merely to *locate* such an island, and so forth.

Ibn A'tham's account thus exemplifies the phenomenon of narrative elaboration over an almost complete historical void. Among the materials transmitted by the tradents responsible for the formation and development of this report, one finds no indication that anything genuine was known about the conquest of Arwād beyond the facts that the island had been taken while Mu'āwiya was governor of Syria and that Junāda ibn Abī Umayya had also been involved. This bare and scanty information hardly made for a satisfactory historical account, and certainly provided nothing of any administrative relevance, didactic merit, or entertainment value. As the demand for more such information grew, with the elaboration of distinctly Islamic social, cultural, and legal institutions and a corresponding increase in demand upon the record of the past for historical details relevant to such concerns, compensation for the almost total dearth of continuously transmitted material—accurate or otherwise—was achieved by recourse to a stock répertoire of *futūḥ* topoi and schemata. On a subject concerning which almost nothing from the era of the conquerors had been known, a fully detailed account thus developed. That this literary edifice is not in and of itself an implausible one does not alter the fact that it is, in reality, entirely spurious.

The Arab-Islamic Tradition: Arwād and Rhodes

As noted already above, Ibn A'tham's *Kitāb al-futūḥ* is well known for its popularizing and imaginative tendencies. It is therefore worth checking to see how the conclusions reached so far will fare when a more "mainstream" historical work is considered. In this respect we are fortunate that an entirely different strand of transmission survives in the account of the capture of Arwād by al-Wāqidī, as reported by al-Ṭabarī:

[131] Cf. the photograph facing 352 above.

> In this year (i.e. in AH 54)—according to what al-Wāqidī claimed—Junāda ibn Abī Umayya conquered an island in the sea, near Constantinople, called Arwād. Muḥammad ibn 'Umar [al-Wāqidī] stated that the Muslims, among them Mujāhid ibn Jabr, resided there for a time—seven years, it is said. [Al-Wāqidī] said: Tubay', son of the wife of Ka'b, said: "Do you see this step (*daraja*)? When it is displaced, we will return home." A strong wind then arose and uprooted (*qala'at*) the step, and there arrived word of Mu'āwiya's death and Yazīd's letter [ordering the Muslims] to return. So we did so. The island was uninhabited after that and fell to ruin, and the Greeks were safe.[132]

This report is also irreconcilable with Theophilus and for the most part ahistorical; but unlike the account of Ibn A'tham it allows us to follow in somewhat clearer terms the process of narrative elaboration that marked the course of its development.

This process can be discerned in the complicated interplay between the chronological details of the report, the figures of Mujāhid ibn Jabr (d. *ca.* 104/722), Tubay' ibn 'Āmir (d. 101/719–20), and the caliph Yazīd ibn Mu'āwiya (d. 64/683), and the episode of the "uprooted" step. First, and despite statements in later literature to the effect that Mujāhid and Tubay' were comrades together in the Arwād campaign,[133] it is extremely unlikely that either Mujāhid or Tubay' could have had anything to do with this expedition, which occurred approximately 72 years before the death of Mujāhid and 69 years prior to the death of Tubay'. Nothing is known about the age of Tubay' upon his death, and in any case such information must be regarded as highly suspect, for the simple reason that very few medieval people, especially in early Islamic times, knew when they had been born; they therefore lacked any basis for a calculation of their age.[134] But even if one wishes to

---

[132] Al-Ṭabarī, *Ta'rīkh*, V, 293:5–11.

[133] See Ibn 'Asākir, *Ta'rīkh madīnat Dimashq*, X, ed. Muḥammad Aḥmad Dahmān (Damascus, 1383/1963), p: 426:10–11; al-Mizzī, *Tahdhīb al-kamāl*, IV, 313:4–6; al-Dhahabī, *Siyar a'lām al-nubalā'*, IV, 413:8.

[134] For a fuller discussion of this problem, see Conrad, "Seven and the *Tasbī'*", 62–72.

work within the parameters of the traditional accounts, the material for Mujāhid raises sufficient grounds for grave doubt. The dates given for his death vary between 100/718 and 108/727; and while—as is usually the case—almost no one knows when he was born, al-Qāsim ibn Sallām (d. 224/838) gives a birth date of 20/641[135] and Ibn Ḥibbān prefers 21/642.[136] At the same time, there is complete agreement on his age: Ibn Jurayj (d. 150/767),[137] al-Haytham ibn ʿAdī (d. 206/821),[138] Yaḥyā ibn ʿAbd Allāh ibn Bukayr (d. 231/845),[139] and Ibn Qutayba (d. 276/889)[140] all agree that he lived to the age of 83 (lunar) years. Leaving aside the problem of how there could be such unanimity on his age when there was such disagreement on when he died and almost complete ignorance of when he had been born, this information implies that at the time of the Arwād campaign Mujāhid was no more than 11 (solar) years old and so could not have been a participant. All of the references—whether in al-Ṭabarī or elsewhere—to Mujāhid and Tubayʿ as comrades in arms during the Arwād campaign must therefore be rejected.

It is not difficult to discover how an error of this kind has arisen, but the nature of the problems and processes confronting us will here divert our investigation into an unexpected line of inquiry. Al-Fasawī (d. 277/890) cites the following report from ʿAbd Allāh ibn Wahb (d. 197/813), who has it from al-Layth ibn Saʿd, who in turn reports on the authority of a certain Rashīd ibn Kaysān:

> We were on Rhodes and our *amīr* was Junāda ibn Abī Umayya al-Azdī. Muʿāwiya ibn Abī Sufyān wrote to us: "Winter is here, and again [I say], winter (*al-shitāʾ thumma al-shitāʾ*); so prepare yourselves for it". Tubayʿ, son of the wife of Kaʿb al-Aḥbār, then said: "You will be recalled back to such-and-so". The people replied: "How are we to be

[135] See the account reported on his authority in al-Fāsī (d. 832/1429), *Al-ʿIqd al-thamīn fī taʾrīkh al-balad al-amīn*, ed. Muḥammad Ḥāmid al-Fiqī *et al.* (Beirut, 1406/1986), VII, 134:7.

[136] Ibn Ḥajar, *Tahdhīb al-tahdhīb*, X, 43:9–10.

[137] Ibn Saʿd, V, 344:11–12; al-Dhahabī, *Siyar aʿlām al-nubalāʾ*, IV, 456:3–4.

[138] Al-Fāsī, *Al-ʿIqd al-thamīn*, VII, 134:4.

[139] Ibn Ḥajar, *Tahdhīb al-tahdhīb*, X, 43:7–8.

[140] *Kitāb al-maʿārif*, ed. Tharwat ʿUkāsha, 2nd ed. (Cairo, 1969), 445:2.

recalled when Mu'āwiya has said in this letter, 'Winter is here, and again [I say], winter?'"[141] Later, a certain high-ranking officer in the army came and said to him: "Because of what you told them about returning, which they do not wish to do, the people are calling you nothing but 'The Liar'". Tubay' then said: "Their authorization will reach them on the such-and-so day of the month of such-and-so, and the portent of this will be that a wind will come and uproot (*taqla'u*) this fig tree (*tīna*) which is in this mosque of theirs". Word of what he had said spread among them, so on the morning of that day they gathered in their mosque to wait for [the fulfillment of his prophecy]. It was a day on which there was no wind, so they waited until they needed to rest and eat, became weary, and so returned to their homes or to their ships. But then in the middle of the day, while some people still remained in the mosque, a great gale (*rīḥ 'iṣāf*) came, swirled around the fig tree, and uprooted it, while the people cried out to each

---

[141]The point here is that the people refuse to believe that Mu'āwiya's warning to prepare for winter could refer, as Tubay' predicts, to a forthcoming order to undertake a voyage. Winter voyages on the Mediterranean were undertakings of great peril, not only because of the risk of ships being overwhelmed in a storm, but also because persistent overcast meant that navigators were deprived of the usual coastal and celestial sightings upon which they relied for knowledge of their precise location—in particular, how close they were to enemy territory and cruising lanes or to dangerous channels or shoals. See Lionel Casson, *Ships and Seamanship in the Ancient World* (Princeton, 1971), 270–72; *idem*, *Travel in the Ancient World* (London, 1974), 150; Goitein, *Mediterranean Society*, I, 316–18; Abraham L. Udovitch, "Time, the Sea and Society: Duration of Commercial Voyages on the Southern Shores of the Mediterranean during the High Middle Ages", in *La navigazione mediterranea nell'alto medioevo* (Spoleto, 1978), 530–33. Udovitch remarks (532) that "I have not found a single example of a *commercial* voyage between Alexandria and North Africa in the eleventh century outside the normal months of the sailing season", i.e. April to late September. For the possible consequences of such a voyage, see the vivid account that Ibn Jubayr (d. 614/1217) gives of his trip from Ceuta to Alexandria in Dhū l-Qa'da 578/March 1183, in his *Riḥla*, ed. William Wright, 2nd ed. by M.J. de Goeje (Leiden, 1907), 36pu–38:1. In the seventh and eighth centuries, this problem led Rhodes to impose a strict ban on winter sailings by commercial vessels; see Walter Ashburner, *The Rhodian Sea Law* (Oxford, 1909), cxlii–cxliii.

> other in their houses: "The fig tree has blown over, the fig tree has blown over!" They came from everywhere until they were gathered together on the beach, and then they saw moving about on the water a sparkling object that finally became clear enough for them to see that it was a ship. It brought them word of the death of Mu'āwiya, news of the rendering of allegiance to Yazīd, his son, and their authorization to return home. They thanked Tubay' and heaped praises upon him, but then said: "Something else yet remains. Winter has arrived, and we fear that our ships will break up". Tubay' replied to them: No mast (*'ūd*) will break nor line snap to harm you until you have arrived back in your country". So they set out, and God—may He be praised and exalted—delivered them home safely.[142]

Tubay' was in later times known as an individual given to speculations on the cataclysmic events (*malāḥim*) that would occur prior to the Last Judgment, and he also had novel explanations, cited on the authority of his famous stepfather Ka'b al-Aḥbār, for various natural phenomena. He is said to have proposed, for example, that the clouds comprise a sieve (*ghirbāl*) that purifies the rain, and that without them the rain would cause any land upon which it fell to decay; and his explanation for why there are bountiful crops in one year and famine in the next was that seeds fall with the rain and then sent up their shoots from the ground.[143] The account we have here implicitly concedes that Tubay' had already become rather notorious for his tales, and the aim of this report is clearly to redeem his reputation by recounting an incident involving a successful prophecy and genuine knowledge of the natural world. But where and when did this particular story originate?

Tubay' was descended from the "southern" tribe of Ḥimyar and was counted by the "Yemenites" of Ḥimṣ as one of their own; but the

[142]Al-Fasawī, *Kitāb al-ma'rifa wa-l-ta'rīkh*, ed. Akram Ḍiyā' al-'Umarī (Baghdad, 1974–75), III, 323:3–324:5. The account is taken from al-Fasawī by Ibn 'Asākir, *Ta'rīkh madīnat Dimashq*, X, 431:18–423:8; and from this work it passes to al-Mizzī, *Tahdhīb al-kamāl*, IV, 316:14–317:15. Cf. also the condensed version in al-Dhahabī, *Siyar a'lām al-nubalā'*, IV, 414:2–8.

[143]See Ibn 'Asākir, *Ta'rīkh madīnat Dimashq*, X, 429ult, 430:11–431:4; al-Mizzī, *Tahdhīb al-kamāl*, IV, 315:1–10; al-Dhahabī, *Siyar a'lām al-nubalā'*, IV, 413:15.

last years of his life were spent in Egypt, he died in Alexandria, and he figures in numerous Egyptian reports concerning, *inter alia*, tales of the ancient prophets and peoples, the history of Alexandria, and matters pertaining to the Last Judgment.[144] Both of the identifiable transmitters of the tale, ʿAbd Allāh ibn Wahb and al-Layth ibn Saʿd, were Egyptians; and one of the primary concerns of the story, the very serious question of a perilous Mediterranean voyage during the stormy months of winter, is also one that would have been of great interest to a Muslim audience in Alexandria, the maritime capital of Egypt. This effort to redeem Tubayʿ's reputation is thus probably an Egyptian one, with the name of Rashīd ibn Kaysān—unknown in any other report and not mentioned in any of the *rijāl* works—serving as a ps.-authority to conceal the true origins of the report.[145]

So far as the date of the tale is concerned, it probably emerged after the deaths of Junāda (*ca.* 80/699), Tubayʿ (101/719–20), and Mujāhid (*ca.* 104/722), and indeed, after the demise of the generation of those Egyptian warriors and seamen who had participated in the early campaigns on Rhodes and in whose lifetimes a fabricator might have feared for the exposure and repudiation of the tale, a possibility that would further impugn, rather than redeem, the reputation of Tubayʿ. On the other hand, that the tale dates from Umayyad times is suggested by its approach to a sensitive issue pertaining to the conquests. The early transmitters conceived of the Arab-Islamic conquests as part of a divine plan, with the conquerors acting as God's agents on earth. God had called on man to believe, but while the Arabs in the barren wastes of Arabia responded to the divine summons, the Greeks—ungrateful for the fair lands, prosperity, and power that God had granted them—rejected His call, corrupted the message of the prophet (Jesus) whom

[144]There are many such traditions from Tubayʿ in Nuʿaym ibn Ḥammād, *Kitāb al-fitan*, index, *s.v.* See also Ibn ʿAbd al-Ḥakam, *Futūḥ Miṣr*, 5:16, 19, 18:3, 7, 18, 19:12, 29:10, 41:10, 42:1, 44:2, 125:5; al-Kindī, *Kitāb al-wulāt*, 182:11–14 (read "Tubayʿ" for "Subayʿ"). Cf. al-Balādhurī, *Ansāb al-ashrāf*, III, ed. ʿAbd al-ʿAzīz al-Dūrī (Wiesbaden, 1978), 85:15–86:3 (from Yūsuf ibn Abī Manīḥ, fl. *ca.* 150/767?); al-Ṭabarī, *Ta'rīkh*, VI, 142:15–17 (from ʿAwāna ibn al-Ḥakam, d. 147/764).

[145]Quoting a *majhūl*, or "unknown person", was a tactic commonly used to conceal the true origins of a forged tradition. See G.H.A. Juynboll, *Muslim Tradition: Studies in Chronology, Provenance and Authorship of Early Ḥadīth* (Cambridge, 1983), esp. 69, 134–60, 158, 203.

God had sent to them, and were, in addition, tyrannical and unjust rulers. God had thus ordained that the Arabs would conquer the Byzantine domains, thereby rewarding the faithful and punishing the unbelievers.[146] But within this conceptual framework a sensitive problem was posed by accounts reporting Muslim defeats or retreats from confrontation with the enemy, since these would apparently stand as contrary to the will of God. Accounts of the Muslim withdrawal from large parts of Syria in the early stages of the al-Yarmūk campaign vividly illustrate the concerns raised by this problem,[147] and our Egyptian treatment of the withdrawal of Muslim forces from Rhodes raises them again. For our storyteller, the argument is that the abandonment of Rhodes has been prefigured in a portent in nature sent by God and predicted and interpreted by an eminent Egyptian Muslim. However, this further implies that the Umayyad caliph Yazīd, as the instrument of divine will, is not to be faulted for forsaking conquered territory. This is, to be sure, not the primary aim of the story; but at a secondary level it clearly does betray thinking along these lines. Such recourse to justification through a scenario of divine foreordainment to defend an Umayyad caliph—and Yazīd, no less—places the likely date for the account prior to or only shortly after the collapse of the Umayyad régime in 132/750. Al-Layth ibn Sa'd (d. 175/791) is therefore probably somewhat too late to be the creator of the story, and is more likely only the first named transmitter of a local Egyptian tale set in circulation by a storyteller (*qāṣṣ*) between about 110/728 (i.e. after the demise of Tubay' and his comrades) and 140/757 (disintegration of Umayyad rule and advent of the 'Abbāsids).[148]

[146]See Conrad, "Al-Azdī's History of the Arab Conquests", 39–40, esp. n. 46. Noth comments on some of the relevant material (*Quellenkritische Studien*, 18–19), but regards it as the product of religious coloring rather than an overarching religious interpretation.

[147]Conrad, "Al-Azdī's History of the Arab Conquests", 44–46.

[148]On storytelling of this kind in the Umayyad period, see the important discussion by Juynboll in his "On the Origins of Arabic Prose: Reflections on Authenticity", in G.H.A. Juynboll, ed., *Studies on the First Century of Islamic Society* (Carbondale and Edwardsville, 1982), 165–68; *idem*, *Muslim Tradition*, 11–14. The implications of a milieu dominated by such storytellers are explored in Patricia Crone, *Meccan Trade and the Rise of Islam* (Oxford, 1987), 214–26. Cf. also the discussion by Leder above, 309–12.

A direct link between this tale and al-Wāqidī's account of the fall of Arwād as cited by al-Ṭabarī is provided by Ibn A'tham. In this last authority's account, Mu'āwiya asks for 'Uthmān's permission to raid Rhodes, a request which, after much reflection upon the perils of sea travel and consultation with the Muslims of Medina, 'Uthmān grants. Mu'āwiya sets sail, defeats the defenders of Rhodes in a sea battle, and proceeds to sack the island (a major portion of the narrative is taken up by a story concerning the riches of Rhodes). The Muslims then make their way back to the shore with their booty and set out to Syria, leaving Rhodes a "desolate ruin" (*kharāb yabāb*). And so the island remains until the caliphate of Mu'āwiya, who repopulates it with Muslim settlers and orders them to take up agriculture. There they remain "for seven years, with neither the Byzantine emperor nor any other ruler of the unbelievers harboring designs on [the island]". Ibn A'tham then introduces Mujāhid himself, who gives his own account of his activities on Rhodes:

> *What Mujāhid said concerning this island*
>
> Mujāhid said: I entered the city of Rhodes in the year 53, and in it we built a mosque, appointed a muezzin to it, and began to hold the ritual prayers. Mujāhid said: One day, when I was teaching him how to recite the Qur'ān, Tubay', son of the wife of Ka'b al-Aḥbār, said to me: "O Mujāhid, it is as if this island had already fallen to ruin and every trace [of habitation] on it had disappeared". I said: "O Tubay', is this island to fall to ruin?" He replied: "The portent for that will be that a great gale (*rīḥ 'iṣāf*) will spring up and blow away this step (*daraja*)". Mujāhid said—By God, we did not have long to wait before the wind came one day: it blew away (*ramat*) that step, and the letter of Yazīd ibn Mu'āwiya reached us from Syria bearing word of the death of Mu'āwiya. So we returned home, and the island fell to ruin [and has remained so] up to this very moment.[149]

This of course has nothing to do with the historical Mujāhid or Tubay', but rather marks a development from the earlier Egyptian

[149] Ibn A'tham, *Kitāb al-futūḥ*, II, 127:6–128:1.

account of the winter voyage and Tubay‘’s prophecy. Numerous and obvious repetitions of terms, phrases, and themes prove that this account is firmly grounded in the old Tubay‘ fable, but equally numerous changes indicate that the account is becoming more elaborate and sophisticated. We are now beyond any effort to tidy up the reputation of Tubay‘: from the beginning of the story he is already a respected Muslim endowed with esoteric insights. His interlocutor is no longer an army officer with the bad news of rumors people are spreading about him, but Mujāhid, who, as a renowned authority on Qur’ānic exegesis, is instructing Tubay‘ on recitation. The problem of the winter voyage has entirely disappeared, and with it the rôles formerly played by the community at large and by Mu‘āwiya’s letter. Our *majhūl*, Rashīd ibn Kaysān, has also made his exit, and instead we have the story narrated by Mujāhid in the first person, a shift sharply highlighting the new version’s more sophisticated (and therefore later) feel for historical evidence and the value of eyewitness testimony, as opposed to the suspicious narration of a *majhūl*. It is also significant that we no longer have to do with a fig tree, but rather with a “step” (*daraja*), which, given the more elaborate formal religious context of the mosque and Qur’ān recitation, is probably a symbol for the pulpit, or *minbar*. This makes for a portent more elegant than that of the uprooted fig tree: when the “step” is blown away, this is a clear sign from God that soon the prayer service address, or *khuṭba*, will no longer be recited on Rhodes—i.e. there will no longer be any Muslims there—and the island will fall to ruin.

There is nothing here that would allow us to suggest a date for this new version, but there are clear conjunctive and separative features indicating that both this account and that recorded by al-Ṭabarī in the name of al-Wāqidī derive from a common source, which has in turn made use of a recasting of the old Tubay‘ fable. This common source is proved by the fact that both later versions have Mujāhid teaching Tubay‘ Qur’ān recitation, both refine the portent by making it a “step” rather than a fig tree, and both conclude that the Muslim departure from Rhodes left it an abandoned ruin, as if there had been no Christian population on the island, or at least none that was not completely displaced by the Arab raid. The two later accounts are unlikely to have arrived at identical changes on such specific points on their own independent initiative. Other alterations, on the other hand, prove that the two versions are not dependent one upon the other. Al-Wāqidī retains the verb *qala'at*, "uprooted", which in the old Tubay' fable had originally referred to the fig tree, while Ibn A'tham's source has noticed that this is awkward in reference to a "step" and so has substituted *ramat*, "threw", "cast aside", now conveying the more appropriate image of something easily blown away by a fierce wind. But the passage of the common source account to al-Wāqidī has also witnessed important changes not found in Ibn A'tham: it is now specified that the island is "near Constantinople" and most importantly of all, Rhodes (Arabic *Rūdus*) has been confused with Arwād.

A vexed problem would seem to be posed by two accounts that in textual terms are closely related to one another and clearly derived from a common source, but yet purport to discuss two entirely different events: in the case of Ibn A'tham, the supposed arrival of Mujāhid on Rhodes in 53/673; and in the case of al-Wāqidī, the conquest of Arwād by Junāda in 54/674. This is cleared up by al-Wāqidī's own version of what happened on Rhodes, a report preserved elsewhere in al-Ṭabarī:

> In this year (i.e. AH 53), Rhodes, an island in the sea, was conquered by Junāda ibn Abī Umayya al-Azdī. The Muslims settled there—according to what Muḥammad ibn 'Umar [al-Wāqidī] related—and took up agriculture and on [Rhodes] acquired property (*amwāl*) and livestock which they grazed round about [the island] and in the evening brought into the citadel (*al-ḥiṣn*). They had a lookout (*nāṭūr*) to warn them of anyone [approaching] by sea pursuing schemes against them, and so remained on guard against [such intruders]. They were most vigorous in their actions against the Greeks, whose movements they obstructed on the sea and whose shipping they pillaged. Mu'āwiya used to lavish supplies and stipends upon them, and the enemy feared them; but when Mu'āwiya died, Yazīd ibn Mu'āwiya recalled them.[150]

[150] Al-Ṭabarī, *Ta'rīkh*, V, 288:5–11.

Confronted by a corpus of disparate material relevant to campaigns and events on various Mediterranean islands, material in which Rhodes and Arwād were named, al-Wāqidī has sought, as was his custom, to combine the available information for each event into a single account.[151] And to this end, of course, he had to decide which information referred to Rhodes and which to Arwād. By comparing his Rhodes and Arwād accounts one can see precisely what has been done. The name of Junāda has been retained in both cases. Rhodes is said to have been "captured" in 53/674, and the passages mentioning the Muslims' daily life, operations against the Greeks, and the recall after the death of Mu'āwiya have been collected into an account of events on Rhodes. On the other hand, everything concerning Mujāhid and Tubay', including the episode of the step and the ruin of the island, has been assigned to an Arwād account. Probably assuming that Arwād was "closer" to the Byzantine heartlands than Rhodes, it has also been assumed that Arwād must have been "near Constantinople" and hence conquered later, in 54/674. Though it is possible that some—or all—of this was the work of one or more of al-Wāqidī's predecessors, such elaboration of new historical detail and even new accounts is typical of material that comes down to us in al-Wāqidī's name.[152] However one explains the division, it is easy to see that it has been extremely arbitrary and not in accord with the true origins of the material in question.

Sorting out these errors should not be seen simply as a task of restoring to Arwād and Rhodes the details and features that properly belong to each, since there is reason to believe that not only al-Wāqidī's Arwād narrative, but also the Rhodes stories from which that narrative evolved, are all artificial composites elaborated from earlier undifferen-

---

[151] On al-Wāqidī's use of the collective *isnād*, see J.M.B. Jones, "Ibn Isḥāq and al-Wāqidī: The Dream of 'Ātika and the Raid to Nakhla in Relation to the Charge of Plagiarism", *BSOAS* 22 (1959), 41–51.

[152] The tendency in modern scholarship has long been to exult in al-Wāqidī's work, apparently because he provides so much information and detail not to be found among any of his predecessors. As we can see here, however, all this must be viewed with great caution. The source-critical problem posed by this feature of his work was first assessed and discussed by J.M.B. Jones, "The Chronology of the *Maghāzī*–a Textual Survey", *BSOAS* 19 (1957), 245–80. For more recent work, see Wansbrough, *Sectarian Milieu*, 76–77; Crone, *Meccan Trade*, 223–24; Lawrence I. Conrad, art. "al-Wāqidī" in *DMA*, XII, 544–45.

tiated fragments in a completely arbitrary fashion. Perhaps the most obvious of the indications pointing to this conclusion is the "ruin of Rhodes", a theme in which the Muslim tradents seem to have taken special interest. Rhodes, an island of almost 1200 square km., was in antiquity a vibrant economic and cultural center. After Alexander's conquests removed trade barriers in the region Rhodes came to dominate the lucrative grain trade, burgeoned into what was arguably the richest of the Greek city states, and controlled considerable mainland territories. Aside from its main urban center at the city of Rhodes, the island had several other towns and was dotted with villages. Though it was not as important in Roman times, the island did maintain much of its former eminence as a cultural center and an entrepôt of Mediterranean trade.[153] Much less is known about it for the Byzantine period. It remained sufficiently important to be the seat for bishops and metropolitans from the fourth century onward,[154] and it was still the seat of a bishopric during the reign of Justinian (527–65).[155] The Persians attacked and captured the city of Rhodes in 620,[156] there are apparently a number of fortresses on the island that date from this time,[157] and John of Nikiu (wr. *ca.* 690) makes Rhodes in September

[153]See H. von Gaertringen, art. "Rhodos" in P/W, *RE*, Supp. V, 731–840; also Cecil Torr, *Rhodes in Ancient Times* (Cambridge, 1885); Hendrik von Gelder, *Geschichte der alten Rhodier* (The Hague, 1900); Lionel Casson, "The Grain Trade of the Hellenistic World", *TAPA* 85 (1954), 168–87; P.M. Fraser and G.E. Bean, *The Rhodian Peraea and Islands* (London, 1954); Hatto H. Schmitt, *Rom und Rhodos* (Munich, 1957); Jones, *The Greek City*, index; *idem*, *Cities of the Eastern Roman Provinces*, 31–32, 48–51, 56, 62, 76–77, 94, 100, 106; Brian Dicks, *Rhodes* (Harrisburg, 1974), 41–68.

[154]On Rhodes as an ecclesiastical center from the Council of Nicaea (325) up until Islamic times, see Evangelos Chrysos, *Die Bischöflisten des V. ökumenischen Konzils (553)* (Bonn, 1966), 17, 27, 98, 146, 162, 165, 178, 187.

[155]In 528 the bishop of Rhodes was a certain Esaias, whom John Malalas (6th c.) and Theophilus vilify as a pederast; see John Malalas, *Chronicle*, trans. Elizabeth Jeffreys, Michael Jeffreys, and Roger Scott (Melbourne, 1986), 253; Theophanes, *Chronographia*, 177:11; Michael, II, 221 (trans.); IV, 296:10–11 (text); *Chronicle of 1234*, I, 191:25.

[156]*Chronicle of 724*, 147:5–7; Agapius, *Kitāb al-'unwān*, II, 335:4–5; Michael, II, 408 (trans.); IV, 408b:15–16 (text); *Chronicle of 1234*, I, 230:7–9; Bar Hebraeus, *Chronicon syriacum*, 95:10–11; *idem*, *Ta'rīkh mukhtaṣar al-duwal*, 156:1–4.

[157]Dicks, *Rhodes*, 68.

641, only a decade before the first Arab raids on the island, a major Byzantine military base and a center where imperial power was sufficiently strong for the régime to send such important imperial figures as Heraclonas and Martina into exile there.[158] The revision of the old maritime code of Rhodes sometime in the seventh or eighth century attests to the continuing commercial importance of the place in the period of concern to us here; and as this code was based on a range of earlier sources, and so suggests a background of continuing generation of maritime (and other commercial) law at Rhodes, it is reasonable to conclude that trade and commerce were also active in the immediately preceding decades as well.[159]

In the 640s, then, the city of Rhodes was in all likelihood still a significant port and urban center, and there were certainly still other towns and villages elsewhere on the island. At the least, there are compelling grounds for concluding that Rhodes could not have declined to such an extent that a single Arab raid would reduce it to a "desolate ruin" devoid of population. Arwād, however, *was* an abandoned ruin after Mu'āwiya ordered its destruction in 29/650. Has an archaic reference to the ruin of some "island" been included among other fragments used to construct accounts of the expedition to Rhodes? Be this as it may, the fact that the *ruwāt* were able to proceed on the assumption that Rhodes could have been rendered desolate and abandoned provides yet another indication that so far as genuinely historical information is concerned, these transmitters at no point had access to any more than sparse and fragmentary material providing little coherent detail.

And what of the dates involved? Ibn A'tham's account of Mujāhid on Rhodes mentions Mu'āwiya asking for the caliph 'Uthmān's permission to raid Rhodes and 'Uthmān consulting with the other Muslims in Medina and finally granting his consent to the expedition. It refers to 'Uthmān's joy at the news of the victory, and has 'Uthmān dividing out the fifth in Medina. It also specifically states that Mu'āwiya became caliph at some time *after* these events.[160] That is, it places the

[158]John of Nikiu, *The Chronicle of John (c. 690* AD*), Coptic Bishop of Nikiu*, trans. Robert Henry Charles (London, 1916), CXX.5, 52; 192, 197. Cf. also Theophanes, *Chronographia*, 330pu–331:5, 341:24–28.

[159]See Ashburner, *The Rhodian Sea Law*, lx-lxxv.

[160]Ibn A'tham, *Kitāb al-futūḥ*, II, 124ult–125:6, 126:14–16, 127:1–2.

sack and "abandonment" of Rhodes during the caliphate of 'Uthmān (23–35/644–56). This would agree with accounts in the Syriac sources and Theophanes (again, indicating their origin in the chronicle of Theophilus of Edessa) dating the attack on Rhodes to AG 965 or AM 6145, i.e. AD 653.[161] We may therefore conclude that this event probably did occur during the caliphate of 'Uthmān, and perhaps in about 32–33/653.[162]

Al-Wāqidī's dating of 53/674 for the attack on Rhodes is thus wrong by two full decades. In explanation of this we may note that in the earliest stages of the elaboration of accounts of Arab naval campaigns in the Mediterranean, there seem to have been in circulation vague and fragmentary references to a Muslim community resident on some island for a period of "seven years". As matters of chronology became more important, the Muslim transmitters were obliged to determine where, within the chronological scheme of things, this period was to be placed. Not surprisingly, they chose a decisive event to mark the end of the period—the death of Mu'āwiya. If one proceeds on the assumption that the beginning of the Muslims' residence on the island referred to a date of conquest, and assigns all this to Rhodes, then by subtracting the "seven years" from the death date of Mu'āwiya, 60/680, one arrives at the conclusion that Rhodes was conquered in 53/673. It was perfectly reasonable for the *ruwāt* to suppose that Yazīd, after his father's death, would have felt the need to withdraw forces loyal to him from advanced island outposts in order to consolidate his political and military position in Syria, and perhaps the new caliph actually did take such action. The conclusions extrapolated from this concerning the conquest of Rhodes, however, are entirely erroneous.

That the false chronology for the conquest and abandonment of Rhodes represents a set of arbitrary conclusions drawn from an assumption of Muslims staying on some island for seven years is a possibility that appears more likely in light of what occurs elsewhere. Among certain authorities independent of al-Wāqidī the abandonment of Rhodes

[161] See Theophanes, *Chronographia*, 345:8–11; Michael, II, 442–43 (trans.); IV, 430:25–31 (text); *Chronicle of 1234*, I, 275:12–19. Cf. also the comment of Dionysius of Tell-Maḥrē in *Chronicle of 1234*, II, 21:7–8.

[162] Cf. Wellhausen, "Kämpfe der Araber mit den Romäern", 419; Caetani, *Annali dell'Islam*, VII, 522–23.

is also pegged to the decisive event of Mu'āwiya's death, but without reference to the "seven years". And in the absence of this detail the date for the conquest of the island does not remain 53/673, but rather becomes 59/679, the year immediately preceding that of Mu'āwiya's death.[163] That is, without the "seven years" detail to suggest otherwise, the transmitters were free to speculate that Rhodes was conquered just before Mu'āwiya's death and then abandoned a year later by Yazīd. In other words, the date of 53/673 for the conquest of Rhodes was not a "fact" transmitted independently from the "seven years" detail; it was a conclusion generated by the latter. And even with such stabilizing elements as a fixed date of conquest and a specified time span for Muslim occupation, confusion could still arise among reports from the same authority. As we have already seen, al-Wāqidī both knew of the "seven years" detail[164] and assigned the date of 53/673 to the conquest of Rhodes. Nevertheless, al-Ṭabarī has another report from him dating the capture of Rhodes to 60/680.[165] And once this is in circulation new accounts derived from it or presuming it soon appear. An unspecified authority of Ibn Taghrībirdī (d. 815/1412) has it that this was the year of "Junāda's entry into Rhodes and the destruction of its houses",[166] and according to al-Layth ibn Sa'd it was in this year that Mu'āwiya died, Yazīd succeeded him, and "the people of Egypt carried foodstuffs to Rhodes".[167] The more reliable evidence dating the expedition to Rhodes to the caliphate of 'Uthmān falsifies, from the start, all of these alternative scenarios so far as a first campaign is concerned. But by examining them in detail it further emerges that there may be little point in seeking to rescue some measure of historicity from such chronologies,

---

[163]See, for example, Ibn 'Abd al-Barr, *Istī'āb*, I, 250:1–4 (from al-Layth ibn Sa'd and al-Walīd ibn Muslim); Ibn 'Asākir, *Ta'rīkh madīnat Dimashq* (Ms.), IV, 16v:28–17r:3 (al-Walīd ibn Muslim), 17r:3–10 (al-Layth ibn Sa'd); = *Tahdhīb*, III, 412:23.

[164]In addition to the passage cited above from al-Ṭabarī, see the report transmitted from al-Wāqidī by his secretary Ibn Sa'd in al-Balādhurī, *Futūḥ al-buldān*, 236:5–6.

[165]Al-Ṭabarī, *Ta'rīkh*, V, 322:3–4.

[166]Ibn Taghrībirdī, *Al-Nujūm al-zāhira fī mulūk Miṣr wa-l-Qāhira* (Cairo, 1348–92/1929–72), I, 154:6. Here Ibn Taghrībirdī is not repeating al-Ṭabarī or any other extant source, and in such cases his information often comes from the great Iraqi compiler al-Madā'inī (d. 228/842).

[167]Khalīfa ibn Khayyāṭ (d. 240/854–55), *Ta'rīkh*, ed. Akram Ḍiyā' al-'Umarī, 2nd ed. (Beirut, 1397/1977), 229:2–4.

e.g. by proposing first and second expeditions, a raid followed by a later occupation, and so forth.[168]

Before leaving the issue of chronology, it is worth noting that an explanation for the "seven years" element in the Rhodes stories can at least be suggested. The period from the Cyprus campaign of 28/648 until the outbreak of the First Civil War in 35/656 is also seven years, and biographical notices of Junāda, as mentioned above, do state that his campaigns ceased when this conflict began. It thus may well be that the "seven years" element springs from undifferentiated statements by early tradents that in their origins concern not Rhodes, but Cyprus, and a time span ending not with the death of Mu'āwiya in 60/680, but with the beginning of his conflict with 'Alī ibn Abī Ṭālib in 35/656.

And what of Junāda and his winter voyage? In the notices for Junāda reference is frequently made to such a voyage, but no authority specifies where it began or where the Muslims went. Thus, while the old Egyptian Tubay' fable discussed above develops the "winter voyage" theme in one direction, the Ḥimṣī Muslim ibn Ziyād (d. *ca*. 140/757), as quoted by the Egyptian Ibn Lahī'a (d. 174/790), elaborates it in an opposite sense:

> Mu'āwiya wrote to him (i.e. Junāda) ordering him to attack an island in the sea (*jazīrat al-baḥr*) with the men he had with him, and this during the winter after the sea was no longer passable.[169] So Junāda said: "O God, obedience is incumbent upon me and upon this sea. We ask you to calm it and to ease our passage over it." They claim that not a single man was killed in the [passage].[170]

Even if we strip away from the Egyptian Tubay' tale the details concerning him, and eliminate from the Ḥimṣī story the elements revolving around the pious Junāda, the remaining cores are utterly at odds: in

---

[168] Much the same occurs elsewhere in the early Arab-Islamic tradition. There are, for example, no fewer than three battles of Badr during the career of the Prophet, and four expeditions and three occupations of the city of Ḥimṣ during the conquest of Syria.

[169] Read *ighlāq* for *ighlāt*.

[170] Ibn 'Asākir, *Ta'rīkh madīnat Dimashq* (Ms.), IV, fol. 16v:10–24 = *Tahdhīb*, III, 412:20–23.

the first Mu'āwiya orders a naval *withdrawal* during the winter, which his men dislike but nevertheless carry out, while in the second Mu'āwiya orders a naval *advance* during the winter, which his men again dislike but execute all the same. The prior material allowing for such discrepancies is not a possibly authentic core account that has later been embellished, but rather only an unhelpful fragment of information asserting that Junāda undertook a winter voyage.

Similar factors are at work in the background to the seemingly incredible statement placing Arwād "near Constantinople", an assertion that in the past has attracted some comment and several unlikely and completely arbitrary explanations. Brooks, apparently unaware that such a place as Arwād does indeed exist, suggested that al-Wāqidī's placement of the island "near Constantinople" and the similarity of his account of the attack on Arwād to his report for the raid on Rhodes indicate that "Arwād" may simply be a mistake for "Rhodes".[171] Wellhausen, followed by Caetani, claimed that "Arwād" meant "Cyzicus"; and Caetani, going even further, advanced the proposition that "Rhodes" means "Crete".[172] For these conclusions, however, no evidence is adduced beyond a statement by Theophanes to the effect that in 670–71 (AM 6162), the Arab commander Faḍāla spent the winter in Cyzicus,[173] a city at the narrow neck of the Kapıdağı promontory on the south side of the Sea of Marmara, about 115 km. from Constantinople. Seybold went even further, and proposed—on the basis of considerations of Arabic orthography alone—that in the reports preserved by al-Balādhurī, al-Ṭabarī, and Yāqūt "Arwād" is a misreading for "Ardāk", i.e. the Greek 'Αρτάκη (modern Erdek), nine km. northwest of Cyzicus.[174] Though attracted by the principle of some

[171] E.W. Brooks, "The Arabs in Asia Minor (641–750), from Arabic Sources", *JHS* 18 (1898), 186.

[172] See Wellhausen, "Kämpfe der Araber mit den Romäern", 425; Leone Caetani, *Chronographia islamica* (Paris, 1912), III, 577, 588.

[173] Theophanes, *Chronographia*, 353:7: καὶ ἐχείμασε Φαδαλᾶς εἰς Κύζικον. This commander was Faḍāla ibn 'Ubayd al-Anṣārī; see Wellhausen, "Kämpfe der Araber mit den Romäern", 422–24.

[174] C.F. Seybold, "I. Osṭādina (Kindī *Usṭādina*, Jāqūt *Usṭādina*) = Konstantinopel. II. Arwād (Belāḏorī, Ṭabarī, Jāqūt) = Artaki, Erdek", *Der Islam* 4 (1913), 152–53. This identification of Arwād with a site "near Constantinople" has recently been embraced by Franz-Christoph Muth in his *Die Annalen von aṭ-Ṭabarī im Spiegel*

confusion between Arwād and Rhodes, Canard, in his own discussion of the problem, would not press the question further and wisely left the matter open.[175]

As already argued above, the evidence should rather lead us to regard the claim that Arwād lies "near Constantinople" simply as one arising within the context of the emergence of many other spurious details as the Rhodes and Arwād materials were being elaborated and in the end arbitrarily separated. There are, however, other possibilities. The capital of Byzantine Cyprus, the main town sacked in Mu'āwiya's campaign of 28/649, was Constantia (ancient Salamis), located on the east coast of the island—i.e. facing Arwād—about nine km. north of the modern town of Famagusta; and Antarados, the mainland Syrian town opposite Arwād, had been renamed Constantia in the fourth century AD. The associations of either of these towns with Arwād could have resulted in an early report or isolated statement locating the island "near Constantia". In either oral or written expression, the Arabic form of this name, Qusṭanṭīya, could easily have been either mistaken for or erroneously "corrected" to Qusṭanṭīnīya, "Constantinople", at some later point. Alternatively, pursuing Brooks' thinking on the matter, it could be argued that originally it was Rhodes that was described as "near Constantinople". This island campaign brought Arab forces closer to the Byzantine capital than any of their other early island expeditions except for that to Cos, and the Arabic sources for Rhodes repeatedly raise such subjects as the raiding of Greek shipping from Rhodes, Muslims watching out for Byzantine counterattacks, the possibility of Greek stratagems and plots, and so forth.[176] Early Rhodes accounts would thus be as likely as others to attract statements claiming not only that the island was "near Constantinople", but also assertions that once the Muslims left the island, "the Greeks were safe". As we have seen, however, in the extant material both of these claims appear in al-Wāqidī's report on Arwād, the location of which was not "near Constantinople"

der europäischen Bearbeitungen (Frankfurt am Main, 1983), 86.

[175] Marius Canard, "Les expéditions des Arabes contre Constantinople dans l'histoire et dans la légende", *JA* 208 (1926), 78–79.

[176] See, for example, al-Balādhurī, *Futūḥ al-buldān*, 236:6–7 (from al-Wāqidī); al-Ṭabarī, *Ta'rīkh*, V, 288:7–10 (from al-Wāqidī); Ibn A'tham, *Kitāb al-futūḥ*, II, 127:4–5.

and the abandonment of which did not render the Byzantine situation "safe".

The arbitrary assignment of Arwād to a site "near" Constantinople had a consequence of particular interest, one that highlights the confusion suggested by the features discussed above. In the history of al-Ṭabarī, Sayf ibn 'Umar reports that Mu'āwiya, wishing to undertake a "sea raid" (*ghazw al-baḥr*), advised the caliph 'Umar ibn al-Khaṭṭāb that the Greeks were in a position very close to Ḥimṣ (referring here to the *jund* of Ḥimṣ, not the city): "In one of the towns of Ḥimṣ the people can hear the barking of the dogs of the Greeks and the crowing of their roosters (*ṣiyāḥ dajājihim*)", adding in a second report: "And the Greeks are directly opposite one of the coastal districts of Ḥimṣ" (*sāḥil min sawāḥil Ḥimṣ*).[177] Sayf has all this in an account of Mu'āwiya's attack on Cyprus in 28/649; but here, surely, we have before us a fragment that originally can only have been meant to refer to Arwād. However, as Arwād had, by Sayf's time, been located "near" Constantinople, this old fragment could not be placed with other Arwād material and was instead arbitrarily assigned to Cyprus. If this explanation is correct, then the assignment of Arwād to a site "near" Constantinople must have occurred already in the mid-second/eighth century, i.e. before the time of al-Wāqidī.

It is not difficult to see how all of this could have occurred. As already suggested, the transmitters involved in the earliest stages in the development of this report had access not to coherent information and reports about the conquests of Arwād, or Rhodes, or Cyprus, or to detailed data that could be discussed and evaluated for their further implications, but rather only to the sketchiest recollection that places by certain names had been taken, that they were islands, and that certain famous early Muslims had been involved. Accounts of the conquest of these islands were thus assembled by collecting references to events referred to as campaigns for some place "in the sea" or on "the island of the sea" or on "islands in the sea", a sea raid "in the land of the Greeks (*arḍ al-Rūm*)", or simply a "sea raid"—in particular, it seems, references in which the names of Junāda, Tubay', or Mujāhid appeared.[178]

[177] Al-Ṭabarī, *Ta'rīkh*, IV, 258:11–15, 259:3–7.

[178] Note, for example, how such material is handled in al-Bukhārī, *Al-Ta'rīkh al-*

These were highly ambiguous reports and allowed for filling gaps and adding new detail through several stages of broad-ranging speculation, which in absolutely arbitrary fashion began to cover a great deal of new ground. The final results were composites consisting of bits of information concerning numerous naval campaigns undertaken by Junāda or at least ascribed to him later, held together with arbitrary transitional schemata and elaborated in consideration of views and issues that in fact reflect later thinking.

In the case of al-Wāqidī's treatment of Arwād, it has been possible to discern the course of this process in some detail. From the era of the conquerors nothing had been transmitted to later generations except for fragmentary and ambiguous recollections that Mu'āwiya, Junāda, Tubay', and Mujāhid had had something to do with campaigns on certain Mediterranean islands, certainly including Cyprus, Rhodes, and Arwād, and perhaps also the raids and campaigns on Crete, Cos, and Sicily. In later Umayyad Egypt, probably in Alexandria, some of these emerged as the historical setting for a specious tale, concerning the Muslims in Rhodes, that was set in circulation in order to promote the reputation of Tubay' ibn 'Āmir. In a later account describing the raid on Rhodes, this anecdote was recast in a much abbreviated form, with Mujāhid introduced into the story and Tubay''s portent changed to a "step", but with the setting remaining on Rhodes. This recasting, now lost, was in turn the basis for two independent versions that survive in the histories of Ibn A'tham and al-Ṭabarī. That in Ibn A'tham reflects some minor changes in wording, but in other respects may be (but cannot be proven to be) largely faithful to the common source. The version in al-Ṭabarī, however, indicates that here further major distortions had occurred: the date of 53/673 is no longer that of Mujāhid's arrival on an island, but that of Junada's conquest of an island, and the entire story has been shifted from Rhodes to Arwād as a result of the arbitrary division of material into accounts describing two different events.

***

kabīr, I.2, 231:13–14 (quoting Mujāhid!); al-Balādhurī, *Futūḥ al-buldān*, 235:12–236:16; al-Ṭabarī, *Ta'rīkh*, V, 288:5 (from al-Wāqidī); Ibn 'Abd al-Barr, *Istī'āb*, I, 250:1–4 (al-Layth ibn Sa'd and al-Walīd ibn Muslim); Ibn 'Asākir, *Ta'rīkh madīnat Dimashq* (Ms.), IV, fol. 16v:10–17v:10 (various reports from Ibn Lahī'a, al-Layth ibn Sa'd, and al-Walīd ibn Muslim).

In several ways the development of al-Wāqidī's account of the fall of Arwād parallels that of the *futūḥ* accounts of the battle of Iṣfahān. As Albrecht Noth demonstrates, this tradition is also discontinuous and seems to have emerged in al-Baṣra near the end of the Umayyad caliphate. Further, in its origins it has nothing to do with Iṣfahān, and instead represents a transfer of material from an earlier tradition for the battle of Nihāwand. And even as a tradition of transmission restored to its original locus, it proves to be an ahistorical tale assembled from the standard répertoire of *futūḥ* topoi, schemata, and motifs.[179] This same process, elaboration of a baseless account which is in part later transferred to another event, is the same one at work in the growth of the Arwād account under discussion here.

Without entering into the question of how much historical information can yet be rescued from the various accounts for Rhodes (or indeed, for the other naval campaigns), it should by now be clear that as an account for events at Arwād, al-Wāqidī's report is absolutely baseless. And it is worth noting that the series of compounding errors that marks the growth of such accounts seems have given the later formal historians cause for distinct discomfort. Al-Ṭabarī, for example, dissociates himself from responsibility for any of al-Wāqidī's conclusions by repeatedly reminding the reader that al-Wāqidī is the one who asserts all this. And Ibn A'tham is quite direct on such problems: in most of his accounts of early Arab naval operations in the Mediterranean, he ends his narrative with the words *wa'llāhu a'lam*, "God knows best", i.e. "whether this is true".[180]

We may finally consider the version of the conquest of Arwād preserved by al-Balādhurī:

> In the year 54, Junāda ibn Abī Umayya conquered Arwād and Mu'āwiya settled Muslims there. Among those who conquered it were Mujāhid and Tubay', son of the wife of Ka'b al-Aḥbār. Mujāhid taught Tubay' to recite the Qur'ān there, although it is said that he taught him to recite the

[179] Albrecht Noth, "Iṣfahān–Nihāwand. Eine quellenkritische Studie zur frühislamischen Historiographie", *ZDMG* 118 (1968), 274–96.

[180] Ibn A'tham, *Kitāb al-futūḥ*, II, 124:14 (Cyprus), 127:5 (Rhodes), 130:12 (battle of Dhāt al-Ṣawārī).

> Qur'ān at Rhodes. Arwād is an island near Constantinople.[181]

This need not long detain our attention, as it is clearly an account which embraces al-Wāqidī's version on almost all points. Al-Balādhurī is aware of the parallel Rhodes material, as is evident from his own account of the raid on Rhodes[182] and from his statement here that for at least some elements of the story there is reason to believe that they occurred on Rhodes, not Arwād. Still, he accepts the assignment of this particular story to Arwād. The report in his *Futūḥ al-buldān* adds nothing to our knowledge of the Arwād campaign, rectifies none of even the extreme distortions and errors committed by past authorities, and instead helps to consecrate what is now an almost entirely spurious account. Arwād is still, for example, "near Constantinople" (*bi-l-qurbi mina l-Qusṭanṭīnīya*), its conquest continues to be associated with Mujāhid and Tubay' and dated to AH 54, and it is still claimed that Mu'āwiya settled Muslims on the island.[183]

Though the Arwād narratives in both al-Balādhurī and al-Ṭabarī were entirely erroneous, they did suit the historical perceptions of their time and so won assent for their historicity. As this assent was simply a manifestation of the general consensus, or *ijmā'*, on Islamic origins and early Islamic history that was emerging in the third/ninth century, these accounts of Arwād seem to have become immune to dispute or repudiation, even in their most obviously mistaken claim: the assertion that Arwād was "near Constantinople". Ibn 'Asākir accepts this in the introductory remarks to his *tarjama* on Tubay',[184] though, as a Damascene with a profound knowledge of earlier Syrian sources and authorities, it is difficult to imagine that he had no knowledge of the

---

[181] *Futūḥ al-buldān*, 236:9–12.

[182] *Ibid.*, 235ult–236:9 (from earlier sources in general, *qālū*, "they said", and from al-Wāqidī in particular).

[183] Stratos (*Byzantium in the Seventh Century*, III, 41–42) uses this report to sustain the argument that after the capture of Arwād the island was not razed but rather settled by the Muslims.

[184] Ibn 'Asākir, *Ta'rīkh madīnat Dimashq*, X, 426:10–11 (this statement is dropped in the *Tahdhīb*, III, 342).

true location of the island. Al-Mizzī[185] and al-Dhahabī[186] both follow him in this error, though again, would al-Dhahabī, another Damascene, never have seen anything more accurate to give him reason for doubt on this point? Ibn al-Athīr (d. 630/1233), who usually summarizes al-Ṭabarī, also follows him in this mistake,[187] and Ibn Kathīr, another Damascene, sidesteps the problem by avoiding any mention of Arwād or Tubay' at all.

Even the geographers had difficulty with Arwād. Al-Idrīsī (wr. 548/1154) correctly locates it off the coast at Ṭarṭūs and speaks of its capture by the forces of Mu'āwiya while he was governor of Syria under 'Uthmān ibn 'Affān.[188] But of all the other geographers only Yāqūt (d. 626/1229) and al-Dimashqī (wr. *ca.* 700/1300) have entries on the place. Yāqūt, though an authority in his field who had travelled extensively in Syria and in fact compiled his great geographical dictionary from the resources of the libraries of Aleppo,[189] follows al-Balādhurī in placing Arwād "near Constantinople" and in all of the other details of his account.[190] Al-Dimashqī, on the other hand, knows the island's location and is sufficiently familiar with the general area to know of the seabed spring. But in describing Arwād itself, he states that it is six miles long and six miles wide.[191]

Emergent Arabic Historiography: the Case of Arwād

Viewing the Arab-Islamic materials for the Arwād campaign more generally, the following conclusions emerge. In historical terms this corpus of material tells us little that does not disintegrate upon closer historiographical inspection. It is beyond doubt that there were numerous

[185] Al-Mizzī, *Tahdhīb al-kamāl*, IV, 313:5–6.

[186] Al-Dhahabī, *Siyar a'lām al-nubalā'*, IV, 413:13.

[187] Ibn al-Athīr, *Al-Kāmil fī l-ta'rīkh* (Beirut, 1385–86/1965–66), III, 497:3–7.

[188] Al-Idrīsī, *Nuzhat al-mushtāq fī ikhtirāq al-āfāq*, ed. E. Cerulli *et al.* (Naples and Rome, 1970–84), III, 375:6–8.

[189] Yāqūt, *Mu'jam al-buldān*, ed. Ferdinand Wüstenfeld (Leipzig, 1866–73), I, 12:4–11.

[190] *Ibid.*, I, 224:6–10.

[191] Al-Dimashqī, *Nukhabat al-dahr*, 120:11–12, 142:14, 207ult–208:4. Cf. n. 10 above.

campaigns and expeditions to various islands in the eastern Mediterranean during the caliphate of 'Uthmān and under the early Umayyads, and where Arwād is concerned the Arabic sources do add one item of information not found in the eastern Christian sources—the name of Junāda ibn Abī Umayya as Mu'āwiya's naval commander. But all the rest represents successive stages of storytelling and the arbitrary elaboration of new detail.

In historiographical terms, however, this material is of considerable importance for the way it clearly illustrates a number of vital issues that must be taken into consideration in any investigation of early Arabic historiography, and indeed, in any attempt to reconstruct events of early Islamic history. In general, these may be reduced to five basic problems.

1) The first is that of discontinuity. Since the beginnings of serious modern scholarship on the Arabic *futūḥ* tradition in the mid-nineteenth century, the explanation for the origins of this tradition has envisaged Arab warriors sitting at evening sessions devoted to narration of their exploits and great victories. For some cases this may well be an accurate characterization, but for the fall of Arwād it is absolutely false. The extant evidence for the tradition on this event allows for only three possible conclusions. First, there were no old warriors sitting around their hearths telling the younger generation of their heroics at Arwād. Or second, if there were, whatever they said was at a very early point almost entirely lost—lost, that is, in the sense that no genuine old report survived to pass into the hands of the later Umayyad tradents to whom we can trace the extant accounts. Or third, the old warriors did tell their stories, these narratives did pass on to the Umayyad *ruwāt*, but then these transmitters ignored the old material and instead chose to circulate baseless accounts generated within their own circles. Each of these alternatives involves extraordinary implications: the first, that the old warriors, in defiance of all we think we know about the ancient "battle-days" (*ayyām*) lore and the continuity of Arabian oral tradition,[192] simply did not relate what must have been an engaging

[192]On the *ayyām*, see Werner Caskel, "Aijām al-'arab. Studien zur altarabischen Epik", *Islamica* 3: Ergänzungsheft (1930), 1–99, esp. 9–34; Aḥmad al-Shā'ib, *Ta'rīkh al-naqā'iḍ*, 2nd ed. (Cairo, 1954), 53–89; Eugen Mittwoch, arts. "Ayyām" in *EI*[1], I, 218–19, and *EI*[2], I (Leiden, 1960), 793–94; Franz Rosenthal, *A His-*

and eventful story; the second, that such stories were not of sufficient interest for later generations to preserve and transmit them; the third, that in Umayyad times there was a broad-ranging practice of discarding old narratives and inventing baseless new ones, and that Umayyad society either did not notice or did not care.

Much more work will be required before these difficulties can be dealt with effectively. But the fact remains that it can be demonstrated in every case that the Arab-Islamic material for the conquest of Arwād does not and cannot consist of accounts passed on from one generation to the next in a continuous tradition beginning with the generation of the Arab conquerors. Instead, the beginnings of the extant tradition for this event must be sought among Umayyad storytellers piecing together narratives with only the barest shreds of genuinely historical information to guide or restrain the process of reconstruction. Indeed, that the final results of this process should be so thoroughly ahistorical provides yet another indication of the fragmentary and undifferentiated material with which the process began. In the case of Ibn Aʿtham's account of

tory of Muslim Historiography, 2nd ed. (Leiden, 1968), 19–21, 66; Geo Widengren, "Oral Tradition and Written Literature among the Hebrews in the Light of Arabic Evidence", *Acta Orientalia* 23 (1959), 232–43; Egbert Meyer, *Der historische Gehalt der Aijām al-ʿArab* (Wiesbaden, 1970), 5–24; Ursula Sezgin, *Abū Miḫnaf. Ein Beitrag zur Historiographie der umaiyadischen Zeit* (Leiden, 1971), 90–91; ʿĀdil Jāsim al-Bayātī, *Al-Shiʿr fī ḥarb Dāḥis wa-l-Ghabrā'* (Najaf, 1972); Noth, *Quellenkritische Studien*, 107, 133, 151; Wansbrough, *Sectarian Milieu*, 25–26; Fred M. Donner, "The Bakr b. Wā'il Tribes and Politics in Northeastern Arabia on the Eve of Islam", *SI* 51 (1980), 8–16; A.A. Duri, *The Rise of Historical Writing among the Arabs*, ed. and trans. Lawrence I. Conrad (Princeton, 1983), 18–20 and index; Conrad, "Abraha and Muḥammad", 228–29, 230–31; al-Bayātī, *Kitāb ayyām al-ʿarab qabla l-Islām* (Beirut, 1407/1987), I, 9–297. The theory according to which the *futūḥ* tradition marks a continuation of the tradition/spirit/style of the *ayyām* rests on slender evidence and requires reconsideration. Arguments on the basis of content and narrative style beg rather than resolve the crucial question of the antiquity of the *ayyām*; and while the existence in pre-Islamic times of "battle-days" poems and lore pertaining to them would not be challenged by this writer, it is to be recalled that it is practically impossible to trace these materials, as we now have them, prior to the collection of Abū ʿUbayda (d. 210/825), again, in the era of al-Wāqidī and other leading compilers. This poses the problem—in view of the conclusions reached above—of determining the form and content of these tales in earlier times, as well as the possibility of their development into their present form in a manner not independent of the *futūḥ*.

Arwād, we have a report that consists entirely of topoi and other stereotyped motifs and contains nothing of historical truth beyond knowledge that Arwād is an island and that Mu'āwiya and Junāda had something to do with its conquest during the caliphate of 'Uthmān. In the case of the Arwād accounts in al-Ṭabarī and al-Balādhurī, it can be shown that these in part originate in storytelling about Tubay' ibn 'Āmir in late Umayyad Egypt, and that the original reference point for most of the material is not even Arwād, but rather Rhodes. In fact, it is likely that in early 'Abbāsid times the arbitrary division of material that led to separate reports for Rhodes and Arwād had not yet occurred. Dim survivals of archaic transmissions about Arwād may perhaps be discerned in the "ruined island" motif and in Sayf's reference to an island so close to the Syrian coast that one could hear its barking dogs and crowing roosters; but this is hardly reassuring, since the former has been displaced to Rhodes and the latter to Cyprus.

Here it is appropriate to consider possible objections to the points outlined above. It could be proposed that the early Arab maritime campaigns may have been a topic of limited interest, and hence that the lack of reliable reports represents a special case with no bearing on the transmission of information concerning events of greater import to the early Muslim community. Or more particularly, it could be asserted that Arwād may have been a place of no significance at the time of the island's capture by Mu'āwiya, and that because of this the old *ruwāt* did not trouble themselves to include it in their tales, and instead concentrated on the more important campaigns and the really great victories they had won—again, implying that patterns evident in the Arabic materials for Arwād are of no broader relevance to the emergence and transmission of the *futūḥ* tradition.

Such objections may easily be dismissed. First, they are sustained not by historiographical argument or assessment of evidence, but rather by arbitrary assertion. Second, the account of Theophilus clearly establishes that Arwād—no mean village in earlier times—remained a base of strategic importance in the reign of 'Uthmān; had this not been the case, why should Mu'āwiya have felt obliged to bring considerable forces to bear to reduce the island, not once, but twice, rather than wait for its inhabitants and garrison to abandon it for want of food and water? With this in mind, there is no reason to suppose that the *ruwāt* of the tribes responsible for the victory would not have been just as interested in transmitting tales about it as other narrators in other tribes were in circulating tales of their victories. And there is surely no reason to believe that, in later times, accounts of Arwād would have suffered a sudden decline in interest and transmission, as compared to events for which accounts do survive. As has been discussed above in several places, the Muslim communities of Syria and Egypt were intensely interested in such subjects as possible Byzantine attacks on their coastal regions and cities, the *jihād* by sea, and matters relating to patrolling and guarding the coasts.[193] Viewed in this social and cultural context, it may be concluded that there is no reason to believe that the Arab victory at Arwād, as a concern of the historical tradition, would have been of significantly less interest than other subjects pertaining to the conquests and other aspects of Syrian history.

Finally, and most importantly, such objections have no bearing on the point of primary interest here. The case of Arwād presents a clear example of how, in a situation of an almost absolute dearth of genuine historical material, detailed narrative accounts could nonetheless develop. Some comparable cases have already been discussed by other scholars, Noth's study of the Iṣfahān–Nihāwand tradition being, as mentioned above, a case with important parallels to the growth of the Arwād tradition.[194] And in his study of the early conquests, Fred M. Donner points to one case in which the tradition allowed for the creation of accounts of a battle that never occurred. In the *futūḥ* tradition for the conquest of Iraq there are accounts of the Battle of the Bridge, a clash with the Sasanians in which the Banū Shaybān were badly defeated. The later Shaybānīs therefore needed a great victory to counterbalance this humiliation and redeem the reputation of their forefathers. The material already in circulation provided no such victory, so the Shaybānīs created one, piecing together from earlier reports of various minor skirmishes a series of entirely spurious accounts, what

[193]The reports expressing these concerns (largely to be found in works of *ḥadīth*) have now been collected and discussed in a very important study by Suliman Bashear, "Apocalyptic and Other Materials on Early Byzantine Wars", *JRAS*, Third Series, 1 (1991), 173–207.

[194]Cf. above, 384.

Donner calls the "Buwayb cycle", describing a battle ("Buwayb") that probably never occurred.[195]

2) A further feature of the Arwād tradition is its instability. Once accounts of the fall of the island come into being, they are not simply transmitted word for word, or even retold in approximately the same sense. Rather, we have before us a series of stages in which an account acquires new details and responds to current notions concerning the scope, themes, utility, and method of history, and what the archaic Islamic past "must have been" or "should have been". Each successive stage thus involves new changes, at times tantamount to generating a new account, which may subsequently respond to the shifting views and conceptions of a later generation, and so forth. Here again parallels may be discerned not only in accounts pertaining to the Arab conquests,[196] but also in the treatment of other topics. Proceeding on the basis of a reinterpretation of the idea of *fatḥ* ("opening" of the sanctuary as opposed to the "conquest" of Mecca) and the rôle of "sanctuary material" in the accounts for the Prophet's conquest of Mecca, G.R. Hawting proposes that the accounts as we now have them may represent the development of early material in which the sanctuary of Mecca was far less prominent, and perhaps absent altogether.[197] The narratives of the Tamīmī delegation to the Prophet, recently analyzed by Ella Landau-Tasseron, amount to a series of highly tendentious family accounts, arbitrary efforts to elucidate possible Qur'ānic allusions to the Banū Tamīm, and a process of sometimes indiscriminate redaction and elaboration that, in the hands of al-Wāqidī, resulted in the conflation of two delegations on different occasions into a single event.[198]

[195] Fred McGraw Donner, *The Early Islamic Conquests* (Princeton, 1981), 198–200.

[196] See Noth, *Quellenkritische Studien*, 174–92. Though the instability of the *futūḥ* tradition is a paramount theme of the work as a whole, this particular section vividly illustrates how accounts of practically unknown and unimportant clashes could be inflated with large amounts of entirely baseless detail and stock motifs.

[197] G.R. Hawting, "Al-Ḥudaybiyya and the Conquest of Mecca: a Reconsideration of the Tradition about the Muslim Takeover of the Sanctuary", *JSAI* 8 (1986), 1–23. Cf. also Claude Gilliot, "Imaginaire social et *maġāzī*: le 'succès décisif' de la Mecque", *JA* 275 (1987), 50–51.

[198] Ella Landau-Tasseron, "Processes of Redaction: the Case of the Tamīmite Delegation to the Prophet Muḥammad", *BSOAS* 49 (1986), 253–70.

Patricia Crone has indicated numerous cases in which the early narrators produced a plethora of utterly irreconcilable accounts of the same event, proceeding in many directions all at the same time, other cases in which early accounts (e.g. in Ibn Isḥāq) appear in lavishly embroidered form in the works of later compilers (such as al-Wāqidī), and yet other instances in which old authentic information seems gradually to have been displaced by later unfounded speculation.[199]

In the case of Arwād, this process seems to have stopped only with the achievement of a general consensus on Islamic origins in the community at large, as signalled, in the field of history, by the appearance of such works as the digests of Ibn Qutayba (the *Kitāb al-ma'ārif*) and al-Balādhurī (his *Futūḥ al-buldān*) and finally the great histories of al-Balādhurī[200] and al-Ṭabarī. In fact, in the introduction to his *Ta'rīkh al-rusul wa-l-mulūk* al-Ṭabarī implicitly appeals to this consensus when he warns his readers that if they encounter in his work anything which they reject or find incomprehensible, the blame for this falls not on al-Ṭabarī himself, but rather on those who transmitted the information to him. The historian's task is not to engage in rational proofs (*ḥujaj al-'uqūl*) or intuitive thinking to discover the truth (*al-istinbāṭ bi-fakr al-nufūs*), he says, but rather to pass material on to others in the same form in which it was handed down to him.[201] This is as much as to say that one accepts those reports to which the community has already given its assent by virtue of the fact that it has transmitted them to current times, and it was the eventual triumph of this attitude that led to the stabilization of the historical tradition in general—history, again, conforming to the expectations of contemporary society. This marks a tremendously important shift in the view of the past prevailing among those who wrote about the past. Hence, if al-Ṭabarī and

---

[199] Crone, *Meccan Trade*, 203–30.

[200] That the *Futūḥ al-buldān* was written some time prior to al-Balādhurī's (never completed) genealogical history, the *Ansāb al-ashrāf*, is certain. See the author's references to the former work in *Ansāb al-ashrāf*, Süleymaniye Kütüphanesi (Istanbul), Ms. Reisülküttap no. 598, fols. 271r:31–32, "I have already given an account of him in the *Book of the Provinces*"; 346r:25, "This is a topic I have already discussed in the book I composed on the affairs of the provinces".

[201] See al-Ṭabarī, *Ta'rīkh*, I, 7:17–8:7; also 58:13–17, where he reiterates his views on this subject.

other formal historians of his era are exponents of a distinct "theory of knowledge",[202] the investigation of what this meant to this generation, in conceptual and methodological terms, does not necessarily lead to conclusions applicable to earlier times.

3) Closely related to the problems of discontinuity and instability, and indeed, a consequence of them, is that of arbitrariness, a recurrent theme in the preceding pages. How does one account for this? On the one hand, the discontinuity of the Arwād tradition, the nearly total absence of genuine historical material, meant that arbitrary guesswork and imposition of new details and conclusions did not encounter the obstacles of eyewitnesses or contemporaries, old warriors who knew better, or the superior testimony of coherent detailed accounts passed on from such sources.

At the same time, the situation confronting the early tradents not only allowed for arbitrary guesswork and elaboration, it demanded it. The primary aim of early "historicizing" was to offer reconstructions authenticated not by the formal historian's adherence to a critical canon for the use of evidence, but rather by the narrator or storyteller's solicitude for factors that often had nothing to do with "factuality" and which could easily brush this consideration aside.[203] His account had to be something his audience would find edifying and/or entertaining; it should be harmonious with that audience's conceptions of the origins of Islam and the early growth of the community; and it had to meet prevailing expectations of what a historical report should be able to offer. If, at a stage when such reports are expected to provide dates, no date is known for the conquest of Arwād, speculation of the most precarious sort will produce one. If, at a time when reports are expected to proffer all sorts of details and minutiae, no one knows where Arwād is or

[202]It is in fact quite difficult to determine the historiographical views of these writers, since they so seldom speak directly to this point and offer in their works materials which have come down to them through processes which—as can be seen here—are often unclear. On al-Ṭabarī in particular, see Henri Loucel, *Les ideés politiques et religieuses d'al-Ṭabarī* (Paris, 1966); Claude Gilliot, "La formation intellectuelle de Tabari (224/5–310/839–923)", *JA* 276 (1988), 203–44.

[203]See Wansbrough, *Sectarian Milieu*, 7–27, although Wansbrough pursues a more limited sense of the process in that he sees the catalytic factor of a key word or polemical idea as crucial to historicization.

how many men or ships Junāda had, conjecture can be made from context, and failing that the required detail can simply be invented: "near Constantinople", "4000 men", "20 ships". If a transmitter thinks of a way to make his story's point more elegantly or more effectively (i.e. in terms of the reactions of a contemporary audience more sophisticated than that to which earlier forms of the account had been offered), the story can be changed accordingly. Thus the uprooted "fig tree" of the old Egyptian Tubay' fable becomes the blown away "step" of the common source underlying Ibn A'tham and al-Wāqidī. If Rhodes is already being referred to as a *kharāb*, a "ruin", why not take advantage of the opportunity for an elegant touch of paronomasia by rewriting to *kharāb yabāb*, a "desolate ruin"? If earlier undifferentiated material seems to relate to island campaigns without specifying which island is meant, the available information can be divided up or reproduced and distributed to supply accounts as needed, in much the same way that "Nihāwand" material was reproduced and transferred to "Iṣfahān", or legal material on the Prophet praying in the Ka'ba came to be attached, after various other possibilities were tried, to accounts of the conquest of Mecca.

Such processes tend to be judged rather harshly in modern scholarship, in which such terminology as "forgery" and "fabrication" abounds. Strictly speaking there is of course truth to such characterizations. But they are problematic in that they divert attention from the fact that, as the examples above clearly illustrate, the discourse among the early *ruwāt* and later among the more formal compilers did not proceed on the assumption that accounts were the inviolate property of a specific author, narrative entities to which no additions or alterations should be made. Nor was the thematic range of the discourse defined so sharply as to confine legitimate discussion to "factual" accounts of "genuine" events and to exclude folklore and edifying but historically baseless anecdotes.[204] This is not to say that there were no bounds beyond

[204] For other discussions apropos of this question, see Noth, *Quellenkritische Studien*, 13, 78; Landau-Tasseron, "Processes of Redaction", 262–63, 270; Crone, *Meccan Trade*, 221; Stefan Leder, "Prosa-Dichtung in der *aḫbār*-Überlieferung. Narrative Analyse einer Satire", *Der Islam* 64 (1987), 6–7; *idem*, "Authorship and Transmission in Unauthored Literature: the *Axbār* Attributed to al-Haiṯam ibn 'Adī", *Oriens* 31 (1988), 71; *idem*, "Features of the Novel in Early Historiography: the Downfall of Xālid al-Qasrī", *Oriens* 32 (1990), 72–96. Cf. also Leder's

which the *ruwāt* could not step, but it does indicate that the tendency to engage in arbitrary elaboration and recasting of received accounts, or in the generation of completely new ones, could go to considerable lengths without attracting rebuke.

4) A crucial feature of the Arwād material is that it is sufficiently clear for us to observe that the process of narrative elaboration proceeded at a rapid pace once an account had been set into circulation. The Egyptian Tubayʻ fable, originally situated on Rhodes, emerged *ca.* 110–40/728–57, and by the time of al-Wāqidī (d. 207/823), less than a century and perhaps only 30–40 years later (depending on when in his lifetime al-Wāqidī handled this material), it had already been excerpted, recast with Mujāhid in attendance, recast again as a narrative related by Mujāhid in the first person, separated from the Rhodes stories, and retold as an incident that occurred on Arwād. It would therefore seem that there could have been hardly any stage in the transmission process at which some substantive change did not occur. In other words, so far as Arwād was concerned it was the rule, not the exception, for a transmitter to reshape or elaborate the material passing through his hands.

5) The problems posed by all of the above would be far less serious for modern researchers were it not for the fact that the process of narrative growth and elaboration produced accounts that to a large extent, and by their very nature, are extremely difficult to penetrate. As an account undergoes successive changes in form and content its origins become increasingly obscure, and as the changes are often so arbitrary it is frequently impossible to discern a particular transmitter's motives or aims, and therefore equally impossible to predict what he had to work with in the first place. And since new forms take shape in accordance with the expectations of an audience of increasing cultural sophistication, they often tend to be increasingly "reasonable" and satisfying in the details they offer and in the way these details are organized and articulated. Convincingness and consistency must therefore be viewed as phenomena of discourse, and not functions of historical truth.[205]

---

comments above, 277–315.

[205] Noth arrives at a similar conclusion from an argument for the secondary character of certain historical themes; see his *Quellenkritische Studien*, 57. Cf. also Wansbrough's discussion of this issue in his *Sectarian Milieu*, 39, where he concludes

To the extent that these matters can be sorted out, it is often not so much because a derivative account betrays the form, agenda, and content of the older one from which it originated or by which its creation was inspired, as because of the testimony brought to bear by external indicators. If other sources (or perhaps the same source) have preserved older accounts attesting to earlier stages in the growth of the tradition, then tracing the development of a formal historical account from old "historicizing" origins can become a task somewhat similar to that of reconstructing the stemma of a manuscript tradition to recover an archetype as close as possible to what was said in the author's autograph.[206] And it is precisely in this respect that materials completely external to the Arab-Islamic literary tradition—non-Islamic literary sources, archaeology, numismatics, epigraphy, and geography—are often so important. They not only assist us in making our way back to that archetype, but also may prove useful in judging its provenance and worth.

The various Arwād narratives serve to illustrate these points. The account in Ibn Aʿtham is in itself a reasonable one. One will immediately notice that it is full of the standard topoi and motifs of the *futūḥ* tradition, but perhaps at the same time, owing to the sheer reasonableness of it all, one will hesitate to dismiss it too quickly. Is it not plausible, for example, that 4000 men, 200 in each of 20 ships, actually did comprise the attacking Arab force? It is only when armed with a map of the Syrian coast and the citations from Theophilus of Edessa that one can make a specific and conclusive case for rejecting Ibn Aʿtham's account in its entirety. The version of the episode of the step that al-Ṭabarī offers is absolutely obscure when viewed in isolation. It is only when we look elsewhere that the origins and intent of this passage become intelligible.

All of this can be seen fairly clearly for the case of Arwād, but to what extent do the problems and paradigms proposed on the basis of the Arwād material apply more generally to the history and historiography of the early medieval Near East?

---

that "authenticity can be as much a result of (successful) narrative technique as of veracity".

[206] Cf. Leder, "Authorship and Transmission", 69, 78. Pressed too far, of course, the analogy quickly breaks down.

First, it can be said that so far as the history of early Arab naval operations is concerned, the problems outlined above are most certainly manifestations of a broader phenomenon. The issue cannot be pursued in detail here, but a vivid illustration may be seen in the attempt by al-Ya'qūbī (d. 284/897) to arrange the various land and sea campaigns of Mu'āwiya into a coherent chronological summary. The impression one gets from this is one of constant sea raiding under numerous commanders to various places "in the sea", but upon closer examination this list clearly attests to a process in which single expeditions that had come to be assigned by various earlier transmitters to different years or different commanders were over time proliferating into multiple expeditions that would accommodate the various attested combinations of dates and commanders.[207] For AH 59, however, the year in which other sources place considerable Arab activity to or from Rhodes, al-Ya'qūbī categorically states, "In that year there was no sea expedition".[208] A similar situation appears in the history of Khalīfa ibn Khayyāṭ (d. 240/854–55), in which citations from the same authority (al-Layth ibn Sa'd) place campaigns to Rhodes in 58/678, 59/679, and 60/680, with the parties responsible being variously named as Akdar, Sa'īd ibn Yazīd, Junāda ibn Abī Umayya al-Azdī, 'Alqama ibn Junāda al-Ḥajrī, 'Alqama ibn al-Akhtham, and "the people of Egypt".[209]

Beyond this limited topic, such difficulties manifest themselves not only in the *futūḥ*,[210] but also in the Arab-Islamic historical tradition more generally. In addition to the other cases cited earlier, it is here worth noting that in a crucially important study of the work of al-Haytham ibn 'Adī (d. 207/822, a contemporary of al-Wāqidī) and its transmission to later times, Stefan Leder has recently demonstrated that even in the generation of al-Ṭabarī's immediate sources and informants the Arab-Islamic tradition still displayed a significant degree of instability so far as the arbitrary elaboration and attribution of old

---

[207] Al-Ya'qūbī, *Ta'rīkh* (Beirut, 1379/1960), II, 239:20–240:17.

[208] *Ibid.*, II, 240:17.

[209] Khalīfa ibn Khayyāṭ, *Ta'rīkh*, 225:10–11, 227:5–8, 229:2–4.

[210] Noth repeatedly stresses the ubiquity of the topoi, schemata, and motifs of the *futūḥ* tradition; see his *Quellenkritische Studien*, 13, 23–24, 48, 59, 101, 157–58, 182–92.

material was concerned.[211] Curiously enough, it proves in the end that the deviations from mere transmission that al-Ṭabarī so categorically rejects in the introduction to his *Ta'rīkh al-rusul wa-l-mulūk* were processes that played a major rôle in shaping the canon that al-Ṭabarī in his own day sought to preserve without further change. And as research on early Islamic historiography proceeds, it is becoming increasingly clear that the sorts of problems discussed above characterize not an author or a topic, but rather a mode of discourse. It would be a serious error to respond to the arguments posed above simply by demoting al-Wāqidī from the ranks of such "good" historians as Ibn Isḥāq to the level of "bad" historians like Sayf ibn 'Umar,[212] or to conclude only that in Umayyad times little was known about the early Arab naval campaigns in the Mediterranean. What we see in the Arwād materials is also to be found among other transmitters and compilers and among the reports for other events; by reason of the considerable external evidence available, the Arwād materials comprise a rare case in which one can clearly see certain ways in which historical discourse was allowed and expected to function in early Islamic society.

This is not to say, however, that all of the early Arabic literary tradition consists of discontinuous unstable material that was rapidly and arbitrarily elaborated to such an extent that one can never penetrate behind it, that if one could it would just be rejected anyway, and that to know anything about the history of the early medieval Near East one must work on the basis of non-Islamic sources, even for the history of Islam. It is a simple and indubitable fact that while it is often possible to prove conclusively that a particular account or corpus of accounts *cannot* be true, and hence (as here) to proceed to analyze in detail the factors at work in a process of baseless and arbitrary elaboration, it is rarely possible to prove that an account or corpus of accounts *must* be true. It is thus the nature of the modes of inquiry currently pur-

[211] Stefan Leder, *Das Korpus al-Haiṯam ibn 'Adī (st. 207/822). Herkunft, Überlieferung, Gestalt früher Texte der Aḫbār Literatur* (Frankfurt, 1991). Also see his "Authorship and Transmission" and "Features of the Novel", and his paper above.

[212] The fallaciousness of such an approach has recently been demonstrated quite clearly by Ella Landau-Tasseron. See her "Sayf ibn 'Umar in Medieval and Modern Scholarship", *Der Islam* 67 (1990), 1–27.

sued in modern research, perhaps more than the nature of the early Arab-Islamic tradition, that is highlighted by a decade of scholarship that has pointed to many of the problems in the Arab-Islamic tradition while failing to vindicate much authentic material.[213]

It should also be obvious that the non-Islamic traditions pose problems of their own, and here it may be observed that in many cases the prevailing consensus of modern scholarship on a source amounts to nothing more than acquiescence in a judgment reached at the turn of the century, when much material was still unknown, historiographical methodology was far less sophisticated, and points now regarded as crucial topics of inquiry were simply taken for granted. It was long believed, for example, that Christian sources written in Greek or Syriac must represent a tradition entirely independent of the Arabic tradition of Islam, the assumption being that such terms as "Greek", "Byzantine", "Hellenic", "Semitic", "Arab", "Syrian", "Christian", "Muslim", "Orthodox", "Monophysite", and so forth, refer to confessional, cultural, social, and linguistic categories which may, even in the very early period of interest to us here, be taken as descriptive primarily of "difference" with respect to other categories, and hence used to sustain equally perilous assumptions about the lack of meaningful contact among the groups so described. But as this writer has elsewhere sought to demonstrate, Syriac writers as early as Theophilus were already using material that can only have come from a nascent Islamic tradition.[214]

It must also be noted that difficulties quite similar to those involved in use of the Arab-Islamic sources emerge in other traditions as well. A vivid illustration of this, one of immediate relevance to matters at issue in these pages, is available in the eastern Christian accounts of the Arab raid on Rhodes. Eastern Christian sources which may all be traced back to Theophilus state that when the Arabs raided Rhodes, they wanted to demolish the great Colossus so they could take the bronze. Unable to destroy the underpinnings of the monument, they

[213]Work that securely vindicates, rather than repudiates, the historicity of early Arabic accounts is extremely difficult, but is nevertheless being pursued. For an excellent example, see Uri Rubin, "Muḥammad's Curse of Muḍar and the Blockade of Mecca", *JESHO* 31 (1988), 249–64.

[214]See Conrad, "Theophanes and the Arabic Historical Tradition", esp. 31–34, on the broader cultural context.

used great cables to topple it; the ruins produced 3000 loads of bronze, which was purchased by a Jew from Edessa.[215] But aside from the fact that there really had been such a thing as the Colossus of Rhodes, Theophilus' story is nonsense from beginning to end. Much of the tale is falsified by ancient accounts of the monument, and a wealth of evidence for late antique and Byzantine Rhodes suggests that the Colossus had disappeared long before the Arab raiders appeared on the scene. The story has significant bearing on views about classical antiquity and pagan culture in late Umayyad and early 'Abbāsid Edessa, where the tale seems to have originated, but tells us nothing about the history of the Arab maritime campaigns in the eastern Mediterranean in the time of the early conquests.[216]

Examples of this kind could be multiplied indefinitely, but here it will suffice to note that the contrast, in terms of historicity, that appears in the pages above between the Arab-Islamic and eastern Christian traditions does not represent a paradigm for which some greater validity is claimed. The events on Arwād occurred in Theophilus' own local region, and it should come as no surprise that among the progeny of those who had left the island there would be many who had heard accounts of the siege. The eastern Christian sources for Arwād thus represent a case that may not be typical, as the example of Theophilus' own account of Rhodes and the alleged Arab destruction of the Colossus clearly reveals.

So far as the history of the early medieval Near East is concerned, the paramount benefit accruing from comparison of one tradition with another is that in many cases one thereby gains access to important external information or insights that would otherwise not emerge. The exercise concedes nothing so far as the question of "better" sources is concerned, since it is clear from the start not only that all have

---

[215]See Theophanes, *Chronographia*, 345:7–10; Constantine Porphyrogenitus (wr. *ca.* 952), *De administrando imperio* XX.7–10; ed. and trans. Gyula Moravcsik and R.J.H. Jenkins, 2nd ed. (Washington, D.C., 1967), 84 (text), 85 (trans.); Cedrenus, *Historia*, I, 755:8–16; Zonaras (wr. after 1118), *Epitome historiarum* XIV.19; ed. Ludwig Dindorf (Leipzig, 1868–75), III, 314:25–29; Michael, II, 442–43 (trans.); IV, 430a:25–31 (text); *Chronicle of 1234*, II, 21:7–8.

[216]See Lawrence I. Conrad, "The Arabs and the Colossus: Syriac Historiography and Secular Culture in Early 'Abbāsid Edessa", forthcoming.

potentially important contributions to make, but also that all pose potentially serious difficulties. Put somewhat differently, all of these traditions can be visualized as narrative landscapes. At the base of each lies a contour of high and low points, with some events related in detail and others entirely ignored, some developments described accurately and others already obscured by tendentious features of one kind or another (folklore, polemic, Heilsgeschichte, etc.). This base contour—had we access to it—would thus pose serious problems of its own. But what lies visible to us, the material to which we have immediate access, is not this level, but rather something "higher up", a later level gradually generated by the successive narrators, transmitters, and compilers that stand between us and the original old material. This visible level has filled in many "low spots", eroded many "peaks", and done a good deal of reshaping in the areas in between. A crucial goal of historiography remains, of course, the determination of the extent to which the present narrative landscape approximates the original one. But knowledge of how and why the later levels have been produced is surely of no less historical importance for our understanding of the generations in which these changes took place, and it remains a fact that in the present state of our knowledge access to "what really happened" can be had only by sifting through the spurious material that conceals it. The ongoing historiographical assessment of the various traditions available for studying the history of the early medieval Near East will undoubtedly continue to arrive at conclusions calling into question various elements of the literary traditions and the customary methods for assessing these materials. But in this regard it may be sufficient to observe, with Noth, that a knowledge of such things as may be learned from the sources must of necessity be accompanied by an appreciation for what these sources cannot teach us and an awareness of the kinds of questions for which they will never offer answers.[217] Progress on the former is illusory unless founded on the latter.

[217] Noth, *Quellenkritische Studien*, 29.

General Index

In the arrangement adopted here, the Arabic definite article (*al-*, *l-*), the transliteration symbols for the Arabic letters *hamza* (') and *'ayn* ('), and distinctions between different letters transliterated by the same Latin character (e.g. *d* and *ḍ*, *o* and *ō*) are ignored for purposes of alphabetization.

and n. 55, 261–62
Abū l-Sā'ib al-Makhzūmī, 289 and n. 40, 290 n. 49
Abū 'Ubayd, 356
Abū 'Ubayd Allāh Kātib al-Mahdī, 260–61
Abū 'Ubayda ibn al-Jarrāḥ, 356
Abū 'Ubayda Ma'mar ibn al-Muthannā, 387–88 n. 192
Acre, Greek raids on, 338 and n. 69
Acts of the Apostles
evidence of *lachnistērion* in, 140, 141 n. 64; 1:12–26, 204 n. 30; 12:17, 196 n. 11; 15:13, 196 n. 11; 21:18, 196 n. 11
Addai
questions addressed to Jacob of Edessa, 190; source for *Gospel of the Twelve Apostles*, 190 and n. 5
administration, Arab
early rôle of Chancery, 217–19 and n. 4, 221 and n. 11; secretaries: education, training, influence, 217–19, 222, 223, 238, 239–41 and n. 53, 256, manuals of instruction, 247 and n. 64, scribes, apprentices distinguished, 254, socio-administrative history, 217–18 and nn. 3–4, use of Greek language, 19
administration, Byzantine
imperial, legal, ecclesiastical: education and training for, 28–30, 83, 85, stimulus for composition, 28–30, 38–39; restructuring in response to Heraclius' campaigns, 83 and n. 8; significance of collapse in ancient cities, 125–26
affliction, physical, a topic in Anastasius of Sinai, 137
Africa, North, *see* North Africa
Against Julian, Ephraem
on rebuilding of Temple, 184–85 and n. 162; on rôle of Christian emperor, 168–69 and nn. 81–85
Agapius
background, origins, 330; on conquest of Arwād, 328–30, 331–32, 347; on invasion of Cyprus, 347; sources used by, 20–21, 331–33 and n. 38, 334, 346, 347, 348
Agathias
absence of references to Arabs, 77; as epigrammatist, 44 n. 78; beliefs, 34–35, 36; characteristics, contents, 27, 31; continuators of, 38–40; debt to Procopius, 25–26 and nn. 2–3, 27; dating of work, 58; diversion from poetry, 30, 32; digressions, 32, 33, 37–38, 50; expertise in military matters of Procopius and, compared, 31–32, 37–38; interest in Franks, 32 and n. 31, 75; military success a stimulus for composition, 72; narration of contemporary events, 46 n. 93; on early Merovingians, 32 n. 31; on Sasanians, 32 and n. 31; origins, education, 36, 68; representation in *Excerpta de legationibus*, 41 n. 58; sententious elements, 40 and n. 53; sources, techniques, 46, 48, 67; treatment of earthquakes, 32–38 and n. 32; work evaluated, 30–38
Aḥmad ibn Yūsuf, 235 n. 43
al-Aḥnaf ibn Qays, 356
'Ā'isha, daughter of Hishām, 232
Akdar, 397
akhbār (sing. *khabar*)
as source for historiography: differing versions, 284, 285–91, 293–306, evaluated, 281–84 and nn. 20–27, 291–93, 314–15, false attribution, 284, unavowed authorship, 284–91; association with poetry, 295, 310; centrality of storytelling, 279; chains of transmitters: described, 280, 281 and n. 15, evaluated, 282, multiplication of versions, 285–91, problem of reliability, 285, character, content, structure, 16–18 and n. 24, 18–19, 278–80 and n. 9, derivation from earlier collections, 280–81 and nn. 11–13, 284–85; development: emergence as discipline in own right, 313–15, expressed through differentiation of versions, 304, refinement of historical perspective during, 304, 306, digest, compilation, narration in, distinguished 279–80 n. 8, 283; evidence of historical method in, 18–19; features, themes: common motifs, 283, depiction of personal characteristics, 310–11, extreme emaciation, 288–89 and n. 37, listing of names, 309–10, ideological considerations, 282–83, interrelation of fact, fiction, sources, 283, 309–12, local tradition, 283, love stories, 288, miracles, legends, 312 and n. 158, moralizing, 311, narrative structure, 294, 307–309, personal involvement of narrator avoided, 307–308, 315, rarity of dialogue, 307–308 and n. 127, use of direct speech, 308 and n. 128; origin of term, 279 and n. 4; *qiṣaṣ* distinguished, 311–12; sources: characteristic of Arabic, 16–18 and n. 24, 18–19, roots in oral tradition, 16–18 and n. 24, 311–12; *see also* alliance of 'Amr and Mu'āwiya
akhbārīyūn, emergence, 313–15
Alexander (martyr), destruction of shrine at Drizipera, 52
Alexander the Great
conquest of Arwād by, 318; in ps.-

tive career, 28–30; trends, changes in nature of, discussed, 45–46 and n. 90; *see also individual authors, works, and related genres*
History, Agathias
continuation in Menander, 40; dating, 31; *see also* Agathias
History, Menander
concentration on diplomacy, 40–42; period covered by, 60, nature of personal comment, 43–45 and n. 74; *see also* Menander
History, Theophylact
dating, 47; *see also* Theophylact
History of Edessa (lost), 325
History of Heraclius, Sebēos, 158 n. 37
Hodēgos, Anastasius of Sinai
dating, 113; modern edition, 111; themes, 115; *see also* Anastasius of Sinai
holy men, *see* asceticism
Holy Spirit, emphasis on, in apocalyptic, 209 and n. 46
homiletic
element of orality, 92; themes common to visual arts and, 101 and n. 68; value as source material, 89–90 and n. 24, 100–101, 112
Hormizd, 53–54
human beings, character differences, a topic in Anastasius of Sinai, 124
Ḥunayn, battle of, 361
al-Ḥusayn ibn 'Alī, 349 n. 90

Iberia, in Theophanes, 38
Ibn 'Abd Rabbih, 247, 306 and n. 125
Ibn Abī 'Atīq, 290–91 and n. 47
Ibn Abī l-Ḥadīd, 296 and n. 76
Ibn Abī Ṭāhir Ṭayfūr, 232, 240, 245–47 and n. 63, 248
Ibn 'Asākir
on Arwād campaign, 35 n. 133, 368 nn. 142–43; on date of conquest of Rhodes, 378 n. 163; on *jihād*, *hijra*, 360 n. 119; on Junāda, 359 n. 117, 379 n. 170; on location of Arwād, 382–83 n. 178; on *Waq'at Ṣiffīn*, 305
Ibn al-Ash'ath, 219 n. 7
Ibn A'tham al-Kūfī
ahistorical material in, 351–58, 362–64 and n. 129; dating questioned, 349 and n. 90, 376–78; Iraqi origins postulated, 348; on conquest of Arwād, 349–59, 372–73; on location of Arwād, 381 n. 176, 382–83 n. 178, 385–86 and n. 184; on *Waq'at Ṣiffīn*, 298 and n. 87, 302–303 and n. 110, 304; origins, sources for, 383, 384 and n. 180, 393–94; topoi, common motifs, 388–89; value as source, 362–64 and n. 128, 388–89
Ibn al-Athīr, 385
Ibn al-Buḥturī, 244
Ibn Da'b, 303 and n. 112
Ibn Ḥamdūn
last date of compilation, 234; hitherto unpublished letters, 225 n. 26; source for 'Abd al-Ḥamīd, 227 n. 32, 233, 248, 249–60
Ibn Hishām, 280 and n. 12
Ibn Isḥāq, 280 and n. 12, 284, 309 and nn. 134, 136, 311
Ibn al-Jawzī, 233, 234, 286 and nn. 31, 33, 288
Ibn Jubayr, 367 n. 141
Ibn Jurayj, 366
Ibn al-Kalbī, Hishām ibn Muḥammad, *see* al-Kalbī
Ibn Kathīr, 224 n. 19, 234, 359 n. 117, 385
Ibn Khaldūn, 234, 248, 249–60
Ibn Khallikān, 223 n. 17, 236 n. 45, 233
Ibn Lahī'a, 379–80, 382–83 n. 178
Ibn al-Marzubān, 290 n. 50, 343 n. 83
Ibn al-Nadīm, 220–21 and nn. 9–11, 223 n. 15, 224, 240, 269 n. 82, 314 n. 165
Ibn Nubāta, 225 n. 28, 234
Ibn Qutayba, 219 n. 7, 289 and n. 38, 299 and nn. 90–91, 366, 392
Ibn al-Qirrīya, 219 n. 7
Ibn Sa'd, 284, 305 n. 122, 309, 378 n. 164
Ibn Sa'īd al-Maghribī, 233, 234, 236 n. 47
Ibn Taghrībirdī, 378 n. 166
Ibrāhīm ibn al-Ḥusayn ibn 'Alī, 305
Ibrāhīm ibn al-Mahdī, 240 n. 53
iconoclasm, iconoclasts
accessibility for study, 81 n. 1; controversies, 93 and n. 40, 102 and n. 73, 104; ill-treatment of Theophanes, 66 n. 182; in North Syria, 337; response to John of Damascus, 87; significance of Byzantine preoccupations, 5, 9; significance for Christian–Muslim relations, 104
al-Idrīsī, 386
illness, Jewish, Christian interpretations of, 144 and n. 72, 145
images, *see* iconoclasm
incest, rebuttal of charges by Gregory of Antioch, 29
instability, historiographical problem in Arabic sources, 391–93
Iraq, surviving literature, 127 and n. 36
Isaozites, 44, 45
Iṣfahān, Arab conquest of, traditions concerning, 384, 390, 393–94
al-Iṣfahānī, Abū l-Faraj, 280–81 n. 13
Ishmael, sons of